THE BEDSIDE BOOK

THE BEDSIDE BOOK

A MISCELLANY

for

THE QUIET HOURS

selected and arranged

by

ARTHUR STANLEY

———

LONDON
VICTOR GOLLANCZ LTD
14 Henrietta Street
W.C.

First published September 1932
Second impression November 1932
Third impression December 1932
Fourth impression December 1932
Fifth impression December 1933
Sixth impression September 1935
Seventh impression October 1936
Eighth impression October 1938
Ninth impression (first cheap edition) November 1939
Tenth impression January 1940
Eleventh impression September 1940
Twelfth impression November 1940

TO
THE OTHER SLEEPERS
IN
"OUR DEN"

INSCRIPTION
FOR AN OLD BED

No tale I tell
Of ill or well,
But this I say:
Night treadeth on day,
And for worst or best,
Right good is rest.

WILLIAM MORRIS

FOREWORD

This book is founded on my belief that a need of my own is probably shared by others. Whether we indulge ourselves in the luxury of reading in bed (like Pepys, reading ourselves asleep) or refrain from it as an objectionable habit, it may be found an advantage to have at hand a book offering a variety of consolation, information and entertainment in that part of our dwelling where we are most free from the invasions of the outside world. The virtuous objector to reading in bed will protest that he goes there to sleep, but even he may one day be sworn of my company ; for there are many people who remain in bed besides those who do not want to get up, and I have had in mind the involuntary bed-user. It is hoped also that this book may sometimes be found useful out of bed—that it may be a friendly companion on journeys by land or sea and on other suitable occasions which the ingenious reader will discover for himself.

I have endeavoured to provide a reasonable variety of matter within the limits of my scheme, which extends in time from the writers of Ancient Egypt to authors now living and in character of material from the Bible to Mr. Punch. While I remain staunch in my loyalty to venerable bed-fellows like Lucretius, Burton, Browne and Montaigne, to whom so many candles have been sacrificed by preceding generations, I have (as will be seen) made other friends both old and new. The maker of a book of this kind is lucky if he satisfies himself : he should not have the effrontery to expect the same satisfaction on the part of his readers. The good anthologist is not so much a guide as a friend, and who can hope to be a friend of all the world ? We begin by overloading our argosies. We pack a great cargo of legacies from the dead and gifts from the living, but we are soon throwing things overboard to lighten the ship, perhaps making flotsam and jetsam of goods for which a ready merchant is waiting at the wharf. But it is not to be supposed that the critics have been reading in bed all these years without discovering some principles to guide the bedside anthologist. They tell us, for example, that the proper bed-book should be continually interesting, un-dramatic, not too exciting, and that it should be one that can be begun anywhere and dropped anywhere. I approve of all these nocturnal regulations, and have endeavoured to obey them. They are stated here in order that my readers may reflect on the frailty of human nature, and have the pleasure of finding out for themselves by means of these tests my errors of inclusion and exclusion.

Sometimes we find the land of sleep as full of briars as this work-a-day world. Perhaps our experience in both depends to some extent on what we bring into them. If so, our last thoughts as we approach the misty frontier should be bright rather than gloomy ; and it may be an advantage to close our eyes at a moment when our minds have been cheered by the gracious companionship of some friendly writer. A good night, then, brother or sister—may the sleep-tide carry you gently to a land of peace, and may you meet only those kindly Dreams that pass the Gate of Horn !

A. S.

8

CONTENTS

9

FIRST PART

§ I CURFEW

Evening, thou that bringest all that bright morning scattered, thou bringest the sheep, the goat, and the child back to its mother.

SAPPHO (Trans. EDWIN M. COX)

For though the day be never so long
At last the bell ringeth to evensong.

STEPHEN HAWES

Ut quotidie sero signe pulsu ad preces Deo fundendas quisque invitaretur, atque occlusis foribus domorum ultra vagari amplius vetitum admoneretur.

ORDER MADE AT SYNOD OF CAEN, 1061

§ I CURFEW ANCIENT AND MODERN

1. CURFEW CUSTOM

Contrary to the general notion, it appears that no " curfew law " was ever enacted in England. There was, however, long before the Norman Conquest a curfew " custom " which was followed by the English as well as by other European peoples as a precaution against fire. There is for example, an old tradition that a curfew bell was rung every evening at Carfax in Oxford during the reign of Alfred the Great and that at its ringing all persons were expected to cover their fires, shut up their houses and go to bed. The medieval Church gave the weight of its authority to this beneficial custom, and somewhat improved upon it when a Synod at Caen (1061), held by the Duke's authority and attended by Bishops, Abbots and Barons, ordered that a bell should be rung every evening, at hearing of which prayer should be offered, and all people should get within their houses and shut their doors. We are told the object in view was " protection from night thieves," and nothing appears to have been said about fires or lights. Thus the old custom became a police regulation and also a call to evening prayer. Doubtless the sanction of the Church facilitated the enforcement of the old English curfew and extended its scope in England after the Norman conquest. But it was not, as has been said so often, a punishment inflicted by William I on a conquered people. If we can believe William of Malmesbury, Henry I allowed the use of candles at court after curfew ; but kings will be kings, or at least they would in those days.

In London, in Edward III's reign, the bells of St. Martin's-le-Grand rang curfew for the closing of the city gates and the shutting of all taverns. Before the end of the 14th century the Great Bell of Bow had become the Common Bell of London, and curfew was then rung by the whole peal of Bow. The Customary Records of London for the year 1495 show that curfew custom was then strictly enforced in the city :—" yf ther be anye paryshe clerke that ryngeth curfewe after the curfewe be ronge at Bowe Chyrche, or Saint Brydes Chyrche, or Saint Gyles without Cripelgat, *all suche to be presented* " (that is, the offending clerk was to be summoned to appear before the Quest—or Court—of Wardmote). Another typical record is furnished by the Articles of Faversham settled in 1531 :—" Imprimis, the sexton, or his sufficient deputy, shall lye in the church steeple ; and at eight o'clock every night shall ring the curfewe by the space of a quarter of an hour, with such bell as of old time hath been accustomed." The curfew was evidently a municipal rather than a state institution.

Curfew is still rung in several English towns and villages throughout the year—in some places at 8 o'clock, in others at 9 o'clock, and this variation of time has existed for at least four centuries. In the Middle Ages curfew ringing began at Michaelmas and ended at Lady Day.

2. CURFEW LAW

The first English " curfew law " (strictly speaking) is probably to be found in the Regulations issued by the Board of Trade during the European War and known as

"The Curfew Order," which sought to reduce the consumption of gas and electricity in order to save coal. By virtue of this order (which came into operation on April 2, 1918) the following provisions applied throughout Great Britain :

No lights to be used in shop fronts.
No hot meals to be served and no food cooked in hotels, restaurants, clubs, or public eating-places between 9-30 p.m. and 5 a.m. and no light to be exhibited in the dining-room of such places after 10 p.m. No gas or electric current to be consumed on the stage or in the auditorium of any place of entertainment between 10-30 at night and 1 p.m. on the following day.

The most recent " curfew law " (which was only of short duration) seems to take us back to Medieval times. This was enacted during the post-war troubles in Ireland when an order of local application was issued on August 30, 1920 by the Competent Military Authority under the Defence of the Realm Regulations requiring that " *every person shall remain indoors between the hours of 10-30 o'clock p.m. and 5 o'clock a.m., unless provided with a Permit in writing.*"

A. S.

ADVICE TO SHEPHERDS

Shepherds all, and maidens fair,
Fold your flocks up, for the air
'Gins to thicken, and the sun
Already his great course has run

See the drew-drops how they kiss
Every little flower that is,
Hanging on their velvet heads,
Like a rope of crystal beads.
See the heavy clouds low falling,
And bright Hesperus down calling
The dead night from underground,
At whose rising, mists unsound,
Damps and vapours fly apace,
Hovering o'er the wanton face
Of these pastures, where they come
Striking dead both bud and bloom.
Therefore from such danger lock
Every one his lovèd flock ;
And let your dogs lie loose without,
Lest the wolf come, as a scout
From the mountain, and ere day
Bear a kid or lamb away ;
Or the crafty, thievish fox
Break upon your simple flocks.
To secure yourselves from these,
Be not too secure in ease.
So shall you good shepherds prove,
And deserve your master's love.
Now, good night ! may sweetest slumbers
And soft silence fall in numbers
On your eyelids : so, farewell ;
Thus I end my evening knell.

JOHN FLETCHER

THE SEVENTH EVENING

" Open, ye everlasting gates ! " they sung ;
" Open, ye Heavens, your living doors ! let in
The great Creator, from his work returned
Magnificent, his six days' work, a World !
Open, and henceforth oft ; for God will deign
To visit oft the dwellings of just men
Delighted, and with frequent intercourse
Thither will send his wingèd messengers
On errands of supernal grace." So sung
The glorious train ascending. He through Heaven,
That opened wide her blazing portals, led
To God's eternal house direct the way—
A broad and ample road, whose dust is gold
And pavement stars, as stars to thee appear
Seen in the Galaxy, that milky way
Which nightly as a circling zone thou seest
Powdered with stars. And now on Earth the seventh
Evening arose in Eden—for the sun
Was set, and twilight from the east came on,
Forerunning night—when at the holy mount
Of Heaven's high-seated top, the imperial throne
Of Godhead, fixed for ever firm and sure,
The Filial Power arrived, and sat him down
With his great Father ; for he also went
Invisible, yet stayed (such privilege
Hath Omnipresence) and the work ordained,
Author and end of all things, and, from work
Now resting, blessed and hallowed the seventh Day,
As resting on that day from all his work ;
But not in silence holy kept : the harp
Had work, and rested not ; the solemn pipe

17

And dulcimer, all organs of sweet stop,
All sounds on fret by string or golden wire,
Tempered soft tunings, intermixed with voice
Choral or unison ; of incense clouds,
Fuming from golden censers, hid the Mount.
Creation and the Six Days' acts they sung.

MILTON (from *Paradise Lost*, Bk. VII)

TO EVENING

Methinks I see thee in the streaky west,
With matron-step slow-moving, while the night
Treads on thy sweeping train ; one hand employ'd
In letting fall the curtain of repose
On bird and beast, the other charg'd for man
With sweet oblivion of the cares of day :
Not sumptuously adorn'd, nor needing aid,
Like homely featur'd night, of clust'ring gems ;
A star or two, just twinkling on thy brow,
Suffices thee ; save that the moon is thine
No less than her's, not worn indeed on high
With ostentatious pageantry, but set
With modest grandeur in thy purple zone,
Resplendent less, but of an ampler round
Come then, and thou shalt find thy vot'ry calm,
Or make me so. Composure is thy gift.

COWPER (from *The Task*)

A NOCTURNAL REVERIE

In such a night, when every louder wind
Is to its distant cavern safe confin'd ;
And only gentle zephyr fans his wings,
And lonely Philomel, still waking, sings ;
Or from some tree, fam'd for the owl's delight,
She, hollowing clear, directs the wand'rer right :
In such a night, when passing clouds give place,
Or thinly vail the Heav'ns mysterious face ;
When in some river, overhung with green,
The waving moon and trembling leaves are seen ;
When freshen'd grass now bears itself upright,
And makes cool banks to pleasing rest invite
Whence springs the woodbind, and the bramble-rose,
And where the sleepy cowslip shelter'd grows ;
Whilst now a paler hue the foxglove takes,
Yet chequers still with red the dusky brakes :
When scatter'd glow-worms, but in twilight fine,
Shew trivial beauties, watch their hour to shine ;
Whilst Salisbury stands the test of every light,
In perfect charms, and perfect virtue bright :
When odours, which declin'd repelling day,
Thro' temp'rate air uninterrupted stray ;
When darken'd groves their softest shadows wear,
And falling waters we distinctly hear ;
When thro' the gloom more venerable shows
Some ancient fabrick, awful in repose,
While sunburnt hills their swarthy looks conceal,
And swelling haycocks thicken up the vale :
When the loos'd horse now, as his pasture leads,
Comes slowly grazing thro' th' adjoining meads,
Whose stealing pace, and lengthen'd shade we fear,

Till torn up forage in his teeth we hear :
When nibbling sheep at large pursue their food,
And unmolested kine re-chew the cud ;
When curlews cry beneath the village-walls,
And to her straggling brood the partridge calls ;
Their shortliv'd jubilee the creatures keep,
Which but endures whilst tyrant man does sleep ;
When a sedate content the spirit feels,
And no fierce light disturbs, whilst it reveals,
But silent musings urge the mind to seek
Something, too high for syllables to speak ;
Till the free soul to a compos'dness charm'd,
Finding the elements of rage disarm'd,
O'er all below a solemn quiet grown,
Joys in th' inferior world, and thinks it like her own :
In such a night let me abroad remain,
Till morning breaks, and all's confus'd again ;
Our cares, our toils, our clamours are renew'd,
Or pleasures, seldom reach'd, again pursu'd.

ANNE, COUNTESS OF WINCHILSEA

SONG FOR THE SPINNING WHEEL

Swiftly turn the murmuring wheel !
Night has brought the welcome hour,
When the weary fingers feel
Help, as if from faery power ;
Dewy night o'ershades the ground ;
Turn the swift wheel round and round !

Now, beneath the starry sky,
Couch the widely-scattered sheep ;—
Ply the pleasant labour, ply !
For the spindle, while they sleep,
Runs with speed more smooth and fine,
Gathering up a trustier line.

Short-lived likings may be bred
By a glance from fickle eyes ;
But true love is like the thread
Which the kindly wool supplies,
When the flocks are all at rest
Sleeping on the mountain's breast.

WORDSWORTH

TO A SKYLARK

Hail to thee, blithe Spirit !
  Bird thou never wert,
That from heaven, or near it,
  Pourest thy full heart
In profuse strains of unpremeditated art.

Higher still and higher
  From the earth thou springest
Like a cloud of fire ;
  The blue deep thou wingest,
And singing still dost soar, and soaring ever singest.

In the golden lightning
  Of the sunken sun,
O'er which clouds are brightening
  Thou dost float and run,
Like an unbodied joy whose race is just begun.

The pale purple even
      Melts around thy flight ;
Like a star of heaven
      In the broad daylight
Thou art unseen, but yet I hear thy shrill delight :

Keen as are the arrows
      Of that silver sphere,
Whose intense lamp narrows
      In the white dawn clear
Until we hardly see, we feel that it is there.

All the earth and air
      With thy voice is loud,
As, when night is bare,
      From one lonely cloud
The moon rains out her beams, and heaven is over-flow'd.

What thou art we know not
      What is most like thee ?
From rainbow clouds there flow not
      Drops so bright to see
As from thy presence showers a rain of melody . . .

Teach me half the gladness
      That thy brain must know ;
Such harmonious madness
      From my lips would flow,
The world should listen then, as I am listening now !

SHELLEY

WHAT THE THRUSH SAID TO THE POET

O thou whose face has felt the Winter's wind,
Whose eye has seen the snow-clouds hung in mist,
And the black elm-tops 'mong the freezing stars,
To thee the Spring will be a harvest time.
O thou, whose only book has been the light
Of supreme darkness which thou feedest on
Night after night when Phoebus was away,
To thee the Spring shall be a triple morn.
O fret not after knowledge—I have none,
And yet my song comes native with the warmth.
O fret not after knowledge—I have none,
And yet the Evening listens. He who saddens
At thought of idleness cannot be idle,
And he's awake who thinks himself asleep.

KEATS

NIGHT

The sun descending in the west,
The evening star does shine ;
The birds are silent in their nest,
And I must seek for mine.
The moon, like a flower
In heaven's high bower,
With silent delight
Sits and smiles on the night.

Farewell, green fields and happy grove,
Where flocks have ta'en delight ;
Where lambs have nibbled, silent move
The feet of angels bright.

Unseen they pour blessing,
And joy without ceasing,
On each bud and blossom,
On each sleeping bosom.

They look in every thoughtless nest,
Where birds are covered warm ;
They visit caves of every beast,
To keep them all from harm.
If they see any weeping
That should have been sleeping,
They pour sleep on their head,
And sit down by their bed.

WILLIAM BLAKE

EVENING IN THE VILLAGE

Now the light o' the west is a-turn'd to gloom,
An' the men be at huome vrom ground ;
An' the bells be a-zenden āl down the Coombe
A muoanen an' dyen sound.
An' the wind is still,
An' the house-dogs da bark,
An' the rooks be a-vled to the elems high an' dark,
An' the water da roar at mill.

An' out droo yander cottage's winder-piane
The light o' the candle da shoot,
An' young Jemmy the blacksmith is down the liane
A-playen his jarmen-flute.

24

An' the miller's man
Da zit down at his ease
'Pon the girt wooden seat that is under the trees,
Wi' his pipe an' his cider can.

Tha'da zay that tis zom'hat in towns to zee
Fresh fiazen vrom day to day:
Tha' mid zee em var me, ef the two or dree
I da love should but smile an' stay.
Zoo gi'e me the sky,
An' the air an' the zun,
An' a huome in the dell wher the water da run,
An' there let me live an' die.

WILLIAM BARNES

MAGDALEN

Magdalen at Michael's gate
    Tirlèd at the pin;
On Joseph's thorn sang the blackbird,
    ' Let her in! Let her in!'

' Hast thou seen the wounds?' said Michael,
    'Know'st thou thy sin?'
' It is evening, evening,' sang the blackbird,
    ' Let her in! Let her in!'

' Yes, I have seen the wounds,
    And I know my sin!'
' She knows it well, well, well,' sang the blackbird,
' Let her in! Let her in!'

25

'Thou bringest no offerings,' said Michael.
  'Nought save sin.'
And the blackbird sang, 'she is sorry, sorry, sorry,
  'Let her in! Let her in!'

When he had sung himself to sleep,
  And night did begin,
One came and open'd Michael's gate,
  And Magdalen went in.

HENRY KINGSLEY

INVOCATION

I am he that walks with the tender and growing
  night,
I call to the earth and sea half-hid by the night.
Press close, bare-bosomed night—press close, magnetic
  nourishing night!
Night of south winds—night of the large few stars.
Still nodding night—mad naked summer night.
Smile, O voluptuous cool-breath'd earth!
Earth of the slumbering and liquid trees!
Earth of departed sunset—earth of the mountains misty-
  topt!
Earth of the vitreous pour of the full moon just tinged with
  blue!
Earth of shine and dark mottling the tide of the river!
Earth of the limpid grey of clouds brighter and clearer for
  my sake!
Far-swooping elbow'd earth—rich apple-blossom'd
  earth—
Smile, for your lover comes.

WALT WHITMAN

LOVE SIGHT

When do I see thee most, belovèd one ?
When in the light the spirits of mine eyes
  Before thy face, their altar, solemnise
The worship of that love thro' thee made known ?
Or when, in the dusk hours (we two alone),
  Close-kissed, and eloquent of still replies
  Thy twilight-hidden glimmering visage lies,
And my soul only sees thy soul its own ?

O love, my love ! if I no more should see
Thyself, nor on the earth the shadow of thee,
  Nor image of thine eyes in any spring,—
How then should sound upon Life's darkening slope
The ground-whirl of the perish'd leaves of Hope,
  The wind of Death's imperishable wing ?

D. G. ROSSETTI

TWILIGHT CALM

    Oh pleasant eventide !
    Clouds on the western side
Grow grey and greyer, hiding the warm sun :
The bees and birds, their happy labours done,
    Seek their close nests and bide.

    Screened in the leafy wood
    The stock-doves sit and brood :
The very squirrel leaps from bough to bough
But lazily ; pauses ; and settles now
    Where once he stored his food.

One by one the flowers close,
    Lily and dewy rose
Shutting their tender petals from the moon :
The grasshoppers are still ; but not so soon
    Are still the noisy crows. . . .

    From far the lowings come
    Of cattle driven home :
From farther still the wind brings fitfully
The vast continual murmur of the sea,
    Now loud, now almost dumb. . . .

    Remote, each single star
    Comes out, till there they are
All shining brightly. How the dews fall damp
While close at hand the glow-worm lights her lamp,
    Or twinkles from afar.

    But evening now is done
    As much as if the sun
Day-giving had arisen in the East—
For night has come ; and the great calm has ceased,
    The quiet sands have run.

CHRISTINA ROSSETTI

VESPERS

O blackbird, what a boy you are !
How you do go it !
Blowing your bugle to that one sweet star—
How you do blow it !

And does she hear you, blackbird boy, so far ?
Or is it wasted breath ?
" Good Lord ! she is so bright
To-night ! "
The blackbird saith.

T. E. BROWN

EVENING

Already evening ! In the duskiest nook
  Of yon dusk corner, under the Death's-head,
  Between the alembics, thrust this legended,
And iron-bound, and melancholy book,
For I will read no longer. The loud brook
  Shelves his sharp light up shallow banks thin-spread
  The slumbrous west grows slowly red, and red :
Up from the ripened corn her silver hook
The moon is lifting : and deliciously
  Along the warm blue hills the day declines :
The first star brightens while she waits for me,
And round her swelling heart the zone grows tight :
  Musing, half-sad, in her soft hair she twines
The white rose, whispering, ' He will come to-night ! '

EARL OF LYTTON

TWILIGHT ON EGDON HEATH

The distant rims of the world and of the firmament
seemed to be a division in time no less than a division in
matter. The face of the heath by its mere complexion

added half an hour to evening; it could in like manner retard the dawn, sadden noon, anticipate the frowning of storms scarcely generated, and intensify the opacity of a moonless midnight to a cause of shaking and dread.

In fact, precisely at this transitional point of its nightly roll into darkness the great and particular glory of the Egdon waste began, and nobody could be said to understand the heath who had not been there at such a time. It could best be felt when it could not clearly be seen, its complete effect and explanation lying in this and the succeeding hours before the next dawn : then, and only then did it tell its true tale. The spot was, indeed, a near relation of night, and when night showed itself an apparent tendency to gravitate together could be perceived in its shades and the scene. The sombre stretch of rounds and hollows seemed to rise and meet the evening gloom in pure sympathy, the heath exhaling darkness as rapidly as the heavens precipitated it. And so the obscurity in the air and the obscurity in the land closed together in a black fraternization towards which each advanced half-way.

The place became full of a watchful intentness now ; for when other things sank brooding to sleep the heath appeared slowly to awake and listen. Every night its Titanic form seemed to await something ; but it had waited thus, unmoved, during so many centuries, through the crises of so many things, that it could only be imagined to await one last crisis—the final overthrow.

It was a spot which returned upon the memory of those who loved it with an aspect of peculiar and kindly congruity. Smiling champaigns of flowers and fruit hardly do this, for they are permanently harmonious only with an existence of better reputation as to its issues than the present. Twilight combined with the scenery of Egdon

Heath to evolve a thing majestic without severity, impressive without showiness, emphatic in its admonitions, grand in its simplicity. The qualifications which frequently invest the façade of a prison with far more dignity than is found in the façade of a palace double its size lent to this heath a sublimity in which spots renowned for beauty of the accepted kind are utterly wanting. Fair prospects wed happily with fair times ; but alas, if times be not fair ! Men have oftener suffered from the mockery of a place too smiling for their reason than from the oppression of surroundings oversadly tinged. Haggard Egdon appealed to a subtler and scarcer instinct, to a more recently learnt emotion, than that which responds to the sort of beauty called charming and fair.

THOMAS HARDY (from *The Return of the Native*)

AN EVENING IN SUSSEX

Ah, Hesperus ! the even falls
From silences to silences,
As when a diver drops at ease
Far down the waters to the halls
Of Thetis and her silver seas,
Beholding through the delicate mist
The colours shifting by degrees
From purple into amethyst.

Across the pure pellucid dale
The shingled spire so darkly stands
Against the gold and crimson bands,
Methinks it were not hard to tell

How points the clock his brazen hands,
Or if the arrow warns us well,
The vane that looks across the lands
The rising winds to sentinel.

Hark in the twilight !—was it sound
Of bell, or bird, or rustling tree ?
It is the children, homeward bound,
Some little comrade they have crowned
The monarch of their revelry ;
Their laughter floats along the hill,
The laughter dies, and all is still.
What horseman comes so late to ride
The solitary stages ? Now
His hoofs are on the steep hill-side,
Now loud and full upon the brow,
Now faintly dying down the hollow :
How many a mile the moon has shown,
Fast dwindling on the friendly stone,
And yet and yet his steed must follow
The road that runs, so white and lone,
Between dark avenues of trees,
Towards the southern villages.

The heavens are like a deep lagoon
In some unfathomable sea,
Where with majestic sail the moon
Sweeps, like a galleon, to the tune
Of oarsmen bending silently.
Her full bright face is clear and cold,
As silver touched with palest gold ;
Her liveried henchmen of the night,
Rose-tinged and gold, and chrysolite,

Move on her errands manifold,
And come and pass and ply their wings
In sweet ethereal wanderings.

Unto what thing shall I compare
So sweet a sight, so strange, so rare,
Or fruit, or flower, or lady fair?
Around her, in a girdling band,
White companies of clouds are spread,
As in the North snow mountains stand,
Encompassing a silver land
Upon a blue lake islanded;
Or moving now before her face,
As babes that in the twilight play
About their mother's feet, nor less
As goats around their shepherdess
In most delightful pastures stray.

The light is on the laurel leaves;
With such a glow it seems to fall
Upon the gables and the eaves,
It looks so pure, so chaste, so holy,
That I could half believe the Hall
Were some old convent mystical,
Haunted by cloistered melancholy.

Come to me, gentle lady mine,
That hast not any part or name
In this our mortal world,—divine
And yet most tender; come the same
As I have seen thee when the beams
Grew softer in the silent grace
Of thy sweet coming; with the face

BB   33

That I have worshipped in my dreams,
Come to me ! 'Tis the hour ; and now
There's something tells me thou art near,
It is thy footfall I can hear ;
Thy lips are pressed upon my brow ;
Thy breath is in the garden scents
That float so softly in the air ;
And all of nature seems to wear
The impress of thy lineaments.

Say not it is the rustling tree,
Whose leaves the soulless breezes stir
Amid the beech-wood ! Come to me !
It is thy voice that bids me be
Thy poet, thine interpreter.
Or if indeed in yon white star,
Where love and life and beauty are
More true, more tender, more intense,
Thy spiritual home I see,
Stretch out thine hand and bear me hence !
O blessèd Lady, take me far
Unto the haunts of innocence !
So for a little space I flee
From my false self, and dwell with thee.

W. J. COURTHOPE

A DAY'S COACHING IN SCOTLAND

Where have I been this perfect summer day,—
Or *fortnight* is it, since I rose from bed,
Devoured that kippered fish, the oatmeal bread,
And mounted to this box ? O bowl away,

Swift stagers, through the dusk ; I will not say
' Enough,' nor care where I have been or be,
Nor know one name of hill, or lake, or lea,
Or moor, or glen ! Were not the clouds at play
Nameless among the hills, and fair as dreams ?
On such a day we must love things, not words,
And memory take or leave them as they are.
On such a day ! What unimagined streams
Are in the world, how many haunts of birds,
What fields and flowers,—and what an evening Star !

EDWARD DOWDEN

THE TRYST

Long are the hours the sun is above,
But when evening comes I go home to my love.

I'm away the daylight hours and more,
Yet she comes not down to open the door.

She does not meet me upon the stair,—
She sits in my chamber and waits for me there.

As I enter the room she does not move :
I always walk straight up to my love ;

And she lets me take my wonted place
At her side, and gaze in her dear dear face.

There as I sit, from her head thrown back
Her hair falls straight in a shadow black.

Aching and hot as my tired eyes be,
She is all that I wish to see.

And in my wearied and toil-dinned ear,
She says all things that I wish to hear.

Dusky and duskier grows the room,
Yet I see her best in the darker gloom.

When the winter eves are early and cold,
The firelight hours are a dream of gold.

And so I sit here night by night,
In rest and enjoyment of love's delight.

But a knock at the door, a step on the stair
Will startle, alas, my love from her chair.

If a stranger comes she will not stay:
At the first alarm she is off and away.

And he wonders, my guest, usurping her throne,
That I sit so much by myself alone.

ROBERT BRIDGES

IN THE CHESTNUT WOODS

Where still Varenna wears her cypress-crown
    At eve amid the chestnut-woods I lay;
The twilight lingered with the little town,
    Then round by Cadenabbia stole away:

The dim woods darkened at the set of day;
Yet where the forest-shadows lowering frown
   Like fairies with their lamps the fire-flies stray,
Lighting their lanterns as the sun goes down.

There in the dusk, in silence resting there,
Was it a Spirit-Voice I heard declare—
   Some Pixy of the Woods that stopped to say—
' Eternal are the skies and infinite;
Eternal are the stars that shine so bright;
   But here a little while the fire-flies play.'

SAMUEL WADDINGTON

THE LATE LARK

A late lark twitters from the quiet skies
And from the west,
Where the sun, his day's work ended,
Lingers as in content,
There falls on the old, gray city
An influence luminous and serene,
A shining peace.
The smoke ascends
In a rosy-and-golden haze. The spires
Shine and are changed. In the valley
Shadows rise. The lark sings on. The sun,
Closing his benediction,
Sinks, and the darkening air
Thrills with a sense of the triumphing night—
Night with her train of stars
And her great gift of sleep.

So be my passing !
My task accomplish'd and the long day done,
My wages taken, and in my heart
Some late lark singing,
Let me be gather'd to the quiet west,
The sundown splendid and serene,
Death.

W. E. HENLEY

IN THE HEART OF THE HILLS

In the warm blue heart of the hills
　My beautiful beautiful one
Sleeps where he laid him down
　Before the journey was done.

All the long summer day
　The ghosts of noon draw nigh,
And the tremulous aspens hear
　The footing of winds go by.

Down to the gates of the sea,
　Out of the gates of the west,
Journeys the whispering river
　Before the place of his rest.

The road he loved to follow
　When June came by his door,
Out through the dim blue haze
　Leads, but allures no more.

The trailing shadows of clouds
  Steal from the slopes and are gone :
The myriad life in the grass
  Stirs, but he slumbers on ;

The inland-wandering tern
  Skriel as they forage and fly ;
His loons on the lonely reach
  Utter their querulous cry

Over the floating lilies
  A dragon-fly tacks and steers ;
Far in the depth of the blue
  A martin settles and veers ;

To every roadside thistle
  A gold-brown butterfly clings ;
But he no more companions
  All the dear vagrant things.

The strong red journeying sun,
  The pale and wandering rain,
Will roam on the hills together
  And find him never again.

Then twilight falls with the touch
  Of a hand that soothes and stills,
And a swamp-robin sings into light
  The lone white star of the hills.

Alone in the dusk he sings,
  And a burden of sorrow and wrong
Is lifted up from the earth
  And carried away in his song.

Alone in the dusk he sings,
    And the joy of another day
Is folded in peace and borne
    On the drift of years away.

But there in the heart of the hills
    My beautiful weary one
Sleeps where I laid him down ;
    And the long sweet night is begun.

BLISS CARMAN

THE END OF THE DAY

I hear the bells at eventide
    Peal slowly one by one,
Near and far off they break and glide,
    Across the stream float faintly beautiful
    The antiphonal bells of Hull ;
The day is done, done, done,
    The day is done.

The dew has gathered in the flowers
    Like tears from some unconscious deep,
The swallows whirl around the towers,
    And light runs out beyond the long cloud bars,
    And leaves the single stars ;
'Tis time for sleep, sleep, sleep,
    'Tis time for sleep.

The hermit thrush begins again,
    Timorous eremite,

That song of risen tears and pain,
  As if the one he loved was far away ;
  ' Alas ! another day—— '
' And now Good-night, Good-night,' ' Good-night.'

DUNCAN C. SCOTT

EVENSONG

Thrush, sing clear, for the spring is here :
Sing, for the summer is near, is near.

All day long thou hast plied thy song,
Hardly hid from the hurrying throng :

Now the shade of the trees is laid
Down the meadow and up the glade :

Now when the air grows cool and rare
Birds of the cloister fall to prayer :

Here is the bed of the patient dead,
Shoulder by shoulder, head by head.

Sweet bells swing in the tower, and ring
Men to worship before their King.

See they come as the grave bells hum,
Restless voices awhile are dumb :

More and more on the sacred floor
Feet that linger about the door :

Sweet sounds swim through the vaulting dim,
Psalm and canticle, vesper hymn.

That is the way that mortals pray :
Which is the sweeter ? Brown bird, say !

Which were best for me ? Both are blest ;
Sing thy sweetest and leave the rest.

A. C. BENSON

CHIMES

Brief, on a flying night,
   From the shaken tower,
A flock of bells take flight,
   And go with the hour.

Like birds from the cote to the gales,
   Abrupt—O hark !
A fleet of bells set sails,
   And go to the dark.

Sudden the cold airs swing
   Alone, aloud,
A verse of bells takes wing
   And flies with the cloud.

ALICE MEYNELL

IN ROMNEY MARSH

As I went down to Dymchurch Wall,
   I heard the South sing o'er the land ;
I saw the yellow sunlight fall
   On knolls where Norman churches stand.

And ringing shrilly, taut and lithe,
  Within the wind a core of sound,
The wire from Romney town to Hythe
  Alone its airy journey wound.

A veil of purple vapour flowed
  And trailed its fringe along the Straits ;
The upper air like sapphire glow'd ;
  And roses fill'd Heaven's central gates.

Masts in the offing wagg'd their tops ;
  The swinging waves peal'd on the shore
The saffron beach, all diamond drops
  And beads of surge, prolong'd the roar.

As I came up from Dymchurch Wall,
  I saw above the Down's low crest
The crimson brands of sunset fall,
  Flicker and fade from out the west.

Night sank : like flakes of silver fire
  The stars in one great shower came down ;
Shrill blew the wind ; and shrill the wire
  Rang out from Hythe to Romney town.

The darkly shining salt sea drops
  Streamed as the waves clashed on the shore ;
The beach, with all its organ stops
  Pealing again, prolong'd the roar.

JOHN DAVIDSON

THE CITY

Full of Zeus the cities : full of Zeus the harbours : full of Zeus are all the ways of men

What domination of what darkness dies this hour,
And through what new, rejoicing, winged, ethereal power
O'erthrown, the cells opened, the heart released from fear
Gay twilight and grave twilight pass. The stars appear
O'er the prodigious, smouldering, dusky, city flare.
The hanging gardens of Babylon were not more fair
Than these blue flickering glades, where childhood in its glee
Re-echoes with fresh voice the heaven-lit ecstasy.
Yon girl whirls like an eastern dervish. Her dance is
No less a god-intoxicated dance than his,
Though all unknowing the arcane fire that lights her feet,
What motions of what starry tribes her limbs repeat.
I, too, firesmitten, cannot linger : I know there lies
Open somewhere this hour a gate to Paradise,
Its blazing battlements with watchers thronged, O where ?
I know not, but my flame-winged feet shall lead me there.
O, hurry, hurry, unknown shepherd of desires,
And with thy flock of bright imperishable fires
Pen me within the starry fold, ere the night falls
And I am left alone below immutable walls.
Or am I there already, and is it Paradise
To look on mortal things with an immortal's eyes ?
Above the misty brilliance the streets assume
A night-dilated blue magnificence of gloom
Like many-templed Nineveh tower beyond tower ;

And I am hurried on in this immortal hour.
Mine eyes beget new majesties : my spirit greets
The trams, the high-built glittering galleons of the streets
That float through twilight rivers from galaxies of light.
Nay, in the Fount of Days they rise, they take their flight,
And wend to the great deep, the Holy Sepulchre.
Those dark misshapen folk to be made lovely there
Hurry with me, not all ignoble as we seem,
Lured by some inexpressible and gorgeous dream.
The earth melts in my blood. The air that I inhale
Is like enchanted wine poured from the Holy Grail.
What was that glimmer then ? Was it the flash of wings
As through the blinded mart rode on the King of Kings ?
O stay, departing glory, stay with us but a day,
And burning seraphim shall leap from out our clay,
And plumed and crested hosts shall shine where men
      have been,
Heaven hold no lordlier court than earth at College Green.
Ah, no, the wizardry is over ; the magic flame
That might have melted all in beauty fades as it came.
The stars are far and faint and strange. The night draws
      down.
Exiled from light, forlorn, I walk in Dublin Town
Yet had I might to lift the veil, the will to dare,
The fiery rushing chariots of the Lord are there,
The whirlwind path, the blazing gates, the trumpets
      blown,
The halls of heaven, the majesty of throne by throne,
Enraptured faces, hands uplifted, welcome sung
By the thronged gods, tall, golden-coloured, joyful,
      young.

GEORGE RUSSELL (" A.E. ")

NOD

Softly along the road of evening,
  In a twilight dim with rose,
Wrinkled with age, and drenched with dew,
  Old Nod, the shepherd, goes.

His drowsy flock streams on before him,
  Their fleeces charged with gold,
To where the sun's last beam leans low
  On Nod the shepherd's fold.

The hedge is quick and green with briar,
  From their sand the conies creep ;
And all the birds that fly in heaven
  Flock singing home to sleep.

His lambs outnumber a noon's roses,
  Yet, when night's shadows fall,
His blind old sheep-dog, Slumber-soon,
  Misses not one of all.

His are the quiet steeps of dreamland,
  The waters of no-more-pain,
His ram's bell rings 'neath an arch of stars,
  " Rest, rest, and rest again."

WALTER DE LA MARR

FAREWELL

Look thy last on all things lovely,
  Every hour. Let no night
Seal thy sense in deathly slumber
    Till to delight

Thou have paid thy utmost blessing ;
Since that all things thou wouldst praise
Beauty took from those who loved them
    In other days.

WALTER DE LA MARE

THE COUNTRY BEDROOM

My room's a square and candle-lighted boat,
In the surrounding depths of night afloat,
My windows are the portholes, and the seas
The sound of rain on the dark apple-trees.

Sea monster-like beneath, an old horse blows
A snort of darkness from his sleeping nose,
Below among drowned daisies. Far off, hark !
Far off one owl amidst the waves of dark.

FRANCES CORNFORD

IN THE COOL OF THE EVENING

I thought I heard Him calling. Did you hear
A sound, a little sound ? My curious ear
Is dinned with flying noises, and the tree
Goes—whisper, whisper, whisper silently
Till all its whispers spread into the sound
Of a dull roar. Lie closer to the ground,
The shade is deep and He may pass us by,
We are so very small, and His great eye,
Customed to starry majesties, may gaze
Too wide to spy us hiding in the maze :

Ah, misery ! the sun has not yet gone
And we are naked : He may look upon
Our crouching shame, may make us stand upright
Burning in terror—O that it were night !
He may not come.... What ? listen, listen, now—
He is here ! lie closer. . . . *Adam, where art thou ?*

JAMES STEPHENS

EVENING SCENTS

No evening scents, I think, have the fascination of the delicate fragrance of the evening primroses, especially that of the commonest variety. Those pale moons irradiate the twilight with their sweet elusive perfumes. Like the flowers themselves their scent as night draws in becomes full of mystery and holds our imagination captive. And the scent of limes, what an exquisite scent this is—as exquisite as the music of the trees. To me the loveliest music in the world is the music of the evening breeze in the lime trees on a July evening. Each one of us, I suppose, dreams their own dreams and reads their own thoughts in the wondrously varied music of trees. Just as with the music of bells. 'He that hears bells will make them sound what he list ; as the soul thinketh, so the bell clinketh.' The sound of the wind amongst beeches is a glorious sound, deep, rich and full. It is magnificent, but it is a song of this earth. The music of limes is a far-away melody reaching to the stars, a music which sweeps our thoughts to those stupendous flowers set by Almighty God in the gardens of space.

ELEANOUR SINCLAIR ROHDE (from
The Scented Garden)

FOREFATHERS

Here they went with smock and crook,
   Toiled in the sun, lolled in the shade,
Here they mudded out the brook
   And here their hatchet cleared the glade.
Harvest-supper woke their wit,
Huntsman's moon their wooings lit.

From this church they led their brides,
   From this church themselves were led
Shoulder-high ; on these waysides
   Sat to take their beer and bread.
Names are gone—what men they were
These their cottages declare.

Names are vanished, save the few
   In the old brown Bible scrawled ;
These were men of pith and thew,
   Whom the city never called ;
Scarce could read or hold a quill,
Built the barn, the forge, the mill.

On the green they watched their sons
   Playing till too dark to see,
As their fathers watched them once,
   As my father once watched me ;
While the bat and beetle flew
On the warm air webbed with dew.

Unrecorded, unrenowned,
   Men from whom my ways begin,
Here I know you by your ground

But I know you not within—
All is mist, and there survives
Not a moment of your lives.

Like the bee that now is blown
 Honey-heavy on my hand,
From the toppling tansy-throne
 In the green tempestuous land,—
I'm in clover now, nor know
Who made honey long ago.

EDMUND BLUNDEN

AT DUSK

Left to the stars the sky,
 Left to the sea the sand,
Softly the small waves drop
 Hand on white hand :
Where murmuring hills are steep
Countless musicians keep
 Tryst, among wild, dim valleys
Lost in sleep.

Their music binds a world
 Of alien fields unknown,
Stirs among cloud-hung peaks
 Lovely and lone.
Far and remote they seem,
Playing their endless theme—
 Thin threads of sound come trembling back,
Dream upon dream.

ENID, COUNTESS OF KINNOULL

THE PRINCE OF SLEEP

I met at eve the Prince of Sleep,
His was a still and lovely face ;
He wandered through a valley steep,
  Lovely in a lonely place.

His garb was grey of lavender,
About his brows a poppy-wreath
Burned like dim coals, and everywhere
  The air was sweeter for his breath.

His twilight feet no sandals wore,
His eyes shone faint in their own flame,
Fair moths that gloomed his steps before
  Seemed letters of his lovely name.

His house is in the mountain ways,
A phantom house of misty walls,
Whose golden flocks at evening graze,
  And witch the moon with muffled calls.

Upwelling from his shadowy springs
Sweet waters shake a trembling sound,
There flit the hoot-owl's silent wings,
  There hath his web the silkworm wound.

Dark in his pools clear visions lurk,
And rosy, as with morning buds,
Along his dales of broom and birk
  Dreams haunt his solitary woods.

I met at eve the Prince of Sleep,
His was a still and lovely face ;
He wandered through a valley steep,
  Lovely in a lonely place.

WALTER RAMAL

THE VALLEY OF BELLS

Monotonous ringing, far away, a solitary bell.
Where? For whom? By whom? There's nobody here
    to tell.
Noon, silent summer noon. The flowers
Droop in the heat. Cloudless, blue, blue sky.
Haze on the convent spire. White, heat haze.
Not a stir on the leaves, not a fluttering butterfly.

Heavy, breathless noon. Even the cows
Sleepy-eyed, cease their tinkling tune
And drowse in the shade of the trees.
All things drowse in the lonely Siesta noon.

Twelve! Listen. Awake, awake peals
The angelus bell. No stir, no answer here.
Pray, pray, an echo rings from the church
Far below. They're pealing and ringing far and near.

Awake, awake. Have you heard, oh idle one?
Why do you dream, lying all day, supine?
Up, up and pray. With your lips to the earth,
Oh, beware, beware, you're drinking the Lotus wine.

Bells, bells, I hear you long ago,
In a far away home, hushing the shrill street cries
In the fetid, smoky air of a northern town;
Pealing and mingling with all its labouring noise.

I'm still in the valley here. They've ceased. But no.
The little convent bell! 'tis late, 'tis late.
Hurry, sister, hurry; the hour is past.
Ring out, little bell. The noon will never wait.

Silence again. Drowsy summer day.
No stir, no answer here. The sun will creep
Soon enough to the western sky. And the bees, hush !
They hum and drone. " Sleep, stranger, sleep."

And still monotonous, far away, a solitary bell.
Why is it ringing now ? There's nobody here to tell.

IRENE HAUGH

SOLITUDE

This is a lonely place,
And old in dreams ; the woods
Fold in their wide embrace
Unravished solitudes.

Here, while still evening falls
And the grey light grows less,
Peace builds the shadowy walls
Of ancient quietness.

Her hands uprear the gloom,
And evermore round me
The vast unshuttered room
Of night grows silently.

She has such mighty guests
To furnish for and keep,
For here old Saturn rests,
And Time comes home to sleep.

R. G. T. COVENTRY

MADONNA OF THE EVENING FLOWERS

All day long I have been working,
Now I am tired.
I call : " Where are you ? "
But there is only the oak tree rustling in the wind.
The house is very quiet,
The sun shines in on your books,
On your scissors and thimble just put down.
But you are not there.
Suddenly I am lonely :
Where are You ?
I go about searching.
Then I see you,
Standing under a spire of pale blue larkspur,
With a basket of roses on your arm.
You are cool, like silver,
And you smile.
I think the Canterbury bells are playing little tunes,
You tell me that the peonies need spraying,
That the columbines have overrun all bounds,
That the pyrus japonica should be cut back and rounded
You tell me these things.
But I look at you, heart of silver,
White heart-flame of polished silver,
Burning beneath the blue steeples of the larkspur,
And I long to kneel instantly at your feet,
While all about us peal the loud, sweet, Te Deums of the
Canterbury bells.

AMY LOWELL

LIGHTS OUT

I have come to the borders of sleep,
The unfathomable deep
Forest where all must lose
Their way, however straight,
Or winding, soon or late ;
They cannot choose

Many a road and track
That, since the dawn's first crack,
Up to the forest brink,
Deceived the travellers
Suddenly now blurs,
And in they sink.

Here love ends,
Despair, ambition ends,
All pleasure and all trouble,
Although most sweet or bitter,
Here ends in sleep that is sweeter
Than tasks most noble.

There is not any book
Or face of dearest look
That I would not turn from now
To go into the unknown
I must enter and leave alone
I know not how.

The tall forest towers;
Its cloudy foliage lowers
Ahead, shelf above shelf;
Its silence I hear and obey
That I may lose my way
And myself.

EDWARD THOMAS

THE MIDLANDS

Black in the summer night my Cotswold hill
  Aslant my window sleeps, beneath a sky
Deep as the bedded violets that fill
  March woods with dusky passion. As I lie
Abed between cool walls I watch the host
  Of the slow stars lit over Gloucester plain,
And drowsily the habit of these most
  Beloved English lands moves in my brain,
While silence holds dominion of the dark,
Save when the foxes from the spinneys bark.

I see the valleys in their morning mist
  Wreathed under limpid hills in moving light,
Happy with many a yeoman melodist;
  I see the little roads of twinkling white
Busy with fieldward teams and market gear
  Of rosy men, cloth-gaitered, who can tell
The many-minded changes of the year,
  Who know why crops and kine fare ill or well;
I see the sun persuade the mist away,
Till town and stead are shining to the day.

I see the wagons move along the rows
 Of ripe and summer-breathing clover-flower,
I see the lissom husbandman who knows
 Deep in his heart the beauty of his power,
As lithely pitched, the full-heaped fork bids on
 The harvest home. I hear the rickyard fill
With gossip as in generations gone,
 While wagon follows wagon from the hill.
I think how, when our seasons all are sealed,
Shall come the unchanging harvest from the field.

I see the barns and comely manors planned
 By men who somehow moved in comely thought,
Who, with a simple shippon to their hand,
 As men upon some godlike business wrought;
I see the little cottages that keep
 Their beauty still where since Plantagenet
Have come the shepherds happily to sleep,
 Finding the loaves and cups of cider set;
I see the twisted shepherds, brown and old,
Driving at dusk their glimmering sheep to fold.

And now the valleys that upon the sun
 Broke from their opal veils, are veil'd again,
And the last light upon the wolds is done,
 And silence falls on flock and fields and men;
And black upon the night I watch my hill,
 And the stars shine, and there an owly wing
Brushes the night, and all again is still,
 And, from this land of worship that I sing,
I turn to sleep, content that from my sires
I draw the blood of England's midmost shires.

                          JOHN DRINKWATER

SWALLOW SONG

O little hearts, beat home, beat home!
   Here is no place to rest;
Night darkens on the falling foam
   And on the fading west.
O little wings, beat home, beat home!
Love may no longer roam.

Oh, Love has touched the fields of wheat,
   And Love has crowned the corn,
And we must follow Love's white feet
   Through all the ways of morn:
Through all the silver roads of air
We pass and have no care.

The silver roads of Love are wide,
O winds that turn, O stars that guide!
Sweet are the ways that Love hath trod
Through the clear skies that reach to God,
But in the cliff-grass Love builds deep
A place where wandering wings may sleep.

MARJORIE PICKTHALL

IN LAMPLIGHT

Now that the chill October day is declining
Pull the blinds, draw each voluminous curtain,
Till the room is full of gloom and of the uncertain
Gleams of firelight on polished edges shining.

Then bring the rosy lamp to its wonted station
On the dark-gleaming table. In that soft splendour
Well-known things of the room, grown deep and tender,
Gather round, a mysterious congregation :
Pallid sheen of the silver, the bright brass fender,
The wine-red pool of carpet, the bowl of roses,
Lustrous-hearted, crimsons and purples looming
From dusky rugs and cushions. Nothing discloses
The unseen walls, but the broken, richly-glooming
Gold of frames and opulent wells of mingling
Dim colours gathered in darkened mirrors. And breaking
The dream-like spell, and your deep chair forsaking
You go, perhaps, to the shelves and, slowly singling
Some old rich-blazoned book, return. But the gleaming
Spells close round you again and you fall to dreaming,
Eyes grown dim, the book on your lap unheeded.

MARTIN ARMSTRONG

FIRST PART
§ II THE EVENING POST

The post is the consolation of life.

VOLTAIRE

Blessed is he who is made happy by the sound of a rat-tat !

THACKERAY

The chief interest of a study of the great letter-writers is that it introduces us, not to literary works, but to persons. This is the triumph of letter-writing, that it keeps a more delicate image alive and presents us with a subtler likeness of the writer than we can find in the more formal achievements of authorship.

SIR WALTER RALEIGH (1861-1922)

§ II THE EVENING POST

LETTERS FROM CICERO

1. *To his friend Atticus* (*in Epirus*) B.C. 60.

Believe me there is nothing at this moment of which I stand so much in need as a man with whom to share all that causes me anxiety ; a man to love me ; a man of sense to whom I can speak without affectation, reserve, or concealment. For my brother is away—that most open-hearted and affectionate of men. Metellus is not a human being, but

"Mere sound and air, a howling wilderness."

While you, who have so often lightened my anxiety and my anguish of soul by your conversation and advice, who are ever my ally in public affairs, my confidant in all private business, the sharer in all my conversations and projects—where are you ? So entirely am I abandoned by all, that the only moments of repose left me are those which are spent with my wife, pet daughter and sweet little Cicero. For as to those friendships with the great, and their artificial attractions, they have indeed a certain glitter in the outside world, but they bring no private satisfaction. And so, after a crowded morning *levée*, as I go down to the forum surrounded by troops of friends, I can find no one out of all that crowd with whom to jest freely, or into whose ear I can breathe a familiar sigh. Therefore I wait for you, I long for you, I even urge on you to come ; for I have many anxieties, many pressing cares, of which I think, if I once had your ears to listen to me, I could un-burden myself in the conversation of a single walk. And of my private anxieties, indeed, I shall conceal all the stings and vexations, and not trust them to this letter and an unknown letter-carrier. These, however—for I don't want you to be made too anxious—are not very painful : yet they are persistent and worrying, and are not put to rest by the advice or conversation of any friend. But in regard to the Republic I have still the same courage and purpose, though it has again and again of its own act eluded treatment. For should I put briefly what has occurred since you left, you would certainly exclaim that the Roman empire cannot be maintained much longer. . . . You now understand in what stormy water we are : and as from what I have written to you in such strong terms you have a view also of what I have not written. Come back to me, for it is time you did. And though the state of affairs to which I invite you is one to be avoided, yet let your value for me so far prevail, as to induce you to come there even in these vexatious circumstances. For the rest I will take care that due warning is given, and a notice put up in all places, to prevent you being entered on the census as absent ; and to get put on the census just before the lustration is the mark of your true man of business. So let me see you at the earliest possible moment. Farewell.

20 January, in the Consulship of Q. Metellus and L. Afranius. (*Written from Rome.*)

2. *To his brother Quintus* (*in Britain*) B.C. 54.

When you receive a letter from me by the hand of an amanuensis, you may be sure that I have not even a little leisure ; when by my own a little. For let me tell you that in regard to causes and trials in court, I have never been closer tied, and that, too, at the most unhealthy season of the year, and in the most oppressively hot weather. . . . How glad I was to get your letter from Britain! I was afraid of the ocean, afraid of the coast of the island. The other parts of the enterprise I do not under-rate; but yet they inspire more hope than fear, and it is the suspense rather than any positive alarm that renders me uneasy. You, however, I can see, have a splendid subject for description, topography, natural features of things and places, manners, races, battles, your commander himself—what themes for your pen! I will gladly, as you request, assist you in the points you mention, and will send you the verses you ask for. But, look you! I think you are keeping me in the dark. Tell me, my dear brother, what Caesar thinks of my verses. For he wrote before to tell me he had read my first book. Of the first part, he said that he had never read anything better even in Greek: the rest, up to a particular passage, somewhat " careless "—that is his word. Tell me the truth is it the subject-matter or the " style " that he does not like? You needn't be afraid: I shall not admire myself one whit the less. On this subject speak like a lover of truth, and with your usual brotherly frankness. (*Written from Rome.*)

LETTERS OF CICERO
(Trans. E. S. SHUCKBURGH)

PLINY TO TACITUS

(*Describing the Eruption of Vesuvius*, 79 A.D.)

Your request that I would send you an account of my uncle's end, so that you may transmit a more exact relation of it to posterity, deserves my acknowledgments; for if his death shall be celebrated by your pen, the glory of it,

I am aware, will be rendered for ever deathless. For notwithstanding he perished, as did whole peoples and cities, in the destruction of a most beautiful region, and by a misfortune memorable enough to promise him a kind of immortality ; notwithstanding he has himself composed many and lasting works ; yet I am persuaded, the mentioning of him in your immortal writings, will greatly contribute to eternize his name. . . . The more willingly do I undertake, nay, solicit, the task you set me.

He was at that time with the fleet under his command at Misenum. On the 24th of August, about one in the afternoon, my mother desired him to observe a cloud of very unusual size and appearance. He had sunned himself, then taken a cold bath, and after a leisurely luncheon was engaged in study. He immediately called for his shoes and went up an eminence from whence he might best view this very uncommon appearance. It was not at that distance discernible from what mountain this cloud issued, but it was found afterwards to be Vesuvius . . .

My uncle, true savant that he was, deemed the phenomenon important and worth a nearer view. He ordered a light vessel to be got ready, and gave me the liberty, if I thought proper, to attend him. I replied I would rather study ; and, as it happened, he had himself given me a theme for composition. As he was coming out of the house he received a note from Rectina, the wife of Bassus, who was in the utmost alarm at the imminent danger (his villa stood just below us, and there was no way to escape but by sea) ; she earnestly entreated him to save her from such deadly peril. He changed his first design and what he began with a philosophical, he pursued with an heroical turn of mind. He ordered large galleys to be launched, and went himself on board one, with the intention of assisting not only Rectina, but many others ; for the villas stand extremely thick upon that beautiful coast. Hastening to the place from whence others were flying, he steered his direct course to the point of danger, and with such freedom from fear, as to be able to make and dictate his observations upon the successive motions and figures of that terrific object.

And now cinders, which grew thicker and hotter the nearer he approached, fell into the ships, then pumice-stones too, with stones blackened, scorched, and cracked by fire, then the sea ebbed suddenly from under them, while the shore was blocked up by landslips from the mountains. . . .

In the meanwhile Mount Vesuvius was blazing in several places with spreading and towering flames, whose refulgent brightness the darkness of the night set in high relief. But my uncle, in order to soothe apprehensions, kept saying that some fires had been left alight by the terrified country people, and what they saw were only deserted villas on fire in the abandoned district. After this he retired to rest . . . On being aroused, he came out, and returned to Pomponianus and the others, who had sat up all night. They consulted together as to whether they should hold out in the house, or wander about in the open. For the house now tottered under repeated and violent concussions, and seemed to rock to and fro as if torn from its foundations. In the open air, on the other hand, they dreaded the falling pumice-stones, light and porous though they were ; yet this, by comparison, seemed the lesser danger of the two ; a conclusion which my uncle arrived at by balancing reasons and the others by balancing fears. They tied pillows upon their heads with napkins ; and this was their whole defence against the showers that fell round them.

It was now day everywhere else, but there a deeper darkness prevailed than in the most obscure night; relieved, however, by many torches and divers illuminations. They thought proper to go down upon the shore to observe from close at hand if they could possibly put out to sea, but they found the waves still run extremely high and contrary. There my uncle having thrown himself down upon a disused sail, repeatedly called for, and drank, a draught of cold water; soon after, flames, and a strong smell of sulphur, which was the forerunner of them dispersed the rest of the company in flight; him they only aroused. He raised himself up with the assistance of two of his slaves, but instantly fell; some unusually gross vapour, as I conjecture, having obstructed his breathing and blocked his windpipe, which was not only naturally weak and constricted, but chronically inflamed. When day dawned again (the third from that he last beheld) his body was found entire and uninjured, and still fully clothed as in life; its posture was that of a sleeping, rather than a dead man.

Meanwhile my mother and I were at Misenum. But this has no connection with history, and your inquiry went no farther than concerning my uncle's death. I will therefore put an end to my letter. Suffer me only to add, that I have faithfully related to you what I was either an eye-witness of myself, or heard at the time, when report speaks most truly. You will select what is most suitable to your purpose; for there is a great difference between a letter, and an history; between writing to a friend, and writing for the public. Farewell.

PLINY THE YOUNGER (*Letters VI*. 16. Trans. W. MELMOTH and W. M. L. HUTCHINSON—Loeb Classical Library)

EGYPTIAN CORRESPONDENCE

Letter from Corbolon to Heraclides (Second Century)

Corbolon to Heraclides, greeting. I send you the key by Horion and the piece of the lock by Onnophris, the camel-driver of Apollonius. I enclosed in the former packet a pattern of white-violet colour. I beg you to be good enough to match it and buy me two drachmas' weight, and send it to me at once by any messenger you can find, for the tunic is to be woven immediately. I received everything you told me to expect by Onnophris safely. I send you by the same Onnophris six quarts of good apples. I thank all the gods to think that I came upon Plution in the Oxyrhynchite nome. Do not think that I took no trouble about the key. The reason is that the smith is a long way from us. I wonder that you did not see your way to let me have what I asked you to send by Corbolon, especially when I wanted it for a festival. I beg you to buy me a silver seal and to send it me with all speed. Take care that Onnophris buys me what Irene's mother told me. I told him that Syntrophus said that nothing more should be given to Amarantus on my account. Let me know what you have given him that I may settle accounts with him. Otherwise I and my son will come for this purpose. I had the large cheeses from Corbolon. I did not however want large ones, but small. Let me know of anything that you want and I will gladly do it. Farewell. Payni the 1st.
—Send me an obol's worth of cake for my nephew.

A Boy's Letter (Second Century)

Theon to his father Theon, greeting. It was a fine thing of you not to take me with you to the city ! If you won't take me with you to Alexandria I won't write you a letter or speak to you or say good-bye to you ; and if you go to Alexandria I won't take your hand nor ever greet you again. That is what will happen if you won't take me. Mother said to Archelaus, " It quite upsets him to be left behind." It was good of you to send me presents . . . on the 12th, the day you sailed. Send me a lyre, I implore you. If you don't, I won't eat, I won't drink ; there now !

To a Wife-Sister (*Second Century*)

Serenus to his beloved sister Isidora, many greetings. Before all else I pray for your health, and every day and evening I perform the act of veneration on your behalf to Thöeris who loves you. I assure you that ever since you left me I have been in mourning, weeping by night and lamenting by day. Since we bathed together on Phaophi 12, I never bathed nor anointed myself until Athur 12. You sent me letters which would have shaken a stone, so much did your words move me. Instantly I answered you and gave the letter sealed to the messenger on the 12th, together with letters for you. . . . See how many times I have sent to you ! Whether you are coming or not, let me know.

Cornelius to Hierax (*Second Century*)

Cornelius to his sweetest son, Hierax, greeting. All our household warmly salutes you and all those with you. Regarding the man about whom you write to me so often, claim nothing until I come to you auspiciously in company with Vestinus and the donkeys. For if the gods will I shall arrive quickly after Mecheir is over, since at present I have urgent affairs on hand. Take care not to offend any of the persons at home, and give your undivided attention to your books, devoting yourself to learning, and then they will bring you profit. Receive by Onnophris the white robes which are to be worn with the purple cloaks, the others you should wear with the myrtle-coloured ones. I shall send you by Anoubas both the money and the monthly supplies and the other pair of scarlet cloaks. You won me over by the dainties, and I will send you the price of these two by Anoubas ; until however Anoubas arrives, you must pay for the provisions of yourself and your household out of your own money, until I send you some. For the month of Tubi there is for yourself what you like, for Phronimus 16 drachmae, for Abascantus and his companions and Myron 9 drachmae, for Secundas 12 drachmae. Send Phronimus to Asclepiades in my name, and let him obtain from him an answer to the letter which I wrote to him, and send it. Let me know what you want. Good-bye, my son.

Invitation to a Festival (*Third Century*)

Greeting, my dear Serenia, from Petosiris. Be sure, dear, to come up on the 20th for the birthday festival of the god, and let me know whether you are coming by boat or by donkey, in order that we may send for you accordingly. Take care not to forget. I pray for your continued health.

OXYRHYNCHUS PAPYRI
(Trans. GRENFELL AND HUNT)

FROM THE EMPEROR JULIAN TO EVAGRIUS, THE RHETORICIAN

(Making him the present of a small estate. Written from Constantinople in the year 362 A.D.)

A small estate of four fields, in Bithynia, was given to me by my grandmother, and this I give as an offering to your affection for me. It is too small to bring a man any great benefit on the score of wealth or to make him appear opulent, but even so it is a gift that cannot wholly fail to please you, as you will see if I describe its features to you one by one. And there is no reason why I should not write in a light vein to you who are so full of the graces and amenities of culture. It is situated not more than twenty stades from the sea, so that no trader or sailor with his chatter and insolence disturbs the place. Yet it is not wholly deprived of the favours of Nereus, for it has a constant supply of fish, fresh and still gasping ; and if you walk up on to a sort of hill away from the house, you will see the sea, the Propontis and the islands, and the city that bears the name of the noble Emperor [Constantinople] ; nor will you have to stand meanwhile on seaweed and brambles, or be annoyed by the filth that is always thrown out on to seabeaches and sands, which is so very unpleasant and even unmentionable ; but you will stand on smilax and thyme and fragrant herbage. Very peaceful it is to lie down there and glance into some book, and then, while resting one's eyes, it is very agreeable to gaze at the ships and the sea. When I was still hardly more than a boy I thought that this was the most delightful summer place, for it has, moreover, excellent springs and a charming bath and garden and

72

trees. When I had grown to manhood I used to long for my old manner of life there and visited it often, and our meetings there did not lack talks about literature. Moreover there is there, as a humble monument of my husbandry, a small vineyard that produces a fragrant, sweet wine, which does not have to wait for time to improve its flavour. You will have a vision of Dionysus and the Graces. The grapes on the vine, and when they are being crushed in the press, smell of roses, and the new made wine in the jars is a " rill of nectar," if one may trust Homer. Then why is not such a vine as this abundant and growing over very many acres ? Perhaps I was not a very industrious gardener. But since my mixing bowl of Dionysus is inclined to soberness, and calls for a large proportion of the nymphs [i.e., of water], I only provided enough for myself and my friends—and they are very few. Well then, I now give this to you as a present, dear heart, and though it be small, as indeed it is, yet it is precious as coming from a friend to a friend, " from home, homeward bound," in the words of the wise poet Pindar. I have written this letter in haste, by lamplight, so that, if I have made any mistakes, do not criticise them severely or as one rhetorician would another.

(From *The Works of the Emperor Julian*. Trans. W. C. WRIGHT—Loeb Classical Library)

SAINT AUGUSTINE TO NEBRIDIUS

I read your letter by lamplight after supper. I had gone to bed, but not (as it happened) to sleep; so I meditated, lying on my bed. These were my inmost thoughts—Augustine talking to Augustine, so to speak—Is it really true, I asked myself, as Nebridius says, that we are happy ? No, indeed ; for he himself would not be so bold as to deny that we are foolish ; and, though fools are not beyond the reach of blessing, we know that we can suffer no greater misfortune than the lack of wisdom—perhaps, indeed, no other misfortune.

Letters (Trans. A. S.)

A 15TH-CENTURY LOVE AFFAIR

(*From the Young Lady's Mother to the Young Gentleman*)

To my worshipful Cousin JOHN PASTON, Be this Bill delivered, &c.

Cousin, I recommend me unto you, Thanking you heartily for the great cheer ye made me, and all my Folks, the last time that I was at Norwich ; and ye promised me, that ye would never break the matter to Margery unto such time, as ye and I were at a point. But ye have made her such an Advocate for you, that I may never have rest night nor day, for calling and crying upon to bring the said matter to effect, &c.

And Cousin, upon Friday is Saint Valentine's day, and every Bird chuseth him a Mate ; and if it like you to come on Thursday at night, and so purvey you, that ye may abide there till Monday, I trust to God, that ye shall so speak to mine husband ; and I shall pray, that we shall bring the matter to a conclusion, &c.

For, Cousin, " it is but a simple Oak,
    " That cuts down at the first stroke."

for ye will be reasonable I trust to God, which have you ever in his merciful keeping, &c.

By your Cousin DAME ELIZABETH BREWS otherwise shall be called by God's Grace. 14th February, 1477.

(*From the Young Lady to the Young Gentleman*)

Unto my right well beloved Valentine, JOHN PASTON, Esquire, be this Bill delivered, &c.

Right reverend and worshipful, and my right well beloved Valentine, I recommend me unto you, full heartily desiring to hear of your welfare, which I beseech Almighty God long for to preserve unto his pleasure, and your heart's desire.

And if it please you to hear of my welfare, I am not in good health of body, nor of heart, nor shall be till I hear from you ; for there knows no creature, what pain that I endure, and for to be dead I dare it not discover.

And my Lady my Mother hath laboured the matter to my father full diligently, but she can no more get than ye know of, for the which God knoweth I am full sorry. But if that ye love me, as I trust verily that ye do, ye will not leave me therefore.

And if ye command me to keep me true wherever
    I go,
I wis I will do all my might you to love, and never
    no mo.

And if my Friends say, that I do amiss,
    They shall not me let so for to do,
Mine heart me bids evermore to love you,
    Truly over all earthly thing,
And if they be never so wrath,
    I trust it shall be better in time coming.

No more to you at this time, but the Holy Trinity have you in keeping ; and I beseech you that this bill be not seen of none earthly Creature save only yourself, &c.

75

And this Letter was endited at Topcroft, with full heavy heart, &c.

By your own,

MARGERY BREWS.

TOPCROFT.

To my Right Well beloved Cousin JOHN PASTON, Esquire, be this Letter delivered, &c.

Right worshipful and well beloved Valentine, in my most humble wise, I recommend me unto you, &c. And heartily I thank you for the letter, which that ye send me by John Beckerton, whereby I understand and know, that ye be purposed to come to Topcroft in short time, and without any errand or matter, but only to have a conclusion of the matter betwixt my father and you, I would be most glad of any Creature alive, so that the matter might grow to effect. And whereas ye say, and if ye come and find the matter no more towards you than ye did aforetime, ye would no more put my father and my Lady my Mother to no cost nor business, for that cause a good while after, which causeth my heart to be full heavy ; and if that ye come, and the matter take to none effect, then should I be much more sorry, and full of heaviness.

And as for myself I have done, and understand in the matter that I can or may, as God knoweth ; and I let you plainly understand, that my father will no more money part withal in that behalf, but an hundred pounds and fifty marks which is right far from the accomplishment of your desire.

Wherefore, if that ye could be content with that Good, and my poor Person, I would be the merriest maiden on ground ; and if ye think nor yourself so satisfied, or that ye might have much more Good, as I have understood

76

by you afore ; good, true, and loving Valentine, that ye take no such labour upon you, as to come more for that matter. But let what is, pass, and never more to be spoken of, as I may be your true Lover and Beadwoman during my life.

No more unto you at this time, but Almighty Jesu preserve you both body and soul, &c.

By your Valentine,
MARGERY BREWS.

TOPCROFT.

(*From the Young Gentleman*)

To my right worshipful Mother MARGARET PASTON.

Right worshipful Mother, after all duties of recommendation, in as humble wise as I can, I beseech you of your daily blessing. Mother, please it you to weet, that the cause that Dame Elizabeth Brews desireth to meet with you at Norwich, and not at Langley, as I appointed with you at my last being at Mawtby, is by my means, for my brother Thomas Jermyn, which knoweth nought of the match, telleth me, that the Causey ere ye can come to Bokenham Ferry is so overflown that there is no man that may scarcely pass it, though he be right well horsed ; which is no meet way for you to pass over, God forbid it. But all things reckoned, it shall be less cost to you to be at Norwich, as for a day or tweyn and pass not, than to meet at Langley, where everything is dear ; and your horse may be sent home again the same Wednesday.

Mother, I beseech you for divers causes, that my Sister Anne may come with you to Norwich ; Mother, the matter is in a reasonable good way, and I trust with God's mercy, and with your good help, that it shall take effect better to mine advantage than I told you of at Norwich ; for I believe there is not a kinder woman living than I shall have to my Mother in law, if the matter take, nor yet a kinder Father in law than I shall have, though he be hard to me as yet.

All the circumstances of the matter, which I trust to tell you at your coming to Norwich, could not be written in three leaves of paper, and ye know my poor head well enough, I may not write long, wherefore I ferry over all things till I may await on you myself. I shall do tun into your place a dozen Ale, and Bread according, against Wednesday. If Sym might be spared it were well done, that he were at Norwich on Wednesday in the morning at market. Dame Elizabeth Brews shall lie at John Cook's ; if it might please you, I would be glad that she might dine in your house on Thursday, for there should you have most secret talking.

And Mother, at the reverence of God, beware that ye be so purveyed for, that ye take no cold by the way towards Norwich, for it is the most perilous March, that ever was seen by any man's days now living ; and I pray to Jesu to preserve you and yours.

Written at Topcroft, the 8th day of March.

Your Son and humble Servant,

JOHN PASTON.

TOPCROFT.

Saturday, 8th of March, 1477.

(From *The Paston Letters*)

FROM THE DUCHESS OF MILAN (BEATRICE D'ESTE) TO THE DUCHESS OF MANTUA (ISABELLA D'ESTE)

Villa Nova, Val di Ticino,

18th March, 1491.

I am now here at Villa Nova, where the loveliness of the country and the balmy sweetness of the air make me think we are already in the month of May, so warm and splendid is the weather we are enjoying ! Every day we go out riding with the dogs and falcons, and my husband and I never come home without having enjoyed ourselves exceedingly in hunting herons and other water-fowl. I cannot say much of the perils of the chase, since game is so plentiful here that hares are to be seen jumping out at every corner—so much so, that often we hardly know which way to turn to find the best sport. Indeed, the eye cannot take in all one desires to see, and it is scarcely possible to count up the number of animals that are to be found in this neighbour-hood. Nor must I forget to tell you how every day Messer Galeazzo and I, with one or two other courtiers, amuse ourselves playing at ball after dinner, and we often talk of your Highness, and wish that you were here. I say all this, not to diminish the pleasure that I hope you will have when you do come by telling you what you may expect to find here, but in order that you may know how well and happy I am, and how kind and affectionate my husband is, since I cannot thoroughly enjoy any pleasure or happiness unless I share it with you. And I must tell you that I have had a whole field of garlic planted for your benefit, so that when you come, we may be able to have plenty of your favourite dishes !

(Trans. JULIA CARTWRIGHT)

A KING'S LOVE LETTERS

(Written by Henry VIII to Anne Boleyn in the year 1528 when the King was seeking a Papal pronouncement annulling his marriage with Katharine of Aragon)

My mistress and friend, my heart and I surrender ourselves into your hands, beseeching you to hold us commended to your favour, and that by absence your affection to us may not be lessened : for it would be a great pity to increase our pain, of which absence produces enough and more than I could ever have thought could be felt, reminding us of a point in astronomy which is this : the longer the days are, the more distant is the sun, and nevertheless the hotter ; so is it with our love, for by absence we are kept a distance from one another, and yet it retains its fervour, at least on my side ; I hope the like on yours, assuring you that on my part the pain of absence is already too great for me ; and when I think of the increase of that which I am forced to suffer, it would be almost intolerable, but for the firm hope I have of your unchangeable affection for me : and to remind you of this sometimes, and seeing that I cannot be personally present with you, I now send you the nearest thing I can to that, namely, my picture set in bracelets, with the whole of the device, which you already know, wishing myself in their place, if it should please you. This is from the hand of your loyal servant and friend,

H. R.

On turning over in my mind the contents of your last letters, I have put myself into great agony, not knowing how to interpret them, whether to my disadvantage, as I understand them in some others, beseeching you earnestly to let me know expressly your whole mind as to the love between us two. It is absolutely necessary for me to obtain this answer, having been for above a whole year stricken with the dart of love, and not yet sure whether I shall fail or find a place in your heart and affection, which last point has prevented me for some time past from calling you my mistress ; because, if you only love me with an ordinary love, that name is not suitable for you, because it denotes a singular love, which is far from common. But if you please to do the office of a true loyal mistress and friend, and to give up yourself body and heart to me, who will be, and have been, your most loyal servant, (if your rigour does not forbid me) I promise you that not only shall the name be given you, but also that I will take you for my only mistress, casting off all others besides you out of my thoughts and affections and serve you only. I beseech you to give an entire answer to this my rude letter, that I may know on what and how far I may depend. And if it does not please you to answer me in writing, appoint some place where I may have it by word of mouth, and I will go thither with all my heart.

No more, for fear of tiring you.

Written by the hand of him who will willingly remain yours,

H. R.

The reasonable request of your last letter, with the pleasure also that I take to know them true, causeth me to send you these news. The legate whom we most desired, arrived at Paris on Sunday or Monday last past, so that I trust by the next Monday to hear of his arrival at Calais ; and then I trust within a while after to enjoy that which I have so long longed for, to God's pleasure, and both our comforts.

No more to you at this present, mine own darling, for lack of time, but that I would you were in mine arms, or I in yours, for I think it long since I kissed you.

Written after the killing of a hart, at eleven of the clock, minding, with God's grace, to-morrow, mighty timely, to kill an other, by the hand, which, I trust, shortly shall be yours.

HENRY R.

FROM SAINT TERESA TO DON FRANCISCO DE SALCEDO, AVILA

Valladolid, Sept. 1568.

Glory be to God, after having written seven or eight unavoidable business letters, a short time remains for me to refresh myself by sending you these few lines telling you what a comfort yours were to me. Do not fancy you are wasting time by writing to me, for I need it occasionally, provided that you do not repeat so often that you are growing old, which cuts me to the heart. As if the lives of young men were guaranteed! Please God, you will live until I die and then I shall ask Him to summon you promptly lest I should be without you in heaven . . .

The 6 ducats you say you would give to see me seem a very dear bargain, but I would pay far more to see you—in fact, you are worth much more, for who sets any value on a poor, insignificant little nun who lives in poverty? *You*, who can give *aloja*,[1] rolls, radishes, and lettuces

_____
[1] A favourite drink in Spain at the time. A. S.

82

from your own garden (and I know that you are the "errand boy" who brings us apples) would naturally fetch a higher price. The *aloja* here is said to be very good, but for want of Francisco de Salcedo we do not know what it tastes like and probably never shall.

I have told Antonia to write to you as I have no time for more. Abide with God !

Your unworthy and sincere servant,

TERESA DE JESUS, *Carmelite*.

A BAD START

(Letter written on board a ship of the Spanish Armada to the Venetian Ambassador in Madrid)

On the 14th of this month, while the Armada was off Cape Finisterre, despatches were sent to his Majesty, and with them I wrote to your Lordship a particular account of our voyage down to that date. After that, partly to meet the galleys which were ordered to wait us in Mugia, a port four leagues distant from the Cape ; partly to take on board some provisions and supplies which the Governor of that Kingdom (Galicia), the Marquis of Seralvo, was to prepare for us, we drew in as far as the island of Cesarga. There, on the 17th, we were joined by the galleys which his Excellency had sent to Corunna for provisions and water, as both were running short ; and to land some sick, who are now in considerable numbers, especially after the storm of the 19th and 20th which the Armada encountered. The flagship, thirty-five others, and almost all the transports and carvels, came into Corunna, before the storm reached its height. The rest of the fleet, partly owing to its falling away to lee, and being unable to make the port, and partly to the dark night which settled down, remained out-side. The night was a tempestuous one, with wind, rain, and a heavy sea. The following day, Monday, the ship of Don Alonzo de Leyva and the flagship of Don Oquendo put into the port of Baris, one much damaged, the other having carried away mainmast, sails, and yards. On Tuesday twelve others arrived at Biucco, among them the *Labbia* uninjured. On Wednesday the Admiral Recalde sailed into Corunna with other twelve ships and two galleys, among them the *Regazzona* uninjured ; yesterday other three. So that up to this hour thirty ships and two galleasses are missing. The storm was one of those great winter storms. It has greatly discouraged the fleet, and above all the commander.

We shall be obliged to wait here till we have news of the missing ships. Some scouts have been sent out this evening to look for them.

Corugna, 24th June 1588.

CALENDAR OF STATE PAPERS
(*Venetian Series, VIII,* 681)

LETTERS FROM DEAN SWIFT

1. *A Letter to " Varina " (Miss Jane Waring)*

April 29, 1696.

MADAM,

Impatience is the most inseparable quality of a lover, and indeed of every person who is in pursuit of a design whereon he conceives his greatest happiness or misery to depend. It is the same thing in war, in courts, and in common business. Everyone who hunts after pleasure, or fame, or fortune, is still restless and uneasy till he has hunted down his game; and all this is not only very natural, but something reasonable too, for a violent desire is little better than a distemper, and therefore men are not to blame in looking after a cure. I find myself hugely infected with this malady, and am easily vain enough to believe it has some very good reasons to excuse it. For indeed, in my case, there are some circumstances which will admit pardon for more than ordinary disquiets. That dearest object upon which all my prospect of happiness entirely depends, is in perpetual danger to be removed for ever from my sight. Varina's life is daily wasting, and though one just and honourable action could furnish health to her, and unspeakable happiness to us both, yet some power that repines at human felicity has that influence to hold her continually doating upon her cruelty, and me upon the cause of it. This fully convinces me of what we are told, that the miseries of man's life are all beaten out on his own anvil. Why was I so foolish to put my hopes and fears into the power or management of another? Liberty is doubtless the most valuable blessing of life; yet we are fond to fling it away on those who have been these five thousand years using us ill. Philosophy advises to keep our desires and prospects of happiness as much as we can in our own breasts, and independent of anything without. He that sends them abroad is likely to have as little quiet as a merchant whose stock depends upon winds, and waves, and pirates, or upon the words and faith of creditors, every whit as dangerous and inconstant as the other . . . Would to God you had treated and scorned me from the beginning. It was your pity

opened the first way to my misfortune ; and now your love
is finishing my ruin. In one fortnight I must take eternal
farewell of Varina, and (I wonder) will she weep at parting,
a little to justify her poor pretences of some affection to
me ? And will my friends still continue reproaching me
for the want of gallantry, and neglecting a close siege ?
How comes it that they all wish us married together, they
knowing my circumstances and yours extremely well, and
I am sure love you too much, if it be only for my sake,
to wish you anything that might cross your interest or
your happiness ?

Surely, Varina, you have but a very mean opinion of the
joys that accompany a true, honourable, unlimited love ;
yet either nature and our ancestors have highly deceived
us, or else all other sublunary things are dross in comparison. Is it possible you can be yet insensible to the prospect
of a rapture and delight so innocent and exalted ? Trust
me, Varina, Heaven has given us nothing else worth the
loss of a thought. Ambition, high appearances, friends,
and fortune, are all tasteless and insipid when they come
in competition ; yet millions of such glorious minutes
are we perpetually losing, for ever losing, irrecoverably
losing, to gratify empty forms and wrong notions, and
affected coldnesses and peevish humour. These are the
unhappy encumbrances which we who are distinguished
from the vulgar do fondly create to torment ourselves.
The only felicity permitted to human life we clog with
tedious circumstances and barbarous formality. By Heaven,
Varina, you are more experienced, and have less virgin
innocence than I. Would not your conduct make one
think you were highly skilled in all the little politic
methods of intrigue ? Love, with the gall of too much
discretion, is a thousand times worse than with none at

all. It is a peculiar part of nature which art debauches, but cannot improve. We have all of us the seeds of it implanted in ourselves, and they require no helps from courts or fortune to cultivate and improve them. To resist the violence of our inclinations in the beginning, is a train of self-denial that may have some pretences to set up for a virtue ; but when they are grounded at first upon reason, when they have taken firm root and grown up to a height, it is folly—folly as well as injustice, to withstand their dictates ; for this passion has a property peculiar to itself, to be most commendable in its extremes, and it is as possible to err in the excess of piety as of love.

These are the rules I have long followed with you, Varina ; and had you pleased to imitate them, we should both have been infinitely happy. The little disguises, and affected contradictions of your sex were all (to say the truth) infinitely beneath persons of your pride and mine ; paltry maxims that they are, calculated for the rabble of humanity. O Varina, how imagination leads me beyond myself and all my sorrows ! It is sunk, and a thousand graves lie open ! No, Madam, I will give you no more of my unhappy temper, though I derive it all from you.

Farewell, Madam, and may love make you a while forget your temper to do me justice. Only remember that, if you still refuse to be mine, you will quickly lose him that has resolved to die as he has lived—all yours

JON. SWIFT.

2. *News for Stella.*

Do you know that about our town we are mowing already and making hay, and it smells so sweet as we walk through the flowery meads ; but the hay-making nymphs are perfect drabs, nothing so clean and pretty as farther in the country. There is a mighty increase of dirty wenches in straw hats since I knew London. I staid at home till five o'clock, and dined with Dean Atterbury : then went by water to Mr. Harley's, where the Saturday club was met, with the addition of the Duke of Shrewsbury. I whispered Lord Rivers, that I did not like to see a stranger among us : and the rogue told it aloud : but Mr. Secretary said, the Duke writ to have leave : so I appeared satisfied, and so we laughed. Mr. Secretary told me the Duke of Buckingham had been talking to him much about me, and desired my acquaintance. I answered, it could not be : for he had not made sufficient advances. Then the Duke of Shrewsbury said, he thought that Duke was not used to make advances. I said I could not help that ; for I always expected advances in proportion to men's quality, and more from a Duke than other men. The Duke replied, that he did not mean anything of his quality ; which was handsomely said enough ; for he meant his pride : and I have invented a notion to believe that nobody is proud. At ten all the company went away ; and from ten till twelve Mr. Harley and I sat together, where we talked through a great deal of matters I had a mind to settle with him, and then walked, in a fine moonshine night, to Chelsea, where I got by one. Lord Rivers conjured me not to walk so late ; but I would, because I had no other way : but I had no money to lose. . .

Morning. I sat up late last night, and waked late to-day ; but will now answer your letter in bed before I go to town, and I will send it to-morrow ; for perhaps you mayn't go so soon to Wexford.—No, you are not out in your number ; the last was Number 14, and so I told you twice or thrice ; will you never be satisfied ? What shall we do for poor Stella ? Go to Wexford, for God's sake : I wish you were to walk there by three miles a-day, with a good lodging at every mile's end. Walking has done me so much good, that I cannot but prescribe it often to poor Stella. . . . O faith, I should be glad to be in the same kingdom with M D., however, although you were at Wexford. But I am kept here by a most capricious fate, which I would break through, if I could do it with decency or honour.—To return without some mark of distinction, would look extremely little : and I would likewise gladly be somewhat richer than I am. I will say no more, but beg you to be easy, till Fortune take her course, and to believe that M D's felicity is the great end I aim at in my pursuits. And so let us talk no more on this subject, which makes me melancholy, and that I would fain divert. Believe me, no man breathing at present has less share of happiness in life than I : I do not say I am unhappy at all, but that everything here is tasteless to me for want of being as I would be. And so a short sigh, and no more of this.

(From *Journal to Stella*)

THOMAS GRAY TO HIS MOTHER

Lyons, Oct. 13, 1739

It is now almost five weeks since I left Dijon, one of the gayest and most agreeable little cities of France, for Lyons its reverse in all these particulars. It is the second in the kingdom in bigness and rank, the streets excessively narrow and nasty ; the houses immensely high and large ; (that, for instance, where we are lodged, has twenty-five rooms on a floor, and that for five stories) it swarms with inhabitants like Paris itself, but chiefly a mercantile people, too much given up to commerce to think of their own, much less of a stranger's diversions. We have no acquaintance in the town, but such English as happen to be passing through here, in their way to Italy and the South, which at present happen to be near thirty in number. It is a fortnight since we set out from hence upon a little excursion to Geneva. We took the longest road, which lies through Savoy, on purpose to see a famous monastery, called the grand Chartreuse, and had no reason to think our time lost. After having travelled seven days very slow (for we did not change horses, it being impossible for a chaise to go post in these roads) we arrived at a little village, among the mountains of Savoy, called Echelles ; from thence we proceeded on horses, who are used to the way, to the mountain of the Chartreuse : It is six miles to the top ; the road runs winding up it, commonly not six feet broad ; on one hand is the rock, with woods of pine trees hanging over head ; on the other, a monstrous precipice, almost perpendicular, at the bottom of which rolls a torrent, that sometimes tumbling among the fragments of stone that have fallen from on high, and sometimes precipitating itself down vast descents with a noise like thunder, which is still made greater by the echo from the mountains on each side, concurs to form one of the most solemn, the most romantic, and the most astonishing scenes I ever beheld : Add to this the strange views made by the craggs and cliffs on the other hand ; the cascades that in many places throw themselves from the very summit down into the vale, and the river below ; and many other particulars impossible to describe ; you will conclude we had no occasion to repent our pains. This place St. Bruno chose to retire to, and upon its very top founded the aforesaid Convent, which is the superior of the whole order. When we came there, the two fathers, who are commissioned to entertain strangers, (for the rest must neither speak one to another, nor to any one else) received us very kindly ; and set before us a repast of dried fish, eggs, butter, and fruits, all excellent in their kind, and extremely neat. They pressed us to spend the night there, and to stay some days with them ; but this we could not do, so they led us about their house, which is, you must think, like a little city ; for there are 100 fathers, besides 300 servants, that make their clothes, grind their corn, press their wine, and do every thing among themselves : The whole is quite orderly and simple ; nothing of finery, but the wonderful decency, and the strange situation, more than supply the place of it. In the evening we descended by the same way, passing through many clouds that were then forming themselves on the mountain's side. Next day we continued our journey by Chamberry, which, though the chief city of the Dutchy, and residence of the king of Sardinia, when he comes into this part of his dominions, makes but a very mean and insignificant appearance ; we lay at Aix, once famous for its hot baths, and the next night at

Anneçy ; the day after, by noon, we got to Geneva. I have not time to say any thing about it, nor of our solitary journey back again.

Turin, Nov. 7, 1739

I am this night arrived here, and have just set down to rest me after eight days tiresome journey : For the three first we have had the same road we before past through to go to Geneva ; the fourth we turned out of it, and for that day and the next travelled rather among than upon the Alps ; the way commonly running through a deep valley by the side of the river Arc, which works itself a passage, with great difficulty and a mighty noise, among vast quantities of rocks, that have rolled down from the mountain tops. The winter was so far advanced, as in great measure to spoil the beauty of the prospect ; however, there was still somewhat fine remaining amidst the savageness and horrour of the place : The sixth we began to go up several of these mountains ; and as we were passing one, met with an odd accident enough : Mr. Walpole had a little fat black spaniel, that he was very fond of, which he sometimes used to set down, and let it run by the chaise side. We were at that time in a very rough road, not two yards broad at most ; on one side was a great wood of pines, and on the other a vast precipice ; it was noon-day, and the sun shone bright, when all of a sudden, from the wood-side, (which was as steep upwards, as the other part was downwards) out rushed a great wolf, came close to the head of the horses, seized the dog by the throat, and rushed up the hill again with him in his mouth. This was done in less than a quarter of a minute ; we all saw it, and yet the servants had not time to draw their pistols, or do any thing to save the dog. If he had not been there, and the creature had thought fit to lay hold of one of the horses, chaise, and we, and all must inevitably have tumbled above fifty fathoms perpendicular down the precipice. The seventh we came to Lanebourg, the last town in Savoy; it lies at the foot of the famous mount Cenis, which is so situated as to allow no room for anyway but over the very top of it. Here the chaise was forced to be pulled to pieces, and the baggage and that to be carried by mules: We ourselves were wrapped up in our furs, and ·seated upon a sort of matted chair, without legs, which is carried upon poles in the manner of a bier and so began to ascend by the help of eight men. It was six miles to the top, where a plain opens itself about as many more in breadth, covered perpetually with very deep snow, and in the midst of that a great lake of unfathomable depth, from whence a river takes its rise, and tumbles over monstrous rocks quite down the other side of the mountain. The descent is six miles more, but infinitely more steep than the going up; and here the men perfectly fly down with you, stepping from stone to stone with incredible swiftness, in places where none but they could go three paces without falling. The immensity of the precipices, the roaring of the river and torrents that run into it, the huge craggs covered with ice and snow, and the clouds below you and about you, are objects it is impossible to conceive without seeing them; and though we had heard many strange descriptions of the scene, none of them at all came up to it. We were but five hours in performing the whole, from which you may judge of the rapidity of the men's motion. We are now got into Piedmont, and stopped a little while at La Ferriere, a small village about three quarters of the way down, but still among the clouds, where we began to hear a new language spoken round about us; at last we got quite down, went through the Pás de Suse, a narrow road among the Alps, defended by two fortresses, and lay at Bossolens : Next evening thro' a fine avenue of nine miles in length, as straight as a line, we arrived at this city.

WILLIAM COWPER TO LADY HESKETH

Olney, Feb. 9, 1786.

My Dear Cousin,

I have been impatient to tell you that I am impatient to see you again . . . And now, my dear, let me tell you once more, that your kindness in promising us a visit has charmed us both—I shall see you again—I shall hear your voice, we shall take walks together ; I will shew you my prospects, the hovel, the alcove, the Ouse, and its banks, every thing that I have described. I anticipate the pleasure of those days not very far distant, and feel a part of it at this moment. Talk not of an inn ! Mention it not for your life ! We have never had so many visitors but we could easily accommodate them all ; though we have received Unwin, and his wife, and his sister, and his son, all at once. My dear, I will not let you come till the end of May, or beginning of June, because before that time my green-house will not be ready to receive us, and it is the only pleasant room belonging to us. When the plants go out, we go in. I line it with mats, and spread the floor with mats ; and there you shall sit with a bed of mignonette at your side, and a hedge of honeysuckles, roses, and jasmine ; and I will make you a bouquet of myrtle every day. Sooner than the time I mention the country will not be in complete beauty. And I will tell you what you shall find at your first entrance. *Imprimis*, as soon as you have entered the vestibule, if you cast a look on either side of you, you shall see on the right hand a box of my making. It is the box in which have been lodged all my Hares, and in which lodges Puss at present. But he, poor fellow, is worn out with age, and promises to die before you can see him. On the right hand, stands a cupboard, the work of the same Author. It was once a dove-cage, but I transformed it. Opposite to you stands a table, which I also made. But a merciless servant having scrubbed it until it became paralytic, it serves no purpose now but of ornament ; and all my clean shoes stand under it. On the left hand, at the farther end of this superb vestibule, you will find the door of the parlour, into which I will conduct you, and where I will introduce you to Mrs. Unwin, unless we should meet her before, and where we will be as happy as the day is long. Order yourself, my Cousin, to the Swan at Newport, and there you shall find me ready to conduct you to Olney . . .

Adieu ! my dearest, dearest Cousin.

The Lodge, Nov. 10, 1787

I have a kitten, my dearest Cousin, the drollest of all creatures that ever wore a cat's skin. Her gambols are not to be described, and would be incredible, if they could. In point of size she is likely to be a kitten always, being extremely small of her age, but time I suppose, that spoils every thing, will make her also a cat. You will see her I hope before that melancholy period shall arrive, for no wisdom that she may gain by experience and reflection hereafter, will compensate the loss of her present hilarity. She is dressed in a tortoise-shell suit, and I know that you will delight in her.

Mrs. Throckmorton carries us to-morrow in her chaise

to Chicheley. The event however must be supposed to depend on elements, at least on the state of the atmosphere, which is turbulent beyond measure. Yesterday it thundered, last night it lightened, and at three this morning I saw the sky as red as a city in flames could have made it. I have a leech in a bottle that foretells all these prodigies and convulsions of nature. No, not as you will naturally conjecture by articulate utterance of oracular notices, but by a variety of gesticulations, which here I have not room to give an account of. Suffice it to say, that no change of weather surprises him, and that in point of the earliest and most accurate intelligence, he is worth all the barometers in the world. None of them all indeed can make the least pretence to foretell thunder—a species of capacity of which he has given the most unequivocal evidence. I gave but sixpence for him, which is a groat more than the market price, though he is in fact, or rather would be, if leeches were not found in every ditch, an invaluable acquisition.

The Lodge, June 27, 1788

For the sake of a longer visit, my dearest Coz, I can be well content to wait. The country, this country at least, is pleasant at all times, and when winter is come, or near at hand, we shall have the better chance for being snug. I know your passion for retirement indeed, or for what we call *deedy* retirement, and the Frogs[1] intending to return to Bath with their mother, when her visit at the Hall is over, you will then find here exactly the retirement in question. I have made in the orchard the best winter-walk in all the parish, sheltered from the east, and from the north-east, and open to the sun, except at his rising, all the day. Then we will have Homer and Don Quixote:

[1] Cowper's friends the Throckmortons. A. S.

96

and then we will have saunter and chat and one laugh more before we die. Our orchard is alive with creatures of all kinds ; poultry of every denomination swarms in it, and pigs, the drollest in the world ! . . .

I must tell you a feat of my dog Beau. Walking by the river-side, I observed some water-lilies floating at a little distance from the bank. They are a large white flower, with an orange coloured eye, very beautiful. I had a desire to gather one, and, having your long cane in my hand, by the help of it endeavoured to bring one of them within my reach. But the attempt proved vain, and I walked forward. Beau had all the while observed me very attentively. Returning soon after toward the same place, I observed him plunge into the river, while I was about forty yards distant from him ; and, when I had nearly reached the spot, he swam to land with a lily in his mouth, which he came and laid at my foot.

Mr. Rose, whom I have mentioned to you as a visitor of mine for the first time soon after you left us, writes me word that he has seen my ballads against the slave-mongers, but not in print. . . . There is but one of them with which I am myself satisfied, though I have heard them all well spoken of. But there are very few things of my own composition, that I can endure to read, when they have been written a month, though at first they seem to me to be all perfection.

Mrs. Unwin, who has been much the happier since the time of your return hither has been in some sort settled, begs me to make her kindest remembrance. Yours, my dear, most truly.

WILLIAM BLAKE TO THOMAS BUTTS

[Postmark Sept. 23, 1800]

DEAR FRIEND OF MY ANGELS,

We are safe arrived at our cottage without accident or
hindrance, tho' it was between eleven and twelve o'clock
at night before we could get home, owing to the necessary
shifting of our boxes and portfolios from one chaise to
another. We had seven different chaises and as many
different drivers. All upon the road was chearfulness and
welcome ; tho' our luggage was very heavy there was no
grumbling at all. We travel'd thro' a most beautiful
country on a most glorious day. Our cottage is more
beautiful than I thought it, and also more convenient, for
tho' small it is well proportion'd, and if I should ever build
a Palace it would be only my cottage enlarged. Please to tell
Mrs. Butts that we have dedicated a chamber for her
service, and that it has a very fine view of the sea. Mr.
Hayley receiv'd me with his usual brotherly affection.
My wife and sister are both very well, and courting Neptune for an embrace, whose terrors this morning made
them afraid, but whose mildness is often equal to his
terrors. The villagers of Felpham are not meer rustics ;
they are polite and modest. Meat is cheaper than in
London, but the sweet air and the voices of winds, trees
and birds, and the odours of the happy ground, makes it a
dwelling for immortals. Work will go on here with God
speed.—A roller and two harrows lie before my window.
I met a plow on my first going out at my gate the first
morning after my arrival, and the Plowboy said to the
Plowman, " Father, the gate is open." I have begun to
work, and find that I can work with greater pleasure than

ever. Hope soon to give you a proof that Felpham is propitious to the Arts.

God bless you ! I shall wish for you on Tuesday evening as usual. Pray give my and my wife and sister's love and respects to Mrs. Butts ; accept them yourself, and believe me, for ever,

Your affectionate and obliged friend,

WILLIAM BLAKE.

Felpham,

Jany. 10, 1802

DEAR SIR,

Your very kind and affectionate letter and the many kind things you have said in it, call'd upon me for an immediate answer ; but it found my wife and myself so ill, and my wife so very ill, that till now I have not been able to do this duty. . . .

But you have so generously and openly desired that I will divide my griefs with you, that I cannot hide what it is now become my duty to explain.—My unhappiness has arisen from a source which, if explor'd too narrowly, might hurt my pecuniary circumstances, as my dependence is on engraving at present, and particularly on the engravings I have in hand for Mr. H. : and I find on all hands great objections to my doing anything but the meer drudgery of business, and intimations that if I do not confine myself to this, I shall not live ; this has always pursu'd me. You will understand by this the source of all my uneasiness. . . . I am not ashamed, afraid, or averse to tell you what ought to be told : that I am under the direction of messengers from Heaven, daily and nightly ; but the nature of such things is not, as some suppose, without trouble or care. Temptations are on the right hand and left ; behind, the sea of time and space roars and follows swiftly ; he who keeps not right onward is lost, and if our footsteps slide in clay, how can we do otherwise than fear and tremble ? but I should not have troubled you with this account of my spiritual state, unless it had been necessary in explaining the actual cause of my uneasiness, into which you are so kind as to enquire ; for I never obtrude such things on others unless question'd, and then I never disguise the truth.—But if we fear to do the dictates of our angels, and tremble at the tasks set before us ; if we refuse to do spiritual acts because of natural fears or natural desires ! Who can describe the dismal torments of such a state !—I too well remember the threats I heard !—" If you, who are organised by Divine Providence for spiritual communion, refuse, and bury your talent in the earth, even tho' you should want natural bread, sorrow and desperation pursues you thro' life, and after death shame and confusion of face to eternity. Every one in eternity will leave you, aghast at the man who was crown'd with glory and honour by his brethren, and betray'd their cause to their enemies. You will be call'd the base Judas who betray'd his friend ! "— Such words would make any stout man tremble, and how then could I be at ease ? But I am now no longer in that state, and now go on again with my task, fearless, and tho' my path is difficult, I have no fear of stumbling while I keep it. . . . Naked we came here, naked of natural things, and naked we shall return ; but while cloth'd with the Divine mercy, we are richly cloth'd in spiritual and suffer all the rest gladly. Pray give my love to Mrs. Butts and your family.

I am, Yours sincerely,
WILLIAM BLAKE.

100

A LETTER FROM CHARLES LAMB

TO JOHN BATES DIBDIN

(A city clerk who had gone to Hastings for his health)

Friday, some day in June, 1826

DEAR D.—My first impulse upon opening your letter was pleasure at seeing your old neat hand, nine parts gentlemanly, with a modest dash of the clerical : my second thought, natural enough this hot weather, am I to answer all this ? why 'tis as long as those to the Ephesians and Galatians put together—I have counted the words for curiosity. But then Paul has nothing like the fun which is ebullient all over yours. I don't remember a good thing (good like yours) from the 1st Romans to the last of the Hebrews. I remember but one Pun in all the Evangely, and that was made by his and our master : Thou art Peter (that is Doctor Rock) and upon this rock will I build &c. ; which sanctifies Punning with me against all gain-sayers. I never knew an enemy to puns who was not an ill-natured man. Your fair critic in the coach reminds me of a Scotchman who assured me that he did not see much in Shakespeare. I replied, I dare say *not*. He felt the equivoke, looked awkward and reddish, but soon returned to the attack, by saying that he thought Burns was as good as Shakespeare : I said that I had no doubt he was—to a *Scotchman*. We exchanged no more words that day.— Your account of the fierce faces in the Hanging, with the presumed interlocution of the Eagle and the Tyger, amused us greatly. You cannot be so very bad, while you can pick mirth off from rotten walls. But let me hear you have escaped out of your oven. May the form of the fourth person who clapt invisible wet blankets about the shoulders of Shadrach, Meschach and Abednego, be with you in the fiery trial. But get out of the frying-pan. Your business, I take it, is bathing, not baking.

Let me hear that you have clamber'd up to Lover's Seat; it is as fine in that neighbourhood as Juan Fernandez, as lonely too, when the fishing boats are not out; I have sat for hours, staring upon a shipless sea. The salt sea is never so grand as when it is left to itself. One cock-boat spoils it. A sea-mew or two improves it. And go to the little church, which is a very protestant Loretto, and seems dropt by some angel for the use of a hermit, which was at once parishioner and a whole parish. It is not too big. Go in the night, bring it away in your portmanteau, and I will plant it in my garden. It must have been erected in the very infancy of British Christianity, for the two or three first converts; yet hath it all the appertenances of a church of the first magnitude, its pulpit, its pews, its baptismal font; a cathedral in a nut-shell. Seven people would crowd it like a Caledonian Chapel. The minister that divides the word there, must give lumping pennyworths. It is built to the text of two or three assembled in my name. It reminds me of the grain of mustard seed. If the glebe land is proportionate, it may yield two potatoes. Tythes out of it could be no more split than a hair. Its first fruits must be its last, for 'twould never produce a couple. It is truly the strait and narrow way, and few there be (of London visitants) that find it. The still small voice is surely to be found there if anywhere. A sounding board is merely there for cere-mony. It is secure from earthquakes, not more from sanctity than size, for 'twould feel a mountain thrown upon it no more than a taper-worm would. Go and see, but not without your spectacles. By the way, there's a capital farm house two thirds of the way to the Lover's Seat, with

incomparable plum cake, ginger beer, etc. Mary bids me
warn you not to read the anatomy of Melancholy in your
present *low way*. You'll fancy yourself a pipkin, or a
headless bear, as Burton speaks of. You'll be lost in
a maze of remedies for a labyrinth of diseasements, a
plethora of cures. Read Fletcher; above all the Spanish
Curate, the Thief or Little Night-walker, the Wit without
Money, and the Lover's Pilgrimage. Laugh and come
home fat. Neither do we think Sir T. Browne quite the
thing for you just at present. Fletcher is as light as Soda
water. Browne and Burton are too strong potions for an
invalid. And don't thumb or dirt the books. Take care
of the bindings. Lay a leaf of silver paper under 'em, as
you read them. And don't smoke tobacco over 'em, the
leaves will fall in and burn or dirty their namesakes. If
you find any dusty atoms of the Indian Weed crumbled
up in the Beaumont and Fletcher they are *mine*. But then,
you know, so is the Folio also. A pipe and a comedy of
Fletcher's the last thing of a night is the best recipe
for light dreams and to scatter away nightmares. *Probatum
est*. But do as you like about the former. Only cut the
Baker's. You will come home else all crust; Rankings must
chip you before you can appear in his counting house.
And my dear Peter Fin Junior, do contrive to see the sea
at least once before you return. You'll be ask'd about it in
the Old Jewry. It will appear singular not to have seen
it. And rub up your Muse, the family Muse, and send us
a rhyme or so. Don't waste your wit upon that damn'd
dry Salter. I never knew but one Dry Salter who could
relish those mellow effusions, and he broke. You knew
Tommy Hill, the wettest of dry salters. Dry Salters, what
a word for this thirsty weather! I must drink after it.
Here's to thee, my dear Dibdin, and to our having you

again snug and well at Colebrooke, but our nearest hopes are to hear again from you shortly. An epistle only a quarter as agreeable as your last, would be a treat.

Yours most truly

C. LAMB.

FIRST PART

§ III A BUNCH OF POPPIES

Yet here, this one night, thou may'st rest with me,
Thy bed green branches. Chestnuts soft have I
And mealy apples, and our fill of cheese.
Already, see, the far-off chimneys smoke,
And deeper grow the shadows of the hills.

C. S. CALVERLEY (after VIRGIL, Eclogue I)

Who shall silence all the airs and madrigals that whisper
softness in chambers?

MILTON (*Areopagitica*)

Oh sleep ! it is a gentle thing,
Beloved from pole to pole !
To Mary Queen the praise be given !
She sent the gentle sleep from Heaven,
That slid into my soul.

COLERIDGE (*The Ancient Mariner*)

§ III A BUNCH OF POPPIES

SONG

Let not the sluggish sleep
Close up thy waking eye,
Until with judgment deep
Thy daily deeds thou try :
He that one sin in conscience keeps
When he to quiet goes,
More venturous is than he that sleeps
With twenty mortal foes.

WILLIAM BYRD

THE LOVER ASKS FOR SLEEP

Come, Sleep, O Sleep ! the certain knot of peace,
   The baiting place of wit, the balm of woe,
The poor man's wealth, the prisoner's release,
   Th' indifferent judge between the high and low :
With shield of proof shield me from out the prease
   Of those fierce darts despair at me doth throw :
O make in me those civil wars to cease ;
   I will good tribute pay, if thou do so,
Take thou of me smooth pillows, sweetest bed,
   A chamber deaf to noise and blind to light,
A rosy garland, and a weary head :
   And if these things, as being thine by right,
Move not thy heavy grace, thou shalt in me,
Livelier than elsewhere, Stella's image see.

SIR PHILIP SIDNEY

TO NIGHT

O Night, the ease of care, the pledge of pleasure,
Desire's best mean, harvest of hearts affected,
The seat of peace, the throne which is erected
   Of human life to be the quiet measure ;
   Be victor still of Phoebus' golden treasure,
Who hath our sight with too much sight infected,
Whose light is cause we have our lives neglected,
   Turning all nature's course to self displeasure.
   These stately stars in their now shining faces,
With sinless sleep, and silence wisdom's mother,
   Witness his wrong, which by thy help is eased.
Thou art, therefore, of these our desert places
   The sure refuge ; by thee and by no other
My soul is blest, sense joy'd, and fortune raised.

SIR PHILIP SIDNEY

SLEEP IN SICKNESS

Care-charming Sleep, thou easer of all woes,
Brother to Death, sweetly thyself dispose
On this afflicted prince : fall like a cloud,
In gentle showers : give nothing that is loud
Or painful to his slumbers ; easy, sweet,
And as a purling stream, thou Son of Night,
Pass by his troubled senses ; sing his pain
Like hollow murmuring wind or silver rain,
Into this prince gently, O gently slide
And kiss him into slumber like a bride.

BEAUMONT AND FLETCHER (from *Valentinian*)

THE EVE OF PHILIPPI

(*Scene—Within the Tent of Brutus*)

BRUTUS : The deep of night is crept upon our talk,
And nature must obey necessity ;
Which we will niggard with a little rest.
There is no more to say ?
CASSIUS :   No more, Good night ;
Early to-morrow will we rise, and hence.
BRUTUS : Lucius ! [*Enter* LUCIUS]—My gown.
    [*Exit* LUCIUS.]—Farewell, good Messala :
Good night, Titinius :—Noble, noble Cassius,
Good night, and good repose.
CASSIUS :   O my dear brother !
This was an ill beginning of the night :
Never come such division 'tween our souls !
Let it not, Brutus.
BRUTUS :   Everything is well.
CASSIUS : Good night, my lord.
BRUTUS :   Good night, good brother.
TITINIUS, MESSALA : Good night, Lord Brutus.
BRUTUS :   Farewell, every one.
        [*Exeunt* CASSIUS, TITINIUS, *and* MESSALA.]
        Re-enter LUCIUS, *with the gown.*
Give me the gown. Where is thy instrument ?
LUCIUS : Here in the tent.
BRUTUS.   What, thou speak'st drowsily ?
Poor knave, I blame thee not ; thou art o'er-watch'd.
Call Claudius, and some other of my men ;
I'll have them sleep on cushions in my tent !
LUCIUS : Varro and Claudius !
        Enter VARRO *and* CLAUDIUS.
VARRO : Calls my lord ?

BRUTUS : I pray you, sirs, lie in my tent and sleep ;
It may be, I shall raise you by-and-by
On business to my brother Cassius.

VARRO : So please you, we will stand and watch your
pleasure.

BRUTUS : I will not have it so ; lie down, good sirs ;
It may be, I shall otherwise bethink me.
Look, Lucius, here's the book I sought for so ;
I put it in the pocket of my gown.

[VARRO *and* CLAUDIUS *lie down*.]

LUCIUS : I was sure your lordship did not give it me.

BRUTUS : Bear with me, good boy, I am much forgetful
Canst thou hold up thy heavy eyes awhile,
And touch thy instrument a strain or two ?

LUCIUS : Ay, my lord, an't please you.

BRUTUS :   It does, my boy :
I trouble thee too much, but thou art willing.

LUCIUS : It is my duty, sir.

BRUTUS : I should not urge thy duty past thy might ;
I know young bloods look for a time of rest.

LUCIUS : I have slept, my lord, already.

BRUTUS : It was well done ; and thou shalt sleep again ;
I will not hold thee long : if I do live,
I will be good to thee. [*Music*]
This is a sleepy tune :—O murderous slumber !
Layest thou thy leaden mace upon my boy,
That plays thee music ?—Gentle knave, good night ;
I will not do thee so much wrong to wake thee.
If thou dost nod, thou break'st thy instrument ;
I'll take it from thee ; and, good boy, good night.
Let me see, let me see ;—is not the leaf turn'd down,
Where I left reading ? Here it is, I think.

SHAKESPEARE (from *Julius Cæsar*)

110

FRIENDSHIP'S CONSOLATION

When to the sessions of sweet silent thought
I summon up remembrance of things past,
I sigh the lack of many a thing I sought,
And with old woes new wail my dear time's waste :
Then can I drown an eye, unused to flow,
For precious friends hid in death's dateless night,
And weep afresh love's long since cancelled woe,
And moan the expense of many a vanished sight :
Then can I grieve at grievances foregone,
And heavily from woe to woe tell o'er
The sad account of fore-bemoanèd moan,
Which I new pay as if not paid before.
    But if the while I think on thee, dear friend,
    All losses are restored and sorrows end.

SHAKESPEARE

TO MUSIQUE, TO BECALME HIS FEVER

Charm me asleep, and melt me so
  With thy Delicious Numbers ;
That being ravisht, hence I goe
  Away in easy slumbers.
    Ease my sick head,
    And make my bed,
  Thou power that canst sever
    From me this ill :
    And quickly still :
    Though thou not kill
      My Fever.

Thou sweetly canst convert the same
    From a consuming fire,
Into a gentle-licking flame,
    And make it thus expire.
        Then make me weep
        My paines asleep ;
    And give me such resposes,
        That I, poore I,
        May think, thereby,
        I live and die
          'Mongst Roses.

Fall on me like a silent dew,
    Or like those Maiden show'rs,
Which, by the peepe of day, doe strew
    A Baptime o're the flowers,
        Melt, melt my paines,
        With thy soft straines ;
    That having ease me given,
        With full delight,
        I leave this light ;
        And take my flight
          For Heaven.

ROBERT HERRICK

THE POET ASKS FOR SLEEP

A flock of sheep that leisurely pass by,
One after one ; the sound of rain, and bees
Murmuring ; the fall of rivers, winds, and seas,
Smooth fields, white sheets of water, and pure sky.
I've thought of all by turns ; and yet do lie
Sleepless ; and soon the small bird's melodies

Must hear first utter'd from my orchard trees,
And the first cuckoo's melancholy cry.
Even thus last night, and two nights more, I lay
And could not win thee, Sleep! by any stealth:
So do not let me wear to-night away:
Without Thee what is all the morning's wealth?
Come, blessèd barrier between day and day,
Dear mother of fresh thoughts and joyous health!

WORDSWORTH

ASIA REPLIES TO THE VOICE IN THE AIR

My soul is an enchanted Boat,
Which, like a sleeping swan, doth float
Upon the silver waves of thy sweet singing;
And thine doth like an angel sit
Beside the helm conducting it,
Whilst all the winds with melody are ringing.
It seems to float ever, for ever,
Upon that many-winding river,
Between mountains, woods, abysses,
A Paradise of wildernesses!
Till, like one in slumber bound,
Borne to the ocean, I float down, around,
Into a sea profound, of ever-spreading sound.

SHELLEY (from *Prometheus Unbound*)

TO SLEEP

O soft embalmer of the still midnight,
Shutting with careful fingers and benign
Our gloom-pleased eyes embowered from the light
Enshaded in forgetfulness divine,

O soothest Sleep ! if so it please thee, close
   In midst of this thine hymn my willing eyes,
Or wait the Amen, ere thy poppy throws
   Around my bed its lulling charities.
   Then save me, or the passèd day will shine
Upon my pillow, breeding many woes ;
   Save me from curious conscience, that still hoards
Its strength for darkness, burrowing like a mole ;
   Turn the key deftly in the oilèd wards,
And seal the hushèd casket of my soul.

KEATS

LAST SONNET

Bright star, would I were steadfast as thou art—
   Not in lone splendour hung aloft the night,
And watching, with eternal lids apart,
   Like Nature's patient sleepless Eremite,
The moving waters at their priestlike task
   Of pure ablution round earth's human shores,
Or gazing on the new soft-fallen mask
   Of snow upon the mountains and the moors.—
No—yet still steadfast, still unchangeable,
   Pillowed upon my fair love's ripening breast,
To feel for ever its soft fall and swell,
   Awake for ever in a sweet unrest ;
Still, still to hear her tender-taken breath,
And so live ever—or else swoon to death.

KEATS

A NIGHT SONG

Oh ! do you wake, or do you sleep
  With window to the full-moon'd sky ?
Oh ! have you lost, or do you keep
  A thought of all the day gone by ?
Or are you dead to all you knew
Of life, the while I live to you ?

May air, o'er wallside roses brought,
  Of charming gardens give you dreams ;
May rustling leaves beguile your thought
  With dreams of walks by falling streams.
And on your lids be light that yields
Bright dream-clouds over daisied fields.

Our meeting hour of yesterday
  To me, now deep in waning night,
Seems all a glory pass'd away
  Beyond a year—time's longsome flight.
Though night seems far too short to weigh
Your words and deeds of yesterday.

While rise or sink the glittering stars
  Above dim woods, or hillock brows,
There, out within the moonpaled bars,
  In darksome bunches sleep your cows.
So sweetly sleep, asleep be they
Until you meet the opening day.

WILLIAM BARNES

NIGHT THOUGHTS

The crackling embers on the hearth are dead ;
  The indoor note of industry is still ;
  The latch is fast ; upon the window-sill
The small birds wait not for their daily bread;
The voiceless flowers—how quietly they shed
  Their nightly odours ; and the household rill
  Murmurs continuous dulcet sounds that fill
The vacant expectation, and the dread
Of listening night. And haply now She sleeps,
  For all the garrulous noises of the air
Are hushed in peace ; the soft dew silent weeps,
  Like hopeless lovers for a maid so fair :—
Oh ! that I were the happy dream that creeps
  To her soft heart, to find my image there.

HARTLEY COLERIDGE

A SUMMING UP

I have lived and I have loved ;
I have waked and I have slept ;
I have sung and I have danced ;
I have smiled and I have wept ;
I have won and wasted treasure ;
I have had my fill of pleasure ;
And all these things were weariness,
And some of them were dreariness.
And all these things, but two things,
Were emptiness and pain :
And Love—it was the best of them ;
And Sleep—worth all the rest of them.

CHARLES MACKAY

SLEEPLESS DREAMS

Girt in dark growths, yet glimmering with one star,
  O night, desirous as the nights of youth !
  Why should my heart within thy spell, forsooth,
Now beat, as the bride's finger-pulses are
Quickened within the girdling golden bar ?
  What wings are these that fan my pillow smooth ?
  And why does Sleep, waved back by Joy and Ruth,
Tread softly round and gaze at me from far ?

Nay, night deep-leaved ! And would Love feign in thee
  Some shadowy palpitating grove that bears
  Rest for man's eyes and music for his ears ?
O lonely night ! art thou not known to me,
A thicket hung with masks of mockery
  And watered with the wasteful warmth of tears ?

D. G. ROSSETTI

INVITATION TO SLEEP

Come, blessed sleep, most full, most perfect, come :
  Come, sleep, if so I may forget the whole ;
  Forget my body and forget my soul,
Forget how long life is and troublesome.
Come, happy sleep, to soothe my heart or numb,
  Arrest my weary spirit or control :
  Till light be dark to me from pole to pole,
And winds and echoes and low songs be dumb
Come, sleep, and lap me into perfect calm,
  Lap me from all the world and weariness :

Come, secret sleep, with thine unuttered psalm,
   Safe sheltering in a hidden cool recess :
Come, heavy dreamless sleep, and close and press
Upon mine eyes thy fingers dropping balm.

CHRISTINA ROSSETTI

LOVE IN DREAMS

Love hath his poppy-wreath,
   Not Night alone.
I laid my head beneath
   Love's lilied throne :
Then to my sleep he brought
   This anodyne—
The flower of many a thought
   And fancy fine :
A form, a face, no more ;
   Fairer than truth ;
A dream from death's pale shore ;
   The soul of youth :
A dream so dear, so deep,
   All dreams above,
That still I pray to sleep—
   Bring Love back, Love !

J. A. SYMONDS

TO SLEEP

O Sleep, O tranquil son of noiseless Night,
   Of humid, shadowy Night ; O dear repose
   For wearied men, forgetfulness of woes
Grievous enough the bloom of life to blight !

Succour this heart that hath outworn delight,
   And knows no rest ; these tirèd limbs compose ;
   Fly to me, Sleep ; thy dusky vans disclose
   Over my languid eyes, then cease thy flight.
Where, where is Silence, that avoids the day ?
   Where the light dreams, that with a wavering tread
   And unsubstantial footing follow thee ?
Alas ! in vain I call thee ; and these grey,
   These frigid shades flatter in vain. O bed,
   How rough with thorns ! O nights, how harsh to me !

                    J. A SYMONDS (from the Italian)

TO THE GENIUS OF ETERNAL SLUMBER

Sleep, thou art named eternal ! Is there then
   No chance of waking in thy noiseless realm ?
   Come there no fretful dreams to overwhelm
The feverish spirits of o'erlaboured men ?
Shall conscience sleep where thou art ; and shall pain
   Lie folded with tired arms around her head ;
   And memory be stretched upon a bed
Of ease, whence she shall never rise again ?
O Sleep, that art eternal ! Say, shall Love
   Breathe like an infant slumbering at thy breast ?
      Shall hope there cease to throb ; and shall the smart
   Of things impossible at length find rest ?
   Thou answerest not. The poppy-heads above
      Thy calm brows sleep. How cold, how still thou art !

                              J. A. SYMONDS

AT NIGHT

Home, home from the horizon far and clear,
    Hither the soft wings sweep ;
Flocks of the memories of the day draw near
    The dovecote doors of sleep.

O, which are they that come through sweetest light
    Of all these homing birds ?
Which with the straightest and the swiftest flight ?
    Your words to me, your words !

ALICE MEYNELL

A PRAYER TO THE BOY-GOD

What sin was mine, sweet, silent boy-god, Sleep,
Or what, poor sufferer, have I left undone,
That I should lack thy guerdon, I alone ?
Quiet are the brawling streams : the shuddering deep
Sinks, and the rounded mountains feign to sleep.
The high seas slumber pillowed on Earth's breast ;
All flocks and birds and beasts are stilled in rest,
But my sad eyes their nightly vigil keep . . .
    O ! if beneath the night some happier swain,
Entwined in loving arms, refuse thy boon
In wanton happiness,—come hither soon,
Come hither, Sleep. Let happier mortals gain
The full embrace of thy soft angel wing :
But touch me with thy wand, or hovering
Above mine eyelids sweep me with thy train.

W. H. FYFE (after STATIUS)

FALSE SLEEP

Ah, Sleep, to me thou com'st not in the guise
Of one who brings good gifts to weary men,
Balm for bruised hearts and fancies alien
To unkind truth, and drying for sad eyes.
I dread the summons to that fierce assize
Of all my foes and woes, that waits me when
Thou mak'st my soul the unwilling denizen
Of thy dim troubled house where unrest lies.

My soul is sick with dreaming, let it rest.
False Sleep, thou hast conspired with Wakefulness,
I will not praise thee, I too long beguiled
With idle tales. Where is thy soothing breast?
Thy peace, thy poppies, thy forgetfulness?
Where is thy lap for me so tired a child?

LORD ALFRED DOUGLAS

THE BAT

In broad daylight
He should not be:
Yet toward and froward,
Froward and toward
He weaves a flight.
Who will guide him back to his cave,
A little bat astray,
Where he'll rest on the breast of night,
Away from day's bright miscreation?
The linnet throbs through the air,
The magpie coquettes with day,
The rook caws " Time to be gone,"
And travels on;

While toward and froward,
Froward and toward,
The bat . . . a fathom
Of flight . . . weaves.

PADRAIC COLUM

BED-TIME

I mind, love, how it ever was this way :
   That I would to my task ; and soon I'd hear
Your little fluttering sigh, and you would say,
   " It's bed-time, dear."

So you would go and leave me at my work ;
   And I would turn to it with steady will,
And wonder why the room had grown so dark,
   The night so chill.

Betimes I'd hear the whisper of your feet
   Upon the stair ; and you would come to me,
All rosy from your dreams, and take your seat
   Upon my knee.

" Poor tired boy ! " you'd say. But I would miss
   The lonely message of your eyes, and so
Proffer the hasty bribery of a kiss,
   And let you go.

But now, dear heart, that you have scaled the stair
   To that dim chamber far above the sun,
I fumble with my futile task, nor care
   To get it done.

For all is empty since you said good-night
  (So spent you were, and weary with the day!)
And on the hearth the ashes of delight
  Lie cold and grey.

Ah, sweet my love, could I but wish you down
  In that white raiment which I know you wear;
And hear once more the rustle of your gown
  Upon the stair;

Could I but have you, drowsily sweet, to say
  The tender little words that once I knew—
How gaily would I put my work away
  And go with you.

RALPH M. JONES

A MEMORY

Each night beside my bed
  My mother sang so tenderly and low,
While I with snuggling head
  Floated away on slumber's quiet flow.—
  There are no songs like hers of long ago.

Each night until I slept
  A little while beside my bed she stayed;
And then away she crept
  While through the fields of wonderland I strayed
  There are no pray'rs like those my mother prayed.

Long years ago, she died.
　　But sometimes when the silence seals the day,
And slumber's dreamful tide
　　Begins to bear me on its homeward way,
　　I think I hear her sing, I hear her pray.

ARTHUR L. SALMON

FALLING ASLEEP

Voices moving about in the quiet house :
Thud of feet and a muffled shutting of doors :
Everyone yawning. Only the clocks are alert.

Out in the night there's autumn-smelling gloom
Crowded with whispering trees ; across the park
A hollow cry of hounds like lonely bells :
And I know that the clouds are moving across the moon ;
The low, red, rising moon. Now herons call
And wrangle by their pool ; and hooting owls
Sail from the wood above pale stooks of oats.

Waiting for sleep, I drift from thoughts like these ;
And where to-day was dream-like, build my dreams.
Music . . . there was a bright white room below,
And someone singing a song about a soldier,
One hour, two hours ago : and soon the song
Will be " *last night* " ; but now the beauty swings
Across my brain, ghost of remembered chords
Which still can make such radiance in my dream
That I can watch the marching of my soldiers,
And count their faces ; faces ; sunlit faces.

Falling asleep . . . the herons, and the hounds. . . .
September in the darkness ; and the world
I've known ; all fading past me into peace.

SIEGFRIED SASSOON

A LITTLE SOUND

A little sound—
Only a little, a little—
The breath in a reed,
A trembling fiddle ;
The trumpet's ring,
The shuddering drum ;
So all the glory, bravery, hush
Of music come.

A little sound—
Only a stir and a sigh
Of each green leaf
Its fluttering neighbour by ;
Oak on to oak,
The wide, dark forest through—
So o'er the watery wheeling world
The night-winds go.

A little sound—
Only a little, a little,
The thin high drone
Of the simmering kettle,
The gathering frost,
The click of needle and thread ;
Mother, the fading wall, the dream,
The drowsy bed.

WALTER DE LA MARE

DON'T FORGET THE VIOLET

For him that may not slepe for sickness set this herbe in water, and at even let him soke well hys fete in the water to the ancles. When he goeth to bed bind of this herbe to his temples, and he shal slepe wel by the grace of God.

ANTHONY ASCHAM (from *A Little Herbal*, 1550)

AN OLD SLEEPING BAG

A Bag to smell unto for melancholy or to cause one to sleep.
Take drie rose leaves, keep them close in a glass which will keep them sweet, then take powder of mints, powder of cloves in a gross powder, and put the same to the rose leaves, then put all these together in a bag, and take that to bed with you, and it will cause you to sleep, and it is good to smell unto at other times.

A New Herbal (1578)

CONCLUSION TO *THE GARDEN OF CYRUS*

But the quincunx of heaven runs low, and 'tis time to close the five ports of knowledge. We are unwilling to spin-out our awaking thoughts into the phantasms of sleep, which often continueth precogitations ; making cables of cobwebs, and wildernesses of handsome groves. Beside Hippocrates hath spoke so little, and the oneirocritical masters have left such frigid interpretations from plants, that there is little encouragement to dream of paradise itself. Nor will the sweetest delight of gardens afford much comfort in sleep ; wherein the dulness of that sense shakes hands with delectable odours; and though in the bed of Cleopatra, can hardly with any delight raise up the ghost of a rose.

Night, which Pagan theology could make the daughter of Chaos, affords no advantage to the description of order: although no lower than that mass can we derive its genealogy. All things began in order, so shall they end, and so shall they begin again; according to the Ordainer of order and mystical mathematics of the city of heaven.

Though Somnus in Homer be sent to rouse up Agamemnon, I find no such effects in these drowsy approaches of sleep. To keep our eyes open longer, were but to act our Antipodes. The huntsmen are up in America, and they are already past their first sleep in Persia. But who can be drowsy at that hour which freed us from everlasting sleep? or have slumbering thoughts at that time, when sleep itself must end, and as some conjecture all shall awake again.

SIR THOMAS BROWNE

COLERIDGE'S COMMENT ON THE FORE-GOING

" *To keep our eyes open longer,*" *etc.* Think you that there ever was such a reason given before for going to bed at midnight; to wit, that if we did not, we should be *acting* the part of our antipodes! And then—" *The Huntsmen are up in America* "—what life, what fancy! Does the whimsical knight give us, thus, the *essence* of gunpowder tea, and call it an *opiate* ?

MS. Notes in a copy of *Browne's Works*

A FEW THOUGHTS ON SLEEP

This is an article for the reader to think of when he or she is warm in bed, a little before he goes to sleep, the clothes at his ear, and the wind moaning in some distant crevice.

" Blessings," exclaimed Sancho, " on him that first invented sleep ! It wraps a man all round like a cloak." It is a delicious moment certainly—that of being well nestled in bed, and feeling that you shall drop gently to sleep. The good is to come, not past : the limbs have been just tired enough to render the remaining in one posture delightful : the labour of the day is done. A gentle failure of the perceptions comes creeping over one : the spirit of consciousness disengages itself more and more, with slow and hushing degrees like a mother detaching her hand from that of her sleeping child ; the mind seems to have a balmy lid closing over it, like the eye ; 'tis closing ;— 'tis more closing ;—'tis closed. The mysterious spirit has gone to take its airy rounds . . .

In the course of the day few people think of sleeping, except after dinner ; and then it is often rather a hovering and nodding on the borders of sleep than sleep itself . . .

The most complete and healthy sleep that can be taken in the day is in summer-time, out in a field. There is, perhaps, no solitary sensation so exquisite as that of slumbering on the grass or hay, shaded from the hot sun by a tree, with the consciousness of a fresh but light air running through the wide atmosphere, and the sky stretching far overhead upon all sides. Earth, and heaven, and a placid humanity seem to have the creation to themselves. There is nothing between the slumberer and the naked and glad innocence of nature.

Next to this, but at a long interval, the most relishing snatch of slumber out of bed is the one which a tired person takes before he retires for the night, while lingering in his sitting-room. The consciousness of being very sleepy, and of having the power to go to bed immediately, gives great zest to the unwillingness to move. Sometimes he sits nodding in his chair ; but the sudden and leaden jerks of the head, to which a state of great sleepiness renders him liable, are generally too painful for so luxurious a moment ; and he gets into a more legitimate posture, sitting sideways with his head on the chair-back, or throwing his legs up at once on another chair, and half reclining. It is curious, however, to find how long an inconvenient posture will be borne for the sake of this foretaste of repose. The worst of it is, that on going to bed the charm sometimes vanishes ; perhaps from the colder temperature of the chamber ; for a fireside is a great opiate.

Speaking of the painful positions into which a sleepy lounger will get himself, it is amusing to think of the more fantastic attitudes that so often take place in bed. If we could add anything to the numberless things that have been said about sleep by the poets, it would be upon this point. Sleep never shows himself a greater leveller. A man in his waking moments may look as proud and self-possessed as he pleases. He may walk proudly, he may sit proudly, he may eat his dinner proudly ; he may shave himself with an air of infinite superiority ; in a word, he may show himself grand and absurd upon the most trifling occasions. But sleep plays the petrifying magician. He arrests the proudest lord as well as the humblest clown in the most ridiculous postures : so that if you could draw a grandee from his bed without waking him, no limb-twisting fool in a pantomime should create wilder laughter. The toy with the string between its legs is hardly a posture-master more extravagant. Imagine a despot lifted up to the gaze of his valets, with his eyes shut, his mouth open, his left hand under his right ear, his other twisted and hanging helplessly before him like an idiot's, one knee lifted up, and the other leg stretched out, or both knees huddled up together ; what a scarecrow to lodge majestic power in ! . . .

Sleep is most graceful in an infant ; soundest, in one who has been tired in the open air ; completest, to the seaman after a hard voyage ; most welcome, to the mind haunted with one idea ; most touching to look at, in the parent that has wept ; lightest, in the playful child ; proudest, in the bride adored.

LEIGH HUNT

A RAILWAY SLEEPER

If the people of Milo did well to put up a statue in gold to the man that invented wheels, so should we also put one up in Portland stone or plaster to the man that invented rails, whose property it is not only to increase the speed and ease of travel, but also to bring on slumber as can no drug : not even poppies gathered under a waning moon. The rails have a rhythm of slight falls and rises . . . they make a loud roar like a perpetual torrent ; they cover up the mind with a veil.

HILAIRE BELLOC (from *The Path to Rome*)

LULLABIES

From Old English Song Books

Retire, my thoughts, unto your rest again,
Your proffered service may incur disdain,
The dice are cast, and if the gamesters please,
I'll take my chance and rest myself at ease.

WEELKES' Madrigalls, 1597

O sleep, fond Fancy, sleep, my head thou tirest
With false delight of that which thou desirest.
Sleep, sleep, I say, and leave my thoughts molesting,
Thy master's head hath need of sleep and resting.

BENNET'S Madrigalls, 1599

Weep you no more, sad fountains ;
   What need you flow so fast ?
Look how the snowy mountains
   Heaven's sun doth gently waste !
But my Sun's heavenly eyes
     View not your weeping,
    That now lies sleeping
Softly, now softly lies
     Sleeping.

Sleep is a reconciling,
   A rest that peace begets ;
Doth not the sun rise smiling
   When fair at even he sets ?
Rest you then, rest, sad eyes !
     Melt not in weeping,
    While she lies sleeping
Softly, now softly lies
     Sleeping.

DOWLAND'S Book of Ayres, 1603

A LOVER'S LULLABY

Sing lullabies, as women do,
  With which they charm their babes to rest ;
And lullaby can I sing too,
  As womanly as can the best.
With lullaby they still the child ;
And, if I be not much beguil'd,
Full many wanton babes have I,
Which must be still'd with lullaby.

First lullaby my youthful years :
  It is now time to go to bed :
For crooked age, and hoary hairs,
  Have wore the haven within mine head.
With lullaby then youth be still,
With lullaby content thy will ;
Since courage quails, and comes behind,
Go sleep, and so beguile thy mind

Next lullaby my gazing eyes,
  Which wonted were to glance apace ;
For ev'ry glass may now suffice
  To shew the furrows in my face.
With lullaby then wink awhile ;
With lullaby your looks beguile ;
Let no fair face, or beauty bright,
Entice you efte with vain delight.

And lullaby my wanton will,
  Let reason's rule now rein thy thought,
Since all too late I find by skill,
  How dear I have thy fancies bought ;

With lullaby now take thine ease,
With lullaby thy doubt appease;
For, trust in this, if thou be still,
My body shall obey thy will.

GEORGE GASCOIGNE

LULLABY FOR TITANIA

FIRST FAIRY

You spotted snakes with double tongue,
   Thorny hedgehogs, be not seen;
Newts, and blind-worms, do no wrong;
   Come not near our fairy queen.

CHORUS

   Philomel with melody
   Sing in our sweet lullaby;
Lulla, lulla, lullaby; lulla, lulla, lullaby!
Never harm, nor spell, nor charm,
   Come our lovely lady nigh!
   So good-night, with lullaby.

SECOND FAIRY

Weaving spiders, come not here;
   Hence, you long-legg'd spinners, hence;
Beetles black, approach not near;
   Worm, nor snail, do no offence.

Philomel with melody
Sing in our sweet lullaby ;
Lulla, lulla, lullaby ; lulla, lulla lullaby .
Never harm, nor spell, nor charm,
Come our lovely lady nigh !
So good-night, with lullaby.

SHAKESPEARE (from *Midsummer Night's Dream*)

GOLDEN SLUMBERS

Golden slumbers kiss your eyes,
Smiles awake you when you rise !
Sleep, pretty wantons ; do not cry,
And I will sing a lullaby :
Rock them, rock them, lullaby !

Care is heavy, therefore sleep you ;
You are care, and care must keep you.
Sleep, pretty wantons ; do not cry,
And I will sing a lullaby :
Rock them, rock them, lullaby !

THOMAS DEKKER

LULLABY FOR WANDERERS

Softly Night's wings closing in have enfolded the mountains,
Hardly a breath is astir in the slumbering trees ;
Snug in the heart of the forest the song-birds are silent—
Rest is at hand for the weary ones—sleep and have ease !

GOETHE (Trans. A. S.)

CRADLE SONG

Sleep, sleep, beauty bright,
Dreaming in the joys of night !
Sleep, sleep ; in thy sleep
Little sorrows sit and weep.

Sweet babe, in thy face
Soft desires I can trace,
Secret joys and secret smiles
Little pretty infant wiles.

As thy softest limbs I feel,
Smiles as of the morning steal
O'er thy cheek, and o'er thy breast
Where thy little heart doth rest.

O, the cunning wiles that creep
In thy little heart asleep !
When thy little heart shall wake,
Then the dreadful light shall break.

WILLIAM BLAKE

A SERENADE

" Lullaby, oh, lullaby ! "
Thus I heard a father cry,
" Lullaby, oh, lullaby !
The brat will never shut an eye ;
Hither come, some power divine !
Close his lids, or open mine ! "

"Lullaby, oh, lullaby!
What the devil makes him cry?
Lullaby, oh, lullaby!
Still he stares—I wonder why,
Why are not the sons of earth
Blind, like puppies, from the birth?"

"Lullaby, oh, lullaby!"
Thus I heard the father cry;
"Lullaby, oh, lullaby!
Mary, you must come and try!—
Hush, oh, hush, for mercy's sake—
The more I sing, the more you wake!"

"Lullaby, oh, lullaby!
Fie, you little creature, fie!
Lullaby, oh, lullaby!
Is no poppy-syrup nigh?
Give him some, or give him all,
I am nodding to his fall!"

"Lullaby, oh, lullaby!
Two such nights, and I shall die!
Lullaby, oh, lullaby!
He'll be bruised, and so shall I,—
How can I from bedposts keep,
When I'm walking in my sleep?"

"Lullaby, oh, lullaby!
Sleep his very looks deny—
Lullaby, oh, lullaby;
Nature soon will stupefy—
My nerves relax,—my eyes grow dim—
Who's that fallen—me or him?"

THOMAS HOOD

SWEET AND LOW

Sweet and low, sweet and low,
  Wind of the western sea,
Low, low, breathe and blow,
  Wind of the western sea !
Over the rolling waters go,
Come from the dying moon, and blow,
  Blow him again to me ;
While my little one, while my pretty one,
    sleeps.

Sleep and rest, sleep and rest,
  Father will come to thee soon :
Rest, rest, on mother's breast,
  Father will come to thee soon ;
Father will come to his babe in the nest,
Silver sails all out of the west
  Under the silver moon :
Sleep, my little one, sleep, my pretty one,
    sleep.

TENNYSON

WILLIE WINKIE

Wee Willie Winkie
  Rins through the toun,
Up stairs and down stairs
  In his nicht-gown,
Tirling at the window,
  Crying at the lock,
  Are the weans in their bed,
  For it's now ten o'clock ? "

Hey, Willie Winkie,
  Are ye coming ben ?
The cat's singing grey thrums
  To the sleeping hen ;
The dog's spelder'd on the floor,
  And disna gie a cheep ;
But here's a waukrife laddie
  That winna fa' asleep.

Onything but sleep, you rogue !
  Glow'ring like the moon,
Rattling in an airn jug
  Wi' an airn spoon,
Rumblin', tumblin' 'round about,
  Crawing like a cock,
Skirlin' like a kenna-what,
  Wauk'nin' sleeping folk.

Hey, Willie Winkie,
  The wean's in a creel !
Wamblin' aff a body's knee
  Like a very eel,
Ruggin' at the cat's lug,
  Rav'llin' a' her thrums—
Hey, Willie Winkie,
  See, there he comes !

Wearied is the mither
  That has a stoorie wean,
A wee stumpie stousie
  That canna rin his lane

138

That has a battle aye wi' sleep,
  Before he'll close an e'e ;
But a kiss fra aff his rosy lips
  Gies strength anew to me.

WILLIAM MILLER

THE WEE CROODLIN' DOO[1]

Will ye no fa' asleep the nicht,
  Ye restless little loun ?
The sun has lang been oot o' sicht
  An' gloamin's dark'nin' doon.
There's claes to mend, the house to clean—
  This nicht I'll no win through,
An' yet ye winna close yer een—
  Ye wee croodlin' doo !

Spurrin' wi' yer restless feet,
  My very legs are sair,
Clautin' wi' yer buffy hands,
  Touslin' mammy's hair.
I've gi'en ye meat wi' sugar sweet,
  Yer little crappie's fu' ;
Cuddle doon, ye stourie loun—
  Ye wee croodlin' doo !

Now, hushaba, my little pet,
  Ye've a' the warld can gi'e ;
Ye're just yer mammy's lammie yet,
  An' daddy's ae e'e.

<hr>

[1] Croodling doo = cooing dove

Will ye never close yer een?
  There's the bogle-boo!
Ye dinna care a single preen,
  Ye wee croodlin' doo!

Twistin' roun' an' roun' again,
  Warslin' aff my lap,
An' pussy on the hearthstane,
  As sound as ony tap;
Dickie birdie gane to rest—
  A' asleep but you,
Nestle into mammy's breast,
  Ye wee croodlin' doo!

Happit cosy, trig, an' sweet,
  Fifty bairns are waur,
An' ye'se get fotties for yer feet
  At the Big Bazaar.
An' ye shall hae a hoodie braw
  To busk yer bonnie broo,
" Cockle shells an' silver bells,"
  My wee croodlin' doo!

Gude be praised, the battle's by,
  An' sleep has won at last,
How still the puddlin' feetie lie,
  The buffy hands at rest!
An' saftly fa's the silken fringe
  Aboon thy een o' blue;
Blessin's on my bonnie bairn—
  My wee croodlin' doo!

JAMES THOMSON (b. 1825)

LULLABY OF A MOUNTAIN WOMAN

(*To an old Irish air*)

Little gold head, my house's candle,
You will guide all wayfarers that walk this mountain.

Little soft mouth that my breast has known,
Mary will kiss you as she passes.

Little round cheek, O silk of the thistle,
Jesus will lay his hand upon you.

Mary's kiss on my child's red mouth,
Christ's little hand on my darling's cheek !

House be still, and ye little grey mice,
Lie close, lie close, lest ye break his slumber.

Moths on the window, fold your wings,
Little black chafers, silence your humming.

Plover and curlew, fly not over my house,
Do not speak, wild barnacle, passing over this mountain.

Things of the mountain that wake in the night-time,
Be still, be still, for my little one sleeps.

PADRAIC H. PEARSE

GOOD NIGHT

Sleep sweetly in this quiet room
O thou—whoe'er thou art—
And let no mournful yesterdays
Disturb thy peaceful heart ;
Nor let to-morrow mar thy rest
With dreams of coming ill.
Thy Maker is thy Changeless Friend :
His love surrounds thee still.
Forget thyself and all the world,
Put out each garish light.
The stars are shining overhead—
Sleep sweetly, then. Good night !

ANONYMOUS

FIRST PART

§ IV LODGINGS FOR THE NIGHT

Matthew, Mark, Luke, and John
Bless the bed that I lie on !
　　Four corners to my bed,
　　Five angels there be spread ;
　　　Two at my head,
　　　Two at my feet,
One at my heart my soul to keep.

The White Paternoster

　Bona sera ai vivi ;
　E riposo ai morti poveri ;
　Bon viaggio ai naviganti ;
　E bona notte a tutti quanti !

Old Song (*15th century*)

　Here my " master " comes : he has poked out all the
house-fires, has looked to all the bolts, has ordered the
whole male and female crew to their chambers ; and
begins to blow my candles out, and says, " Time, Sir
George, to go to bed ! Twelve o'clock ! "

　" Bless me ! So indeed it is." And I close my book, and
go to my rest, with a blessing on those around me now
asleep.

THACKERAY (*The Virginians*)

§ IV LODGINGS FOR THE NIGHT

DISCOUNT FOR CASH

A few days afterwards we set out on our return to Florence. We lay one night at a place on this side Chioggia, on the left hand as you go toward Ferrara. Here the host insisted upon being paid before we went to bed, and in his own way ; and when I observed that it was the custom everywhere else to pay in the morning, he answered : " I insist on being paid overnight, and in my own way." I retorted that men who wanted everything their own way ought to make a world after their own fashion, since things were differently managed here. Our host told me not to go on bothering his brains, because he was determined to do as he had said. Tribolo stood trembling with fear, and nudged me to keep quiet, lest they should do something worse to us ; so we paid them in the way they wanted, and afterwards we retired to rest. We had, I must admit, the most capital beds, new in every particular, and as clean as they could be. Nevertheless I did not get one wink of sleep, because I kept on thinking how I could revenge myself. At one time it came into my head to set fire to his house ; at another to cut the throats of four fine horses which he had in the stable ; I saw well enough that it was easy for me to do all this ; but I could not see how it was easy to secure myself and my companion. At last I resolved to put my things and my comrade's on board the boat ; and so I did. When the towing-horses had been harnessed to the cable, I ordered the people not to stir before I returned, for I had left a pair of slippers in my bedroom. Accordingly I went back

to the inn and called our host, who told me he had nothing to do with us, and that we might go to Jericho. There
was a ragged stable-boy about, half asleep, who . . . asked
me for a tip, and I gave him a few Venetian coppers, and
told him to make the barge man wait till I had found
my slippers and returned. I went upstairs, took out a little
knife as sharp as a razor, and cut the four beds that I
found there into ribbons. I had the satisfaction of knowing
I had done a damage of more than fifty crowns. Then I ran
down to the boat with some pieces of the bed-covers in
my pouch, and bade the bargee start at once without
delay. We had not gone far before my gossip Tribolo
said that he had left behind some little straps belonging
to his carpet-bag, and that he must be allowed to go back
for them. I answered that he need not take thought for a
pair of little straps, since I could make him as many big
ones as he liked. He told me I was always joking, but that
he must really go back for his straps. Then he began
ordering the bargee to stop, while I kept ordering him to
go on. Meanwhile I informed my friend what kind of trick
I had played our host, and showed him specimens of the
bed-covers and other things, which threw him into such a
quaking fright that he roared out to the bargee : " On with
you, on with you, as quick as you can ! " and never thought
himself quite safe until we reached the gates of Florence.

When we arrived there, Tribolo said : " Let us bind our
swords up, for the love of God ; and play me no more of
your games, I beg ; for all this while I've felt as though my
guts were in the saucepan." I made answer : " Gossip
Tribolo, you need not tie your sword up, for you have
never loosed it " ; and this I said at random, because I
never once had seen him act the man upon that journey.
When he heard the remark, he looked at his sword and

cried out : " In God's name, you speak true ! Here it is tied, just as I arranged it before I left my house." My gossip deemed that I had been a bad travelling companion to him, because I resented affronts and defended myself against folk who would have done us injury. But I deemed that he had acted a far worse part with regard to me by never coming to my assistance at such pinches. Let him judge between us who stands by and has no personal interest in our adventures.

BENVENUTO CELLINI (from *Autobiography*—
Trans. J. A. SYMONDS)

ADVICE FROM A TUDOR DOCTOR

Whole men of what age or complexion soever they be of, should take their natural rest and sleep in the night : and to eschew meridial sleep. But if need should compel a man to sleep after his meat : let him make a pause, and then let him stand and lean and sleep against a cupboard, or else let him sit upright in a chair and sleep. To bedward be you merry or have merry company about you, so that to bedward no anger nor heaviness, sorrow nor pensifulness do trouble or disquiet you. In the night let the windows of your house, especially of your chamber, be closed. When you be in your bed lie a little while on your left side, and sleep on your right side. Let your night cap be of scarlet : and this I do advertise you, to cause to be made a good thick quilt of cotton, or else of pure flocks or of clean wool, and let the covering of it be of white fustian, and lay it on the feather-bed that you do lie on ; and in your bed lie not too hot nor too cold, but in a temperance.

Old ancient Doctors of Physic say seven hours of sleep in summer and nine in winter is sufficient for any man ; but I do think that sleep ought to be taken as the complexion of man is. When you do rise in the morning, rise with mirth and remember God.

ANDREW BORDE (from *A Compendious Regyment*, 1557)

CHARGING THE WATCH

DOGBERRY : Are you good men and true ?

VERGES : Yea, or else it were pity but they should suffer salvation, body and soul.

DOGBERRY : Nay, that were a punishment too good for them, if they should have any allegiance in them, being chosen for the prince's watch.

VERGES : Well, give them their charge, neighbour Dogberry.

DOGBERRY : First, who think you the most desartless man to be constable ?

FIRST WATCH : Hugh Otecake, sir, or George Seacole ; for they can write and read.

DOGBERRY : Come hither, neighbour Seacole. God hath blessed you with a good name : to be a well-favoured man is the gift of fortune ; but to write and read comes by nature.

SECOND WATCH : Both which, master constable,—

DOGBERRY : You have : I knew it would be your answer. Well, for your favour, sir, why, give God thanks, and make no boast of it ; and for your writing and reading, let that appear when there is no need of such vanity. You are thought here to be the most senseless and fit man for the constable of the watch ; therefore bear you the lantern. This is your charge : you shall comprehend all vagrom men ; you are to bid any man stand, in the prince's name.

SECOND WATCH : How if a' will not stand ?

DOGBERRY : Why, then, take no note of him, but let him go ; and presently call the rest of the watch together, and thank God you are rid of a knave.

VERGES : If he will not stand when he is bidden, he is none of the prince's subjects.

DOGBERRY : True, and they are to meddle with none but the prince's subjects. You shall also make no noise in the streets ; for for the watch to babble and to talk is most tolerable and not to be endured.

WATCH : We will rather sleep than talk : we know what belongs to a watch.

DOGBERRY : Why, you speak like an ancient and most quiet watchman ; for I cannot see how sleeping should offend : only, have a care that your bills be not stolen. Well, you are to call at all the ale-houses, and bid those that are drunk get them to bed.

WATCH : How if they will not ?

DOGBERRY : Why, then, let them alone till they are sober : if they make you not then the better answer, you may say they are not the men you took them for.

WATCH : Well, sir.

DOGBERRY : If you meet a thief, you may suspect him, by virtue of your office, to be no true man ; and, for such kind of men, the less you meddle or make with them, why, the more is for your honesty.

WATCH : If we know him to be a thief, shall we not lay hands on him ?

DOGBERRY : Truly, by your office, you may ; but I think they that touch pitch will be defiled : the most peaceable way for you, if you do take a thief, is to let him show himself what he is, and steal out of your company.

VERGES : You have been always called a merciful man, partner.

DOGBERRY : Truly, I would not hang a dog by my will, much more a man who hath any honesty in him.

VERGES : If you hear a child cry in the night, you must call to the nurse and bid her still it.

WATCH : How if the nurse be asleep and will not hear us ?

DOGBERRY : Why, then, depart in peace, and let the child wake her with crying ; for the ewe that will not hear her lamb when it baes will never answer a calf when he bleats.

VERGES : 'Tis very true.

DOGBERRY : This is the end of the charge . . . Well, masters, good night : an there be any matter of weight chances, call up me : keep your fellows' counsels and your own ; and good night. Come, neighbour.

WATCH : Well, masters, we hear our charge : let us go sit here upon the church-bench till two, and then all to bed.

SHAKESPEARE (from *Much Ado about Nothing*)

ANGLERS AT HODDESDON

PISCATOR : 'Tis enough, honest scholar, come let's to supper. Come, my friend Coridon, this trout looks lovely, it was twenty-two inches when it was taken, and the belly of it looked some part of it as yellow as a marigold, and part of it as white as a lily, and yet, methinks, it looks better in this good sauce.

CORIDON : Indeed, honest friend, it looks well, and tastes well, I thank you for it, and so does my friend Peter, or else he is to blame.

PETER : Yes, and so I do, we all thank you, and when we

have supped, I will get my friend Coridon to sing you a song, for requital.

CORIDON: I will sing a song, if anybody will sing another; else, to be plain with you, I will sing none: I am none of those that sing for meat, but for company: I say, *'Tis merry in hall, when men sing all.*

PISCATOR: I'll promise you I'll sing a song that was lately made at my request by Mr. William Basse, one that hath made the choice songs of The Hunter in his Career, and of Tom of Bedlam, and many others of note; and this that I will sing is in praise of angling.

CORIDON: And then mine shall be the praise of a countryman's life; what will the rest sing of?

PETER: I will promise you, I will sing another song in praise of angling to-morrow night; for we will not part till then, but fish to-morrow, and sup together, and the next day every man leave fishing, and fall to his business.

VIATOR: 'Tis a match; and I will provide you a song or a catch against then too, that shall give some addition of mirth to the company; for we will be merry.

PISCATOR: 'Tis a match, my masters; let's e'en say grace, and turn to the fire, drink the other cup to wet our whistles, and so sing away all sad thoughts. Come on, my masters, who begins? I think it best to draw cuts and avoid contention.

PETER: It is a match. Look the shortest cut falls to Coridon.

CORIDON: Well, then, I will begin: for I hate contention. (CORIDON *sings*.) ...

PISCATOR: Well sung, Coridon, this song was sung with metal, it was choicely fitted to the occasion; I shall love you for it as long as I know you: I would you were a brother of the Angle, for a companion that is cheerful and free from swearing and scurrilous discourse, is worth gold. I'll love such mirth as does not make friends ashamed to look upon one another next morning : nor men (that cannot well bear it) to repent the money they spend when they be warmed with drink : and take this for a rule, you may pick out such times and such companions, that you may make yourselves merrier for a little than a great deal of money : for then it is the company and not the charge that makes the feast : and such a companion you prove, I thank you for it. But I will not compliment you out of the debt that I owe you, and therefore I will begin my song, and wish it may be as well liked. (PISCATOR sings.) . . .

CORIDON : Well sung, brother, you have paid your debt in good coin. We anglers are all beholden to the good man that made this song : come, hostess, give us more ale, and let's drink to him. And now let's every one go to bed, that we may rise early ; but first let's pay our reckoning, for I will have nothing to hinder me in the morning, for I will prevent the sun-rising.

PETER : A match. Come, Coridon, you are to be my bed-fellow. I know, brother, you and your scholar will lie together. But where shall we meet to-morrow night ? for my friend Coridon and I will go up the water towards Ware.

PISCATOR : And my scholar and I will go down towards Waltham.

CORIDON : Then let's meet here, for here are fresh sheets that smell of lavender ; and I am sure we cannot expect better meat or better usage.

PETER : 'Tis a match. Goodnight to everybody !

PISCATOR : And so say I.

VIATOR : And so say I.

IZAAK WALTON (from *The Compleat Angler*)

1668. *June* 11 (*Thursday*). By a happy mistake, and that looked like an adventure, we were carried out of our way to a town where we would lye, since we could not go so far as we would. And there with great difficulty come about ten at night to a little inn, where we were fain to go into a room where a pedlar was in bed, and made him rise; and there wife and I lay, and in a truckle-bed Betty Turner and Willett.[1] But good beds, and the master of the house a sober, understanding man, and I had good discourse with him about this country's matters, as wool, and corne, and other things. By and by to bed, glad of this mistake, because, it seems, had we gone on as we intended, we could not have passed with our coach, and must have lain on the Plain all night.

12*th* (*Friday*). Up, finding our beds good, but lousy; which made us merry.

Diary of Samuel Pepys

ROBINSON MAKES THE BEST OF IT

What to do with myself at night I knew not, nor indeed where to rest, for I was afraid to lie down on the ground, not knowing but some wild beast might devour me, though, as I afterwards found, there was really no need for those fears.

However, as well as I could, I barricaded myself round with the chest and boards that I had brought on shore, and made a kind of hut for that night's lodging. As for food,

---

[1] These were the daughter of Pepys' " Cozen Turner " and Mrs. Pepys' maid. The truckle or trundle bed was a low bedstead on wheels, which was run under the principal bed when not in use. A. S.

I yet saw not which way to supply myself, except that I had seen two or three creatures like hares run out of the wood where I shot the fowl.

I now began to consider that I might yet get a great many things out of the ship which would be useful to me, and particularly some of the rigging and sails, and such other things as might come to land ; and I resolved to make another voyage on board the vessel, if possible . . .

Having got my second cargo on shore—though I was fain to open the barrels of powder, and bring them by parcels, for they were too heavy, being large casks—I went to work to make me a little tent with the sail and some poles which I cut for that purpose : and into this tent I brought everything that I knew would spoil either with rain or sun ; and I piled all the empty chests and casks up in a circle round the tent, to fortify it from any sudden attempt, either from man or beast.

When I had done this, I blocked up the door of the tent with some boards within, and an empty chest set up on end without ; and spreading one of the beds upon the ground, laying my two pistols just at my head, and my gun at length by me, I went to bed for the first time, and slept very quietly all night.

DEFOE (from *Robinson Crusoe*)

LIBERTY HALL

Scene 1. *Room in an Alehouse*

(MARLOW, HASTINGS, TONY LUMPKIN AND LANDLORD.)

MARLOW : This house promises but a poor reception ; though perhaps the landlord can accommodate us.

LANDLORD : Alack, master ! we have but one spare bed in the whole house.

TONY : And, to my knowledge, that's taken up by three lodgers already. (*After a pause, in which the rest seem disconcerted.*) I have it. Don't you think, Stingo, our land-lady could accommodate the gentlemen by the fireside, with—three chairs and a bolster ?

HASTINGS : I hate sleeping by the fireside.

MARLOW : And I detest your three chairs and a bolster.

TONY : You do, do you ?—then, let me see—what if you go on a mile farther, to the Buck's Head ; the Old Buck's Head, on the hill, one of the best inns in the whole country ?

HASTINGS : O ho ! so we have escaped an adventure for this night, however.

LANDLORD (*apart to* TONY) : Sure, you ben't sending them to your father's as an inn, be you ?

TONY : Mum, you fool you. Let them find that out. (*To them*) You have only to keep on straight forward, till you come to a large old house by the road side. You'll see a pair of large horns over the door. That's the sign. Drive up the yard and call stoutly about you.

HASTINGS : Sir, we are obliged to you. The servants can't miss the way ?

TONY : No, no ; but I tell you, though, the landlord is rich, and going to leave off business ; so he wants to be thought a gentleman, saving your presence, he ! he ! He'll be for giving you his company ; and, ecod ! if you mind him, he'll persuade you that his mother was an alderman, and his aunt a justice of peace.

LANDLORD : A troublesome old blade, to be sure ; but he keeps as good wines and beds as any man in the whole country.

MARLOW : Well, if he supplies us with these, we shall want no further connection. We are to turn to the right did you say ?

TONY : No, no ; straight forward, I'll just step myself, and show you a piece of the way. (*To the* LANDLORD Mum !

Scene 2. Mr. Hardcastle's House

(*Enter* HARDCASTLE.)

HARDCASTLE : Gentlemen, once more you are heartily welcome. Which is Mr. Marlow ? Sir, you are heartily welcome. It's not my way, you see, to receive my friends with my back to the fire. I like to give them a hearty reception in the old style at my gate. I like to see their horses and trunks taken care of.

MARLOW (*aside*) : He has got our names from the servants already. (*To him*) We approve your caution and hospitality, sir. (*To* HASTINGS) I have been thinking, George, of changing our travelling dresses in the morning. I am grown confoundedly ashamed of mine.

HARDCASTLE : I beg, Mr. Marlow, you'll use no ceremony in this house.

HASTINGS : I fancy, Charles, you're right : the first blow is half the battle. I intend opening the campaign with the white and gold.

HARDCASTLE : Mr. Marlow—Mr. Hastings—gentlemen —pray, be under no restraint in this house. This is Liberty Hall, gentlemen. You may do just as you please here.

MARLOW : Yet, George, if we open the campaign too fiercely at first, we may want ammunition before it is over. I think to reserve the embroidery to secure a retreat.

HARDCASTLE : Your talking of a retreat, Mr. Marlow, puts me in mind of the Duke of Marlborough, when we went to besiege Denain. He first summoned the garrison——

MARLOW : Don't you think the *ventre d'or* waistcoat will do with the plain brown ?

HARDCASTLE : He first summoned the garrison, which might consist of about five thousand men——.

HASTINGS : I think not : brown and yellow mix but very poorly.

HARDCASTLE : I say, gentlemen, as I was telling you, he summoned the garrison, which might consist of about five thousand men——

MARLOW : The girls like finery.

HARDCASTLE : Which might consist of about five thousand men, well appointed with stores, ammunition, and other implements of war. Now, says the Duke of Marlborough to George Brooks, that stood next to him—you must have heard of George Brooks—I'll pawn my dukedom, says he, but I take that garrison without spilling a drop of blood. So——

MARLOW : What, my good friend, if you gave us a glass of punch in the meantime, it would help us to carry on the siege with vigour.

HARDCASTLE : Punch, sir ! (*Aside*) This is the most unaccountable kind of modesty I ever met with.

MARLOW : Yes, sir, punch. A glass of warm punch, after our journey, will be comfortable. This is Liberty Hall, you know.

GOLDSMITH (from *She Stoops to Conquer*)

THE DIFFICULTY OF GETTING UP

I talked of the difficulty of rising in the morning. Dr. Johnson told me " that the learned Mrs. Carter, at that period when she was eager in study, did not awake as early as she wished, and she therefore had a contrivance, that, at a certain hour, her chamber-light should burn a string to which a heavy weight was suspended, which then fell with a strong sudden noise : this roused her from sleep, and then she had no difficulty in getting up." But I said *that* was my difficulty ; and wished there could be some medicine invented which would make one rise without pain, which I never did, unless after lying in bed a very long time. Perhaps there may be something in the stores of Nature which could do this. I have thought of a pully to raise me gradually ; but that would give me pain, as it would counteract my internal inclination. I would have something that can dissipate the *vis inertiæ*, and give elasticity to the muscles. As I imagine that the human body may be put, by the operation of other substances, into any state in which it has ever been ; and as I have experienced a state in which rising from bed was not disagreeable, but easy, nay, sometimes agreeable ; I suppose that this state may be produced, if we knew by what. We can heat the body, we can cool it ; we can give it tension or relaxation ; and surely it is possible to bring it into a state in which rising from bed will not be a pain.

BOSWELL (from *Life of Samuel Johnson*)

A little light food at intervals during the night is said to be a cure for insomnia. A small table by the bedside would accommodate a dish of the following

HERBACEOUS TREAT

To make this condiment, your poet begs
The pounded yellow of two hard-boil'd eggs ;
Two boil'd potatoes, pass'd through kitchen sieve,
Smoothness and softness to the salad give ;
Let onion atoms lurk within the bowl,
And, half-suspected, animate the whole.
Of mordant mustard add a single spoon,
Distrust the condiment that bites so soon ;
But deem it not, thou man of herbs, a fault,
To add a double quantity of salt ;
Four times the spoon with oil from Lucca brown,
And twice with vinegar procured from town ;
And, lastly, o'er the flavoured compound toss
A magic soupçon of anchovy sauce.
Oh, green and glorious ! Oh, herbaceous treat !
'Twould tempt the dying anchorite to eat :
Back to the world he'd turn his fleeting soul,
And plunge his fingers in the salad-bowl !
Serenely full, the epicure would say,
Fate cannot harm me, I have dined to-day

SYDNEY SMITH

A FERRYMAN'S HUT

Loch Katrine, August 27, 1803

We caroused our cups of coffee, laughing like children at the strange atmosphere in which we were : the smoke came in gusts, and spread along the walls and above our heads in the chimney, where the hens were roosting like light clouds in the sky. We laughed and laughed again, in spite of the smarting of our eyes, yet had a quieter pleasure in observing the beauty of the beams and rafters gleaming between the clouds of smoke. They had been crusted over and varnished by many winters, till, where the firelight fell upon them, they were as glossy as black rocks on a sunny day cased in ice. When we had eaten our supper we sate about half an hour, and I think I had never felt so deeply the blessing of a hospitable welcome and a warm fire. When I went to bed, the mistress, desiring me to " go ben," attended me with a candle, and assured me that the bed was dry, though not " sic as I had been used to." . . .

The walls of the whole house were of stone unplastered. It consisted of three apartments—the cow-house at one end, the kitchen or house in the middle, and the spence at the other end. The rooms were divided, not up to the rigging, but only to the beginning of the roof, so that there was a free passage for light and smoke from one end of the house to the other.

I went to bed some time before the family. The door was shut between us, and they had a bright fire, which I could not see ; but the light it sent up among the varnished rafters and beams, which crossed each other in almost as intricate and fantastic a manner as I have seen the under-boughs of a large beech-tree withered by the depth of the shade above, produced the most beautiful effect that can be conceived. It was like what I should suppose an underground cave or temple to be, with a dripping or moist roof, and the moonlight entering in upon it by some means or other, and yet the colours were more like melted gems. I lay looking up till the light of the fire faded away, and

the man and his wife and child had crept into their bed at
the other end of the room. I did not sleep much, but passed
a comfortable night, for my bed, though hard, was warm
and clean : the unusualness of my situation prevented me
from sleeping. I could hear the waves beat against the
shore of the lake ; a little " syke " close to the door made a
much louder noise ; and when I sate up in my bed I could
see the lake through an open window-place at the bed's
head. Add to this, it rained all night.

DOROTHY WORDSWORTH

(from Recollections of a Tour made in Scotland)

TWO FALLACIES

1. *That we should rise with the lark*

At what precise minute that little airy musician doffs
his night gear, and prepares to tune up his unseasonable
matins, we are not naturalists enough to determine. But
for a mere human gentleman—that has no orchestra
business to call him from his warm bed to such prepos-
terous exercises—we take ten, or half after ten (eleven, of
course, during this Christmas solstice), to be the very
earliest hour at which he can begin to think of abandoning
his pillow. To think of it, we say ; for to do it in earnest,
requires another half hour's good consideration. Not but
there are pretty sun-risings, as we are told, and such like
gawds, abroad in the world, in summer time especially,
some hours before what we have assigned ; which a
gentleman may see, as they say, only for getting up. But,
having been tempted once or twice, in earlier life, to

assist at those ceremonies, we confess our curiosity abated. We are no longer ambitious of being the sun's courtiers, to attend at his morning levees. We hold the good hours of the dawn too sacred to waste them upon such observances ; which have in them, besides, something Pagan and Persic. To say truth, we never anticipated our usual hour, or got up with the sun (as 'tis called), to go a journey or upon a foolish whole day's pleasuring, but we suffered for it all the long hours after in listlessness and headaches ; Nature herself sufficiently declaring her sense of our presumption, in aspiring to regulate our frail waking courses by the measures of that celestial and sleepless traveller. We deny not that there is something sprightly and vigorous, at the outset especially, in these break-of-day excursions. It is flattering to get the start of a lazy world ; to conquer death by proxy in his image. But the seeds of sleep and mortality are in us ; and we pay usually in strange qualms, before night falls, the penalty of the unnatural inversion. Therefore, while the busy part of mankind are fast huddling on their clothes, are already up and about their occupations, content to have swallowed their sleep by wholesale ; we chose to linger a-bed, and digest our dreams. It is the very time to re-combine the wandering images, which night in a confused mass presented ; to snatch them from forgetfulness ; to shape, and mould them. Some people have no good of their dreams. Like fast feeders, they gulp them too grossly, to taste them curiously. We love to chew the cud of a fore-gone vision : to collect the scattered rays of a brighter phantasm, or act over again, with firmer nerves, the sadder nocturnal tragedies ; to drag into daylight a struggling and half-vanishing nightmare ; to handle and examine the terrors, or the airy solaces. We have too much respect for these spiritual communications, to let them go so lightly. We are not so stupid, or so careless, as that Imperial forgetter of his dreams, that we should need a seer to remind us of the form of them. They seem to us to have as much significance as our waking concerns ; or rather to import us more nearly as more nearly we approach by years to the shadowy world whither we are hastening. We have shaken hands with the world's business ; we have done with it ; we have discharged ourself of it. Why should we get up ? we have neither suit to solicit nor affairs to manage. The drama has shut in upon us at the fourth act. We have nothing here to expect, but in a short time a sick bed, and a dismissal. We delight to anticipate death by such shadows as night affords. We are already half acquainted with ghosts. We were never much in the world. Disappointment early struck a dark veil between us and its dazzling illusions. Our spirits showed grey before our hairs. The mighty changes of the world already appear as but the vain stuff out of which dramas are composed. We have asked no more of life than what the mimic images in play-houses present us with. Even those types have waxed fainter. Our clock appears to have struck. We are SUPERANNUATED. In this dearth of mundane satisfaction, we contract politic alliances with shadows. It is good to have friends at court. The abstracted media of dreams seem no ill introduction to that spiritual presence, upon which in no long time we expect to be thrown. We are trying to know a little of the usages of that colony ; to learn the language, and the faces we shall meet with there, that we may be the less awkward at our first coming among them. We willingly call a phantom our fellow, as knowing we shall soon be of their dark companionship. Therefore, we cherish dreams. We try to spell in them the alphabet of the invisible world ; and think we know already, how it shall be with us. Those uncouth shapes, which, while we clung to flesh and blood, affrighted us, have become familiar. We feel attenuated into their meagre essences, and have given the hand of half-way approach to incorporeal being. We once thought life to be something ; but it has unaccountably fallen from us before its time. Therefore we choose to dally with visions. The sun has no purposes of ours to light us to. Why should we get up ?

2. *That we should lie down with the lamb*

We could never quite understand the philosophy of this arrangement, or the wisdom of our ancestors in sending us for instructions to these woolly bedfellows. A sheep, when it is dark, has nothing to do but to shut his silly eyes, and sleep if he can. Man found out long sixes.— Hail candle-light ! without disparagement to sun or moon, the kindliest luminary of the three—if we may not rather style thee their radiant deputy, mild viceroy of the moon ! —We love to read, talk, sit silent, eat, drink, sleep, by candle-light. They are everybody's sun and moon. This is our peculiar and household planet. Wanting it, what savage unsocial nights must our ancestors have spent, wintering in caves and unillumined fastnesses ! They must have lain about and grumbled at one another in the dark. What repartees could have passed, when you must have felt about for a smile, and handled a neighbour's cheek to be sure that he understood it ? This accounts for the seriousness of the elder poetry. It has a sombre cast (try Hesiod or Ossian) derived from the tradition of those unlantern'd nights. Jokes came in with candles. We wonder how they saw to pick up a pin, if they had any. How did they sup? what a melange of chance carving they must have made of it!—here one had got a leg of a goat, when he wanted a horse's shoulder—there another had dipt his scooped palm in a kid-skin of wild honey, when he meditated right mare's milk. There is neither good eating nor drinking in fresco. Who, even in these civilised times, has never experienced this, when at some economic table he has commenced dining after dusk, and waited for the flavour till the lights came? The senses absolutely give and take reciprocally. Can you tell pork from veal in the dark? or distinguish Sherris from pure Malaga? Take away the candle from the smoking man; by the glimmering of the left ashes, he knows that he is still smoking, but he knows it only by an inference; till the restored light, coming in aid of the olfactories, reveals to both senses the full aroma. Then how he redoubles his puffs! how he burnishes!—There is absolutely no such thing as reading, but by a candle. We have tried the affectation of a book at noon-day in gardens, and in sultry arbours; but it was labour thrown away. Those gay motes in the beam come about you, hovering and teazing, like so many coquets, that will have you all to their self, and are jealous of your abstractions. By the midnight taper, the writer digests his meditations. By the same light we must approach to their perusal, if we would catch the flame, the odour. It is a mockery, all that is reported of the influential Phoebus. No true poem ever owed its birth to the sun's light. They are abstracted works:

" *Things that were born, when none but the still night*
And his dumb candle, saw his pinching throes."

Marry, daylight—daylight might furnish the images, the crude material ; but for the fine shapings, the true turning and filing (as mine author hath it) they must be content to hold their inspiration of the candle. The mild internal light that reveals them, like fires on the domestic hearth, goes out in the sunshine. Night and silence call out the starry fancies. Milton's Morning Hymn on Paradise, we would hold a good wager, was penned at midnight ; and Taylor's richer description of a sunrise smells decidedly of the taper. Even ourself, in these our humbler lucubrations, tune our best measured cadences (Prose has her cadences) not unfrequently to the charm of the drowsier watchman, " blessing the doors " ; or the wild sweep of winds at midnight. Even now a loftier speculation than we have yet attempted courts our endeavours. We would indite something about the Solar System.—*Betty, bring the candles !*

CHARLES LAMB (from *Popular Fallacies*)

A TRAVELLER IN THE EAST

1. *My First Night*

We had ridden on for some two or three hours—the stir and bustle of our commencing journey had ceased—the liveliness of our little troop had worn off with the declining day, and the night closed in as we entered the great Servian forest. Through this our road was to last for more than a hundred miles. Endless and endless now on either side the tall oaks closed in their ranks, and stood gloomily lowering over us, as grim as an army of giants

166

with a thousand years' pay in arrear. One strived, with listening ear, to catch some tidings of that forest-world within—some stirring of beasts, some night-bird's scream ; but all was quite hushed, except the voice of the cicadas that peopled every bough, and filled the depths of the forest through and through with one same hum everlasting—more stilling than very silence. . .

Long before midnight we reached the hamlet in which we were to rest for the night ; it was made up of about a dozen clay huts standing upon a small tract of ground hardly won from the forest. . . . The burdens unstrapped from the pack-saddles very quickly furnished our den : a couple of quilts spread upon the floor with a carpet-bag at the head of each, became capital sofas. . . . Soon there was tea before us, with all its welcome fragrance ; and as we reclined on the floor we found that a portmanteau was just the right height for a table. The duty of candlesticks was ably performed by a couple of intelligent natives : the rest of the villagers stood by the open doorway at the lower end of the room, and watched our banquet with grave and devout attention.

The first night of your first campaign (though you be but a mere peaceful campaigner) is a glorious time in your life. It is so sweet to find one's self free from the stale civilisation of Europe ! Oh, my dear ally, when first you spread your carpet in the midst of these Eastern scenes, do think for a moment of those your fellow-creatures that dwell in squares, and streets, and even (for such is the fate of many !) in actual country-houses ; think of the people that are " presenting their compliments," and " request-ing the honour," and " much regretting "—of those that are pinioned at dinner-tables, or stuck up in ball-rooms, or cruelly planted in pews—ay, think of these, and so remembering how many poor devils are living in a state of utter respectability, you will glory the more in your own delightful escape.

But, with all its charms, a mud floor (like a mercenary match) does certainly promote early rising. Long before daybreak we were up and had breakfasted ; afterwards there was nearly a whole tedious hour to endure, whilst the horses were laden by torch-light ; but this had an end, and then our day's journey began.

2. *My First Bivouac*

We heard at a little distance the brawling of a rivulet, and on the banks of this it was determined to establish our bivouac ; we soon found the stream, and following its course for a few yards came to a spot which was thought to be fit for our purpose. . . .

My servants busied themselves in unpacking the baggage, as though we had arrived at an hotel—Shereef and his helpers unsaddled their cattle. We had left Tiberias without the slightest idea that we were to make our way to Jerusalem along the desolate side of the Jordan, and my servants (generally provident in those matters) had brought with them only, I think, some unleavened bread, and a rocky fragment of goat's-milk cheese. These treasures were produced. Tea, and the contrivances for making it, were always a standing part of my baggage. My men gathered in circle round the fire. The Nazarene was in a false position, from having misled us so strangely, and he would have shrunk back, poor devil, into the cold and outer darkness, but I made him draw near, and share the luxuries of the night. My quilt and my pelisse were spread, and the rest of my people had all their *capotes* or pelisses, or robes of some sort, which furnished their couches. The men gathered in circle, some kneeling, some sitting, some lying reclined around our common hearth. Sometimes on one, sometimes on another, the flickering light would glare more fiercely. Sometimes it was the good Shereef that seemed the foremost as he sat with venerable beard, the image of manly piety—unknowing of all geography, unknowing where he was, or whither he might go, but trusting in the goodness of God, and the clenching power of fate, and the good star of the Englishman. Sometimes, like marble, the classic face of the Greek Mysseri would catch the sudden light, and then again, by turns, the ever perturbed Dthemetri, with his odd Chinaman's eye, and bristling, terrier-like moustache, shone forth illustrious.

I always liked the men who attended me on these Eastern travels, for they were all of them brave, cheery-hearted fellows, and, although their following my career brought upon them a pretty large share of those toils and hardships which are so much more amusing to gentlemen than to servants, yet not one of them ever uttered or hinted a syllable of complaint, or even affected to put on an air of resignation. I always liked them, but never perhaps so much as when they were thus grouped together under the light of the bivouac fire. I felt towards them as my comrades, rather than as my servants, and took delight in breaking bread with them, and merrily passing the cup. . . .

At length we thought it well to seek for sleep. Our plans were laid for keeping up a good watch through the night. My quilt, and my pelisse, and my cloak were spread out so that I might lie spokewise, with my feet towards the central fire. I wrapped my limbs daintily round, and gave myself orders to sleep like a veteran soldier. But my attempt to sleep upon the earth that God gave me was more new and strange than I had fancied it. I had grown used to the scene which was before me whilst I was sitting or reclining by the side of the fire ; but now that I laid myself down at full length, it was the deep, black mystery of the heavens that hung over my eyes—not an earthly thing in the way from my own very forehead right up to the end of all space. I grew proud of my boundless bed-chamber. I might have " found sermons " in all this greatness (if I had I should surely have slept), but such was not then my way. If this cherished Self of mine had built the universe, I should have dwelt with delight on " the wonders of creation." As it was, I felt rather the vainglory of my promotion, from out of mere rooms and houses, into the midst of that grand, dark, infinite palace.

And then, too, my head, far from the fire, was in cold latitudes, and it seemed to me strange that I should be lying so still and passive, whilst the sharp night-breeze walked free over my cheek, and the cold damp clung to my hair, as though my face grew in the earth, and must bear with the footsteps of the wind and the falling of the dew, as meekly as the grass of the field. And so, when, from time to time, the watch quietly and gently kept up the languishing fire, he seldom, I think, was unseen to my restless eyes. Yet, at last, when they called me, and said that the morn would soon be dawning, I rose from a state of half-oblivion, not much unlike to sleep, though sharply qualified by a sort of vegetable's consciousness of having been growing still colder and colder for many and many an hour.

A. W. KINGLAKE (from *Eothen*)

Tom had never been in London, and would have liked to have stopped at the Belle Savage, where they had been put down by the Star, just at dusk, that he might have gone roving about those endless, mysterious, gas-lit streets, which, with their glare and hum and moving crowds excited him so that he couldn't talk even. But as soon as he found that the Peacock arrangement would get him to Rugby by twelve o'clock in the day, whereas otherwise he wouldn't be there till the evening, all other plans melted away; his one absorbing aim being to become a public schoolboy as fast as possible, and six hours sooner or later seeming to him of the most alarming importance.

Tom and his father had alighted at the Peacock, at about seven in the evening, and having heard with unfeigned joy the paternal order at the bar of steaks and oyster-sauce for supper in half-an-hour, and seen his father seated cosily by the bright fire in the coffee-room, with the paper in his hand, Tom had run out to see about him, had wondered at all the vehicles passing and repassing, and had fraternised with the boots and ostler, from whom he ascertained that the Tally-ho was a tip-top goer, ten miles an hour including stoppages, and so punctual, that all the road set their clocks by her.

Then being summoned to supper, he had regaled himself in one of the bright little boxes of the Peacock coffee-room, on the beef-steak and unlimited oyster-sauce, and brown stout (tasted then for the first time—a day to be marked for ever by Tom with a white stone); had at first attended to the excellent advice which his father was bestowing on him from over his glass of steaming brandy-and-water, and then begun nodding, from the united effects of the stout, the fire, and the lecture. Till the Squire observing Tom's state, and remembering that it was nearly nine o'clock, and that the Tally-ho left at three, sent the little fellow off to the chambermaid, with a shake of the hand (Tom having stipulated in the morning before starting, that kissing should now cease between them) and a few parting words. Tom was carried off by the chambermaid in a brown study, from which he was roused in a clean little attic, by that buxom person calling him a little darling, and kissing him as she left the room ; which indignity he was too much surprised to resent.

THOMAS HUGHES (*Tom Brown's School Days*)

THE SARACEN'S HEAD

" I say," remonstrated Bob Sawyer, looking in at the coach window, as they pulled up before the door of the Saracen's Head, Towcester, " this won't do, you know."

" Bless me," said Mr. Pickwick, just awakening from a nap, " I'm afraid you're wet."

" Oh, you are, are you ? " returned Bob. " Yes, I am a little that way. Uncomfortably damp, perhaps."

Bob did look dampish, inasmuch as the rain was streaming from his neck, elbows, cuffs, skirts and knees ; and his whole apparel shone so with the wet that it might have been mistaken for a full suit of prepared oilskin.

" I *am* rather wet," said Bob, giving himself a shake, and casting a little hydraulic shower around, like a Newfoundland dog just emerged from the water.

" I think it's quite impossible to go on to-night," interposed Ben.

"Out of the question, sir," remarked Sam Weller, coming to assist in the conference; "it's a cruelty to animals, sir, to ask 'em to do it. There's beds here, sir," said Sam, addressing his master, "everything clean and comfortable. Wery good little dinner, sir, they can get ready in half an hour—pair of fowls, sir, and a weal cutlet; French beans, 'taturs, tart, and tidiness. You'd better stop vere you are, sir, if I might recommend. Take adwice, sir, as the doctor said."

The host of the Saracen's Head opportunely appeared at this moment, to confirm Mr. Weller's statement relative to the accommodation of the establishment, and to back his entreaties with a variety of dismal conjectures regarding the state of the roads, the doubt of fresh horses being to be had at the next stage, the dead certainty of its raining all night, the equally mortal certainty of its clearing up in the morning, and other topics of inducement familiar to innkeepers.

"Well," said Mr. Pickwick; "but I must send a letter to London by some conveyance, so that it may be delivered the very first thing in the morning, or I must go forward at all hazards."

The landlord smiled his delight. Nothing could be easier than for the gentleman to inclose a letter in a sheet of brown paper, and send it on, either by the mail or the night coach from Birmingham. If the gentleman were particularly anxious to have it left as soon as possible, he might write outside, "To be delivered immediately," which was sure to be attended to; or "pay the bearer half-a-crown extra for instant delivery," which was surer still.

"Very well," said Mr. Pickwick, "then we will stop here."

" Lights in the Sun, John ; make up the fire ; the gentlemen are wet ! " cried the landlord. " This way, gentlemen ; don't trouble yourselves about the postboy now, sir.
I'll send him to you when you ring for him, sir. Now,
John, the candles."

DICKENS (from *Pickwick Papers*)

DISTURBANCES AT HEILBRONN

We were in bed by ten, for we wanted to be up and
away on our tramp homeward with the dawn. I hung
fire, but Harris went to sleep at once. I hate a man who
goes to sleep at once ; there is a sort of indefinable something about it which is not exactly an insult, and yet is an
insolence ; and one which is hard to bear, too. I lay there
fretting over this injury, and trying to go to sleep ; but the
harder I tried the wider awake I grew. I got to feeling
very lonely in the dark, with no company but an undigested
dinner. My mind got a start by-and-by, and began to
consider the beginning of every subject which has ever
been thought of ; but it never went further than the
beginning : it was touch and go ; it fled from topic to
topic with a frantic speed. At the end of an hour my head
was in a perfect whirl, and I was dead tired, fagged out.

The fatigue was so great that it presently began to make
some head against the nervous excitement ; while imagining myself wide awake, I would really doze into momentary unconsciousnesses, and come suddenly out of
them with a physical jerk which nearly wrenched my
joints apart—the delusion of the instant being that I was
tumbling backwards over a precipice. After I had fallen
over eight or nine precipices and thus found out that

174

one half of my brain had been asleep eight or nine times without the wide-awake, hard-working other half suspecting it, the periodical unconsciousnesses began to extend their spell gradually over more of my brain-territory, and at last I sank into a drowse which grew deeper and deeper and was doubtless just on the very point of becoming a solid, blessed, dreamless stupor, when—what was that?

My dulled faculties dragged themselves partly back to life, and took a receptive attitude. Now out of an immense, a limitless distance, came a something which grew and grew, and approached, and presently was recognisable as a sound—it had rather seemed to be a feeling, before. This sound was a mile away, now—perhaps it was the murmur of a storm; and now it was nearer—not a quarter of a mile away; was it the muffled rasping and grinding of distant machinery? No, it came still nearer; was it the measured tramp of a marching troop? But it came nearer still, and still nearer—and at last it was right in the room: it was merely a mouse gnawing the woodwork. So I had held my breath all that time for such a trifle.

Well, what was done could not be helped; I would go to sleep at once and make up the lost time. That was a thoughtless thought. Without intending it—hardly knowing it—I fell to listening intently to that sound, and even unconsciously counting the strokes of the mouse's nutmeg-grater. Presently I was deriving exquisite suffering from this employment, yet maybe I could have endured it if the mouse had attended steadily to his work; but he did not do that; he stopped every now and then, and I suffered more while waiting and listening for him to begin again than I did while he was gnawing. Along at first I was mentally offering a reward of five—six—seven—ten dollars for that mouse ; but towards the last I was offering rewards which were entirely beyond my means. I close-reefed my ears—that is to say, I bent the flaps of them down, and furled them into five or six folds, and pressed them against the hearing-orifice—but it did no good : the faculty was so sharpened by nervous excitement that it was become a microphone, and could hear through the overlays without trouble.

My anger grew to a frenzy. I finally did what all persons before me have done, clear back to Adam—resolved to throw something. I reached down and got my walking-shoes, then sat up in bed and listened, in order to exactly locate the noise. But I couldn't do it ; it was as unlocatable as a cricket's noise ; and where one thinks that that is, is always the very place where it isn't. So I presently hurled a shoe at random, and with a vicious vigour. It struck the wall over Harris's head and fell down on him ; I had not imagined I could throw so far. It woke Harris, and I was glad of it until I found he was not angry ; then I was sorry. He soon went to sleep again, which pleased me ; but straightway the mouse began again, which roused my temper once more. I did not want to wake Harris a second time, but the gnawing continued until I was compelled to throw the other shoe. This time I broke a mirror—there were two in the room—I got the largest one of course. Harris woke again, but did not complain, and I was sorrier than ever. I resolved that I would suffer all possible torture before I would disturb him a third time.

The mouse eventually retired, and by-and-by I was sinking to sleep, when a clock began to strike ; I counted till it was done, and was about to drowse again when another clock began ; I counted ; then the two great Rathhaus clock angels began to send forth soft, rich, melodious blasts from their long trumpets. I had never heard anything that was so lovely, or weird, or mysterious —but when they got to blowing the quarter-hours, they seemed to me to be overdoing the thing.

MARK TWAIN (from *A Tramp Abroad*)

THE ENGLISH INN

1. *The Open Arms*

A night in a good inn gives repose a quality of stimulus. Sleep and food have here a flavour that is absent from sleep and food at a friend's house. The inn waits at the end of the journey as certainly as your friend's house ; yet its shelter and food come always with an agreeable sensation of accident and surprise. Too, you have at your inn all that your friend can give you, with many more conveniences and a wider range of entertainment ; and with all this you are yet at the full centre of fluid life. In your friend's house you are shut away, but in the inn you are a looker-on at goings and comings ; you are in contact with the present and you touch hands with the wraiths of the past and the substantial mementoes of their days ; and from your seat in the lounge you view the world as through a loophole of retreat. I begrudge my sixpence or shilling for the inspection of the mansions of the great, with their Keep Off the Grass and Please Do Not Touch ; I consider five pounds a trifle for the privilege of spending a night at the George of Glastonbury, the Feathers of Ludlow, the Lygon Arms of Broadway, or the Spread Eagle of Thame, where I am free to look and touch, and to walk unhindered up lordly staircases and to command a retinue of servitors. The ordinary Englishman's home is not in any sense—and never was—his castle. An officer or bailiff with the proper warrant may enter it when he chooses. But the Englishman's inn—say, the Angel, at Grantham, or the King Arthur, at Tintagel—is a castle, and every sojourner is its lord. He may feel its traditions in his blood as certainly as the children of a great house feel the traditions of their territory.

Your old inn is a many-pointed star, at each point touching great event or pleasing anecdote. A single inn may evoke memories of Izaak Walton, Charles I, Walter Scott, Drunken Barnaby, Bolingbroke, George Borrow, Jonathan Swift; and all these memories and traditions are yours. Isn't it worth five pounds to sit down to dinner with that company, or to trip over that same unseen stair in the dark passages that sent Celia Fiennes to her hands and knees? Or to use that room at the Angel, Grantham, where Richard signed Buckingham's death-warrant in 1483; or sleep in that oaken four-poster at the Saracen's Head, Southwell, where Charles slept his last night of freedom before surrendering to the Scotch; or to sleep in the rooms where slept those shadowy but urgently-living creatures of our novelists? . . To get the full savour of an old inn you should come to it at night, and best of all a winter night, or twilight, when the mists are rising and the soul is low, and a log fire and a dinner seem to be the twin stars of human aspiration. All of us know those moments, and that is why inns were made—to stand upon the pilgrim's way with an understanding smile for the pilgrim's weakness. They are a sign to us to shed austerity and vigilance, and to meet and mingle with our fellows; to turn from our various occasions, lofty or low, and to ease our common needs and common anxieties in kindly communion.

THOMAS BURKE (from *The Book of the Inn*)

2. *The Inn of the Future*

The more general means of transit will be the air, and there will be special air hotels. As distance will be a mere matter of minutes, they will occur only at wide intervals in such places as popular taste may dictate. They will be large and modern. The inn has adapted itself to many changes, but it will not be able to adapt itself to this. As soon as the air becomes everybody's road, those inns that happen to be in the selected spots will be able to do nothing but pull down and rebuild in accordance with the new idea. Those that are outside the air-track will have to close, and possibly become, as many did in the railway-age, private houses . . .

And so, farewell the inn. There may be some who will regret its passing, but life is a series of adjustments, of getting used to what is, while we are still regretting what was ; and before we know where we are we shall be wondering how we ever put up with its easy, intimate homeliness. We shall congratulate ourselves on having escaped out of the Dark Ages. The old will tell tales of having cans of hot water brought to their bedrooms. They will tell of going four days without a bath, despite thirty desperate dashes to the bath-room. They will tell how, if you wanted a meal, you had to take it within a given two hours fixed by the inn, or go without. They will tell of the standardised lunch. They will tell of the game of Bedroom Bell, played between guest and ser-vants, the game being to see who gave way first, the

Ringer or the Rung; a game that guests seldom won. They will tell of the desiccated drawing-rooms for Ladies Only. And the young will sit and wonder why the old fools were so spineless and so rooted in custom as to accept these things.

THOMAS BURKE (from *The English Inn*)

NIGHT CAPS

If your Landlord does not know his business, you can teach him the following method of making

INN KEEPERS' PUNCH

Dissolve about seven ounces of lump sugar in one pint of boiling water, add forty grains of citric acid, seven or eight drops of essence of lemon, and (when well mixed) half of a pint of rum, a quarter of a pint of brandy, and a glass of sherry.

If you are a Prohibitionist, you may like to know about a cold weather temperance drink with a kick in it – not sufficient to throw you off your balance. It is called

STINGER

Its ingredients are :—2 lbs. Loaf Sugar, ½ oz. Essence of Cayenne, ½ oz. Essence of Ginger, ½ oz. Tartaric Acid, 3 Lemons—rind and juice. Peel the lemons and boil the rind for ten minutes in half a pint of water. Strain and add the rest of the ingredients with two quarts of boiling water. Stir until all is dissolved. This makes about four bottles of concentrated essence to be taken in the proportion of about two tablespoonfuls to a tumbler of hot water.

OXFORD NIGHT CAPS

IN(N)S AND OUTS OF THE LAW

(*By a Solicitor*)

Assuming you are a traveller, an innkeeper is bound to receive you at any hour of day or night if he has a vacant bedroom, and you arrive "in proper condition" and are able and willing to pay a reasonable sum for your accommodation. If all the bedrooms are occupied, it will not do to say you don't object to sleep in the coffee-room ; you must go away. You can properly be denied the use of a vacant bedroom if you are a chimney sweep in your business costume, if you are drunk, or if you bring a large dog and refuse to be parted from him.

An innkeeper must take good care of his guests' person and property and must indemnify his guest for injury to the person or theft of goods if he or his servants have been careless in the matter. If you are beaten by another guest, that is your own affair ; and if you hang your watch on the stairs or decorate with your jewels the dressing-table of an unlocked bedroom, your landlord will not be responsible for such eccentricities. The rights of the inn are attached to your sacred office of " traveller." If you stay long enough to abandon this character, the landlord can turn you out.

It has been decided that a lady in " rational " dress has no claim against an innkeeper who refuses to serve her in the coffee-room, provided he offers to serve her in the bar parlour (*R. v. Sprague*, 1899). It does not appear that a lady in " irrational " dress would have any stronger claim.

A NIGHT OUT IN THE DOLOMITES

(*A True Story*)

About 6 o'clock on a September evening we found ourselves in the wild and beautiful valley of Angoraz at the foot of the Passo di Miel, which leads up to the great Pala Plateau. We had seen no reason why two girls should not pass on foot in one day from the Val di San Lucano to San Martino in the Val di Castrozza ; but through a series of mishaps we had lost about three hours of precious daylight. The most difficult part of our journey was yet to come, and the sinking sun warned us that San Martino would be beyond our reach. We decided to spend the night at the Club Hut on the Rosetta Pass.

After a stiff climb up very steep and slippery slabs of rock we reached the top of the pass about 7 o'clock, and another quarter of an hour brought us to the signpost on the edge of the wide stone-covered Plateau. From this point our way was supposed to be sufficiently marked with painted stakes and heaps of stones (locally called " Stone Men.") We found these of little use, for the evening clouds were now down, hugging the peaks which should have been our landmarks and sweeping in bewildering drifts along the level of the Plateau. The whole region appeared to be a mass of limestone slabs and loose stones. To the south-west a momentary break in the clouds showed us the foot of a small glacier on our left front. From the bearings we had taken earlier in the day I felt sure that our way lay across the foot of that glacier. My companion thought differently ; and, as she had been there before and I had not, I gave in. We set off in the opposite direction, climbing and descending what seemed to be an interminable series of hillocks. The stakes and Stone Men seemed to lead us in all directions, and were more a hindrance than a help. After a while the clouds broke, and we saw a mountain straight ahead which we knew was not in our direction. We turned back. Daylight was now fading, but the Plateau began to slope downwards, which was encouraging. We found more way-marks, but soon lost them in the gathering darkness. Our frequent shouts received no reply.

We were now nearly dead beat, and agreed that we could not possibly go on. We clambered into a gully, where a tiny snow-drift promised a supply of water—a welcome discovery, as we had long since thrown out our water to lighten our packs. Thankful to get rid of my rucsac and sit down, I lost no time in getting out the spirit lamp, lighting it, boiling the kettle and making tea. It was now about 9 o'clock. We decided to spend the night in the gully, although it seemed very stony and un-attractive. We tried to clear a space to lie on, but whenever we moved a sharp stone we found a sharper one under-neath. Huddled close together for warmth and covered by our rain-coats, we spent a restless night, neither of us sleeping for more than a few minutes at a time. These snatches of sleep were, in my case, filled with vivid pic-tures of the day—our fruitless search for breakfast at

5.30 a.m., the late arrival of the carriage, the detour to Agordo to obtain breakfast and provisions, the broken bridge at Taibon, the long trudge in stifling heat up the San Lucano valley, the welcome shelter of the pine woods, the wooden bowls full of creamy milk at the alpine dairy, the little meadow bright with gentians and pansies, the steep rocks of the Pass, the all-embracing clouds and the wilderness of stones.

Even had our beds been more comfortable, we should have been wakened by the cold. We were wet as well as cold, for our clothing had been saturated by the damp mist. Before midnight a bitter wind came whistling through the gully. Winds were busy in the upper air also, making bright moments in the sky. At one time we watched the Great Bear being chased by swift clouds, at another we admired the lovely jewels of the Milky Way hanging above our heads. At frequent intervals we boiled our precious kettle. We did not hesitate to mix our drinks, but used everything we had—tea, chocolate, milk, brandy—and just as day was beginning to dawn, we had a final beverage comprising all that was left of my nice strong English peppermints. Thus we disposed of the last of our snow-water and the last of our methylated spirit. In the faint light, as we gathered our scattered belongings together, I saw the dry bottom of our little pool—it gave me a shock. It was lined with the dirtiest of dirt! Stiff and tired, though warmed and refreshed by our peppermint soup, we started off once more. My companion, climbing first out of the gully, cried " Cima Rosetta ! ", and joining her I saw straight ahead a jagged Dolomite peak rising above the mist. In front of us lay the path to the Hut, not a stone's throw away.

BERTHA SMITH

SEA-LODGINGS

I. *A Leith Sloop* (1776)

I made my way, by Linlithgow, to Edinburgh, and got on board a Leith sloop bound for Newcastle. We had no sooner got down the Firth of Forth to the open sea than we met a heavy swell, and presently encountered a violent gale which soon tore our sails to shivers, drove us far out of sight of land, and put our crew in a great bustle and dilemma. In this small vessel the crew and passengers amounted to twenty-six. For these latter there was no accommodation. The boat upon deck was full of the sick, covered by an old sail, and the rest were obliged to sit or lie down in any corner where they could find room. The first night was a sickly, suffocating one ; and for three more nights and three days there was little or no amendment of our situation. On board this sloop there were only two beds that were not stowed with goods ; and, from my wanting rest so long before I left Edinburgh, I crept into one of them as soon as I could, but found it so low that I could not lie on my side or easily turn over. So I could get no sleep ; and, to mend the matter, I had not been long in this wretched bed till an infant was put in beside me, its mother being dismally sick in the boat upon deck ; and the child fell exclusively into my charge. I nursed it as well as I could during the whole voyage; and I think, had I not done so, it must have died.

THOMAS BEWICK

II. *An American Trader* (1840)

(a) Roughing it off the Horn

The decks were covered with snow, and there was a constant driving of sleet. In fact, Cape Horn had set in with good earnest. In the midst of all this, and before it became dark, we had all the studding-sails to make up and stow away, and then to lay aloft and rig in all the booms fore and aft, and coil away the tacks, sheets, and halyards. This was pretty tough work for four or five hands, in the face of a gale which almost took us off the yards, and with ropes so stiff with ice that it was almost impossible to bend them. I was nearly half an hour out on the end of the fore yard, trying to coil away and stop down the top-mast studding-sail tack and lower halyards. It was after dark when we got through, and we were not a little pleased to hear four bells struck, which sent us below for two hours, and gave us each a pot of hot tea with our cold beef and bread, and, what was better yet, a suit of thick, dry clothing, fitted for the weather, in place of our thin clothes, which were wet through and now frozen stiff.

This sudden turn, for which we were so little prepared, was as unacceptable to me as to any of the rest ; for I had been troubled for several days with a slight tooth-ache, and this cold weather, and wetting and freezing were not the best things in the world for it.

When we went on deck at eight bells, it had stopped snowing, and there were a few stars out, but the clouds were still black, and it was blowing a steady gale. Just before midnight, I went aloft and sent down the mizen royal yard, and had the good luck to do it to the satisfaction of the mate, who said it was done " out of hand and shipshape." The next four hours below were but little relief to me, for I lay awake in my berth, the whole time, from the pain in my face, and heard every bell strike, and at four o'clock, turned out with the watch, feeling little spirit for the hard duties of the day. Bad weather and hard work at sea can be borne up against very well, if one only has spirit and health ; but there is nothing brings a man down, at such a time, like bodily pain and want of sleep. There was, however, too much to do to allow time to think ; for the gale of yesterday, and the heavy seas we met with a few days before, while we had yet ten degrees more southing to make, had convinced the captain that we had something before us which was not to be trifled with, and orders were given to send down the long top-gallant masts. It was an interesting sight to see our noble ship, dismantled of all her top-hamper of long tapering masts and yards, and boom pointed with spear-head, which ornamented her in port ; and all that canvas, which a few days before had covered her like a cloud, from the truck to the water's edge, spreading far out beyond her hull on either side, now gone ; and she, stripped, like a wrestler for the fight. It corresponded, too, with the desolate character of her situation ;—alone, as she was, battling with storms, wind, and ice, at this extremity of the globe, and in almost constant night.

(b) Full Sail at Night

One night, while we were in the tropics, I went out to the end of the flying-jib-boom, upon some duty, and, having finished it, turned round, and lay over the boom for a long time, admiring the beauty of the sight before me. Being so far out from the deck, I could look at the ship, as at a separate vessel ;—and there rose up from the water, supported only by the small black hull, a pyramid of canvas, spreading out far beyond the hull, and towering up almost, as it seemed in the indistinct night air, to the clouds. The sea was as still as an inland lake ; the light trade wind was gently and steadily breathing from astern ; the dark blue sky was studded with the tropical stars ;

there was no sound but the rippling of the water under the stem ; and the sails were spread out, wide and high ; the two lower studding-sails stretching, on each side, far beyond the deck ; the top-mast studding-sails, like wings to the top-sails ; the top-gallant studding-sails spreading fearlessly out above them ; still higher, the two royal studding-sails, looking like two kites flying from the same string ; and highest of all, the little sky-sail, the apex of the pyramid, seeming actually to touch the stars, and to be out of reach of human hand. So quiet, too, was the sea, and so steady the breeze, that if these sails had been sculptured marble, they could not have been more motionless. Not a ripple upon the surface of the canvas ; not even a quivering of the extreme edges of the sail—so perfectly were they distended by the breeze. I was so lost in the sight, that I forgot the presence of the man who came out with me, until he said (for he too, rough old man-of-war's-man as he was, had been gazing at the show,) half to himself, still looking at the marble sails— " How quietly they do their work ! "

R. H. DANA (from *Two Years Before the Mast*)

III. *An Atlantic Liner* (1925)

He explored the steamer. It was to him, the mechanic, the most sure and impressive mechanism he had ever seen; more satisfying than a Rolls, a Delauney-Belleville, which to him had been the equivalents of a Velasquez. He marvelled at the authoritative steadiness with which the bow mastered the waves; at the powerful sweep of the lines of the deck and the trim stowing of cordage. He admired the first officer, casually pacing the bridge. He wondered that in this craft which was, after all, but a floating iron egg-shell, there should be the roseate music-room, the smoking-room with its Tudor fireplace—solid and terrestrial as a castle—and the swimming-pool, green-lighted water washing beneath Roman pillars. He climbed to the boat deck, and some never-realised desire for sea-faring was satisfied as he looked along the sweep of gang-ways, past the huge lifeboats, the ventilators like giant saxophones, past the lofty funnels serenely dribbling black woolly smoke, to the forward mast. The snow-gusts along the deck, the mysteriousness of this new world but half seen in the frosty lights, only stimulated him. He shivered and turned up his collar, but he was pricked to imagina-tiveness, standing outside the wireless-room, by the crackle of messages springing across bleak air-roads ocean-bounded to bright snug cities on distant plains.

" I'm at sea ! "

He tramped down to tell Fran—he was not quite sure what it was that he wanted to tell her, save that steamers were very fine things indeed, and that ahead of them, in the murk of the horizon, they could see the lanes of England.

She, in their cabin with its twin brass beds, its finicking imitations of grey-blue French prints on the panelled walls, was amid a litter of shaken-out frocks, heaps of shoes, dressing gowns, Coty Powder, three gift copies of *The Perennial Bachelor*, binoculars, steamer letters, steamer telegrams, the candy and the Charles & Company baskets of overgrown fruit and tiny conserves with which they were to help out the steamer's scanty seven meals a day, his dress-shirts (of which he was to, and certainly would not, put on a fresh one every evening), and French novels (which she was to, and certainly wouldn't, read in a stately, aloof, genteel manner every day on deck). . . .

Round and round the deck. The long stretch on the starboard side, filled with deck chairs, with rug-wadded passengers turning a pale green as the sea rose, with wind-ruffled magazines, cups left from teatime, and children racing with toy carts. The narrow passage aft, where the wind swooped on them, pushing them back, and the steamer dipped so that they had to labour uphill, bending forward, their limbs of lead. But, as they toiled, a glimpse of ship mysteries that were stirring to land-bound imaginations. They looked down into a hatchway—someone said there were half a dozen Brazilian cougars being shipped down there—and along a dizzy aerial gangway to the after-deck and the wheelhouse and a lone light in the weaving darkness. They saw the last glimmer of the streaky wake stretching back to New York. . . .

He awoke, bewildered, at two in the morning. The storm had come ; the steamer was pitching abominably. . . . He lay awake. In the watery light from the transom he saw the sheen of her silver toilet things on the dresser. He thought of this tremendous steamer, pounding the waves. He thought of the modern miracle of the radio, up above, of the automatic electric steering apparatus. Yet on the bridge were sailors, unautomatic, human, eternal. The ship, too, was eternal, as a vehicle of man's old voyaging. Its creaking seemed to him like the creaking of an ancient Greek trireme.

But while his thoughts reached out thus for things heroic, he heard her placid breathing and he smelled not the sea gale but perfume that came from little crystal vials among her silver toilet-things that were vaster than the hull of the steamer, stronger than the storm.

He felt that he would never sleep again.

He closed his great fist, tight. Then it relaxed, and he was asleep.

SINCLAIR LEWIS (from *Dodsworth*)

" SHOWING A LEG "

In Nelson's time, when His Majesty's ships were in harbour, ladies were allowed to sleep on board. The sailors were required to get up at the usual hour, but the ladies might please themselves. A nice problem of discipline thus arose. A solution was found in the fact that the ladies wore their stockings in bed, while the men slept bare-footed. If (as usually happened) all the sailors did not appear punctually on deck, it was necessary for the Boatswain to search for defaulters. He went along the bunks calling out " Show a leg ! show a leg." The owner of a bare leg was promptly dealt with ; but any leg wearing a stocking was allowed to return where it came from, and doubtless the Boatswain would apologize to the lady in nautical terms. Evidently our sailors, being such innocent fellows, never thought of borrowing the ladies' stockings.

A. S.

BAD COMPANIONS

1. *Pulex Irritans*

This is the Latin name for the homely English flea. Those who are fond of French phrases may call him *pousse-pour-tous*. His love of dirt and darkness suggests that he is not a person of culture, but he has his luxurious side, being also fond of warmth, cosiness and quiet situations. Though a great believer in indoor exercise, he is no fresh air fiend. If you keep your windows and doors wide open and lie on your bed quite naked in a thorough draught, he will keep away from you all night, but he will not accept responsibility for any inconvenience caused to you by such arrangements. Long ago he paid us the compliment of giving up his wings in order to cultivate our society and that of other mammals. His athletic powers, which attracted the attention of Socrates, are very considerable. It is true that he can jump into the air to a height sixty-four times his length, his record on the level being two hundred times his length ; but these figures become less impressive if we remember his length is only about one-sixteenth of an inch and that of his wife (truly his " better half ") one-tenth of an inch. As a race the P.I. are highly intelligent, and our grandparents often paid sixpence to see one of their teams drawing a dainty coach. They are nimble folk and make very lively companions, but it is a mistake to cultivate their society, as they have been known to abuse human hospitality in a distressing manner, causing the most pain to those with whom they are most familiar. There is nothing P.I. likes better (after meals) than a game of hide-and-seek, and he seldom gives in until he is compelled to rest by pressure from a piece of soap. The average life of the P.I. is only about five weeks ; but he lives merrily, if not long.

2. *Cimex Lectularius*

There is little to be said in favour of the C.L. His appearance, his odour, his habits and his pet name— bug—are all equally unattractive. Let us say at once that he is not really an Englishman. We are told he was introduced into England in the time of Charles II, an event which marks the extremity of the English taste for foreign importations in the 17th century. For diet the C.L. prefers human blood, but at a pinch will nibble at grain, seed, flour and soft woods such as deal. Apparently he has no objection to long waits between meals, and has been known to live for twelve months without food. He is a night-worker, spending his days lazily in cracks and crevices. His nature is bloodthirsty and his influence degrading. He is worthy of capital punishment, and this sentence should be executed on all his household. You must find out his residence and insert a soothing mixture into all its apertures, say soft soap and paraffin. Benzine is good also, but dangerous, being inflammable. Boiling water will do ; but it must be really boiling, not merely hot.

Early in March is said to be the best time for a bug-hunt, but few people will hesitate to poach in the close season. As a counter-attraction for the C.L. you may hang a bunch of pepperwort on your bedstead, but it is long odds he will like you better.

3. *Anopheles*

This name suggests some Greek hero of the Trojan war, and seems rather high-sounding for a small insect. Those who have travelled in Italy will perhaps remember the mosquito as *Signora Zanzara*, a name which suits this little lady very well. She is truly an enemy of Sleep ; for, if her bites do not keep you awake, her trumpetings probably will. It is said that the purpose of her shrill note is to call her mate and let him know where she is ; but why must this love business be conducted in our bedrooms ? Signor Zanzara is not so good a buzzer. Jove-like he drinks nectar (of flowers), and he is a fruit-eater. He seems to have some little respect for human beings ; but perhaps his principles are vegetarian. When in a country which you have to share with the Zanzare, undress with your windows tightly closed, put out the light before you open them, and beware of careless servants who overlook holes in the mosquito curtains or draw them shutting an enemy inside.

The little mosquito has had the audacity to dispute with man for possession of a considerable portion of the earth's surface. Indeed we surrendered large tracts of territory to these little pests, who were in a fair way to become conquerors of the tropical world. It looked as if it was possible for the mosquito in its capacity of malaria-carrier to have destroyed the human race. It was found there were only two ways of stamping out malaria —to exterminate man or to exterminate the mosquito. Naturally we desired to adopt the latter alternative. The issue was decided in 1897 when Sir Ronald Ross found the malaria organism in the stomach of a dapple-winged mosquito. This was one of the greatest discoveries ever made by man ; compared with it Columbus' discovery of America resembles the finding of sixpence in the gutter.

It is only fair to the mosquitoes to say that their bite is normally harmless in itself. They have no malicious motive—they merely want some food—and the microbe is introduced incidentally. If they are carrying it, they cannot help passing it on. After all, they take the risk of getting something unpleasant from us. That was a sad ending to the story in Goldsmith's *Elegy* :—

> " The man recovered of the bite,
> The dog it was that died."

A. S.

CONCERNING BITES

1. *Prevention*

Rub into the skin of the exposed parts of your body the following mixture :—

> Naphtha — 4 parts.
> Oil of citronella — 1 part.
> Oil of eucalyptus — 1 part.
> Oil of peppermint — 1 part.

2. *Cure*

The reaction of human beings to bites and curative applications varies greatly, but most people will obtain relief if they apply Tincture of Iodine to the afflicted spot soon after the bite has been received.

A. S.

A NIGHTLY ARMOUR

Against small foes that fly, creep, crawl, and/or bite

Make a bag of strongest artificial silk about seven feet long and about three feet wide with casing for running string at top. Cut out a piece of same material of size and shape suitable for hood, making one casing along edges of top and sides (for running string to draw round face) and another casing along bottom edge (for running string to draw round neck). Stitch lower edge of hood to top of bag at centre of back. Insert running strings. Provide a piece of mosquito netting sufficient to cover the face loosely and amply. Before getting into the bag remove boots or shoes and any other apparel or decorations you may be wearing likely to cause damage. Otherwise, clothing may be worn according to taste, provided there is room for it. If you intend to use other coverings, such as bedclothes, you will (unless you are a Sack Race Blue) place the bag in position beneath these before getting into it, otherwise you would have to perform certain difficult movements. These might be very amusing, but it would be wasteful to provide such entertainment in the absence of spectators. Examine the bag carefully before you get in. It may be already inhabited. When in the bag place the face netting loosely over your face and tuck in the edges underneath the hood. Then draw tight and securely fasten the neck strings and face strings of the hood. The edges of the netting should then be amply covered. Lastly, draw tight and securely fasten the neck strings of the bag, keeping your hands well inside while doing so. You can then lie down and go to sleep. When you wish to get up in the morning untie the strings, remove the face netting and get out of the bag delicately. Thoroughly shake netting, bag and hood, examine them carefully and remove any foreign bodies discovered. Then fold or roll up bag, hood and netting and cover and keep secure till next required. This contrivance is equally suitable for indoor and outdoor use. It has been tested many times in varying climates and found efficient. It is not fool-proof, and any user relying upon it without following strictly all the above instructions is liable to be punished with bites *according to taste*.

A. S.

A BASKET OF BUGS

I believe I am the only surviving basket-maker who, during the 'sixties and early 'seventies, made, in the ordinary course of his work, the wicker bug-traps then surviving in use in middle-class families. Such, as I remember, were placed in every bed in my great-grandfather's house in Whitechapel and in my grandfather's house in Spital-fields. In order to preserve specimens of this quaint instrument I made one for exhibition in our Cambridge Museum of Archæology and Ethnology, and another for the London Museum of Pestology.... The trap was placed behind the bolster and between it and the head of the bed—the iron bed had not then been invented. The little anthropophagi after their nightly meal would retire to digest between the interstices of the wicker trap. The housemaid in the morning would take the trap into the yard or garden and shake out the victims, who would meet a violent death under her feet. She would then replace the trap in position for the following night's service.

THOMAS OKEY (from *A Basketful of Memories*)

EXECUTION IN THE PALACE

Among the records preserved in the College of Pestology (52 Bedford Square, W.C.) is a receipt for two guineas paid in July 1827 to the Bug-Destroyer to His Majesty King George IV for destroying bugs in four bedsteads.

A. S.

THE ACCOMPANIMENT

The soloist engaged in such an exquisite performance as the act of sleeping should be provided with a fitting and harmonious accompaniment. Your ordinary sleeper will very likely share the opinion of the crusty old gentleman who, being asked by the barber how he liked his hair cut, replied " In silence." But more finished performers will have it that the beauty of sleep is intensified by certain sounds heard first consciously, then subconsciously. The sound of a storm at night is exhilarating to some, but many find such a powerful orchestra too violent an accompaniment. Lesser winds make sweeter music for most of us, using trees for instruments. Poplars near a house will send on windy nights a soothing pattering sound through the open windows. Wind in pine trees is to some of us a sobbing melancholy sound—to others, more fortunate, it may be a pleasing croon. For ourselves, we sleep most happily on a rainy night ; for there is a spout from the roof close to our bedroom window down which the rain slips very pleasantly, making a soothing sound like *googly-goo*. The sound of the sea will be pleasing to some, though we ourselves have often been kept awake by that melancholy roar which retreating waves send up from a pebbly beach. But it is surely pleasant to sleep by a quiet river. What a lovely sleep we had once at Landeck in Tyrol ! The tall windows were thrown open, and our eyes shut themselves unwillingly against a wide sky glittering with stars. Below us the living waters of the Inn went by melodiously all night long like dancers dancing in tune. It is likely that all audible sounds give form and colour to our dreams, no matter how little we remember them when we awake.

If you are unaccustomed to sleep in the open air, you will do wisely to make a careful survey of your surroundings before settling down. If you are in the neighbourhood of cows, you will find that their grazing, which seems such a quiet affair in daytime, sounds at night exactly like stout sheets being torn asunder. Again, hotels at Railway Junctions, though very convenient for the catching of early trains, are often impossible sleeping-places. Goods traffic is much handled at night, and the clash of waggons meeting each other is no less startling than the shrieks of locomotives. You will probably hear plenty of both. Our sleep, however, may become attuned to anything by custom. The kindly owner of a noisy factory, which was working at night, had in his employment a mechanic who lived near and was seriously ill. A message was sent to the man's wife to say that night-work would be stopped if that would make the patient sleep better. " If they stop the works," she said ; " he won't sleep a wink."

A. S.

SOLVITUR AMBULANDO

There is nothing more conducive to sleep than fresh air and exercise. If Sleep refuses her gift because during the day you have withheld these offerings, it is never too late to make amends. Don't go to bed just yet, or if already there get up, dress yourself and go for a short walk. If it be dark, wet and windy, good and well ; groping through the darkness and battling with wind and rain will make you more fit for sleep. If the moon be shining clearly out of a windless sky, the quiet beauty of the night will give you almost a foretaste of sleep. In any case you will very likely add something notable to your experiences. The night-walker is at least sure of one reward—a comforting feeling of superiority to the " folk in housen." Don't go far, don't walk fast, and go to bed at once when you return.

A. S.

BOOKS AT NIGHT

The great moment of the day is come. One stands watching the last sweep of violet into dun above the line of the hill, one sees how the flowers are falling one and all into a grey mist of confusion through which the little evening wind faintly whispers. Beyond the gate on the rough among the bracken, that has been amber-coloured all day and now is stretching a pale cloud to the horizon, two farmers are talking :

" Well, good-night."

" Good-night."

Now the only sound in all the world is the running stream, you turn down the path, open the door, find your way by the light of the fire to the lamp, light it, and then turn. The books crowd in upon you, they are pressing, urgent, upon every side. As you stand by one of the bookcases there is a glorious instant of indecision that you would prolong if nature would but allow it, then the book, almost without deliberate consciousness, is in your hand, your chair is drawn to the blaze, and with a sigh of content you are off and away. So, as the House has my Books and my Books have me, this last prayer to their presiding god :

Command the Roofe, great Genius, and from thence
Into this house powre downe thy influence,
That through each room a golden pipe may run
Of living water by thy Benizon.
Fulfill the Larders, and with strengthening bread
Be ever more these Bynns replenished.
Next, like a Bishop consecrate my ground,
That luckie Fairies here may dance their Round :
And after that, lay downe some silver pence,
The Master's charge and care to recompence.
Charme then the chambers ; make the beds for ease
More than for peavish pining sicknesses.
Fix the foundation fast, and let the Roofe
Growold with time, but yet keepe weather-proofe.

HUGH WALPOLE (from *Reading*)

WHAT SIR HARRY THINKS

It's nice to get up in the morning when the sun begins to
    shine,
At four or five or six o'clock in the good old summer time ;
But when the snow is snowing, and it's murky overhead—
It's nice to get up in the morning—but it's nicer to lie
    in your bed !

SIR HARRY LAUDER

MORNING

'Tis the hour when white-horsed Day
Chases Night her mares away ;
When the Gates of Dawn (they say)
    Phoebus opes :

And I gather that the Queen
May be uniformly seen,
Should the weather be serene,
　　On the slopes.

When the ploughman, as he goes
Leathern-gaitered o'er the snows,
From his hat and from his nose
　　Knocks the ice ;
And the panes are frosted o'er,
And the lawn is crisp and hoar,
As has been observed before
　　Once or twice.

When arrayed in breastplate red
Sings the robin, for his bread,
On the elmtree that hath shed
　　Every leaf ;
While, within, the frost benumbs
The still sleepy schoolboy's thumbs,
And in consequence his sums
　　Come to grief.

But when breakfast-time hath come,
And he's crunching crust and crumb,
He'll no longer look a glum
　　Little dunce ;
But be brisk as bees that settle
On a summer rose's petal :
Wherefore, Polly, put the kettle
　　On at once.

                              C. S. CALVERLEY

SECOND PART

§ I SMALL TALK IN THE CARAVANSERAI

§ 1. Little Playthings

§ 2. These from the Land of *Nods*

A halt on the journey, a rest, a drink from the well, and the caravan moves on at the setting of the stars.

OMAR KHAYYÁM

" The time has come," the Walrus said,
    " To talk of many things :
Of shoes—and ships—and sealing wax—
    Of cabbages—and kings——"

LEWIS CARROLL (*Through the Looking-glass*)

§ 1. LITTLE PLAYTHINGS

WASSAIL

The old English merrymakings on New Year's Eve were of very ancient origin. The Head of the House assembled his family around a bowl of spiced ale (comically called " Lamb's Wool "). After the Head had drunk the health of all, the bowl was passed round and each person before drinking said the Saxon words *waes hdl* (i.e. " be whole "=" be well "=" good health "). The children of the poor carried round the neighbourhood a bowl decorated with ribbons, begging the means of filling it with " Lamb's Wool." They announced their presence with

A WASSAIL SONG

" Here we come a wassailing,
    Among the leaves so green,
Here we come a wandering,
    So fair to be seen.

Love and joy come to you,
And to you your wassail too,
And God bless you and send you
        a happy New Year !

We are not daily beggars,
    That beg from door to door ;
But we are neighbours' children,
    Whom you have seen before.

Here we have a little purse
    Of stretching leather skin,
A little from your money bags
    Would line it well within.

So bring us out a table,
    And spread it with a cloth ;
And bring us out a mouldy cheese,
    And some of your Christmas loaf.

God bless the master of this house,
    Likewise the mistress too,
And all the little children,
    That round the table go !

Love and joy come to you,
And to you your wassail too,
And God bless you and send you
        a happy New Year ! ”

The Loving Cup filled with sweetened and spiced wine handed round at the Feasts of the City of London Companies is the true descendant of the Wassail Bowl ; but those who wish for a proper wassailing after the old style will take note of the following

RECIPE

Put into a bowl ½lb. of Lisbon sugar ; pour on it 1 pint of warm beer ; grate a nutmeg and some ginger into it ; add 5 additional pints of beer ; stir well ; sweeten to taste ; cover up and keep covered for 3 hours ; then add 4 thin slices of toasted bread and 4 roasted apples which will float pleasantly on the top. You can then begin wassailing, or, if you prefer to bottle the mixture and drink it unceremoniously, it will be ready for use in a few days in an effervescent state.

A. S.

A FOURTEENTH CENTURY DISH

Take hens and pork, and boil them together. Take the flesh and hew it small, and grind it all to dust. Take grated bread, and mix it with the broth, and add to it yolks of eggs. Boil it, and put therein powder of ginger sugar, saffron, and salt—and look that it be stiff.

Cookery Book of King Richard II

SLEEPING AND WAKING:

(*Love and love*)

Sleep, wayward thoughts, and rest you with my Love.
  Let not my Love be with my love dis-eased.
Touch not, proud hands, lest you her anger move,
  But pine you with my longings long displeased.
Thus while she sleeps I sorrow for her sake,
So sleeps my Love, and yet my love doth wake . .

My love doth rage, and yet my Love doth rest.
  Fear in my love, and yet my Love secure.
Peace in my Love, and yet my love oppressed,

Impatient yet of perfect temperature.
Sleep, dainty Love, while I sigh for thy sake.
So sleeps my Love, and yet my love doth wake.

From DOWLAND'S *Booke of Ayres*, 1597

GET BORN ON A SUNDAY

Sunday's child is full of grace,
Monday's child is full in the face,
Tuesday's child is solemn and sad,
Wednesday's child is merry and glad,
Thursday's child is inclined to thieving,
Friday's child is free in giving,
Saturday's child works hard for his living.

A Cornish Rhyme

ROMANCE

My mother said that I never should
Play with the gipsies in the wood.
I told my mother that if I could
I'd play with the gipsies in the wood.
I went to the sea, but couldn't get across,
So I paid ten shillings for an old blind horse.
I jumped on his back, was off in a crack,
And came at last to the woodman's track.
The wood was dark and the grass was green.
Up came Sally with a tambourine.

Old English Game Song

BIBO AND CHARON

When Bibo thought fit from the world to retreat,
As full of champagne as an egg's full of meat,
He wak'd in the boat ; and to Charon he said,
He would be row'd back, for he was not yet dead,
" Trim the boat, and sit quiet," stern Charon replied,
" You may have forgot, you were drunk when you died."

MATTHEW PRIOR

STELLA'S BIRTHDAY
(1720)

All travellers at first incline
Where'er they see the fairest sign,
And if they find the chambers neat,
And like the liquor and the meat,
Will call again, and recommend
The Angel Inn to every friend.
And though the painting grows decay'd,
The house will never lose its trade :
Nay, though the treach'rous tapster, Thomas,
Hangs a new Angel two doors from us,
As fine as daubers' hands can make it,
In hopes that strangers may mistake it,
We think it both a shame and sin
To quit the true old Angel Inn.
    Now this is Stella's case in fact,
An angel's face a little crack'd.
(Could poets or could painters fix
How angels look at thirty-six :)

This drew us in at first to find
In such a form an angel's mind;
And every virtue now supplies
The fainting rays of Stella's eyes.
See, at her levee crowding swains,
Whom Stella freely entertains
With breeding, humour, wit, and sense,
And puts them to so small expense;
Their minds so plentifully fills,
And makes such reasonable bills,
So little gets for what she gives,
We really wonder how she lives!
And had her stock been less, no doubt
She must have long ago run out.

    Then who can think we'll quit the place,
When Doll hangs out a newer face;
Or stop and light at Chloe's Head,
With scraps and leavings to be fed.

    Then, Chloe, still go on to prate
Of thirty-six and thirty-eight;
Pursue your trade of scandal picking,
Your hints that Stella is no chicken.
Your innuendoes when you tell us
That Stella loves to talk with fellows;
And let me warn you to believe
A truth, for which your soul should grieve:
That should you live to see the day
When Stella's locks must all be grey,
When age must print a furrowed trace
On every feature of her face;
Though you and all your senseless tribe,
Could art, or time, or nature bribe
To make you look like beauty's queen

And hold for ever at fifteen;
No bloom of youth can ever blind
The cracks and wrinkles of your mind;
All men of sense will pass your door,
And crowd to Stella's at fourscore.

SWIFT

A GENTLE ECHO ON WOMAN

(*In the Doric Manner*)

SHEPHERD. Echo, I ween, will in the wood reply,
   And quaintly answer questions : shall I try?
ECHO.   Try.
SHEPHERD : What must we do our passion to express?
ECHO.   Press.
SHEPHERD. How shall I please her, who ne'er loved
      before?
ECHO.   Be Fore.
SHEPHERD : What moves women when we them address?
ECHO :   A dress.
SHEPHERD : Say, what can keep her chaste whom I adore?
ECHO :   A door.
SHEPHERD : If music softens rocks, love tunes my lyre.
ECHO :   Liar.
SHEPHERD : Then teach me, Echo, how shall I come by
      her.
ECHO :   Buy her.
SHEPHERD : When bought, no question I shall be her
      dear?

ECHO :　　　　　　　Her deer.

SHEPHERD : But deer have horns : how must I keep her under ?

ECHO :　　　　　　　Keep her under.

SHEPHERD : But what can glad me when she's laid on bier ?

ECHO :　　　　　　　Beer.

SHEPHERD : What must I do when women will be kind ?

ECHO :　　　　　　　Be kind.

SHEPHERD : What must I do when women will be cross ?

ECHO :　　　　　　　Be cross.

SHEPHERD : Lord, what is she that can so turn and wind ?

ECHO :　　　　　　　Wind.

SHEPHERD : If she be wind, what stills her when she blows ?

ECHO :　　　　　　　Blows.

SHEPHERD : But if she bang again, still should I bang her ?

ECHO :　　　　　　　Bang her.

SHEPHERD : Is there no way to moderate her anger ?

ECHO :　　　　　　　Hang her.

SHEPHERD : Thanks, gentle Echo ! right thy answers tell What woman is and how to guard her well.

ECHO :　　　　　　　Guard her well.

SWIFT

SOMETHING ABOUT NOTHING

I am now trying an experiment very frequent among modern authors, which is to write upon nothing ; when the subject is utterly exhausted, to let the pen still move on : by some called the ghost of wit, delighting to walk after the death of its body. And to say the truth, there seems to be no part of knowledge in fewer hands than that of discerning when to have done. By the time that an author has written out a book he and his readers are become old acquaintance, and grow very loth to part ; so that I have sometimes known it to be in writing as in visiting, where the ceremony of taking leave has employed more time than the whole conversation before. The conclusion of a treatise resembles the conclusion of human life, which has sometimes been compared to the end of a feast, where few are satisfied to depart ; for men will sit down after the fullest meal, though it be only to doze or to sleep out the rest of the day. But in this latter I differ extremely from other writers ; and shall be too proud if, by all my labours, I can have anyways contributed to the repose of mankind in times so turbulent and unquiet as these. Neither do I think such an employment so very alien from the office of a wit as some would suppose. For, among a very polite nation in Greece, there were the same temples built and consecrated to Sleep and the Muses ; between which two deities they believed the strictest friendship was established.

SWIFT (from *Tale of a Tub*)

MRS. MARY BLAIZE

Good people all, with one accord,
    Lament for Madam Blaize,
Who never wanted a good word—
    From those who spoke her praise.

A Comb

I am white at the neck as Susannah the fair,
Tho' my body sometimes is all cover'd with hair ;
As a flounder am flat, as a beetle am blind,
Yet good services do to the race of mankind ;
The copses and coverts I traverse each day,
To drive from their holds and destroy beasts of prey ;
Having two rows of teeth for engagement design'd,
They all fly before me like chaff before wind ;
Now tell but my name, ye mammas or misses,
And those who stand by shall reward you with kisses.

A Pair of Shoes

Tho' good fellows we are,
We can't hope to be sav'd ;
From our very first day,
To our last we're enslav'd,
Our office is hardest,
And food sure the worst,

Being crammed with raw flesh,
Till we're ready to burst ;
Tho' low in our state,
Ev'n Kings we support ;
And at balls have
The principal share of the sport.

A Doll

Like Lady Patch, in diff'rent dress,
    I either sex can ape ;
And like her, all mankind confess,
    Have comeliness and shape ;

Had she the innocence of me,
    And I her air and parts,
She would a perfect goddess be,
    And I should gain more hearts.

A Fan

Come hear and see a tawdry thing,
Fluttering with expanded wing ;
Like the lark that upward tends,
And like her too, when she descends
Toss'd by the owner to and fro,
Her beauty and its own to show ;
Suff'ring much at ball and play
And working ev'ry holiday ;
But what is still more strange to tell,
When by Belinda manag'd well,
Its pow'r th' admiring youth perplexes,
For her it cools, but burns Alexis.

From *A New Riddle Book*, 1778

SOME OLD RHYMES

The Wish

Oh that I were where I would be !
Then should I be where I am not ;
But where I am, there I must be,
And where I would be I can not.

If

If all the world was apple-pie
   And all the sea was ink,
And all the trees were bread and cheese,
   What should we do for drink?
It's enough to make an old man
   Scratch his head and think.

A Candle Burning

Little Nan Etticoat
In a white petticoat
And a red nose:
The longer she stands
The shorter she grows.

ANONYMOUS

KITTY OF COLERAINE

As beautiful Kitty one morning was tripping,
   With a pitcher of milk from the fair of Coleraine,
When she saw me she stumbled, the pitcher it tumbled,
   And all the sweet butter-milk watered the plain.

O, what shall I do now, 'twas looking at you, now,
   Sure, sure, such a pitcher I'll not meet again.
'Twas the pride of my dairy, O, Barney M'Leary,
   You're sent as a plague to the girls of Coleraine.

I sat down beside her—and gently did chide her,
  That such a misfortune should give her such pain,
A kiss then I gave her—before I did leave her,
  She vowed for such pleasure she'd break it again.

'Twas hay-making season, I can't tell the reason,
  Misfortunes will never come single,—that's plain,
For, very soon after poor Kitty's disaster,
  The devil a pitcher was whole in Coleraine.

E. LYSAGHT

HOUSEHOLD HINTS

Luncheon for an Invalid

Put bread crumbs and red currant, or any other jelly,
alternately into a tumbler, and when nearly half full, fill
it up with milk.

The Bustard

will probably thrive well on the same food as the turkey.
It is seldom reared ; but, as its flesh has ever been considered most delicious, it appears particularly worthy of
the attention of those who aim at variety and novelty.

FOR AUTHORS DESIRING IMMORTALITY

How to make Permanent Ink

Rub down, in a small mortar, 5 scruples of lunar caustic,
with one drachm of gumarabic, 1 scruple of sap green, and
one ounce of rain water.

From MRS. DALGAIRNS' *Practice of Cookery, &c.,* 1829

SAFE EXERCISES

Miss Blofield, Professor of the Terpsichorean Positions, exercises in families and schools where dancing cannot be conscientiously admitted. Miss B. begs to state that her system of exercises may be practised with perfect safety, on account of the great gentleness of the method pursued.

Advertisement in 1834

FAITHLESS SALLY BROWN

Young Ben he was a nice young man,
   A carpenter by trade ;
And he fell in love with Sally Brown,
   That was a lady's maid.

But as they fetch'd a walk one day,
   They met a press-gang crew ;
And Sally she did faint away,
   Whilst Ben he was brought to.

The Boatswain swore with wicked words,
   Enough to shock a saint,
That though she did seem in a fit,
   'Twas nothing but a feint.

" Come, girl," said he, " hold up your head,
   He'll be as good as me ;
For when your swain is in our boat,
   A boatswain he will be."

So when they'd made their game of her,
  And taken off her elf,
She rous'd, and found she only was
  A coming to herself.

" And is he gone, and is he gone ? "
  She cried, and wept outright :
" Then I will to the water-side,
  And see him out of sight."

A waterman came up to her,
  " Now, young woman," said he,
" If you weep on so, you will make
  Eye-water in the sea."

" Alas ! they've taken my beau Ben,
  To sail with old Benbow " ;
And her woe began to run afresh,
  As if she'd said, Gee woe !

Says he, " They've only taken him
  To the Tender-ship, you see " ;
" The Tender-ship," cried Sally Brown,
  " What a hard-ship that must be ! "

" Oh ! would I were a mermaid now,
  For then I'd follow him ;
But—Oh ! I'm not a fish-woman,
  And so I cannot swim.

" Alas ! I was not born beneath
  The virgin and the scales,
So I must curse my cruel stars,
  And walk about in Wales."

Now Ben had sail'd to many a place
    That's underneath the world ;
But in two years the ship came home,
    And all her sails were furl'd.

But when he call'd on Sally Brown,
    To see how she got on,
He found she'd got another Ben,
    Whose Christian name was John.

" Oh, Sally Brown, Oh, Sally Brown,
    How could you serve me so,
I've met with many a breeze before,
    But never such a blow ! "

Then reading on his 'bacco box,
    He heav'd a heavy sigh,
And then began to eye his pipe,
    And then to pipe his eye.

And then he tried to sing, " All's Well,"
    But could not, though he tried ;
His head was turn'd, and so he chew'd
    His pigtail till he died.

His death, which happened in his berth,
    At forty-odd befell ;
They went and told the sexton, and
    The sexton toll'd the bell.

THOMAS HOOD

THE BRUTES

I think I could turn and live with animals, they are so
    placid and self-contain'd ;
I stand and look at them sometimes half the day long.
They do not sweat and whine about their condition ;
They do not lie awake in the dark and weep for their
    sins ; . . .
Not one is dissatisfied—not one is demented with the
    mania of owning things ; . . .
Not one is respectable or industrious over the whole earth.

WALT WHITMAN (from *Song of Myself*)

AN OXFORD IDYLL

Ah little mill, you're rumbling still,
    Ah sunset flecked with gold !
Ah deepening tinge, ah purple fringe
    Of lilac as of old !
Ah hawthorn hedge, ah light-won pledge
    Of kisses warm and plenty,
When she was true, and twenty-two,
    And I was two-and-twenty.
I don't know how she broke her vow—
    She said that I was " horty " ;
And there's the mill a-goin' still,
    And I am five-and-forty.
And sooth to tell, 'twas just as well,
    Her aitches were uncertain ;
Her ways though nice, not point-device ;
    Her father liked his " Burton."

But there's a place you cannot trace,
　　So spare the fond endeavour—
A cloudless sky, where Kate and I
　　Are twenty-two for ever.

T. E. BROWN

ENGLISH MADE IN GERMANY

Inscription on a receptacle for cigar-ash

NOTIS !

Every defilement of the carpet with cigar-ash is forbidden to the severest. He who nevertheless finds himself guilty of such a one will be punished irrevocably with house-arrest.

(From a German-made article, 19th century)

INSCRIPTION ON A MEMORIAL TABLET NEAR MÜRREN

Erected in memory of Miss —— who was killed by lightning on this spot by her sorrowing sister.

(Copied on the spot)

FOOTNOTES TO HISTORY (1914–1918)

Mr. Punch watches the Great War

THE BULL-DOG BREED

Scene : The English shore.

OFFICER : " Now, my lad, do you know what you are placed here for ? "

RECRUIT : " To prevent the henemy from landin', Sir."

OFFICER : " And do you think that you could prevent him landing all by yourself ? "

RECRUIT : " Don't know, Sir, I'm sure. But I'd have a dam good try ! "

Punch (Sept. 30, 1914)

THE SKEELY SKIPPER

FIRST TRAWLER SKIPPER (to friend who is due to sail by next tide) : " Are ye takin' any precautions against these submarines, Jock ? "

SECOND SKIPPER : " Ay ! Although I've been in the habit o' carryin' my bits o' bawbees wi' me, I went an' bankit them this mornin', an' am no takin' ma best oilskins or ma noo seaboots."

FIRST SKIPPER : " Oh, you're a' richt, then. Ye'll have practically naethin' tae lose but yer life."

Punch (July 14, 1915)

TIME AND TASTE

THE PESSIMIST (morbidly) : " I tell yer wot it is. This ere War's goin' to last five years."

THE OTHER : " Why not make it fifty, and *thoroughly* enjoy yourself ? "

Punch (July 21, 1915)

SHOPPING IN FRANCE

SUBALTERN : " Donnez-moi, s'il vous plait, du pain, de la beurre et de la fromage, pour la messe."

MADAME : " Pour la messe ! Mon Dieu, quelle religion ! "

Punch (July 21, 1915)

MAKING THE MOST OF IT

COSTER'S LADY (pointing to a friend who has just passed) : " Yes, she's off to the cinema again, and I don't blame her. Make the most of it, I say. Who knows ? We may be 'aving peace upon us at any moment ! "

Punch (August 25, 1915)

FAITH IN THE FORCE

MISTRESS : " Well, Cook, if you and the other maids are at all nervous of the Zeppelins, you can have your beds removed into the basement."

COOK : " No, thank you, ma'am. We have every confidence in the policeman at the gate."

Punch (March 10, 1915)

AN AWKWARD SITUATION

YOUNG LADY VISITOR (at private hospital) : " Can I see Lieutenant Barker, please ? "

MATRON : " We do not allow ordinary visiting. May I ask if you are a relative ? "

YOUNG LADY (boldly) : " Oh, yes ! I'm his sister."

MATRON : " Dear me. I'm very glad to meet you. I'm *his mother*."

Punch (April 5, 1916)

PET OF THE PLATOON : " I didn't half tell off our Sergeant just now. I called him a knock-kneed, pigeon-toed, swivel-eyed monkey, and said he ought to go to a night school."

ECSTATIC CHORUS : " And what did he say ? "

BILL (after a pause) : " Well, as a matter of fac', I don't think he quite heard me."

Punch (January 24, 1917)

FIDO DOES (WITHOUT) HIS BIT

ANGRY LADY (on being told that Fido's favourite biscuits are now unobtainable) : " Nothing but these ! Really this war is getting beyond a joke ! "

Punch (August 15, 1917)

CIRCUMSTANCES ALTER CASES

MEDICAL OFFICER (London practitioner in private life, addressing military patient) : " Would you come to me with such a trivial complaint in private life ? "

PRIVATE : " No, Sir. I should send for you."

Punch (August 21, 1918)

SOME THOUGHTS ON EXAMINATIONS

Doctor Johnson said that questioning is not the mode of conversation among gentlemen. Doctor Johnson left Oxford without a degree.

The brilliant man who did not know and the learned

man who did not think met in the Second Class and
disliked each other. The poet sat in the Third and
laughed.

The nightingale got no prize at the poultry show.

WISHES AT A GARDEN PARTY

I wish I loved the Human Race ;
I wish I loved its silly face ;
I wish I liked the way it walks ;
I wish I liked the way it talks ;
And when I'm introduced to one
I wish I thought *What Jolly Fun* !

SIR WALTER RALEIGH (1861–1922)
(from *Laughter from a Cloud*)

RÉCHAUFFÉ FIN DE SIÈCLE

(*from a novel published in* 1897)

Love, alas ! when smitten with the sword of indifference,
dieth soon, but once struck on the tunnelled cheek of
secrecy with the hand of pity there leaves a scar of indelible
intolerance, until wiped out for ever with the curative
balsam of battled freedom . . .

" Speak ! Irene ! Wife ! Woman ! Do not sit in silence
and allow the blood that now boils in my veins to ooze
through cavities of unrestrained passion and trickle down
to drench me with its crimson hue ! " . . .

It was at this stage, too, that Lady Dunfern was made to taste of the dish of fanciful wish in which she often dipped her slender fingers to sprinkle her body of dishonesty. She got time now to brood over her actions of silly execution and hatch them with heated hunger . . .

She had at last been cast on the mercy of a world of icy indifference to facts of long standing, and made to taste of the stagnant waters of pity, which flung their muddy drops of rancid rascality on the face of dogmatic dread . . .

He was tempted to invest in the polluted stocks of magnified extension, and when their banks seemed swollen with rotten gear, gathered too often from the winds of wilful wrong, how the misty dust blinded his sense of sight and drove him through the field of fashion and feeble effeminacy, which he once never meant to tread, landing him on the slippery rock of smutty touch, to wander into its hidden cavities of ancient fame . . .

AMANDA M'KITTRICK ROS
(from *Irene Iddesleigh*)

ABSIT NOMEN !

Rebecca flung about the town
Without a thought of settling down.
Her features most distinctly classy
Began to grow a little *passé*.
She vowed to husband her resources,
And summoned all her female forces
To advertise her hand and heart
Upon the London marriage mart.
Although her charms were slightly aged,
Rebecca soon became engaged.
Charles suited well her dearest fancy,

229

And was indeed a fine fiancy.
Her rivals incommoded were—
(Whatever could he see in her ?)
Bewitching were her smiles and prattles
When Charles produced his list of chattels,
And told without the slightest swank
The size of his account at Bank,
Described his country seat at Wantage
With grounds laid out to great advantage,
His diamonds with frequent facets,
His cellars full of liquid assets,
His car that ran like a torpedo,
His yacht at Cannes, his house at Lido.
They motored, dined, and danced and swam,
They rowed on Isis, Thames and Cam ;
They flew abroad for winter sports,
They sunbathed in the shortest shorts.
But when the wedding day approached
Fear in Rebecca's heart encroached.
A fly was in the festive ointment—
She failed to keep her church appointment.
It was, she said, a rotten shame
She should be asked to change her name.
Her friends might call her jilt or flirt—
She could not marry Mr. Dyrt.

ANONYMOUS

NANNY

I sing a long-neglected dame.
Let plays and poets all proclaim
The wonder of the Mother's name,
   And even that of Granny ;

Let others tell with loud hurrahs
The general praises of papas—
I hymn the Mother of Mammas,
   I sing the British Nanny.
Not every pink and girlish thing
   That pushes round a pram,
The ancient rock-like NURSE I sing,
   Britannia's virgin dam,
That, old as mountains and as stout,
From child to child is passed about
Till childless yet, she passes out,
   The lonely British Nanny.

For she it was that from the first
Refused to judge us by our worst;
We might be yelling fit to burst—
   She crooned a cheerful ditty;
Our very aunts could not deny
That we were small and ugly fry,
But she with fond prophetic eye
   Maintained that we were pretty.
Alone of all the human race
   She took the kind of view
Of our importance, brain and face,
   That we would have men do;
And I can never quite forget
No other person I have met
Considered me a perfect pet,
   So here's a health to Nanny!

The artless prattle of a child
Drives everybody nearly wild,
And who that for an hour beguiled
   A babe however clever

For all the riches of the rich
Would undertake a life in which
They lived at that exacting pitch
   Ten hours a day for ever ?
Though even in the mother's joys
   A grander cycle dawns
When we grow more like little boys
   And less like little prawns,
Our Nanny, in a nobler strain,
Would have us at our worst remain,
A babe for ever pink and plain,
   Herself for ever Nanny.

Alas ! the twig becomes a bough ;
We do not need a Nanny now ;
Forgetting her who showed us how,
   We walk to death or glory ;
And whether Fate blows cold or hot,
Whatever women shape our lot,
It's safe to say a Nurse will not
   Be mentioned in the story.
Some other baby far away
   Is hers to soothe or slap.
Some Nelson's in the bath to-day,
   Some Shelley in her lap ;
And when I think on this small star
How many mighty men there are,
I call for wine and drain a jar
   To England's noble Nannies.

A. P. HERBERT

VERSES THAT RHYME

(if read as intended)

There was a young fellow of *St. Bartholomew's*
Whose car went by fits and by *St. Startholomew's*
   Till a chap named *St. John*
   Overhauled the *t. John*
And fitted it out with spare *St. Partholomew's*.

ANONYMOUS

A LIMERICK

There was once a young rascal called Denny
Who sold all his clothes for a penny ;
   When the folk went to church
   He was left in the lurch,
But he said I shall go without any.

ANONYMOUS

TEMPER

" Blow out the light," they said, they said
   (She'd got to the very last page) ;
" Blow out the light," they said, they said,
" It's dreadfully wicked to read in bed " ;
Her eyes grew black and her face grew red
   And she blew in a terrible rage.

She put out the moon, she did, she did,
   So frightfully hard she blew,
She put out the moon, she did, she did ;
Over the sky the darkness slid,
The stars all scuttled away and hid—
   (A very wise thing to do).

But please don't whisper the tale about,
   She'd get into trouble, she would ;
Please don't whisper the tale about,
If anyone else should ever find out
She'd get into trouble without a doubt,
   And now she's *ever* so good.

ROSE FYLEMAN

§ 2. THESE FROM THE LAND OF *NODS*

> Our good Homer sometimes nods.
>
> HORACE (*Ars Poetica*)

MORTAL STARS

O eyes, O mortal stars,
   The authors of my harms,
That in slumbering wage wars
   To kill me with sweet charms ;
If closed you do annoy me,
Being open you'd destroy me.

From *Ferrabosco's Ayres*, 1609

THE SLUGGARD

'Tis the voice of the sluggard ; I hear him complain,
" You have wak'd me too soon, I must slumber again."
As the door on its hinges, so he on his bed,
Turns his sides, and his shoulders, and his heavy head.

" A little more sleep, and a little more slumber,"
Thus he wastes half his days and his hours without
    number ;
And when he gets up, he sits folding his hands,
Or walks about sauntering, or trifling he stands.

I pass'd by his garden, and saw the wild brier,
The thorn and the thistle grow broader and higher ;
The clothes that hang on him are turning to rags ;
And his money still wastes till he starves or he begs.

I made him a visit, still hoping to find
He had took better care for improving his mind :
He told me his dreams, talk'd of eating and drinking ;
But scarce reads his Bible, and never loves thinking.

Said I then to my heart, " Here's a lesson for me,"
That man's but a picture of what I might be ;
But thanks to my friends for their care in my breeding ;
Who taught me betimes to love working and reading.

ISAAC WATTS

THE SAINT PURSUED

Hark ! she bids all her friends adieu ;
Some angel calls her to the spheres ;
Our eyes the radiant saint pursue
Through liquid telescopes of tears.

ISAAC WATTS (from lines
On the sudden death of Mrs. Mary Peacock)

POOR SOUTH

Poor South ! Her books get fewer and fewer,
She was never much given to literature.

J. GORDON COOGLER

A WORD FOR THE WORM

O may Thy powerful word
   Inspire the feeble worm
To rush into Thy kingdom, Lord,
   And take it as by storm.

          From *The Wesleyan Hymn-Book*

TO GENTLE READERS

And now, kind friends, what I have wrote,
   I hope you will pass o'er,
And not criticise as some have done
   Hitherto herebefore.

          JULIA MOORE

A POETICAL THOUGHT

O Moon, when I gaze on thy beautiful face,
Careering along through the boundaries of space,
The thought has often come into my mind
If I ever shall see thy glorious behind.

          ANONYMOUS

A WARNING TO TOURISTS

But most avoid Italia's coast,
Where ev'ry sentiment is lost,
Where Treach'ry reigns, and base Disguise,
And Murder—looking to the skies,
While sordid Selfishness appears
In low redundancy of fears.
O ! What can Music's voice bestow
Of sculptur'd grace, or Titian glow,
To recompense the feeling mind
For British virtues left behind ?

ANONYMOUS (*c.* 1790)

PAOLO AND FRANCESCA

Twice had he seen her since the Prince was gone,
On some small matter needing unison ;
Twice linger'd, and convers'd, and grown long friends
But not till now where no one else attends.—
" May I come in ? " said he :—it made her start,—
That smiling voice ;—she colour'd, press'd her heart
A moment, as for breath, and then with free
And usual tone said,—" O yes, certainly."

LEIGH HUNT (from *The Story of Rimini*)

A CRITICISM OF LEIGH HUNT

O crimini !
What a nimini-pimini
Story of Rimini !

THEODORE HOOK (from *Letter from a Cockney*)

DIABOLUS EX MACHINA

Now, when the rustic wears the social smile,
Released from day and its attendant toil,
And draws his household round their evening fire,
And tells the oft-told tales that never tire :
Or where the town's blue turrets dimly rise,
And manufacture taints the ambient skies,
The pale mechanic leaves the labouring loom,
The air-pent hold, the pestilential room,
And rushes out, impatient to begin
The stated course of customary sin :
Now, now, my solitary way I bend
Where solemn groves in awful state impend,
And cliffs, that boldly rise above the plain,
Bespeak, blest Clifton, thy sublime domain.

HENRY KIRKE WHITE (from *Clifton Grove*)

A GOOD GOER

To horse ! to horse ! my coal-black steed
  Paws the ground and snuffs the air !
There's not a foal of Arab's breed
  More knows what he must bear ;
On the hill he will not tire,
Swifter as it waxes higher ;
In the march he will not slacken,
On the plain be overtaken,
In the wave he will not sink,
Nor pause at the brook's side to drink ;

In the race he will not pant,
In the combat he'll not faint;
On the stones he will not stumble
Time nor toil will make him humble;
In the stall he will not stiffen,
But be wingèd as a griffin,
Only flying with his feet:
And will not such a voyage be sweet?

BYRON (from *The Deformed Transformed*)

A PUZZLER

" Now, little Edward, say why so :
My little Edward, tell me why."—
" I cannot tell, I do not know."—
" Why, this is strange," said I.

WORDSWORTH (from *Anecdote for Fathers*)

ENOUGH OF IT

And thus continuing, she said,
" I had a son, who many a day
Sailed on the sea ; but he is dead ;
In Denmark he was cast away ;
And I have travelled far as Hull to see
What clothes he might have left, or other property."

WORDSWORTH (from *The Sailor's Mother*)

A NASTY PUSH

By that lake whose gloomy shore
Skylark never warbles o'er,
Where the cliff hangs high and steep,
Young St. Kevin stole to sleep.
" Here at least," he calmly said,
" Woman ne'er shall find my bed."
Ah ! the good Saint little knew
What that wily sex can do . . .
Even now, while calm he sleeps,
Kathleen o'er him leans and weeps.
Fearless, she had tracked his feet
To this rocky wild retreat ;
And when morning met his view,
Her mild glances met it too.
Ah ! your Saints have cruel hearts !
Sternly from his bed he starts,
And with rude, repulsive shock,
Hurls her from the beetling rock.

THOMAS MOORE (from *Irish Melodies*)

A QUESTION

Little girl, have you finished your daily employ
  With industry, patience and care ?
If so, lay your head on your pillow with joy,
  No thorn to disturb shall be there.

JANE TAYLOR (1804)

CHARLES AND THE INSECTS

1. *The Bee*

Ah, cruel Charles, how could'st thou take
    Captive that bee, amid the flow'r,
Which gaily left its home to make
    Sweet honey at the morning hour . . .

O, thou hast crushed, hard-hearted boy,
    The little weak industrious thing ;
How could'st thou wantonly destroy—
    Ha ! dost thou feel its venom'd sting ?

Well may'st thou shriek, weep, pout, and low'r,
    That hadst no pity on the bee—
Tho' but an insect it had pow'r
    To make thee rue thy cruelty.

2. *The Moth*

When Charles with his loved parents sat
In social and amusing chat,
Candles shone bright, bright glow'd the fire,
And Lydia touch'd the tuneful lyre.

And now as loud the sweet harp rung,
And Charles with his fond sister sung,
A sprightly moth its wings outspread
And humm'd and buzz'd around each head . . .

She hovers round and round the light,
Nor dreams its glare is deadly bright,
Then darts amid the flame, most blest,
To bask in such a Phoenix' nest . . .

Lydia and Charles, O, be aware,
That pleasure often proves a gilded snare :
The flames of vice, tho' clad in lovely tints most bright,
Are but the guide to realms of everlasting night.

J. F. PENNIE (1822)

THE FEMALE FRIEND

In this imperfect, gloomy scene
    Of complicated ill,
How rarely is a day serene,
    The throbbing bosom still !
Will not a beauteous landscape bright,
    Or music's soothing sound,
Console the heart, afford delight,
    And throw sweet peace around ?
They may, but never comfort lend
Like an accomplish'd female friend ! . . .

As orbs revolve and years recede,
    As seasons onward roll,
The fancy may on beauties feed,
    With discontented soul !
A thousand objects bright and fair
    May for a moment shine,
Yet many a sigh and many a tear
    But mark their swift decline ;
While lasting joys the man attend
Who has a faithful female friend !

CORNELIUS WHUR (1837)

SECOND PART

§II A LIGHT REPAST

Dost thou think, because thou art virtuous, there shall be no more cakes and ale?

SHAKESPEARE (*Twelfth Night*)

I live in a constant endeavour to fence against the evils of life by mirth, being firmly persuaded that every time a man smiles—but much more so when he laughs—it adds something to this Fragment of Life.

STERNE (Dedication of *Tristram Shandy*)

Damn braces! Bless relaxes!
I hate scarce smiles. I love laughing.

BLAKE

§ II A LIGHT REPAST

TO HIS COY MISTRESS

Had we but world enough, and time,
This coyness, lady, were no crime.
We would sit down, and think which way
To walk, and pass our long love's day.
Thou by the Indian Ganges' side
Should'st rubies find : I by the tide
Of Humber would complain. I would
Love you ten years before the Flood,
And you should, if you please, refuse
Till the conversion of the Jews.
My vegetable love should grow
Vaster than empires, and more slow.
An hundred years should go to praise
Thine eyes, and on thy forehead gaze :
Two hundred to adore each breast :
But thirty thousand to the rest ;
An age at least to every part,
And the last age should shew your heart.
For, lady, you deserve this state,
Nor would I love at lower rate.
   But at my back I always hear
Time's wingèd chariot hurrying near :
And yonder all before us lie
Deserts of vast eternity.
Thy beauty shall no more be found ;
Nor, in thy marble vault, shall sound
My echoing song ; then worms shall try
That long-preserv'd virginity :

And your quaint honour turn to dust,
And into ashes all my lust.
The grave's a fine and private place,
But none, I think, do there embrace,
 Now, therefore, while the youthful hue
Sits on thy skin like morning dew,
And while thy willing soul transpires
At every pore with instant fires,
Now let us sport us while we may ;
And now, like amorous birds of prey,
Rather at once our Time devour,
Than languish in his slow-chapt power.
Let us roll all our strength and all
Our sweetness up into one ball,
And tear our pleasures with rough strife
Thorough the iron gates of life.
Thus, though we cannot make our Sun
Stand still, yet we will make him run.

MARVELL

AFTERNOON TEA IN 1816

 Some innuendoes more had pass'd,
Till out the scandal came at last.
" Come then, I'll tell you something more,"
Says she,—" Eliza, shut the door.—
I would not trust a creature here,
For all the world, but you, my dear.
Perhaps it's false—I wish it may,
—But let it go no further, pray."
" O," says mamma, " You need not fear,
We never mention what we hear."

" Indeed we shall not, Mrs. G."
Says I, again, impatiently :
And so, we drew our chairs the nearer,
And whispering, lest the child should hear her,
She told a tale, at least too *long*,
To be repeated in a song ;
We, panting every breath between,
With curiosity and spleen.
And how we did enjoy the sport !
And echo every faint report,
And answer every candid doubt,
And turn her motives inside out,
And holes in all her virtues pick,
Till we were sated, almost sick.
  —Thus having brought it to a close,
In great good humour, we arose.
Indeed, 'twas more than time to go,
Our boy had been an hour below.
So, warmly pressing Mrs. G.
To fix a day to come to tea,
We muffled up in cloke and plaid,
And trotted home behind the lad.

JANE TAYLOR

JUAN'S EDUCATION

But that which Donna Inez most desired,
  And saw into herself each day before all
The learned tutors whom for him she hired,
  Was, that his breeding should be strictly moral :

249

Much into all his studies she enquired,
    And so they were submitted first to her, all,
Arts, sciences, no branch was made a mystery
To Juan's eyes, excepting natural history.

The languages, especially the dead,
    The sciences, and most of all the abstruse.
The arts, at least all such as could be said
    To be the most remote from common use,
In all these he was much and deeply read ;
    But not a page of any thing that's loose,
Or hints continuation of the species,
Was ever suffer'd, lest he should grow vicious.

His classic studies made a little puzzle,
    Because of filthy loves of gods and goddesses,
Who in the earlier ages raised a bustle,
    But never put on pantaloons or bodices ;
His reverend tutors had at times a tussle,
    And for their Aeneids, Iliads, and Odysseys,
Were forced to make an odd sort of apology,
For Donna Inez dreaded the Mythology. . . .

Juan was taught from out the best edition,
    Expurgated by learned men, who place,
Judiciously, from out the schoolboy's vision,
    The grosser parts ; but fearful to deface
Too much their modest bard by this omission,
    And pitying sore his mutilated case,
They only add them all in an appendix,
Which saves, in fact, the trouble of an index. . . .

The Missal too (it was the family Missal)
      Was ornamented in a sort of way
Which ancient mass-books often are, and this all
      Kinds of grotesques illumined ; and how they,
Who saw the figures on the margin kiss all,
      Could turn their optics to the text and pray,
Is more than I know—but Don Juan's mother
Kept this herself, and gave her son another.

Sermons he read, and lectures he endured,
      And homilies, and lives of all the saints ;
To Jerome and to Chrysostom inured,
      He did not take such studies for restraints ;
But how faith is acquired, and then ensured,
      So well not one of the aforesaid paints
As Saint Augustine in his fine Confessions,
Which make the reader envy his transgressions.

This, too, was a seal'd book to little Juan—
      I can't but say that his mamma was right,
If such an education was the true one.
      She scarcely trusted him from out her sight ;
Her maids were old, and if she took a new one
      You might be sure she was a perfect fright,
She did this during even her husband's life—
I recommend as much to every wife.

                              BYRON (from *Don Juan*)

THE MERMAID TAVERN

Souls of poets dead and gone,
What Elysium have ye known,
Happy field or mossy cavern,
Choicer than the Mermaid Tavern?
Have ye tippled drink more fine
Than mine host's Canary wine?
Or are fruits of Paradise
Sweeter than those dainty pies
Of venison? O generous food!
Dressed as though bold Robin Hood
Would, with his Maid Marian,
Sup and bowse from horn and can.

I have heard that on a day
Mine host's sign-board flew away,
Nobody knew whither, till
An astrologer's old quill
To a sheepskin gave the story,
Said he saw you in your glory,
Underneath a new old sign
Sipping beverage divine,
And pledging with contented smack
The Mermaid in the Zodiac!

Souls of poets dead and gone,
What Elysium have ye known,
Happy field or mossy cavern,
Choicer than the Mermaid Tavern?

KEATS

GRANDPAPA

This is a portrait. Here one can
   Descry those purely human features
Whereby, since first the world began,
Man has with ease distinguished Man
   From humbler fellow-creatures
And seldom, whatso'er his shape,
Mistaken him for Dog or Ape.

Inspect this subject well, and note
   The whiskers centrally divided,
The silken stock about his throat,
The loose but elegant frock-coat,
   The boots (elastic-sided),
And you'll at once remark : "Ah, ha !
" This must, of course, be Grandpapa ! "

'Tis he, of feudal types the last,
   By all his peers revered, respected ;
His lines in pleasant places cast
Where churls saluted as he pass'd
   And maidens genuflected,
And, if he chanced to meet the Vicar,
The latter's pulse would beat the quicker. . . .

In politics it was his rule
   To be broadminded but despotic ;
In argument he kept quite cool
Knowing a man to be a fool
   And most unpatriotic
Who differed from the views that he
Had cherished from the age of three.

I well remember, as a child,
    How much his moods perplexed and awed me
At times irate, at others mild,
Alternately he frowned and smiled,
    Would censure or applaud me,
And either pat me on the head
Or send me screaming off to bed.

If I was late for morning pray'rs
    I saw dire retribution looming ;
Though stealthily I crept downstairs
And knelt and smelt the study chairs
    While Grandpa's voice kept booming,
I knew I should be soundly trounced
After the Blessing was pronounced.

Once I recall—a sad affair—
    When, as a child of years still tender,
I chanced to sit in *his* armchair,
He seized me roughly by the hair
    And flung me in the fender.
He had such quaint impulsive ways ;
I didn't sit again for days.

Dear Grandpapa—I see him yet,
    My friend, philosopher and guide, too,
A personality, once met,
One could not possibly forget,
    Though lots of people tried to—
Founder of a distinguished line,
And worthy ancestor of mine !

HARRY GRAHAM (from *Strained Relations*)

" Give me that helmet, friend," said the knight, "for if I understand anything of adventures, I descry one yonder that obliges me to arm."

The gentleman in green, hearing this, looked about to see what was the matter, but could perceive nothing but a waggon, which made towards them ; and by the little flags about it, he judged it to be one of the king's carriages, and so he told Don Quixote. . . . By this time the waggon was come up with them, attended only by the carter, mounted on one of the mules, and another man that sat on the forepart of the waggon. Don Quixote making up to them, " Whither go ye, friends ? " said he. " What waggon is this ? What do you convey in it ? And what is the meaning of these colours ? "—" The waggon is mine," answered the waggoner: " I have there two brave lions, which the general of Oran is sending to the king our master, and these colours are to let the people understand that what goes here belongs to him. . . " What ! " said Don Quixote, with a scornful smile, " lion whelps against me ! Against me those puny beasts ! . . . In despite of those enchanters that have sent them to try me, I will make the creatures know, in the midst of this very field, who Don Quixote de la Mancha is." . . Then turning about to the keeper, " Sirrah ! you rascal you," said he, " either open your cages immediately, or I vow to God, I will pin thee to the waggon with this lance."— " Good sir," cried the waggoner, seeing this strange apparition in armour so resolute, "for mercy's sake, do but let me take out our mules first, and get out of harm's way with them as fast as I can, before the lions get out ; for if they should once set upon the poor beasts, I should be undone for ever; for alas! that cart and they are all I have in the world to get a living with." . .

Sancho, hearing this, came up to his master with tears in his eyes, and begged him not to go about this fearful undertaking . . "Good your worship," cried he, " I peeped even now through the grates of the cage, and I am sure I saw the claw of a true lion, and such a claw as makes me think the lion that owns it must be as big as a mountain." "Alas, poor fellow!" said Don Quixote, "thy fear will make him as big as half the world. Retire, Sancho, and leave me, and if I chance to fall here, thou knowest our old agreement; repair to Dulcinea—I say no more." . .

Now while the keeper took time to open the foremost cage, Don Quixote stood debating with himself, whether he had best make his attack on foot or on horseback; and upon mature deliberation, he resolved to do it on foot, lest Rozinante, not used to lions, should be put into disorder. Accordingly he quitted his horse, threw aside his lance, grasped his shield, and drew his sword; then advancing with a deliberate motion, and an undaunted heart, he posted himself just before the door of the cage, commending himself to heaven, and afterwards to his lady Dulcinea. . .

The keeper observing the posture Don Quixote had put himself in, and that it was not possible for him to prevent letting out the lions, without incurring the resentment of the desperate knight, set the door of the foremost cage wide open, where the male lion lay, who appeared of a monstrous bigness and of a hideous frightful aspect. The first thing he did was to roll and turn himself round in his cage; in the next place, he stretched out one of his paws, put forth his claws, and roused himself. After that he gaped and yawned for a good while, and showed his dreadful fangs, and then thrust out half a yard of broad tongue, and with it licked the dust out of his eyes and face. Having done this, he thrust his head quite out of the cage, and stared about with his eyes that looked like two live coals of fire; a sight and motion enough to have struck terror into temerity itself. But Don Quixote only regarded it with attention, wishing his grim adversary would leap out of his hold, and come within his reach, that he might exercise his valour, and cut the monster piece-meal. To this height of extravagance had his folly transported him; but the generous lion, more gentle than arrogant, taking no notice of his vapouring and bravadoes, after he had looked about him a while, turned his tail, and having showed Don Quixote his posteriors, very contentedly lay down again in his apartment.

Don Quixote, seeing this, commanded the keeper to rouse him with his pole, and force him out whether he would or no. " Not I, indeed, sir," answered the keeper: " I dare not do it for my life; for if I provoke him, I am sure to be the first he will tear to pieces. Let me advise you, sir, to be satisfied with your day's work . . . You have shown enough the greatness of your courage. No man is obliged to do more than challenge his enemy, and wait for him in the field. If he comes not, that is his own fault, and the scandal is his, as the honour the challenger's."

" 'Tis true," replied Don Quixote. " Come, shut the cage-door, honest friend, and give me a certificate under thy hand, in the amplest form thou canst devise, of what thou hast seen me perform; how thou didst open the cage for the lion; how I expected his coming, and he did not come out; how, upon his not coming out then, I staid his own time, and instead of meeting me, he turned tail and lay down. I am obliged to do no more. So,

IB   257

enchantments, avaunt ! and heaven prosper truth, justice, and knight-errantry ! Shut the door, as I bid thee, while I make signs to those that ran away from us, and get them to come back, that they may have an account of this exploit from thy own mouth."

The keeper obeyed, and at last Sancho observed the signal of the white flag, and calling out to the rest, " Hold," cried he, " my master calls to us ; I will be hanged if he has not got the better of the lions."

At this they all faced about, and, recovering a little from their fright, they leisurely rode back and came up to the waggon.

" Well, Sancho," said Don Quixote to his squire, " what dost thou think of this ? Can enchantment prevail over true fortitude ? No, these magicians may perhaps rob me of success, but never of my invincible greatness of mind."

CERVANTES (Trans. P. A. MOTTEUX)

A MIDNIGHT REVEL

(*Enter Sir Toby Belch and Sir Andrew Aguecheek*)

SIR TO. : Approach, Sir Andrew : not to be a-bed after midnight is to be up betimes ; and ' diluculo surgere,' thou know'st,—

SIR AND. : Nay, by my troth, I know not : but I know, to be up late is to be up late.

SIR TO. : A false conclusion : I hate it as an unfilled can. To be up after midnight and to go to bed then, is early : so that to go to bed after midnight is to go to bed betimes. Does not our life consist of the four elements ?

SIR AND.: Faith, so they say; but I think it rather consists of eating and drinking.

SIR TO.: Thou'rt a scholar; let us therefore eat and drink. Marian, I say! a stoup of wine!

(Enter Clown)

SIR AND.: Here comes the fool, i' faith.

CLO.: How now, my hearts! did you never see the picture of ' we three ' ?

SIR TO.: Welcome, ass! Now let's have a catch.

SIR AND.: By my troth, the fool has an excellent breast. I had rather than forty shillings I had such a leg, and so sweet a breath to sing, as the fool has. In sooth, thou wast in very gracious fooling last night, when thou spokest of Pigrogromitus, of the Vapians passing the equinoctial of Queubus: 'twas very good, i' faith. I sent thee sixpence for thy leman: hadst it?

CLO.: I did impeticos thy gratillity; for Malvolio's nose is no whipstock; my lady has a white hand, and the Myrmidons are no bottle-ale houses.

SIR AND.: Excellent! why, this is the best fooling, when all is done. Now, a song!

SIR TO.: Come on; there is sixpence for you: let's have a song.

SIR AND.: There's a testril of me too: if one knight give a——

CLO.: Would you have a love-song, or a song of good life?

SIR TO.: A love-song, a love-song.

SIR AND.: Ay, ay: I care not for good life.

CLO. [*Sings.*]

> *O Mistress mine, where are you roaming?*
> *O, stay and hear ; your true love's coming,*
>   *That can sing both high and low :*

> Trip no further, pretty sweeting ;
> Journeys end in lovers meeting,
> Every wise man's son doth know.

SIR AND. : Excellent good, i' faith.
SIR TO. : Good, good.
CLO. [*Sings.*]

> What is love ? 'tis not hereafter ;
> Present mirth hath present laughter ;
> What's to come is still unsure ;
> In delay there lies no plenty ;
> Then come kiss me, sweet and twenty,
> Youth's a stuff will not endure.

SIR AND. : A mellifluous voice, as I am true knight.
SIR TO. : A contagious breath.
SIR AND. : Very sweet and contagious i' faith.
SIR TO. : To hear by the nose, it is dulcet in contagion.
But shall we make the welkin dance indeed ? shall we
rouse the night-owl in a catch that will draw three souls
out of one weaver ? shall we do that ?
SIR AND. : An you love me, let's do't : I am dog at a
catch.
CLO. : By'r lady, sir, and some dogs will catch well.
SIR AND. : Most certain. Let our catch be ' Thou
knave.'
CLO. : ' Hold thy peace, thou knave,' knight ? I shall be
constrained in't to call thee knave, knight.
SIR AND. : 'Tis not the first time I have constrained one
to call me knave. Begin, fool ; it begins ' Hold thy peace.'
CLO. : I shall never begin if I hold my peace.
SIR AND. : Good, i' faith. Come, begin.

[*They sing a catch.*]

(Enter Maria)

MAR. : What a caterwauling do you keep here ! If my lady have not called up her steward Malvolio and bid him turn you out of doors, never trust me.

SIR TO. : My lady's a Cataian, we are politicians, Malvolio's a Peg-a-Ramsey, and ' Three merry men we be.' Am not I consanguineous ? am I not of her blood ? Tillyvally. Lady ! [*Sings.*] '*There dwelt a man in Babylon, lady, lady !* '

CLO. : Beshrew me, the knight's in admirable fooling.

SIR AND. : Ay, he does well enough if he be disposed, and so do I too : he does it with a better grace, but I do it more natural.

SIR TO. : [*Sings.*] ' *O, the twelfth day of December,*'—

MAR. : For the love o' God, peace !

(Enter Malvolio)

MAL. : My masters, are you mad ? or what are you ? Have you no wit, manners, nor honesty, but to gabble like tinkers at this time of night ? Do ye make an alehouse of my lady's house, that ye squeak out your coziers' catches without any mitigation or remorse of voice ? Is there no respect of place, persons, nor time in you ?

SIR TO. : We did keep time, sir, in our catches. Sneck up !

MAL. : Sir Toby, I must be round with you. My lady bade me tell you, that, though she harbours you as her kinsman, she's nothing allied to your disorders. If you can separate yourself and your misdemeanours, you are welcome to the house ; if not, an it would please you to take leave of her, she is very willing to bid you farewell.

SIR TO. : ' *Farewell, dear heart, since I must needs be gone.*'

MAR. : Nay, good Sir Toby.

CLO. : ' *His eyes do show his days are almost done.*'

MAL. : Is't even so ?

SIR TO. : ' *But I will never die.* '
CLO. : Sir Toby, there you lie.
MAL. : This is much credit to you.
SIR TO. : ' *Shall I bid him go ?* '
CLO. : ' *What an if you do ?* '
SIR TO. : ' *Shall I bid him go, and spare not ?* '
CLO. : ' *O no, no, no, no, you dare not.* '
SIR TO. : Out o' tune, sir : ye lie. Art any more than a
steward ? Dost thou think, because thou art virtuous,
there shall be no more cakes and ale ?
CLO. : Yes, by Saint Anne, and ginger shall be hot i' the
mouth too.
SIR TO. : Thou'rt i' the right. Go, sir, rub your chain
with crumbs. A stoup of wine, Maria !
MAL. : Mistress Mary, if you prized my lady's favour at
any thing more than contempt, you would not give means
for this uncivil rule : she shall know of it, by this hand.
[*Exit.*]

MAR. : Go shake your ears.
SIR AND. : 'Twere as good a deed as to drink when a
man's a-hungry, to challenge him the field, and then to
break promise with him and make a fool of him.
SIR TO. : Do't, knight : I'll write thee a challenge ; or
I'll deliver thy indignation to him by word of mouth.
MAR. : Sweet Sir Toby, be patient for to-night : since
the youth of the count's was today with my lady, she is
much out of quiet. For Monsieur Malvolio, let me alone
with him : if I do not gull him into a nayword, and make
him a common recreation, do not think I have wit enough
to lie straight in my bed : I know I can do it . . . For this
night, to bed, and dream on the event. Farewell. [*Exit.*]
SIR TO. : Good night, Penthesilea.
SIR AND. : Before me, she's a good wench.

SIR TO.: She's a beagle, true-bred, and one that adores me : what o' that ?

SIR AND.: I was adored once too.

SIR TO.: Let's to bed, knight. Thou hadst need send for more money.

SIR AND.: If I cannot recover your niece, I am a foul way out.

SIR TO.: Send for money, knight : if thou hast her not i' the end, call me cut.

SIR AND.: If I do not, never trust me, take it how you will.

SIR TO.: Come come, I'll go burn some sack ; 'tis too late to go to bed now : come, knight ; come, knight.

SHAKESPEARE (from *Twelfth Night*)

REMINISCENCES

(*Sir John Falstaff, Justice Shallow and Silence*)

FAL.: I am glad to see you, by my troth, Master Shallow.

SHAL.: O, Sir John, do you remember since we lay all night in the windmill in Saint George's field ?

FAL.: No more of that, good Master Shallow, no more of that.

SHAL.: Ha ! 'twas a merry night. And is Jane Nightwork alive ?

FAL.: She lives, Master Shallow.

SHAL.: She never could away with me.

FAL.: Never, never ; she would always say she could not abide Master Shallow.

SHAL.: By the mass, I could anger her to the heart. She was then a *bona-roba*. Doth she hold her own well ?

FAL. : Old, old, Master Shallow.

SHAL. : Nay, she must be old ; she cannot choose but be old ; certain she's old ; and had Robin Nightwork by old Nightwork before I came to Clement's Inn.

SIL. : That's fifty-five years ago.

SHAL. : Ha, cousin Silence, that thou hadst seen that that this knight and I have seen ! Ha, Sir John, said I well ?

FAL. : We have heard the chimes at midnight, Master Shallow.

SHAL. : That we have, that we have, that we have.

SHAKESPEARE (from *Henry IV*, *Part* 2)

A SAILOR'S WOOING

Scene—A Room in Foresight's House
(*Enter Ben, a young sailor, and Prue, a country girl*)

BEN : Come, mistress, will you please to sit down ? for an you stand astern a that'n, we shall never grapple together.—Come, I'll haul a chair ; there, an you please to sit I'll sit by you.

PRUE : You need not sit so near one ; if you have anything to say I can hear you farther off, I an't deaf.

BEN : Why, that's true, as you say ; nor I an't dumb ; I can be heard as far as another ;—I'll heave off to please you.—(*Sits further off.*) An we were a league asunder, I'd undertake to hold discourse with you, an 'twere not a main high wind indeed, and full in my teeth. Look you, forsooth, I am, as it were, bound for the land of matrimony ; 'tis a voyage, d'ye see, that was none of my seeking, I was commanded by father, and if you like of it mayhap

264

I may steer into your harbour. How say you, mistress?
The short of the thing is, that if you like me, and I like
you, we may chance to swing in a hammock together.

Prue : I don't know what to say to you, nor I don't care
to speak with you at all.

Ben : No? I'm sorry for that.—But pray, why are you so
scornful?

Prue : As long as one must not speak one's mind, one
had better not speak at all, I think, and truly I won't tell
a lie for the matter.

Ben : Nay, you say true in that, 'tis but a folly to lie:
for to speak one thing, and to think just the contrary way,
is, as it were, to look one way and row another. Now, for
my part, d'ye see, I'm carrying things above board, I'm
not for keeping anything under hatches,—so that if you
ben't as willing as I, say so a' God's name, there's no harm
done. Mayhap you may be shamefaced? some maidens,
tho'f they love a man well enough, yet they don't care to
tell'n so to's face : if that's the case, why silence gives
consent.

Prue : But I'm sure it is not so, for I'll speak sooner than
you should believe that ; and I'll speak truth, though one
should always tell a lie to a man ; and I don't care, let my
father do what he will ; I'm too big to be whipped ; so I'll
tell you plainly I don't like you, nor love you at all, nor
never will, that's more : so, there's your answer for you ;
and don't trouble me no more, you ugly thing!

Ben : Look you, young woman, you may learn to give
good words however, I spoke you fair, d'ye see, and civil.—
As for your love or your liking, I don't value it of a rope's
end ;—and mayhap I like you as little as you do me.—
What I said was in obedience to father ; gad, I fear a
whipping no more than you do. But I tell you one thing,

if you should give such language at sea you'd have a cat o' nine-tails laid across your shoulders. Flesh! who are you? You heard t'other handsome young woman speak civilly to me, of her own accord : whatever you think of yourself, gad, I don't think you are any more to compare to her than a can of small beer to a bowl of punch.

PRUE : Well, and there's a handsome gentleman, and a fine gentleman, and a sweet gentleman, that was here, that loves me, and I love him ; and if he sees you speak to me any more he'll thrash your jacket for you, he will, you great sea-calf!

BEN : What, do you mean that fair-weather spark that was here just now? will he thrash my jacket ?—let'n— let'n. But an he comes near me, mayhap I may giv'n a salt eel for's supper, for all that. What does father mean to leave me alone as soon as I come home, with such a dirty dowdy? Sea-calf! I an't calf enough to lick your chalked face, you cheese-curd, you!—Marry thee ! 'oons, I'll marry a Lapland witch as soon, and live upon selling contrary winds and wrecked vessels.

PRUE : I won't be called names, nor I won't be abused thus, so I won't. If I were a man (*Cries*), you durst not talk at this rate ;—no, you durst not, you stinking tar-barrel ! . . .

BEN : Tar-barrel ? let your sweetheart there call me so if he'll take your part, your Tom Essence, and I'll say something to him ; gad, I'll lace his musk doubtlet for him ! I'll make him stink ! he shall smell more like a weasel than a civet cat afore I ha' done with 'en.

(*Enter Mrs. Foresight and Mrs. Frail*)

MRS. FORE. : Bless me, what's the matter, miss ? What, does she cry ?—Mr. Benjamin, what have you done to her ?

266

BEN : Let her cry : the more she cries, the less she'll—she has been gathering foul weather in her mouth, and now it rains out at her eyes.

MRS. FORE. : Come, miss, come along with me, and tell me, poor child.

MRS. FRAIL : Lord, what shall we do ? there's my brother Foresight and Sir Sampson coming.—Sister, do you take miss down into the parlour, and I'll carry Mr. Benjamin into my chamber, for they must not know that they are fallen out.—Come, sir, will you venture yourself with me ?

(Looking kindly at him)

BEN : Venture, mess, and that I will, though 'twere to sea in a storm.

(Exeunt)

CONGREVE (from *Love for Love*)

DOCTOR JOHNSON AND THE PIG

I told him, in one of my latest visits to him, of a wonderful learned pig, which I had seen at Nottingham ; and which did all that we have observed exhibited by dogs and horses. The subject amused him. ' Then,' said he, ' the pigs are a race unjustly calumniated. *Pig* has, it seems, not been wanting to *man*, but *man* to *pig*. We do not allow time for his education, we kill him at a year old.' Mr. Henry White, who was present, observed that if this instance had happened in or before Pope's time, he would not have been justified in instancing the swine as the lowest degree of groveling instinct. Dr. Johnson seemed pleased with the observation, while the person who made it proceeded to remark that great torture must have been employed ere the indocility of the animal could have been subdued.—'Certainly,' said the Doctor, 'but (turning to me) how old is your pig?' I told him three years old. 'Then,' said he, 'the pig has no cause to complain; he would have been killed the first year if he had not been educated.'

ANNA SEWARD (from BOSWELL'S *Life of Johnson*)

MR. JORROCKS ARRIVES

The clear bright beauty of the day, combined with the attraction of a stranger coming to fill so important a situation as master of fox-hounds, drew many to the Datton railway station who were previously unacquainted even with the name of 'Jorrocks'. . .

All the flys, hack horses, donkeys, and ponies, were bespoke as usual; and many set out at noon to secure good berths at the station. . . Precisely at three-quarters of a minute before three, a wild shrill whistle, that seemed to issue from the bowels of the earth and to run right up into mid-air, was heard at the back of Shavington Hill, and, in an instant, the engine and long train rounded the base, the engine smoking and snorting like an exasperated crocodile. Nearer and nearer it comes with a thundering sort of hum that sounds throughout the country. The wondering ploughman stops his team. The cows and sheep stand staring with astonishment, while the horses take a look, and then gallop about the fields, kicking up their heels and snorting with delight. The guard's red coat on the engine is visible—next his gold hatband appears—

now we read the 'Hercules' on the engine, and anon it pulls up with a whiff, a puff, and a whistle, under the slate-covered shed, to give the Hercules his water, and set down and take up passengers and goods. Seven first-class passenger carriages follow the engine, all smart, clean, and yellow, with appropriate names on each door panel—The Prince Albert, Queen Victoria, and the Prince of Wales, The Venus, The Mercury, The Comet, and The Star; next come ten second-class ones, green, with covered tops and half-covered sides, but in neither set is there anything at all like the Jorrocks party. Cattle-pens follow, holding sheep, swine, donkeys, and poultry; then come an open platform with a broken britzka, followed by a curious looking nondescript one horse vehicle, containing a fat man in a low-crowned hat, and a versatio, or re-versible coat, with the preferable side outwards. Along with him were two ladies muffled up in cloaks, and at the back was a good looking servant-maid. From the bottom of the carriage swung a couple of hams, and a large warm-ing pan. 'Pray is Mr. Jorrocks here?' inquired the elegant M.C., who had persuaded the station-master to let him in upon the line, riding his white charger near the door of the first-class carriage, and raising his hat as he spoke; but getting no answer, he continued his interrogatory down the whole set until he came to the end, when casting a despairing glance at the cattle pens, he was about to wheel round, when the gentleman in the versatio coat, in a very stentorian voice, roared out, 'I say, Sir! Bain't this the 'Andley Cross station?' 'It is, Sir,' replied Captain Doleful, in his most dignified manner, 'The Datton station for Handley Cross at least.'

'Then I want to land,' responded the same sweet voice.

'Here's a gentleman wants to be down,' observed

Captain Doleful to the scarlet-coated guard, who came bustling past with a pen of Cochin-Chinas to put upon the train.

' Yes, a gentleman and two ladies,' roared our friend ; ' Mister and Missis Jorrocks in fact, and Miss Jorrocks ! ' . . .

Thereupon the Captain beckoned the guard, and Mr. Jorrocks, standing up in the vehicle, looking very like a hay-stack with a hat on the top, bounded to the ground. Mrs. Jorrocks, in a black velvet bonnet lined with pink satin, and her body all shrouded in a sea green silk cloak, then accepted the offer of the Captain's arm, and descended with caution and due state, while Belinda, with the spring of youth and elasticity in her limbs, bounded on to the foot-way beyond the rail. Benjamin, who was asleep in the horse-box, being considerately kicked awake by Mr. Jorrocks, the porters cut off the last joints of the train, when away it went, hissing and snorting through the quiet country, leaving our party to the undisturbed observation of the Handley Cross company.

ROBERT SMITH SURTEES (from *Handley Cross*)

THE BRUISERS OF ENGLAND

Let no one sneer at the bruisers of England—what were the gladiators of Rome, or the bullfighters of Spain, in its palmiest days, compared to England's bruisers ? Pity that ever corruption should have crept in amongst them—but of that I wish not to talk ; let us still hope that a spark of the old religion, of which they were the priests, still lingers in the breasts of Englishmen. There they come, the bruisers, from far London, or from wherever else they might chance to be at the time, to the great rendezvous in the old city; some came one way, some another: some of tip-top reputation came with peers in their chariots, for glory and fame are such fair things that even peers are proud to have those invested therewith by their sides; others came in their own gigs, driving their own bits of blood, and I heard one say: " I have driven through at a heat the whole hundred and eleven miles, and only stopped to bait twice." Oh, the blood-horses of old England! but they, too, have had their day—for everything beneath the sun there is a season and a time.

So the bruisers of England are come to be present at the grand fight speedily coming off; there they are met in the precincts of the old town, near the field of the chapel, planted with tender saplings at the restoration of sporting Charles, which are now become venerable elms, as high as many a steeple; there they are met at a fitting rendezvous, where a retired coachman, with one leg, keeps an hotel and a bowling-green. I think I now see them upon the bowling-green, the men of renown, amidst hundreds of people with no renown at all, who gaze upon them with timid wonder. Fame, after all, is a glorious thing, though it lasts only for a day. There's Cribb, the champion of England, and perhaps the best man in England; there he is, with his huge massive figure, and face wonderfully like that of a lion. There is Belcher, the younger, not the mighty one, who is gone to his place, but the Teucer Belcher, the most scientific pugilist that ever entered a ring, only wanting strength to be, I won't say what. He appears to walk before me now, as he did that evening, with his white hat, white greatcoat, thin genteel figure, springy step, and keen, determined eye. Crosses him, what a contrast! grim, savage, Shelton, who has a civil word for nobody, and a hard blow for anybody—hard! one blow, given with the proper play of his athletic arm, will unsense a giant. Yonder individual, who strolls about with his hands behind him, supporting his brown coat lappets, under-sized, and who looks anything but what he is, is the king of the light weights, so called—Randall! the terrible Randall, who has Irish blood in his veins ; not the better for that, nor the worse ; and not far from him is his last antagonist, Ned Turner, who, though beaten by him, still thinks himself as good a man, in which he is, perhaps, right, for it was a near thing ; and " a better shentleman," in which he is quite right, for he is a Welshman. But how shall I name them all? they were there by dozens, and all tremendous in their way. There was Bulldog Hudson, and fearless Scroggins, who beat the conqueror of Sam the Jew. There was Black Richmond— no, he was not there, but I knew him well ; he was the most dangerous of blacks, even with a broken thigh. There was Purcell, who could never conquer till all seemed over with him. There was—what! shall I name thee last ? ay, why not ? I believe that thou art the last of all that strong family still above the sod, where mayst thou long continue—true piece of English stuff, Tom of Bedford— sharp as Winter, kind as Spring.

Hail to thee, Tom of Bedford, or by whatever name it may please thee to be called, Spring or Winter. Hail to thee, six-foot Englishman of the brown eye, worthy to have carried a six foot bow at Flodden, where England's yeomen triumphed over Scotland's king, his clans and chivalry. Hail to thee, last of England's bruisers, after all the many victories which thou hast achieved—true English victories, unbought by yellow gold ; need I recount them ? nay, nay ! they are already well known to fame—sufficient to say that Bristol's Bull and Ireland's Champion were vanquished by thee, and one mightier still, gold itself, thou didst overcome ; for gold itself strove in vain to deaden the power of thy arm ; and thus thou didst proceed till men left off challenging thee, the un-vanquishable, the incorruptible. 'Tis a treat to see thee, Tom of Bedford, in thy " public " in Holborn way, whither thou hast retired with thy well-earned bays. 'Tis Friday night, and nine by Holborn clock. There sits the yeoman at the end of his long room, surrounded by his friends ; glasses are filled, and a song is the cry, and a song is sung well suited to the place ; it finds an echo in every heart—fists are clenched, arms are waved, and the portraits of the mighty fighting men of yore, Broughton, and Slack, and Ben, which adorn the walls, appear to smile grim approbation, whilst many a manly voice joins in the chorus.

GEORGE BORROW (from *Lavengro*)

NEWS FROM THE FRONT (1812)

" You must remember, Captain, time's passing ; the placards are all out ; must be at press before one o'clock to-night ; the morning edition is everything with us. You were at the first parallel, I think ? "

" Devil a bit o' me knows. Just ring that bell near you ; them's elegant oysters ; and you're not taking your drop of liquor ; here's a toast for you ; ' May——' whoop—raal Carlingfords upon my conscience. See now, if I won't hit that little black chap up there, the first shot."

Scarcely were the words spoken, when a little painted

bust of Shakespeare fell in fragments on the floor as an oyster shell laid him low.

A faint effort at a laugh at the eccentricities of his friend was all the poor editor could accomplish, while Mike's triumph knew no bounds.

" Didn't I tell you ? But come now, are you ready ? Give the pen a drink, if you won't take one yourself."

" I'm ready, quite ready," responded the editor.

" Faith, and it's more nor I am. See now, here it is : The night was murthering dark ; you could not see a stim."

" Not see a—a what ? "

" A stim ! bad luck to you ; don't you know English ? Hand me the hot water. Have you that down yet ? "

" Yes. Pray proceed."

" The Fifth Division was orthered up bekase they were fighting chaps ; the Eighty-eighth was among them ; the Rangers—oh ! upon my soul, we must drink the Rangers. Here, devil a bit o' me will go on till we give them all the honours—hip—begin."

" Hip," sighed the luckless editor, as he rose from his chair, obedient to the command.

" Hurra—hurra—hurra ! Well done ! there's stuff in you yet, ould foolscap ! the little bottle's empty—ring again, if you plaze."

" Really, Mr. Free, I see no prospect of our ever getting done."

" The saints in heaven forbid," interrupted Mike piously ; " the evening's young, and drink plenty ; here, now, make ready ! "

The editor once more made a gesture of preparation.

" Well, as I was saying," resumed Mike, " it was pitch dark when the columns moved up, and a cold raw night with a little thin rain falling. Have you that down ? "

"Yes. Pray go on."

"Well, just as it might be here at the corner of the trench I met Doctor Quill. 'They're waiting for you, Misther Free,' says he, 'down there. Picton's asking for you.' 'Faith, and he must wait,' says I . . ."

"But, my dear sir," interposed Mr. Meekins, "pray *do* remember this is somewhat irrelevant. In fifteen minutes it will be 12 o'clock."

"I know it, ould boy, I know it. I see what you're at. You were going to observe how much better we'd be for a broiled bone." . .

"Nothing of the kind, I assure you. I protest that here we are for two hours at work, and we haven't got to the foot of the great breach."

"And wasn't the army three months and a half in just getting that far, with a battering train, and mortars, and the finest troops ever were seen ? and there you sit, a little fat creature, with your pen in your hand, grumbling that you can't do more than the whole British army. Take care you don't provoke me to beat you ; for I am quiet till I am roused. But, by the Rock O' Cashel——"

"For mercy's sake, Mr. Free——"

"Well, sit down then, and don't be bothering me about sieges, and battles, and things you know nothing about."

"I protest," rejoined Mr. Meekins, "that, had you not sent to my office intimating your wish to communicate an account of the siege, I never should have thought of intruding myself upon you. Once for all, sir, . . . I would beg you to recollect that, on the faith of your message to me, I have announced an account of the storming of Ciudad Rodrigo for our morning edition. Are you prepared, may I ask, for the consequences of my disappointing ten thousand readers ? "

" It's little I care for one of them. I never knew much of reading myself."

" If you think to make a jest of me——" interposed Mr. Meekins, reddening with passion.

" A jest of you ! Troth, it's little fun I can get out of you ; you're as tiresome a creature as ever I spent an evening with. See, now, I told you before not to provoke me : we'll have a little more drink ; ring the bell : who knows but you'll turn out better by-and-by ? "

CHARLES LEVER (from *Charles O'Malley*)

BOB SAWYER'S PARTY

" Does Mr. Sawyer live here ? " said Mr. Pickwick, when the door was opened.

" Yes," said the girl, " first floor. It's the door straight afore you, when you gets to the top of the stairs." Having given this instruction, the handmaid, who had been brought up among the aboriginal inhabitants of South-wark, disappeared, with the candle in her hand, down the kitchen stairs : perfectly satisfied that she had done everything that could possibly be required of her under the circumstances.

Mr. Snodgrass, who entered last, secured the street door, after several ineffectual efforts, by putting up the chain ; and the friends stumbled upstairs, where they were received by Mr. Bob Sawyer, who had been afraid to go down, lest he should be waylaid by Mrs. Raddle.

" How are you ? " said the discomfited student. " Glad to see you—take care of the glasses." This caution was addressed to Mr. Pickwick, who had put his hat in the tray.

"Dear me," said Mr. Pickwick, "I beg your pardon."

"Don't mention it, don't mention it," said Bob Sawyer. "I'm rather confined for room, here, but you must put up with all that, when you come to see a young bachelor. Walk in. You've seen this gentleman before, I think?" Mr. Pickwick shook hands with Mr. Benjamin Allen, and his friends followed his example. They had scarcely taken their seats when there was another double knock.

"I hope that's Jack Hopkins!" said Mr. Bob Sawyer. "Hush. Yes, it is. Come up, Jack; come up."

A heavy footstep was heard upon the stairs, and Jack Hopkins presented himself. He wore a black velvet waistcoat, with thunder-and-lightning buttons; and a blue striped shirt, with a white false collar.

"You're late, Jack?" said Mr. Benjamin Allen.

"Been detained at Bartholomew's," replied Hopkins.

"Anything new?"

"No, nothing particular. Rather a good accident brought into the casualty ward."

"What was that, sir?" inquired Mr. Pickwick.

"Only a man fallen out of a four pair of stairs' window; —but it's a very fair case—very fair case indeed."

"Do you mean that the patient is in a fair way to recover?" inquired Mr. Pickwick.

"No," replied Hopkins carelessly. "No, I should rather say he wouldn't. There must be a splendid operation though, to-morrow—magnificent sight if Slasher does it."

"You consider Mr. Slasher a good operator?" said Mr. Pickwick.

"Best alive," replied Hopkins. "Took a boy's leg out of the socket last week—boy ate five apples and a gingerbread cake—exactly two minutes after it was all over, boy said he wouldn't lie there to be made game of, and he'd tell his mother if they didn't begin."

"Dear me!" said Mr. Pickwick, astonished.

"Pooh! That's nothing, that ain't," said Jack Hopkins. "Is it, Bob?"

"Nothing at all," replied Mr. Bob Sawyer.

"By the bye, Bob," said Hopkins, with a scarcely perceptible glance at Mr. Pickwick's attentive face, "we had a curious accident last night. A child was brought in, who had swallowed a necklace."

"Swallowed what, sir?" interrupted Mr. Pickwick.

"A necklace," replied Jack Hopkins. "Not all at once, you know, that would be too much—*you* couldn't swallow that, if the child did—eh, Mr. Pickwick, ha! ha!" Mr. Hopkins appeared highly gratified with his own pleasantry; and continued. "No, the way was this. Child's parents were poor people who lived in a court. Child's eldest sister bought a necklace; common necklace, made of large black wooden beads. Child, being fond of toys, cribbed the necklace, hid it, played with it, cut the string, and swallowed a bead. Child thought it capital fun, went back next day, and swallowed another bead."

"Bless my heart," said Mr. Pickwick, "what a dreadful thing! I beg your pardon, sir. Go on."

"Next day, child swallowed two beads; the day after that, he treated himself to three, and so on, till in a week's time he had got through the necklace—five-and-twenty beads in all. The sister, who was an industrious girl, and seldom treated herself to a bit of finery, cried her eyes out at the loss of the necklace: looked high and low for it;

but, I needn't say, didn't find it. A few days afterwards, the family were at dinner—baked shoulder of mutton, and potatoes under it—the child, who wasn't hungry, was playing about the room, when suddenly there was heard a devil of a noise, like a small hailstorm. 'Don't do that, my boy,' said the father. 'I ain't doin' nothing,' said the child. 'Well, don't do it again,' said the father. There was a short silence, and then the noise began again, worse than ever. 'If you don't mind what I say, my boy,' said the father, 'you'll find yourself in bed, in something less than a pig's whisper.' He gave the child a shake to make him obedient, and such a rattling ensued as nobody ever heard before. 'Why, dam'me, it's *in* the child!' said the father, 'he's got the croup in the wrong place!' 'No, I haven't, father,' said the child, beginning to cry, 'it's the necklace; I swallowed it, father.'—The father caught the child up, and ran with him to the hospital; the beads in the boy's stomach rattling all the way with the jolting; and the people looking up in the air, and down in the cellars, to see where the unusual sound came from. He's in the hospital now," said Jack Hopkins, "and he makes such a devil of a noise when he walks about, that they're obliged to muffle him in a watchman's coat, for fear he should wake the patients!"

"That's the most extraordinary case I ever heard of," said Mr. Pickwick, with an emphatic blow on the table.

"Oh, that's nothing," said Jack Hopkins; "is it, Bob?"

"Certainly not," replied Mr. Bob Sawyer.

"Very singular things occur in our profession, I can assure you, sir," said Hopkins.

"So I should be disposed to imagine," replied Mr. Pickwick.

.   .   .   .

After supper, another jug of punch was put upon the table, together with a paper of cigars, and a couple of bottles of spirits. . .

"Now, Betsy," said Mr. Bob Sawyer, with great suavity, and dispersing at the same time, the tumultuous little mob of glasses the girl had collected in the centre of the table : "now, Betsy, the warm water. Be brisk, there's a good girl."

"You can't have no warm water," replied Betsy.

"No warm water !" exclaimed Mr. Bob Sawyer.

"No," said the girl, with a shake of the head which expressed a more decided negative than the most copious language could have conveyed. "Missis Raddle said you warn't to have none."

The surprise depicted on the countenances of his guests imparted new courage to the host.

"Bring up the warm water instantly—instantly !" said Mr. Bob Sawyer, with desperate sternness.

"No. I can't," replied the girl ; "Missis Raddle raked out the kitchen fire afore she went to bed, and locked up the kittle."

"Oh, never mind ; never mind. Pray don't disturb yourself about such a trifle," said Mr. Pickwick, observing the conflict of Bob Sawyer's passions, as depicted in his countenance, "cold water will do very well."

"Oh, admirably," said Mr. Benjamin Allen.

"My landlady is subject to some slight attacks of mental derangement," remarked Bob Sawyer with a ghastly smile ; "and I fear I must give her warning."

"No, don't," said Ben Allen.

"I fear I must," said Bob with heroic firmness. "I'll pay her what I owe her, and give her warning to-morrow morning." Poor fellow! how devoutly he wished he could! . .

" Now," said Jack Hopkins, " just to set us going again, Bob, I don't mind singing a song." And Hopkins, incited thereto, by tumultuous applause, plunged himself at once into " The King, God bless him," which he sang as loud as he could, to a novel air, compounded of the " Bay of Biscay " and " A Frog he would." The chorus was the essence of the song ; and, as each gentleman sang it to the tune he knew best, the effect was very striking indeed.

It was at the end of the chorus to the first verse, that Mr. Pickwick held up his hand in a listening attitude, and said, as soon as silence was restored :

" Hush! I beg your pardon. I thought I heard somebody calling from upstairs."

A profound silence immediately ensued ; and Mr. Bob Sawyer was observed to turn pale.

" I think I hear it now," said Mr. Pickwick. " Have the goodness to open the door."

The door was no sooner opened than all doubt on the subject was removed.

" Mr. Sawyer! Mr. Sawyer! " screamed a voice from the two-pair landing.

" It's my landlady," said Bob Sawyer, looking round him with great dismay. " Yes, Mrs. Raddle."

" What do you mean by this, Mr. Sawyer? " replied the voice, with great shrillness and rapidity of utterance. " Ain't it enough to be swindled out of one's rent, and money lent out of pocket besides, and abused and insulted by your friends that dares to call themselves men : without having the house turned out of the window, and noise enough made to bring the fire-engines here, at two o'clock in the morning?—Turn them wretches away."

"You ought to be ashamed of yourselves," said the voice of Mr. Raddle, which appeared to proceed from beneath some distant bed-clothes.

"Ashamed of themselves!" said Mrs. Raddle. "Why don't you go down and knock 'em every one downstairs? You would if you was a man."

"I should if I was a dozen men, my dear," replied Mr. Raddle, pacifically, "but they've the advantage of me in numbers, my dear."

"Ugh, you coward!" replied Mrs. Raddle, with supreme contempt. "*Do* you mean to turn them wretches out, or not, Mr. Sawyer?"

"They're going, Mrs. Raddle, they're going," said the miserable Bob. "I am afraid you'd better go," said Mr. Bob Sawyer to his friends. "I *thought* you were making too much noise."

"It's a very unfortunate thing," said the prim man. "Just as we were getting so comfortable too! . . It's hardly to be borne—hardly to be borne, is it?"

"Not to be endured," replied Jack Hopkins; "let's have the other verse, Bob. Come, here goes!"

"No, no, Jack, don't," interposed Bob Sawyer; "it's a capital song, but I am afraid we had better not have the other verse. They are very violent people, the people of the house."

"Shall I step upstairs, and pitch into the landlord?" inquired Hopkins, "or keep on ringing the bell, or go and groan on the staircase? You may command me, Bob."

"I am very much indebted to you for your friendship and good nature, Hopkins," said the wretched Mr. Bob

Sawyer, " but I think the best plan to avoid any further dispute is for us to break up at once."

" Now, Mr. Sawyer ! " screamed the shrill voice of Mrs. Raddle, " *are* them brutes going ? "

DICKENS (from Pickwick Papers)

DINNER BY PROXY

" Is that the little gentleman from Blunderstone ? "

" Yes, ma'am," I said.

" What name ? " inquired the lady.

" Copperfield, ma'am," I said.

" That won't do," returned the lady. " Nobody's dinner is paid for here, in that name."

" Is it Murdstone, ma'am ? " I said.

" If you're Master Murdstone," said the lady, " why do you go and give another name first ? "

I explained to the lady how it was, who then rang a bell, and called out, " William ! show the coffee-room ! " upon which a waiter came running out of a kitchen on the opposite side of the yard to show it, and seemed a good deal surprised when he found he was only to show it to me.

It was a large, long room with some large maps in it. I doubt if I could have felt much stranger if the maps had been real foreign countries, and I cast away in the middle of them. I felt it was taking a liberty to sit down, with my cap in my hand, on the corner of the chair nearest the door ; and when the waiter laid a cloth on purpose for me, and put a set of castors on it, I think I must have turned red all over with modesty.

He brought me some chops and vegetables, and took the covers off in such a bouncing manner that I was afraid I must have given him some offence. But he greatly relieved my mind by putting a chair for me at the table, and saying, very affably, " Now six-foot ! come on ! "

I thanked him, and took my seat at the board ; but found it extremely difficult to handle my knife and fork with anything like dexterity, or to avoid splashing myself with the gravy, while he was standing opposite, staring so hard, and making me blush in the most dreadful manner every time I caught his eye. After watching me into the second chop, he said :

" There's half a pint of ale for you. Will you have it now ? "

I thanked him and said " Yes." Upon which he poured it out of a jug into a large tumbler, and held it up against the light, and made it look beautiful.

" My eye ! " he said. " It seems a good deal, don't it ? "

" It does seem a good deal," I answered with a smile. For it was quite delightful to me to find him so pleasant. He was a twinkling-eyed, pimple-faced man, with his hair standing upright all over his head ; and as he stood with one arm a-kimbo, holding up the glass to the light with the other hand, he looked quite friendly.

" There was a gentleman here, yesterday," he said— " a stout gentleman, by the name of Topsawyer—perhaps you know him ? "

" No," I said, " I don't think——"

" In breeches and gaiters, broad-brimmed hat, grey coat, speckled choker," said the waiter.

" No," I said bashfully, " I haven't the pleasure——"

" He came in here," said the waiter, looking at the light through the tumbler, " ordered a glass of this ale—

would order it—I told him not—drank it, and fell dead. It was too old for him. It oughtn't to be drawn ; that's the fact."

I was very much shocked to hear of this melancholy accident, and said I thought I had better have some water.

" Why, you see," said the waiter, still looking at the light through the tumbler, with one of his eyes shut up, " our people don't like things being ordered and left. It offends 'em. But *I'll* drink it, if you like. I'm used to it, and use is everything. I don't think it'll hurt me, if I throw my head back, and take it off quick. Shall I ? "

I replied that he would much oblige me by drinking it, if he thought he could do it safely, but by no means otherwise. When he did throw his head back, and take it off quick, I had a horrible fear, I confess, of seeing him meet the fate of the lamented Mr. Topsawyer, and fall lifeless on the carpet. But it didn't hurt him. On the contrary, I thought he seemed the fresher for it.

" What have we got here ? " he said, putting a fork into my dish. " Not chops ? "

" Chops," I said.

" Lord bless my soul ! " he exclaimed, " I didn't know they were chops. Why, a chop's the very thing to take off the bad effects of that beer ! Ain't it lucky ? "

So he took a chop by the bone in one hand, and a potato in the other, and ate away with a very good appetite, to my extreme satisfaction. He afterwards took another chop, and another potato ; and after that another chop and another potato. When he had done, he brought me a pudding, and having set it before me, seemed to ruminate, and to become absent in his mind for some moments.

" How's the pie ? " he said, rousing himself.

" It's a pudding," I made answer.

" Pudding ! " he exclaimed. " Why, bless me, so it is ! What ! " looking at it nearer. " You don't mean to say it's a batter-pudding ! "

" Yes, it is indeed."

" Why, a batter-pudding," he said, taking up a table-spoon, " is my favourite pudding ! Ain't that lucky. Come on, little 'un, and let's see who'll get most."

The waiter certainly got most. He entreated me more than once to come in and win, but what with his table-spoon to my tea-spoon, his despatch to my despatch, and his appetite to my appetite, I was left far behind at the first mouthful, and had no chance with him. I never saw anyone enjoy a pudding so much, I think ; and he laughed, when it was all gone, as if his enjoyment of it lasted still.

DICKENS (from *David Copperfield*)

CHILDREN AT A WEDDING

Flora had a great scarlet and gold church service. As soon as she opened it, she disconcerted me by saying aloud, to an imaginary female friend, " My dear, there is going to be a collection ; and I have left my purse on the piano."

At this time, also, Gus, seeing that the business was well begun, removed to the further end of the pew, sat down on the hassock, and took from his trousers' pocket a large tin trumpet.

I broke out all over in a cold perspiration as I looked at him. He saw my distress, and putting it to his lips, puffed out his cheeks. Flora administered comfort to me. She

286

said, " You are looking at that foolish boy. Perhaps he
won't blow it, after all. He mayn't if you don't look at him.
At all events, he probably won't blow it till the organ
begins ; and then it won't matter so much." . .

I wish those dear children (not meaning them any harm)
had been, to put it mildly, at play on the village green, that
blessed day.

When I looked at Gus again, he was still on the hassock,
threatening propriety with his trumpet. I hoped for the
best. Flora had her prayer-book open, and was playing
the piano on each side of it, with her fingers. After a time
she looked up at me, and said out loud—

" I suppose you have heard that Archy's cat has
kittened ? "

I said, " No."

" Oh, yes, it has," she said. " Archy harnessed it to his
meal cart, which turns a mill, and plays music when the
wheels go round ; and it ran downstairs with the cart ;
and we heard the music playing as it went ; and it kittened
in the wood-basket immediately afterwards ; and Alwright
says she don't wonder at it ; and no more do I ; and the
steward's room boy is going to drown some. But you
mustn't tell Archy, because, if you do, he won't say his
prayers ; and if he don't say his prayers, he will—etc.,
etc." Very emphatically, and in a loud tone of voice.

This was very charming. If I could only answer for
Gus, and keep Flora busy, it was wildly possible that we
might pull through. If I had not been a madman, I should
have noticed that Gus had disappeared.

He had. And the pew door had never opened, and I was
utterly unconscious. Gus had crawled up, on all fours,
under the seat of the pew, until he was opposite the
calves of his sister's legs, against which calves, *horresco*

referens, he put his trumpet and blew a long shrill blast. Flora behaved very well and courageously. She only gave **one** long, wild shriek, as from a lunatic in a padded cell at Bedlam, and then, hurling her prayer-book at him, she turned round and tried to kick him in the face.

This was the culminating point of my misfortunes. After this, they behaved better.

HENRY KINGSLEY (from *Ravenshoe*)

A BLACK AFFAIR

The skipper was the first to discover the mischief, and he came on deck and published the news in a voice which struck a chill to all hearts.

" Where's that black devil got to ? " he yelled.

" Anything wrong, sir ? " asked Sam anxiously.

" Come and look here," said the skipper. He led the way to the cabin, where the mate and one of the crew were already standing, shaking their heads over the parrot.

" What do you make of that ? " demanded the skipper fiercely.

" Too much dry food, sir," said Sam, after due deliberation.

" Too much what ? " bellowed the skipper.

" Too much dry food," repeated Sam firmly. " A parrot—a grey parrot—wants plenty o' sop. If it don't get it, it moults."

" It's had too much *cat*," said the skipper fiercely, " and you know it, and overboard it goes."

" I don't believe it was the cat, sir," interposed the other man ; " it's too soft-hearted to do a thing like that."

288

" You can shut your jaw," said the skipper reddening. " Who asked you to come down here at all ? "

" Nobody saw the cat do it," urged the mate.

The skipper said nothing, but, stooping down, picked up a tail feather from the floor, and laid it on the table. He then went on deck followed by the others, and began calling, in seductive tones, for the cat. No reply forthcoming from the sagacious animal, which had gone into hiding, he turned to Sam, and bade him call it.

" No, sir, I won't 'ave no 'and in it," said the old man. " Putting aside my liking for the animal, *I'm* not going to 'ave anything to do with the killing of a black cat."

" Rubbish ! " said the skipper.

" Very good, sir," said Sam, shrugging his shoulders, " you know best, o' course. You're eddicated and I'm not, an' p'raps you can afford to make a laugh o' such things. I knew one man who killed a black cat an' he went mad. There's something very pecooliar about that cat o' ours."

" It knows more than we do," said one of the crew, shaking his head. " That time you—I mean we—ran the smack down, that cat was expecting of it 'ours before. It was like a wild thing."

" Look at the weather we've 'ad—look at the trips we've made since he's been aboard," said the old man. " Tell me it's chance if you like, but I *know* better."

The skipper hesitated. He was a superstitious man even for a sailor, and his weakness was so well known that he had become a sympathetic receptacle for every ghost story, which, by reason of its crudeness or lack of corroboration, had been rejected by other experts. He was a perfect reference library for omens, and his interpretations of dreams had gained for him a widespread reputation.

"That's all nonsense," he said, pausing uneasily; "still, I only want to be just. There's nothing vindictive about me, and I'll have no hand in it myself. Joe, just tie a lump of coal to that cat and heave it overboard."

"Not me," said the cook, following Sam's lead, and working up a shudder. "Not for fifty pun in gold. I don't want to be haunted."

"The parrot's a little better now, sir," said one of the men, taking advantage of his hesitation, "he's opened one eye."

"Well, I only want to be just," repeated the skipper. "I won't do anything in a hurry, but, mark my words, if the parrot dies that cat goes overboard."

Contrary to expectations, the bird was still alive when London was reached, though the cook, who from his connection with the cabin had suddenly reached a position of unusual importance, reported great loss of strength and irritability of temper. It was still alive, but failing fast on the day they were to put to sea again; and the fo'c'sl in preparation for the worst, stowed their pet away in the paint-locker and discussed the situation.

Their council was interrupted by the mysterious behaviour of the cook, who, having gone out to lay in a stock of bread, suddenly broke in upon them more in the manner of a member of a secret society than a humble but useful unit of a ship's company.

"Where's the cap'n?" he asked in a hoarse whisper, as he took a seat on the locker with the sack of bread between his knees.

"In the cabin," said Sam, regarding his antics with some disfavour. "What's wrong, cookie?"

"What d'yer think I've got in here," asked the cook, patting the bag.

The obvious reply to this question was, of course, bread; but as it was known that the cook had departed specially to buy some, and that he could hardly ask a question involving such a simple answer, nobody gave it.

"It come to me all of a sudden," said the cook, in a thrilling whisper. "I'd just bought the bread and left the shop, when I see a big black cat, the very image of ours, sitting on a doorstep. I just stooped down to stroke its 'ed when it come to me."

"They will sometimes," said one of the seamen.

"I don't mean that," said the cook, with the contempt of genius. "I mean the idea did. Ses I to myself, 'You might be old Satan's brother by the look of you; an' if the cap'n wants to kill a cat, let it be you,' I ses. And with that, before it could say Jack Robinson, I picked it up by the scruff o' the neck and shoved it in the bag."

"What, all in along of our bread?" said the previous interrupter in a pained voice.

"Some of yer are 'ard ter please," said the cook, deeply offended.

"Don't mind him, cook," said the admiring Sam. "You're a masterpiece, that's what you are."

"Of course, if any of you've got a better plan——" said the cook generously.

"Don't talk rubbish, cook," said Sam; "fetch the two cats out and put 'em together."

"Don't mix 'em," said the cook warningly; "for you'll never know which is which agin if you do."

He cautiously opened the top of the sack and produced his captive, and Satan, having been relieved from his prison, the two animals were carefully compared.

"They're as like as two lumps o' coal," said Sam

slowly. " Lord, what a joke on the old man. I must tell the mate o' this ; he'll enjoy it."

" It'll be all right if the parrot don't die," said the dainty pessimist, still harping on his pet theme. " All that bread spoilt, and two cats aboard."

" Don't mind what he ses," said Sam; "you're a brick, that's what you are. I'll just make a few holes in the lid o' the boy's chest, and pop old Satan in. You don't mind, do you, Billy ? "

" Of course he don't," said the other men indignantly.

Matters being thus agreeably arranged, Sam got a gimlet, and prepared the chest for the reception of its tenant, who, convinced that he was being put out of the way to make room for a rival, made a frantic fight for freedom.

" Now get something 'eavy and put on the top of it," said Sam, having convinced himself that the lock was broken ; " and, Billy, put the noo cat in the paint-locker till we start ; it's home-sick."

The boy obeyed, and the understudy was kept in durance vile until they were off Limehouse, when he came on deck and nearly ended his career there and then by attempting to jump over the bulwark into the next garden. For some time he paced the deck in a perturbed fashion, and then, leaping on the stern, mewed plaintively as his native city receded farther and farther from his view.

" What's the matter with old Satan," said the mate, who had been let into the secret. " He seems to have something on his mind."

" He'll have something round his neck presently," said the skipper grimly.

The prophecy was fulfilled some three hours later, when he came up on deck ruefully regarding the remains of a bird whose vocabulary had once been the pride of its native town. He threw it overboard without a word, and then, seizing the innocent cat, who had followed him under the impression that it was about to lunch, produced half a brick attached to a string, and tied it round his neck. The crew, who were enjoying the joke immensely, raised a howl of protest.

"The *Skylark*'ll never have another like it, sir," said Sam solemnly. "That cat was the luck of the ship."

"I don't want any of your old woman's yarns," said the skipper brutally. "If you want the cat, go and fetch it."

He stepped aft as he spoke, and sent the gentle stranger hurtling through the air. There was a "plomp" as it reached the water, a bubble or two came to the surface, and all was over.

"That's the last o' that," he said turning away.

The old man shook his head. "You can't kill a black cat for nothing," said he, "mark my words!"

.   .   .   .

The night, which had been dirty, cleared somewhat, and the bright crescent of the moon appeared above a heavy bank of clouds, as the cat, which had by dint of using its back as a lever at length got free from that cursed chest, licked its shapely limbs, and came up on deck. After its stifling prison, the air was simply delicious.

"Bob!" yelled the skipper suddenly.

"Ay, ay, sir!" said the look-out, in a startled voice.

"Did you mew?" inquired the skipper.

"Did I *wot*, sir?" cried the astonished Bob.

"Mew," said the skipper sharply, "like a cat?"

"No, sir," said the offended seaman. "What 'ud I want to do that for?"

"I don't know what you want to for," said the skipper,

looking round him uneasily. " There's some more rain coming, Bob."

" Ay, ay, sir," said Bob.

" Lot o' rain we've had this summer," said the skipper, in a meditative bawl.

" Ay, ay, sir," said Bob. " Sailing-ship on the port bow, sir."

The conversation dropped, the skipper, anxious to divert his thoughts, watching the dark mass of sail as it came plunging out of the darkness into the moonlight until it was abreast of his own craft. His eyes followed it as it passed his quarter, so that he saw not the stealthy approach of the cat which came from behind the companion, and sat down close by him. For over thirty hours the animal had been subjected to the grossest indignities at the hands of every man on board the ship except one. That one was the skipper, and there is no doubt but that its subsequent behaviour was a direct recognition of that fact. It rose to its feet, and crossing over to the unconscious skipper, rubbed its head affectionately and vigorously against his leg.

From simple causes great events do spring. The skipper sprang four yards, and let off a screech which was the subject of much comment on the barque which had just passed. When Bob, who came shuffling up at the double, reached him he was leaning against the side, incapable of speech, and shaking all over.

" Anything wrong, sir ? " inquired the seaman anxiously, as he ran to the wheel.

The skipper pulled himself together a bit, and got closer to his companion.

" Believe me or not, Bob," he said at length, in trembling accents, " just as you please, but the ghost of that

—— cat, I mean the ghost of that poor affectionate animal which I drowned, and which I wish I hadn't, came and rubbed itself up against my leg."

" Which leg ? " inquired Bob, who was ever careful about details.

" What the blazes does it matter which leg ? " demanded the skipper, whose nerves were in a terrible state. " Ah, look—look there ! "

The seaman followed his outstretched finger, and his heart failed him as he saw the cat, with its back arched, gingerly picking its way along the side of the vessel.

" I can't see nothing," he said doggedly.

.   .   .   .

" Can't you see anything, cook ? " demanded the skipper.

" It may be fancy, sir," faltered the cook, lowering his eyes, " but it does seem to me as though I can see a little misty sort o' thing there. Ah, now it's gone."

" No, it ain't," said the skipper. " The ghost of Satan's sitting there. The case seems to have fallen on its tail. It appears to be howling something dreadful."

The men made a desperate effort to display the astonishment suitable to such a marvel, whilst Satan, who was trying all he knew to get his tail out, cursed freely. How long the superstitious captain of the *Skylark* would have let him remain there will never be known, for just then the mate came on deck and caught sight of it before he was quite aware of the part he was expected to play.

" Why the devil don't you lift the thing off the poor brute," he yelled, hurrying up towards the case.

" What, can *you* see it, Dick ? " said the skipper impressively, laying his hand on his arm.

" *See* it ? " retorted the mate. " D'ye think I'm blind ? Listen to the poor brute. I should—oh ! "

He became conscious of the concentrated significant gaze of the crew. Five pairs of eyes speaking as one, all saying " idiot " plainly, the boy's eyes conveying an expression too great to be translated.

Turning, the skipper saw the bye-play, and a light slowly dawned upon him. But he wanted more, and he wheeled suddenly to the cook for the required illumination.

The cook said it was a lark. Then he corrected himself and said it wasn't a lark, then he corrected himself again and became incoherent. Meantime the skipper eyed him stonily, while the mate released the cat and good-naturedly helped to straighten its tail.

It took fully five minutes of unwilling explanation before the skipper could grasp the situation. He did not appear to fairly understand it until he was shown the chest with the ventilated lid ; then his countenance cleared, and, taking the unhappy Billy by the collar, he called sternly for a piece of rope.

W . W . J A C O B S (from *A Black Affair*)

SUMMER SORROWS OF THE SUPER-RICH

In the course of each summer it is my privilege to do some visiting in the class of the super-rich. By this I mean the kind of people who have huge estates at such fashionable places as Nagahucket, and Dogblastit, and up near Lake Owatawetness, where the country is so beautifully wild that it costs a thousand dollars an acre. . . .

Now you would think that the people who live in these great places are happy. They are not. They have troubles of which you and I and the ordinary people never dream. They come out to the wilderness to rough it, and to snatch a brief four months' vacation between the strain of the Riviera and the pressure of New York, and then, right in the happiest season of the summer, they come up against desperate problems. . . .

Problem No. 1. What to do to amuse the butler in the evening ?

It seems that he doesn't play bridge. The butler who was here last year was always quite content if he could be provided with a game of bridge, and except for a run to New York now and then and a trip to see his brother in Vancouver in the middle of the summer, he stayed on the place without a break and seemed quite satisfied.

But the new man Jennings doesn't care for cards. He says quite frankly that it is not a matter of conscience and that he doesn't mind cards in the house, but that they simply don't interest him. So what can one do ?

Problem No. 2. How to get the chauffeur's collars starched ?

It appears that there have been very great difficulties at Dogblastit about this. It is very hard to get the kind of gloss that Ransome likes on his collars. There is, of course, an electric laundry in the basement of Dogblastit itself, but unfortunately the laundry maids who do the work in it will not undertake any collars over 11 inches long. They say they simply won't undertake them.

The experiment was made of bringing up a laundress from Boston, but it was found that she wouldn't undertake to starch anything at such a high altitude. She can only do her work at from 500 to 800 feet above the sea. Beyond that, she said, she could do nothing.

They tried also sending Ransome's collars by express to New York, but this was quite unsatisfactory, because the express people threw them about so roughly. More than once they were seen actually throwing the packet of Ransome's collars right from the platform of Dogblastit station into the express car. The only feasible thing up to now has been to have Ransome take one of the cars and drive his collars either to New York or to Philadelphia. The objection is that it takes up so much of his time, especially as he always likes to drive his boots over to Burlington, Vermont, once a week, where he can get them properly treated.

Problem No. 3. What to get for the cook to read on Sunday ?

The trouble is, she doesn't care for fiction. She evidently is a woman of literary culture, somehow, because she said one day that she had read the whole of Shakespeare and thought it very good. In the library of Dogblastit itself, which is a really beautiful room done in Japanese oak with leaded windows to represent the reading room of a settler's cabin, there are practically no books that suit the cook. In fact, there are nothing but the Blue Book (one needs that to look up people in) and the Pink Book and the Red Book, and of course the Automobile Rude Book and then some Guide Books such as *The Perfect Bartender*, and the *Gentleman's Collar* and *Cocktails for All Occasions*.

Beyond that there are, of course, all the new books—the new fiction—because there is a standing order with Spentano to send up fifty pounds of new fiction by express once a week. None of the guests of the house ever care to read any book more than three weeks old, as they are quite worthless for conversation.

An order was sent to Boston for the Harvard Classics, but the cook says she doesn't care for the way they are selected. The only compromise so far is to get her books about the South Seas. She says she is just crazy over the South Sea literature. So we have given her *Six Weeks in the Marquesas Islands* and *Four Days in Fiji, Half Hours in Hoo-Poo*. But all that will only last her less than seven weeks, and after that we don't know what to do. . .

My visits with my fashionable friends have been so much disturbed by perpetual conversation on these problems that I have decided to give them up altogether and to get back into my own class of society. I have some friends, real ones, who have a wooden house on an island where there is no electric light within twenty miles and where they use rain water out of a barrel.

They have coal-oil lanterns to see by; they wear flannel collars and they pass the soap from one room to another as it is needed. The men cut the firewood, as required, and never keep more than half an hour's supply on hand, and the girls do all the work because help can't be got and they know ten different ways of cooking canned salmon.

I am going back there.

STEPHEN LEACOCK (from *Winnowed Wisdom*)

The burglar stepped inside the window quickly, and then he took his time. A burglar who respects his art always takes his time before taking anything else.

The house was a private residence. By its boarded front door and untrimmed Boston ivy the burglar knew that the mistress of it was sitting on some ocean-side piazza telling a sympathetic man in a yachting cap that no one had ever understood her sensitive, lonely heart. He knew by the light in the third-story front windows, and by the lateness of the season, that the master of the house had come home, and would soon extinguish his light and retire. For it was September of the year and of the soul, in which season the house's good man comes to consider roof gardens and stenographers as vanities, and to desire the return of his mate and the more durable blessings of decorum and the moral excellencies.

The burglar lighted a cigarette. The guarded glow of the match illuminated his salient points for a moment. He belonged to the third type of burglars.

This third type has not yet been recognised and accepted. The police had made us familiar with the first and second. Their classification is simple. The collar is the distinguishing mark.

When a burglar is caught who does not wear a collar he is described as a degenerate of the lowest type, singularly vicious and depraved, and is suspected of being the desperate criminal who stole the handcuffs out of Patrolman Hennessy's pocket in 1878 and walked away to escape arrest.

The other well-known type is the burglar who wears a collar. He is always referred to as a Raffles in real life. He is invariably a gentleman by daylight, breakfasting in a dress suit, and posing as a paper-hanger, while after dark he plies his nefarious occupation of burglary. His mother is an extremely wealthy and respected resident of Ocean Grove, and when he is conducted to his cell he asks at once for a nail file and the *Police Gazette.* He always has a wife in every State in the Union and fiancées in all the Territories, and the newspapers print his matrimonial gallery out of their stock of cuts of the ladies who were cured by only one bottle after having been given up by five doctors, experiencing great relief after the first dose.

The burglar wore a blue sweater. He was neither a Raffles nor one of the chefs from Hell's Kitchen. The police would have been baffled had they attempted to classify him. They have not yet heard of the respectable, unassuming burglar who is neither above nor below his station.

This burglar of the third class began to prowl. He wore no masks, dark lanterns, or gum shoes. He carried a 38-calibre revolver in his pocket, and he chewed peppermint gum thoughtfully.

The furniture of the house was swathed in its summer dust protectors. The silver was far away in safe-deposit vaults. The burglar expected no remarkable " haul." His objective point was that dimly lighted room where the master of the house should be sleeping heavily after whatever solace he had sought to lighten the burden of his loneliness. A " touch " might be made there to the extent of legitimate fair, professional profits—loose money, a watch, a jewelled stick-pin—nothing exorbitant or beyond reason. He had seen the window left open and had taken the chance.

The burglar softly opened the door of the lighted room.

The gas was turned low. A man lay in the bed asleep. On the dresser lay many things in confusion—a crumpled roll of bills, a watch, keys, three poker chips, crushed cigars, a pink silk hair bow, and an unopened bottle of bromo-seltzer for a bulwark in the morning.

The burglar took three steps toward the dresser. The man in the bed suddenly uttered a squeaky groan and opened his eyes. His right hand slid under his pillow, but remained there.

"Lay still," said the burglar in conversational tone. Burglars of the third type do not hiss. The citizen in the bed looked at the round end of the burglar's pistol and lay still.

"Now hold up both your hands," commanded the burglar.

The citizen had a little, pointed, brown-and-grey beard, like that of a painless dentist. He looked solid, esteemed, irritable, and disgusted. He sat up in bed and raised his right hand above his head.

"Up with the other one," ordered the burglar. "You might be amphibious and shoot with your left. You can count two, can't you? Hurry up, now."

"Can't raise the other one," said the citizen with a contortion of his lineaments.

"What's the matter with it?"

"Rheumatism in the shoulder."

"Inflammatory?"

"Was. The inflammation has gone down."

The burglar stood for a moment or two, holding his gun on the afflicted one. He glanced at the plunder on the dresser and then, with a half-embarrassed air back at the man in the bed. Then he, too, made a sudden grimace.

"Don't stand there making faces," snapped the

citizen, bad-humouredly. " If you've come to burgle why don't you do it ? There's some stuff lying around."

" 'Scuse me," said the burglar, with a grin ; " but it just socked me one, too. It's good for you that rheumatism and me happens to be old pals. I got it in my left arm, too. Most anybody but me would have popped you when you wouldn't hoist that left claw of yours."

" How long have you had it ? " inquired the citizen.

" Four years. I guess that ain't all. Once you've got it, it's you for a rheumatic life—that's my judgment."

" Ever try rattlesnake oil ? " asked the citizen interestedly.

" Gallons," said the burglar. " If all the snakes I've used the oil of was strung out in a row they'd reach eight times as far as Saturn, and the rattles could be heard at Valparaiso, Indiana, and back."

" Some use Chiselum's Pills," remarked the citizen.

" Fudge ! " said the burglar. " Took 'em five months. No good. I had some relief the year I tried Finkelham's Extract, Balm of Gilead poultices, and Pott's Pain Pulverizer ; but I think it was the buckeye I carried in my pocket what done the trick."

" Is yours worse in the morning or at night ? " asked the citizen.

" Night," said the burglar ; " just when I'm busiest. Say, take down that arm of yours—I guess you won't— Say ! did you ever try Blickerstaff's Blood Builder ? "

" I never did. Does yours come in paroxysms or is it a steady pain ? "

The burglar sat down on the foot of the bed and rested his gun on his crossed knee.

" It jumps," said he. " It strikes me when I ain't looking for it. I had to give up second-story work because

I got stuck sometimes half-way up. Tell you what—I don't believe the bloomin' doctors know what is good for it."

" Same here. I've spent a thousand dollars without getting any relief. Yours swell any ? "

" Of mornings. And when it's goin' to rain—great Christopher ! "

" Me, too," said the citizen. " I can tell when a streak of humidity the size of a tablecloth starts from Florida on its way to New York. And if I pass a theatre where there's an ' East Lynne ' matinée going on, the moisture starts my left arm jumping like a toothache."

" It's undiluted—hades ! " said the burglar.

" You're dead right," said the citizen.

The burglar looked down at his pistol and thrust it into his pocket with an awkward attempt at ease.

" Say, old man," he said constrainedly, " ever try opodeldoc ? "

" Slop ! " said the citizen angrily. " Might as well rub on restaurant butter."

" Sure," concurred the burglar. " It's a salve suitable for little Minnie when the kitty scratches her finger. I'll tell you what ! We're up against it. I only find one thing that eases her up. Hey ? Little old sanitary, ameliorating, lest-we-forget Booze. Say—this job's off—'scuse me—get on your clothes and let's go out and have some. 'Scuse the liberty, but—ouch ! There she goes again ! "

" For a week," said the citizen, " I haven't been able to dress myself without help. I'm afraid Thomas is in bed, and——"

" Climb out ! " said the burglar, " I'll help you get into your duds."

The conventional returned as a tidal wave and flooded the citizen. He stroked his brown-and-grey beard.

" It's very unusual——" he began.

" Here's your shirt," said the burglar, " fall out. I know a man who said Omberry's Ointment fixed him in two weeks so he could use both hands in tying his four-in-hand."

As they were going out the door the citizen turned and started back.

" Liked to forgot my money," he explained ; " laid it on the dresser last night."

The burglar caught him by the right sleeve.

" Come on," he said, bluffly. " I ask you. Leave it alone. I've got the price. Ever try witch hazel and oil of wintergreen ? "

O. HENRY (from *Sixes and Sevens*)

THE OLDEST JOKE

Many investigators have speculated as to the character of the first joke ; and as speculation must our efforts remain. But I personally have no doubt whatever as to the subject-matter of that distant pleasantry ; it was the face of the other person involved. I don't say that Adam was caustic about Eve's face or Eve about Adam's : that is improbable. Nor does matrimonial invective even now ordinarily take this form. But after a while, after cousins had come into the world, the facial jest began ; and by the time of Noah and his sons the riot was in full swing. In every rough and tumble among the children of Ham,

Shem, and Japheth, I feel certain that crude and candid personalities fell to the lot, at any rate, of the little Shems.

So was it then; so is it still to-day. No jests are so rich as those that bear upon the unloveliness of features not our own. The tiniest street urchins in dispute always—sooner or later—devote their retorts to the distressing physiognomy of the foe. Not only are they conforming to the ancient convention, but they show sagacity too, for to sum up an opponent as " Face," " Facey," or " Funny Face," is to spike his gun. There is no reply but the cowardly *tu quoque*. He cannot say, " My face is not comic, it is handsome "; because that does not touch the root of the matter. The root of the matter is your opinion of his face as deplorable.

Not only is the recognition of what is odd in an opponent's countenance of this priceless value in ordinary quarrels among the young and the ill-mannered (just as abuse of the opposing counsel is the best way of covering the poverty of one's own case at law), but the music-hall humorist has no easier or surer road to the risibilities of most of his audience. Jokes about faces never fail, and are never threadbare. Sometimes I find myself listening to one who has been called—possibly the label was self-imposed—the Prime Minister of Mirth, and he invariably enlarges upon the quaintness of somebody's features, often, for he is the soul of impartiality, his own; and the first time, now thirty years ago, that I ever entered a music-hall (the tiny stuffy old Oxford at Brighton, where the chairman with the dyed hair—it was more purple than black—used to sit amid a little company of bloods whose proud privilege it was to pay for his refreshment), another George, whose surname was Beauchamp, was singing about a siren into whose clutches he had or had not fallen, who had

an indiarubber lip
Like the rudder of a ship.

—So you see there is complete continuity.

But the best example of this branch of humour is beyond all question that of the Two Macs, whose influence, long though it is since they eclipsed the gaiety of the nation by vanishing, is still potent. Though gone they still jest : or, at any rate, their jests did not all vanish with them : the incorrigible veneration for what is antique displayed by low comedians takes care of that. " I saw your wife at the masked ball last night," the first Mac would say, in his rich brogue. " My wife was at the ball last night," the other would reply in a brogue of deeper richness, " but it wasn't a masked ball." The first Mac would then express an overwhelming surprise, as he countered with the devastating question, " Was *that* her face ? "

" You're not two-faced, anyway. I'll say that for you," was the apparently magnanimous concession made by one comedian to another in a recent farcical play. The other was beginning to express his gratification when the speaker continued : " If you were, you wouldn't have come out with that one." Again, you observe, there is no answer to this kind of attack. Hence, I suppose, its popularity. And yet, perhaps, to take refuge in a smug sententiousness, and remark crisply, " Handsome is as handsome does," should now and then be useful. But it requires some self-esteem.

There is no absolute need, however, for the face joke to be applied to others to be successful. Since, in spite of the complexion creams, " plumpers," and nose-machines advertised in the papers, faces will continue to be here and there somewhat Gothic, the wise thing for their owners is to accept them and think of other things, or console themselves before the unflattering mirror with the memory of those mortals who have been both quaint-looking and gifted. Wiser still perhaps to make a little capital out of the affliction. Public men who are able to make a jest of the homeliness of their features never lose by it. President Wilson's public recital of the famous lines on his countenance (which I personally find not impossibly unprepossessing) did much to increase his popularity.

> As a beauty I am not a star,
> There are others more handsome by far.
>   But my face, I don't mind it,
>   For I keep behind it ;
> It's the people in front get the jar.

And an English bishop, or possibly dean, came, at last, very near earth when in a secular address he repeated his retort to the lady who had commented upon his extraordinary plainness : " Ah, but you should see my brother." There is also the excellent story of the ugly man before the camera, who was promised by the photographer that he should have justice done to him. " Justice ! " he exclaimed. " I don't want justice ; I want mercy."

The great face joke, as I say, obviously came first. Because there were in the early days none of the materials for the other staple quips—such as alcohol, and sausages, and wives' mothers. Faces, however, were always there. And not even yet have the later substitutes ousted it. Just as Shakespeare's orator, " When he is out," spits, so does the funny man, in similar difficulties, if he is wise, say, " Do you call that a face ? " and thus collects his thoughts for fresh sallies. If all " dials " were identical, Mr. George Graves, for example, would be a stage bankrupt ; for, resourceful as he is in the humour of quizzical disapproval, the vagaries of facial oddity are his foundation stone.

Remarkable as are the heights of grotesque simile to which all the Georges have risen in this direction, it is, oddly enough, to the other and gentler sex that the classic examples (in my experience) belong. At a dinner-party given by a certain hospitable lady who remained something of an *enfant terrible* to the end of her long life, she drew the attention of one of her guests, by no means too cautiously, to the features of another guest, a bishop of great renown. " Isn't his face," she asked, in a deathless sentence, " like the inside of an elephant's foot ? " I have not personally the honour of this divine's acquaintance, but all my friends who have met or seen him assure me that the similitude is exact. Another lady, happily still living, said of the face of an acquaintance, that it was " not so much a face, as a part of her person which she happened to leave uncovered, by which her friends were able to recognise her." A third, famous for her swift analyses, said that a certain would-be beauty might have a title to good looks but for a " rush of teeth to the head." I do not quote these admirable remarks merely as a proof of woman's natural kindliness, but to show how even among the elect—for all three speakers are of more than common culture—the face joke holds sway.

E. V. LUCAS (from *Mixed Vintages*)

THE MATCH-MAKER

The grill-room clock struck eleven with the respectful unobtrusiveness of one whose mission in life is to be ignored. When the flight of time should really have rendered abstinence and migration imperative the lighting apparatus would signal the fact in the usual way.

Six minutes later Clovis approached the supper-table, in the blessed expectancy of one who has dined sketchily and long ago.

" I'm starving," he announced, making an effort to sit down gracefully and read the menu at the same time.

" So I gathered," said his host, " from the fact that you were nearly punctual. I ought to have told you that I'm a Food Reformer. I've ordered two bowls of bread-and-milk and some health biscuits. I hope you don't mind."

Clovis pretended afterwards that he didn't go white above the collar-line for the fraction of a second.

" All the same," he said, " you ought not to joke about such things. There really are such people. I've known people who've met them. To think of all the adorable things there are to eat in the world, and then to go through life munching sawdust and being proud of it."

" They're like the Flagellants of the Middle Ages, who went about mortifying themselves."

" They had some excuse," said Clovis. " They did it to save their immortal souls, didn't they ? You needn't tell me that a man who doesn't love oysters and asparagus and good wines has got a soul, or a stomach either. He's simply got the instinct for being unhappy highly developed."

Clovis relapsed for a few golden moments into tender

intimacies with a succession of rapidly disappearing oysters.

" I think oysters are more beautiful than any religion," he resumed presently. " They not only forgive our un-kindness to them ; they justify it, they incite us to go on being perfectly horrid to them. Once they arrive at the supper-table they seem to enter thoroughly into the spirit of the thing. There's nothing in Christianity or Buddhism that quite matches the sympathetic unselfish-ness of an oyster. Do you like my new waistcoat ? I'm wearing it for the first time to-night."

" It looks like a great many others you've had lately, only worse. New dinner waistcoats are becoming a habit with you."

" They say one always pays for the excesses of one's youth ; mercifully that isn't true about one's clothes. My mother is thinking of getting married."

" Again ! "

" It's the first time."

" Of course, you ought to know. I was under the impres-sion that she'd been married once or twice at least."

" Three times, to be mathematically exact. I meant that it was the first time she'd thought about getting married ; the other times she did it without thinking. As a matter of fact, it's really I who am doing the thinking for her in this case. You see, it's quite two years since her last husband died."

" You evidently think that brevity is the soul of widowhood."

" Well, it struck me that she was getting moped, and beginning to settle down, which wouldn't suit her a bit. The first symptom that I noticed was when she began to complain that we were living beyond our income. All decent people live beyond their incomes nowadays, and those who aren't respectable live beyond other people's. A few gifted individuals manage to do both."

" It's hardly so much a gift as an industry."

" The crisis came," returned Clovis, " when she suddenly started the theory that late hours were bad for one, and wanted me to be in by one o'clock every night. Imagine that sort of thing for me, who was eighteen on my last birthday."

" On your last two birthdays, to be mathematically exact."

" Oh, well, that's not my fault. I'm not going to arrive at nineteen as long as my mother remains at thirty-seven. One must have some regard for appearances."

" Perhaps your mother would age a little in the process of settling down."

" That's the last thing she'd think of. Feminine reformations always start in on the failings of other people. That's why I was so keen on the husband idea."

" Did you go as far as to select the gentleman, or did you merely throw out a general idea, and trust to the force of suggestion ? "

" If one wants a thing done in a hurry one must see to it oneself. I found a military Johnny hanging round on a loose end at the club, and took him home to lunch once or twice. He's spent most of his life on the Indian frontier building roads, and relieving famines and minimizing earthquakes, and all that sort of thing that one does do on frontiers. He could talk sense to a peevish cobra in fifteen native languages, and probably knew what to do if you found a rogue elephant on your croquet-lawn ; but he was shy and diffident with women. I told my mother privately that he was an absolute woman-hater ; so, of course, she laid herself out to flirt all she knew, which isn't a little."

" And was the gentleman responsive ? "

" I hear he told some one at the club that he was looking out for a Colonial job, with plenty of hard work, for a young friend of his, so I gather that he has some idea of marrying into the family."

" You seem destined to be the victim of the reformation, after all."

Clovis wiped the trace of Turkish coffee and the beginnings of a smile from his lips, and slowly lowered his dexter eyelid. Which, being interpreted, probably meant " I *don't* think ! "

" SAKI " (from *The Chronicles of Clovis*)

SPORT AT THE RACES

The races had by this time begun with a competition known as the " Hop, Step, and Lep " ; this, judging by the yells was a highly interesting display, but as it was conducted between two impervious rows of onlookers, the aristocracy on the fish-boxes saw nothing save the occasional purple face of a competitor, starting into view above the wall of backs like a jack-in-the-box. For me, however, the odorous sanctuary of the fish-boxes was not to be. I left it guarded by Slipper with a cart-whip of flail-like dimensions, as disreputable an object as could be seen out of low comedy, with someone's old white cords on his bandy legs, butcher boots three sizes too big for him, and a black eye. The small boys fled before him ; in the glory of his office he would have flailed his own mother off the fish-boxes had occasion served.

I had an afternoon of decidedly mixed enjoyment. My stewardship blossomed forth like Aaron's rod, and added to itself the duties of starter, handicapper, general referee, and chucker-out, besides which I from time to time strove with emissaries who came from Philippa with messages about water and kettles. Flurry and I had to deal single-handed with the foot-races (our brothers in office being otherwise engaged at Mr. Sheehy's), a task of many difficulties, chiefest being that the spectators all swept forward at the word " Go ! " and ran the race with the competitors, yelling curses, blessings, and advice upon them, taking short cuts over anything and everybody, and mingling inextricably with the finish. By fervent applications of the whips, the course was to some extent purged for the quarter-mile, and it would, I believe, have been a triumph of handicapping had not an unforeseen disaster overtaken the favourite—old Mrs. Knox's bath-chair boy. Whether, as was alleged, his braces had or had not been tampered with by a rival was a matter that the referee had subsequently to deal with in the thick of a free fight ; but the painful fact remained that in the course of the first lap what were described as " his galluses " abruptly severed their connection with the garments for whose safety they were responsible, and the favourite was obliged to seek seclusion in the crowd.

The tug-of-war followed close on this *contretemps*, and had the excellent effect of drawing away, like a blister, the inflammation set up by the grievances of the bath-chair boy. I cannot at this moment remember of how many men each team consisted ; my sole aim was to keep the numbers even, and to baffle the volunteers, who, in an ecstasy of sympathy, attached themselves to the tail of the rope at moments when their champions weakened. The rival forces dug their heels in and tugged in an uproar that drew forth the innermost line of customers from Mr. Sheehy's porter tent, and even attracted " the quality " from the haven of the fish-boxes, Slipper, in the capacity of Squire of Dames, pioneering Lady Knox through the crowd with the cart-whip, and with language whose nature was providentially veiled, for the most part, by the din. The tug-of-war continued unabated. One team was getting the worst of it, but hung doggedly on, sinking lower and lower till they gradually sat down ; nothing short of the trump of judgment could have conveyed to them, that they were breaking rules, and both teams settled down by slow degrees on to their sides, with the rope under them, and their heels still planted in the ground, bringing about complete deadlock. I do not know the record duration for a tug-of-war, but I can certify that the Cullinagh and Knockranny teams lay on the ground at full tension for half-an-hour, like men in apoplectic fits, each man with his respective adherents howling over him, blessing him, and adjuring him to continue.

With my own nauseated eyes I saw a bearded country-man, obviously one of Mr. Sheehy's best customers, fling himself on his knees beside one of the combatants, and kiss his crimson and streaming face in a rapture of en-couragement. As he shoved unsteadily past me on his return journey to Mr. Sheehy's, I heard him informing a friend that " he cried a handful over Danny Mulloy, when he seen the poor brave boy so shtubborn, and, indeed, he couldn't say why he cried."

" For good-nature, ye'd cry," suggested the friend.

" Well, just that, I suppose," returned Danny Mulloy's

admirer resignedly ; " indeed, if it was only two cocks ye seen fightin' on the road, yer heart'd take part with one o' them ! "

I had begun to realise that I might as well abandon the tug-of-war and occupy myself elsewhere, when my wife's much harassed messenger brought me the portentous tidings that Mrs. Yeates wanted me at the tent at once. When I arrived I found the tent literally bulging with Philippa's guests ; Lady Knox, seated on a hamper, was taking off her gloves, and loudly announcing her desire for tea, and Philippa, with a flushed face and a crooked hat, breathed into my ear the awful news that both the cream and the milk had been forgotten.

" But Flurry Knox says he can get me some," she went on ; " he's gone to send people to milk a cow that lives near here. Go out and see if he's coming."

I went out and found, in the first instance, Mrs. Cadogan, who greeted me with the prayer that the divil might roast Julia McCarthy, that legged it away to the races like a wild goose, and left the cream afther her on the servants' hall table. " Sure, Misther Flurry's gone looking for a cow, and what cow would there be in a backwards place like this ? And look at me shtriving to keep the kettle simpering on the fire, and not as much coals undher it as'd redden a pipe ! "

" Where's Mr. Knox ? " I asked.

" Himself and Slipper's galloping the counthry like the deer. I believe it's to the house above they went, sir."

I followed up a rocky hill to the house above, and there found Flurry and Slipper engaged in the patriarchal task of driving two brace of coupled and spancelled goats into a shed.

" It's the best we can do," said Flurry briefly ; " there

isn't a cow to be found, and the people are all down at the sports. Be d——d to you, Slipper, don't let them go from you!" as the goats charged and doubled like football players.

"But goats' milk!" I said, paralysed by horrible memories of what tea used to taste like at Gib.

"They'll never know it!" said Flurry, cornering a venerable nanny; "here, hold this divil, and hold her tight!"

I have no time to dwell upon the pastoral scene that followed. Suffice it to say, that at the end of ten minutes of scorching profanity from Slipper, and incessant warfare with the goats, the latter had reluctantly yielded two small jugfuls, and the dairymaids had exhibited a nerve and skill in their trade that won my lasting respect.

"I knew I could trust *you*, Mr. Knox!" said Philippa, with shining eyes, as we presented her with the two foaming beakers. I suppose a man is never a hero to his wife, but if she could have realised the bruises on my legs, I think she would have reserved a blessing for me also.

What was thought of the goats' milk I gathered symptomatically from a certain fixity of expression that accompanied the first sip of the tea, and from observing that comparatively few ventured on second cups. I also noted that, after a brief conversation with Flurry, Miss Sally poured hers secretly on to the grass.

E. Œ. SOMERVILLE AND MARTIN ROSS
(from *The Irish R.M.*)

" O illustrious person," said Kai Lung very earnestly, " this is evidently an unfortunate mistake. Doubtless you were expecting some exalted Mandarin to come and render you homage, and were preparing to overwhelm him with gratified confusion by escorting him yourself to your well-appointed abode. Indeed, I passed such a one on the road, very richly apparelled, who inquired of me the way to the mansion of the dignified and upright Lin Yi. By this time he is perhaps two or three li towards the east."

" However distinguished a Mandarin he may be, it is fitting that I should first attend to one whose manners and accomplishments betray him to be of the Royal House," replied Lin Yi, with extreme affability. " Precede me, therefore, to my mean and uninviting hovel, while I gain more honour than I can reasonably bear by following closely in your elegant footsteps, and guarding your Imperial person with this inadequate but heavily-loaded weapon."

Seeing no chance of immediate escape, Kai Lung led the way, instructed by the brigand, along a very difficult and bewildering path, until they reached a cave hidden among the crags. Here Lin Yi called out some words in the Miaotze tongue, whereupon a follower appeared, and opened a gate in the stockade of prickly mimosa which guarded the mouth of the den. Within the enclosure a fire burned, and food was being prepared. At a word from the chief, the unfortunate Kai Lung found his hands seized and tied behind his back, while a second later a rough hemp rope was fixed round his neck, and the other end tied to an overhanging tree.

Lin Yi smiled pleasantly and critically upon these preparations, and when they were complete dismissed his follower.

"Now we can converse at our ease and without restraint," he remarked to Kai Lung. "It will be a distinguished privilege for a person occupying the important public position which you undoubtedly do ; for myself, my instincts are so degraded and low-minded that nothing gives me more gratification than to dispense with ceremony."

To this Kai Lung made no reply, chiefly because at that moment the wind swayed the tree, and compelled him to stand on his toes in order to escape suffocation.

"It would be useless to try to conceal from a person of your inspired intelligence that I am indeed Lin Yi," continued the robber. "It is a dignified position to occupy, and one for which I am quite incompetent. In the sixth month of the third year ago, it chanced that this unworthy person, at that time engaged in commercial affairs at Knei Yang, became inextricably immersed in the insidious delights of quail-fighting. Having been entrusted with a large number of taels with which to purchase elephants' teeth, it suddenly occurred to him that if he doubled the number of taels by staking them upon an exceedingly powerful and agile quail, he would be able to purchase twice the number of teeth, and so benefit his patron to a large extent. This matter was clearly forced upon his notice by a dream, in which he perceived one whom he then understood to be the benevolent spirit of an ancestor in the act of stroking a particular quail, upon whose chances he accordingly placed all he possessed. Doubtless evil spirits had been employed in the matter ; for, to this person's great astonishment the quail in question failed in a very discreditable manner at the encounter. Unfortunately, this person had risked not only the money which had been entrusted to him, but all that he had himself become possessed of by some years of honourable toil and assiduous courtesy as a professional witness in law cases. Not doubting that his patron would see that he was himself greatly to blame in confiding so large a sum of money to a comparatively young man of whom he knew little, this person placed the matter before him, at the same time showing him that he would suffer in the eyes of the virtuous if he did not restore this person's savings, which but for the presence of the larger sum, and a generous desire to benefit his patron, he would never have risked in so uncertain a venture as that of quail-fighting. Although the facts were laid in the form of a dignified request instead of a demand by legal means, and the reasoning carefully drawn up in columns on fine parchment by a very illustrious writer, the reply which this person received showed him plainly that a wrong view had been taken of the matter, and that the time had arrived when it became necessary for him to make a suitable rejoinder by leaving the city without delay."

" It was a high-minded and disinterested course to take," said Kai Lung with great conviction, as Lin Yi paused. " Without doubt evil will shortly overtake the avaricious-souled person at Knei Yang."

" It has already done so," replied Lin Yi. " While passing through this forest in the season of Many White Vapours, the spirits of his bad deeds appeared to him in misleading and symmetrical shapes and drew him out of the path and away from his bowmen. After suffering many torments, he found his way here, where, in spite of our continual care, he perished miserably and in great bodily pain. . . . But I cannot conceal from myself, in spite of your distinguished politeness, that I am becoming intolerably tiresome with my commonplace talk."

"On the contrary," replied Kai Lung, "while listening to your voice I seemed to hear the beating of many gongs of the finest and most polished brass. I floated in the Middle Air, and for the time I even became unconscious of the fact that this honourable appendage, though fashioned, as I perceive, out of the most delicate silk, makes it exceedingly difficult for me to breathe."

"Such a thing cannot be permitted," exclaimed Lin Yi, with some indignation, as with his own hands he slackened the rope, and, taking it from Kai Lung's neck, fastened it round his ankle. "Now, in return for my uninviting confidences, shall not my senses be gladdened by a recital of the titles and honours borne by your distinguished family? Doubtless, at this moment many Mandarins of the highest degree are anxiously awaiting your arrival at Knei Yang, perhaps passing the time by outdoing one another in protesting the number of taels each would give rather than permit you to be tormented by fire-brands, or even to lose a single ear."

"Alas!" replied Kai Lung, "never was there a truer proverb than that which says, ' It is a mark of insincerity of purpose to spend one's time in looking for the sacred Emperor in the low-class tea-shops.' Do Mandarins or the friends of Mandarins travel in mean garments and unattended? Indeed, the person who is now before you is none other than the outcast Kai Lung, the story-teller, one of degraded habits and no very distinguished or reputable ancestors. His friends are few, and mostly of the criminal class; his wealth is not more than some six or eight cash, concealed in his left sandal; and his entire stock-in-trade consists of a few unendurable and badly told stories, to which, however, it is his presumptuous intention shortly to add a dignified narrative of the high-born Lin Yi, setting out his domestic virtues and the honour which he has reflected upon his house, his valour in war, the destruction of his enemies, and, above all, his great benevolence and the protection which he extends to the poor and those engaged in the distinguished arts."

" The absence of friends is unfortunate," said Lin Yi thoughtfully, after he had possessed himself of the coins indicated by Kai Lung, and also of a much larger amount concealed elsewhere among the story-teller's clothing.

ERNEST BRAMAH (from *The Wallet of Kai Lung*)

SECOND PART

§ III STAR DUST

Bright thoughts are the gems of noble minds.

SIR THOMAS BROWNE

The true harvest of my daily life is somewhat as intangible and indescribable as the tints of morning or
evening. It is a little star-dust caught, a segment of the
rainbow which I have clutched.

THOREAU (*Walden*)

" Can you emit sparks ? " said the cat to the ugly
duckling in the fairy tale, and the poor abashed creature
had to admit that it could not.

A. BIRRELL (*Res Judicatae*)

§ III STAR DUST

THOUGHTS WORTH REMEMBERING

Others, too, having done what men may, have borne what men must.

Speech of Nicias to the Athenian Army

Wise men learn more from fools than fools learn from wise men.

CATO

We cannot prevent the black birds of evil from flying over our heads, but we can prevent them from building their nests in our hair.

Chinese Proverb

He who goes to the hills goes to his mother.

Indian Saying

Of law there can be no less acknowledged than that her seat is in the bosom of God, her voice the harmony of the world, all things in heaven and earth do her homage,—the very least in feeling her care, and the greatest as not exempted from her power.

HOOKER

Man is a name of honour for a king.

CHAPMAN

What a deal of cold business doth a man mis-spend the better part of life in ! In scattering compliments, tendering visits, gathering and venting news, following feasts and plays, making a little winter-love in a dark corner.

BEN JONSON

Old friends are best. King James used to call for his old shoes : they were easiest for his feet.

King James said to the fly, Have I three kingdoms, and thou must needs fly into my eye ?

SELDEN

Only the actions of the just
Smell sweet and blossom in their dust.

SHIRLEY

Act nothing in furious passion ; it's putting to sea in a storm.

Almost twenty years since, I heard a profane jest, and still remember it. How many pious passages of a far later date have I forgotten ! It seems my soul is like a filthy pond, wherein fish die soon, and frogs live long.

Some admiring what motives to mirth infants meet with in their silent and solitary smiles, have resolved (how truly I know not) that then they converse with angels.

THOMAS FULLER

No man can make another man to be his slave, unless he hath first enslaved himself to life and death, to pleasure and pain, to hope or fear ; command these passions, and you are freer than the Parthian Kings.

Stay but till to-morrow, and your present sorrow will be weary, and will lie down to rest.

JEREMY TAYLOR

A man that should call every thing by its right name, would hardly pass the streets without being knocked down as a common enemy.

Hope is generally a wrong guide, though it is very good company by the way.

The best party is but a kind of conspiracy against the rest of the nation.

LORD HALIFAX

You will never enjoy the world aright till the sea itself floweth in your veins, till you are clothed with the heavens and crowned with the stars.

THOMAS TRAHERNE

Friendship is to be purchased only by friendship. A man may have authority over others ; but he can never have their heart but by giving his own.

BISHOP WILSON (1663–1755)

In faith and hope the world will disagree,
But all mankind's concern is charity.

. . . .

Is there no bright reversion in the sky
For those who greatly think, or bravely die ?

POPE

Statesmen and beauties are very rarely sensible of the gradations of their decay ; and, too sanguinely hoping to shine on in their meridian, often set with contempt and ridicule.

Cunning is the dark sanctuary of incapacity.

LORD CHESTERFIELD

The English have a hundred religions, but only one sauce.

VOLTAIRE

There is nothing so ridiculous that has not at some time been said by some philosopher.

GOLDSMITH

There is more pleasure in building castles in the air than on the ground.

GIBBON

If the world were good for nothing else, it is a fine subject for speculation.

HAZLITT

God created man in his image, and man has not been slow in returning the compliment.

HEINE

Our dead are never dead to us until we have forgotten them ; they can be injured by us, they can be wounded.

GEORGE ELIOT

We need examples of people who, leaving Heaven to decide whether they are to rise in the world, decide for themselves that they will be happy in it, and have resolved to seek not greater wealth but simple pleasure, not higher future but deeper felicity—to make the first of possessions self-possession.

RUSKIN

There is no room for sweeping denunciations or trenchant criticisms in the dealings of a world whose falsehoods and veracities are separated by so very thin a barrier.

BISHOP STUBBS (1825–1901)

Business is really more agreeable than pleasure ; it interests the whole mind, the aggregate nature of man more continuously, and more deeply. But it does not *look* as if it did.

WALTER BAGEHOT

To himself every one is an immortal ; he may know that he is going to die, but he can never know that he is dead.

SAMUEL BUTLER (1835–1902)

Vulgarity is an inadequate conception of the art of living.

BISHOP CREIGHTON

Education is an admirable thing, but it is well to remember from time to time that nothing that is worth knowing can be taught.
The soul is born old but grows young. That is the comedy of life. The body is born young and grows old. That's life's tragedy.

OSCAR WILDE

The soul is dyed the colour of its leisure thoughts.

DEAN INGE

The difficult is that which can be done immediately, the impossible that which takes a little longer.

NANSEN

Whoever it was who searched the heavens with his telescope and found no God would not have found the human mind if he had searched the brain with a microscope.

Truth is a jewel which should not be painted over ; but it may be set to advantage and shown in a good light.

Life is not a spectacle or a feast ; it is a predicament.

To understand oneself is the classic form of consolation ; to elude oneself is the romantic.

GEORGE SANTAYANA

JOTTINGS BY LEONARDO

Who injures others regards not himself.

Why does the eye see a thing more clearly in dreams than the imagination when awake ?

In rivers, the water that you touch is the last of what has passed and the first of that which comes : so with time present.

Thou, O God, dost sell unto us all good things at the price of labour.

As a well-spent day brings happy sleep, so life well used brings happy death.

Note-Books of Leonardo da Vinci

(Trans. E. McCURDY)

SOME PROVERBS

The best preacher is the heart ; the best teacher is time ; the best book is the world ; the best friend is God.

Before fording the river, do not curse the alligator's mother.

If fate throws a knife at you, there are two ways of catching it—by the blade and by the handle.

The dogs bark but the caravan passes.

God does not smite with both hands.

If the weather is fine, take your cloak ; if it rains, do as you please.

Hope is a good breakfast but a bad supper.

The gods sell all things at a fair price.

No man can be happy without a friend, nor be sure of him till he's unhappy.

Genius is one part inspiration and three parts perspiration.

Do right, and fear no man ; don't write, and fear no woman.

By the road called Straight we come to the house called Beautiful.

He who speaks the truth must have one foot in the stirrup.

No one but God and I knows what is in my heart.

The stars make no noise.

Night is a good herdsman, she brings all creatures home.

From poverty to profusion is a hard journey, but the way back is easy.

You can count the number of apples on one tree, but you cannot count the number of trees in one apple.

HOT AND COLD

She is my joy, she is my care and woe,
She is my pain, she is my ease therefor
She is my death, she is my life also,

She is my salve, she is my wound so sore :
In fine, she hath the hand and knife
That both may save and end my life.

EDWARD DE VERE, EARL OF OXFORD

THE BEST OF SHYLOCK

TUBAL : There came divers of Antonio's creditors in my
company to Venice. . . One of them showed me a ring
that he had of your daughter for a monkey.
SHYLOCK : Out upon her ! Thou torturest me, Tubal. It
was my turquoise. I had it of Leah when I was a bachelor !
I would not have given it for a wilderness of monkeys.

SHAKESPEARE (from *Merchant of Venice*)

OTHER SHAKESPEARIAN ITEMS

There was a star danced, and under that was I born.
Cousins, God give you joy !

(From *Much Ado About Nothing*)

A good leg will fall ; a straight back will stoop ; a black
beard will turn white ; a curled pate will grow bald ;
a fair face will wither ; a full eye will wax hollow : but a
good heart, Kate, is the sun and the moon ; or rather
the sun and not the moon ; for it shines bright and never
changes, but keeps his course truly.

(From *Henry V*)

Weariness
Can snore upon the flint, when resty sloth
Finds the down pillow hard.

(From *Cymbeline*)

They say miracles are past : and we have our philosophical
persons to make modern and familiar things supernatural
and causeless. Hence is it that we make trifles of terrors,
ensconcing ourselves into seeming knowledge, when we
should submit ourselves to an unknown fear.

(From *All's Well that Ends Well*)

Let never day nor night unhallow'd pass,
But still remember what the Lord hath done.

(From 2 *Henry VI*)

To Thee I do commend my watchful soul
Ere I let fall the windows of mine eyes :
Sleeping and waking, O, defend me still !

(From *Richard III*)

ELIZABETHAN CRITICISM

1. *Homage to Chaucer*

Truly I know not, whether to mervaile more, either
that he in that mistie time, could see so clearly, or that
wee in this cleare age, walke so stumblingly after him.

SIR PHILIP SIDNEY

2. *Satirical Observations on certain " lines in Mr. Shakespeare's vayne "*

Ey marry, Sir, these have some life in them ! Let this
duncified worlde esteeme of Spencer and Chaucer, I'le

worshipp sweet Mr. Shakespeare and to honour him will lay his Venus and Adonis under my pillowe, as we reade of one (I doe not well remember his name, but I am sure he was a Kinge), slept with Homer under his bed's heade.

ANONYMOUS (from *The Returne from Parnassus*,
a play acted by students of St. John's College,
Cambridge, 1601)

CORYATE DISCOVERS THE FORK

I observed a custom in all those Italian cities and towns through the which I passed, that is not used in any other country that I saw in my travels. The Italians do always at their meals use a little fork when they cut their meat. The reason of this their curiosity is, because the Italian cannot by any means endure to have his dish touched with fingers, seeing all men's fingers are not alike clean.

THOMAS CORYATE (from *Crudities*, 1611)

GIPSY SONG

The faery beam upon you,
The stars to glister on you ;
  A moon of light
  In the noon of night,
Till the fire-drake hath o'ergone you !
The wheel of fortune guide you,
The boy with the bow beside you ;
  Run aye in the way
  Till the bird of day,
And the luckier lot betide you !

BEN JONSON

INFORMATIONS OF BEN JONSON TO W. D.

when he came to Scotland on foot

That Shakspear wanted Arte :

That he told Cardinal depperon at his being in France anno 1613 who shew him his translations of Virgill that they were naught :

Shakspear in a play brought in a number of men saying they had suffered Shipwrack in Bohemia wher yr is no sea neer by some 100 miles :

S. P. Sidney was no pleasant man in countenance, his face being spoiled with Pimples :

Queen Elizabeth never saw herself after she became old in a true Glass. they painted her & sometymes would vermilion her nose, she had allwayes about Christmas evens set dice, that threw sixes or five, & she knew not they were other, to make her win & esteame herself fortunate :

A Cook, who was of ane evill lyfe, when a minister told him he would to hell, askt what torment was yr, being answered fyre, fire (said he) that is my Playfellow.

From *Notes made by William Drummond of Hawthornden,* 1619

HOW SHAKESPEARE STRUCK A CONTEMPORARY

Hee was (indeed) honest, and of an open, and free nature : had an excellent *Phantsie* ; brave notions, and gentle expressions : wherein he flow'd with that facility that sometime it was necessary he should be stop'd.

BEN JONSON (from *Discoveries,* 1641)

IF ALL BE TRUE

If all be true that I do think,
There are five reasons we should drink;
Good wine; a friend; or being dry;
Or lest we should be by and by;
Or any other reason why.

HENRY ALDRICH

NIGHT-WORK

Now Mayors and Shrieves are hush'd and satiate lay,
Yet eat in dreams, the custard of the day;
While pensive poets painful vigil keep,
Sleepless themselves, to give their readers sleep.

POPE (from The Dunciad)

TWO RIVERS

Says Tweed to Till—
" What gars ye rin sae still ? "
Says Till to Tweed—
" Though ye rin with speed
And I rin slaw,
For ae man that ye droon
I droon twa."

ANONYMOUS

AN UNSATISFACTORY POSITION

" I wish I had not known so much of this affair," added
my uncle Toby, " or that I had known more of it."

STERNE (from Tristram Shandy)

A BLOCK IN PICCADILLY

I have been twice going to stop my coach in Piccadilly (and the same has happened to Lady Aylesbury), thinking there was a mob; and it was only nymphs and swains sauntering or trudging. T'other morning, i.e. at two o'clock, I went to see Mrs. Garrick and Miss Hannah More at the Adelphi, and was stopped five times before I reached Northumberland House; for the tides of coaches, chariots, curricles, phaetons, &c., are endless. Indeed, the town is so extended, that the breed of chairs is almost lost; for Hercules and Atlas could not carry anybody from one end of this enormous capital to the other.

HORACE WALPOLE (from Correspondence)

HORACE'S CHOICE

I had rather be put into the round-house for a wrong-headed quarrel, than sup quietly at eight o'clock with my grandmother.

HORACE WALPOLE

EPIGRAM ON BEAUTY

You say that Celia's face combines
  The lily and the rose;
True, on her cheek the former pines,
  The latter tips her nose.

ANONYMOUS (18th Century)

337

TWO HEADS BETTER THAN ONE

See, one physician, like a sculler, plies,
The patient lingers and by inches dies.
But two physicians, like a pair of oars,
Waft him more swiftly to the Stygian shores.

ANONYMOUS

SAYINGS OF SAMUEL JOHNSON

Whoever thinks of going to bed before twelve o'clock is a scoundrel.

The happiest part of a man's life is what he passes lying awake in bed in the morning.

Hope is itself a species of happiness, and, perhaps, the chief happiness which this world affords.

Sir, when a man is tired of London, he is tired of life ; for there is in London all that life can afford.

If a man does not make new acquaintance as he advances through life, he will soon find himself left alone. A man, Sir, should keep his friendship in constant repair.

Sorrow is a kind of rust of the soul, which every new idea contributes in its passage to scour away.

Grief is a species of idleness.

Small debts are like small shot ; they are rattling on every side, and can scarcely be escaped without a wound ; great debts are like cannon ; of loud noise, but little danger.

The highest panegyric that private virtue can receive is the praise of servants.

BOSWELL (from *Life of Johnson*)

GOOD SHOTS FROM A WITTY CAN(N)ON

A Welcome Gift

I thank God, who has made me poor, that he has made me merry.

Improvement in Modern Travel

The Scotchman now eats his porridge at home in the morning and scratches himself in Piccadilly ere set of sun.

Sleepy Sermons

Is sin to be taken from men, as Eve was from Adam, by casting them into a deep slumber ?

SYDNEY SMITH

SOME CURES FOR THE BLUES

1. Live as well as you dare.
2. Go into the shower-bath.
3. Amusing books.
4. Be as busy as you can.
5. See as much as you can of those friends who respect and like you.
6. Compare your lot with that of other people.
7. Be as much as you can in the open air without fatigue.
8. Don't be too severe upon yourself.

SYDNEY SMITH (from Correspondence)

EAU DE COLOGNE

In Köln, a town of monks and bones,
And pavements fang'd with murderous stones,
And rags, and hags, and hideous wenches ;
I counted two and seventy stenches,
All well defined, and several stinks !
Ye Nymphs that reign o'er sewers and sinks,
The river Rhine, it is well known,
Doth wash your city of Cologne ;
But tell me, Nymphs ! what power divine
Shall henceforth wash the river Rhine ?

COLERIDGE

SOUVENIR

Jenny kiss'd me when we met,
    Jumping from the chair she sat in ;
Time, you thief ! who love to get
    Sweets into your list, put that in.
Say I'm weary, say I'm sad ;
    Say that health and wealth have miss'd me ;
Say I'm growing old, but add—
    Jenny kiss'd me !

LEIGH HUNT

POETRY

Poetry awakens and enlarges the mind by a thousand
unapprehended combinations of thought. It lifts the veil
from the hidden beauty of the world. The great secret of

morals is love ; or a going out of our own nature, and an identification of ourselves with the beautiful which exists in thought, action, or person, not our own. A man to be greatly good must imagine intensely and comprehensively; he must put himself in the place of another and of many others ; the pains and pleasures of his species must become his own. The great instrument of moral good is the imagination. Poetry enlarges the circumference of the imagination and strengthens the faculty which is the organ of the moral nature of man, in the same manner as exercise strengthens a limb.

SHELLEY (from *A Defence of Poetry*)

WHY NOT ?

My brain is dull, my sight is foul,
  I cannot write a verse, or read,—
Then Pallas, take away thine Owl,
  And let us have a Lark instead.

THOMAS HOOD

SAYINGS OF EMERSON

In every work of genius we recognise our own rejected thoughts ; they come back to us with a certain alienated majesty.

Let us treat the men and women well : treat them as if they were real : perhaps they are.

It is always so pleasant to be generous, though very vexatious to pay debts.

Our chief want in life is, somebody who shall make us do what we can.

THE NIGHT SHADOWS

A wonderful fact to reflect upon, that every human creature is constituted to be that profound secret and mystery to every other. A solemn consideration, when I enter a great city by night, that every one of those darkly clustered houses encloses its own secret; that every room in every one of them encloses its own secret; that every beating heart in the hundreds of thousands of breasts there, is, in some of its imaginings, a secret to the heart nearest it! . . . In any of the burial-places of this city through which I pass, is there a sleeper more inscrutable than its busy inhabitants are, in their innermost personality, to me, or than I am to them?

DICKENS (from *Tale of Two Cities*)

EPITAPH IN DERRY CATHEDRAL ON A YOUNG CURATE WHO DIED DURING AN EPIDEMIC OF TYPHUS

Down through our crowded lanes and closer air,
O friend, how beautiful thy footsteps were!
When through the fever's waves of fire they trod,
A form was with thee like the Son of God.

'Twas but one step for those victorious feet
From their day's walk unto the golden street ;
And they who watch'd that walk so bright and brief
Have marked this marble with their hope and grief.

ARCHBISHOP ALEXANDER

DISTICHS

I

Wisely a woman prefers to a lover a man who neglects her,
This one may love her some day, some day the lover will
not.

II

Maidens, why do you worry in choosing whom you shall
marry,
Choose whom you may, you'll find you've got somebody
else !

JOHN HAY

A MEMORY OF " CUMMY "

(*Stevenson's Nurse*)

How well I remember her lifting me out of bed, carrying me to the window, and showing me one or two lit
windows up in Queen Street across the dark belt of
gardens ; where also, we told each other, there might be
sick little boys and their nurses waiting, like us, for the
morning.

R. L. STEVENSON (from *Memories and Portraits*)

343

Of those who have thus survived themselves most completely, left a sort of personal seduction behind them in the world, and retained, after death, the art of making friends, Montaigne and Samuel Johnson certainly stand first.

If your morals make you dreary, depend upon it they are wrong.

There is no duty we so much underrate as the duty of being happy.

Absences are a good influence in love and keep it bright and delicate.

No man is useless while he has a friend.

To-morrow's travel will carry you, body and mind, into some different parish of the infinite.

THE NIGHT HAS A THOUSAND EYES

The night has a thousand eyes,
    And the day but one;
Yet the light of the bright world dies
    With the dying sun.

The mind has a thousand eyes,
    And the heart but one;
Yet the light of a whole life dies
    When love is done.

F. W. BOURDILLON

SEEING BETWEEN THE LINES

What we have inherited from our fathers and mothers is not all that walks in us ! There are all sorts of dead ideas and lifeless old beliefs. They have no tangibility, but they haunt us all the same and we cannot get rid of them. Whenever I take up a newspaper I seem to see Ghosts gliding between the lines.

IBSEN (from *Ghosts*)

ONE WORLD

The worlds in which we live are two—
The world " I am " and the world " I do."
The worlds in which we live at heart are one,—
The world " I am " the fruit of " I have done " ;
And underneath these worlds of flower and fruit
The world " I love " the only living root.

H. VAN DYKE

GOOD COUNSEL

To awaken each morning with a smile brightening my face ; to greet the day with reverence for the opportunities it contains ; to approach my work with a clean mind ; to hold ever before me, even in the doing of little things, the Ultimate Purpose toward which I am working ; to

345

meet men and women with laughter on my lips and love in my heart ; to be gentle, kind, and courteous through all the hours ; to approach the night with weariness that ever woos sleep and the joy that comes from work well done—this is how I desire to waste wisely my days.

THOMAS DEKKER

Give me a man that is not dull,
When all the world with rifts is full ;
But unamazed dares clearly sing,
Whenas the roof's a-tottering ;
And, though it falls, continues still
Tickling the cittern with his quill.

ROBERT HERRICK

My soul, sit thou a patient looker-on ;
Judge not the play before the play is done.
Her plot hath many changes ; every day
Speaks a new scene ; the last act crowns the play.

FRANCIS QUARLES

Though all the winds of doctrine were let loose to play upon the Earth, so Truth be in the field, we do injuriously to misdoubt her strength. Let her and Falsehood grapple. Whoever knew Truth put to the worse in a free and open encounter ?

MILTON

What I spent I had,
What I saved I lost,
What I gave I have.

Old German Motto

Honey and the honeycomb, roses and violets, are yet in the Earth. The Sun and Moon yet reign in Heaven, and the lesser lights keep up their pretty twinklings. Meats and drinks, sweet sights and sweet smells, a country walk, spring and autumn, follies and repentance, quarrels and reconcilements, have all a sweetness by turns.

CHARLES LAMB

It is hard to believe long together that anything is worth while unless there is some eye to kindle in common with our own, some brief word uttered now and then to imply that what is infinitely precious to us is precious alike to another mind.

GEORGE ELIOT

A CAPITAL LETTER

(from a School-boy to his Uncle)

S.O.S., L.S.D., R.S.V.P.

ANONYMOUS

A CHILD'S PRAYER

Make me, dear Lord, polite and kind
　　To every one, I pray.
And may I ask you how you find
　　Yourself, dear Lord, to-day?

JOHN BANISTER TABB

A BAD LOT

From Witches, Warlocks and Wurricoes,
From Ghoulies, Ghosties and Long-leggity Beasties,
From all Things that go bump in the night—
　　Good Lord deliver us!

A Cornish Litany

SECOND PART

§ IV DREAMLAND

There are two Gates of the dark Underworld. Through the Horn Gate kindly and true Visions throng unhindered ; but by that other, fashioned of glistening Ivory, go forth Dreams false and evil.

VIRGIL (Aeneid, Bk. VI)

Saint Francis and Saint Benedict
Blesse thys House from Wicked Wight,
From the Nightmare and the Goblin that is hight !
Goodfellow Robin keepe it
From all evil Spirites, Fayries, Wezles, Bats and Ferryts,
From Curfew Time till the next Prime !

An Old House-Blessing

§ 1. DREAM POETRY

FAUSTUS' VISION OF HELEN

Was this the face that launched a thousand ships
And burnt the topless towers of Ilium ?
Sweet Helen, make me immortal with a kiss.
Her lips suck forth my soul ; see where it flies !—
Come, Helen, come, give me my soul again.
Here will I dwell, for heaven is in these lips,
And all is dross that is not Helena.
I will be Paris, and for love of thee,
Instead of Troy, shall Wittenberg be sacked :
And I will combat with weak Menelaus,
And wear thy colours on my plumèd crest :
Yea, I will wound Achilles in the heel,
And then return to Helen for a kiss,
Oh, thou art fairer than the evening air
Clad in the beauty of a thousand stars ;
Brighter art thou than flaming Jupiter
When he appeared to hapless Semele :
More lovely than the monarch of the sky
In wanton Arethusa's azured arms ;
And none but thou shall be my paramour.

MARLOWE (from *Faustus*)

SLEEP SIGHT

How would, I say, mine eyes be blessèd made
By looking on thee in the living day,
When in dead night thy fair imperfect shade

Through heavy sleep on sightless eyes doth stay ?
All days are nights to see, till I see thee,
And nights bright days, when dreams do show me thee.

SHAKESPEARE (from *Sonnet XLIII*)

TO THE MEMORY OF HIS SECOND WIFE[1]

Methought I saw my late espousèd Saint
　Brought to me like Alcestis from the grave,
　Whom Jove's great Son to her glad Husband gave,
　Rescu'd from death by force though pale and faint.
Mine as whom washt from spot of child-bed taint
　Purification in the old Law did save,
　And such as yet once more I trust to have
　Full sight of her in Heaven without restraint,
Came vested all in white, pure as her mind :
　Her face was vail'd, yet to my fancied sight,
　Love, sweetness, goodness, in her person shin'd
So clear, as in no face with more delight.
　But O as to embrace me she enclin'd
　I wak'd, she fled, and day brought back my night.

MILTON

DREAMS

Dreams are but interludes which Fancy makes ;
When monarch Reason sleeps, this mimic wakes :
Compounds a medley of disjointed things,
A mob of cobblers, and a court of kings :

---

[1] As Milton had become blind some years before his second marriage, this was the first time he *saw* his second wife, who died soon after giving birth to a daughter. A. S.

Light fumes are merry, grosser fumes are sad:
Both are the reasonable soul run mad;
And many monstrous forms in sleep we see,
That neither were, nor are, nor e'er can be.
Sometimes forgotten things long cast behind
Rush forward in the brain, and come to mind.
The nurse's legends are for truths received,
And the man dreams but what the boy believed.
Sometimes we but rehearse a former play,
The night restores our actions done by day;
As hounds in sleep will open for their prey.
In short, the farce of dreams is of a piece,
Chimeras all; and more absurd or less.

DRYDEN (from *The Cock and the Fox*)

ST. CATHERINE ASLEEP

You pleasing dreams of love and sweet delight,
Appear before this slumbering Virgin's sight:
Soft visions set her free
From mournful piety;
Let her sad thoughts from heaven retire;
And let the melancholy love
Of those remoter joys above
Give place to your more sprightly fire;
Let purling streams be in her fancy seen,
And flowery meads and vales of cheerful green;
And in the midst of deathless groves
Soft sighing wishes lie,
And smiling hopes fast by,
And just beyond them ever-laughing loves.

DRYDEN (from *Tyrannic Love*)

A THOUGHT OF BEAUTY

A thing of beauty is a joy for ever :
Its loveliness increases ; it can never
Pass into nothingness ; but still will keep
A bower quiet for us, and a sleep
Full of sweet dreams, and health, and quiet breathing.

KEATS (from Endymion)

BOAT-SONG OF THE HIGHLANDERS IN CANADA

Listen to me as when you heard our father
   Sing long ago the songs of other shores,
Listen to me and then in chorus gather
   All your deep voices as you pull your oars—
   Fair these broad meads, these hoary woods are grand,
   But we are exiles from our native land.

From the lone shieling of the misty island
   Mountains divide us and the waste of seas ;
Yet still the blood is strong, the heart is Highland,
   And we in dreams behold the Hebrides.

ANONYMOUS

DREAM-PEDLARY

If there were dreams to sell,
   What would you buy ?
Some cost a passing bell ;
   Some a light sigh,
That shakes from Life's fresh crown
Only a rose-leaf down.
If there were dreams to sell,
Merry and sad to tell,
And the crier rang the bell,
   What would you buy ?

A cottage lone and still,
   With bowers high,
Shadowy, my woes to still,
   Until I die.
Such pearl from Life's fresh crown
Fain would I shake me down.
Were dreams to have at will,
This would best heal my ill,
   This would I buy.

THOMAS LOVELL BEDDOES

PRAYER IN SLEEP

Prayer goeth forth in sleep as true
And pauseless as the pulses do.

ELIZABETH BARRETT BROWNING

THE BLESSÈD DAMOZEL

The blessèd damozel leaned out
    From the gold bar of Heaven ;
Her eyes were deeper than the depth
    Of waters stilled at even ;
She had three lilies in her hand,
    And the stars in her hair were seven.

Her robe, ungirt from clasp to hem,
    No wrought flowers did adorn,
But a white rose of Mary's gift,
    For service meetly worn ;
Her hair that lay along her back
    Was yellow like ripe corn.

Her seemed she scarce had been a day
    One of God's choristers ;
The wonder was not yet quite gone
    From that still look of hers ;
Albeit, to them she left, her day
    Had counted as ten years.

(To *one* it is ten years of years.
    . . . Yet now, and in this place,
Surely she leaned o'er me—her hair
    Fell all about my face . . .
Nothing : the autumn-fall of leaves.
    The whole year sets apace.)

It was the rampart of God's house
    That she was standing on ;
By God built over the sheer depth

The which is Space begun ;
So high, that looking downward thence
   She scarce could see the sun.

It lies in Heaven, across the flood
   Of ether, as a bridge.
Beneath, the tides of day and night
   With flame and darkness ridge
The void, as low as where this earth
   Spins like a fretful midge.

Around her, lovers, newly met
   'Mid deathless love's acclaims,
Spoke evermore among themselves
   Their heart-remembered names ;
And the souls mounting up to God
   Went by her like thin flames.

And still she bowed herself and stooped
   Out of the circling charm,
Until her bosom must have made
   The bar she leaned on warm,
And the lilies lay as if asleep
   Along her bended arm.

From the fixed place of Heaven she saw
   Time like a pulse shake fierce
Through all the worlds. Her gaze still strove
   Within the gulf to pierce
Its path ; and now she spoke as when
   The stars sang in their spheres.

The sun was gone now; the curled moon
    Was like a little feather
Fluttering far down the gulf; and now
    She spoke through the still weather.
Her voice was like the voice the stars
    Had when they sang together.

(Ah sweet! Even now, in that bird's song,
    Strove not her accents there,
Fain to be hearkened? When those bells
    Possessed the mid-day air,
Strove not her steps to reach my side
    Down all the echoing stair?)

D. G. ROSSETTI

DREAMS

It looks as if in dreams the soul was free,
    No bodily limit checks its absolute play;
Then why doth it not use its liberty,
    And clear a certain way
To further truth beyond the actual sea?

It is not so; for when, with loosened grip,
    The warder sense unlocks the visible hold,
Then will my soul from forth its chamber slip,
    An idiot blithe and bold,
And into vacancy of folly skip;

Or aimless wander on the poppied floor
   Of gaudy fields, or, scarce upon the street,
Return unto the grim, familiar door,
   And, coward, crave retreat,
As who had never been outside before.

What boots it that I hold the chartered space,
   If I but fill it with th' accustomed forms,
And load its breathless essence with the trace
   Of casual-risen storms,
And drag my chain along the lovely place ?

O, but if God would make a deep suspense,
   And draw me perfect from th' adhesive sheath :
If all the veils and swathings of pretence,
   Dropt from me, sunk beneath,
Then would I get me very far from hence.

I'd come to Him with one swift arrow-dart,
   Aimed at the zenith of th' o'erbrooding blue ;
Straight to the centre of His awful heart
   The flight long-winged and true
Should bear me rapt through all the spheres that part.

But as it is, it is a waste of rest.
   God uses not the occasion : on the rock
Stands prone my soul, a diver lean undrest,
   And looks, and fears the shock,
And turns and hides its shame with some poor sorry jest.

T. E. BROWN

A DREAM

Beneath the loveliest dream there coils a fear :
Last night came she whose eyes are memories now ;
Her far-off gaze seemed all forgetful how
Love dimmed them once, so calm they shone and clear.
" Sorrow," I said, " has made me old, my dear ;
'Tis I, indeed, but grief can change the brow :
Beneath *my* load a seraph's neck might bow,
Vigils like mine would blanch an angel's hair."
Oh, then I saw, I saw the sweet lips move !
I saw the love-mists thickening in her eyes—
I heard a sound as if a murmuring dove
Felt lonely in the dells of Paradise ;
But when upon my neck she fell, my love,
Her hair smelt sweet of whin and woodland spice.

T. WATTS-DUNTON

AD AMICAM

When from the blossoms of the noiseful day
  Unto the hive of sleep and hushèd gloom
Throng the dim-wingèd dreams—what dreams are they
  That with the wildest honey hover home ?
Oh, they that have from many thousand thoughts
  Stolen the strange sweet of ever-blossomy you,
A thousand fancies in fair-coloured knots
  Which you are inexhausted meadow to.
Ah, what sharp heathery honey, quick with pain,
  Do they bring home ! It holds the night awake
To hear their lovely murmur in my brain ;

And Sleep's wings have a trouble for your sake.
Day and you dawn together : for, at end,
  With the first light breaks the first thought—
    " My friend ! "

FRANCIS THOMPSON

RENOUNCEMENT

I must not think of thee ; and, tired yet strong,
  I shun the thought that lurks in all delight—
  The thought of thee—and in the blue Heaven's height,
And in the sweetest passage of a song.

Oh, just beyond the fairest thoughts that throng
  This breast, the thought of thee waits, hidden yet
    bright ;
  But it must never, never come in sight ;
I must stop short of thee the whole day long.

But when sleep comes to close each difficult day,
  When night gives pause to the long watch I keep,
    And all my bonds I needs must loose apart.

Must doff my will as raiment laid away,—
  With the first dream that comes with the first sleep
    I run, I run, I am gathered to thy heart.

ALICE MEYNELL

SONG

She comes not when Noon is on the roses—
    Too bright is Day.
She comes not to the Soul till it reposes
    From work and play.

But when Night is on the hills, and the great Voices
    Roll in from sea.
By starlight and by candlelight and dreamlight
    She comes to me.

HERBERT TRENCH

PROMISE

Be not so desolate
Because thy dreams have flown
And the hall of the heart is empty
And silent as stone,
As age left by children
Sad and alone.

Those delicate children,
Thy dreams, still endure :
All pure and lovely things
Wend to the Pure.
Sigh not : unto the fold
Their way was sure.

Thy gentlest dreams, thy frailest,
Even those that were
Born and lost in a heart-beat,

Shall meet thee there.
They are become immortal
In shining air.

The unattainable beauty
The thought of which was pain,
That flickered in eyes and on lips
And vanished again :
That fugitive beauty
Thou shalt attain.

The lights innumerable
That led thee on and on,
The Masque of Time ended,
Shall glow into one.
It shall be with thee for ever
Thy travel done.

GEORGE RUSSELL ("A. E.")

TO L. H. B. (1894–1915)

Last night for the first time since you were dead
I walked with you, my brother, in a dream.
We were at home again beside the stream
Fringed with tall berry bushes, white and red.
" Don't touch them : they are poisonous," I said.
But your hand hovered, and I saw a beam
Of strange, bright laughter flying around your head ;
And as you stooped I saw the berries gleam,
" Don't you remember ? We called them Dead Man's
    Bread."

I woke and heard the wind moan and the roar
Of the dark water tumbling on the shore.
Where—where is the path of my dream for my eager feet ?
By the remembered stream my brother stands
Waiting for me with berries in his hands.
" These are my body. Sister, take and eat."

KATHERINE MANSFIELD

COUNTING SHEEP

Half-awake I walked
A dimly-seen sweet hawthorn lane
Until sleep came ;
I lingered at a gate and talked
A little with a lonely lamb.
He told me of the great still night,
Of calm starlight,
And of the lady moon, who'd stoop
For a kiss sometimes ;
Of grass as soft as sleep, of rhymes
The tired flowers sang :
The ageless April tales
Of how, when sheep grew old,
As their faith told,
They went without a pang
To far green fields, where fall
Perpetual streams that call
To deathless nightingales.
    And then I saw, hard by,
A shepherd lad with shining eyes,
And round him, gathered one by one
Countless sheep, snow-white ;

More and more they crowded
With tender cries,
Till all the field was full
Of voices and of coming sheep.
Countless they came, and I
Watched, until deep
As dream-fields lie
I was asleep.

WILLIAM KERR

§ 2. PROSE

ARTEMIDORUS ON DREAMS

A dream is a motion of fiction of the soul in a diverse form, signifying either good or evil to come.

Thus :—

1. To have the head of a lion, a wolf, a panther, or elephant instead of his own, is good : for he which attempteth things beyond his power, and hath this dream shall attain unto great dignity and honour. Many desiring offices and places of honour after this dream have obtained them. To dream you have the head of a dog, horse or ass, or such four-footed beast, is servitude, pain and misery. To have a bird's head argues one shall not stay long in this country.

2. To see a great fish in the sea is good for no man, the dolphin excepted ; but out of the sea every fish and great monster is good, for they can hurt no more, nor save themselves : and therefore besides that our dream signifies that our enemies cannot hurt us. Notwithstanding, the dolphin being out of the sea is not good, but signifieth the death of some of our good friends.

3. To see all the stars clear and fair is good for a traveller and for all business. Such stars as vanish and go out of the sky is poverty and forsaking to the rich ; for you must imagine that the sky signifieth the house of him that dreams. To eat the stars is not good, except to astrologers and sooth-sayers.

4. Mixed or compounded dreams are very doubtful, and cannot be easily understood or expounded, which is a great grief to many.

Dreams are notable means of discovering our own

inclinations. The wise man learns to know himself, as well by the night's black mantle as the scorching beams of the day : in sleep we have the naked and natural thoughts of our souls : outward objects interpose not, either to shuffle in occasional cogitations, or hale out the included fancy. The mind is then shut up in the burrow of the body. The Indians, when their kings went to their sleep used to pray that they might have happy dreams and withal consult well for their subjects' benefit; as if the night had been a time wherein they might grow good and wise. And certainly the wise man is the wiser for his sleeping, if he can order well in the day,—and every dream the eyeless night presents him is to be counted of. Dreams may to a wise observer be of special benefit. I would neither depend upon any to incur a prejudice, nor yet cast any away in a prodigal neglect and scorn. I find it of one that, having been troubled with the paining spleen, he dreamt if he opened a certain vein between two of his fingers he should be cured, which he awaking did, and amended. But indeed I would rather believe this than to be drawn to practice after it.

(Trans. R. WOOD)

KING MILINDA ASKS ABOUT DREAMS

" Venerable Nâgasena, when a man dreams a dream, is he awake or asleep ? "

" Neither the one, O king, nor yet the other. But when his sleep has become light, and he is not yet fully conscious, in that interval it is that dreams are dreamt. When a man is in deep sleep, O king, his mind has returned home like a bird that has re-entered its nest, and a mind thus shut in does not act. A mind hindered in its action knows not evil and good, and he who knows not has no dreams. Just, O king, as in the darkness and gloom, where no light is, no shadow will fall even on the most burnished mirror, so when a man is in deep sleep his mind has returned into itself and acts not, knowing neither good nor evil. As the mirror, O king, are you to regard the body, as the darkness sleep, as the light the mind."

"Venerable Nâgasena, is there a beginning, a middle, and an end of sleep?"

"Yes, O king, there is. The feeling of oppression and inability in the body—of weakness, slackness, inertness—that is the beginning, of sleep. The light "monkey's sleep" in which a man still guards his scattered thoughts —that is the middle of sleep. When the mind has entered into itself—that is the end of sleep. And it is in the middle stage that dreams are dreamt. Just, O king, as when a man self-restrained with collected thoughts, stedfast in the faith, unshaken in wisdom, plunges deep into the woods far from the sound of strife, and thinks over some subtle matter, he there, tranquil and at peace, will master the meaning of it—just so a man still watchful, not fallen into sleep, but dozing will dream a dream.

The Questions of King Milinda (Trans. from the
Pâli by T. W. RHYS DAVIDS)

THE SACRED SLEEP

The soul has a twofold life, a lower and a higher. In sleep that soul is freed from the constraint of the body, and enters, as one emancipated, on its divine life of intelligence. Then, as the noble faculty which beholds objects as they are—the objects in the world of intelligence—stirs within, and awakens to its power, who can be surprised that the mind, which contains in itself the principles of all that happens, should, in this its state of liberation, discern the future in those antecedent principles which will make that future what it is to be? The nobler part of the soul is thus united by abstraction to higher natures, and becomes a participant in the wisdom and foreknowledge of the gods.

Recorded examples of this are numerous and well authenticated; instances occur, too, every day. Numbers of sick, by sleeping in the temple of Aesculapius, have had their cure revealed to them in dreams vouchsafed by the god. Would not Alexander's army have perished but for a dream in which Dionysus pointed out the means of safety? Was not the siege of Aphutis raised through a dream sent by Jupiter Ammon to Lysander? The night-time of the body is the day-time of the soul.

IAMBLICHUS

ST. AUGUSTINE RELATES A DREAM

It chanced at Carthage that the rhetorician Eulogius, who had been my disciple in that art, being (as he himself, after our return to Africa, told us the story) in course of lecturing to his disciples on Cicero's rhetorical books, as he looked over the portion of reading which he was to deliver on the following day, fell upon a certain passage, and not being able to understand it, was scarce able to sleep for the trouble of his mind: in which night, as he dreamed, I expounded to him that which he did not understand; nay, not I, but my likeness, while I was unconscious of the thing and far away beyond sea, it might be

369

doing, or it might be dreaming, some other thing, and not in the least caring for his cares. In what way these things come about I know not; but in what way soever they come, why do we not believe it comes in the same way for a person in a dream to see a dead man, as it comes that he sees a living man? both, no doubt, neither knowing nor caring who dreams of their images, or where or when.

From *De Cura pro Mortuis Habenda* (Oxford Library of the Fathers, XVII)

A MYSTERY OF SLEEP

There yet live in my memory the images of such things, as my ill custom there fixed; which haunt me, strengthless when I am awake : but in sleep, not only so as to give pleasure, but even to obtain assent, and what is very like reality. Yea, so far prevails the illusion of the image, in my soul and in my flesh, that, when asleep, false visions persuade to that which when waking, the true cannot. Am I not then myself, O Lord my God! And yet there is so much difference betwixt myself and myself, within that moment wherein I pass from waking to sleeping, or return from sleeping to waking ! Where is reason then, which, awake, resisteth such suggestions ? And should the things themselves be urged on it, it remaineth unshaken. Is it clasped up with the eyes ? is it lulled asleep with the senses of the body ? And whence is it that often even in sleep we resist, and mindful of our purpose, and abiding most chastely in it, yield no assent to such enticement ? And yet so much difference there is, that when it happeneth otherwise, upon waking we return to peace of conscience : and by this very difference discover that we did not, what yet we be sorry that in some way it was done in us.

Confessions of St. Augustine (Trans. E. B. PUSEY)

THE HAPPY DREAMER

I thank God for my happy dreams, as I do for my good rest ; for there is a satisfaction in them unto reasonable desires, and such as can be content with a fit of happiness ; and surely it is not a melancholy conceit to think we are all asleep in this World, and that the conceits of this life are as meer dreams to those of the next, as the Phantasms of the night to the conceits of the day. There is an equal delusion in both, and the one doth but seem to be the emblem or picture of the other : we are somewhat more than our selves in our sleeps, and the slumber of the body seems to be but the waking of the soul. It is the ligation of sense, but the liberty of reason ; and our waking conceptions do not match the Fancies of our sleeps. At my Nativity my Ascendant was the watery sign of Scorpius ; I was born in the Planetary hour of Saturn, and I think I have a piece of that Leaden Planet in me. I am no way facetious, nor disposed for the mirth and galliardise of company ; yet in one dream I can compose a whole Comedy, behold the action, apprehend the jests, and laugh my self awake at the conceits thereof. Were my memory as faithful as my reason is then fruitful, I would never study but in my dreams ; and this time also would I chuse for my devotions : but our grosser memories have then so little hold of our abstracted understandings, that they forget the story, and can only relate to our awaked souls, a confused and broken tale of that that hath passed. Aristotle, who hath written a singular Tract *Of Sleep*, hath not, methinks, thoroughly defined it ; nor yet Galen, though he seem to have corrected it ; for those Noctambuloes and night-walkers, though in their sleep, do yet injoy the action of their senses. We must therefore say that there is something in us that is not in the jurisdiction of Morpheus ; and that those abstracted and estatick souls do walk about in their own corps, as spirits with the bodies they assume, wherein they seem to hear, see, and feel, though indeed the Organs are destitute of sense, and their natures of those faculties that should inform them. Thus it is observed, that men sometimes, upon the hour of their departure, do speak and reason above themselves ; for then the soul, beginning to be freed from the ligaments of the body, begins to reason like her self, and to discourse in a strain above mortality.

We term sleep a death ; and yet it is waking that kills us, and destroys those spirits that are the house of life. 'Tis indeed a part of life that best expresseth death ; for every man truely lives, so long as he acts his nature, or some way makes good the faculties of himself. Themistocles, therefore, that slew his Soldier in his sleep, was a merciful Executioner : 'tis a kind of punishment the mildness of no laws hath invented : I wonder the fancy of Lucan and Seneca did not discover it. It is that death by which we may be literally said to dye daily ; a death which Adam dyed before his mortality ; a death whereby we live a middle and moderating point between life and death : in fine, so like death, I dare not trust it without my prayers, and an half adieu unto the World, and take my farewell in a Colloquy with God.

SIR THOMAS BROWNE (from *Religio Medici*)

Now I saw in my dream, that by this time the pilgrims were got over the Enchanted Ground, and entering into the country of Beulah whose air was very sweet and pleasant, the way lying directly through it, they solaced themselves there for a season. Yea, here they heard continually the singing of birds, and saw every day the flowers appear in the earth, and heard the voice of the turtle in the land. In this country the sun shineth night and day ; wherefore this was beyond the Valley of the Shadow of Death, and also out of the reach of Giant Despair, neither could they from this place so much as see Doubting Castle. Here they were within sight of the city they were going to, also here met them some of the inhabitants thereof ; for in this land the Shining Ones commonly walked, because it was upon the borders of heaven, So I saw, that as I went on, there met them two men, in raiment that shone like gold ; also their faces shone as the light.

These men asked the pilgrims whence they came ; and they told them. They also asked them where they had lodged, what difficulties and dangers, what comforts and pleasures they had met in the way ; and they told them. Then said the men that met them, You have but two difficulties more to meet with, and then you are in the city.

Christian then, and his companion, asked the men to go along with them; so they told them they would But, said they, you must obtain it by your own faith. So I saw in my dream that they went on together, until they came in sight of the gate.

Now, I further saw, that betwixt them and the gate was a river, but there was no bridge to go over ; the river was very deep. At the sight, therefore, of this river, the pilgrims were much stunned; but the men that went with them said, You must go through, or you cannot come at the gate. Then they took courage, and the enemy was after that as still as a stone, until they were gone over. Christian therefore presently found ground to stand upon, and so it followed that the rest of the river was but shallow. Thus they got over. . .

Now you must note that the city stood upon a mighty hill, but the pilgrims went up that hill with ease, because they had these two men to lead them up by the arms; also, they had left their mortal garments behind them in the river, for though they went in with them, they came out without them. They, therefore, went up here with much agility and speed, though the foundation upon which the city was framed was higher than the clouds. They, therefore, went up through the regions of the air, sweetly talking as they went, being comforted, because they safely got over the river, and had such glorious companions to attend them.

Now while they were thus drawing towards the gate, behold a company of the heavenly host came out to meet them. . There came out also at this time to meet them, several of the King's trumpeters, clothed in white and shining raiment, who, with melodious noises and loud, made even the heavens to echo with their sound. These trumpeters saluted Christian and his fellow with ten thousand welcomes from the world; and this they did with shouting, and sound of trumpet.

This done, they compassed them round on every side; some went before, some behind, and some on the right hand, some on the left (as it were to guard them through the upper regions), continually sounding as they went, with melodious noise, in notes on high : so that the very sight was to them that could behold it, as if heaven itself was come down to meet them. Thus, therefore, they walked on together ; and as they walked, ever and anon these trumpeters, even with joyful sound, would, by mixing their music with looks and gestures, still signify to Christian and his brother, how welcome they were into their company, and with what gladness they came to meet them ; and now were these two men, as it were, in heaven, before they came at it, being swallowed up with the sight of angels, and with hearing of their melodious notes. Here also they had the city itself in view, and they thought they heard all the bells therein to ring, to welcome them thereto. But above all, the warm and joyful thoughts that they had about their own dwelling there, with such company, and that for ever and ever. Oh, by what tongue or pen can their glorious joy be expressed ! And thus they came up to the gate.

Now I saw in my dream that these two men went in at the gate : and lo, as they entered, they were transfigured, and they had raiment put on that shone like gold. There were also that met them with harps and crowns, and gave them to them—the harps to praise withal, and the crowns in token of honour. Then I heard in my dream that all the bells in the city rang again for joy.

BUNYAN (from *The Pilgrim's Progress*)

READING VIRGIL IN BED

After the lassitude of a day, spent in the strolling manner, which is usual with men of pleasure in this town, and with a head full of a million of impertinencies, which had danced round it for ten hours together, I came to my lodging, and hastened to bed. My valet-de-chambre knows my university-trick of reading there ; and he, being a good scholar for a gentleman, ran over the names of Horace, Tibullus, Ovid, and others, to know which I would have. Bring Virgil, said I ; and, if I fall asleep, take care of the candle. I read the Sixth Book over with the most exquisite delight, and had gone half through it a second time, when the pleasant ideas of Elysian fields, deceased worthies walking in them, sincere lovers enjoying their languishment without pain, compassion for the unhappy spirits who had mispent their short day-light, and were exiled from the seats of bliss for ever ; I say, I was deep again in my reading, when this mixture of images had taken place of all others in my imagination before, and lulled me into a dream, from which I am just awake, to my great disadvantage. The happy mansions of Elysium, by degrees, seemed to be wafted from me, and the very traces of my late waking thoughts began to fade away, when I was cast by a sudden whirlwind upon an island, encompassed with a roaring and troubled sea, which shaked its very centre, and rocked its inhabitants as in a cradle. The islanders lay on their faces without offering to look up, or hope for preservation ; all her harbours were crowded with mariners, and tall vessels of war lay in danger of being driven to pieces on her shores. Bless me, said I, why have I lived in such a manner, that the convulsion of nature should be so terrible to me, when I feel in myself that the better part of me is to survive it ? Oh ! may that be in happiness.

STEELE (from The Tatler)

ON DREAMS

Our dreams are great instances of that activity which is natural to the human soul, and which it is not in the power of sleep to deaden or abate. When the man appears tired and worn out with the labours of the day, this active part in his composition is still busied and unwearied. When the organs of sense want their due repose and necessary reparations, and the body is no longer able to keep pace with that spiritual substance to which it is united, the soul exerts herself in her several faculties, and continues in action till her partner is again qualified to bear her company. In this case dreams look like the relaxations and amusements of the soul, when she is disencumbered of her machine ; her sports and recreations, when she has laid her charge asleep.

In the second place, dreams are an instance of that agility and perfection which is natural to the faculties of the mind, when they are disengaged from the body. The soul is clogged and retarded in her operations, when she acts in conjunction with a companion that is so heavy and unwieldy in its motions. But in dreams it is wonderful to observe with what a sprightliness and alacrity she exerts herself. The slow of speech make unpremeditated harangues, or converse readily in languages that they are but little acquainted with. The grave abound in pleasantries, the dull in repartees and points of wit. There is not a more painful action of the mind than invention ; yet in dreams it works with that ease and activity, that we are not sensible when the faculty is employed. . .

There is another circumstance, which, methinks, gives us a very high idea of the nature of the soul, in regard to what passes in dreams : I mean that innumerable multitude and variety of ideas which then arise in her. Were that active watchful being only conscious of her own existence at such a time, what a painful solitude would her hours of sleep be? Were the soul sensible of her being alone in her sleeping moments after the same manner that she is sensible of it while awake, the time would hang very heavy on her, as it often actually does when she dreams that she is in such solitude.

But this observation I only make by the way. What I would here remark, is that wonderful power in the soul of producing her own company on these occasions. She converses with numberless beings of her own creation, and is transported into ten thousand scenes of her own raising. She is herself the theatre, the actors, and the beholder. This puts me in mind of a saying which I am infinitely pleased with, and which Plutarch ascribes to Heraclitus, "That all men, whilst they are awake, are in one common world; but that each of them, when he is asleep, is in a world of his own." The waking man is conversant in the world of nature; when he sleeps he retires to a private world that is particular to himself. There seems something in this consideration that intimates to us a natural grandeur and perfection in the soul, which is rather to be admired than explained.

I must not omit that argument for the excellency of the soul, which I have seen quoted out of Tertullian, namely its power of divining in dreams. That several such divinations have been made, none can question who believes the holy writings, or who has but the least degree of a common historical faith; there being innumerable instances of this nature in several authors, both ancient and modern, sacred and profane. Whether such dark presages, such visions of the night, proceed from any latent power in the soul during this her state of abstraction, or from any communication with the Supreme Being, or from any operation of subordinate spirits, has been a great dispute among the learned;—the matter of fact is, I think, incontestable, and has been looked upon as such by the greatest writers, who have never been suspected either of superstition or enthusiasm.

I do not suppose that the soul in these instances is entirely loose and unfettered from the body; it is sufficient, if she is not so far sunk and immersed in matter, nor entangled and perplexed in her operations with such motions of blood and spirits, as when she actuates the machine in its waking hours. The corporeal union is slackened enough to give the mind more play. The soul seems gathered within herself, and recovers that spring which is broke and weakened, when she operates more in concert with the body.

The speculations I have here made, if they are not arguments, they are at least strong intimations not only of the excellency of a human soul, but of its independence on the body; and if they do not prove, do at least confirm those two great points, which are established by many other reasons that are altogether unanswerable.

ADDISON (from *The Spectator*)

DREAMS OF MEN AND ANIMALS

Seeking the cause of our dreams—what it is that makes our former sensations repeat themselves—we notice that we do not dream during profound sleep, for then we are completely unconscious, asleep without and within. But our inner consciousness falls asleep last and wakens first, because it is more lively, more active, and more easily disturbed than our outer consciousness. Consequently it is during periods of light or incomplete sleep that we dream, renewing our former sensations, especially those on which we have reflected in our waking hours. Then our inner consciousness, unable to operate on actual sensations while our outer consciousness is quiescent, concerns itself with past sensations. The most vivid will be those which have been most frequently apprehended, and the more vivid the sensation the more extraordinary will be the scene presented. Hence our dreams are very often either terrifying or extremely pleasant.

Our outer consciousness need not be entirely dormant in order that our inner consciousness should operate—it is enough that it be quiescent. Although we are accustomed to give ourselves up as a matter of course to expected sleep, we do not always readily do so. Our bodies, relaxed and extended, may be quite motionless ; our eyes under their closed lids see nothing in the darkness ; our ears tell us nothing, so quiet is our chamber, so silent is the night ; —we are entirely at rest, yet no part of us is entirely lulled. Then, when we have no thoughts, our outer consciousness being inactive, our inner consciousness assumes control, and presents us with grotesque images and tumbling shadows. We become spectators in sleep's theatre. If we are in good health we receive pleasant impressions, but otherwise it is different—we see old hags and dreadful ghosts which seem to speak to us and which succeed one another with startling rapidity. It is like a magic lantern show which fills our brain then empty of other images, and these phantoms are the more lively, the more numerous and the more unpleasant in proportion as our faculties are out of order, our nerves upset and our bodies enfeebled ; for the effects of real sensations being greater in illness than in health, the images of such sensations which the renewal of these effects produces must also be more vivid and more unpleasant.

We remember our dreams just as we remember actual sensations that we have recently received, and the only difference here between the lower animals and ourselves is that we are able to distinguish between dream sensations and actual sensations. Into this operation of our memory (which involves a comparison) the idea of time enters. The lower animals, however, being unable to make this comparison, cannot distinguish between their dreams and their actual experiences ; so that to them all that they have dreamt appears to have actually happened.

BUFFON (from *Sur la Nature des Animaux*—

Trans. A.S.)

BOCCACCIO'S DREAM

Scarcely had I closed my eyes, if indeed time can be reckoned any more in sleep than in heaven, when my Fiammetta seemed to have led me into the meadow. . . I sprang to embrace her.

" Do not spill the water ! Ah ! you have spilt a part of it."

I then observed in her hand a crystal vase. A few drops were sparkling on the sides and running down the rim : a few were trickling from the base and from the hand that held it.

" I must go down to the brook," said she, " and fill it again as it was filled before."

What a moment of agony was this to me ! Could I be

certain how long might be her absence? She went: I was following: she made a sign for me to turn back: I disobeyed her only an instant: yet my sense of disobedience, increasing my feebleness and confusion, made me lose sight of her. In the next moment she was again at my side with the cup quite full. I stood motionless: I feared my breath might shake the water over. I looked her in the face for her commands—and to see it—to see it so calm, so beneficent, so beautiful. I was forgetting what I had prayed for, when she lowered her head, tasted of the cup, and gave it me. I drank; and suddenly sprang forth before me, many groves and palaces and gardens, and their statues and their avenues, and their labyrinths of alaternus and bay, and alcoves of citron, and watchful loopholes in the retirements of impenetrable pomegranate. Farther off, just below where the fountain slipt away from its marble hall and guardian gods, arose, from their beds of moss and drosera and darkest grass, the sisterhood of oleanders, fond of tantalising with their bosomed flowers and their moist and pouting blossoms the little shy rivulet, and of covering its face with all the colours of the dawn. My dream expanded and moved forward. I trod again the dust of Posilipo, soft as the feathers in the wings of Sleep. I emerged on Baia; I crossed her innumerable arches; I loitered in the breezy sunshine of her mole; I trusted the faithful seclusion of her caverns, the keepers of so many secrets; and I reposed on the buoyancy of her tepid sea. Then Naples, and her theatres and her churches and grottoes and dells and forts and promontories, rushed forward in confusion, now among soft whispers, now among sweetest sounds, and subsided, and sank, and disappeared. Yet a memory seemed to come fresh from every one: each had time enough for its tale, for its pleasure, for its reflection, for its pang. As I mounted with silent steps the narrow staircase of the old palace, how distinctly did I feel against the palm of my hand the coldness of that smooth stonework, and the greater of the cramps of iron in it!

" Ah me! is this forgetting? " cried I anxiously to Fiammetta.

" We must recall these scenes before us," she replied : " such is the punishment of them. Let us hope and believe that the apparition, and the compunction which must follow it, will be accepted as the full penalty, and that both will pass away almost together."

I feared to lose anything attendant on her presence : I feared to approach her forehead with my lips : I feared to touch the lily on its long wavy leaf in her hair, which filled my whole heart with fragrance. Venerating, adoring, I bowed my head at last to kiss her snow-white robe, and trembled at my presumption. And yet the effulgence of her countenance vivified while it chastened me. I loved her—I must not say *more* than ever—*better* than ever ; it was Fiammetta who had inhabited the skies. As my hand opened toward her,

" Beware! " said she, faintly smiling ; " beware, Giovanni! Take only the crystal ; take it, and drink again."

" Must all be then forgotten? " said I sorrowfully.

" Remember your prayer and mine, Giovanni. Shall both have been granted—O how much worse than in vain ? "

Although the water gave me strength and comfort, and somewhat of celestial pleasure, many tears fell around the border of the vase as she held it up before me, exhorting me to take courage, and inviting me with more than exhortation to accomplish my deliverance. She came nearer, more tenderly, more earnestly ; she held the dewy globe with both hands, leaning forward, and sighed and shook her head, drooping at my pusillanimity. It was only when a ringlet had touched the rim, and perhaps the water (for a sunbeam on the surface could never have given it such a golden hue) that I took courage, clasped it, and exhausted it. Sweet as was the water, sweet as was the serenity it gave me—alas ! that also which it moved away from me was sweet !

" This time you can trust me alone," said she, and parted my hair, and kissed my brow. Again she went toward the brook ; again my agitation, my weakness, my doubt, came over me : nor could I see her while she raised the water, nor knew I whence she drew it. When she returned, she was close to me at once : she smiled : her smile pierced me to the bones : it seemed an angel's. She sprinkled the pure water on me ; she looked most fondly ; she took my hand ; she suffered me to press hers to my bosom, but, whether by design I cannot tell, she let fall a few drops of the chilly element between.

" And now, O my beloved ! " said she, " we have consigned to the bosom of God our earthly joys and sorrows. The joys can not return, let not the sorrows. These alone would trouble my repose among the blessed."

" Trouble thy repose ! Fiammetta ! Give me the chalice ! " cried I—" not a drop will I leave in it, not a drop."

" Take it ! " said that soft voice. " O now most dear Giovanni ! I know thou hast strength enough ; and there is but little—at the bottom lies our first kiss."

" Mine ! didst thou say, beloved one ? and is that left thee still ? "

384

" *Mine*," said she, pensively ; and as she abased her head, the broad leaf of the lily hid her brow and her eyes ; the light of heaven shone through the flower.

" O Fiammetta ! Fiammetta ! " cried I in agony, " God is the God of mercy, God is the God of love—can I, can I ever ? ". I struck the chalice against my head, unmindful that I held it ; the water covered my face and my feet. I started up, not yet awake, and I heard the name of Fiammetta in the curtains.

W. S. LANDOR (from *The Pentameron*)

NIGHT-FANCIES

My night-fancies have long ceased to be afflictive. I confess an occasional nightmare ; but I do not, as in early youth, keep a stud of them. Fiendish faces, with the extinguished taper, will come and look at me ; but I know them for mockeries, even while I cannot elude their presence, and I fight and grapple with them. For the credit of my imagination, I am almost ashamed to say how tame and prosaic my dreams are grown. They are never romantic, seldom even rural. They are of architecture and of buildings—cities abroad, which I have never seen and hardly have hope to see. I have traversed, for the seeming length of a natural day, Rome, Amsterdam, Paris, Lisbon —their churches, palaces, squares, market-places, shops, suburbs, ruins, with an inexpressible sense of delight— a map-like distinctness of trace, and a daylight vividness of vision, that was all but being awake.—I have formerly travelled among the Westmoreland fells—my highest

Alps,—but they are objects too mighty for the grasp of my dreaming recognition ; and I have again and again awoke with ineffectual struggles of the inner eye, to make out a shape, in any way whatever, of Helvellyn. Methought I was in that country, but the mountains were gone. The poverty of my dreams mortifies me. There is Coleridge, at his will can conjure up icy domes, and pleasure-houses for Kubla Khan, and Abyssinian maids, and songs of Abara . . . to solace his night solitudes—when I cannot muster a fiddle. Barry Cornwall has his tritons and his nereids gambolling before him in nocturnal visions, and proclaiming sons born to Neptune—when my stretch of imaginative activity can hardly, in the night season, raise up the ghost of a fish-wife. To set my failures in somewhat a mortifying light—it was after reading the noble Dream of this poet, that my fancy ran strong upon these marine spectra ; and the poor plastic power, such as it is, within me set to work to humour my folly in a sort of dream that very night. Methought I was upon the ocean billows at some sea nuptials, riding and mounted high with the customary train sounding their conchs before me (I myself, you may be sure, the *leading god*), and jollily we went careering over the main, till just where Ino Leucothea should have greeted me (I think it was Ino) with a white embrace, the billows gradually subsiding fell from a sea roughness to a sea calm, and thence to a river motion, and that river (as happens in the familiarisation of dreams) was no other than the gentle Thames, which landed me in the wafture of a placid wave or two, alone, safe and inglorious, somewhere at the foot of Lambeth palace.

The degree of the soul's creativeness in sleep might furnish no whimsical criterion of the quantum of poetical

386

faculty resident in the same soul waking. An old gentleman, a friend of mine, and a humorist, used to carry this notion so far, that when he saw any stripling of his acquaintance ambitious of becoming a poet, his first question would be,—" Young man, what sort of dreams have you ? " I have so much faith in my old friend's theory, that when I feel that idle vein returning upon me, I presently subside into my proper element of prose, remembering those eluding nereids, and that inauspicious inland landing.

CHARLES LAMB

A POET'S DREAM

The fifth canto of Dante pleases me more and more—it is that one in which he meets with Paolo and Francesca. I had passed many days in rather a low state of mind, and in the midst of them I dreamt of being in that region of Hell. The dream was one of the most delightful enjoyments I ever had in my life. I floated about the whirling atmosphere (as it is described) with a beautiful figure to whose lips mine were joined, as it seemed for an age—and in the midst of all this cold and darkness I was warm— even flowery tree tops sprung up and we rested on them sometimes with the lightness of a cloud, till the wind blew us away again. I tried a Sonnet upon it—there are fourteen lines but nothing of what I felt in it—O that I could dream it every night !

KEATS (from a Letter written
at Wentworth Place in 1819)

387

THE VISION

How frequently does his form visit my mind's eye in slumber and in wakefulness, in the light of day, and in the night watches; but last night I saw him in his beauty and his strength; he was about to speak, and my ear was on the stretch, when at once I awoke, and there was I alone, and the night storm was howling amidst the branches of the pines which surround my lonely dwelling : " Listen to the moaning of the pine, at whose root thy hut is fastened,"— a saying that, of wild Finland, in which there is wisdom ; I listened, and thought of life and death.

GEORGE BORROW (from *Lavengro*)

THE QUEEN'S CROQUET-GROUND

(*part of Alice's dream*)

When the procession came opposite to Alice, they all stopped and looked at her, and the Queen said severely, " Who is this ? " She said it to the Knave of Hearts, who only bowed and smiled in reply.

" Idiot ! " said the Queen, tossing her head impatiently ; and, turning to Alice, she went on, " What's your name, child ? "

" My name is Alice, so please your Majesty," said Alice very politely ; but she added, to herself, " Why, they're only a pack of cards, after all. I needn't be afraid of them ! "

" And who are *these* ? " said the Queen, pointing to the three gardeners who were lying round the rose-tree ;

for, you see, as they were lying on their faces, and the pattern on their backs was the same as the rest of the pack, she could not tell whether they were gardeners, or soldiers, or courtiers, or three of her own children.

"How should *I* know?" said Alice, surprised at her own courage. "It's no business of *mine*."

The Queen turned crimson with fury, and, after glaring at her for a moment like a wild beast, began screaming, "Off with her head! Off——"

"Nonsense!" said Alice, very loudly and decidedly, and the Queen was silent.

The King laid his hand upon her arm, and timidly said "Consider, my dear : she is only a child!"

The Queen turned angrily away from him, and said to the Knave "Turn them over!"

The Knave did so, very carefully, with one foot.

"Get up!" said the Queen in a shrill, loud voice, and the three gardeners instantly jumped up, and began bowing to the King, the Queen, the royal children, and everybody else.

"Leave off that!" screamed the Queen. "You make me giddy." And then, turning to the rose-tree, she went on, "What *have* you been doing here?"

"May it please your Majesty," said Two, in a very humble tone, going down on one knee as he spoke, "we were trying——"

"*I* see!" said the Queen, who had meanwhile been examining the roses. "Off with their heads!" and the procession moved on, three of the soldiers remaining behind to execute the unfortunate gardeners, who ran to Alice for protection.

"You shan't be beheaded!" said Alice, and she put them into a large flower-pot that stood near. The three soldiers wandered about for a minute or two, looking for them, and then quietly marched off after the others.

" Are their heads off ? " shouted the Queen.

" Their heads are gone, if it please your Majesty ! " the soldiers shouted in reply.

" That's right ! " shouted the Queen. " Can you play croquet ? "

The soldiers were silent, and looked at Alice, as the question was evidently meant for her.

" Yes ! " shouted Alice.

" Come on, then ! " roared the Queen, and Alice joined the procession, wondering very much what would happen next.

" It's—it's a very fine day ! " said a timid voice at her side. She was walking by the White Rabbit, who was peeping anxiously into her face.

" Very," said Alice :—" Where's the Duchess ? "

" Hush ! hush ! " said the Rabbit in a low, hurried tone. He looked anxiously over his shoulder as he spoke, and then raised himself upon tiptoe, put his mouth close to her ear, and whispered " She's under sentence of execution."

" What for ? " said Alice.

" Did you say ' What a pity ' ? " the Rabbit asked.

" No, I didn't," said Alice : " I don't think it's at all a pity. I said ' What for ? ' "

" She boxed the Queen's ears——" the Rabbit began. Alice gave a little scream of laughter. " Oh, hush ! " the Rabbit whispered in a frightened tone. " The Queen will hear you ! You see she came rather late, and the Queen said——"

" Get to your places ! " shouted the Queen in a voice of

thunder, and people began running about in all directions, tumbling up against each other ; however, they got settled down in a minute or two, and the game began.

LEWIS CARROLL (from *Alice in Wonderland*)

TWO DREAMS

1. *The Pig in the Dining-Room*

Mrs. Atlay, wife of a late Bishop of Hereford, dreamed one night that there was a pig in the dining-room of the palace. She came downstairs, and in the hall told her governess and children of the dream before family prayers. When these were over, nobody who was told the story having left the hall in the interval, she went into the dining-room and there was the pig. It was proved to have escaped from the sty after Mrs. Atlay got up.

2. *The Lost Cheque*

Mr. A., a barrister, sat up one night to write letters, and about half-past twelve went out to put them in the post. On undressing he missed a cheque for a large sum, which he had received during the day. He hunted everywhere in vain, went to bed, slept, and dreamed that he saw the cheque curled round an area railing not far from his own door. He woke, got up, dressed, walked down the street and found his cheque in the place he had dreamed of. In his opinion he had noticed it fall from his pocket as he walked to the letter-box, without consciously remarking it and his deeper memory awoke in slumber.

ANDREW LANG (from *A Book of Dreams and Ghosts*)

THIRD PART

§ I   THE ANCIENT WORLD

I know nothing can conduce more to letters than to examine the writings of the Ancients. They opened the gates, and made the way that went before us.

BEN JONSON

We go to our favourite classical author, as it were for conversation with a friend ; and we discover that these benevolent antique minds reflect our own thoughts, but in a richer maturity. Their friendship never fails us, and their serene philosophy brings us reconciliation—and how often do we need it !—with mankind and with ourselves.

SAINTE-BEUVE

§ 1. EGYPT AND THE EAST

THE COMING FORTH BY DAY

(*Hymn to the Rising Sun*)

" Homage to thee, O Rā, when thou risest. Thou art adored by me when thy beauties are before mine eyes, and when thy radiance falleth upon my body. Thou stridest over the heavens in peace, and all thy foes are cast down ; the never-resting stars sing hymns of praise unto thee, and the stars which rest, and the stars which never fail glorify thee as thou sinkest to rest in the horizon of Manu, O thou who art beautiful at morn and at eve, O thou lord who livest and art established, O my lord !

" Homage to thee, O thou who art Rā when thou risest, and Ten when thou settest in beauty. Thou risest and shinest on the back of thy mother Nut, O thou who art crowned king of the gods ! Nut doeth homage unto thee, and everlasting and never-changing order embraceth thee at morn and at eve. Thou stridest over the heaven, being glad of heart, and the Lake of Testes is content thereat. . . Rā hath a fair wind ; the boat goeth forth and sailing along it cometh into port. The gods of the south and of the north, of the west and of the east, praise thee, O thou divine substance, from whom all forms of life come into being. Thou sendest forth the word, and the earth is flooded with silence, O thou only One, who didst dwell in heaven before ever the earth and the mountains came into existence. O Runner, O Lord, O only One, thou maker of things which are, thou hast fashioned the tongue of the company of the gods, thou hast produced whatsoever cometh forth from the waters, and thou springest up from them over the flooded land of the Lake of Horus. Let me snuff the air which cometh forth from thy nostrils, and the north wind which cometh forth from thy mother Nut. O make thou to be glorious my shining form, O Osiris, make thou to be divine my soul! Thou art worshipped in peace, O lord of the gods, thou art exalted by reason of thy wondrous works. Shine thou with thy rays of light upon my body day by day, upon me, Osiris the scribe, the teller of the divine offerings of all the gods, the overseer of the granary of the lords of Abydos, the royal scribe in truth who loveth thee; Ani, victorious in peace. . .

"Hail, thou Disk, thou lord of rays, who risest on the horizon day by day! Shine thou with thy beams of light upon the face of Osiris Ani, who is victorious; for he singeth hymns of praise unto thee at dawn, and he maketh thee to set at eventide with words of adoration. May the soul of Osiris Ani, the triumphant one, come forth with thee into heaven, may he cleave his path among the never-resting stars. . .

"Homage to thee, O thou who risest in thy horizon as Rā, thou reposest upon law which changeth not nor can it be altered. Thou passest over the sky, and every face watcheth thee and thy course, for thou hast been hidden from their gaze. Thou dost shew thyself at dawn and at eventide day by day. The boat, wherein is thy Majesty, goeth forth with might; thy beams shine upon all faces; the number of thy red and yellow rays cannot be known, nor can thy bright beams be told. The lands of the gods, and the eastern lands of Punt must be seen, ere that which is hidden in thee may be measured. Alone and by thyself thou dost manifest thyself when thou comest into being above the sky. May Ani advance, even as thou dost

advance ; may he never cease to go forward, even as thy
Majesty ceaseth not to go forward, even though it be for
a moment; for with strides dost thou in one little moment
pass over the spaces which would need hundreds of
thousands and millions of years for man to pass over ;
this thou doest, and then dost thou sink to rest. Thou
puttest an end to the hours of the night, and thou dost
count them, even thou ; thou endest them in thine own
appointed season, and the earth becometh light. Thou
settest thyself before thy handiwork in the likeness of Rā ;
thou risest in the horizon " . . .

And the god saith :—
" Thou shalt come forth into heaven, thou shalt pass
over the sky, thou shalt be joined unto the starry deities.
. . . Thou shalt behold Horus on the standing-place of the
pilot of the boat, and Thoth and Maāt shall stand one
upon each side of him. All the gods shall rejoice when they
behold Rā coming in peace to make the hearts of the
shining ones to live, and Osiris Ani, victorious, the
scribe of the divine offerings of the lords of Thebes, shall
be along with them ! "

From *The Book of the Dead*
(Trans. SIR E. A. WALLIS BUDGE)

A SONG FROM PALESTINE

*(Sung during the arraying of the Bride before leaving
her parents' house)*

' O Sabha, Darling, 'tis to thee we sing :
    In lyric song our voices rise and fall.
We hear thy Father calling, Sabha, Dear,
    We hear thy Father's gentle loving call.

' O Sabha of the trustful sable eyes,
  Eyes dark as night, so calm, so deep, so rare :
We hear thy Brother call thee, Sabha, Dear—
  We hear thy Brother call thee, Sabha, Fair.

' O Sabha of the rippling golden hair ;
  Gold, living gold, its every curling tress :
Let not our sorrow cloud thy faithful heart,
  Let not our sorrow that dear heart distress.

' With softest sound of rhythmic melody
  The anklets tinkle on thy Mother's feet.
Sabha, we hear thy Father's Brother call,
  We hear thy Father's Brother call thee, Sweet.

' The anklets tinkle, Sabha, on thy feet,
  Making soft melody within the hall.
Sabha, we hear thy Mother's Brother call—
  O Love, we hear thy Mother's Brother call.

' We clasp the bracelet on thy white round arm,
  Less round and white the silvery moon appears.
Thine eyes are tenderer than the camel's eyes,
  And hers compare with liquid wells of tears.

' Behold the scarlet shoes upon thy feet,
  Each dainty foot lost in a dainty shoe,
Fair as the moon as full thy face is fair.
  More fair than moon thy form, more pure than
    dew,

398

'I clasp these priceless gems around thy neck,
    They hide the Breast so far more dear to me ;
My steed, my camel for thy sake I'd sell,
    My choicest treasure I'd pour out for thee.'

From DALMAN'S *Palästinischer Diwan*
(Trans. H. BARNES)

FROM THE PERSIAN

On her delicate cheeks the ringlets flutter with the breath of my sigh, in the same manner that the reflexion of the hyacinth in the water quivers with the blowing of the breeze. When she walks there is a pleasant tremor of the body from head to foot, just like the quivering of the roses on a tender rose-branch.

My sweetheart has entered the hut, and the bird of my heart has remained bewildered. The candle is put into the lantern, and the moth is left outside fluttering.

Take care, the sleep of non-existence will overtake you at last ; for the coming and going of the breath is but the rocking of the cradle.

When the wind waves thy dark ringlets, thy rosy face glows still more. One may say, it has in hand a fan of raven's feather, and by the movement of the fan it makes the fire blaze.

Translated by M. N. KUKA

THE GUEST

The householder, when the day's work is finished, shall rest awhile in the evening. He shall sit before his dwelling, during the time required for the milking of a cow, in readiness for the arrival of an unexpected guest.

From a Hindu Law-Book

The reward for honouring a guest is heavenly bliss and immunity from misfortunes. The householder shall converse kindly with his guest and gladden him with milk and eatables. He shall offer to his guest a room, a bed, a mattress, a pillow with a cover, and ointment and what else may be necessary. The reception of guests is an everlasting sacrifice offered by the householder. He who entertains guests for one night obtains earthly happiness, a second night gains the middle air, a third heavenly bliss, a fourth the world of unsurpassable happiness. Many nights procure endless worlds. A guest who can repeat the whole Veda (together with the supplementary books) is worthy to receive a cow.

From *Aphorisms on the Sacred Laws of the Hindus*
(Trans. GEORG BÜHLER)

THE INDIAN'S PRAYER

O Supreme Ruler, all-pervading and all-supporting, O endowed Messengers of God, make our wills wise rulers of our thoughts and deeds that we may abide in happiness. Let winds be favourable to us. Let the seas send forth soft vapours to form clouds sweet as honey. And on land make the herbs and plants to flourish for our well-being. Let day and night be pleasant to us. Let our father, the Sun, pour down happiness. May the Almighty Lord Indra, owner of heaven and the wide regions, the great Creator, be gracious to us and give us peace.

From the *Rigveda*

INDIAN APHORISMS

The sage who excludes from his mind external objects, who restrains senses, mind and understanding, from whom desire, fear and wrath have departed is, indeed, for ever released from birth and death. He, knowing the great Lord of all worlds and the Friend of all beings, attains tranquillity.

From *Bhagavadgîtâ* (Trans. K. T. TELANG)

Health is the greatest of gifts, contentment the best riches ; trust is the best of relationships. He who has tasted the sweetness of solitude and tranquillity is free from fear and free from sin, while he tastes the sweetness of drinking in the law. He who walks in the company of fools suffers a long way ; company with fools, as with an enemy, is always painful ; company with the wise is pleasure, like meeting with kinsfolk. Therefore, one ought to follow the wise, the learned, the much enduring, the dutiful, the elect : one ought to follow such a good and wise man, as the moon follows the path of the stars.

From *Dhammapada* (Trans. F. MAX MÜLLER)

A DREAM IN WINTER

Cold, cold the year draws to its end,
The crickets and grasshoppers make a doleful chirping.
The chill wind ceases its violence.
My wandering love has no coat to cover him.
He gave his embroidered furs to the Lady of Lo,
But from me his bedfellow he is quite estranged.
Sleeping alone in the depth of the long night
In a dream I thought I saw the light of his face.
My dear one thought of our old joys together,
He came in his chariot and gave me the front reins.
I wanted so to prolong our play and laughter,
To hold his hand and go back with him in his coach.
But when he had come he would not stay long,
Nor stop to go with me to the Inner Chamber.
Truly without the falcon's wings to carry me
How can I rival the flying wind's swiftness?
I go and lean at the gate and think of my grief,
My falling tears wet the double gates.

From the Chinese, 1st Century B.C.
(Trans. A. WALEY)

HOW GOES THE NIGHT?

How goes the night?
Midnight has still to come.
Down in the court the torch is blazing bright;
I hear far off the throbbing of the drum.

How goes the night?
The night is not yet gone.

I hear the trumpets blowing on the height :
The torch is paling in the coming dawn.

How goes the night ?
The night is past and done.
The torch is smoking in the morning light,
The dragon banner floating in the sun.

From the Chinese, 9th Century B.C.
(Trans. HELEN WADDELL)

FROM AN OLD PILLOW-BOOK

One has been expecting someone, and rather late at
night there is a stealthy tapping at the door. One sends a
maid to see who it is, and lies waiting, with some slight
flutter of the breast. But the name one hears when she returns is that of someone completely different, who does
not concern one at all. Of all depressing experiences, this
is by far the worst. . . .

Of course, what I really like is a house where there is no
fuss about the front gate, and no one particularly minds
whether it is midnight or morning. Then one can go out to
the front of the house and talk to whoever it may be—
perhaps one of the princes, or of the lords attached to his
Majesty's service—sit all through a winter's night with
the shutters open, and after the guest has gone, watch him
make his way into the distance. If he leaves just at daybreak, this is very agreeable, particularly if he plays upon
his flute as he goes. Then, when he is out of sight, one does

not hurry to go to bed, but discusses the visitor with some-one, reviews the poems he made, and so gradually falls to sleep.

SEI SHŌNAGON, 10th Century

(Trans. A. WALEY)

THE RIVER OF HEAVEN

He is coming, my long-desired lord, whom I have been waiting to meet here, on the banks of the River of Heaven. . . . The moment of loosening my girdle is nigh.

Over the Rapids of the Everlasting Heaven, floating in his boat, my lord will doubtless deign to come to me this very night.

From the day that the autumn wind began to blow (I kept saying to myself), "Ah, when shall we meet ? "—but now my beloved, for whom I waited and longed, has come indeed !

On the River of Heaven, at the place of the august ferry, the sound of the water has become loud : perhaps my long-awaited lord will soon be coming in his boat.

When I see the water-grasses of the River of Heaven bend in the autumn wind (I think to myself) : " The time for our meeting seems to have come."

When I feel in my heart a sudden longing for my hus-band, then on the River of Heaven the sound of the rowing of the night-boat is heard, and the plash of the oars resounds.

When autumn comes, and the river-mists spread over the Heavenly Stream, I turn toward the river and long ; and the nights of my longing are many !

Hikoboshi and Tanabata-tsumé are to meet each other

to-night ;—ye waves of the River of Heaven, take heed that ye do not rise !

On the River of Heaven a sound of plashing can be distinctly heard : is it the sound of the rippling made by Hikoboshi quickly rowing his boat ?

Perhaps this evening shower is but the spray flung down from the oar of Hikoboshi, rowing his boat in haste.

From to-morrow alas ! after having put my jewel-bed in order, no longer reposing with my lord, I must sleep alone !

Oh, ferryman, make speed across the stream !—my lord is not one who can come and go twice in a year !

From the Japanese (Trans. LAFCADIO HEARN)

WHEN EVENING COMES

When evening comes
I will leave the door open beforehand and
        then wait
For him who said he would come
To meet me in my dreams.

By way of pretext
I said " I will go
And look at
The condition of the bamboo fence " ;
But it was really to see you !

From the Japanese (YAKAMOCHI, d. 785 A.D.
                            —Trans. A. WALEY)

§2. GREECE

PRIAM GOES TO ACHILLES

And the messenger of Zeus stood beside Priam and spake softly unto him, and trembling came upon his limbs : " Be of good cheer in thy heart, O Priam son of Dardanos, and be not dismayed for anything, for no evil come I hither to forebode to thee, but with good will. I am the messenger of Zeus to thee, who, though he be afar off, hath great care and pity for thee. The Olympian biddeth thee ransom noble Hector and carry gifts to Achilles that may gladden his heart : go thou alone, let none other of the Trojans go with thee. Only let some elder herald attend on thee to guide the mules and the smooth-wheeled waggon to carry back to the city the dead man whom noble Achilles slew. Let not death be in thy thought, nor any fear ; such guide shall go with thee, even the slayer of Argus, who shall lead thee until his leading bring thee to Achilles. . ."

Then the old man made haste to go up into his car, and drave forth from the doorway and the echoing portico. In front the mules drew the four-wheeled wain, and wise Idaios drave them ; behind came the horses which the old man urged with the lash at speed along the city : and his friends all followed lamenting loud as though he were faring to his death. And when they were come down from the city and were now on the plain, then went back again to Ilios his sons and marriage kin. But the two coming forth upon the plain were not unbeheld of far-seeing Zeus. But he looked upon the old man and had compassion on him, and straightway spake unto Hermes his dear son : " Hermes, since unto thee especially is it dear to companion men, and thou hearest whomsoever thou wilt, go forth and so guide Priam to the hollow ships of the Achaians that no man behold or be aware of him, among all the Danaans' host, until he come to the son of Peleus."

Thus spake he, and the Messenger, the slayer of Argus, was not disobedient unto his word. . . When they were come to the towers and trench of the ships, there were the sentinels just busying them about their supper. Then the Messenger, the slayer of Argus, shed sleep upon them all, and straightway opened the gates and thrust back the bars, and brought within Priam and the splendid gifts upon his wain and spake aloud : " Old sire, go thou in and clasp the knees of Peleus' son, and entreat him for his father's sake and his mother's of the lovely hair and for his child's sake that thou mayest move his soul."

Thus Hermes spoke, and departed unto high Olympus. But Priam leapt from the car to the earth, and left Idaios in his place ; he stayed to mind the horses and mules ; but the old man made straight for the house where Achilles dear to Zeus was wont to sit. And therein he found the man himself, and his comrades sate apart. But they were unaware of great Priam as he came in, and so stood he anigh and clasped in his hands the knees of Achilles, and kissed his hands, terrible, man-slaying, that slew many of Priam's sons. And as when a grievous curse cometh upon a man who in his own country hath slain another and escapeth to a land of strangers, to the house of some rich man, and wonder possesseth them that look on him—so Achilles wondered when he saw godlike Priam, and the rest wondered likewise, and looked upon one another. Then Priam spake and entreated him, saying : " Bethink thee, O Achilles like to gods, of thy father that is of like years with me, on the grievous pathway of old age. Him haply are the dwellers round about entreating evilly, nor is there any to ward from him ruin and bane. Nevertheless while he heareth of thee as yet alive he rejoiceth in his heart, and hopeth withal day after day that he shall see his dear son returning from Troy-land. But I, I am utterly unblest, since I begat sons the best men in wide Troyland, but declare unto thee that none of them is left. He who was yet left and guarded city and men, him slewest thou but now as he fought for his country, even Hector. For his sake come I unto the ships of the Achaians that I may win him back from thee, and I bring with me untold ransom. Yea, fear thou the gods, Achilles, and have compassion on me, even me, bethinking thee of thy father. Lo, I am yet more piteous than he, and have braved what none other man on earth have braved before, to stretch forth my hand toward the face of the slayer of my sons."

Thus spake he, and stirred within Achilles desire to make lament for his father. And he touched the old man's hand and gently moved him back. And as they both bethought them of their dead, so Priam for man-slaying Hector wept sore as he was fallen before Achilles feet, and Achilles wept for his own father, and now again for Patroklos, and their moan went up throughout the house. But when noble Achilles had satisfied him with lament, and the desire thereof departed from his heart and limbs, straightway he sprang from his seat, and raised the old man by his hand, pitying his hoary head and hoary beard, and spake unto him winged words and said : " Ah hapless ! many ill things verily thou hast endured in thy heart. How durst thou come alone to the ships of Achaians and to meet the eyes of the man who hath slain full many of thy brave sons ? of iron verily is thy heart.

But come then set thee on a seat, and we will let our sorrows lie quiet in our hearts, for all our pain, for no avail cometh of chill lament. This is the lot the gods have spun for miserable men, that they should live in pain; yet themselves are sorrowless. . . Keep courage, and lament not unabatingly in thy heart. For nothing wilt thou avail by grieving for thy son, neither shalt thou bring him back to life or ever some new evil come upon thee."

Then made answer unto him the old man, godlike Priam : " Bid me not to a seat, O fosterling of Zeus, so long as Hector lieth uncared for at the huts, but straightway give him back that I may behold him with mine eyes ; and accept thou the great ransom that we bring. So mayest thou have pleasure thereof, and come unto thy native land, since thou hast spared me from the first."

Then fleet-footed Achilles looked sternly upon him and said : " No longer chafe me, old sire ; of myself am I minded to give Hector back to thee, for there came to me a messenger from Zeus, even my mother who bare me, daughter of the Ancient One of the Sea. . . Thy son, old sire, is given back as thou wouldest and lieth on a bier and with the break of day thou shalt see him thyself as thou carriest him " . . .

Now all other gods and warriors lords of chariots slumbered all night, by soft sleep overcome. But not on the Helper Hermes did sleep take hold as he sought within his heart how he should guide forth king Priam from the ships unespied of the trusty sentinels. And he stood above his head and spake a word to him : " Old sire, no thought then hast thou of any evil, seeing thou yet sleepest among men that are thine enemies, for that Achilles spared thee. Truly now hast thou won back thy dear son, and at great price. But for thy life will thy sons thou hast left behind be offered threefold ransom, if but Agamemnon Atreus' son be aware of thee, and aware be all the Achaians."

Thus spake he, and the old man feared, and roused the herald. And Hermes yoked the horses and mules for them, and himself drave them lightly through the camp, and none was aware of them.

But when they came to the ford of the fair-flowing river, (even eddying Xanthos, begotten of immortal Zeus) then Hermes departed up to high Olympus, and Morning of the saffron robe spread over all the earth. And they with wail and moan drave the horses to the city, and the mules drew the dead. Nor marked them any man or fair-girdled woman until Kassandra, peer of golden Aphrodite, having gone up upon Pergamos, was aware of her dear father as he stood in the car, and the herald that was crier to the town. Then beheld she him that lay upon the bier behind the mules, and thereat she wailed and cried aloud throughout all the town : " O men and women of Troy, come ye hither and look upon Hector, if ever while he was alive ye rejoiced when he came back from battle, since great joy was he to the city and all the folk."

Thus spake she, nor was man or woman left within the city, for upon all came unendurable grief. And near the gates they met Priam bringing home the dead. First bewailed him his dear wife and lady mother, as they cast them on the fair-wheeled wain and touched his head ; and around them stood the throng and wept.

From HOMER'S *Iliad*, Bk. XXIV.
(Trans. LANG, LEAF and MYERS)

ULYSSES AND NAUSICAA

Now when they were come to the beautiful stream of the river, where truly were the unfailing cisterns, and bright water welled up free from beneath, and flowed past, enough to wash the foulest garments clean, there the girls unharnessed the mules from under the chariot, and turning them loose they drove them along the banks of the eddying river to graze on the honey-sweet clover. Then they took the garments from the wain, in their hands, and bore them to the black water, and briskly trod them down in the trenches, in busy rivalry. Now when they had washed and cleansed all the stains, they spread all out in order along the shore of the deep even where the sea, in beating on the coast, washed the pebbles clean. Then having bathed and anointed them well with olive oil, they took their mid-day meal on the river's banks, waiting till the clothes should dry in the brightness of the sun. Anon, when they were satisfied with food, the maidens and the princess, they fell to playing at ball, casting away their tires, and among them Nausicaa of the white arms began the song. And even as Artemis, the archer, moveth down the mountain, either along the ridges of lofty Taygetus or Erymanthus, taking her pastime in the chase of boars and swift deer, and with her the wild wood-nymphs disport them, the daughters of Zeus, lord of the Aegis, and Leto is glad at heart, while high over all she rears her head and brows, and easily may she be known—but all are fair ; even so the girl unwed outshone her maiden company.

But when now she was about going homewards, after yoking the mules and folding up the goodly raiment, then grey-eyed Athene turned to other thoughts, that so

Odysseus might awake, and see the lovely maiden, who should be his guide to the city of the Phaeacian men. So then the princess threw the ball at one of her company; she missed the girl, and cast the ball into the deep eddying current, whereat they all raised a piercing cry. Then the goodly Odysseus awoke and sat up, pondering in his heart and spirit:

"Woe is me! to what men's land am I come now? say, are they froward, and wild, and unjust, or are they hospitable, and of godfearing mind? How shrill a cry of maidens rings round me, of the nymphs that hold the steep hill-tops, and the river-springs, and the grassy water meadows! It must be, methinks, that I am near men of human speech. Go to, I myself will make trial and see."

Therewith the goodly Odysseus crept out from under the coppice, having broken with his strong hand a leafy bough from the thick wood, to hold athwart his body, that it might hide his nakedness withal. And forth he sallied like a lion mountain-bred, trusting in his strength, who fares out blown and rained upon, with flaming eyes; amid the kine he goes or amid the sheep or in the track of the wild deer; yea, his belly bids him go even to the good homestead to make assay upon the flocks. Even so Odysseus was fain to draw nigh to the fair-tressed maidens, all naked as he was, such need had come upon him. But he was terrible in their eyes, being marred with the salt sea foam, and they fled cowering here and there about the jutting spits of shore. And the daughter of Alcinous alone stood firm, for Athene gave her courage of heart, and took all trembling from her limbs. So she halted and stood over against him, and Odysseus considered whether he should clasp the knees of the lovely maiden, and so make

412

his prayer, or should stand as he was, apart, and beseech her with smooth words, if haply she might show him the town, and give him raiment. And as he thought within himself, it seemed better to stand apart, and beseech her with smooth words, lest the maiden should be angered with him if he touched her knees : so straightway he spake a sweet and cunning word :

" I supplicate thee, O queen, whether thou art a goddess or a mortal! If indeed thou art a goddess of them that keep the wide heaven ; to Artemis, then, the daughter of great Zeus, I mainly liken thee, for beauty and stature and shapeliness. But if thou art one of the daughters of men who dwell on earth, thrice blessed are thy father and thy lady mother, and thrice blessed thy brethren. Surely their souls ever glow with gladness for thy sake, each time they see thee entering the dance, so fair a flower of maidens. But he is of heart the most blessed beyond all other who shall prevail with gifts of wooing, and lead thee to his home. Never have mine eyes beheld such an one among mortals, neither man nor woman ; great awe comes upon me as I look on thee. Yet in Delos once I saw as goodly a thing : a young sapling of a palm tree springing by the altar of Apollo. For thither too I went, and much people with me, on that path where my sore troubles were to be. Yea, and when I looked there upon, long time I marvelled in spirit,—for never grew there yet so goodly a shoot from ground,—even in such wise as I wonder at thee, lady, and am astonied and do greatly fear to touch thy knees, though grievous sorrow is upon me. Yesterday, on the twentieth day, I escaped from the wine-dark deep, but all that time continually the wave bare me, and the vehement winds drave, from the isle Ogygia. And now some god has cast me on this shore, that here too, methinks, some evil may betide me : for I trow not that trouble will cease ; the gods ere that time will yet bring many a thing to pass. But, queen, have pity on me, for after many trials and sore to thee first of all am I come, and of the other folk, who hold this city and land, I know no man. Nay show me the town, give me an old garment to cast about me, if thou hadst, when thou camest here, any wrap for the linen. And may the gods grant thee all thy heart's desire : a husband and a home, and a mind at one with his may they give—a good gift, for there is nothing mightier and nobler than when man and wife are of one heart and mind in a house, a grief to their foes, and to their friends great joy, but their own hearts know it best."

Then Nausicaa of the white arms answered him, and said : " Stranger, forasmuch as thou seemest no evil man nor foolish—and it is Olympian Zeus himself that giveth weal to men, to the good and to the evil, to each one as he will, and this thy lot doubtless is of him, and so thou must in anywise endure it :—and now, since thou hast come to our city and our land, thou shalt not lack raiment, nor aught else that is the due of a hapless suppliant, when he has met them who can befriend him. And I will show thee the town, and name the name of the people. The Phaeacians hold this city and land, and I am the daughter of Alcinous, great of heart, on whom all the might and force of the Phaeacians depend."

Thus she spake, and called to her maidens of the fair tresses : " Halt, my maidens, whither flee ye at the sight of a man ? Ye surely do not take him for an enemy ? That mortal breathes not, and never will be born, who shall come with war to the land of the Phaeacians, for they are very dear to the gods. Far apart we live in the wash of the waves, the outermost of men, and no other mortals are conversant with us. Nay, but this man is some helpless one come hither in his wanderings, whom now we must kindly entreat, for all strangers and beggars are from Zeus, and a little gift is dear. So, my maidens, give the stranger meat and drink, and bathe him in the river, where withal is a shelter from the winds."

So she spake, but they had halted and called each to the other, and they brought Odysseus to the sheltered place, and made him sit down, as Nausicaa bade them, the daughter of Alcinous, high of heart. Beside him they laid a mantle, and a doublet for raiment, and gave him soft olive oil in the golden cruse, and bade him wash in the streams of the river. . .

Then they went apart and told all to their lady. But with the river water the goodly Odysseus washed from his skin the salt scurf that covered his back and broad shoulders, and from his head he wiped the crusted brine of the barren sea. But when he had washed his whole body, and anointed him with olive oil, and had clad himself in the raiment that the unwedded maidens gave him, then Athene, the daughter of Zeus, made him greater and more mighty to behold, and from his head caused deep curling locks to flow, like the hyacinth flower. . .

Then to the shore of the sea went Odysseus apart, and sat down, glowing in beauty and grace, and the princess marvelled at him.

From HOMER'S Odyssey, Bk. VI.
(Trans. BUTCHER and LANG)

It was these men and their like who made Athens great. With them, as with few among Greeks, words cannot exaggerate the deeds that they have done. Such an end as we have here seems indeed to show us what a good life is, from its first signs of power to its final consummation. For even where life's previous record showed faults and failures it is just to weigh the last brave hour of devotion against them all. There they wiped out evil with good and did the city more service as soldiers than they did her harm in private life. There no hearts grew faint because they loved riches more than honour ; none shirked the issue in the poor man's dream of wealth. All these they put aside to strike a blow for the city. Counting the quest to avenge her honour as the most glorious of all ventures, and leaving Hope, the uncertain goddess, to send them what she would, they faced the foe as they drew near him in the strength of their own manhood ; and when the shock of battle came, they chose rather to suffer the uttermost than to win life by weakness. So their memory has escaped the reproaches of men's lips, but they bore instead on their bodies the marks of men's hands, and in a moment of time, at the climax of their lives, were rapt away from a world filled, for their dying eyes, not with terror but with glory.

Such were the men who lie here and such the city that inspired them. We survivors may pray to be spared their bitter hour, but must disdain to meet the foe with a spirit less triumphant. Let us draw strength, not merely from twice-told arguments—how fair and noble a thing it is to show courage in battle—but from the busy spectacle of our great city's life as we have it before us day by day, falling in love with her as we see her, and remembering that all this greatness she owes to men with the fighter's daring, the wise man's understanding of his duty, and the good man's self-discipline in its performance—to men who sacrificed their lives as the best offerings on her behalf. So they gave their bodies to the commonwealth and received, each for his own memory, praise that will never die, and with it the grandest of all sepulchres, not that in which their mortal bones are laid, but a home in the minds of men, where their glory remains fresh to stir to speech or action as the occasion comes by. For the whole earth is the sepulchre of famous men ; and their story is not graven only on stone over their native earth, but lives on far away, without visible symbol, woven into the stuff of other men's lives. For you now it remains to rival what they have done.

Therefore I do not mourn with the parents of the dead who are here with us. I will rather comfort them. For they know that they have been born into a world of manifold chances and that he is to be accounted happy to whom the best lot falls—the best sorrow, such as is yours to-day, or the best death, such as fell to these, for whom life and happiness were cut to the self-same measure. I know it is not easy to give you comfort. I know how often in the joy of others you will have reminders of what was once your own, and how men feel sorrow, not for the loss of what they have never tested, but when something that has grown dear to them has been snatched away. But you must keep a brave heart in the hope of other children, those who are still of age to bear them. For the newcomers will help you to forget the gap in your own circle, and will help the city to fill up the ranks of its workers and its soldiers. For no man is fitted to give fair and honest advice in council if he has not, like his fellows, a family at stake in the hour of the city's danger. To you who are past the age of vigour I would say : count the long years of happiness so much gain to set off against the brief space that yet remains, and let your burden be lightened by the glory of the dead. For the love of honour alone is not staled by age, and it is by honour, not, as some say, by gold, that the helpless end of life is cheered.

THUCYDIDES (*History*, Bk. II—
Trans. A. E. ZIMMERN)

A TALK BY THE RIVER

PHAEDRUS : Where shall we sit and read ?
SOCRATES : Let us turn aside here and go along the Ilissus; then we can sit down quietly wherever we please.
PHAEDRUS : I am fortunate, it seems, in being barefoot ; you are so always. It is easiest then for us to go along the brook with our feet in the water, and it is not unpleasant, especially at this time of the year and the day.
SOCRATES : Lead on then, and look out for a good place where we may sit.
PHAEDRUS : Do you see that very tall plane tree ?
SOCRATES : What of it ?
PHAEDRUS : There is shade there and moderate breeze and grass to sit on, or, if we like, to lie down on.
SOCRATES : Lead the way.
PHAEDRUS : Tell me, Socrates, is it not from some place along here by the Ilissus that Boreas is said to have carried off Oreithyia ?
SOCRATES : Yes, that is the story.

PHAEDRUS : Well, is it from here ? The streamlet looks very pretty and pure and clear and fit for girls to play by.

SOCRATES : No, the place is about two or three furlongs farther down, where you cross over to the precinct of Agra. . . But, my friend, while we were talking, is not this the tree to which you were leading us ?

PHAEDRUS : Yes, this is it.

SOCRATES : By Hera, it is a charming resting place. For this plane tree is very spreading and lofty, and the tall and shady willow is very beautiful, and it is in full bloom, so as to make the place most fragrant ; then, too, the spring is very pretty as it flows under the plane tree, and its water is very cool, to judge by my foot. And it seems to be a sacred place of some nymphs and of Achelous, judging by the figurines and statues. Then again, if you please, how lovely and perfectly charming the breeziness of the place is ! and it resounds with the shrill summer music of the chorus of cicadas. But the most delightful thing of all is the grass, as it grows on the gentle slope, thick enough to be just right when you lay your head on it. So you have guided the stranger most excellently, dear Phaedrus.

PHAEDRUS : You are an amazing and most remarkable person. For you really do seem exactly like a stranger who is being guided about, and not like a native. You don't go away from the city, out over the border, and it seems to me you don't go outside the walls at all.

SOCRATES : Forgive me, my dear friend. You see, I am fond of learning. Now the country places and the trees won't teach me anything, and the people in the city do. But you seem to have found the charm to bring me out. For as people lead hungry animals by shaking in front of them a branch of leaves or some fruit, just so, I think, you, by holding before me discourses in books, will lead me all over Attica and wherever else you please. So now that I have come here, I intend to lie down, and do you choose the position in which you think you can read most easily, and read. . . We have plenty of time, apparently ; and besides, the locusts seem to be looking down upon us as they sing and talk with each other in the heat. Now if they should see us not conversing at mid-day, but, like most people, dozing, lulled to sleep by their song because of our mental indolence, they would quite justly laugh at us, thinking that some slaves had come to their resort and were slumbering about the fountain at noon like sheep. But if they see us conversing and sailing past them unmoved by the charm of their Siren voices, perhaps they will be pleased and give us the gift which the gods bestowed on them to give to men.

PHAEDRUS : What is this gift ? I don't seem to have heard of it.

SOCRATES : It is quite improper for a lover of the Muses never to have heard of such things. The story goes that these locusts were once men, before the birth of the Muses, and when the Muses were born and song appeared, some of the men were so overcome with delight that they sang and sang, forgetting food and drink, until at last unconsciously they died. From them the locust tribe afterwards arose, and they have this gift from the Muses, that from the time of their birth they need no sustenance, but sing continually, without food or drink, until they die, when they go to the Muses and report who honours each of them on earth. They tell Terpsichore of those who have honoured her in dances, and make them dearer to her ; they gain the favour of Erato for the poets of love, and that of the other Muses for their votaries, according to their various ways of honouring them ; and to

Calliope, the eldest of the Muses, and to Urania who is next to her, they make report of those who pass their lives in philosophy and who worship these Muses who are most concerned with heaven and with thought divine and human and whose music is the sweetest. So for many reasons we ought to talk and not sleep in the noontime.
PHAEDRUS : Yes, we ought to talk.

A PRAYER OF SOCRATES

Grant to me that I may be made beautiful in my soul within, and that all external possessions be in harmony with my inner man. May I consider the wise man rich, and may I have such wealth as only the self-restrained man can bear or endure.

From PLATO'S *Phaedrus* (Trans. H. N. FOWLER—
Loeb Classical Library)

REST OUT OF DOORS

So, I and Eucritus and the fair Amyntichus, turned aside into the house of Phrasidamus, and lay down with delight in beds of sweet tamarisk and fresh cuttings from the vines, strewn on the ground. Many poplars and elm-trees were waving over our heads, and not far off the running of the sacred water from the cave of the nymphs warbled to us : in the shimmering branches the sun-burnt grasshoppers were busy with their talk, and from afar the little owl cried softly out of the tangled thorns of the blackberry ; the larks were singing and the hedge-birds, and the turtle-dove moaned ; the bees flew round and round the fountains, murmuring softly ; the scent of late summer and of the fall of the year was everywhere ; the pears fell from the trees at our feet, and apples in number rolled down at our sides, and the young plum-trees were bent to the earth with the weight of their fruit.

THEOCRITUS (*Idyll* VII—
Trans. WALTER PATER)

SAYINGS OF EPICTETUS

It is not easy to gain the attention of effeminate young men, for you cannot take custard by a hook.

How do we act in a voyage ? What is in my power ? To choose the pilot, the sailors, the day, the time of day. Afterwards comes a storm. What have I to care for ? My part is performed. The subject belongs to another, to the pilot. But the ship is sinking : what then have I to do ? That which alone I can do : I am drowned, without fear, without clamour, or accusing God ; but as one who knows that what is born must likewise die. For I am not eternity, but a man ; a part of the whole, as an hour is of the day. I must come like an hour, and like an hour must pass away. What signifies it whether by drowning or by a fever ? For, in some way or other, pass I must.

You see that Caesar hath procured us a profound peace ; there are neither wars nor battles, nor great robberies nor piracies, but we may travel at all hours, and sail from east to west. But can Caesar procure us peace from a fever too ? From a shipwreck ? From a fire ? From an earthquake ? From a thunderstorm ? Nay, even from love ? He cannot. From grief ? From envy ? No, not from any one of these. But the doctrine of philosophers promises to procure us peace from these too. And what doth it say ? " If you will attend to me, O mortals, wherever you are, and whatever you are doing, you shall neither grieve nor be angry, nor be compelled nor restrained ; but you shall live impassive, and free from all." Shall not he who enjoys this peace, proclaimed, not by Caesar (for how should he have it to proclaim ?) but by God, through reason, be contented when he is alone reflecting and considering : " To me there can now no ill happen ; there is no thief nor earthquake. All is full of peace, all full of tranquillity ; every road, every city, every assembly. My neighbour, my companion, unable to hurt me."

Ought we not when we are digging and ploughing and eating to sing this hymn to God ?—" Great is God, who has given us such implements with which we shall cultivate the earth : great is God, who has given us hands, the power of swallowing, a stomach, imperceptible growth, and the power of breathing while we sleep." This is what we ought to sing on every occasion, and to sing the greatest and most divine hymn for giving us the faculty of comprehending these things and using a proper way. I am a rational creature, and I ought to praise God : this is my work ; I do it, nor will I desert this post, so long as I am allowed to keep it ; and I exhort you to join in this same song.

(Trans. E. CARTER)

(*Note by the Author* :—The following matter is intended to have an attraction independent of any originality of subject. This attraction is in the veiled reference underlying all the details of my narrative ; they parody the cock-and-bull stories of ancient poets, historians, and philosophers. As I have no truth to put on record, having lived a very humdrum life, I fall back on falsehood—but falsehood of a more consistent variety ; for I now make the only true statement you are to expect—that I am a liar. My subject is, then, what I have neither seen, experienced, nor been told, what neither exists nor could conceivably do so.)

1. *The Land of Vines*

Starting on a certain date from the Pillars of Heracles, I sailed with a fair wind into the Atlantic. The motives of my voyage were a certain intellectual restlessness, a passion for novelty, a curiosity about the limits of the ocean and the peoples who might dwell beyond it. This being my design, I provisioned and watered my ship on a generous scale. My crew amounted to fifty, all men whose interests, as well as their years, corresponded with my own. I had further provided a good supply of arms, secured the best navigator to be had for money, and had the ship—a sloop—specially strengthened for a long and arduous voyage.

For a day and a night we were carried quietly along by the breeze, with land still in sight. But with the next day's dawn the wind rose to a gale, with a heavy sea and dark sky ; we found ourselves unable to take in sail. We surrendered ourselves to the elements, let her run, and were storm-driven for more than eleven weeks. On the eightieth day the sun came out quite suddenly, and we found ourselves close to a lofty wooded island, round which the waves were murmuring gently, the sea having almost fallen by this time. We brought her to land, disembarked, and after our long tossing lay a considerable time idle on shore ; we at last made a start, however, and leaving thirty of our number to guard the ship I took the other twenty on a tour of inspection.

We had advanced half a mile inland through woods, when we came upon a brazen pillar, inscribed in Greek characters—which however were worn and dim—"Heracles and Dionysus reached this point." Not far off were two footprints on rock ; one might have been an acre in area, the other being smaller ; and I conjecture that the latter was Dionysus's, and the other Heracles's ; we did obeisance, and proceeded. Before we had gone far, we found ourselves on a river which ran wine ; it was very like Chian ; the stream full and copious, even navigable in parts. This evidence of Dionysus's sojourn was enough to convince us that the inscription on the pillar was authentic. Resolving to find the source, I followed the river up, and discovered, instead of a fountain, a number of huge vines covered with grapes ; from the root of each there issued a trickle of perfectly clear wine, the joining of which made the river. It was well stocked with great fish, resembling wine both in colour and taste ; catching and eating some, we at once found ourselves intoxicated ; and indeed when opened the fish were full of wine-lees ; presently it occurred to us to mix them with ordinary water fish, thus diluting the strength of our spirituous food.

We now crossed the river by a ford, and came to some

vines of a most extraordinary kind. Out of the ground came a thick well-grown stem; but the upper part was a woman, complete from the loins upward. They were like our painters' representations of Daphne in the act of turning into a tree just as Apollo overtakes her. From the finger-tips sprang vine twigs, all loaded with grapes; the hair of their heads was tendrils, leaves, and grape-clusters. They greeted us and welcomed our approach, talking Lydian, Indian, and Greek, most of them the last. They went so far as to kiss us on the mouth; and whoever was kissed staggered like a drunken man. But they would not permit us to pluck their fruit, meeting the attempt with cries of pain. Some of them made further amorous advances; and two of my comrades who yielded to these solicitations found it impossible to extricate themselves again from their embraces; the man became one plant with the vine, striking root beside it; his fingers turned to vine twigs, the tendrils were all round him, and embryo grape-clusters were already visible on him.

We left them there and hurried back to the ship, where we told our tale, including our friends' experiment in viticulture. Then after taking some casks ashore and filling them with wine and water we bivouacked near the beach, and next morning set sail before a gentle breeze.

2. *The Isle of Dreams*

Very soon we seemed quite close to the Isle of Dreams, though there was a certain dimness and vagueness about its outline; but it had something dreamlike in its very nature; for as we approached it it receded, and seemed to get further and further off. At last we reached it and sailed into Slumber, the port, close to the ivory gates where stands the temple of the Cock. It was evening when we landed, and upon proceeding to the city we saw many strange dreams. But I intend first to describe the city, as it has not been done before ; Homer indeed mentions it, but gives no detailed description.

The whole place is embowered in wood, of which the trees are poppy and mandragora, all thronged with bats ; this is the only winged thing that exists there. A river, called the Somnambule, flows close by, and there are two springs at the gates, one called Wakenot, and the other Nightlong. The rampart is lofty and of many colours, in the rainbow style. The gates are not two, as Homer says, but four, of which two look on to the plain Stupor ; one of them is of iron, the other of pottery, and we were told that these are used by the grim, the murderous, and the cruel. The other pair face the sea and port, and are of horn—it was by this that we had entered—and of ivory. On the right as you enter the city stands the temple of Night, which deity divides with the Cock their chief allegiance ; the temple of the latter is close to the port. On the left is the palace of Sleep. He is the governor, with two lieutenants, Nightmare, son of Whimsy, and Flittergold, son of Fantasy. A well in the middle of the market-place goes by the name of Heavyhead ; beside which are the temples of Deceit and Truth. In the market also is the shrine in which oracles are given, the priest and prophet, by special appointment from Sleep, being Antiphon the dream-interpreter.

The dreams themselves differed widely in character and appearance. Some were well-grown, smooth-skinned, shapely, handsome fellows, other rough, short, and ugly ; some apparently made of gold, others of common cheap stuff. Among them some were found with wings, and other strange variations ; others again were like the mummers in a pageant, tricked out as kings or gods or what not. Many of them we felt that we had seen in our world, and sure enough these came up and claimed us as old acquaintance ; they took us under their charge, found us lodgings, entertained us with lavish kindness, and, not content with the magnificence of this present reception, promised us royalties and provinces. Some of them also took us to see our friends, doing the return trip all in the day.

For thirty days and nights we abode there—a very feast of sleep.

LUCIAN (Trans. H. W. FOWLER and
F. G. FOWLER)

APOLLONIUS AND KING PORUS

While they were thus talking, the strain of the hymn sung to the flute fell upon their ears, and Apollonius asked the king what was the meaning of their ode. " The Indians," he answered, " sing their admonitions to the king, at the moment of his going to bed ; and they pray that he may have good dreams, and rise up propitious and affable towards his subjects." " And how," said Apollonius, " do you, O king, feel in regard to this matter ? For it is yourself I suppose that they honour with their pipes." " I don't laugh at them," he said, " for I must allow it because of the law, although I do not require any admonition of the kind : for in so far as a king behaves himself with moderation and integrity, he will bestow, I imagine, favours on himself rather than on his subjects."

After this conversation they laid themselves down to repose ; but when the day dawned, the king himself went to the chamber in which Apollonius and his companions were sleeping, and gently stroking the bed he addressed the sage, and asked him what he was thinking about. " For," he said, " I don't imagine you are asleep, since you drink water and despise wine." Said the other : " Then you don't think that those who drink water go to sleep ? " " Yes," said the king, " they sleep, but with a very light sleep, which just sits upon the tips of their eyelids, as we say, but not upon their minds." " Nay, with both do they sleep," said Apollonius, "and perhaps more with the mind than with the eyelids. For unless the mind is thoroughly composed, the eyes will not admit of sleep either. For note how madmen are not able to go to sleep because their mind leaps with excitement, and their thoughts run coursing hither and thither, so that their glances are full of fury and morbid impulse, like those of the dragons who never sleep. . . But those who drink water, as I do, see things as they really are, and they do not record in fancy things that are not ; and they go to bed with a clear, pure soul and welcome sleep, and are neither buoyed up by the bubbles of their own private luck, nor scared out of their wits by any adversity. For the soul meets both alternatives with equal calm, if it be sober and not overcome by either feeling ; and that is why it can sleep a delightful sleep untouched by the sorrows which startle others from their couches.

And more than this, as a faculty of divination by means of dreams, which is the divinest and most godlike of human faculties, the soul detects the truth all the more

429

easily when it is not muddied by wine, but accepts the message unstained and scans it carefully. Anyhow, the explainers of dreams and visions, those whom the poets call interpreters of dreams, will never undertake to explain any vision to anyone without having first asked the time when it was seen. For if it was at dawn and in the sleep of morning-tide, they calculate its meaning on the assumption that the soul is then in a condition to divine soundly and healthily, because by then it has cleansed itself of the stains of wine. But if the vision was seen in the first sleep or at midnight, when the soul is still immersed in the lees of wine and muddied thereby, they decline to make any suggestions, if they are wise. . . And I could mention many oracles, held in repute by Greeks and barbarians alike, where the priest utters his responses from the tripod after imbibing water and not wine. So you may consider me also as a fit vehicle of the god, O king, along with all who drink water. For we are rapt by the nymphs and are bacchantic revellers in sobriety."

From PHILOSTRATUS' *Life of Apollonius* (Trans.
F. C. CONYBEARE—Loeb Classical Library)

DAPHNIS AND CHLOE

It was the beginning of spring, and all the flowers of the lawns, meadows, valleys and hills were now blowing. All was fresh and green. Now was there humming of bees, and chanting of melodious birds, and skipping of newborn lambs ; the bees hummed in the meadows, the birds warbled in the groves, the lambs skipt on the hills. And now, when such a careless joy had filled those blest and happy fields, Daphnis and Chloe, as delicate and young folks will, would imitate the pleasant things they heard and saw. Hearing how the birds did chant it, they began to carol too, and seeing how the lambs skipt, tript their light and nimble measures. Then, to emulate the bees, they fall to cull the fairest flowers; some of which in toysome sport they cast in one another's bosoms, and of some platted garlands for the Nymphs; and always keeping near together, had and did all things in common; for Daphnis often gathered in the straggling sheep, and Chloe often drove the bolder venturous goats from the crags and precipices; and sometimes to one of them the care of both the flocks was left while the other did intend some pretty knack or toysome play.

For all their sports were sports of children and of shepherds. Chloe, scudding up and down and here and there picking up the windlestraws, would make in plats a cage for a grasshopper, and be so wholly bent on that, that she was careless of her flocks. Daphnis on the other side having cut the slender reeds and bored the quills or intervals between the joints, and with his soft wax joined and fitted one to another, took no care but to practise or devise some tune even from morning to the twilight. Their wine and their milk and whatsoever was brought from home to the fields, they had still in common. And a man might sooner see all the cattle separate from one another than he should Chloe and Daphnis asunder.

But while they are thus playing away their time to sweeten pleasure, afterwards Love in good earnest kindled up this fire. A wolf that had a kennel of whelps was come often ravenous upon the neighbouring fields, and had borne away from other flocks many cattle, because she needed much prey to keep herself and those cubs. The villagers therefore meet together, and in the night they dig ditches a fathom wide and four fathom deep ; of the earth flung up they scatter the more part all abroad at a good distance, and laying over-cross the chasm long, dry, and rotten sticks, they strow them over with the earth that did remain, to make the ground like it was before ; that if a hare do but offer to run there, she cannot choose but break those rods that were as brittle as the stubble, and then does easily make it known that that indeed was not true, but only counterfeited soil. Many such trap-ditches were now digged in the mountains and the fields ; yet they could not take this wolf (for she could perceive them because of the sophistic and commentitious ground), but many of their sheep and goats were there destroyed, and there wanted but a little that Daphnis too was not slain. And it was on this chance.

Two he-goats were exasperated to fight, and the shock was furious. One of them, by the violence of the very first butt, had one of his horns broke. Upon the pain and grief of that, all in a fret, and mighty chafe he betakes himself to flight, but the victor, pursuing him close, would not let him take breath. Daphnis was vexed to see the horn broke and that kind of malapertness of the goat. Up he catches a cudgel, and pursues the pursuer. But as it frequently happens when one hastes away as fast as possibly he can and the other with ardency pursues, there was no certain prospect of the things before them, but into the trap-ditch both fall, first the goat, then Daphnis. And indeed it was only this that served to save poor Daphnis, that he flundered down to the bottom a-cock-horse on the rough goat. There in a lamentable case he lay, waiting if perchance it might be somebody to draw him out. Chloe seeing the accident, away she flies to the

432

ditch, and finding he was alive, calls for help to a herdsman of the adjoining fields. When he was come, he
bustled about for a long cord, which holding, Daphnis
might be drawn up ; but finding none, Chloe in a tearing
haste pulls off her stomacher or breastband, gives him it
to let down, and standing on the pitbrim, they both began
to draw and hale ; and Daphnis, holding fast by it, nimbly
followed Chloe's line, and so ascended to the top. They
drew up too the wretched goat, which now had both his
horns broke (so fiercely did the revenge of the vanquished
pursue him); and they gave him to the herdsman to sacrifice, as a reward of the rescue and redemption of their
lives. And if anybody missed him at home, they would say
it was an invasion of wolves. And so returned to see after
their sheep and goats.

And when they had found that all were feeding orderly,
both goats and sheep, sitting down upon the trunk of an
oak they began curiously to search whether he had hurt
any limb in that terrible fall. But nothing was hurt,
nothing bloodied ; only his hair and the rest of his body
were dirtied by mud and the soil which covered over and
hid the trap. And therefore they thought it best before the
accident was made known to Lamo and Myrtale, that he
should wash himself in the cave of the Nymphs.

And coming there together with Chloe, he gave her his
scrip and his shirt to hold, and standing by the spring fell
to washing himself from top to toe. Now his hair was long
and black, and his body all brown and sunburnt, insomuch that the one seemed to have taken colour from the
shadow of the tother ; and to Chloe's eye he seemed of a
sweet and beautiful aspect, and when she wondered that
she had not deemed him such before, she thought it must
be the washing that was the cause of it. And when she

433

washed his back and shoulders the flesh yielded so softly and gently to her hand, that again and again she privily touched herself to see if hers were more delicate than his. Sunset now coming on, they drove home their flocks, and that night there was but one thing in Chloe's mind, and that the wish she might see Daphnis at his washing again.

When they came out to pasture in the morning, and Daphnis, sitting down under the oak where they were wont, played his pipe and watched the flocks that lay around as if to listen to the music of it, Chloe, sitting close by, although she looked well after her sheep, looked better after Daphnis. And piping there, he seemed again to her goodly and beautiful to look to, and wondering again, she thought the cause must be the music ; and so, when he was done, took the pipe from him and played, if haply she herself might be as beautiful. Then she asked him if he would come again to the bath, and when she persuaded him, watched him at it ; and as she watched, put out her hand and touched him ; and before she went home had praised his beauty, and that praise was the beginning of love.

LONGUS (Trans. GEORGE THORNLEY, revised by
J. M. EDMUNDS—Loeb Classical Library)

THE SPINNING WOMAN

Morning and evening, sleep she drove away,
  Old Platthis,—warding hunger from the door,
And still to wheel and distaff hummed her lay
  Hard by the gates of Eld, and bent and hoar ;
Plying her loom until the dawn was grey,
  The long course of Athene did she tread :

With withered hand by withered knee she spun
   Sufficient for the loom of goodly thread,
Till all her work and all her days were done.
   And in her eightieth year she saw the wave
   Of Acheron,—old Platthis,—kind and brave.

LEONIDAS (Trans. A. LANG)

LITTLE POEMS FROM THE GREEK ANTHOLOGY

(Trans. F. A. WRIGHT)

TO ASTER

Thou gazest on the stars ·
   Would I might be,
O star of mine, the skies
With myriad eyes
   To gaze on thee.

PLATO

EPITAPH ON TIMAS: A GIRL WHO DIED BEFORE HER MARRIAGE DAY

Behold the dust of Timas dead ;
   She knew not wedlock's hour,
For ere that day her golden head
   Passed to the Dark Maid's bower.
Yea, she has gone, and all her comrades fair
Have shorn with flashing steel the radiance of
   their hair.

SAPPHO

A Dedication

Old Satyra and Melo bring
The Muses dear their offering :
Melo the flute that oft did please
Her father Antigenides
Whereon her lips would swiftly race,
And with it, see, this boxwood case.
To Satyra this pipe belongs,
Sweet minstrel of a lover's songs,
Companion of the evening revel
Fast bound with wax to make it level,
With it content she played through all the night
Till the sun came and smote the doors with light.

LEONIDAS

Spring Song

Now swallows build beneath the eaves,
And shape anew their rounded home ;
Now meadows smile with tender leaves,
And know that spring has come.

Now is the hour for ships to go,
And lightly o'er the billows leap ;
While winter winds no longer blow
Or vex the ocean deep.

Come then, ye shipmen, hoist the sail,
And from its nest the anchor haul ;
Coil the wet ropes and take the gale ;
Lo I, Priapus, call.

ANTIPATER

EPITAPHS AND EPIGRAMS FROM THE GREEK ANTHOLOGY

(Trans. J. W. MACKAIL)

I. *Epitaphs*

Philip his father laid here the twelve-years-old child, his high hope, Nicoteles.

I am the tomb of one shipwrecked ; but sail thou ; for even while we perished, the other ships sailed on over the sea.

Mariner, ask not whose tomb I am here, but be thine own fortune a kinder sea.

I am the grave of Biton, O wayfarer ; and if leaving Torone thou goest even to Amphipolis, tell Nicagoras that the wind from Strymon at the setting of the Kids lost him his only son.

I, Brotachus of Gortyna, a Cretan, lie here, not having come hither for this, but for traffic.

I, Dionysius of Tarsus, lie here at sixty, having never married ; and I would that my father had not.

Thou who passest on the path, if haply thou dost mark this monument, laugh not, I pray thee, though it is a dog's grave ; tears fell for me, and the dust was heaped above me by a master's hands, who likewise engraved these words on my tomb.

No longer, poor partridge migrated from the rocks, does thy woven house hold thee in its thin withies, nor under the sparkle of fresh-faced Dawn dost thou ruffle up the edges of thy basking wings ; the cat bit off thy head, but the rest of thee I snatched away, and she did not fill her greedy jaw ; and now may the earth cover thee not lightly but heavily, lest she drag out thy remains.

II. *Epigrams*

I know that I am mortal and ephemeral ; but when I scan the multitudinous circling spirals of the stars, no longer do I touch earth with my feet, but sit with Zeus himself, and take my fill of the ambrosial food of gods.

If that which bears all things bears thee, bear thou and be borne ; but if thou art indignant and vexest thyself, even so that which bears all things bears thee.

SONG OF THE TROZENIAN WOMEN

(Phædra, unable to avoid her destiny, has gone to hang herself in the Castle)

Could I take me to some cavern for mine hiding,
   In the hill-tops where the Sun scarce hath trod ;
Or a cloud make the home of mine abiding,
   As a bird among the bird-droves of God !
     Could I wing me to my rest amid the roar
     Of the deep Adriatic on the shore,

Where the waters of Eridanus are clear,
  And Phaëthon's sad sisters by his grave
Weep into the river, and each tear
    Gleams, a drop of amber, in the wave.

To the strand of the Daughters of the Sunset,
  The Apple-tree, the singing and the gold;
Where the mariner must stay him from his onset,
  And the red wave is tranquil as of old;
    Yea, beyond that Pillar of the End
    That Atlas guardeth, would I wend;
Where a voice of living waters never ceaseth
  In God's quiet garden by the sea,
And Earth, the ancient life-giver, increaseth
  Joy among the meadows, like a tree.

EURIPIDES (from *Hippolytus*—
Trans. G. MURRAY)

HERACLITUS

They told me, Heraclitus, they told me you were dead,
They brought me bitter news to hear and bitter tears to
    shed.
I wept as I remember'd how often you and I
Had tired the sun with talking and sent him down the sky.

And now that thou art lying, my dear old Carian guest,
A handful of grey ashes, long, long ago at rest,
Still are thy pleasant voices, thy nightingales, awake;
For Death, he taketh all away, but them he cannot take.

CALLIMACHUS, Ep. II (Trans. WILLIAM CORY)

§3. ROME

SLEEP AND DEATH

Sleep occurs when the substance of the soul has been disturbed throughout the several members, and has partly seceded from the body (as being driven forth abroad,) and has partly, as being more concentrated, retreated into the interior of the body ; for then, at length, when the frame is in this state, the limbs are relaxed and lose their power. Since there is no doubt but that this our vital sense exists in us by means of the soul, which sense when sleep hinders from being exerted, we must then suppose that our soul is disturbed, and expelled from the body ; but not wholly, for if it were all withdrawn, the body would lie steeped in the eternal cold of death, as, in that case, no part of the soul would remain latent in the members, (concealed, as fire lies hidden under thick ashes,) whence the sense might be suddenly rekindled throughout the limbs, and flame, as it were, rise from secret heat.

But by what means this change from wakefulness to sleep is produced, and how the soul may be disturbed, and the body languish, I will explain. Do you, my friend take care that I may not pour out my words to the winds.

In the first place, it necessarily happens that the body since it is touched by the breezes of the air to which it is exposed, must be externally assailed and harassed by the frequent impulse of that air; and, for this reason, almost all animated bodies are covered with hide, or even with shells, or with hard skin, or bark. This same air, likewise, impinges on the interior part of the body of animals, when, as they breathe, it is drawn in and respired. For which reason, when the body is affected from both causes, and when assaults penetrate through the small pores of our frame to its primary parts and first elements, a labefactation, as it were, takes place by degrees throughout our members; for the positions of the elements of the body and mind are disturbed, so that part of the soul is drawn forth from them, and part retires hidden into the interior; part also, dispersed throughout the limbs, cannot remain united together, nor perform its ordinary motions mutually with other parts; for nature obstructs the communications and passages, and therefore, the motions of the atoms being changed, sense wholly fails. And since there remains nothing that can, as it were, prop up the limbs, the body becomes weak, and all its members languish; the arms and the eye-lids fall, and the hams often subside with a sinking lassitude, and relax their strength.

When the mind and body are merely at rest together in sleep, no one will feel concern for himself and his life; for, for our parts, our sleep might thus be eternal; nor does any care for ourselves affect us; and yet, at that season, the atoms, throughout our limbs, withdraw to no great distance from sensible motions, and the man who is suddenly roused from sleep quickly recollects himself. Death, then, we must consider to be of far less concern to us, if less can be than that which we see to be nothing. For a greater separation of the atoms of matter takes place in death, nor does any man awake when once the cold pause of life has overtaken him. . . . Why do you groan and weep at the thought of death? For if your past and former life has been an object of gratification to you, and all your blessings have not, as if poured into a leaky vessel, flowed away and

441

been lost without pleasure, why do you not, O unreasonable man, retire like a guest satisfied with life, and take your undisturbed rest with resignation? But if those things, of which you have had the use, have been wasted and lost, and life is offensive to you, why do you seek to incur further trouble, which may all again pass away and end in dissatisfaction? . . Yield then, with submissive feelings, to that which is stronger than thou; for it is necessary. . . The matter of which thou art made is wanted by nature that succeeding generations may grow up from it; all which, however, when they have passed their appointed term of life, will follow thee; and so have other generations, before these, fallen into destruction; and other generations, not less certainly than thyself, will fall. Thus shall one thing never cease to rise from another; and thus is life given to none in possession, but to all only for use.

LUCRETIUS (from *De Rerum Natura*—
Trans. J. S. WATSON)

THE BEGINNING OF MUSIC

To imitate with the mouth the liquid voices of birds was practised long before men could play melodious tunes, and delight the ear with music. The whistling of the zephyr through the empty reeds first taught the rustics to blow through hollow stalks. Then by degrees they learned the sweet plaintive notes, which the pipe, pressed by the fingers of the players, pours forth—the pipe, which is now found through all the pathless groves and woods and glades, through the solitary haunts and divine resting-places of the shepherds. (Thus time by degrees suggests every discovery, and skill evolves it into the regions of light and fame.) These melodies softened the hearts of those swains, and delighted them when they were satisfied with food ; for then every thing affords pleasure.

LUCRETIUS (from *De Rerum Natura*—
Trans. J. S. WATSON)

SULPICIA'S BIRTHDAY

Juno of the birthday, receive the holy piles of incense which the accomplished maid's soft hand now offers thee. To-day she is thine wholly ; most joyfully she has decked herself for thee, to stand before thy altar a sight for all to see. 'Tis in thee, goddess, she bids us find the reason for this apparelling. Yet there is one that in secret she desires to please. Then, hallowed one, be kind, and let none pluck apart the lovers : but forge, I prithee, like fetters for the youth. Thus shalt thou match them well. There is no maid that he, or man that she might serve more fitly. And may no watchful guard surprise their wooings, but Love suggest a thousand ways for his outwitting. Bow assent and come in all the sheen of purple palla. They are making offering to thee, holy goddess, thrice with cake and thrice with wine, and the mother eagerly enjoins upon her child what she must pray for. But she, now mistress of herself, sues for another thing in the silence of her heart. She burns as the altar burns with the darting flames, nor, even purple; another hoards up wealth, and broods over the gold he has buried in the earth; one is amazed and dazzled at the eloquence of the Rostra; one the applause of commons and patricians, redoubled as it is along the rows of the theatre, sets agape with the shock of joy; some delight to steep themselves in brother's blood, and exchange for a place of exile their homes and pleasant thresholds, and seek a fatherland that lies beneath another sun. The husbandman with his crooked plough furrows the soil; from this comes the work for the year; by this he maintains his country and little grandsons, by this his herds of oxen, and his bullocks that have served him well. And there is never a time of rest; for either in fruits the season richly abounds, or in the offspring of cattle, or in the sheaf of Ceres' stalk, and loads the furrows with increase, and overflows the barns. Then winter comes; in the olive-mill is bruised the berry of Sicyon, the swine come home, well satisfied with mast, the forest gives the fruit of the arbutus, and Autumn drops his various produce, and on the sunny cliffs the mellowing vintage basks.

Meanwhile his dear children hang about his lips, his stainless house preserves its purity; his cows hang down their udders fraught with milk, and fat kids on the smiling lawn with levelled horns against each other strive. The sire himself keeps holy-day, and stretched along the grass, where is a kindled altar in the midst and his companions wreathe the wine-bowl, with a libation invokes thee, O Father of the wine-press, and for the masters of his cattle sets upon an elm the target, for a match at the flying dart, and their wondrous hardy limbs they strip for the rustic wrestling bout. This life of yore the antique Sabines lived, and Remus too, and his brother; so, I ween, brave

Etruria grew, and Rome became the beauty of the world ;
and, one within herself, encompassed with her bulwarks
seven heights. Likewise, before the Cretan king held
sceptred sway, and before an impious age banqueted on
slaughtered bullocks, this was the life that Saturn passed
on earth, the monarch of the golden age ; nor yet too had
they heard the clarion blare, nor sword-blades ring, when
placed on anvils hard.

But we in our career have traversed o'er a vast expanse
of plain, and now 'tis time to loosen from the yoke our
horses' smoking necks.

> From VIRGIL's *Georgics*, Bk. II
>   (Trans. J. LONSDALE and S. LEE)

WINTER NIGHT

See, deep in glistening snow Soracte stands ;
No more the straining woods their load uphold,
The streams are frozen with the piercing cold ;
Pile on the hearth the chill-dispersing brands,
Pour out the Sabine wine, four winters old.

Leave to the gods all else ; when they allay
The winds that battle on the seething seas,
The ancient ashes and the cypress trees
Will shake no longer ; count as gain each day
That Fortune grants ; but never think to tease

Its secret from to-morrow. Now, ere yet
Morose old age thy bloom of beauty stain,
Sweet love and dances thou must not disdain,
Nor shun the places where most oft are met
Whispers of tenderness, when night again

Brings back the trysting hour, and laughs betray
The merry maid in some far corner hid,
Whose ring or bracelet has been snatched, in play
Which she invites, while feigning to forbid.

HORACE, *Odes*, I. 9 (Trans. F. COUTTS
and W. H. POLLOCK)

THE ROMAN PEASANT

How happy in his low degree,
How rich, in humble poverty, is he,
Who leads a quiet country life ;
Discharg'd of business, void of strife,
And from the griping scrivener free ! . .
Sometimes beneath an ancient oak,
Or on the matted grass he lies :
No God of Sleep he need invoke ;
The stream, that o'er the pebbles flies,
With gentle slumber crowns his eyes.
The wind that whistles through the sprays,
Maintains the concert of the song :
And hidden birds with native lays
The golden sleep prolong.
But when the blast of winter blows,
And hoary frost invests the year,
Into the naked woods he goes,
And seeks the tusky boar to rear,
With well-mouth'd hounds and pointed
spear ! . .

Amidst his harmless, easy joys,
   No anxious care invades his health,
Nor love his peace of mind destroys,
   Nor wicked avarice of wealth.
But, if a chaste and pleasing wife,
To ease the business of his life,
Divides with him his household care,
Such as the Sabine matrons were,
Such as the swift Apulian's bride,
   Sunburnt and swarthy though she be,
Will fire for winter nights provide,
   And—without noise—will oversee
   His children and his family :
And order all things till he come,
Sweaty and overlabour'd, home.

            DRYDEN (after **HORACE**, *Epode* 2)

A CAPTIVE OF LOVE

What makes my bed seem hard, seeing it is soft ?
Or why slips down the coverlet so oft ?
Although the nights be long, I sleep not though
My sides are sore with tumbling to and fro.
Were Love the cause, it's like I should descry him ;
Or lies he close, and shoots where none can spy him ?
'Twas so he struck me with a slender dart ;
'Tis cruel Love turmoils my captive heart.
Yielding or struggling, do we give him might ?
Let's yield : a burden easily borne is light !

         MARLOWE (after **OVID**, *Elegies*, I. 2)

THE NOISES OF ROME

Why am I brought so oft, and by what charm,
To dry Nomentum and this humble farm ?
For poor men, Sparsus, who would find a space
For sleep or thinking, Rome affords no place.
You claim to think ; but all deny your right,
By morn schoolmasters, baker's men by night ;
Armies of copper-smiths, a thousand strong,
Go hammer, hammer, hammer, all day long.
Your money-changers here, a lazy horde,
Rattle gold coins upon their dirty board ;
There ponderous mallets, pounding Spanish rock
For lumps of gold, the midnight chamber shock.
Add to the noise Bellona's drunken crew,
The shipwrecked mariner, the begging Jew,
Ay, and blind beggars, selling matches, too !
He who can tell how many clamours keep
The weary Roman from his noonday sleep
Can count the brazen instruments as soon
Of those who beat their gongs to help the Moon.
You, Sparsus, of these plagues can nothing tell,
Who, far-removed, in dainty villa dwell,
And on the slumbering hills look down at home,
To see your farm and vineyards both in Rome.
Your grapes are large as what Falernum stores ;
Your house so spacious you may drive indoors ;
No noise breaks in upon your sleep at night ;
By day naught wakes you but admitted light.
For me the laughter of the passing crowd,
All Rome beneath my bedroom, shrill and loud,
Disgust me with some ever fresh alarm :
Hence, when I wish to sleep, I seek this farm.

MARTIAL—(XII. 57—Trans. W. J. COURTHOPE)

Antonius being thus inclined, the last and extremest mischief of all other (to wit, the love of Cleopatra) lighted on him, who did waken and stir up many vices yet hidden in him, and were never seen to any : and if any spark of goodness or hope of rising were left him, Cleopatra quenched it straight, and made it worse than before. The manner how he fell in love with her was this. Antonius, going to make war with the Partians, sent to command Cleopatra to appear personally before him when he came into Cilicia, to answer unto such accusations as were laid against her, being this : that she had aided Cassius and Brutus in their war against him. The messenger sent unto Cleopatra, to make this summons unto her, was called Dellius ; who when he had thoroughly considered her beauty, the excellent grace and sweetness of her tongue, he nothing mistrusted that Antonius would do any hurt to so noble a lady, but rather assured himself, that within few days she should be in great favour with him. Thereupon he did her great honour, and persuaded her to come into Cilicia, as honourably furnished as she could possible ; and bade her not to be afraid at all of Antonius, for he was a more courteous lord than any that she had ever seen. Cleopatra on the other side, believing Dellius' words, and guessing by the former access and credit she had with Julius Caesar and C. Pompey (the son of Pompey the Great) only for her beauty, she began to have good hope that she might more easily win Antonius. For Caesar and Pompey knew her when she was but a young thing, and knew not then what the world meant : but now she went to Antonius at the age when a woman's beauty is at the prime, and she also of best judgment. So she furnished herself with a world of gifts, store of gold and silver, and of riches and other sumptuous ornaments, as is credible enough she might bring from so great a house, and from so wealthy and rich a realm as Egypt was. But yet she carried nothing with her wherein she trusted more than in herself, and in the charms and enchantment of her passing beauty and grace. Therefore, when she was sent unto by divers letters, both from Antonius himself and also from his friends, she made so light of it, and mocked Antonius so much, that she disdained to set forward otherwise, but to take her barge in the river of Cydnus; the poop whereof was of gold, the sails of purple, and the oars of silver, which kept stroke in rowing after the sound of the music of flutes, howboys, citherns, viols, and such other instruments as they played upon in the barge. And now for the person of her self, she was laid under a pavilion of cloth of gold of tissue, apparelled and attired like the goddess Venus, commonly drawn in picture: and hard by her, on either hand of her, pretty fair boys apparelled as painters do set forth god Cupid, with little fans in their hands, with the which they fanned wind upon her. Her ladies and gentlewomen also, the fairest of them, were apparelled like the nymphs Nereids (which are the mermaids of the waters) and like the Graces; some steering the helm, others tending the tackle and ropes of the barge, out of the which there came a wonderful passing sweet savour of perfumes, that perfumed the wharf's side, pestered with innumerable multitudes of people. Some of them followed the barge all along the river-side: others also ran out of the city to see her coming in. So that in the end, there ran such multitudes of people one after another to see her, that Antonius was left post alone in the market-place, in his imperial seat, to give audience: and there went a rumour in the people's mouths, that the goddess Venus was come to play with the god Bacchus, for the general good of all Asia. When Cleopatra landed, Antonius sent to invite her to supper to him. But she sent him word again, he should do better rather to come and sup with her. Antonius therefore, to shew himself courteous unto her at her arrival, was contented to obey her, and went to supper to her : where he found such passing sumptuous fare, that no tongue can express it. But amongst all other things he most wondered at the infinite number of lights and torches hanged on the top of the house, giving light in every place, so artificially set and ordered by devices, some round, some square : that it was the rarest thing to behold that eye could discern, or that ever books could mention. The next night Antonius, feasting her, contended to pass her in magnificence and fineness ; but she overcame him in both. So that he himself began to scorn the gross service of his house, in respect of Cleopatra's sumptuousness and fineness. And when Cleopatra found Antonius' jests and slents to be but gross and soldier-like, in plain manner, she gave it him finely, and without fear taunted him thoroughly. Now her beauty (as it is reported) was not so passing as unmatchable of other women, nor yet such as upon present view did enamour men with her : but so sweet was her company and conversation, that a man could not possibly but be taken. And besides her beauty, the good grace she had to talk and discourse, her courteous nature that tempered her words and deeds, was a spur that pricked to the quick. Furthermore, besides all these, her voice and words were marvellous pleasant : for her tongue was an instrument of music to divers sports and pastimes, the which she easily turned into any language that pleased her. She spake unto few barbarous people by interpreter, but made them answer her self, or at the least the most part of them ; as the Æthiopians, the Arabians, the Troglodytes, the Hebrews, the Syrians, the Medes, and the Parthians, and to many others also, whose languages she had learned. Whereas divers of her progenitors, the kings of Egypt, could scarce learn the Egyptian tongue only, and many of them forgot to speak the Macedonian.

Now Antonius was so ravished with the love of Cleopatra, that though his wife Fulvia had great wars, and much ado with Caesar for his affairs, and that the army of the Parthians (the which the king's lieutenants had given to the only leading of Labienus) was now assembled in Mesopotamia, ready to invade Syria ; yet (as though all this had nothing touched him) he yielded himself to go with Cleopatra unto Alexandria, where he spent and lost in childish sports (as a man might say) and idle pastimes, the most precious thing a man can spend (as Antiphon saith), and that is, time. For they made an order between them, which they called *Amimetobian* (as much to say, no life comparable and matchable with it), one feasting each other by turns, and in cost exceeding all measure and reason.

From PLUTARCH'S *Lives*

(Trans. SIR THOMAS NORTH
from the French of AMYOT)

SOME MEDITATIONS OF MARCUS AURELIUS CONCERNING HIMSELF

Betimes in the morning say to thy selfe, This day I shall have to doe with an idle curious man, with an unthankfull man, a railer, a crafty, false, or an envious

man ; an unsociable uncharitable man. All these ill
qualities have hapned unto them, through ignorance of
that which is truly good and truly bad. But I that understand the nature of that which is good, that it onely is to
be desired, and of that which is bad, that it onely is truly
odious and shameful : who know moreover, that this
transgressor, whosoever he be, is my kinsman, not by the
same blood and seed, but by participation of the same
reason, and of the same divine particle ; How can I either
be hurt by any of those, since it is not in their power to
make me incurre anything that is truly reproachfull ?

Let it be thy earnest and incessant care as a Romane and
a man to performe whatsoever it is that thou art about,
with true and unfained gravity, naturall affection, freedome
and justice : and as for all other cares, and imaginations,
how thou mayest ease thy minde of them. Which thou
shalt doe ; if thou shalt goe about every action as thy last
action, free from all vanitie, all passionate and wilfull
aberration from reason, and from all hypocrisie, and selfe-
love, and dislike of those things, which by the fates or
appointment of God have hapned unto thee.

If thou shalt finde any thing in this mortall life better
then righteousnesse, then truth, temperance, fortitude,
and in generall better then a minde contented both with
those things which according to right and reason shee
doth, and in those, which without her will and knowledge
happen unto thee by the Providence ; If I say, thou canst
finde out any thing better then this ; apply thy selfe unto
it with thy whole heart, and that which is best whereso-
ever thou dost finde it, injoy freely.

They seeke for themselves private retiring places, as countrey villages, the sea shoare, mountains ; yea thou thy selfe art wont to long much after such places. But all this thou must know proceeds from simplicitie in the highest degree. At what time soever thou wilt, it is in thy power, to retire into thy selfe, and to bee at rest, and free from all businesses.

Whatsoever is now present, and from day to day hath its existence ; all objects of memories, and the mindes and memories themselves, incessantly consider, all things that are, have their being by change, and alteration. Use thy selfe therefore often to meditate upon this, that the Nature of the Universe delights in nothing more, then in altering those things that are, and in making others like unto them. So that wee may say, that whatsoever is, is but as it were the seed of that which shall be.

Let this be thy only joy, and thy only comfort, from one sociable kinde action without intermission to passe unto another, God being ever in thy minde.

Hee that seeth the things that are now, hath seene all that either was ever, or ever shall be, for all things are of one kinde ; and all like one unto another. Meditate often upon the connexion of all things in the world ; and upon the mutuall relation that they have one unto another.

How all things upon Earth are pesle mesle ; and how miraculously things contrary one to another, concurre to the beautie and perfection of this Universe.

Remember, that to change thy minde upon occasion, and to follow him that is able to rectifie thee, is equally ingenuous, as to finde out at the first what is right and just, without helpe.

O my soule, the time I trust will be when thou shalt be good, simple, single, more open and visible then that body by which it is inclosed. Thou wilt one day be sensible of their happinesse, whose end is love.

In the morning when thou findest thyselfe unwilling to rise, consider with thyselfe presently it is to goe about a mans worke that I am stirred up. Am I then yet unwilling to goe about that, for which I myselfe was borne and brought forth into this world? Or was I made for this, to lay me downe, and make much of myself in a warme bed?

From *The Golden Book*
(Trans. MERIC CASAUBON, 1634)

§ 4. GÖTTERDÄMMERUNG

That ancient world perished ; and all the while, side by side with it, a new world was growing up ... Even through the long swoon of art which is usually thought of as following the darkness of the third century, the truth was that art was transforming itself into new shapes and learning a new language. The last wisdom of the Neo-Platonic philosophy was barely said when the Church of the Holy Wisdom rose in Constantinople, the most perfect work of art that has yet been known in organic beauty of design and splendour of ornament ; and when Justinian by his closure of the schools of Athens marked off, as by a precise line, the end of the ancient world, in the Greek monasteries of Athos new types of beauty were being slowly wrought out which passed outward from land to land, transfiguring the face of the world as they went.

It is only in the growth and life of that new world that the decay and death of the old can be regarded with equanimity, or can in a certain sense be historically justified ; for Greek civilization was and still is so incomparable that its loss might otherwise fill the mind with despair, and seem to be the last irony cast by fate against the idea of human progress. But it is the law of all Nature, from her highest works to her lowest, that life only comes by death ; " she replenishes one thing out of another," in the words of the Roman poet, " and does not suffer anything to be begotten before she has been recruited by the death of something else."

J. W. MACKAIL (from Introduction to *Selections from the Greek Anthology*)

B.C. AND A.D.

Soles occidere et redire possunt:
Nobis, cum semel occidit brevis lux,
Nox est perpetua una dormienda.

CATULLUS, V.

Behold, I shew you a mystery ! The trumpet shall sound,
and the dead shall be raised incorruptible ; for this mortal
must put on immortality. Then shall be brought to pass
the saying that is written : " Death is swallowed up in
victory."

I CORINTHIANS (A.V.)

THIRD PART

§ II ROMANCE AND FAIRIES

So whan I saw I might not slepe
Til now late, this other nyght
Upon my bedde I sat upryght
And bad oon rechė me a book,
A ròmaunce, and he hit me took
To rede, and dryve the nyght away.

CHAUCER

Sweet friends, to bed ! . . .
To bed ; 'tis almost fairy time.

SHAKESPEARE (*Midsummer Night's Dream*)

§11 ROMANCE AND FAIRIES

THE SEVEN SLEEPERS

Among the insipid legends of ecclesiastical history, I am tempted to distinguish the memorable fable of the Seven Sleepers; whose imaginary date corresponds with the reign of the younger Theodosius and the conquest of Africa by the Vandals. When the emperor Decius persecuted the Christians, seven noble youths of Ephesus concealed themselves in a spacious cavern in the side of an adjacent mountain; where they were doomed to perish by the tyrant, who gave orders that the entrance should be firmly secured with a pile of huge stones. They immediately fell into a deep slumber, which was miraculously prolonged, without injuring the powers of life, during a period of one hundred and eighty-seven years. At the end of that time, the slaves of Adolius, to whom the inheritance of the mountain had descended, removed the stones, to supply materials for some rustic edifice; the light of the sun darted into the cavern, and the seven sleepers were permitted to awake. After a slumber, as they thought, of a few hours, they were pressed by the calls of hunger; and resolved that Jamblichus, one of their number, should secretly return to the city, to purchase bread for the use of his companions. The youth (if we may still employ that appellation) could no longer recognise the once familiar aspect of his native country; and his surprise was increased by the appearance of a large cross, triumphantly erected over the principal gate of Ephesus. His singular dress and obsolete language confounded the baker, to whom he offered an ancient medal of Decius as the current coin of the empire ; and Jamblichus, on the suspicion of a secret treasure, was dragged before the judge. Their mutual inquiries produced the amazing discovery that two centuries were almost elapsed since Jamblichus and his friends had escaped from the rage of a Pagan tyrant. The bishop of Ephesus, the clergy, the magistrates, the people, and, as it is said, the emperor Theodosius himself, hastened to visit the cavern of the Seven Sleepers ; who bestowed their benediction, related their story, and at the same instant peaceably expired. The origin of this marvellous fable cannot be ascribed to the pious fraud and credulity of the *modern* Greeks, since the authentic tradition may be traced within half a century of the supposed miracle. James of Sarug, a Syrian bishop, who was born only two years after the death of the younger Theodosius, has devoted one of his two hundred and thirty homilies to the praise of the young men of Ephesus. Their legend before the end of the sixth century was translated from the Syriac into the Latin language, by the care of Gregory of Tours. The hostile communions of the East preserve their memory with equal reverence ; and their names are honourably inscribed in the Roman, the Abyssinian, and the Russian calendar. Nor has their reputation been confined to the Christian world. This popular tale, which Mahomet might learn when he drove his camels to the fairs of Syria, is introduced, as a divine revelation, into the Koran. The story of the Seven Sleepers has been adopted, and adorned, by the nations, from Bengal to Africa, who profess the Mahometan religion ; and some vestiges of a similar tradition have been discovered in the remote extremities of Scandinavia. This easy and universal belief, so expressive of the sense of mankind, may be ascribed to the genuine merit of the fable itself. We imperceptibly advance from youth to age without observing the gradual but incessant change of human affairs, and, even in our larger experience of history, the imagination is accustomed, by a perpetual series of causes and effects, to unite the most distant revolutions. But, if the interval between two memorable æras could be instantly annihilated—if it were possible, after a momentary slumber of two hundred years, to display the *new* world to the eyes of a spectator who still retained a lively and recent impression of the *old*—his surprise and his reflections would furnish the pleasing subject of a philosophical romance.

> GIBBON (from *Decline and Fall of the Roman Empire*, Ch. 33)

THE MARRIAGE OF PSYCHE

Men sailed no longer to Paphos, to Cnidus or Cythera, to the presence of the goddess Venus ; her sacred rites were neglected, her images stood uncrowned, the cold ashes were left to disfigure her forsaken altars. It was to a maiden that men's prayers were offered, to a human countenance they looked, in propitiating so great a godhead : when the girl went forth in the morning they strewed flowers on her way, and the victims proper to that unseen goddess were presented as she passed along. This conveyance of divine worship to a mortal kindled meantime the anger of the true Venus. " Lo ! now the ancient parent of nature," she cried, " the fountain of all elements ! Behold me, Venus, benign mother of the world, sharing my honours with a mortal maiden, while my name, built up in heaven, is profaned by the mean things of earth !

Shall a perishable woman bear my image about with her ? In vain did the shepherd of Ida prefer me ! Yet shall she have little joy, whosoever she be, of her usurped and unlawful loveliness ! " Thereupon she called to her that winged, bold boy, of evil ways, who wanders armed by night through men's houses, spoiling their marriages ; and stirring yet more by her speech his inborn wantonness, she led him to the city and showed him Psyche as she walked.

" I pray thee," she said, " give thy mother a full revenge. Let this maid become the slave of an unworthy love." Then, embracing him closely, she departed to the shore and took her throne upon the crest of the wave. And lo ! at her unuttered will, her ocean-servants are in waiting : the daughters of Nereus are there singing their song, and Portunus, and Salacia, and the tiny charioteer of the dolphin, with a host of Tritons leaping through the billows. And one blows softly through his sounding seashell, another spreads a silken web against the sun, a third presents the mirror to the eyes of his mistress, while the others swim side by side below, drawing her chariot. Such was the escort of Venus as she went upon the sea.

Psyche meantime, aware of her loveliness, had no fruit thereof. All people regarded and admired, but none sought her in marriage. It was but as upon the finished work of the craftsman that they gazed upon that divine likeness. Her sisters, less fair than she, were happily wedded. She, even as a widow, sitting at home, wept over her desolation, hating in her heart the beauty in which all men were pleased.

And the king, supposing that the gods were angry, inquired of the oracle of Apollo, and Apollo answered him thus : " Let the damsel be placed on the top of a certain mountain, adorned as for the bed of marriage and of death. Look not for a son-in-law of mortal birth ; but for that evil serpent-thing, by reason of whom even the gods tremble and the shadows of Styx are afraid."

So the king returned home and made known the oracle to his wife. For many days she lamented, but at last the fulfilment of the divine precept was urgent upon her, and the company was made ready to conduct the maiden to her deadly bridal. And now the nuptial torch gathers dark smoke and ashes ; the pleasant sound of the pipe changes into a cry ; the marriage hymn concludes in a sorrowful wailing. Below her yellow wedding-veil the bride shook away her tears : insomuch that the whole city was afflicted together at the ill-luck of the stricken house.

But the mandate of the god impelled the hapless Psyche to her fate, and, those solemnities being ended, the funeral of the living soul goes forth, all the people following. Psyche, bitterly weeping, assists not at her marriage but at her own obsequies, and while the parents hesitate to accomplish a thing so unholy the daughter cries to them : " Wherefore torment your luckless age by long weeping ? This was the prize of my extraordinary beauty ! When all people celebrated us with divine honours, and with one voice named the *New Venus*, it was then ye should have wept for me as one dead. Now at last I understand that that one name of Venus has been my ruin. Lead me and set me upon the appointed place. I am in haste to submit to that well-omened marriage, to behold that goodly spouse. Why delay the coming of him who was born for the destruction of the whole world ? "

She was silent, and with firm step went on the way. And they proceeded to the appointed place on a steep mountain, and left there the maiden alone, and took their way homewards dejectedly. The wretched parents, in their close-shut house, yielded themselves to perpetual night ; while to Psyche, fearful and trembling and weeping sore upon the mountain-top, comes the gentle Zephyrus. He lifts her gently, and, with vesture floating on either side, bears her by his own soft breathing over the windings of the hills, and sets her lightly among the flowers in the bosom of a valley below.

Psyche, in those delicate grassy places, lying sweetly on her dewy bed, rested from the agitation of her soul and arose in peace. And lo ! a grove of mighty trees, with a fount of water, clear as glass, in the midst ; and hard by the water, a dwelling-place, built not by human hands but by some divine cunning. One recognized, even at the entering, the delightful hostelry of a god. Golden pillars sustained the roof, arched most curiously in cedar-wood and ivory. The walls were hidden under wrought silver :—all tame and woodland creatures leaping forward to the visitor's gaze. Wonderful indeed was the craftsman, divine or half-divine, who by the subtlety of his art had breathed so wild a soul into the silver. The very pavement was distinct with pictures in goodly stones. In the glow of its precious metal the house is its own daylight, having no need of the sun. Well might it seem a place fashioned for the conversation of gods with men !

Psyche, drawn forward by the delight of it, came near, and her courage growing, stood within the doorway. One by one, she admired the beautiful things she saw ; and, most wonderful of all ! no lock, no chain, nor living guardian protected that great treasure-house. But as she gazed there came a voice—a voice, as it were unclothed of its bodily vesture—" Mistress ! " it said, " all these things are thine. Lie down, and relieve thy weariness, and rise again for the bath when thou wilt. We thy servants, whose voice thou hearest, will be beforehand with our service, and a royal feast shall be ready."

And Psyche understood that some divine care was providing, and, refreshed with sleep and the bath, sat down to the feast. Still she saw no one; only she heard words falling here and there, and had voices alone to serve her. And the feast being ended, one entered the chamber and sang to her unseen, while another struck the chords of a harp, invisible with him who played on it. Afterwards, the sound of a company singing together came to her, but still so that none was present to sight; yet it appeared that a great multitude of singers was there.

And the hour of evening inviting her, she climbed into the bed; and as the night was far advanced, behold a sound of a certain clemency approaches her. Then, fearing for her maidenhood, in so great solitude, she trembled, and more than any evil she knew dreaded that she knew not. And now the husband, that unknown husband, drew near, and ascended the couch, and made her his wife; and lo! before the rise of dawn he had departed hastily. And the attendant voices ministered to the needs of the newly married. And so it happened with her for a long season.

WALTER PATER (from *Marius the Epicurean*)

THE DEAD AT CLONMACNOIS
(*From the Irish*)

In a quiet water'd land, a land of roses,
    Stands Saint Kieran's city fair;
And the warriors of Erin in their famous generations
    Slumber there.

There beneath the dewy hillside sleep the noblest
    Of the clan of Conn,
Each below his stone with name in branching Ogham
    And the sacred knot thereon.

There they laid to rest the seven Kings of Tara,
    There the sons of Cairbrè sleep—
Battle-banners of the Gael that in Kieran's plain of
        crosses
    Now their final hosting keep.

And in Clonmacnois they laid the men of Teffia,
    And right many a lord of Breagh ;
Deep the sod above Clan Creidè and Clan Conaill,
    Kind in hall and fierce in fray.

Many and many a son of Conn the Hundred-fighter
    In the red earth lies at rest ;
Many a blue eye of Clan Colman the turf covers,
    Many a swan-white breast.

T. W. ROLLESTON

THE LITTLE BLACK ROSE

The little black rose shall be red at last ;
What made it black but the March wind dry,
And the tear of the widow that fell on it fast ?
It shall redden the hills when June is nigh.

The Silk of the Kine shall rest at last ;
What drove her forth but the dragon-fly ?

In the golden vale she shall feed full fast
With her mild gold horn and slow dark eye.

The wounded wood dove lies dead at last !
The pine long bleeding it shall not die !
This song is secret—mine ear it passed
In a wind on the plains at Athenry.

AUBREY DE VERE

THE COMPLAINT OF TROILUS FOR CRESSIDA REMOVED TO THE GRECIAN CAMP

On morwe, as sone as day bigan to clere,
This Troilus gan of his slep t'abreyde,
And to Pandàre, his ownè brother dere,
' For love of God,' full pitousliche he seyde,
' As go we sen the paleis of Criseyde :
For sin we yit may han no morè feste,
So lat us sen her paleis at the leste ! ' . .

Therwith whan he was war and gan biholde
How shet was every window of the place,
As frost, him thoughte, his hertè gan to colde ;
For-which with chaungèd dedlich palè face,
Withouten word he forth-by gan to pace ;
And, as God wolde, he gan so fastè ride,
That no wight of his contenaunce espi'de.

Than seide he thus : ' O paleis desolat,
O hous, of houses whilom best y-hight,
O paleis empty and disconsolat,
O thou lantèrne of which queynt is the light,
O paleis, whilom day that now art night,
Wel oughtestow to falle, and I to dye,
Sin she is went that wont was us to gye !

' O paleis, whilom crowne of houses alle,
Enluminèd with sonne of allè blisse !
O ring, fro which the ruby is out-falle,
O cause of wo, that cause hast been of lisse !
Yit, sin I may no bet, fayn wolde I kisse
Thy coldè dorès, dorste I for this route :
And far-wel shrine, of which the seynt is oute ! ' . .

Fro thennèsforth he rideth up and down,
And everything com him to rèmembraunce
As he rod for-by places of the town
In which he whilom hadde al his plesàunce.
' Lo, yonder saw I last my lady daunce !
And in that templè with her ẏen clere
Me caughtè first my rightè lady dere ! ' . .

Upon the wallès faste ek wolde he walke,
And on the Grekès cost he woldè see,
And to himself right thus he woldè talke,
' Lo, yonder is myn ownè lady free !
Or ellès yonder ther the tentès be !
And thennèscom'th this eir that is so swote,
That in my soule I fele it doth me bote !

' And, hardily, this wind, that more and more
Thus stoundemele encresseth in my face,
Is of my lady's depè sikès sore !
I preve it thus, for in non other space
Of al this town, save only in this place,
Fele I no wind that souneth so lik peyne :
It seith, " Allas ! why twinnèd be we tweyne ? " '

CHAUCER (from Troilus and Cressida)

THE GOOD OLD TIMES

In tholdè dayès of the Kyng Arthòur,
Of which that Britons speken greet honòur,
All was this land fulfild of faèrye.
The elf queene with hir joly compaignye
Dauncèd ful ofte in many a grenè mede.
This was the olde opinion as I rede,—
I speke of manye hundred yeres ago,—
But now kan no man se none elvès mo.

CHAUCER (from Wife of Bath's Tale)

THE END OF A GREAT LOVE STORY

Then came Sir Bors de Ganis, and said, My Lord Sir
Launcelot, what think ye for to do, now to ride in this
realm ? wit thou well ye shall find few friends. Be as be
may, said Sir Launcelot, keep you still here, for I will
forth on my journey, and no man nor child shall go with
me. So it was no boot to strive, but he departed and rode

westerly, and there he sought a seven or eight days, and at the last he came to a nunnery, and then was queen Guenever ware of Sir Launcelot as he walked in the cloister, and when she saw him there she swooned thrice, that all the ladies and gentlewomen had work enough to hold the queen up. So when she might speak, she called ladies and gentlewomen to her, and said, Ye marvel, fair ladies, why I make this fare. Truly, she said, it is for the sight of yonder knight that yonder standeth : wherefore, I pray you all, call him to me. When Sir Launcelot was brought to her, then she said to all the ladies, Through this man and me hath all this war been wrought, and the death of the most noblest knights of the world ; for through our love that we have loved together is my most noble lord slain. Therefore, Sir Launcelot, wit thou well I am set in such a plight to get my soul's health ; and yet I trust, through God's grace, that after my death to have a sight of the blessed face of Christ, and at doomsday to sit on his right side, for as sinful as ever I was are saints in heaven. Therefore, Sir Launcelot, I require thee and beseech thee heartily, for all the love that ever was betwixt us, that thou never see me more in the visage ; and I command thee on God's behalf, that thou forsake my company, and to thy kingdom thou turn again and keep well thy realm from war and wrack. For as well as I have loved thee, mine heart will not serve me to see thee ; for through thee and me is the flower of kings and knights destroyed. Therefore, Sir Launcelot, go to thy realm, and there take thee a wife, and live with her with joy and bliss, and I pray thee heartily pray for me to our Lord, that I may amend my mis-living. Now, sweet madam, said Sir Launcelot, would ye that I should return again unto my country, and there to wed a lady ? Nay, madam, wit you well that shall I never do : for I shall never be so false to you of that I have promised, but the same destiny that ye have taken you to, I will take me unto, for to please Jesu, and ever for you I cast me specially to pray. If thou wilt do so, said the queen, hold thy promise; but I may never believe but that thou wilt turn to the world again. Well, madam, said he, ye say as pleaseth you, yet wist you me never false of my promise, and God defend but I should forsake the world as ye have done. For in the quest of the Sancgreal I had forsaken the vanities of the world, had not your lord been. And if I had done so at that time with my heart, will, and thought, I had passed all the knights that were in the Sancgreal, except Sir Galahad my son. And therefore, lady, sithen ye have taken you to perfection, I must needs take me to perfection of right. For I take record of God, in you I have had mine earthly joy. And if I had found you now so disposed, I had cast me to have had you into mine own realm.

But sithen I find you thus disposed, I insure you faithfully I will ever take me to penance, and pray while my life lasteth, if that I may find any hermit either grey or white that will receive me. Wherefore, madam, I pray you kiss me, and never no more. Nay, said the queen, that shall I never do, but abstain you from such works. And they departed. But there was never so hard an hearted man, but he would have wept to see the dolour that they made. For there was lamentation as they had been stung with spears, and many times they swooned. And the ladies bare the queen to her chamber, and Sir Launcelot awoke, and went and took his horse, and rode all that day and all that night in a forest, weeping. And at the last he was ware of an hermitage and a chapel stood betwixt two cliffs, and then he heard a little bell ring to mass, and thither he rode and alight, and tied his horse to the gate, and heard mass, . . and there he served God day and night with prayers and fastings. And thus upon a night there came a vision to Sir Launcelot, and charged him, in remission of his sins, to haste him unto Almesbury,— And by then thou come there, thou shalt find queen Guenever dead : and therefore take thy fellows with thee, and purvey them of an horse bier, and fetch thou the corpse of her, and bury her by her husband the noble king Arthur. So this vision came to Launcelot thrice in one night.

Then Sir Launcelot rose up or day, and told the hermit. It were well done, said the hermit, that ye made you ready, and that ye disobey not the vision. Then Sir Launcelot took his seven fellows with him, and on foot they went from Glastonbury to Almesbury, the which is little more than thirty miles. And thither they came within two days, for they were weak and feeble to go. And when Sir Launcelot was come to Almesbury, within the nunnery, queen Guenever died but half an hour before. . . Then Sir Launcelot saw her visage, but he wept not greatly, but sighed. And so he did all the observance of the service himself, both the Dirige, and on the morn he sang mass. And there was ordained an horse bier : and so with an hundred torches ever burning about the corpse of the queen, and ever Sir Launcelot with his eight fellows went about the horse bier singing and reading many an holy orison, and frankincense upon the corpse incensed. Thus Sir Launcelot and his eight fellows went on foot from Almesbury unto Glastonbury : and when they were come to the chapel and the hermitage, there she had a Dirige with great devotion. And on the morn the hermit, that sometime was Bishop of Canterbury, sang the mass of

Requiem with great devotion : and Sir Launcelot was the first that offered, and then all his eight fellows. And then she was wrapped in cered cloth of Raines, from the top to the toe in thirty fold, and after she was put in a web of lead, and then in a coffin of marble. And when she was put in the earth, Sir Launcelot swooned, and lay long still, and never after eat but little meat, nor drank, till he was dead. . . So at a season of the night they went all to their beds, for they all lay in one chamber. And so after midnight, against day, when Sir Bors and his fellows came to his bed they found him stark dead, and he lay as he had smiled, and the sweetest savour about him that ever they felt. Then was there weeping and wringing of hands, and the greatest dole they made that ever made men. And on the morn the bishop did his mass of Requiem ; and after the bishop and all the nine knights put Sir Launcelot in the same horse bier that queen Guenever was laid in tofore that she was buried : and so the bishop and they altogether went with the corpse of Sir Launcelot daily, till they came to Joyous Gard, . . and ever they had a hundred torches burning about him ; and so within fifteen days they came to Joyous Gard. And there they laid his corpse in the body of the quire, and sang and read many psalters and prayers over him and about him ; and ever his visage was laid open and naked, that all folk might behold him ; for such was the custom in those days, that all men of worship should so lie with open visage till that they were buried. And right thus as they were at their service, there came Sir Ector de Maris, that had seven year sought all England, Scotland, and Wales, seeking his brother Sir Launcelot.

And when Sir Ector heard such noise and light in the quire of Joyous Gard, he alight and put his horse from him, and came into the quire, and there he saw men sing and weep. And they all knew Sir Ector, but he knew not them. Then went Sir Bors unto Sir Ector, and told him how there lay his brother Sir Launcelot dead. And then Sir Ector threw his shield, sword, and helm from him ; and when he beheld Sir Launcelot's visage he fell down in a swoon. And when he awaked it were hard any tongue to tell the doleful complaints that he made for his brother. Ah, Launcelot, he said, thou were head of all christian knights ; and now I dare say, said Sir Ector, thou Sir Launcelot, there thou liest, that thou were never matched of earthly knight's hand ; and thou were the courtiest knight that ever bare shield ; and thou were the truest friend to thy lover that ever bestrode horse ; and thou were the truest lover of a sinful man that ever loved woman ; and thou were the kindest man that ever strake with sword ; and thou were the goodliest person ever came among press of knights ; and thou was the meekest man and the gentlest that ever ate in hall among ladies ; and thou were the sternest knight to thy mortal foe that ever put spear in the rest.

SIR THOMAS MALORY (from *Le Morte Darthur*)

THE ESCAPE OF NICOLETTE

It befel in the fair summer time, in the month of May, when the long days are warm and the nights are blissful and still, that Nicolette lay on her bed, and watched the moon shine clear through her window, and likewise heard the nightingale sing in the garden. Then was she mindful of her friend Aucassin whom she loved so well. Now the old woman who guarded her slept full soundly; so she arose and tired herself in a goodly tunic of silk that she had at hand, and took up napkins and sheets of the bed and knotted one to the other, and very featly she made a rope as long as she could and tied it to a pillar of the window. Therewith she let herself down unto the ground and caught her raiment in both hands, behind and before, and tucked it up because there was much dew on the grass, and so made her way through the moonlit garden.

Her locks were fair and curly, her eyes bright and smiling, her face of a good length, her nose high and well set, her lips more red than cherry or rose in summer, her teeth white and small; her breasts so firm that they bore up her tunic as they had been two large nuts; so slim she was that your two hands might have girdled her waist, and the daisy-flowers that brake beneath her toes and bent above them seemed black against her feet, so very white was this maiden.

Quietly she unlocked the postern gate and passed into the streets of Beaucaire, and keeping within the shadows of the houses (for the moon shone very clearly) she went on till that she came to the tower where Aucassin was shut up. She crouched behind one of the pillars, and putting her ear to a chink in the wall, heard Aucassin making a great dole and sorrowing for his sweet friend.

When she had listened to him long enough she began to speak.

Now Aucassin was filled with dismay when he heard Nicolette tell how she would go away to another land, because his father hated her. " Fair sweet friend," said he, " indeed you shall not go away, for that would kill me."

While he was so saying, the town watch were searching the streets with their swords drawn under their cloaks.

Now the sentinel on the tower (who was a gallant man and kindly withal) heard them talking of Nicolette and saying that she must be put to death.

"Alas!" he thought, "what a pity to slay so fair a maiden! It were a kindness to make her ware of this danger."

And very cleverly the sentinel began to sing. Now his song was a warning to Nicolette, but the watch took it for an old ballad that he sang to himself.

"Ah!" said Nicolette, "may the souls of your father and mother have sweet repose, because of those gentle and gracious words. If it so please God, I shall now make myself safe."

So she wrapped her cloak full closely about her, and crouching in the deep shadow deftly hid herself until the watch had passed. Then she tarried no longer, but took leave of her dear Aucassin, and, climbing the castle wall which was of a great age and partly broken, so came to a narrow place between the high wall and the steep moat. Now the moat was of a great depth and full of darkness, and Nicolette was sorely afraid.

"Alas!" thought she, "if I fall in this perilous place I shall break my neck, and if I go back I shall be taken to prison as soon as the sun shines."

So she made the sign of the cross, and slid down to the bottom of the moat, which was dried up. Her dainty feet and her fair hands were sorely cut and bruised, but she faced the other side bravely and clomb up with much pain, and came at length to the top. At a bowshot from the moat lay a great forest, and hither Nicolette made her way. Now in this forest dwelt beasts of a savage kind and baneful serpents, and at first she feared to enter it, thinking these would devour her. Then she remembered the terrible Count of Beaucaire. If she went back to the town she would be taken to his prison, and perchance afterwards she would be burned to death. So she entered the great forest, and, lying down in a bushy place, she fell asleep. When she awoke the birds were singing gaily all round her, and she was ware of a company of herd boys who had driven their beasts into the forest and were eating their breakfast at a beautiful spring near by. Nicolette arose and ran towards them.

"Fair youths," she called out, "may God have you in His keeping!"

"And may God bless you also!" replied one who was more ready of tongue than the others.

Then Nicolette begged them that they seek out Aucassin, the son of Count Garin of Beaucaire, and have him to come hunting in that forest, for that he would find there a beast he would not lose the chance of taking for all the wealth in the world.

Aucassin and Nicolette (from the Old French
—Trans. A. S.)

HOW BRUIN THE BEAR WAS SPED OF REYNARD THE FOX

Now is Bruin gone on his way toward the Fox in a stout mood, which supposed well that the Fox should not have beguiled him. As he came in a dark wood in a forest where Reynard had a bypath when he was hunted, there beside was a high mountain and land, and there must Bruin go over in the middle for to go to Maleperduys. For

Reynard had many a dwelling place, but the Castle of Maleperduys was the best and the safest burrow that he had. There lay he in, when he had need and was in any dread or fear. Now when Bruin was come to Maleperduys, he found the gate fast shut. Then went he before the gate, and sat upon his tail, and called : " Reynard, be ye at home ? I am Bruin. The King hath sent me for you that you should come to Court, for to plead your cause. He hath sworn there by his God, come ye not or bring I you not with me for to abide such right and sentence as shall be there given, it shall cost you your life. He will hang you or set you on the rack. Reynard, do by my counsel, and come to the Court."

Reynard lay within the gate, as he oft was wont to do, for the warmth of the sun. When Reynard heard Bruin, then went he inward into his hole. For Maleperduys was full of holes—here one hole and there another, and yonder another—narrow, crooked and long, with many ways to go out, which he opened and shut after that he had need. When he had brought any prey home, or wist that any sought him for his misdeeds and trespasses, then he ran and hid him from his enemies into his secret chambers that they could not find him : by which he deceived many a beast that sought him. And then thought Reynard in himself how he might best bring the Bear to trouble, and that *he* abode in credit.

In this thought Reynard came out, and said : " Bruin, uncle, ye be welcome ! I heard you well before, but I was in mine evensong—therefore have I the longer tarried a little. Dear uncle, he hath done to you no good service, and I owe him no thanks that hath sent you over this long hill ; for I see that ye be also weary that the sweat runneth down by your cheeks. It was no need : I had nevertheless come to Court to-morrow; and I sorrow now the less, for your wise counsel shall well help me in the Court. And could the King find none less messenger but you for to send hither? That is great wonder. For, next the King, ye be the most gentle, and richest of levies and of land. I would well that we were now at the Court, but I fear me that I shall not well know how to go thither, for I have eaten so much new food that methinketh my belly will break or cleave asunder, and because the food was new I ate the more."

Then spake the Bear : " Dear nephew, what food have ye eaten that made you so full ? "

" Dear uncle, what I ate, what might it help you if I told you ? I ate but simple food. A poor man is no Lord, that may ye know, uncle, by me. We poor folk must eat oftimes such as we gladly would not eat if we had better. They were great honeycombs; which I must needs eat for hunger. They have made my belly so great that I can nowhere endure."

Bruin then spake anon : " Alas, Reynard, what say ye ! Set ye so little by honey ? I prize and love it above all food. Dear Reynard, help me that I might get a deal of this honey, and as long as I live I shall be to you a true friend, and abide by you, as far as ye help me that I may have a part of this honey."

" Bruin, uncle, I would have supposed that ye had jested therewith."

" So help me God, Reynard, nay. I should not gladly jest with you."

Then spake the red Reynard : " Is it then earnest, that ye love so well the honey ? I shall see that you have so much that ten of you should not eat it at one meal, might I get therewith your friendship."

"Not we ten, Reynard nephew!" said the Bear. "How should that be? Had I all the honey that is between this and Portugal, I should well eat it alone."

Reynard said: "What say ye, uncle? Hereby dwelleth a husbandman named Lantfert, which hath so much honey that ye could not eat it in seven years; which ye shall have in your hold if ye will be to me friendly and helping against mine enemies in the King's Court."

Then promised Bruin the Bear to him that, if he might have his belly full, he would truly be to him before all other a faithful friend.

Hereof laughed Reynard the knave, and said: "If ye would have seven amber barrels full, I shall well get them, and help you to have them." These words pleased the Bear so well, and made him so much to laugh that he could not well stand.

Then thought Reynard: "This is good luck; I shall lead him thither that he shall laugh *by measure*."

Reynard said then: "This matter may not be long delayed. I must pain myself for you. Ye shall well understand the very favour and goodwill that I bear toward you. I know none in all my lineage that I now would labour for thus sore."

That thanked him the Bear, and thought he tarried long.

"Now, uncle, let us go a good pace, and follow ye me. I shall make you to have as much honey as ye may bear." The Fox meant, of good strokes; but the caitiff marked not what the Fox meant; and they went so long together that they came unto Lantfert's yard. Then was Sir Bruin merry.

Now hark of Lantfert. If it is true what men say,

Lantfert was a strong carpenter of great timber, and had brought the day before into his yard a great oak, which he begun to cleave. And, as men be accustomed, he had smitten two wedges therein one after the other, in such wise the oak was wide open. Whereof Reynard was glad, for he had found it exactly as he wished, and said to the Bear all laughing : " See now well sharply to it ! In this tree is so much honey that it is *without measure.* Try if ye can come therein ; and eat but little, for, though the honeycombs be sweet and good, yet beware that ye eat not too many, but take of them *by measure,* that ye catch no harm in your body ; for, sweet uncle, I should be blamed if they did you any harm."

" What, Reynard, cousin, trouble yourself not for me ! Ween ye that I were a fool ? "

" *Measure* is good in all food," Reynard said. " Ye say truth. Wherefore should I trouble myself ? Go to the end, and creep therein ! "

Bruin the Bear hasted sore toward the honey, and trode in with his two foremost feet, and put his head over his ears into the cleft of the tree. And Reynard sprang lightly and brake out the wedges of the tree. Then helped the Bear neither flattering ne chiding : he was fast shut in the tree. Thus hath the nephew, with deceit, brought his uncle in prison in the tree, in such wise as he could not get out with might ne with craft, head ne foot.

What profiteth Bruin the Bear that he strong and hardy is ? That may not help him. He saw well that he was beguiled. He began to howl, and to bellow, and scratched with the hinder feet, and made such a noise and rumour that Lantfert came out hastily, and knew nothing what this might be ; and brought in his hand a sharp hook. Bruin the Bear lay in the cleft of the tree in great fear and

dread, and held fast his head, and nipped both his fore-
feet. He struggled, he wrestled, and cried ; and all was for
naught. He wist not how he might get out.

WILLIAM CAXTON (from *Reynard the Fox*—
modernised by W. S. STALLYBRASS)

THOMAS OF ERCILDOUNE
(who slept for seven years)

True Thomas lay on Huntley bank ;
    A ferlie spied he wi' his ee ;
There he saw a lady bright
    Come riding doun by the Eildon Tree.

Her skirt was o' the grass green silk,
    Her mantle o' the velvet fine ;
At ilka tett o' her horse's mane,
    Hung fifty siller bells and nine.

True Thomas he pu'd aff his cap,
    And louted low doun on his knee :
' Hail to thee, Mary, Queen of Heaven !
    For thy peer on earth could never be.'

' O no, O no, Thomas,' she said,
    ' That name does not belong to me ;
I'm but the Queen o' fair Elfland,
    That hither have come to visit thee.

' Harp and carp, Thomas,' she said ;
    ' Harp and carp along wi' me ;

And if ye dare to kiss my lips,
  Sure of your body I shall be.'

' Betide me weal, betide me woe,
  That weird shall never daunten me.'
Syne he has kiss'd her on the lips,
  All underneath the Eildon Tree.

' Now ye maun go wi' me,' she said,
  ' Now, Thomas, ye maun go wi' me ;
And ye maun serve me seven years,
  Through weal or woe as may chance to be.

She's mounted on her milk-white steed,
  And she's ta'en Thomas up behind ;
And aye, whene'er her bridle rang,
  The steed gaed swifter than the wind.

O they rade on, and farther on,
  The steed gaed swifter than the wind ;
Until they reach'd a desert wide,
  And living land was left behind.

' Now, Thomas, light doun, light doun,' she said,
  ' And lean your head upon my knee ;
Abide ye there a little space,
  And I will show you ferlies three.

' O see ye not yon narrow road,
  So thick beset wi' thorns and briars ?
That is the Path of Righteousness,
  Though after it but few enquires.

' And see ye not yon braid, braid road,
    That lies across the lily leven ?
That is the Path of Wickedness,
    Though some call it the road to Heaven.

' And see ye not yon bonny road
    That winds about the ferny brae ?
That is the road to fair Elfland,
    Where thou and I this night maun gae.

' But, Thomas, ye sall haud your tongue,
    Whatever ye may hear or see ;
For speak ye word in Elfin-land,
    Ye'll ne'er win back to your ain countrie.'

O they rade on, and further on,
    And they waded rivers abune the knee ;
And they saw neither sun nor moon,
    But they heard the roaring of a sea. . .

Syne they came to a garden green,
    And she pu'd an apple frae a tree :
' Take this for thy wages, Thomas,' she said ;
    ' It will give thee the tongue that can never lee.'

' My tongue is my ain,' then Thomas he said ;
    ' A gudely gift ye wad gie to me !
I neither dought to buy or sell
    At fair or tryst where I might be.

' I dought neither speak to prince or peer,
    Nor ask of grace from fair ladye ! '—
' Now haud thy peace, Thomas,' she said,
    ' For as I say, so must it be.'

He has gotten a coat of the even cloth,
    And a pair o' shoon of the velvet green ;
And till seven years were come and gane,
    True Thomas on earth was never seen.

ANONYMOUS

THE FAIRY FROLIC

All sing :

By the moon we sport and play,
With the night begins our day :
As we dance the dew doth fall :
Trip it, little urchins all !
Lightly as the little bee,
Two by two, and three by three :
And about go we, and about go we ! ..

First Fairy :

I do come about the copse
Leaping upon flowers' tops ;
Then I get upon a fly,
She carries me above the sky,
And trip and go.

Second Fairy :

When a dewdrop falleth down,
And doth light upon my crown,
Then I shake my head and skip,
And about I trip.

All sing :
Round about, round about, in a fine ring a,
Thus we dance, thus we dance and thus we sing a ;
Trip and go, to and fro, over this green a,
All about, in and out, for our brave Queen a.

ANONYMOUS (from *The Maid's Metamorphosis*, 1600)

FAIRY PUNISHMENT

Pinch him, pinch him, black and blue,
Saucy mortals must not view
What the Queen of Stars is doing,
Nor pry into our fairy wooing.
  Pinch him blue—
  And pinch him black—
  Let him not lack
Sharp nails to pinch him blue and red
Till sleep has rocked his addle head.
For the trespass he hath done,
Spots o'er all his flesh shall run.

     JOHN LYLY (from *Endymion*)

SONG OF THE FAIRY QUEEN

Hark all you ladies that do sleep !
The Fairy Queen Proserpina
Bids you awake and pity them that weep !
  You may do in the dark
  What the day doth forbid ;
  Fear not the dogs that bark,
  Night will have all hid.

But, if you let your lovers moan,
The Fairy Queen Proserpina
Will send abroad her fairies every one
      That shall pinch black and blue
      Your white hands and fair arms,
      That did not kindly rue
      Your paramours' harms.

In myrtle arbours on the downs
The Fairy Queen Proserpina
This night by moonshine, leading merry rounds,
      Holds watch with sweet Love,
      Down the dale, up the hill,
      No plaints nor griefs may move
      Their holy vigil.

All you that will hold watch with Love,
The Fairy Queen Proserpina
Will make you fairer than Diana's dove.
      Roses red, lilies white,
      And the clear damask hue
      Shall on your cheeks alight.
      Love will adorn you.

All you that love or loved before !
The Fairy Queen Proserpina
Bids you increase that loving humour more !
      They that have not yet fed
      On delight amorous—
      She vows that they shall lead
      Apes in Avernus.

ANONYMOUS, 16th century

She is the fairies' midwife, and she comes
In shape no bigger than an agate-stone
On the fore-finger of an alderman,
Drawn with a team of little atomies
Athwart men's noses as they lie asleep;
Her waggon-spokes made of long spinners' legs,
The cover of the wings of grasshoppers,
The traces of the smallest spider's web,
The collars of the moonshine's watery beams,
Her whip of cricket's bone, the lash of film,
Her waggoner a small grey-coated gnat,
Not half so big as a round little worm
Prick'd from the lazy finger of a maid;
Her chariot is an empty hazel-nut
Made by the joiner squirrel or old grub,
Time out o' mind the fairies' coachmakers.
And in this state she gallops night by night
Through lovers' brains, and then they dream of love;
O'er courtiers' knees, that dream on court'sies straight,
O'er lawyers' fingers, who straight dream on fees,
O'er ladies' lips, who straight on kisses dream,
Which oft the angry Mab with blisters plagues,
Because their breaths with sweetmeats tainted are:
Sometime she gallops o'er a courtier's nose,
And then dreams he of smelling out a suit;
And sometime comes she with a tithe-pig's tail
Tickling a parson's nose as a' lies asleep,
Then dreams he of another benefice:
Sometime she driveth o'er a soldier's neck,
And then dreams he of cutting foreign throats,
Of breaches, ambuscadoes, Spanish blades,

Of healths five-fathom deep ; and then anon
Drums in his ear, at which he starts and wakes,
And being thus frighted swears a prayer or two
And sleeps again.

SHAKESPEARE (from *Romeo and Juliet*)

NEWS OF THE DUKE

They say he is already in the Forest of Arden, and a
many merry men with him ; and there they live like the
old Robin Hood of England ; they say many young
gentlemen flock to him every day, and fleet the time
carelessly, as they did in the golden world.

SHAKESPEARE (from *As You Like It*)

HOBGOBLINS, &c.

A bigger kind there is of them called with us hobgoblins,
and Robin Goodfellows, that would in those superstitious
times grind corn for a mess of milk, cut wood, or do any
manner of drudgery work. They would mend old irons in
those Æolian isles of Lipari, in former ages, and have been
often seen and heard. Tholosanus calls them Trullos and
Getulos, and saith, that in his days they were common in
many places of France. Dithmarus Bleskenius, in his description of Iceland, reports for a certainty, that almost in
every family they have yet some such familiar spirits ; and
Fœlix Malleolus affirms as much, that these Trolli or
Telchines are very common in Norway, and seem to do

drudgery work ; to draw water, dress meat, or any such thing. Another sort of these there are, which frequent forlorn houses, which the Italians call foliots, most part innoxious. They will make strange noises in the night, howl sometimes pitifully, and then laugh again, cause great flame and sudden lights, fling stones, rattle chains, shave men, open doors and shut them, fling down platters, stools, chests, sometimes appear in the likeness of hares, crows, black dogs, etc.

ROBERT BURTON (from *Anatomy of Melancholy*)

COMUS LEADS IN THE REVELLERS

The star that bids the shepherd fold
Now the top of heaven doth hold ;
And the gilded car of day
His glowing axle doth allay
In the steep Atlantic stream :
And the slope sun his upward beam
Shoots against the dusky pole,
Pacing toward the other goal
Of his chamber in the east.
Meanwhile, welcome joy and feast,
Midnight shout and revelry,
Tipsy dance and jollity.
Braid your locks with rosy twine,
Dropping odours, dropping wine.
Rigour now is gone to bed ;
And Advice with scrupulous head,
Strict Age, and sour Severity,
With their grave saws, in slumber lie.

We, that are of purer fire,
Imitate the starry quire,
Who, in their nightly watchful spheres,
Lead in swift round the months and years.
The sounds and seas, with all their finny drove,
Now to the moon in wavering morrice move ;
And on the tawny sands and shelves
Trip the pert fairies and the dapper elves.
By dimpled brook and fountain-brim,
The wood-nymphs, decked with daisies trim,
Their merry wakes and pastimes keep :
What hath night to do with sleep ?

MILTON (from *Comus*)

ADVICE FROM A GHOST

'Tis late and cold, stir up the fire ;
Sit close and draw the table nigher ;
Be merry and drink wine that's old,
A hearty medicine 'gainst a cold.
Your beds of wanton down the best,
Where you shall tumble to your rest.
Call for the best the house may ring,
Sack, white, and claret let them bring,
And drink apace, whilst breath you have ;
You'll find but cold drink in the grave ;
Plover, partridge for your dinner,
And a capon for the sinner,
You shall find ready when you're up,
And your horse shall have his sup.
Welcome, welcome, shall fly round,
And I shall smile, though underground.

JOHN FLETCHER (from *The Lover's Progress*)

THE FAIRY'S FUNERAL

I was walking alone in my garden ; there was great stillness among the branches and flowers, and more than common sweetness in the air ; I heard a low and pleasant sound, and I knew not whence it came. At last I saw the broad leaf of a flower move, and underneath I saw a procession of creatures, of the size and colour of green and grey grasshoppers, bearing a body laid out on a rose-leaf, which they buried with songs, and then disappeared. It was a fairy funeral.

WILLIAM BLAKE (from GILCHRIST'S
Life of Blake)

THE OLD GODS

For the stricken heart of Love
This visible nature, and this common world,
Is all too narrow ; yea, a deeper import
Lurks in the legend told my infant years
Than lies upon that truth we live to learn ;
For fable is Love's world, his home, his birth-place ;
Delightedly dwells he 'mong fays and talismans,
And spirits ; and delightedly believes
Divinities, being himself divine
The intelligible forms of ancient poets,
The fair humanities of old religion,
The Power, the Beauty, and the Majesty,
That had her haunts in dale, or piny mountain,
Or forest by slow stream, or pebbly spring,
Or chasms, and wat'ry depths ; all these have vanish'd.
They live no longer in the faith of reason !

But still the heart doth need a language, still
Doth the old instinct bring back the old names,
And to yon starry world they now are gone,
Spirits or gods, that used to share this earth
With man as with their friend.

SCHILLER (from *The Piccolomini*—
Trans. COLERIDGE)

KILMENY

' Kilmeny, Kilmeny, where have you been ?
Long hae we sought baith holt and den ;
By linn, by ford, and green-wood tree,
Yet you are halesome and fair to see.
Where gat you that joup o' the lily scheen ?
That bonnie snood of the birk sae green ?
And these roses, the fairest that ever were seen ?
Kilmeny, Kilmeny, where have you been ? ' . .

 In yon green-wood there is a waik,
And in that waik there is a wene,
 And in that wene there is a maike,
That neither has flesh, blood nor bane ;
And down in yon green-wood he walks his lane.

In that green wene Kilmeny lay,
Her bosom happ'd wi' flowerets gay ;
But the air was soft and the silence deep,
And bonnie Kilmeny fell sound asleep.
She kenn'd nae mair, nor open'd her e'e,
Till waked by the hymns of a far countrye . .

They clasped her waist and her hands sae fair,
They kiss'd her cheek and they kemed her hair,
And round came many a blooming fere,
Saying, ' Bonny Kilmeny, ye're welcome here ! ' ..

They bore her away, she wist not how,
For she felt not arm nor rest below ;
But so swift they wain'd her through the light,
'Twas like the motion of sound or sight ;
They seem'd to split the gales of air,
And yet nor gale nor breeze was there.
Unnumber'd groves below them grew,
They came, they pass'd, and backward flew,
Like floods of blossoms gliding on,
In moment seen, in moment gone.
O, never vales to mortal view
Appear'd like those o'er which they flew !
That land to human spirits given,
The lowermost vales of the storied heaven ;
From thence they can view the world below,
And heaven's blue gates with sapphires glow,
More glory yet unmeet to know.
They bore her far to a mountain green,
To see what mortal never had seen ;
And they seated her high on a purple sward,
And bade her heed what she saw and heard,
And note the changes the spirits wrought,
For now she lived in the land of thought ..

With distant music, soft and deep,
They lull'd Kilmeny sound asleep ;
And when she awaken'd, she lay her lane,
All happ'd with flowers, in the green-wood wene.

When seven lang years had come and fled,
When grief was calm, and hope was dead ;
When scarce was remember'd Kilmeny's name,
Late, late in a gloamin' Kilmeny came hame ! . .

When a month and a day had come and gane,
Kilmeny sought the green-wood wene ;
There laid her down on the leaves sae green,
And Kilmeny on earth was never mair seen.
But O, the words that fell from her mouth
Were words of wonder, and words of truth !
But all the land were in fear and dread,
For they kendna whether she was living or dead.
It wasna her hame, and she couldna remain ;
She left this world of sorrow and pain,
And return'd to the land of thought again.

JAMES HOGG

PROUD MAISIE

Proud Maisie is in the wood,
    Walking so early ;
Sweet Robin sits on the bush,
    Singing so rarely.

" Tell me, thou bonny bird,
    When shall I marry me ? "
" When six braw gentlemen
    Kirkward shall carry ye."

"Who makes the bridal bed,
  Birdie say truly?"
"The grey-headed sexton
  That delves the grave duly.

"The glow-worm o'er grave and stone
  Shall light thee steady;
The owl from the steeple sing
  'Welcome, proud lady.'"

SIR WALTER SCOTT

MUSIC AT SEA

Around, around, flew each sweet sound,
Then darted to the Sun;
Slowly the sounds came back again,
Now mixed, now one by one.

Sometimes a-dropping from the sky
I heard the sky-lark sing;
Sometimes all little birds that are,
How they seemed to fill the sea and air
With their sweet jargoning!

And now 'twas like all instruments,
Now like a lonely flute;
And now it is an angel's song
That makes the heavens be mute.

It ceased ; yet still the sails made on
A pleasant noise till noon,
A noise like of a hidden brook
In the leafy month of June,
That to the sleeping woods all night
Singeth a quiet tune.

COLERIDGE (from *The Ancient Mariner*)

LA BELLE DAME SANS MERCI

' O what can ail thee, knight-at-arms,
   Alone and palely loitering ?
The sedge is wither'd from the lake,
   And no birds sing.

' O what can ail thee, knight-at-arms,
   So haggard and so woe-begone ?
The squirrel's granary is full,
   And the harvest's done.

' I see a lily on thy brow
   With anguish moist and fever dew ;
And on thy cheek a fading rose
   Fast withereth too.'

' I met a lady in the meads,
   Full beautiful—a faery's child,
Her hair was long, her foot was light,
   And her eyes were wild.

501

' I made a garland for her head,
    And bracelets too, and fragrant zone ;
She look'd at me as she did love,
    And made sweet moan.

' I set her on my pacing steed
    And nothing else saw all day long,
For sideways would she lean, and sing
    A faery's song.

' She found me roots of relish sweet,
    And honey wild and manna dew,
And sure in language strange she said,
    " I love thee true ! "

' She took me to her elfin grot,
    And there she wept and sigh'd full sore ;
And there I shut her wild, wild eyes
    With kisses four.

' And there she lullèd me asleep,
    And there I dream'd—Ah ! woe betide !
The latest dream I ever dream'd
    On the cold hill's side.

' I saw pale kings and princes too,
    Pale warriers, death-pale were they all ;
Who cried—" La belle Dame sans Merci
    Hath thee in thrall ! "

' I saw their starved lips in the gloam
    With horrid warning gapèd wide,
And I awoke and found me here
    On the cold hill's side.

' And this is why I sojourn here
    Alone and palely loitering,
Though the sedge is wither'd from the lake,
    And no birds sing.'

KEATS

THE DEATH OF THE PHOENIX

O'er the broad nest her silver wings
Shook down their wasteful glitterings ;
Her brinded neck high-arched in air
Like a small rainbow faded there ;
But brighter glowed her plumy crown
Mouldering to golden ashes down ;
With fume of sweet woods, to the skies,
Pure as a Saint's adoring sighs,
Warm as a prayer in Paradise,
Her life-breath rose in sacrifice !
The while with shrill triumphant tone
Sounding aloud, aloft, alone,
Ceaseless her joyful deathwail she
Sang to departing Araby !
  Deep melancholy wonder drew
Tears from my heartspring at that view.
Like cresset shedding its last flare
Upon some wistful mariner,
The Bird, fast blending with the sky,
Turned on me her dead-gazing eye
Once—and as surge to shallow spray
Sank down to vapoury dust away !

GEORGE DARLEY (from *Nepenthe*)

JOHNNIE KIGARROW

My brother and I went down to Wales,
And listened by night to the Welshman's tales :
I was but seven and he was ten.
We sat on the knees of the farmer's men
After the whole day's work was done ;
And I was friends with the farmer's son.
His hands were rough, his arms were strong,
His mouth was merry and loud for song :
Each night, when set by the ingle-wall,
He was the merriest man of them all.
I would catch at his beard and say
All the things I had done in the day—
Tumbled boulders over the force,
Swum in the river and fired the gorse—
' Half the side of the hill ! ' quoth I :—
' Tut ! ' cried he, ' and didn't you die ?
How was it, then, you saved your marrow ?
Didn't you meet with Johnnie Kigarrow ? '
' No ! ' said I, ' and who will he be ?
And what will be Johnnie Kigarrow to me ? '
The farmer's son said under his breath,
' Johnnie Kigarrow may be your death !
Listen you here, and keep you still—
Johnnie Kigarrow bides under the hill ;
Twloch barrow stands over his head ;
He shallows the river to make his bed :
Boulders roll when he stirs a limb ;
And the gorse on the hills belongs to him !
And if so be one fires his gorse,
He's out of his bed, and he mounts his horse.

Off he sets : at the first long stride
He is halfway over the mountain side :
At a second stride he's across the barrow,
And has you fast, has Johnnie Kigarrow ! '

Half I laughed and half I feared,
As I upped and tugged at the strong man's beard,
And bragged as brave as a boy could be—
' So ? ' but, you see, 'he didn't catch *me* ! '

Fear took hold of me : what had I done ?
High as the roof rose the farmer's son :
How the sight of him froze my marrow !
' I,' he cried, ' am Johnnie Kigarrow ! '

Well, you wonder, what was the end ?
Never forget ;—he'd called me ' friend ' !
Mighty of limb, and hard, and brown :
Quickly he laughed, and set me down.
' Heh ! ' said he, ' but the squeak was narrow,
Not to be caught by Johnnie Kigarrow ! '

Now, I hear, after years gone by,
Nobody knows how he came to die.
He strode out one night of storm :
' Get you to bed, and keep you warm ! '
Out into darkness so went he :
Nobody knows where his bones may be.

Only I guess—if tongue let go
Truth that once—how perhaps *I* know.
Twloch river and Twloch barrow
Cover the sleep of Johnnie Kigarrow.

LAURENCE HOUSMAN

505

THE STOLEN CHILD

Where dips the rocky highland
Of Sleuth Wood in the lake,
There lies a leafy island
Where flapping herons wake
The drowsy water rats ;
There we've hid our faery vats,
Full of berries,
And of reddest stolen cherries.
Come away, O human child !
To the waters and the wild
With a faery, hand in hand,
For the world's more full of weeping than
    you can understand.

Where the wave of moonlight glosses
The dim grey sands with light,
Far off by farthest Rosses
We foot it all the night,
Weaving olden dances,
Mingling hands and mingling glances
Till the moon has taken flight ;
To and fro we leap
And chase the frothy bubbles,
While the world is full of troubles
And is anxious in its sleep.
Come away, O human child !
To the waters and the wild
With a faery, hand in hand,
For the world's more full of weeping than
    you can understand.

Where the wandering water gushes
From the hills above Glen-Car,
In pools among the rushes
That scarce could bathe a star,
We seek for slumbering trout
And whispering in their ears
Give them unquiet dreams ;
Leaning softly out
From ferns that drop their tears
Over the young streams,
Come away, O human child !
To the waters and the wild
With a faery, hand in hand,
For the world's more full of weeping than
you can understand.

Away with us he's going,
The solemn-eyed :
He'll hear no more the lowing
Of the calves on the warm hillside
Or the kettle on the hob
Sing peace into his breast,
Or see the brown mice bob
Round and round the oatmeal-chest.
For he comes, the human child,
To the waters and the wild
With a faery, hand in hand,
From a world more full of weeping than
he can understand.

W. B. YEATS

THE TWILIGHT OF THE FAIRIES

The new Spirit of Chivalry made a shift to support itself for a time, when reason was but dawning, as we may say, and just about to gain the ascendant over the portentous spectres of the imagination. Its growing splendour, in the end, put them all to flight, and allowed them no quarter even amongst the poets . . . Thus at length the magic of the old romances was perfectly dissolved. They began with reflecting an image indeed of the feudal manners, but an image magnified and distorted by unskilful designers. Common sense being offended with these perversions of truth and nature (still accounted the more monstrous, as the antient manners, they pretended to copy after, were now disused, and of most men forgotten) the next step was to have recourse to *allegories*. . . . Under this form the tales of faery kept their ground, and even made their fortune at Court, where they became for two or three reigns the ordinary entertainment of our princes. But reason, in the end (assisted however by party and religious prejudices), drove them off the scene, and would endure these *lying wonders*, neither in their own proper shape, nor as masked in figures.

Henceforth, the taste of wit and poetry took a new turn, and fancy, that had wantoned it so long in the world of fiction, was now constrained, against her will, to ally herself with strict truth, if she would gain admittance into reasonable company. What we have gotten by this revolution, you will say, is a great deal of good sense. What we have lost, is a world of fine fabling ; the illusion of which is so grateful to the *Charmed Spirit* ; that, in spite of philosophy and fashion, *Faery* Spenser still ranks highest among the Poets—I mean with all those who are either come of that house or have any kindness for it.

RICHARD HURD, Bishop of Worcester
(from *Letters on Chivalry and Romance*, 1762)

THIRD PART

§ III FRIENDS OLD AND NEW

Life is to be fortified by many friendships.

SYDNEY SMITH

Intercourse with books is my comfort in solitude. For diverting my troublesome fancies there is no resource like that of books ; they easily turn my thoughts to themselves and drive out the others. They always receive me with the same welcome.

MONTAIGNE

§ III FRIENDS OLD AND NEW

§ 1. OUT-OF-DOOR POEMS

BARLEY-BREAK

(The Elizabethan form of ' Prisoners' Base ')

Now is the month of maying,
When merry lads are playing,
Each with his bonny lass,
Upon the greeny grass.

The Spring clad all in gladness,
Doth laugh at Winter's sadness,
And to the bag-pipe's sound
The nymphs tread out their ground.

Fie then ! why sit we musing,
Youth's sweet delight refusing ?
Say, dainty nymphs, and speak,
Shall we play barley-break ?

ANONYMOUS (1595)

SONG OF AUTOLYCUS

When daffodils begin to peer,
  With heigh ! the doxy over the dale,
Why, then comes in the sweet o' the year ;
  For the red blood reigns in the winter's pale.

The white sheet bleaching on the hedge,
 With heigh! the sweet birds, O how they sing!
Doth set my pugging tooth on edge;
 For a quart of ale is a dish for a king...

Jog on, jog on, the foot-path way,
 And merrily hent the stile-a:
A merry heart goes all the day,
 Your sad tires in a mile-a.

SHAKESPEARE (from *Winter's Tale*)

THOUGHTS IN A GARDEN

How vainly men themselves amaze
To win the palm, the oak, or bays,
And their uncessant labours see
Crown'd from some single herb or tree,
Whose short and narrow-vergèd shade
Does prudently their toils upbraid;
While all the flowers and trees do close
To weave the garlands of repose.

Fair Quiet, have I found thee here,
And Innocence thy sister dear!
Mistaken long, I sought you then
In busy companies of men:
Your sacred plants, if here below,
Only among the plants will grow:
Society is all but rude
To this delicious solitude...

What wondrous life in this I lead !
Ripe apples drop about my head ;
The luscious clusters of the vine
Upon my mouth do crush their wine ;
The nectarine and curious peach
Into my hands themselves do reach ;
Stumbling on melons, as I pass,
Ensnared with flowers, I fall on grass.

Meanwhile the mind, from pleasure less,
Withdraws into its happiness ;
The mind, that ocean where each kind
Does straight its own resemblance find ;
Yet it creates, transcending these,
Far other worlds, and other seas ;
Annihilating all that's made
To a green thought in a green shade.

MARVELL

DAFFODILS

I wandered lonely as a cloud
That floats on high o'er vales and hills,
When all at once I saw a crowd,
A host, of golden daffodils ;
Beside the lake, beneath the trees,
Fluttering and dancing in the breeze.

Continuous as the stars that shine
And twinkle on the milky way,
They stretched in never-ending line
Along the margin of a bay :

Ten thousand saw I at a glance,
Tossing their heads in sprightly dance.

The waves beside them danced ; but they
Out-did the sparkling waves in glee :
A poet could not but be gay,
In such a jocund company ;
I gazed—and gazed—but little thought
What wealth the show to me had brought :

For oft, when on my couch I lie
In vacant or in pensive mood,
They flash upon that inward eye
Which is the bliss of solitude ;
And then my heart with pleasure fills,
And dances with the daffodils.

WORDSWORTH

HYMN TO PAN

O thou, whose mighty palace roof doth hang
From jagged trunks, and overshadoweth
Eternal whispers, glooms, the birth, life, death
Of unseen flowers in heavy peacefulness ;
Who lovest to see the Hamadryads dress
Their ruffled locks where meeting hazels darken ;
And through whole solemn hours dost sit, and hearken
The dreary melody of bedded reeds—
In desolate places, where dank moisture breeds

The pipy hemlock to strange overgrowth,
Bethinking thee, how melancholy loth
Thou wast to lose fair Syrinx—do thou now,
By thy love's milky brow,
By all the trembling mazes that she ran,
Hear us, great Pan !

O thou, for whose soul-soothing quiet turtles
Passion their voices cooingly 'mong myrtles,
What time thou wanderest at eventide
Through sunny meadows, that outskirt the side
Of thine enmossèd realms : O thou, to whom
Broad-leavèd fig-trees even now foredoom
Their ripened fruitage ; yellow-girted bees
Their golden honey-combs ; our village leas
Their fairest-blossomed beans and poppied corn ;
The chuckling linnet its five young unborn,
To sing for thee ; low-creeping strawberries
Their summer coolness ; pent-up butterflies
Their freckled wings ; yea, the fresh-budding year
All its completions—be quickly near,
By every wind that nods the mountain pine,
O forester divine !

Thou, to whom every Faun and Satyr flies
For willing service ; whether to surprise
The squatted hare while in half-sleeping fit ;
Or upward ragged precipices flit
To save poor lambkins from the eagle's maw ;
Or by mysterious enticement draw
Bewildered shepherds to their path again ;
Or to tread breathless round the frothy main

And gather up all fancifullest shells
For thee to tumble into Naiads' cells,
And, being hidden, laugh at their out-peeping;
Or to delight thee with fantastic leaping,
The while they pelt each other on the crown
With silvery oak-apples, and fir-cones brown—
By all the echoes that about thee ring,
Hear us, O satyr king!

O Hearkener to the loud-clapping Shears,
While ever and anon to his shorn peers
A ram goes bleating: Winder of the Horn,
When snouted wild-boars, routing tender corn,
Anger our huntsmen: Breather round our farms,
To keep off mildews, and all weather harms:
Strange Ministrant of undescribèd sounds,
That come a-swooning over hollow grounds,
And wither drearily on barren moors:
Dread Opener of the Mysterious Doors
Leading to universal knowledge—see,
Great Son of Dryope,
The many that are come to pay their vows,
With leaves about their brows!

Be still the unimaginable lodge
For solitary thinkings: such as dodge
Conception to the very bourne of heaven,
Then leave the naked brain! be still the leaven,
That spreading in this dull and clodded earth,
Gives it a touch ethereal—a new birth!
Be still a symbol of immensity;
A firmament reflected in a sea;

An element filling the space between ;
An unknown—but no more ! We humbly screen
With uplift hands our foreheads, lowly bending,
And, giving out a shout most heaven-rending,
Conjure thee to receive our humble Paean
Upon thy Mount Lycean !

KEATS (from *Endymion*)

LINDEN LEA

'Ithin the woodlands, flow'ry gleäded,
 By the woak tree's mossy moot,
The sheenèn grass bleädes, timber-sheäded,
 Now do quiver under voot ;
An' birds do whissle auver head,
An' water's bubblèn in its bed,
An' there vor me the apple tree
Do leän down low in Linden Lea.

When leaves that leätely wer a-springèn
 Now do feäde 'ithin the copse,
An' painted birds do hush ther zingèn
 Up upon the timber's tops ;
An' brown-leaf'd fruit's a-turnèn red,
In cloudless zunsheen, auver head,
Wi' fruit vor me, the apple tree
Do leän down low in Linden Lea.

Let other vo'k meäke money vaster
 In the aïr o' dark-room'd towns,
I don't dread a peevish meäster ;
 Though noo man do heed my frowns,

517

I be free to goo abrode,
Or teäke ageän my hwomeward road
To where, vor me, the apple tree
Do leän down low in Linden Lea.

WILLIAM BARNES

FOUR DUCKS ON A POND

Four ducks on a pond,
A grass-bank beyond,
A blue sky of spring,
White clouds on the wing ;
What a little thing
To remember for years—
To remember with tears !

WILLIAM ALLINGHAM

MAY-DAY ON MAGDALEN TOWER

Morn of the year, of day and May the prime !
How fitly do we scale the steep dark stair
Into the brightness of the matin air
To praise with chanted hymn and echoing chime,
Dear Lord of Light, thy lowlihead sublime
That stooped erewhile our life's frail weed to wear !
Sun, cloud, and hill, all things Thou framest so fair,
With us are glad and gay, greeting the time.

The college of the lily leaves her sleep ;
   The grey tower rocks and trembles into sound,
     Dawn-smitten Memnon of a happier hour ;
Through faint-hued fields the silver waters creep ;
   Day grows, birds pipe, and robed anew and crowned,
     Green Spring trips forth to set the world aflower.

SIR HERBERT WARREN

MARCH THOUGHTS FROM ENGLAND

O that I were lying under the olives,
Lying alone among the anemones !
Shell-colour'd blossoms they bloom there and scarlet,
Far under stretches of silver woodland,
Flame in the delicate shade of the olives.

O that I were lying under the olives !
Grey grows the thyme on the shadowless headland,
The long low headland, where white in the sunshine
The rocks run seaward. It seems suspended
Lone in an infinite gulf of azure.

There were I lying under the olives,
Might I behold come following seaward,
Clear brown shapes in a world of sunshine,
A russet shepherd, his sheep too, russet.
Watch them wander the long grey headland
Out to the edge of the burning azure.
O that I were lying under the olives !
So should I see the far-off cities
Glittering low by the purple water,
Gleaming high on the purple mountain ;
See where the road goes winding southward.

It passes the valleys of almond blossom,
Curves round the crag o'er the steep-hanging orchards,
Where almond and peach are aflush 'mid the olives—
Hardly the amethyst sea shines through them—
Over it cypress on solemn cypress
Lead to the lonely pilgrimage places. . .

Would I were listening under the olives !
So should I see in an airy pageant
A proud chivalrous pomp sweep by me ;
Hear in high courts the joyous ladies
Devising of Love in a world of lovers ;
Hear the song of the Lion-hearted,
A deep-voiced song—and O ! perchance,
Ghostly and strange and sweet to madness,
Rudel sing the Lady of Tripoli.

MARGARET L. WOODS

THE WAY THROUGH THE WOODS

They shut the road through the woods
   Seventy years ago.
Weather and rain have undone it again,
   And now you would never know
There was once a road through the woods
   Before they planted the trees.
It is underneath the coppice and heath,
   And the thin anemones.
   Only the keeper sees
That, where the ring-dove broods,
   And the badgers roll at ease,
There was once a road through the woods.

Yet, if you enter the woods
  Of a summer evening late,
When the night-air cools on the trout-ringed pools
  Where the otter whistles his mate,
(They fear not men in the woods
  Because they see so few)
You will hear the beat of a horse's feet
  And the swish of a skirt in the dew,
  Steadily cantering through
The misty solitudes,
  As though they perfectly knew
The old lost road through the woods . .
But there is no road through the woods.

RUDYARD KIPLING

IN A MEADOW

  This is the place
Where far from the unholy populace
The daughter of Philosophy and Sleep
  Her court doth keep,
Sweet Contemplation. To her service bound
  Hover around
The little amiable summer airs,
  Her courtiers.

  The deep black soil
Makes mute her palace-floors with thick trefoil;
The grasses sagely nodding overhead
  Curtain her bed;

521

And lest the feet of strangers overpass
   Her walls of grass,
Gravely a little river goes his rounds
    To beat the bounds.

   No bustling flood,
To make a tumult in her neighbourhood,
But such a stream as knows to go and come
   Discreetly dumb.
Therein are chambers tapestried with weeds
   And screen'd with reeds ;
For roof the waterlily-leaves serene
   Spread tiles of green.

   The sun's large eye
Falls soberly upon me where I lie ;
For delicate webs of immaterial haze
   Refine his rays.
The air is full of music none knows what,
   Or half-forgot ;
The living echo of dead voices fills
   The unseen hills.

   I hear the song
Of cuckoo answering cuckoo all day long ;
And know not if it be my inward sprite
   For my delight
Making remember'd poetry appear
   As sound in the ear :
Like a salt savour poignant in the breeze
   From distant seas.

Dreams without sleep,
And sleep too clear for dreaming and too deep ;
And Quiet very large and manifold
   About me roll'd ;
Satiety, that momentary flower,
   Stretch'd to an hour :
These are her gifts which all mankind may use,
   And all refuse.

J. S. PHILLIMORE

WASHING DAY

The washing hangs upon the line,
Between the prunus and the arch
(Where tender leaves of rambler thrust),
On this gay day in middle March.

The washing bellies in the breeze,
Across the clothes blue shadows go,
Above the house the lark sings high,
Before me, see, two aprons blow.

To watch the patterns move criss-cross,
Cast from the branches of the pear ;
For symphony the song of birds,
And daffodils beside my chair ;—

These are the simple joys of life ;
With rippling clothes put out to dry,
Reflecting cleanliness and light
Beneath a wide and changing sky.

THEODORA ROSCOE

TEWKESBURY ROAD

It is good to be out on the road, and going one knows not
    where,
  Going through meadow and village, one knows not
    whither nor why ;
Through the grey light drift of the dust, in the keen cool
    rush of the air,
  Under the flying white clouds, and the broad blue lift
    of the sky ;

And to halt at the chattering brook, in the tall green fern
    at the brink
  Where the harebell grows, and the gorse, and the fox-
    gloves purple and white ;
Where the shy-eyed delicate deer troop down to the pools
    to drink,
  When the stars are mellow and large at the coming on of
    the night.

O ! to feel the warmth of the rain and the homely smell of
    the earth
  Is a tune for the blood to jig to, a joy past power of
    words ;
And the blessed green comely meadows seem all a-ripple
    with mirth
  At the lilt of the shifting feet, and the dear wild cry of
    the birds.

JOHN MASEFIELD

THE STARLING LAKE

My sorrow that I am not by the little dūn
By the lake of the starlings at Rosses under the hill,
And the larks there, singing over the fields of dew,
Or evening there and the sedges still.
For plain I see now the length of the yellow sand,
And Lissadell far off and its leafy ways,
And the holy mountain whose mighty heart
Gathers into it all the coloured days.
My sorrow that I am not by the little dūn
By the lake of the starlings at evening when all is still,
And still in whispering sedges the herons stand.
'Tis there I would nestle at rest till the quivering moon
Uprose in the golden quiet over the hill.

SEUMAS O'SULLIVAN

§ 2. INDOOR POEMS

TO LADY ANNE FITZPATRICK,

when about five years old, with a present of shells (1772)

O nymph, compar'd with whose young bloom
    Hebe's herself an ancient fright;
May these gay shells find grace and room
    Both in your baby-house and sight!
Shells! What are shells? you ask, admiring
    With stare half pleasure half surprise;
And fly with nature's art, enquiring
    In dear mamma's all-speaking eyes.

Shells, fairest Anne, are playthings, made
   By a brave god call'd Father Ocean,
Whose frown from pole to pole's obey'd,
   Commands the waves, and stills their motion.
From that old sire a daughter came,
   As like mamma, as blue to blue ;
And, like mamma, the sea-born dame
   An urchin bore, not unlike you.
For him fond grand-papa compels
   The floods to furnish such a state
Of corals and of cockleshells,
   Would turn a little lady's pate.
The chit has tons of bawbles more ;
   His nurs'ry's stuff'd with doves and sparrows ;
And litter'd is its azure floor
   With painted quivers, bows, and arrows.
Spread, spread your frock ; you must be friends ;
   His toys shall fill your lap and breast :
To-day the boy this sample sends,
   And some years hence he'll send the rest.

HORACE WALPOLE, EARL OF ORFORD

THE SPIRIT OF BEAUTY

Spirit of beauty, that dost consecrate
   With thine own hues all thou dost shine upon
   Of human thought or form, where art thou gone ?
Why dost thou pass away and leave our state,
This dim vast vale of tears, vacant and desolate ?
     Ask why the sunlight not for ever
     Weaves rainbows o'er yon mountain river ;

Why aught should fail and fade that once is shown ;
　　Why fear and dream and death and birth
　　Cast on the daylight of this earth
　　Such gloom ; why man has such a scope
For love and hate, despondency and hope.

No voice from some sublimer world hath ever
　　To sage or poet these responses given :
　　Therefore the names of Demon, Ghost, and Heaven,
Remain the records of their vain endeavour ;
Frail spells, whose uttered charm might not avail to sever,
　　From all we hear and all we see,
　　Doubt, chance, and mutability.
Thy light alone, like mists o'er mountains driven,
　　Or music by the night wind sent
　　Through strings of some still instrument,
　　Or moonlight on a midnight stream,
Gives grace and truth to life's unquiet dream.

Love, Hope, and Self-esteem, like clouds, depart
　　And come, for some uncertain moments lent.
　　Man were immortal, and omnipotent,
Didst thou, unknown and awful as thou art,
Keep with thy glorious train firm state within his heart.
　　Thou messenger of sympathies,
　　That wax and wane in lover's eyes ;
Thou, that to human thought art nourishment,
　　Like darkness to a dying flame !
　　Depart not as thy shadow came :
　　Depart not—lest the grave should be,
Like life and fear, a dark reality.

* * * * * *

The day becomes more solemn and serene
   When noon is past : there is a harmony
   In autumn, and a lustre in its sky,
Which through the Summer is not heard or seen,
As if it could not be, as if it had not been !
     Thus let thy power, which like the truth
     Of Nature on my passive youth
Descended, to my onward life supply
     Its calm, to one who worships thee,
     And every form containing thee,
     Whom, SPIRIT fair, thy spells did bind
To fear himself, and love all human kind.

      SHELLEY (from *Hymn to Intellectual Beauty*)

TO MR. AND MRS. ——, A SON

Out of the deep, my child, out of the deep,
Where all that was to be, in all that was,
Whirl'd for a million aeons thro' the vast
Waste dawn of multitudinous-eddying light—
Out of the deep, my child, out of the deep,
Thro' all this changing world of changeless law,
And every phase of ever-heightening life,
And nine long months of antenatal gloom,
With this last moon, this crescent—her dark orb
Touch'd with earth's light—thou comest, darling boy ;
Our own ; a babe in lineament and limb
Perfect, and prophet of the perfect man ;
Whose face and form are hers and mine in one,
Indissolubly married like our love ;

Live, and be happy in thyself, and serve
This mortal race thy kin so well, that men
May bless thee as we bless thee, O young life
Breaking with laughter from the dark ; and may
The fated channel where thy motion lives
Be prosperously shaped, and sway thy course
Along the years of haste and random youth
Unshatter'd ; then full-current thro' full man ;
And last in kindly curves, with gentlest fall,
By quiet fields, a slowly-dying power,
To that last deep where we and thou are still.

TENNYSON (from *De Profundis*)

THE POPE SPEAKS OF POMPILIA

First of the first,
Such I pronounce Pompilia, then as now
Perfect in whiteness : stoop thou down, my child,
Give one good moment to the poor old Pope
Heart-sick at having all his world to blame—
Let me look at thee in the flesh as erst,
Let me enjoy the old clean linen garb,
Not the new splendid vesture ! Armed and crowned,
Would Michael, yonder, be, nor crowned nor armed,
The less pre-eminent angel ? Everywhere
I see in the world the intellect of man,
That sword, the energy his subtle spear,
The knowledge which defends him like a shield—
Everywhere ; but they make not up, I think,
The marvel of a soul like thine, earth's flower
She holds up to the softened gaze of God !

It was not given Pompilia to know much,
Speak much, to write a book, to move mankind,
Be memorized by who records my time.
Yet if in purity and patience, if
In faith held fast despite the plucking fiend,
Safe like the signet stone with the new name
That saints are known by,—if in right returned
For wrong, most pardon for worst injury,
If there be any virtue, any praise—
Then will this woman-child have proved—who knows ?—
Just the one prize vouchsafed unworthy me,
Seven years a gardener of the untoward ground
I till,—this earth, my sweat and blood manure
All the long day that barrenly grows dusk :
At least one blossom makes me proud at eve
Born 'mid the briers of my enclosure ! Still
(Oh, here as elsewhere, nothingness of man!)
Those be the plants, imbedded yonder South
To mellow in the morning, those made fat
By the master's eye, that yield such timid leaf,
Uncertain bud, as product of his pains !
While—see how this mere chance-sown cleft-nursed seed
That sprang up by the wayside 'neath the foot
Of the enemy, this breaks all into blaze,
Spreads itself, one wide glory of desire
To incorporate the whole great sun it loves
From the inch-height whence it looks and longs ! My
    flower,
My rose I gather for the breast of God.

BROWNING (from *The Ring and the Book*)

A CHILD'S LAUGHTER

All the bells of heaven may ring,
All the birds of heaven may sing,
All the wells on earth may spring,
All the winds on earth may bring
   All sweet sounds together;
Sweeter far than all things heard,
Hand of harper, tone of bird,
Sound of woods at sundown stirred,
Welling water's winsome word,
   Wind in warm wan weather.

One thing yet there is, that none
Hearing ere its chime be done
Knows not well the sweetest one
Heard of man beneath the sun,
   Hoped in heaven hereafter;
Soft and strong and loud and light,
Very sound of very light
Heard from morning's rosiest height,
When the soul of all delight
   Fills a child's clear laughter.

Golden bells of welcome rolled
Never forth such notes, nor told
Hours so blithe in tones so bold,
As the radiant mouth of gold
   Here that rings forth heaven.
If the golden-crested wren
Were a nightingale—why, then,
Something seen and heard of men
Might be half as sweet as when
   Laughs a child of seven.

SWINBURNE

A COSMIC OUTLOOK

Onward :—thro' baffled hopes, thro' bootless prayers,
With strength that sinks, with high task half begun,
Things great desired, things lamentable done,
Vows writ in water, blows that beat the air.
Oh ! I have guessed the end ; the end is fair.
Not with these weak limbs is thy last race run ;
Not all thy vision sinks with this low sun ;
Not all thy spirit swoons in this despair.
Look how thine own soul, throned where all is well,
Smiles to regard thy days disconsolate ;
Yea ; since herself she wove the worldly spell,
Doomed thee for lofty gain to low estate ;—
Sown with thy fall a seed of glory fell ;
Thy heaven is in thee, and thy will thy fate.

F. W. H. MYERS

TO MILTON—BLIND

He who said suddenly, " Let there be light ! "
To thee the dark deliberately gave ;
That those full eyes might undistracted be
By this beguiling show of sky and field,
This brilliance, that so lures us from the Truth.
He gave thee back original night, His own
Tremendous canvas, large and blank and free,
Where at each thought a star flashed out and sang.
O blinded with a special lightning, thou
Hadst once again the virgin Dark ! and when
The pleasant flowery sight, which had deterred

Thine eyes from seeing, when this recent world
Was quite withdrawn; then burst upon thy view
The elder glory; space again in pangs,
And Eden odorous in the early mist,
That heaving watery plain that *was* the world;
Then the burned earth, and Christ coming in clouds.
Or rather a special leave to thee was given
By the high power, and thou with bandaged eyes
Wast guided through the glimmering camp of God.
Thy hand was taken by angels who patrol
The evening, or are sentries to the dawn,
Or pace the wide air everlastingly.
Thou wast admitted to the presence, and deep
Argument heardest, and the large design
That brings this world out of the woe to bliss.

STEPHEN PHILLIPS

THE FAIR CHIVALRY

Ah, see the fair chivalry come, the companions of Christ!
White Horsemen, who ride on white horses, the Knights
    of God!
They, for their Lord and their Lover who sacrificed
All save the sweetness of treading where He first trod!

These, through the darkness of death, the dominion of
    night,
Swept, and they woke in white places at morning tide:
They saw with their eyes, and sang for joy of the sight,
They saw with their eyes the Eyes of the Crucified.

Now, whithersoever He goeth, with Him they go :
White Horsemen, who ride on white horses, oh, fair to
    see !
They ride, where the Rivers of Paradise flash and flow,
White Horsemen, with Christ their Captain : for ever He !

LIONEL JOHNSON

WISHES FOR WILLIAM

These things I wish you for our friendship's sake :
A sunburnt thatch, a door to face the sun
At westering, the noise of homing rooks,
A kind, old, lazy chair, a courtly cat
To rub against your knees,
Shelves of well-chosen books—
I wish you these.

I wish you friends whose wisdom makes them kind,
Well leisured friends to share your evening's peace,
Friends who can season knowledge with a laugh.
A hedge of lavender, a patch of thyme,
With sage and marjoram and rosemary,
A damask rosebush and a hive of bees,
And cabbages that hold the morning dew,
A blackbird in the orchard boughs—all these
And—God bless you.

Children, no matter whose, to wait for you
With flower faces at your garden gate,
And one to watch the clock with eager eyes,
Saying, " He's late—he's late."

W. M. LETTS

§3. LOVE POEMS

THE APPEAL:

An Earnest Suit to his Unkind Mistress, not to Forsake him

And wilt thou leave me thus?
Say nay, say nay, for shame!
To save thee from the blame
Of all my grief and grame.
And wilt thou leave me thus?
    Say nay! say nay!

And wilt thou leave me thus,
That hath loved thee so long
In wealth and woe among:
And is thy heart so strong
As for to leave me thus?
    Say nay! say nay!

And wilt thou leave me thus,
That hath given thee my heart
Never for to depart
Neither for pain nor smart:
And wilt thou leave me thus?
    Say nay! say nay!

And wilt thou leave me thus,
And have no more pitye
Of him that loveth thee?
Alas, thy cruelty!
And wilt thou leave me thus?
    Say nay! say nay!

SIR THOMAS WYATT

535

THE SHIP OF LOVE

My galley, chargèd with forgetfulness,
   Through sharpè seas in winter nights doth pass
   'Tween rock and rock ; and eke my foe, alas,
   That is my lord, steereth with cruelness :
And every hour, a thought in readiness,
   As though that death were light in such a case,
   An endless wind doth tear the sail apace
   Of forcèd sighs and trusty fearfulness.
A rain of tears, a cloud of dark disdain,
   Have done the wearied cords great hinderance ;
   Wreathèd with error and with ignorance,
The stars be hid that lead me to this pain ;
   Drowned is reasòn, that should be my comfòrt,
   And I remain despairing of the port.

                           SIR THOMAS WYATT

THE ROYAL LOVER

I grieve, yet dare not shew my discontent,
   I love, and yet am forc'd to seem to hate ;
I do, yet dare not say I ever meant,
   I seem stark mute, but inwardly do prate.
     I am, and not, I freeze, and yet am burn'd,
     Since from myself my other self I turn'd.

My care is like my shadow in the sun,
   Follows me flying, flies when I pursue it ;
Stands and lies by me, does what I have done ;
   This too familiar care doth make me rue it.
     No means I find to rid him from my breast,
     Till by the end of things it be supprest.

Some gentler passions steal into my mind,
  For I am soft, and made of melting snow ;
Or, be more cruel, love, and so be kind,
  Let me or float or sink, be high or low ;
    Or let me live with some more sweet content,
    Or die, and so forget what love e'er meant.

QUEEN ELIZABETH (from *Ashmol. Mus. MSS.*
6989–781)

LOVE THE FULFILMENT

Love is life's end (an end, but never ending)
  All joys, all sweets, all happiness awarding ;
Love is life's wealth (ne'er spent, but ever spending),
  More rich by giving, taking by discarding ;
Love's life's reward, rewarded in rewarding :
    Then from thy wretched heart fond care remove ;
    Ah ! should thou live but once love's sweets to prove,
    Thou wilt not love to live unless thou live to love.

ANONYMOUS (from *Brittain's Ida,* 1628)

THE LOVER PLAINETH IN WINTER

O western wind, when wilt thou blow
  That the small rain down can rain ?
Christ, that my love were in my arms
  And I in my bed again !

ANONYMOUS (16th Century)

DESIRE

1. *Lullaby*

"Sleep, baby mine," Desire's nurse Beauty singeth ;
"Thy cries, O baby, set mine head on aching."
The babe cries, "Way ! thy love doth keep me waking."

"Lully, lully, my babe ! Hope cradle bringeth
Unto my children, always good rest taking."
The babe cries "Way ! thy love doth keep me waking."

"Since, baby mine, from me thy watching springeth,
Sleep then a little ; pap Content is making."
The babe cries "Nay ! for that abide I waking."

2. *Complaint*

Thou blind man's mark, thou fool's self-chosen snare,
Fond fancy's scum, and dregs of scattered thought :
Band of all evils ; cradle of causeless care ;
Thou web of will, whose end is never wrought :
Desire ! Desire ! I have too dearly bought,
With price of mangled mind, thy worthless ware ;
Too long, too long, asleep thou hast me brought,
Who should my mind to higher things prepare.
But yet in vain thou hast my ruin sought ;
In vain thou mad'st me to vain things aspire ;
In vain thou kindlest all thy smoky fire ;
For Virtue hath this better lesson taught,—
Within myself to seek my only hire,
Desiring nought but how to kill Desire.

3. *Farewell*

Leave me, O Love, which reachest but to dust ;
And thou, my mind, aspire to higher things ;
Grow rich in that which never taketh rust ;
Whatever fades, but fading pleasure brings.
Draw in thy beams, and humble all thy might
To that sweet yoke, where lasting freedoms be ;
Which breaks the clouds, and opens forth the light
That doth both shine, and give us sight to see.
O take fast hold ; let that light be thy guide
In this small course which birth draws out to death,
And think how evil becometh him to slide,
Who seeketh heav'n and comes of heav'nly breath.
Then farewell, world ; thy uttermost I see :
Eternal Love, maintain thy Life in me.

SIR PHILIP SIDNEY

THE TRUE BEAUTY

O how much more doth beauty beauteous seem
By that sweet ornament which truth doth give !
The Rose looks fair, but fairer we it deem
For that sweet odour which doth in it live.
The Canker-blooms have full as deep a dye
As the perfumèd tincture of the Roses,
Hang on such thorns, and play as wantonly
When summer's breath their maskèd buds discloses :

But—for their virtue only is their show—
They live unwoo'd and unrespected fade,
Die to themselves. Sweet Roses do not so;
Of their sweet deaths are sweetest odours made.
   And so of you, beauteous and lovely youth,
   When that shall vade, my verse distils your truth.

SHAKESPEARE

ETERNAL LINES

Shall I compare thee to a Summer's day?
Thou art more lovely and more temperate:
Rough winds do shake the darling buds of May,
And Summer's lease hath all too short a date:
Sometime too hot the eye of heaven shines,
And often is his gold complexion dimm'd;
And every fair from fair sometime declines,
By chance or nature's changing course untrimm'd:
But thy eternal Summer shall not fade
Nor lose possession of that fair thou owest;
Nor shall Death brag thou wanderest in his shade,
When in eternal lines to time thou growest:
   So long as men can breathe, or eyes can see,
   So long lives this, and this gives life to thee.

SHAKESPEARE

A NIGHT OF WAITING

Good night, good rest ! Ah, neither be my share :
She bade good night that kept my rest away ;
And daff'd me to a cabin hang'd with care,
To descant on the doubts of my decay.
   " Farewell," quoth she, " and come again to-morrow " :
   Fare well I could not, for I supp'd with sorrow.

Yet at my parting sweetly did she smile,
In scorn or friendship, nill I conster whether :
May be she joy'd to jest at my exile,
May be again to make me wander thither :
   " Wander," a word for shadows like myself,
   As take the pain, but cannot pluck the pelf.

Lord, how mine eyes throw gazes to the east !
My heart doth charge the watch ; the morning rise
Doth cite each moving sense from idle rest.
Not daring trust the office of mine eyes,
   While Philomela sings, I sit and mark,
   And wish her lays were tunèd like the lark ;

For she doth welcome daylight with her ditty,
And drives away at last dark dreaming night ;
The night so pack'd, I post unto my pretty ;
Heart hath his hope and eyes their wishèd sight ;
   Sorrow made solace, solace mix'd with sorrow ;
   For why ? She sigh'd, and bade me come to-morrow.

Were I with her, the night would post too soon ;
But now are minutes added to the hours ;
To spite me now, each minute seems a moon ;
Yet not for me—Shine sun to succour flowers !
  Pack night, peep day ; good day, of night now borrow ;
  Short, night, to-night, and length thyself, to-morrow !

ANONYMOUS (from *The Passionate Pilgrim*, 1599)

NOBLE LOVE

It is the counterpoise that minds
To fair and virtuous things inclines ;
It is the gust we have and sense
Of every noble excellence ;
It is the pulse by which we know
Whether our souls have life or no ;
And such a soft and gentle fire
As kindles and inflames desire ;
Until it all like incense burns
And unto melting sweetness turns.

RICHARD FLECKNOE

HIGH AND LOW

Were I as base as is the lowly plain,
And you, my love, as high as heaven above,
Yet should the thoughts of me your humble swain
Ascend to heaven in honour of my love.

Were I as high as heaven above the plain,
And you, my love, as humble and as low
As are the deepest bottoms of the main,
Wheresoe'er you were, with you my love should go.
Were you the earth, dear love, and I the skies,
My love should shine on you like to the sun,
And look upon you with ten thousand eyes,
Till heaven waxed blind, and till the world were done.
　Wheresoe'er I am, below, or else above you,
　Wheresoe'er you are, my heart shall truly love you.

J. SYLVESTER (1602)

MY LADY'S TEARS

　I saw my Lady weep,
And Sorrow proud to be advancèd so
In those fair eyes where all perfections keep.
　Her face was full of woe ;
But such a woe (believe me) as wins more hearts
Than Mirth can do with her enticing parts.

　Sorrow was there made fair,
And Passion wise ; Tears a delightful thing ;
Silence beyond all speech, a wisdom rare :
　She made her sighs to sing,
And all things with so sweet a sadness move
As made my heart at once both grieve and love.

O fairer than aught else
The world can show, leave off in time to grieve !
Enough, enough : your joyful look excels :
   Tears kill the heart, believe.
O strive not to be excellent in woe,
Which only breeds your beauty's overthrow.

From JOHN DOWLAND'S *Third and Last*
                        Book of Songs or Airs, 1603

THE THOUGHT

If you do love as well as I,
Then every minute from your heart
   A thought doth part ;
And wingèd with desire doth fly
Till it hath met, in a straight line,
   A thought of mine
So like to yours, we cannot know
Whether of both doth come, or go,
   Till we define
Which of us two, that thought doth owe.

I say then, that your thoughts which pass,
Are not so much the thoughts you meant,
   As those I sent :
For as my image in a glass
Belongs not to the glass you see,
   But unto me ;
So when your fancy is so clear
That you would think you saw me there,
   It needs must be
That it was I did first appear.

Likewise, when I send forth a thought,
My reason tells me, 'tis the same
  Which from you came,
And which your beauteous image wrought.
Thus while our thoughts by turns do lead,
  None can precede ;
And thus, while in each other's mind
Such interchangèd forms we find,
  Our loves may plead
To be of more than vulgar kind.

May you then often think on me,
And by that thinking know 'tis true
  I thought on you ;
I in the same belief will be :
While, by this mutual address,
  We will possess
A love must live, when we do die,
Which rare and secret property
  You will confess,
If you do love as well as I.

LORD HERBERT OF CHERBURY

SONGS

I.

O were my Love yon lilac fair,
 Wi' purple blossoms to the spring,
And I a bird to shelter there,
 When wearied on my little wing ;

How I wad mourn when it was torn
　　By autumn wild and winter rude !
But I wad sing on wanton wing
　　When youthfu' May its bloom renew'd.

O gin my Love were yon red rose
　　That grows upon the castle wa',
And I mysel a drap o' dew
　　Into her bonnie breast to fa' ;
O there, beyond expression blest,
　　I'd feast on beauty a' the night ;
Seal'd on her silk-saft faulds to rest,
　　Till fley'd awa' by Phoebus' light.

2.

O, wert thou in the cauld blast
　　On yonder lea, on yonder lea,
My plaidie to the angry airt,
　　I'd shelter thee, I'd shelter thee.
Or did Misfortune's bitter storms
　　Around thee blaw, around thee blaw,
Thy bield should be my bosom
　　To share it a', to share it a'.

Or were I in the wildest waste,
　　Sae black and bare, sae black and bare,
The desert were a Paradise,
　　If thou wert there, if thou wert there.
Or were I monarch of the globe,
　　Wi' thee to reign, wi' thee to reign,
The brightest jewel in my crown
　　Wad be my queen, wad be my queen.

BURNS

ROSE AYLMER

Ah, what avails the sceptred race !
    Ah, what the form divine,
What every virtue, every grace !
    Rose Aylmer, all were thine.

Rose Aylmer, whom these wakeful eyes
    May weep, but never see,
A night of memories and sighs
    I consecrate to thee.

W. S. LANDOR

AMOR OMNIA VINCIT

Our love is not a fading, earthly flower :
Its wingèd seed dropped down from Paradise,
And, nursed by day and night, by sun and shower,
Doth momently to fresher beauty rise :
To us the leafless autumn is not bare,
Nor winter's rattling boughs lack lusty green.
Our summer hearts make summer's fulness, where
No leaf, or bud, or blossom may be seen :
For nature's life in love's deep life doth lie,
Love,—whose forgetfulness is beauty's death,
Whose mystic key these cells of Thou and I
Into the infinite freedom openeth,
And makes the body's dark and narrow grate
The wind-flung leaves of Heaven's palace-gate.

JAMES RUSSELL LOWELL

A BIRTHDAY

My heart is like a singing bird
   Whose nest is in a watered shoot ;
My heart is like an apple-tree
   Whose boughs are bent with thickset fruit :
My heart is like a rainbow shell
   That paddles in a halcyon sea ;
My heart is gladder than all these
   Because my love is come to me.

Raise me a dais of silk and down ;
   Hang it with vair and purple dyes ;
Carve it in doves and pomegranates,
   And peacocks with a hundred eyes ;
Work it in gold and silver grapes,
   In leaves and silver fleurs-de-lys ;
Because the birthday of my life
   Is come, my love is come to me.

CHRISTINA ROSSETTI

THE SOURCE OF LOVE

My eyes for beauty pine,
   My soul for Goddès grace :
No other care nor hope is mine
   To heaven I turn my face.

One splendour thence is shed
   From all the stars above :
'Tis namèd when God's name is said,
   'Tis Love, 'tis heavenly Love.

And every gentle heart,
   That burns with true desire,
Is lit from eyes that mirror part
   Of that celestial fire.

ROBERT BRIDGES

SONG

The nightingale has a lyre of gold,
   The lark's is a clarion call,
And the blackbird plays but a boxwood flute,
   But I love him best of all.

For his song is all of the joy of life,
   And we in the mad, spring weather,
We two have listened till he sang
   Our hearts and lips together.

W. E. HENLEY

NIGHT IS FALLEN

Night is fallen within, without,
   Come, Love, soon !
I am weary of my doubt.
The golden fire of the Sun is out,
   The silver fire of the Moon.

   Love shall be
   A child in me

When they are cinders grey,
With the earth and with the sea,
With the star that shines on thee,
And the night and day.

MARY E. COLERIDGE

THE HAPPY NIGHT

I have loved to-night; from love's last bordering steep
  I have fallen at last with joy and forgotten the shore;
  I have known my love to-night as never before,
I have flung myself in the deep, and drawn from the deep,
And kissed her lightly, and left my belovèd to sleep.
  And now I sit in the night and my heart is still:
  Strong and secure; there is nothing that's left to will,
There is nothing to win but only a thing to keep.

And I look to-night, completed and not afraid,
  Into the windy dark where shines no light;
And care not at all though the darkness never should fade,
  Nor fear that death should suddenly come to-night.
Knowing my last would be surely my bravest breath,
I am happy to-night: I have laughed to-night at death.

J. C. SQUIRE

§4. PROSE

TWO KINDS OF HUNTING

1. *Hunting by Water*

Fishing is a kind of hunting by water, be it with nets, weeles, baits, angling, or otherwise, and yields all out as much pleasure to some men as dogs or hawks, when they draw their fish upon the bank. James Dubravius, that Moravian, in his book telleth how, travelling by the highway side in Silesia, he found a nobleman, " booted up to the groins," wading himself, pulling the nets, and labouring as much as any fisherman of them all : and when some belike objected to him the baseness of his office, he excused himself, " that if other men might hunt hares, why should not he hunt carps ? " Many gentlemen in like sort with us will wade up to the arm-holes upon such occasions, and voluntarily undertake that to satisfy their pleasure, which a poor man for a good stipend would scarce be hired to undergo. Plutarch speaks against all fishing, " as filthy, base, illiberal employment, having neither wit nor perspicacity in it, nor worth the labour." But he that shall consider the variety of baits for all seasons, and pretty devices which our anglers have invented, peculiar lines, false flies, several sleights, etc., will say, that it deserves like commendation, requires as much study and perspicacity as the rest, and is to be preferred before many of them. Because hawking and hunting are very laborious, much riding, and many dangers accompany them ; but this is still and quiet : and if so be the angler catch no fish, yet he hath a wholesome walk to the brookside, pleasant shade by the sweet silver streams ; he hath good air, and sweet smells of fine fresh meadow flowers, he hears the melodious harmony of birds, he sees the swans, herons, ducks, waterhorns, coots, etc., and many other fowl, with their brood, which he thinketh better than the noise of hounds, or blast of horns, and all the sport that they can make.

2. *Hunting the Dear*

'Tis most true, many gentlewomen are so nice, they scorn all suitors, crucify their poor paramours, and think nobody good enough for them, as dainty to please as Daphne herself. One while they will not marry, as they say at least (when as they intend nothing less), another while not yet, when 'tis their only desire, they rave upon it. She will marry at last, but not him : he is a proper man indeed, and well qualified, but he wants means : another of her suitors hath good means, but he wants wit ; one is too old, another too young, too deformed, she likes not his carriage : a third too loosely given, he is rich, but base born : she will be a gentlewoman, a lady, as her sister is, as her mother is : she is all out as fair, as well brought up, hath as good a portion, and she looks for as good a match, as Matilda or Dorinda : if not, she is resolved as yet to tarry, so apt are young maids to boggle at every object, so soon won or lost with every toy, so quickly diverted, so hard to be pleased. In the meantime, one suitor pines away, languisheth in love, another sighs and grieves, she cares not. They take a pride to prank up themselves, to make young men enamoured to dote on them, and to run mad for their sakes. All suit and service is too little for them, presents too base. As Atalanta they must be overrun, or not won. Many young men are as obstinate, and as curious in their choice, as tyrannically proud, insulting, deceitful, false-hearted, as irrefragable and peevish on the other side, Narcissus-like. Echo wept and wooed him by all means above the rest, Love me for pity, or pity me for love, but he was obstinate, " he would rather die than give consent." Psyche ran whining after Cupid, but he rejected her nevertheless. Thus many lovers do hold out so long, doting on themselves, stand in their own light, till in the end they come to be scorned and rejected, as Narcissus was himself. They begin to be contemned themselves of others, as he was of his shadow, and take up with a poor curate, or an old serving-man at last, that might have had their choice of right good matches in their youth. Yet this is a common humour, will not be left, and cannot be helped.

ROBERT BURTON (from *Anatomy of Melancholy*)

OLD SONGS

PISCATOR : Look, under that broad *Beech tree* I sate down, when I was last this way a fishing, and the birds in the adjoyning Grove seemed to have a friendly contention with an Eccho, whose dead voice seemed to live in a hollow tree, near to the brow of that Primrose-hill ; there I sate viewing the silver-streams glide silently towards their center, the tempestuous Sea, yet sometimes opposed by rugged roots and pebble stones which broke their waves and turned them into foam : and sometimes I beguil'd time by viewing the harmless Lambs, some leaping securely in the cool shade, whilst others sported themselves in the chearful Sun ; and saw others craving comfort from the swoln Udders of their bleating Dams. . . As I left this place, and entered into the next field, a second pleasure entertained me, 'twas a handsome milk-maid, that had not yet attain'd so much age and wisdom as to load her mind with any fears of many things that will never be (as too many men too often do) but she cast away all care, and sung like a *Nightingale* : her voice was good, and the Ditty fitted for it ; 'twas that smooth song which was made by *Kit Marlow*, now at least fifty years ago ; and the Milk-maid's Mother sung an answer to it, which was made by Sir *Walter Rawleigh* in his younger days. They were old fashioned Poetry, but choicely good, I think much better than the strong lines that are now in fashion in this critical age. Look yonder ! on my word, yonder they both be a milking again : I will give her the *Chub*, and perswade them to sing those two songs to us.

IZAAK WALTON (from *The Compleat Angler*)

THE WARFARING CHRISTIAN

Good and evil we know in the field of this world grow up together almost inseparably ; and the knowledge of good is so involved and interwoven with the knowledge of evil, and in so many cunning resemblances hardly to be discerned, that those confused seeds which were imposed upon Psyche as an incessant labour to cull out, and sort asunder, were not more intermixed. It was from out the rind of one apple tasted, that the knowledge of good and evil, as two twins cleaving together, leaped forth into the world. And perhaps this is that doom which Adam fell into of knowing good and evil, that is to say of knowing good by evil. As therefore the state of man now is ; what wisdom can there be to choose, what continuance to forbear without the knowledge of evil ? He that can apprehend and consider vice with all her baits and seeming pleasures, and yet abstain, and yet distinguish, and yet prefer that which is truly better, he is the true warfaring Christian. I cannot praise a fugitive and cloistered virtue, unexercised and unbreathed, that never sallies out and sees her adversary, but slinks out of the race, where that immortal garland is to be run for, not without dust and heat. Assuredly we bring not innocence into the world, we bring impurity much rather ; that which purifies us is trial, and trial is by what is contrary.

MILTON (from *Areopagitica*)

THE NEGLECT OF PREACHING

I shall produce certain instances to show the great neglect of preaching now among us.

These may be reduced under two heads. First, men's absence from the service of the church ; and secondly, their misbehaviour when they are here.

The first instance of men's neglect is in their frequent absence from the church.

There is no excuse so trivial that will not pass upon some men's consciences to excuse their attendance at the public worship of God. Some are so unfortunate as to be always indisposed on the Lord's day, and think nothing so unwholesome as the air of a church. Others have their affairs so oddly contrived, as to be always unluckily prevented by business. With some it is a great mark of wit and deep understanding to stay at home on Sundays. Others again discover strange fits of laziness, that seize them particularly on that day, and confine them to their beds. Others are absent out of mere contempt of religion. And, lastly, there are not a few who look upon it as a day of rest, and therefore claim the privilege of their cattle, to keep the Sabbath by eating, drinking, and sleeping, after the toil and labour of the week. Now in all this the worst circumstance is, that these persons are such whose companies are most required, and who stand most in need of a physician.

Secondly, Men's great neglect and contempt of preaching appear by their misbehaviour when at church.

If the audience were to be ranked under several heads, according to their behaviour when the word of God is delivered, how small a number would appear of those who receive it as they ought! How much of the seed then sown would be found to fall by the wayside upon stony ground, or among thorns ; and how little good ground there would be to take it ! A preacher cannot look round from the pulpit without observing that some are in a perpetual whisper, and by their air and gesture give occasion to suspect that they are in those very minutes defaming their neighbour. Others have their eyes and imagination constantly engaged in such a circle of objects, perhaps to gratify the most unwarrantable desires, that they never once attend to the business of the place ; the sound of the preacher's words does not so much as once interrupt them. Some have their minds wandering among idle, worldly, or vicious thoughts. Some lie at catch to ridicule whatever they hear, and with much wit and humour provide a stock of laughter by furnishing themselves from the pulpit. But of all misbehaviour, none is comparable to that of those who come here to sleep. Opium is not so stupefying to many persons as an afternoon sermon. Perpetual custom hath so brought it about that the words of whatever preacher become only a sort of uniform sound at a distance, than which nothing is more effectual to lull the senses. For that it is the very sound of the sermon which bindeth up their faculties is manifest from hence because they all awake so very regularly as soon as it ceaseth, and with much devotion receive the blessing.

SWIFT (from *A Sermon on Sleeping in Church*)

A RAMBLE FROM RICHMOND TO LONDON

I lay one night last week at Richmond ; and being restless, not out of dissatisfaction, but a certain busy inclination one sometimes has, I rose at four in the morning, and took boat for London, with a resolution to rove by boat and coach for the next four-and-twenty hours, till the many different objects I must needs meet with should tire my imagination, and give me an inclination to a repose more profound than I was at that time capable of. I beg people's pardon for an odd humour I am guilty of, and was often that day, which is saluting any person whom I like, whether I know him or not. This is a particularity would be tolerated in me, if they considered that the greatest pleasure I know I receive at my eyes, and that I am obliged to an agreeable person for coming abroad into my view, as another is for a visit of conversation at their own houses.

The hours of the day and night are taken up in the cities of London and Westminster, by people as different from each other as those who are born in different centuries. Men of six o'clock give way to those of nine, they of nine to the generation of twelve ; and they of twelve disappear, and make room for the fashionable world, who have made two o'clock the noon of the day.

When we first put off from shore, we soon fell in with a fleet of gardeners, bound for the several market ports of

557

London; and it was the most pleasing scene imaginable to see the cheerfulness with which those industrious people plied their way to a certain sale of their goods. The banks on each side are as well peopled, and beautified with as agreeable plantations, as any spot on the earth; but the Thames itself, loaded with the product of each shore, added very much to the landscape. It was very easy to observe by their sailing, and the countenances of the ruddy virgins, who were supercargoes, the parts of the town to which they were bound. There was an air in the purveyors for Covent-garden, who frequently converse with morning rakes, very unlike the seeming sobriety of those bound for Stocks-market.

Nothing remarkable happened in our voyage; but I landed with ten sail of apricot-boats, at Strand-bridge, after having put in at Nine-Elms, and taken in melons, consigned by Mr. Cuffe, of that place, to Sarah Sewell and Company, at their stall in Covent-garden. We arrived at Strand-bridge at six of the clock, and were unloading; when the hackney-coachmen of the foregoing night took their leave of each other at the Dark-house, to go to bed before the day was too far spent. . .

The day of people of fashion began now to break, and carts and hacks were mingled with equipages of show and vanity; when I resolved to walk it out of cheapness; but my unhappy curiosity is such, that I find it always my interest to take coach; for some odd adventure among beggars, ballad-singers, or the like, detains and throws me into expense. It happened so immediately: for at the corner of Warwick-street, as I was listening to a new ballad, a ragged rascal, a beggar who knew me, came up to me, and began to turn the eyes of the good company upon me, by telling me he was extremely poor, and should die in the street for want of drink, except I immediately would have the charity to give him sixpence to go into the next ale-house and save his life. He urged, with a melancholy face, that all his family had died of thirst. All the mob have humour, and two or three began to take the jest ; by which Mr. Sturdy carried his point, and let me sneak off to a coach. As I drove along, it was a pleasing reflection to see the world so prettily checkered since I left Richmond, and the scene still filling with children of a new hour. This satisfaction increased as I moved towards the city ; and gay signs, well-disposed streets, magnificent public structures and wealthy shops adorned with contented faces, made the joy still rising till we came into the centre of the city, and centre of the world of trade, the Exchange of London. As other men in the crowds about me were pleased with their hopes and bargains, I found my account in observing them, in attention to their several interests. I, indeed, looked upon myself as the richest man that walked the Exchange that day ; for my benevolence made me share the gains of every bargain that was made. . . When I came to my chambers, I writ down these minutes ; but was at a loss what instruction I should propose to my reader from the enumeration of so many insignificant matters and occurrences ; and I thought it of great use, if they could learn with me to keep their minds open to gratification, and ready to receive it from any thing it meets with. This one circumstance will make every face you see give you the satisfaction you now take in beholding that of a friend ; will make every object a pleasing one ; will make all the good which arrives to any man an increase of happiness to yourself.

STEELE (from the *Spectator*)

" I was born " (says he) " on the side of a mountain, near a little village of Peru, and made a voyage to England in an ingot, under the convoy of Sir Francis Drake. I was, soon after my arrival taken out of my Indian habit, refined, naturalised, and put into the British mode, with the face of Queen Elizabeth on one side, and the arms of the country on the other. Being thus equipped, I found in me a wonderful inclination to ramble, and visit all parts of the new world into which I was brought. The people very much favoured my natural disposition, and shifted me so fast from hand to hand, that before I was five years old, I had travelled into almost every corner of the nation. But in the beginning of my sixth year, to my unspeakable grief, I fell into the hands of a miserable old fellow, who clapped me into an iron chest, where I found five hundred more of my own quality who lay under the same confinement. The only relief we had, was to be taken out and counted over in the fresh air every morning and evening. After an imprisonment of several years, we heard somebody knocking at our chest, and breaking it open with a hammer. This we found was the old man's heir, who, as his father lay a-dying, was so good as to come to our release : he separated us that very day. What was the fate of my companions I know not ; as for myself, I was sent to the apothecary's shop for a pint of sack. The apothecary gave me to an herb-woman, the herb-woman to a butcher, the butcher to a brewer, and the brewer to his wife, who made a present of me to a nonconformist preacher. After this manner I made my way merrily through the world; for, as I told you before, we shillings love nothing so much as travelling. I sometimes fetched in a shoulder of mutton, sometimes a play-book, and often had the satisfaction to treat a Templar at a twelvepenny ordinary or carry him, with three friends, to Westminster Hall.

" In the midst of this pleasant progress which I made from place to place, I was arrested by a superstitious old woman, who shut me up in a greasy purse, in pursuance of a foolish saying, ' That while she kept a Queen Elizabeth's shilling about her, she should never be without money.' I continued here a close prisoner for many months, till at last I was exchanged for eight and forty farthings.

" I thus rambled from pocket to pocket till the beginning of the civil wars, when to my shame be it spoke, I was employed in raising soldiers against the king : for being of a very tempting breadth, a sergeant made use of me to inveigle country fellows, and list them in service of the parliament.

" As soon as he had made one man sure, his way was to oblige him to take a shilling of a more homely figure, and then practise the same trick upon another. Thus I continued doing great mischief to the crown, till my officer, chancing one morning to walk abroad earlier than ordinary, sacrificed me to his pleasures, and made use of me to seduce a milk-maid. This wench bent me, and gave me to her sweetheart applying more properly than she intended the usual form of, ' To my love and from my love.' This ungenerous gallant, marrying her within a few days after, pawned me for a dram of brandy, and drinking me out next day, I was beaten flat with a hammer, again set a-running.

" After many adventures, which it would be tedious to relate, I was sent to a young spendthrift, in company with the will of his deceased father. The young fellow, who I found was very extravagant, gave great demonstrations of joy at the receiving of the will ; but opening it, he found himself disinherited and cut off from the possession of a fair estate, by virtue of my being made a present to him. This put him into such a passion, that after having taken me in his hand, and cursed me, he squirred me away from him as far as he could fling me. I chanced to light in an unfrequented place under a dead wall, where I lay undiscovered and useless, during the usurpation of Oliver Cromwell.

" About a year after the king's return, a poor cavalier that was walking there about dinner-time, fortunately cast his eye upon me, and, to the great joy of us both, carried me to a cook's shop, where he dined upon me, and drank the king's health. When I came again into the world, I found that I had been happier in my retirement than I thought, having probably, by that means, escaped wearing a monstrous pair of breeches.[1]

" Being now of great credit and antiquity, I was rather looked upon as a medal than an ordinary coin ; for which reason a gamester laid hold of me and converted me to a counter, having got together some dozens of us for that use. We led a melancholy life in his possession, being busy at those hours wherein current coin is at rest, and partaking the fate of our master, being in a few moments valued at a crown, a pound, or a sixpence, according to the situation in which the fortune of the cards placed us. I had at length the good luck to see my master break, by which means I was again sent abroad under my primitive denomination of a shilling.

" I shall pass over many other accidents of less moment,

[1] A fancied resemblance, from the disposition of the arms of England and Ireland on Commonwealth coins. A. S.

and hasten to that fatal catastrophe, when I fell into the hands of an artist, who conveyed me under ground, and with an unmerciful pair of shears, cut off my titles, clipped my brims, retrenched my shape, rubbed me to my inmost ring, and, in short, so spoiled and pillaged me, that he did not leave me worth a groat. You may think what a confusion I was in, to see myself thus curtailed and disfigured. I should have been ashamed to have shown my head, had not all my old acquaintance been reduced to the same shameful figure, excepting some few that were punched through the belly. In the midst of this general calamity, when everybody thought our misfortune irretrievable, and our case desperate, we were thrown into the furnace together, and (as it often happens with cities rising out of a fire) appeared with greater beauty and lustre than we could ever boast of before. What has happened to me since this change of sex which you now see, I shall take some other opportunity to relate. In the meantime, I shall only repeat two adventures, as being very extraordinary, and neither of them having ever happened to me above once in my life. The first was, my being in a poet's pocket, who was so taken with the brightness and novelty of my appearance, that it gave occasion to the finest burlesque poem in the British language, entitled from me, ' The Splendid Shilling.' [1] The second adventure, which I must not omit, happened to me in the year 1703, when I was given away in charity to a blind man; but indeed this was by a mistake, the person who gave me having heedlessly thrown me into the hat among a pennyworth of farthings."

ADDISON (from the Tatler)

---

[1] By John Phillips. A. S.

As long as the cruelty of Maximin was confined to the illustrious senators, or even to the bold adventurers who in the court or army expose themselves to the caprice of fortune, the body of the people viewed their sufferings with indifference, or perhaps with pleasure. But the tyrant's avarice, stimulated by the insatiate desires of the soldiers, at length attacked the public property. Every city of the empire was possessed of an independent revenue, destined to purchase corn for the multitude, and to supply the expenses of the games and entertainments. By a single act of authority, the whole mass of wealth was at once confiscated for the use of the Imperial treasury. The temples were stripped of their most valuable offerings of gold and silver, and the statues of gods, heroes, and emperors, were melted down and coined into money. These impious orders could not be executed without tumults and massacres, as in many places the people chose rather to die in defence of their altars, than to behold in the midst of peace their cities exposed to the rapine and cruelty of war. The soldiers themselves, among whom this sacrilegious plunder was distributed, received it with a blush ; and, hardened as they were in acts of violence, they dreaded the just reproaches of their friends and relations. Throughout the Roman world a general cry of indignation was heard, imploring vengeance on the common enemy of human kind ; and at length, by an act of private oppression, a peaceful and unarmed province was driven into rebellion against him.

The procurator of Africa was a servant worthy of such a master, who considered the fines and confiscations of the rich as one of the most fruitful branches of the Imperial revenue. An iniquitous sentence had been (A.D. 237, April) pronounced against some opulent youths of that country, the execution of which would have stripped them of far the greater part of their patrimony. In this extremity, a resolution that must either complete or prevent their ruin, was dictated by despair. A respite of three days, obtained with difficulty from the rapacious treasurer, was employed in collecting from their estates a great number of slaves and peasants, blindly devoted to the commands of their lords, and armed with the rustic weapons of clubs and axes. The leaders of the conspiracy, as they were admitted to the audience of the procurator, stabbed him with the daggers concealed under their garments, and, by the assistance of their tumultuary train, seized on the little town of Thysdrus, and erected the standard of rebellion against the sovereign of the Roman empire. They rested their hopes on the hatred of mankind against Maximin, and they judiciously resolved to oppose to that detested tyrant, an emperor whose mild virtues had already acquired the love and esteem of the Romans, and whose authority over the province would give weight and stability to the enterprise. Gordianus, their proconsul, and the object of their choice, refused, with unfeigned reluctance, the dangerous honour, and begged with tears that they would suffer him to terminate in peace a long and innocent life, without staining his feeble age with civil blood. Their menaces compelled him to accept the Imperial purple, his only refuge indeed against the jealous cruelty of Maximin ; since, according to the reasoning of tyrants, those who have been esteemed worthy of the throne deserve death, and those who deliberate have already rebelled.

The family of Gordianus was one of the most illustrious

of the Roman senate. On the father's side, he was descended from the Gracchi; on his mother's from the emperor Trajan. A great estate enabled him to support the dignity of this birth, and, in the enjoyment of it, he displayed an elegant taste and beneficent disposition. The palace in Rome, formerly inhabited by the great Pompey, had been, during several generations, in the possession of Gordian's family. It was distinguished by ancient trophies of naval victories, and decorated with the works of modern painting. His villa on the road to Praeneste was celebrated for baths of singular beauty and extent, for three stately rooms of an hundred feet in length, and for a magnificent portico, supported by two hundred columns of the four most curious and costly sorts of marble. The public shows exhibited at his expense, and in which the people were entertained with many hundreds of wild beasts and gladiators, seemed to surpass the fortune of a subject; and whilst the liberality of other magistrates was confined to a few solemn festivals in Rome, the magnificence of Gordian was repeated, when he was aedile, every month in the year, and extended, during his consulship, to the principal cities of Italy. He was twice elevated to the last-mentioned dignity, by Caracalla and by Alexander; for he possessed the uncommon talent of acquiring the esteem of virtuous princes without alarming the jealousy of tyrants. His long life was innocently spent in the study of letters and the peaceful honours of Rome; and, till he was named proconsul of Africa by the voice of the senate and the approbation of Alexander, he appears prudently to have declined the command of armies and the government of provinces. As long as that emperor lived, Africa was happy under the administration of his worthy representative; after the barbarous Maximin had usurped the throne, Gordianus alleviated the miseries which he was unable to prevent. When he reluctantly accepted the purple, he was above fourscore years old ; a last and valuable remains of the happy age of the Antonines, whose virtues he revived in his own conduct and celebrated in an elegant poem of thirty books. With the venerable proconsul, his son, who had accompanied him into Africa as his lieutenant, was likewise declared emperor. His manners were less pure, but his character was equally amiable with that of his father. Twenty-two acknowledged concubines, and a library of sixty-two thousand volumes, attested the variety of his inclinations, and from the productions which he left behind him, it appears that the former as well as the latter were designed for use rather than ostentation. The Roman people acknowledged in the features of the younger Gordian the resemblance of Scipio Africanus, recollected with pleasure that his mother was the grand-daughter of Antoninus Pius, and rested the public hope on those latent virtues which had hitherto, as they fondly imagined, lain concealed in the luxurious indolence of a private life.

EDWARD GIBBON (from *Decline and Fall of the Roman Empire*)

THE ENGLISH MAIL-COACH
(1805—1815)

From eight p.m., to fifteen or twenty minutes later, imagine the mails assembled on parade in Lombard Street, where, at that time, and not in St. Martin's-le-Grand, was seated the General Post-Office. In what exact strength we mustered I do not remember ; but, from the length of each separate *attelage*, we filled the street, though a long one, and though we were drawn up in double file. On *any* night the spectacle was beautiful. The absolute perfection of all the appointments about the carriages and the harness, their strength, their brilliant cleanliness, their beautiful simplicity—but, more than all, the royal magnificence of the horses—were what might first have fixed the attention. Every carriage, on every morning in the year, was taken down to an official inspector for examination—wheels, axles, linchpins, pole, glasses, lamps, were all critically probed and tested. Every part of every carriage had been cleaned, every horse had been groomed, with as much rigour as if they belonged to a private gentleman ; and that part of the spectacle offered itself always. But the night before us is a night of victory ; and, behold ! to the ordinary display, what a heart-shaking addition !— horses, men, carriages, all are dressed in laurels and flowers, oak-leaves and ribbons. The guards, as being officially his Majesty's servants, and of the coachmen such as are within the privilege of the post-office, wear the royal liveries of course ; and as it is summer (for all the *land* victories were naturally won in summer), they wear, on this fine evening, these liveries exposed to view without any covering of upper coats. Such a costume, and the elaborate arrangement of the laurels in their hats, dilate their hearts, by giving to them openly a personal connection with the great news, in which already they have the general interest of patriotism. That great national sentiment surmounts and quells all sense of ordinary distinctions. Those passengers who happen to be gentlemen are now hardly to be distinguished as such except by dress ; for the usual reserve of their manner in speaking to the attendants has on this night melted away. One heart, one pride, one glory, connects every man by the transcendent bond of his national blood. The spectators, who are numerous beyond precedent, express their sympathy with these fervent feelings by continual hurrahs. Every moment are shouted aloud by the post-office servants, and summoned to draw up, the great ancestral names of cities known to history through a thousand years—Lincoln, Winchester, Portsmouth, Gloucester, Oxford, Bristol, Manchester, York, Newcastle, Edinburgh, Glasgow, Perth, Stirling, Aberdeen—expressing the grandeur of the empire by the antiquity of its towns, and the grandeur of the mail establishment by the diffusive radiation of its separate missions. Every moment you hear the thunder of lids locked down upon the mail-bags. That sound to each individual mail is the signal for drawing off, which process is the finest part of the entire spectacle. Then come the horses into play. Horses! can these be horses that bound off with the action and gestures of leopards? What stir!—what sea-like ferment!—what a thundering of wheels!—what a trampling of hoofs!—what a sounding of trumpets!

THOMAS DE QUINCEY

THE GREAT MOMENT

" I want to tell you something," I said : " I want to tell you all."

" Speak, Lucy ; come near ; speak ! . ."

Before I had half done, he held both my hands, he consulted my eyes with a most piercing glance : there was

569

something in his face which tended neither to calm nor to put me down; he forgot his own doctrine, he forsook his own system of repression when I most challenged its exercise. I think I deserved strong reproof: but when have we our deserts? I merited severity; he looked indulgence. To my very self I seemed imperious and unreasonable; he smiled, betraying delight. Warm, jealous, and haughty, I knew not till now that my nature had such a mood: he gathered me near his heart. I was full of faults; he took them and me all home. For the moment of utmost mutiny he reserved the one deep spell of peace...

We walked back to the Rue Fossetti by moonlight—such moonlight as fell on Eden—shining through the shades of the Great Garden, and haply gilding a path glorious for a step divine—a Presence nameless. Once in their lives some men and women go back to these first fresh days of our great Sire and Mother—taste that grand morning's dew—bathe in its sunrise.

CHARLOTTE BRONTË (from *Villette*)

THE DEATH OF A BIRD

The bird, however hard the frost may be, flies briskly to his customary roosting-place, and, with beak tucked into his wing, falls asleep. He has no apprehensions; only the hot blood grows colder and colder, the pulse feebler as he sleeps, and at midnight, or in the early morning, he drops from his perch—dead.

Yesterday he lived, and moved, responsive to a thousand external influences, reflecting earth and sky in his small brilliant brain as in a looking-glass; also he had a various language, the inherited knowledge of his race, and the faculty of flight, by means of which he could shoot, meteor-like, across the sky, and pass swiftly from place to place ; and with it such perfect control over all his organs, such marvellous certitude in all his motions, as to be able to drop himself plumb down from the tallest tree-top, or out of the void air, on to a slender spray, and scarcely cause its leaves to tremble. Now, on this morning, he lies stiff and motionless; if you were to take him up and drop him from your hand, he would fall to the ground like a stone or a lump of clay—so easy and swift is the passage from life to death in wild nature! But he was never miserable.

W. H. HUDSON (from *Birds in Town and Village*)

GOOD COMPANY

It is enough to lie on the sward in the shadow of green boughs, to listen to the songs of summer, to drink in the sunlight, the air, the flowers, the sky, the beauty of all. Or upon the hill-tops to watch the white clouds rising over the curved hill-lines, their shadows descending the slope. Or on the beach to listen to the sweet sigh as the smooth sea runs up and recedes. It is lying beside the immortals, in-drawing the life of the ocean, the earth, and the sun.

I want to be always in company with these, with earth, and sun, and sea, and stars by night. The pettiness of house-life—chairs and tables—and the pettiness of observances, the petty necessity of useless labour, useless because productive of nothing, chafe me the year through.

I want to be always in company with the sun, and sea, and earth. These, and the stars by night, are my natural companions.

RICHARD JEFFERIES (from *The Story of my Heart*)

IN ENGLAND NOW

Every morning, early, through the misty air of spring, she walked over the fields (to St. Chad's). The path was familiar and beloved ; past the mill, through flats of mare's-tail and king-cup steeped in moist, marshy odours. At this early hour the millpond lay tranced as in the quiet of evening. On its glassy flats the roach rose lazily with sucking dimples that spread to rings. Sometimes the burning blue of a kingfisher that haunted the willow-roots passed with a flash that brought her heart into her mouth. Above the pool a field of cowslips. The low sun raked their pale clusters with a keener fire ; their gusty vinous odour mounted to her brain. Then the edge of the larch-wood, piercingly green, younger than anything on earth. Within its curved shadow dew lay late ; the cropped turf was bloomed with it ; and there, unconscious of her coming, crouched the little huddled shapes of rabbits nibbling against time. It was almost as if they could hear her smile. Suddenly the nibbling ceased ; the warm bodies lay like scattered stones. One drummed his feet, and all vanished with a clumsy, unhurried reluctance. They did not seem very much afraid of her. She was sorry that they mistrusted her at all. Couldn't they see, the silly things, that she loved them.

FRANCIS BRETT YOUNG (from *Portrait of Clare*)

THIRD PART

§ IV TRAVELLERS' JOY

" How many miles to Babylon ? "
" Three score and ten."
" Can I get there by candle-light ? "
" Yes ! If your legs are long."

Old English Game Song

In every land thy feet may tread
Time like a veil is round thy head.
Only the land thou seek'st with me
Never hath been nor yet shall be.

SIR HENRY NEWBOLT

TO BABYLON BY CANDLELIGHT

It is by candlelight one enters Babylon; and all roads lead to Babylon, provided it is by candlelight one journeys. It was by candlelight that John Milton read Diodorus, and by the Third Book he had voyaged beyond the Cape of Hope and now was past Mozambic, and already felt freshly blowing on his face

> *Sabean odours from the spicie shore*
> *Of Arabie the blest.*

It was by candlelight that the sea coast of Bohemia was discovered, and the finding of it made a winter's tale. Baghdad is not a city to be seen by day; candlelight is the only illumination for all Arabian nights.

One sees most by candlelight, because one sees little. There is a magic ring, and in it all things shine with a yellow shining, and round it wavers the eager dark. This is the magic of the lyrics of the twelfth century in France, lit candles in "a casement ope at night," starring the dusk in Babylon; candles flare and gutter in the meaner streets, Villon's lyrics, these; candles flame in its cathedral-darkness, Latin hymns of the Middle Ages, of Thomas of Celano and Bernard of Morlaix. For if Babylon has its Quartier Latin, it has also its Notre Dame. The Middle Ages are the Babylon of the religious heart.

Every literature has its Babylon. Or rather, like that other Babylon, not of the spirit, Babylon is one, and all nations have drunk of her wine. She, too, is the haven desired of "everyone that saileth any whither" by reason of her costliness, her merchandise of gold and precious stones and pearls, of fine linen and purple and silk and scarlet, thyine wood and ivory, cinnamon and incense, wine and souls of men ; and this Babylon too will have fallen when the sound of the flute is no more heard in her, and " the light of a candle shall shine no more at all." All languages are spoken in Babylon, yet with the same accent ; here are gateways of the Moors in Spain, Venetian waterways, streets of Old Paris, and over all the undiscerning twilight. All men meet in Babylon who go on pilgrimages, for all roads end in Babylon, the Road of the San Grael, the Road of the Secret Rose.

HELEN WADDELL (from Introduction to
Lyrics from the Chinese)

THE INTERIOR OF CATHAY

Upon leaving the capital and travelling ten miles, you come to a river named Pulisangan, which discharges itself into the ocean, and is navigated by many vessels entering from thence, with considerable quantities of merchandise. Over this river there is a very handsome bridge of stone, perhaps unequalled by any other in the world. Its length is three hundred paces, and its width eight paces ; so that ten mounted men can, without inconvenience, ride abreast. It has twenty-four arches, supported by twenty-five piers erected in the water, all of serpentine stone, and built with great skill.

On each side, and from one extremity to the other, there is a handsome parapet, formed of marble slabs and pillars arranged in a masterly style. At the beginning of the ascent the bridge is something wider than at the summit, but from the part where the ascent terminates, the sides run in straight lines and parallel to each other. Upon the upper level there is a massive and lofty column, resting upon a tortoise of marble, and having near its base a large figure of a lion, with a lion also on the top. Towards the slope of the bridge there is another handsome column or pillar, with its lion, at the distance of a pace and a half from the former; and all the spaces between one pillar and another, throughout the whole length of the bridge, are filled up with slabs of marble, curiously sculptured, and mortised into the next adjoining pillars, forming altogether a beautiful spectacle. These parapets serve to prevent accidents that might otherwise happen to passengers.

Upon leaving the fortress of Thaigin, and travelling about twenty miles, you come to a river called the Karamoran [Yellow River], which is of such magnitude, both in respect to width and depth, that no solid bridge can be erected upon it. Its waters are discharged into the ocean. On its banks are many cities and castles, in which a number of trading people reside, who carry on an extensive commerce. The country bordering upon it produces ginger, and silk also in large quantities.

Of birds the multitude is incredible, especially of pheasants, which are sold at the rate of three for the value of a Venetian groat. Here likewise grows a species of large cane, in infinite abundance, some of a foot and others a foot and a half in circumference, which are employed by the inhabitants for a variety of useful purposes.

Having crossed this river and travelled three days' journey, you arrive at a city named Ka-chan-fu, whose inhabitants are idolaters. They carry on a considerable traffic, and work at a variety of manufactures. The country produces in great abundance silk, ginger, and many drugs that are nearly unknown in our part of the world. Here they weave gold tissues, as well as every other kind of silken cloth. We shall speak in the next place of the noble and celebrated city of Ken-zan-fu, in the kingdom of the same name.

Departing from Ka-chan-fu, and proceeding eight days' journey in a westerly direction, you continually meet with cities and commercial towns, and pass many gardens and cultivated grounds, with abundance of the mulberry-tree that contributes to the production of silk. The inhabitants in general worship idols, but there are also found here Nestorian Christians, Turkomans, and Saracens.

The wild beasts of the country afford excellent sport and a variety of birds also are taken.

At the end of eight days you arrive at the city of Ken-zan-fu, which was anciently the capital of an extensive, noble, and powerful kingdom, the seat of many kings, highly descended and distinguished in arms. At the present day it is governed by a son of the Great Khan, named Mangalu, upon whom his father has conferred the sovereignty.

It is a country of great commerce, and eminent for its manufactures. Raw silk is produced in large quantities, and tissues of gold and every other kind of silk are woven there. At this place likewise they prepare every article necessary for the equipment of an army. All species of provisions are in abundance, and to be procured at a moderate price. . .

In a plain, about five miles from the city, stands a beautiful palace belonging to King Mangalu, embellished with many fountains and rivulets, both within and on the outside of the buildings. There is also a fine park, surrounded by a high wall, with battlements, enclosing an extent of five miles, where all kinds of wild animals, both beasts and birds, are kept for sport. In its centre is this spacious palace, which, for symmetry and beauty, cannot be surpassed. It contains many marble halls and chambers, ornamented with paintings and beaten gold and the finest azure. Mangalu, pursuing the footsteps of his father, governs his principality with strict equity, and is beloved by his people. He also takes much delight in hunting and hawking.

Travelling westward three days, from the residence of Mangalu, you still find towns and castles, whose inhabitants subsist by commerce and manufactures, and where there is an abundance of silk. At the end of these three days you enter upon a region of mountains and valleys, which lie within the province of Kun-kin.

This tract, however, has no want of inhabitants, who are worshippers of idols and cultivate the earth. They live also by the chase, the land being much covered with woods. In these are found many wild beasts, such as tigers, bears, lynxes, fallow-deer, antelopes, stags, and many other animals, which are made to turn to good account. This region extends to the distance of twenty days' journey, during which the way lies entirely over mountains and through valleys and woods, but containing towns where travellers may find convenient accommodation.

From *Travels of Marco Polo*
(Trans. MARSDEN and KOMROFF)

And now will I tell you of lands and countries and isles that are beyond the land of Cathay ; And therefore he that will go from Cathay to Inde . . . shall go through a kingdom that is called Cadile, the which is a great land. And there groweth a manner of fruit great as gourds, and when it is ripe they open it and find therein a beast with flesh and blood, and bone, and it is like to a little lamb without wool. And men of that country eat that beast and the fruit also. And that is a great marvel. . .

In this land also are great apples of noble smell and noble savour, and men may find of them on a cluster an hundred and more and the leaves of the trees are two foot long and some longer. And in that country are trees bearing gariofles and nutmegs, and great nuts of Inde, and other divers spiceries. And there are vines that bear so great bobbs of grapes that a strong man may uneasily bear one of them.

And in that land are many griffins, more than in any country else. And some men say they have the shape of an eagle before, and behind the shape of a lion, and sickerly they say sooth.

.   .   .

I, John Maundeville Knight (although I be unworthy) have passed many lands and many isles and countries and searched many full strange places, and have been in many a full good honourable company, and now I am comen home, maugre myself, to rest, for gowts that me distreynen and put an end to my labour, against my will God knoweth.

SIR JOHN MANDEVILLE (from *Voiage and Travaile* —Cotton MS., c. 1400)

CONVERSATION FOR FLEMISH TRAVELLERS

(14th Century)

GUEST : God be here, dame !

HOSTESS : Fellow, ye be welcome.

GUEST : May I have a bed here within ?—May I here be lodged ?

HOSTESS : Yea, well and cleanly, even though were ye twelve, all on horseback.

GUEST : Nay, but we three. Is there to eat here within ?

HOSTESS : Yea, enough, God be thanked.

GUEST : Bring it to us. Give hay to the horses, and straw them well ; but see that they be watered. . .
Dame, what owe we ? We have been well eased.

HOSTESS : We shall reckon to-morrow, and shall pay also, that ye shall hold you pleased.

GUEST : Bring us to sleep ; we been merry.

HOSTESS : Well, I go. Ye shall rest. Janet light the candle ; and lead them there above ; and bear them hot water for to wash their feet ; and cover them with cushions ; see that the stable be well shut.

From a Flemish Phrase-Book compiled at Bruges
(Trans. WM. CAXTON)

ERASMUS TRAVELS IN GERMANY

I left Bâle relaxed and worn out as one out of favour with the gods. The river part of my journey was well enough, save for the heat of the sun. We dined at Breisach. Dinner abominable. Foul smells and flies in swarms. We were kept waiting half an hour while the precious banquet was preparing. There was nothing that I could eat, every dish filthy and stinking. At night we were turned out of the boat into a village—the name I forget, and I would not write it if I remembered. It nearly made an end of me. There were sixty of us to sup together in a tavern, a medley of human animals in one small heated room. It was ten o'clock, and, oh! the dirt and the noise, especially after the wine had begun to circulate. The cries of the boatmen woke us in the morning. I hurry on board unsupped and unslept. At nine we reached Strasburg, when things mended a little. From Strasburg we went on to Speyer. My English horse had broken down, a wretch of a blacksmith having burnt his foot with a hot shoe. I escaped the inn at Speyer and was entertained by my friend the Dean. Two pleasant days with him, thence in a carriage to Worms and so on to Mentz, where I was again lodged by a Cathedral canon. So far things had gone tolerably with me. The smell of the horses was disagreeable and the pace was slow, but that was the worst. At a village further on I call on my friend Christopher, the wine-merchant, to his great delight. On his table I saw the works of Erasmus. He invited a party to meet me, sent the boatmen a pitcher of wine and promised to let them off the customs duty as a reward for having brought him so great a man. Imagine a wine-merchant reading my books and given to the study of the Muses. Christ said the publicans and harlots would go into the kingdom of heaven before the Pharisees. Priests and monks live for their bellies, and vintners take to literature. But, alas, the red wine which he sent to the boatmen took the taste of the bargeman's wife, a red-faced sot of a woman. She drank it to the last drop, and then flew to arms and almost murdered a servant wench with oyster-shells. Then she rushed on deck, tackled her husband, and tried to pitch him overboard. There is vinal energy for you !

At the hotel at Cologne I ordered breakfast at ten o'clock, with a carriage and pair to be ready immediately after. I went to church, came back to find no breakfast, and a carriage not to be had. My horse being disabled, I tried to hire another. I was told this could not be done either. I saw what it meant. I was to be kept at Cologne, and I did not choose to be kept; so I ordered my poor nag to be saddled, lame as he was, with another for my servant, and I started on a five hours' journey for the Count of New Eagle. I had five pleasant days with the Count, whom I found a young man of sense. A carriage had been ordered for me for the next morning. The Count would not take leave of me overnight, meaning to see me before I started. The night was wild. I rose before dawn to finish off some work. At seven, the Count not appearing, I sent to call him. He came, and protested that I must not leave his house in such weather. I must have lost half my mind when I went to Cologne. My evil genius now carried off the other half. Go I would, in an open carriage, with wind enough to tear up oak-trees. It came from the south and charged with pestilence. Towards evening wind changed to rain. I reached Aix shaken to pieces by the bad roads. I should have done better on my lame horse.

Letter of ERASMUS (1518)

ENGLAND AS SEEN BY FOREIGNERS IN QUEEN ELIZABETH'S TIME

1. A Dutch Physician, 1560

At my first arrival at Dover, and so along my journey toward London, which I dispatched partly upon horseback and partly by water, I saw and noted many things able to ravish and allure any man in the world, with desire to travel and see that so noble a country. Frankly to utter what I think of the incredible courtesy and friendliness in speech and affability used in this famous realm, I must needs confess it doth surmount and carry away the prick and price of all others. And beside this, the neat cleanliness, the exquisite fineness, the pleasant and delightful furniture in every point for household, wonderfully rejoiced me; their chambers and parlours strawed over with sweet herbs refreshed me; their nosegays finely intermingled with sundry sorts of fragrant flowers in their bedchambers and privy rooms, with comfortable smell cheered me up and entirely delighted all my senses. And this do I think to be the cause that Englishmen, living by such wholesome and exquisite meat, and in so wholesome and healthful air be so fresh and clean coloured: their faces, eyes and countenance carrying with it and representing a portly grace and comeliness, giveth out evident tokens of an honest mind; in language very smooth and allective, but yet seasoned and tempered within the limits and bonds of moderation, not bombasted with any unseemly terms or enforced with any clawing flatteries or allurements. At their tables although they be very sumptuous, and love to have good fare, yet neither use they to overcharge themselves with excess of drink, neither thereto greatly provoke and urge others, but suffer every man to drink in such measure as best pleaseth himself, which drink being either Ale or Beer, most pleasant in taste and wholesomely relished, they fetch not from foreign places, but have it among themselves brewed. As touching their populous and great haunted cities, the fruitfulness of their ground and soil, their lively springs and mighty rivers, their great herds and flocks of cattle, their mysteries and art of weaving and cloth-making, their skilfulness in shooting, it is needless here to discourse— seeing the multitude of merchants exercising the traffic and art of merchandise among them, and ambassadors also sent thither from foreign Princes, are able abundantly to testify that nothing needful and expedient for man's use and commodity lacketh in that most noble island.

LEVINUS LEMNIUS
(from *The Touchstone of Complexions*)

2. An Antwerp Merchant, 1575

The people are bold, courageous, ardent, and cruel in war, fiery in attack and having little fear of death; they are not vindictive, but very inconstant, rash, vain-glorious, light, and deceiving, and very suspicious, especially of foreigners, whom they despise. They are full of courtly and affected manners and words, which they take for gentility, civility, and wisdom. They are eloquent and very hospitable ; they feed well and delicately, and eat a great deal of meat ; and as the Germans pass the bounds of sobriety in drinking, these do the same in eating, for which the fertility of the country affords them sufficient means, although in general the fruits have not such strength and virtue as in France or the Netherlands for the want of hot sun. Even the grass, as the herbalists say, is not so nourishing, whereby the meat is in consequence softer and not so firm, although they have a great abundance of it ; but it is well-tasted enough.

The people are not so laborious and industrious as the Netherlanders or French, and the most toilsome, difficult, and skilful works are chiefly performed by foreigners as among the idle Spaniards. They have a great many sheep which bear fine wool, of which for these 200 years they have learnt to make fine cloth. They keep many lazy servants, and also many wild animals for their pleasure, rather than trouble themselves to cultivate the land. The island which they inhabit is very large, and abounds with fish ; they have likewise the best harbours in Christendom. They are also rich in ships ; nevertheless they do not catch as many fish as they require, so that they are obliged to buy more from their neighbours ; but they do catch a great quantity of herrings, of which they send away every year more than five or six hundred lasts to Italy and elsewhere. . .

Although the women there are entirely in the power of their husbands except for their lives, yet they are not kept so strictly as they are in Spain or elsewhere. . . They are well-dressed, fond of taking it easy, and commonly leave the care of household matters and drudgery to their servants. They sit before their doors, decked out in fine clothes, in order to see and be seen by the passers-by. . The rest of their time they employ in walking and riding, in playing at cards or otherwise, in visiting their friends and keeping company, conversing with their equals (whom they term *gosseps*) and their neighbours, and making merry with them at child-births, christenings, churchings, and funerals ; and all this with the permission and knowledge of their husbands, as such is the custom.

The women are beautiful, fair, well-dressed and modest, which is seen there more than elsewhere, as they go about the streets without any covering either of huke or mantle, hood, veil, or the like. Married women only wear a hat both in the street and in the house; those unmarried go without a hat, although ladies of distinction have lately learnt to cover their faces with silken masks or vizards, and feathers,—for indeed they change very easily, and that every year, to the astonishment of many.

EMANUEL VAN METEREN
(from *History of the Netherlands*)

3. A Brandenburg Lawyer, 1598

The soil is fruitful and abounds with cattle, which inclines the inhabitants rather to feeding than ploughing, so that near a third part of the land is left uncultivated for grazing. The climate is most temperate at all times, and the air never heavy, consequently maladies are scarcer, and less physic is used there than anywhere else. . . The general drink is ale, which is prepared from barley, and is excellently well tasted, but strong and what soon fuddles. . .

The English are serious like the Germans, lovers of show; followed wherever they go by whole troops of servants, who wear their masters' arms in silver fastened to their left arms, and are not undeservedly ridiculed for wearing tails hanging down their backs. They excel in dancing and music, for they are active and lively, though of a thicker make than the French; they cut their hair close on the middle of the head, letting it grow on either side; they are good sailors and better pirates, cunning, treacherous, and thievish; above 300 are said to be hanged annually at London; beheading with them is less infamous than hanging; they give the wall as the place of honour: hawking is the common sport with the gentry. They are more polite in eating than the French, consuming less bread but more meat, which they roast in perfection; they put a great deal of sugar in their drink; their beds are covered with tapestry, even those of farmers; they are often molested with the scurvy, said to have first crept into England with the Norman Conquest; their houses are commonly of two stories, except in London, where they are of three and four, though but seldom of four; they are built of wood, those of the richer sort with bricks, their roofs are low, and where the owner has money, covered with lead. They are powerful in the field, successful against their enemies, impatient of anything like slavery; vastly fond of great noises that fill the ear, such as the firing of cannon, drums, and the ringing of bells, so that in London it is common for a number of them that have got a glass in their heads to go up into some belfry, and ring the bells for hours together, for the sake of exercise. If they see a foreigner very well made, or particularly handsome, they will say, " It is a pity he is not an Englishman."

PAUL HENTZNER
(from *Itinerary of Travels in England*, etc.)

I

Northward Ho !

(An account of the First Voyage of Master John Davis undertaken in June, 1585, for the Discovery of the North West Passage)

The 19th of July we fell into a great whirling and brustling of a tide, setting to the northwards ; and sailing about half a league we came into a very calm sea, which bent to the south-south-west. Here we heard a mighty great roaring of the sea, as if it had been the breach of some shore, the air being so foggy and full of thick mist, that we could not see the one ship from the other, being a very small distance asunder ; so the captain and the master, being in distrust how the tide might set them, caused the *Moonshine* to hoist out her boat and to sound, but they could not find ground in three hundred fathoms and better. Then the captain, master, and I went towards the breach to see what it should be, giving charge to our gunners that at every blast they should shoot off a musket shot, to the intent we might keep ourselves from losing them ; then coming near to the breach, we met many islands of ice floating, which had quickly compassed us about. Then we went upon some of them, and did perceive that all the roaring which we heard was caused only by the rolling of this ice together. Our company seeing us not to return according to our appointment, left off shooting muskets and began to shoot falconets, for they feared some mishap had befallen us ; but before night we came aboard again, with our boat laden with ice, which made very good fresh water. Then we bent our course toward the north, hoping by that means to double the land.

The 20th, as we sailed along the coast, the fog brake up, and we discovered the land, which was the most deformed, rocky, and mountainous land that ever we saw, the first sight whereof did show as if it had been in form of a sugar loaf, standing to our sight above the clouds, for that it did show over the fog like a white liste [edge] in the sky, the tops altogether covered with snow, and the shore beset with ice a league off into the sea, making such irksome noise as that it seemed to be the true pattern of desolation, and after the same our captain named it the land of desolation.

The 21st the wind came northerly and overblew, so that we were constrained to bend our course south again, for we perceived that we were run into a very deep bay, where we were almost compassed with ice, for we saw very much towards the north-north-east, west, and south-west ; and this day and this night we cleared ourselves of the ice, running south-south-west along the shore.

Upon Thursday, being the 22nd of this month, about three of the clock in the morning, we hoisted out our boat, and the captain, with six sailors, went towards the shore, thinking to find a landing-place, for the night before we did perceive the coast to be void of ice to our judgment ; and the same night we were all persuaded that we had seen a canoe rowing along the shore, but afterwards we fell in some doubt of it, but we had no great reason so to do. The captain, rowing towards the shore willed the master to bear in with the land after him ; and before he came near the shore, by the space of a league, or about two miles, he found so much ice that he could not get to land by any means. Here our mariners put to their lines to see if they could get any fish, because there were so many seals upon the coast, and the birds did beat upon the water, but all was in vain : the water about this place was very black and thick, like to a filthy standing pool ; we sounded, and had ground in 120 fathoms. While the captain was rowing to the shore our men saw woods upon the rocks, like to the rocks of Newfoundland, but I could not discern them ; yet it might be so very well, for we had wood floating upon the coast every day, and the *Moonshine* took up a tree at sea not far from the coast, being sixty foot of length and fourteen handfuls about, having the root upon it. After this, the captain came aboard, the weather being very calm and fair, we bent our course toward the south with intent to double the land.

The 23rd we coasted the land which did lie east-north-east and west-south-west.

The 24th, the wind being very fair at east, we coasted the land which did lie east and west, not being able to come near the shore by reason of the great quantity of ice. At this place, because the weather was somewhat cold by reason of the ice, and the better to encourage our men, their allowance was increased. The captain and the master took order that every mess, being five persons, should have half a pound of bread and a can of beer every morning to breakfast. The weather was not very cold, but the air was moderate, like to our April weather in England. When the wind came from the land or the ice it was somewhat cold, but when it came off the sea it was very hot.

The 25th of this month we departed from sight of this land at six of the clock in the morning, directing our course to the north-westward, hoping in God's mercy to find our desired passage, and so continued above four days.

The 29th of July we discovered land in 64 degrees 15 minutes of latitude, bearing north-east from us. The wind being contrary to go to the north-westwards, we bare in with this land to take some view of it, being utterly void of the pester of ice, and very temperate. Coming near the coast we found many fair sounds and good roads for shipping, and many great inlets into the land, whereby we judged this land to be a great number of islands standing together. Here, having moored our barque in good order we went on shore upon a small island to seek for water and wood. Upon this island we did perceive that there had been people, for we found a small shoe and pieces of leather sewed with sinews and a piece of fur, and wool like to beaver. Then we went upon another island on the other side of our ships, and the captain, the master, and I, being got up to the top of a high rock, the people of the country having espied us made a lamentable noise, as we thought, with great outcries and screechings : we, hearing them, thought it had been the howling of wolves. At last I hallooed again, and they likewise cried; then we, perceiving where they stood—some on the shore, and one rowing in a canoe about a small island fast by them—we made a great noise, partly to allure them to us and partly to warn our company of them. Whereupon M. Bruton and the master of his ship, with others of their company, made great haste towards us, and brought our musicians with them from our ship, purposing either by force to rescue us, if needs should so require, or with courtesy to allure the people. When they came unto us we caused our musicians to play, ourselves dancing and making many signs of friendship. At length there came ten canoes from the other islands, and two of them came so near the shore where we were that they talked with us, the other being in their boats a pretty way off. Their pronunciation was very hollow through the throat, and their speech such as we could not understand, only we allured them by friendly embracings and signs of courtesy. At length one of them, pointing up to the sun with his hand, would presently strike his breast so hard that we might hear the blow. This he did many times before he would any way trust us. Then John Ellis, the master of the *Moonshine*, was appointed to use his best policy to gain their friendship, who struck his breast and pointed to the sun after their order, which when he had divers times done they began to trust him, and one of them came on shore, to whom we threw our caps, stockings, and gloves, and such others things as then we had about us, playing with our music, and making signs of joy, and dancing. So the night coming we bade them farewell, and went aboard our barques.

JOHN JANES
(from HAKLUYT'S *Principal Navigations,* etc.)

2

A Worthy Fight

Performed in the voyage from Turkey by five ships of London, against eleven galleys and two frigates of the King of Spain's, at Pantalarea, within the Straits, Anno 1586

The merchants of London, being of the incorporation for the Turkey trade, having received intelligences and advertisements from time to time that the King of Spain, grudging at the prosperity of this kingdom, had not only of late arrested all English ships, bodies, and goods in

Spain, but also, maligning the quiet traffic which they used, to and in the dominations and provinces under the obedience of the Great Turk, had given orders to the captains of his galleys in the Levant to hinder the passage of all English ships, and to endeavour by their best means to intercept, take, and spoil them, their persons and goods; they hereupon thought it their best course to set out their fleet for Turkey in such strength and ability for their defence that the purpose of their Spanish enemy might the better be prevented, and the voyage accomplished with greater security to the men and ships. For which cause, five tall and stout ships appertaining to London, and intending only a merchant's voyage, were provided and furnished with all things belonging to the seas, the names whereof were these :—

1. The *Merchant Royal*, a very brave and goodly ship, and of great report.
2. The *Toby*.
3. The *Edward Bonaventure*.
4. The *William and John*.
5. The *Susan*.

These five departing from the coast of England in the month of November, 1585, kept together as one fleet till they came as high as the isle of Sicily, within the Levant. And there, according to the order and direction of the voyage, each ship began to take leave of the rest, and to separate himself, setting his course for the particular port whereunto he was bound. . . But before they divided themselves, they altogether consulted of and about a certain and special place for their meeting again after the lading of their goods at their several ports. And in conclusion, the general agreement was to meet at Zante, an island near to the main continent of the west part of

Morea, well known to all the pilots, and thought to be the fittest place for their rendezvous. . .

It fell out that the *Toby*, which was bound for Constantinople, had made such good speed, and gotten such good weather, that she first of all the rest came back to the appointed place of Zante, and not forgetting the former conclusion, did there cast anchor, attending the arrival of the rest of the fleet, which accordingly (their business first performed) failed not to keep promise. . .

Thus in good order they left Zante and the Castle of Grecia, and committed themselves again to the seas, and proceeded in their course and voyage in quietness, without sight of any enemy till they came near to Pantalarea, an island so called betwixt Sicily and the coast of Africa ; into sight whereof they came the 13th day of July, 1586. And the same day, in the morning, about seven of the clock, they descried thirteen sails in number, which were of the galleys lying in wait of purpose for them in and about that place. As soon as the English ships had spied them, they, by-and-bye, according to a common order, made themselves ready for a fight. In the meantime, the galleys more and more approached the ships, and in their banners there appeared the arms of the isles of Sicily and Malta, being all as then in the service and pay of the Spaniard. Immediately both the Admirals of the galleys sent from each of them a frigate to the Admiral of our English ships, which being come near them, the Sicilian frigate first hailed them, and demanded of them whence they were ; they answered that they were of England, the arms whereof appeared in their colours. Whereupon the said frigate expostulated with them, and asked why they delayed to send or come with their captains and pursers to Don Pedro de Leiva, their General, to acknowledge their duty and obedience to him, in the name of the Spanish king, lord of those seas. Our men replied and said that they owed no such duty nor obedience to him, and therefore would acknowledge none. . . They also demanded of the frigate whence she and the rest of the galleys were. The messenger answered, " We are of Malta, and for mine own part, my name is Cavalero. These galleys are in service and pay to the King of Spain, under the conduct of Don Pedro de Leiva, a nobleman of Spain who hath been commanded hither by the king with this present force and army of purpose to intercept you. You shall there-fore," quoth he, " do well to repair to him to know his pleasure ; he is a nobleman of good behaviour and courtesy, and means you no ill." The captain of the English Admiral, whose name was Master Edward Wilk-inson, replied and said, " We purpose not at this time to make trial of Don Pedro his courtesy, whereof we are suspicious and doubtful, and not without good cause " ; using withal good words to the messenger, and willing him to come aboard him, promising security and good usage, that thereby he might the better know the Spaniard's mind. Whereupon he indeed left his frigate and came aboard him, whom he entertained in friendly sort, and caused a cup of wine to be drawn for him, which he took, and began, with his cap in his hand and with reverent terms, to drink to the health of the Queen of England, speaking very honourably of Her Majesty, and giving good speeches of the courteous usage and entertainment that he himself had received in London. . . At the last he entreated to have the merchant of the Admiral carried by him as a messenger to the General, that so he might be satisfied and assured of their minds by one of their own company. But Master Wilkinson would agree to no such thing ; although Richard Rowit, the merchant himself, seemed willing to be employed in that message, and laboured by reasonable persuasions to induce Master Wilkinson to grant it—as hoping to be an occasion by his presence and discreet answers to satisfy the General, and thereby to save the effusion of Christian blood, if it should grow to a battle. And he seemed so much the more willing to be sent, by how much deeper the oaths and protestations of this Cavalero were, that he would (as he was a true knight and a soldier) deliver him back again in safety to his company. Albeit, Master Wilkinson, who, by his long experience, had received sufficient trial of Spanish inconstancy and perjury, wished him in no case to put his life and liberty in hazard upon a Spaniard's oath ; but at last, upon much entreaty, he yielded to let him go to the General, thinking indeed that good speeches and answers of reason would have contented him, whereas, otherwise, refusal to do so might peradventure have provoked the more discontentment.

Master Rowit, therefore, passing to the Spanish General, the rest of the galleys, having espied him, thought, indeed, that the English were rather determined to yield than to fight, and therefore came flocking about the frigate, every man crying out. . . And the Spanish General, being come to the galley wherein he was, showed himself to Master Rowit in his armour, his guard of soldiers attending upon him, in armour also, and began to speak very proudly in this sort : " Thou Englishman, from whence is your fleet ? Why stand ye aloof off ? know ye not your duty to the Catholic king, whose person I here represent ? Where are your bills of lading, your letters, passports, and the chief of your men ? Think ye my attendance in these seas to be in vain, or my person to no purpose?" .. These words of the Spanish General were not so outrageously pronounced, as they were mildly answered by Master Rowit, who told him that they were all merchantmen, using traffic in honest sort, and seeking to pass quietly, if they were not urged further than reason. .. And as touching his commandment aforesaid for the acknowledging of duty in such particular sort, he told him that, where there was no duty owing there none should be performed, assuring him that their whole company and ships in general stood resolutely upon the negative, and would not yield to any such unreasonable demand, joined with such imperious and absolute manner of commanding. " Why, then," said he, " if they will neither come to yield, nor show obedience to me in the name of my king, I will either sink them or bring them to harbour ; and so tell them from me." With that the frigate came away with Master Rowit, and brought him aboard to the English Admiral again, according to promise, who was no sooner entered in but by-and-bye defiance was sounded on both sides. The Spaniards hewed off the noses of the galleys, that nothing might hinder the level of the shot ; and the English, on the other side, courageously prepared themselves to the combat, every man, according to his room, bent to perform his office with alacrity and diligence. In the meantime a cannon was discharged from out the Admiral of the galleys, which being the onset of the fight, was presently answered by the English Admiral with a culverin ; so the skirmish began, and grew hot and terrible. There was no powder nor shot spared, each English ship matched itself in good order against two Spanish galleys, besides the inequality of the frigates on the Spanish side. . . . Thus the fight continued furious and sharp, and doubtful a long time to which part the victory would incline, till at last the Admiral of the galleys of Sicily began to warp from the fight, and to hold up her side for fear of sinking, and after her went also two others in like case, whom all the sort of them enclosed, labouring by all their means to keep them above water, being ready by the force of English shot which they had received to perish in the seas. And what slaughter was done among the Spaniards the English were uncertain, but by a probable conjecture apparent afar off they supposed their loss was so great that they wanted men to continue the charging of their pieces; whereupon with shame and dishonour, after five hours spent in the battle, they withdrew themselves. And the English, contented in respect of their deep lading rather to continue their voyage than to follow in the chase, ceased from further blows, with the loss of only two men slain amongst them all, and another hurt in his arm, whom Master Wilkinson, with his good words and friendly promises did so comfort that he nothing esteemed the smart of his wound, in respect of the honour of the victory and the shameful repulse of the enemy.

Thus, with dutiful thanks to the mercy of God for His gracious assistance in that danger, the English ships proceeded in their navigation. And coming as high as Algiers, a port town upon the coast of Barbary, they made for it, of purpose to refresh themselves after their weariness, and to take in such supply of fresh water and victuals as they needed. They were no sooner entered into the port but immediately the king thereof sent a messenger to the ships to know what they were. With which messenger the chief master of every ship repaired to the king, and acquainted him not only with the state of their ships in respect of merchandise, but with the late fight which they had passed with the Spanish galleys, reporting every particular circumstance in word as it fell out in action; whereof the said king showed himself marvellous glad, entertaining them in the best sort, and promising abundant relief of all their wants; making general proclamation in the city, upon pain of death, that no man, of what degree or state soever he were, should presume either to hinder them in their affairs or to offer them any manner of injury in body or goods; by virtue whereof they despatched all things in excellent good sort with all favour and peaceableness.

The English, having received this good justice at the king's hands, and all other things that they wanted or could crave for the furnishing of their ships, took their leave of him, and of the rest of their friends that were resident in Algiers, and put out to sea, looking to meet with the second army of the Spanish king, which waited for them about the mouth of the Strait of Gibraltar, which they were of necessity to pass. But coming near to the said strait, it pleased God to raise, at that instant, a very dark and misty fog, so that one ship could not discern another if it were forty paces off, by means whereof, together with the notable fair Eastern winds that then blew most fit for their course, they passed with great speed through the strait, and might have passed, with that good gale, had there been five hundred galleys to withstand them and the air never so clear for every ship to be seen. But yet the Spanish galleys had a sight of them, when they were come within three English miles of the town, and made after them with all possible haste; and although they saw that they were far out of their reach, yet in a vain fury and foolish pride, they shot off their ordnance and made a stir in the sea as if they had been in the midst of

them, which vanity of theirs ministered to our men notable matter of pleasure and mirth, seeing men to fight
with shadows and to take so great pains to so small
purpose.

But thus it pleased God to deride and delude all the
forces of that proud Spanish king, which he had provided
of purpose to distress the English ; who, notwithstanding,
passed through both his armies,—in the one, little hurt,
and in the other, nothing touched, to the glory of His
immortal name, the honour of our prince and country,
and the just commendation of each man's service performed in that voyage.

PHILIP JONES
(from HAKLUYT'S *Principal Navigations*, etc.)

OF TRAVELLING IN GENERAL

For my part, I think variety to be the most pleasing
thing in the world, and the best life to be, neither con-
templative alone, nor active altogether, but mixed of both.
God would have made eternal spring, had he not known,
that the divers seasons would be not only most profitable
to the works of nature, but also most pleasant to his
creatures, while the cold winter makes the temperate
spring more wished. Such is the delight of visiting foreign
countries, charming all our senses with most sweet variety.
They seem to me most unhappy, and no better than prisoners, who from the cradle to old age, still behold the
same walls, faces, orchards, pastures, and objects of the
eye, and still hear the same voices and sounds beat in
their ears ; not the song of the cuckoo, nor the craking
of the crows, nor the howling of wolves, nor the bellowing

of oxen, nor the bleying of sheep, no nor the sweet voices of larks and nightingales, if they be shut up in a cage, do so much please us at home, as the variety of all, composed of divers tunes, delights us in the fields abroad. In like sort, it is manifest that all the other senses are not so much pleased with any thing, as variety. They are in some measure happy, who having but one house, yet have change of chambers, to remove as the season of the year changeth : but I judge lawyers and officers more happy, who have their terms to live in the city, and their vacations to return into the country, so often (as it were) renewing their marriage days : and of all, I judge the nomads most happy, (the comparison holding in other things) who live in tents, and so by removing, not only escape the heat of summer, the cold of winter, the want of pastures, all diseases, and all unpleasing things, but at their pleasure, enjoy all commodities of all places.

Let us imitate the storks, swallows, and cranes, which like the nomads yearly fetch their circuits, and follow the sun, without suffering any distemper of the seasons. The fixed stars have not such power over inferior bodies as the wandering planets. Running water is sweet, but standing pools stink : take away idleness, and the bait of all vice is taken away. Men were created to move, as birds to fly ; what they learn by nature, that reason joined to nature teacheth us. Nothing can be added to the worthy praises of him as the poet saith :

> *Who many men's manners hath seen,*
> *And hath in many cities been.*

In one word, I will say what can be said upon this subject ; every soil is to a valiant man his own country, as the sea to the fishes. We are citizens of the whole world, yea,

not of this world, but of that to come. All our life is a pilgrimage. God for his only begotten Son's sake (the true
Mercury of travellers) bring us that are here strangers
safely into our true country.

FYNES MORYSON (from *Itinerary*, 1617)

THE ROAD TO THE HIGHLANDS

The road which we travelled had become wild and
open as soon as we had left Glasgow a mile or two behind
us, and was growing more dreary as we advanced. Huge
continuous heaths spread before, behind, and around us
in hopeless barrenness, now level and interspersed with
swamps, green with treacherous verdure, or sable with
turf, or, as they call them in Scotland, peat-bogs, and now
swelling into huge heavy ascents, which wanted the dignity
and form of hills, while they were still more toilsome to the
passenger. There were neither trees nor bushes to relieve
the eye from the russet livery of absolute sterility. The
very heath was of that stinted, imperfect kind which has
little or no flower, and affords the coarsest and meanest
covering, which, as far as my experience enables me to
judge, Mother Earth is ever arrayed in. Living thing
we saw none, except occasionally a few straggling sheep
of a strange diversity of colours, as black, bluish, and
orange. The sable hue predominated, however, in their
faces and legs. The very birds seemed to shun these
wastes,—and no wonder, since they had an easy method of
escaping from them ; at least, I only heard the monotonous
and plaintive cries of the lapwing and curlew, which my
companions denominated the peasweep and whaup. . .

The few miserable hovels that showed some marks of human habitation were now of still rarer occurrence ; and at length, as we began to ascend an uninterrupted swell of moorland, they totally disappeared. The only exercise which my imagination received was when some particular turn of the road gave us a partial view, to the left, of a large assemblage of dark-blue mountains stretching to the north and north-west, which promised to include within their recesses a country as wild, perhaps, but certainly differing greatly in point of interest, from that which we now travelled. The peaks of this screen of mountains were as wildly varied and distinguished as the hills which we had seen on the right were tame and lumpish ; and while I gazed on this Alpine region I felt a longing to explore its recesses. . .

The road, which had ascended for six or seven English miles, began now to descend for about the same space, through a country which, neither in fertility or interest, could boast any advantage over that which we had passed already, and which afforded no variety, unless when some tremendous peak of a Highland mountain appeared at a distance. We continued, however, to ride on without pause ; and even when night fell and overshadowed the desolate wilds which we traversed, we were, as I understood from Mr. Jarvie, still three miles and a bittock distant from the place where we were to spend the night.

The night was pleasant, and the moon afforded us good light for our journey. Under her rays, the ground over which we passed assumed a more interesting appearance than during the broad daylight, which discovered the extent of its wasteness. The mingled light and shadows gave it an interest which naturally did not belong to it, and, like the effect of a veil flung over a plain woman, irritated our curiosity on a subject which had in itself nothing gratifying.

The descent, however, still continued, turned, winded, left the more open heaths, and got into steeper ravines, which promised soon to lead us to the banks of some brook or river, and ultimately made good their presage. We found ourselves at length on the bank of a stream which rather resembled one of my native English rivers than those I had hitherto seen in Scotland. It was narrow, deep, still, and silent; although the imperfect light, as it gleamed on its placid waters, showed also that we were now among the lofty mountains which formed its cradle. "That's the Forth," said the Bailie, with an air of reverence which I have observed the Scotch usually pay to their distinguished rivers. . .

The Forth, however, as far as the imperfect light permitted me to judge, seemed to merit the admiration of those who claimed an interest in its stream. A beautiful eminence of the most regular round shape, and clothed with copsewood of hazels, mountain-ash, and dwarf-oak, intermixed with a few magnificent old trees, which, rising above the underwood, exposed their forked and bared branches to the silver moonshine, seemed to protect the sources from which the river sprung. If I could trust the tale of my companion,—which, while professing to disbelieve every word of it, he told under his breath, and with an air of something like intimidation,—this hill, so regularly formed, so richly verdant, and garlanded with such a beautiful variety of ancient trees and thriving copsewood, was held by the neighbourhood to contain, within its unseen caverns, the palaces of the fairies : a race of airy beings, who formed an intermediate class between men and demons, and who, if not positively malignant to humanity, were yet to be avoided and feared, on account of their capricious, vindictive, and irritable disposition.

" They ca' them," said Mr. Jarvie, in a whisper, " *Daoine Schie*, whilk signifies, as I understand, men of peace,—meaning thereby to make their gude-will. And we may e'en as weel ca' them that too, Mr. Osbaldistone ; for there's nae gude in speaking ill o' the laird within his ain bounds." But he added presently after, on seeing one or two lights which twinkled before us, " It's deceits o' Satan, after a', and I fearna to say it ; for we are near the manse now, and yonder are the lights in the Clachan of Aberfoil."

SIR WALTER SCOTT (from *Rob Roy*)

JOHNSON AND BOSWELL IN THE WESTERN ISLES

Glenelg, September 1, 1773.

It grew dusky, and we had a very tedious ride for what was called five miles, but I am sure would measure ten. We had no conversation. I was riding forward to the inn at Glenelg, on the shore opposite to Skye, that I might take proper measures before Dr. Johnson, who was now advancing in dreary silence, Hay leading his horse, should arrive. Vass also walked by the side of his horse, and Joseph followed behind ; as therefore he was thus attended, and seemed to be in deep meditation, I thought there could be no harm in leaving him for a little while. He called me back with a tremendous shout, and was really in a passion with me for leaving him. I told him my intentions, but he was not satisfied, and said, " Do you know, I should as soon have thought of picking a pocket as doing so."—BOSWELL : " I am diverted with you, sir."—JOHNSON : " Sir, I could never be diverted with incivility : doing such a thing makes one lose confidence in him who has done it, as one cannot tell what he may do next." His extraordinary warmth confounded me so much that I justified myself but lamely to him, yet my intentions were not improper. . .

We came on to the inn at Glenelg. There was no provender for our horses, so they were sent to grass, with a man to watch them. A maid showed us up-stairs into a room damp and dirty, with bare walls, a variety of bad smells, a coarse black greasy fir table, and forms of the same kind ; and out of a wretched bed started a fellow from his sleep, like Edgar in *King Lear*: " Poor Tom's a-cold." . .

Our bad accommodation here made me uneasy and almost fretful. Dr. Johnson was calm. I said he was so from vanity.—JOHNSON : " No, sir, it is from philosophy." It pleased me to see that the Rambler could practise so well his own lessons.

I resumed the subject of my leaving him on the road, and endeavoured to defend it better. He was still violent upon that head, and said, " Sir, had you gone on, I was thinking that I should have returned with you to Edinburgh, and then have parted from you, and never spoken to you more."

I sent for fresh hay, with which we made beds for ourselves, each in a room equally miserable. Like Wolfe, we had " a choice of difficulties." Dr. Johnson made things easier by comparison. At Macqueen's last night, he observed, that few were so well lodged in a ship. To-night, he said, we were better than if we had been upon the hill. He lay down buttoned up in his great coat : I had my sheets spread on the hay, and my clothes and great coat laid over me by way of blankets.

Thursday, September 2.

I had slept ill. Dr. Johnson's anger had affected me much. I considered that without any bad intention I might suddenly forfeit his friendship, and was impatient to see him this morning. I told him how uneasy he had made me by what he had said, and reminded him of his own remark at Aberdeen, upon old friendships being hastily broken off. He owned he had spoken to me in a passion ; that he would not have done what he had threatened ; and that if he had he should have been ten times worse than I ; that forming intimacies would indeed be " limning the water," were they liable to such sudden dissolution ; and he added, " Let's think no more on't."

Skye, September 12.

Miss Flora Macdonald (for so I shall call her) told me she heard upon the mainland, as she was returning home about a fortnight before, that Mr. Boswell was coming to Skye, and one Mr. Johnson, a young English buck, with him. He was highly entertained with this fancy. Giving an account of the afternoon which we passed, at Anoch, he said, " I, being a *buck*, had miss in to make tea."—He was rather quiescent to-night, and went early to bed. I was in a cordial humour, and promoted a cheerful glass. The punch was excellent. Honest Mr. Macqueen observed that I was in high glee, " my *governor* being gone to bed." . . . I slept in the same room with Dr. Johnson. Each had a neat bed, with tartan curtains, in an upper chamber.

The room where we lay was a celebrated one. Dr. Johnson's bed was the very bed in which the grandson of the unfortunate King James the Second lay, on one of the nights after the failure of his rash attempt in 1745–6, while he was eluding the pursuit of the emissaries of Government, which had offered thirty thousand pounds as a reward for apprehending him. To see Dr. Samuel Johnson lying in that bed, in the Isle of Skye, in the house of Miss Flora Macdonald, struck me with such a group of ideas as it is not easy for words to describe, as they passed through the mind. He smiled, and said, " I have had no ambitious thoughts in it." . . . At breakfast he said he would have given a good deal rather than not have lain in that bed. I owned he was the lucky man ; and observed, that without doubt it had been contrived between Mrs. Macdonald and him. She seemed to acquiesce, adding, " You know young *bucks* are always favourites of the ladies." He spoke of Prince Charles being here, and asked Mrs. Macdonald " *Who* was with him ? We were told, madam, in England, there was one Miss Flora Macdonald with him." She said, "They were very right"; and perceiving Dr. Johnson's curiosity, though he had delicacy enough not to question her, very obligingly entertained him with a recital of the particulars which she herself knew of that escape, which does so much honour to the humanity, fidelity, and generosity of the Highlanders. Dr. Johnson listened to her with placid attention, and said, " All this should be written down."

Ostig, September 29.

After a very good sleep, I rose more refreshed than I had been for some nights. We were now at but a little distance from the shore, and saw the sea from the windows, which made our voyage seem nearer. Mr. Macpherson's manners and address pleased us much. He appeared to be a man of such intelligence and taste as to be sensible of the extraordinary powers of his illustrious guest. He said to me : " Dr. Johnson is an honour to mankind ; and, if the expression may be used, is an honour to religion."

Col, who had gone yesterday to pay a visit at Camus-cross, joined us this morning at breakfast. Some other gentlemen also came to enjoy the entertainment of Dr. Johnson's conversation. The day was windy and rainy, so that we had just seized a happy interval for our journey last night. We had good entertainment here, better accommodation than at Corrichatachin, and time enough to ourselves. The hours slipped along imperceptibly. We talked of Shenstone. Dr. Johnson said he was a good layer-out of land, but would not allow him to approach excellence as a poet. He said, he believed he had tried to read all his Love Pastorals, but did not get through them. . . . He was this afternoon full of critical severity, and dealt about his censures on all sides. . .

While he was in this mood, I was unfortunate enough, simply perhaps, but I could not help thinking, undeservedly, to come within " the whiff and wind of his fell sword." I asked him, if he had ever been accustomed to wear a night-cap. He said, " No." I asked, if it was best not to wear one.—JOHNSON : " Sir, I had this custom by chance, and perhaps no man shall ever know whether it is best to sleep with or without a night-cap."—Soon afterwards, he was laughing at some deficiency in the Highlands and said, " One might as well go without shoes and stockings."—Thinking to have a little hit at his own deficiency, I ventured to add, "Or without a night-cap, sir."

But I had better have been silent ; for he retorted directly. " I do not see the connection there (laughing). Nobody before was ever foolish enough to ask whether it was best to wear a night-cap or not. This comes of being a little wrong-headed."—He carried the company along with him ; and yet the truth is, that if he had always worn a night-cap, as is the common practice, and found the Highlanders did not wear one, he would have wondered at their barbarity ; so that my hit was fair enough.

BOSWELL (from *Journal of a Tour to the Hebrides*)

EXCURSIONS AT GRASMERE

Sunday, 27th June, 1800.—After tea we rowed down to Loughrigg Fell, visited the white foxglove, gathered wild strawberries, and walked up to view Rydale. We lay a long time looking at the lake ; the shores all dim with the scorching sun. The ferns were turning yellow, that is here and there one was quite turned. We walked round by Benson's wood home. The lake was now most still, and reflected the beautiful yellow and blue and purple and grey colours of the sky. We heard a strange sound in the Bainriggs wood, as we were floating on the water ; it *seemed* in the wood, but it must have been above it, for presently we saw a raven very high above us. It called out, and the dome of the sky seemed to echo the sound. It called again and again as it flew onwards, and the mountains gave back the sound, seeming as if from their centre ; a musical bell-like answering to the bird's hoarse voice. We heard both the call of the bird, and the echo, after we could see him no longer.

Friday Evening, 29*th August,* 1800.—We walked over the hill by the firgrove. I sate upon a rock, and observed a flight of swallows gathering together high above my head. They flew towards Rydale. We walked through the wood over the stepping-stones. The lake of Rydale very beautiful, partly still. John and I left Wm. to compose an inscription ; that about the path. We had a very fine walk by the gloomy lake. There was a curious yellow reflection in the water, as of corn fields. There was no light in the clouds from which it appeared to come.

(*Saturday Morning,* 30*th August.*)— . . . William finished his Inscription of the Pathway, then walked in the wood ; and when John returned, he sought him, and they bathed together. I read a little of Boswell's *Life of Johnson.* I went to lie down in the orchard. I was roused by a shout that Anthony Harrison was come. We sate in the orchard till tea time. Drank tea early, and rowed down the lake, which was stirred by breezes. We looked at Rydale, which was soft, cheerful, and beautiful. We then went to peep into Langdale. The Pikes were very grand. We walked back to the view of Rydale, which was now a dark mirror. We rowed home over a lake still as glass, and then went to George Mackareth's to hire a horse for John. A fine moonlight night. The beauty of the moon was startling, as it rose to us over Loughrigg Fell. We returned to supper at 10 o'clock.

DOROTHY WORDSWORTH (from *Journals*)

THE BRUGES-GHENT CANAL

Nothing can be more refreshing than to float thus at ease, the awning screening us from the sun, and the pleasant breezes fanning our temples ; . . . cottages constantly varying the shores, which are particularly gay at this season, interspersed with fruit-tree blossom and the broom flower ; goats tethered on the grassy banks, under the thin line of elms ; a village with a pretty church, midway on the journey ; . . . the air delightfully refreshed by the rain ; the banks, again low, allow the eye to stretch beyond the avenue ; corn looking well, rich daisy-clad pastures, and here alive with grasshoppers ; large village on both sides of the canal, bridge between, from which letters are dropped into the barge, as we pass, by means of a shoe. A sale at a Thames-like château; we take on purchasers with their bargains—chests of drawers, bed and chamber furniture of all sorts—barge crowded ; Catholic priests do not scruple to interlard their conversation with oaths ; the three Towers of Ghent, seen through the misty air in the distance under the arch of the canal bridge, give a fine effect to this view ; drawing nearer and gliding between villages and châteaux, the architecture looks very rich.

MARY WORDSWORTH
(from *Journal of a Tour in Belgium*, 1823)

SEVILLE

As it was my intention to remain at Seville for some months, I determined to hire a house, in which I conceived I could live with more privacy, and at the same time more economically than in a posada. It was not long before I found one in every respect suited to me. It was situated in the Plazuela de la Pila Seca, a retired part of the city, in the neighbourhood of the cathedral, and at a short distance from the gate of Xeres; and in this house, on the arrival of Antonio and the horses, which occurred within a few days, I took up my abode.

I was now once more in beautiful Seville, and had soon ample time and leisure to enjoy its delights and those of the surrounding country; unfortunately, at the time of my arrival, and indeed for the next ensuing fortnight, the heaven of Andalusia, in general so glorious, was overcast with black clouds, which discharged tremendous showers of rain, such as few of the Sevillians, according to their own account, had ever seen before. This extraordinary weather had wrought no little damage in the neighbourhood, causing the Guadalquivir, which, during the rainy season, is a rapid and furious stream, to overflow its banks and to threaten an inundation. It is true that intervals were occurring when the sun made his appearance from his cloudy tabernacle, and with his golden rays caused everything around to smile, enticing the butterfly forth from the bush, and the lizard from the hollow tree, and I invariably availed myself of these intervals to take a hasty promenade.

O how pleasant it is, especially in springtide, to stray along the shores of the Guadalquivir. Not far from the city, down the river, lies a grove called Las Delicias, or the Delights. It consists of trees of various kinds, but more especially of poplars and elms, and is traversed by long shady walks. This grove is the favourite promenade of the Sevillians, and there one occasionally sees assembled whatever the town produces of beauty or gallantry. There wander the black-eyed Andalusian dames and damsels,

614

clad in their graceful silken mantillas ; and there gallops the Andalusian cavalier, on his long-tailed thick-maned steed of Moorish ancestry. As the sun is descending, it is enchanting to glance back from this place in the direction of the city ; the prospect is inexpressibly beautiful. Yonder in the distance, high and enormous, stands the Golden Tower, now used as a toll-house, but the principal bulwark of the city in the time of the Moors. It stands on the shore of the river like a giant keeping watch, and is the first edifice which attracts the eye of the voyager as he moves up the stream to Seville. On the other side, opposite the tower, stands the noble Augustine convent, the ornament of the faubourg of Triana, whilst between the two edifices rolls the broad Guadalquivir, bearing on its bosom a flotilla of barks from Catalonia and Valencia. Farther up is seen the bridge of boats which traverses the water. The principal object of this prospect, however, is the Golden Tower, where the beams of the setting sun seem to be concentrated as in a focus, so that it appears built of pure gold, and probably from that circumstance received the name which it now bears. Cold, cold must the heart be which can remain insensible to the beauties of this magic scene, to do justice to which the pencil of Claude himself were barely equal. Often have I shed tears of rapture whilst I beheld it, and listened to the thrush and the nightingale piping forth their melodious songs in the woods, and inhaled the breeze laden with the perfume of the thousand orange gardens of Seville.

GEORGE BORROW (from *The Bible in Spain*)

THE ISLE OF APHRODITE

(*Cyprus*)

The isle is beautiful : from the edge of the rich, flowery fields on which I trod, to the midway sides of the snowy Olympus, the ground could only here and there show an abrupt crag or a high straggling ridge that upshouldered itself from out of the wilderness of myrtles, and of a thousand bright-leaved shrubs that twined their arms together in lovesome tangles. The air that came to my lips was warm and fragrant as the ambrosial breath of the goddess, infecting me—not (of course) with a faith in the old religion of the isle, but with a sense and apprehension of its mystic power—a power that was still to be obeyed— obeyed by me ; for why otherwise did I toil on with sorry horses to " where, for HER, the hundred altars glowed with Arabian incense, and breathed with the fragrance of garlands ever fresh " ?

I passed a sadly disenchanting night in the cabin of a Greek priest—not a priest of the goddess, but of the Greek Church : there was but one humble room, or rather shed, for man, and priest, and beast. The next morning I reached Baffa (Paphos), a village not far distant from the site of the temple. There was a Greek husbandman there who (not for emolument, but for the sake of the protection and dignity which it afforded) had got leave from the man at Limesol to hoist his flag as a sort of deputy-provision-ary-subvice-pro-acting-consul of the British sovereign. The poor fellow instantly changed his Greek head-gear for the cap of consular dignity, and insisted upon accompanying me to the ruins. I would not have stood this if I could have felt the faintest gleam of my yesterday's pagan piety, but I had ceased to dream, and had nothing to dread from any new disenchanters.

The ruins (the fragments of one or two prostrate pillars) lie upon a promontory, bare and unmystified by the gloom of surrounding groves. My Greek friend in his consular cap stood by, respectfully waiting to see what turn my madness would take now that I had come at last into the presence of the old stones. If you have no taste for research, and can't affect to look for inscriptions, there is some awkwardness in coming to the end of a merely sentimental pilgrimage, when the feeling which impelled you has gone : in such a strait you have nothing to do but to laugh the thing off as well as you can—and, by-the-bye, it is not a bad plan to turn the conversation (or rather allow the natives to turn it) towards the subject of hidden treasures. This is a topic on which they will always speak with eagerness ; and if they can fancy that you, too, take an interest in such matters, they will not only begin to think you perfectly sane, but will even perhaps give you credit for some more than human powers of forcing dark Earth to show you its hoards of gold.

When we returned to Baffa, the vice-consul seized a club, with the quietly determined air of a brave man resolved to do some deed of note. He went into the yard adjoining his cottage, where there were some thin, thoughtful, canting cocks, and serious, low-church-looking hens, respectfully listening, and chickens of tender years so well brought up as scarcely to betray in their conduct the careless levity of youth. The vice-consul stood for a moment quite calm—collecting his strength ; then suddenly he rushed into the midst of the congregation and began to deal death and destruction on all sides ; he spared neither sex nor age. The dead and dying were immediately removed from the field of slaughter, and in less than an hour, I think, they were brought to the table, deeply buried in mounds of snowy rice.

A. W. KINGLAKE (from Eothen)

THE ARABIAN DAYS

Damascus Prepares for the Pilgrimage

There is every year a new stirring of this goodly Oriental city in the days before the Haj ; so many strangers are passing in the bazaars, of outlandish speech and clothing from far provinces. The more part are of Asia Minor, many of them bearing overgreat white turbans that might weigh more than their heads : the most are poor folk of a solemn countenance, which wander in the streets seeking the bakers' stalls, and I saw that many of the Damascenes could answer them in their own language. The town is moved in the departure of the great Pilgrimage of the Religion and again at the home-coming, which is made a public spectacle ; almost every Moslem household has some one of their kindred in the caravan.

In the markets there is much taking up in haste of wares for the road. The tent-makers are most busy in their street, overlooking and renewing the old canvas of hundreds of tents, of tilts and the curtains for litters ; the curriers in their bazaar are selling apace the water-skins and leathern buckets and saddle-bottes, *matara* or *zemzemîeh* ; the carpenters' craft are labouring in all haste for the Haj, the most of them mending litter-frames.

The Good Traveller

The traveller must be himself, in men's eyes, a man worthy to live under the bent of God's heaven, and were it without a religion : he is such who has a clean human heart and long-suffering under his bare shirt ; it is enough, and though the way be full of harms, he may travel to the ends of the world. Here is a dead land, whence, if he die not, he shall bring home nothing but a perpetual weariness in his bones. The Semites are like to a man sitting in a cloaca to the eyes, and whose brows touch heaven. Of the great antique humanity of the Semitic desert, there is a moment in every adventure, wherein a man may find to make his peace with them, so he know the Arabs. The sour Wahaby fanaticism has in these days cruddled the hearts of the nomads, but every Beduin tent is sanctuary in the land of Ishmael (so there be not in it some cursed Jael). If the outlandish person come alone to strange nomad booths, let him approach boldly, and they will receive him.

The Red House

Before the sunset we came to our white tents pitched beside the ruinous kella, without door and commonly abandoned. Dàr-el-Hamra, " the red house." Ruddy is that earth and the rocks whereof this water-castle is built. High and terrible it showed in the twilight in this desolation of the world.

Sun and Moon

The summer's night at end, the sun stands up as a crown of hostile flames from that huge covert of inhospitable sandstone bergs ; the desert day dawns not little and little, but it is noontide in an hour. The sun, entering as a tyrant upon the waste landscape, darts upon us a torment of fiery beams, not to be remitted till the far-off evening.—No matins here of birds ; not a rock partridge-cock, calling with blithesome chuckle over the extreme waterless desolation. Grave is that giddy heat upon the crown of the head; the ears tingle with a flickering shrillness, a subtle crepitation it seems, in the glassiness of this sun-stricken nature : the hot sand-blink is in the eyes, and there is little refreshment to find in the tents' shelter ; the worsted booths leak to this fiery rain of sunny light. Mountains looming like dry bones through the thin air stand far around about us : the savage flank of Ybba Moghrair, the high spire and ruinous stacks of el-Jebâl, Chebàd, the coast of Helwàn ! Herds of weak nomad camels waver dispersedly, seeking pasture in the midst of this hollow fainting country, where but lately the swarming locusts have fretted every green thing. This silent air burning about us we endure breathless till the assr : when the dazing Arabs in the tents revive after their heavy hours. The lingering day draws down to the sun-setting ; the herdsmen, weary of the sun, come again with the cattle, to taste in their menzils the first sweetness of mirth and repose.—The day is done, and there rises the nightly freshness of this purest mountain air : and then to the cheerful song and the cup at the common fire. The moon rises ruddy from that solemn obscurity of jebel like a mighty beacon :—and the morrow will be as this day, days deadly drowned in the sun of the summer wilderness.

CHARLES DOUGHTY
(from *Travels in Arabia Deserta*)

AN AUSTRALIAN ROBINSON

I found myself on my legs upon the beach, though hardly able to move from exhaustion of mind and body. When at length I had recovered sufficiently to walk about, I made a hasty survey of the little island or sandbank upon which I found myself. Thank God, I did not realise at that moment that I should have to spend a soul-killing *two and a half years* on that desolate, miscroscopical strip of sand ! . .

The great thing was to ward off the dull agony, the killing depression, and manias generally. Fortunately I was of a very active disposition, and as a pastime I took to gymnastics, even as I had at Montreux. I became a most proficient tumbler and acrobat, and could turn two or three somersaults on dashing down from the sloping roof of my hut ; besides, I became a splendid high jumper, with and without pole. Another thing I interested myself in was the construction of a sun-dial. . .

I also played the part of Neptune in a very extraordinary way. I used to wade out to where the turtles were, and on catching a big six-hundred pounder, I would calmly sit astride on his back. Away would swim the startled creature, mostly a foot or so below the surface. When he dived deeper I simply sat far back on the shell, and then he was forced to come up. I steered my queer steeds in a curious way. When I wanted my turtle to turn to the left, I simply thrust my foot into his right eye, and *vice-versâ* for the contrary direction. My two big toes placed simultaneously over both his optics caused a halt so abrupt as almost to unseat me. Before the wet season commenced I put a straw thatch on the roof of my hut, as before stated, and made my quarters as snug as possible. And it was a very necessary precaution, too, for sometimes it rained for days at a stretch. It never kept me indoors, however, and I took exercise just the same, as I didn't bother about clothes, and I rather enjoyed the shower bath. I was always devising means of making life more tolerable, and amongst other things I made a sort of swing, which I found extremely useful in beguiling time. I would also practise jumping with long poles. One day I captured a young pelican, and trained him to accompany me in my walks and help me in my fishing operations. He also acted as a decoy. Frequently I would hide myself in some grass, whilst my pet bird walked a few yards away to attract his fellows. Presently he would be joined by a whole flock, many of which I shot with my bow and arrows, or lassoed. But for my dog—my almost human Bruno—I think I must have died. I used to talk to him just as though he were a human being. We were absolutely inseparable. I preached long sermons to him from Gospel texts. I told him in a loud voice all about my early life and school-days at Montreux ; I recounted to him my adventures from the fatal meeting with Poor Peter Jensen in Singapore ; I sang little *chansons* to him, and among these he had his favourites as well as those he disliked cordially. If he did not care for a song, he would set up a pitiful howl.

LOUIS DE ROUGEMONT (from *Adventures*)

A DESCENT INTO ITALY

1. *Above Val Tellina*

Our evening drive was swift and exciting. An impetuous horse whirled us down a steep vine-clad hill, rounding the zigzags at a pace which made perils by mountains sink into insignificance compared to the perils by road. Near a beautiful waterfall tumbling from the opposite hills, the Malero was leapt by a bold arch, and for some time we ran along a terrace, high above the strong glacier torrent.

From the last brow overlooking the Val Tellina the eye rests on one of those wonderful landscapes which tell the southward-bound traveller that he has reached his goal and is at last in Italy.

The great barrier is crossed, and the North is all behind us. The face of the earth, nay the very nature of the air, has changed, colours have a new depth, shadows a new sharpness. From the deep-green carpet of the smooth valley to the crowns of the sunset-flushed hills, all is wealth and luxuriance. No more pines stand stiff in regimental ranks to resist the assaults of winter and rough weather. No mountain rhododendrons collect all their strength in a few tough short shoots, and push themselves forward like hardy skirmishers of the vegetable world into the very abode of snow. Here the " green things of the earth " are all at home and at peace, not as in some high Graubünden valley waging unequal war in an enemy's country. The beeches cluster in friendly companies on the hills. The chestnut-forest rejoicing in a green old age spreads out into the kindly air broad, glossy branches, the vines toss their long arms here and there in sheer exuberance of life. Even on the roadside wall the lizards run in and out amongst beds of cyclamen and tenderest ferns and mosses. The hills seem to stand back and leave room for the sunshine; and the broad, shining town of Sondrio, girt by towers and villas, wears, after the poor hamlets of the mountains, a stately air, as if humanity too shared in the general well-being.

Near Cevio the landscape takes a more romantic character. The valley-walls close in and bend, and huge knobs of ruddy-grey rock thrust themselves forward. The river, confined to a narrow bed, alternately lies still in pools, whose depth of blue no comparison can express, or rushes off over the white boulders in a clear sparkling dance. Chestnut-trees hang from the crags overhead ; higher on the hills every ledge is a stripe of verdure fringed with the delicate shapes of the birch and larch. In the far distance a snow-peak in the range above Val Leventina gleams behind the folds of the nearer mountains. . . . The waters at our feet are transparent depths of colour, half sapphire and half emerald, indescribable, and, the moment the eye is taken away, inconceivable, so that every glance becomes a fresh surprise. In the foreground on either bank of the stream are frescoed walls and mossy house-roofs ; beyond is a summer-house supported by pillars, and a heavily laden peach-orchard lit with a blaze of sunflowers. At the gate of Val Bavona a white village glistens from amidst its vineyards. Sheer above it two bold granite walls rise out of the verdure, and form the entrance to a long avenue of great mountain shapes. Behind these foremost masses the hills fall valley-wards in noble and perfectly harmonious lines. Each upper cliff flows down into a slope of chestnut-muffled boulders in a curve, the classical beauty of which is repeated by the vine-tendrils at its feet. In the distance the snows of the Basodine seen through the sunny haze gleam, like a golden halo, on the far-off head of the mountain.

Is human interest wanted to give completeness and a motive to the picture ? As daylight faded I have watched the swinging torches and low chaunt of those who carried the Host to some passing soul. In the morning-glow I have seen a white-robed procession pour slowly with banners and noise of bells from the yet dark village, then suddenly issuing into the sunshine, surge, a living wave of brightness, over the high-arched bridges.

D. W. FRESHFIELD (from *Italian Alps*)

NIGHT IN VENICE

Night in Venice ! Night is nowhere else so wonderful, unless it be in winter among the high Alps. But the nights of Venice and the nights of the mountains are too different in kind to be compared.

There is the ever-recurring miracle of the full moon rising, before day is dead, behind San Giorgio, spreading a path of gold on the lagoon, which black boats traverse with the glow-worm lamp upon their prow ; ascending the cloudless sky and silvering the domes of the Salute ; pouring vitreous sheen upon the red lights of the Piazzetta ; flooding the Grand Canal, and lifting the Rialto higher in ethereal whiteness ; piercing but penetrating not the murky labyrinth of *rio* linked with *rio* through which we wind in light and shadow, to reach once more the level glories and the luminous expanse of heaven beyond Misericordia.

This is the melodrama of Venetian moonlight ; and if a single impression of the night has to be retained from one visit to Venice, those are fortunate who chance upon a full moon of fair weather. Yet I know not whether some quieter and soberer effects are not more thrilling. To-night, for example, the waning moon will rise late through veils of *scirocco*. Over the bridges of San Cristoforo and San Gregorio, through the deserted Calle di Mezzo, my friend and I walk in darkness, pass the marble basements of the Salute, and push our way along its Riva to the point of the Dogana. We are out at sea alone, between the Canal-ozzo and the Giudecca. A moist wind ruffles the water and cools our forehead. It is so dark that we can only see San Giorgio by the light reflected on it from the Piazzetta. The same light climbs the Campanile of St. Mark, and shows the golden angel in a mystery of gloom. The only noise that reaches us is a confused hum from the Piazza. Sitting and musing there, the blackness of the water whispers in our ears a tale of death. And now we hear a splash of oars, and gliding through the darkness comes a single boat. One man leaps upon the landing-place without a word and disappears. There is another wrapped in a military cloak asleep. I see his face beneath me, pale and quiet. The *barcaruolo* turns the point in silence. From the darkness they came; into the darkness they have gone. It is only an ordinary incident of coastguard service. But the spirit of the night has made a poem of it.

Even tempestuous and rainy weather, though melan-choly enough, is never sordid here. There is no noise from carriage traffic in Venice, and the sea-wind preserves the purity and transparency of the atmosphere. It had been raining all day, but at evening came a partial clearing. I went down to the Molo, where the large reach of the lagoon was all moon-silvered, and San Giorgio Maggiore dark against the bluish sky, and Santa Maria della Salute domed with moon-irradiated pearl, and the wet slabs of the Riva shimmering in moonlight, the whole misty sky, with its clouds and stellar spaces, drenched in moonlight, nothing but moonlight sensible except the tawny flare of gas-lamps and the orange lights of gondolas afloat upon the waters. On such a night the very spirit of Venice is abroad. We feel why she is called Bride of the Sea.

Take yet another night. There had been a representation of Verdi's *Forza del Destino* at the Teatro Malibran. After midnight we walked homeward through the Merceria, crossed the Piazza, and dived into the narrow *calle* which leads to the *traghetto* of the Salute. It was a warm moist starless night, and there seemed no air to breathe in those narrow alleys. The gondolier was half asleep. Eustace called him as we jumped into his boat, and rang our *soldi* on the gunwale. Then he arose and turned the ferro round, and stood across towards the Salute. Silently, insensibly, from the oppression of confinement in the airless streets to the liberty and immensity of the water and the night we passed. It was but two minutes ere we touched the shore and said good-night, and went our way and left the ferryman. But in that brief passage he had opened our souls to everlasting things—the freshness, and the darkness, and the kindness of the brooding, all enfolding night above the sea.

J. A. SYMONDS (from *A Venetian Medley*)

THE GLAMOUR OF THE SEA

1. *The East*

" And this is how I see the East. I have seen its secret places and have looked into its very soul ; but now I see it always from a small boat, a high outline of mountains, blue and far in the morning ; like faint mist at noon ; a jagged

627

wall of purple at sunset. I have the feel of the oar in my hand, the vision of a scorching blue sea in my eyes. And I see a bay, a wide bay, smooth as glass and polished like ice, shimmering in the dark. A red light burns far off upon the gloom of the land, and the night is soft and warm. We drag at the oars with aching arms, and suddenly a puff of wind, a puff faint and tepid and laden with strange odours of blossoms, of aromatic wood, comes out of the still night—the first sigh of the East on my face. That I can never forget. It was impalpable and enslaving, like a charm, like a whispered promise of mysterious delight. . . . When I opened my eyes again the silence was as complete as though it had never been broken. I was lying in a flood of light, and the sky had never looked so far, so high, before. I opened my eyes and lay without moving.

" And then I saw the men of the East—they were looking at me. The whole length of the jetty was full of people. I saw brown, bronze, yellow faces, the black eyes, the glitter, the colour of an Eastern crowd. And all these beings stared without a murmur, without a sigh, without a movement. They stared down at the boats, at the sleeping men who at night had come to them from the sea. Nothing moved. The fronds of palms stood still against the sky. Not a branch stirred along the shore, and the brown roofs of hidden houses peeped through the green foliage, through the big leaves that hung shining and still like leaves forged of heavy metal. This was the East of the ancient navigators, so old, so mysterious, resplendent and sombre, living and unchanged, full of danger and promise. And these were the men. I sat up suddenly. A wave of movement passed through the crowd from end to end, passed along the heads, swayed the bodies, ran along the jetty like a ripple on the water, like a breath of wind on a field—and all was still again. I see it now—the wide sweep of the bay, the glittering sands, the wealth of green infinite and varied, the sea blue like the sea of a dream, the crowd of attentive faces, the blaze of vivid colour—the water reflecting it all, the curve of the shore, the jetty, the high-sterned outlandish craft floating still, and the three boats with the tired men from the West sleeping, unconscious of the land and the people and of the violence of sunshine. They slept thrown across the thwarts, curled on bottom-boards, in the careless attitudes of death. The head of the old skipper, leaning back in the stern of the long-boat, had fallen on his breast, and he looked as though he would never wake. Farther out old Mahon's face was upturned to the sky, with the long white beard spread out on his breast, as though he had been shot where he sat at the tiller ; and a man, all in a heap in the bows of the boat, slept with both arms embracing the stem-head and with his cheek laid on the gunwale. The East looked at them without a sound.

" I have known its fascination since ; I have seen the mysterious shores, the still water, the lands of brown nations, where a stealthy Nemesis lies in wait, pursues, overtakes so many of the conquering race, who are proud of their wisdom, of their knowledge, of their strength. But for me all the East is contained in that vision of my youth. It is all in that moment when I opened my young eyes on it. I came upon it from a tussle with the sea—and I was young—and I saw it looking at me. And this is all that is left of it ! Only a moment ; a moment of strength, of romance, of glamour—of youth ! . . . A flick of sunshine upon a strange shore, the time to remember, the time for a sigh, and—good-bye !—Night—Good-bye . . . ! "

He drank.

" Ah ! The good old time—the good old time. Youth and the sea. Glamour and the sea ! The good, strong sea, the salt, bitter sea, that could whisper to you and roar at you and knock your breath out of you."

He drank again.

" By all that's wonderful it is the sea, I believe, the sea itself—or is it youth alone ? Who can tell ? But you here —you all had something out of life : money, love—whatever one gets on shore—and, tell me, wasn't that the best time, that time when we were young at sea ; young and had nothing, on the sea that gives nothing, except hard knocks—and sometimes a chance to feel your strength— that only—what you all regret ? "

And we all nodded at him : the man of finance, the man of accounts, the man of law, we all nodded at him over the polished table that like a still sheet of brown water reflected our faces, lined, wrinkled ; our faces marked by toil, by deceptions, by success, by love ; our weary eyes looking still, looking always, looking anxiously for something out of life, that while it is expected is already gone— has passed unseen, in a sigh, in a flash—together with the youth, with the strength, with the romance of illusions.

2. *The Old River*

The day was ending in a serenity of still and exquisite brilliance. The water shone pacifically ; the sky, without a speck, was a benign immensity of unstained light ; the very mist on the Essex marshes was like a gauzy and radiant fabric, hung from the wooded rises inland, and draping the low shores in diaphanous folds. Only the gloom to the west, brooding over the upper reaches, became more sombre every minute, as if angered by the approach of the sun.

And at last, in its curved and imperceptible fall, the sun sank low, and from glowing white changed to a dull red without rays and without heat, as if about to go out suddenly, stricken to death by the touch of that gloom brooding over a crowd of men.

Forthwith a change came over the waters, and the serenity became less brilliant but more profound. The old river in its broad reach rested unruffled at the decline of day, after ages of good service done to the race that peopled its banks, spread out in the tranquil dignity of a waterway leading to the uttermost ends of the earth. We looked at the venerable stream not in the vivid flush of a short day that comes and departs for ever, but in the august light of abiding memories. And indeed nothing is easier for a man who has, as the phrase goes, " followed the sea " with reverence and affection, than to evoke the great spirit of the past upon the lower reaches of the Thames. The tidal current runs to and fro in its unceasing service, crowded with memories of men and ships it had borne to the rest of home or to the battles of the sea. It had known and served all the men of whom the nation is proud, from Sir Francis Drake to Sir John Franklin, knights all, titled and untitled —the great knights-errant of the sea. It had borne all the ships whose names are like jewels flashing in the night of time, from the *Golden Hind* returning with her round flanks full of treasure, to be visited by the Queen's Highness and thus pass out of the gigantic tale, to the *Erebus* and *Terror*, bound on other conquests—and that never returned. It had known the ships and the men. They had sailed from Deptford, from Greenwich, from Erith—the adventurers and the settlers ; kings' ships and the ships

of men on 'Change ; captains, admirals, the dark " inter-
lopers " of the Eastern trade, and the commissioned
" generals " of East India fleets. Hunters for gold or pur-
suers of fame, they all had gone out on that stream, bearing
the sword, and often the torch, messengers of the might
within the land, bearers of a spark from the sacred fire.
What greatness had not floated on the ebb of that river
into the mystery of an unknown earth ! . . . The dreams of
men, the seed of commonwealths, the gems of empires.

The sun set ; the dusk fell on the stream, and lights
began to appear along the shore. The Chapman light-
house, a three-legged thing erect on a mud-flat, shone
strongly. Lights of ships moved in the fairway—a great
stir of lights going up and going down. And farther west
on the upper reaches the place of the monstrous town was
still marked ominously on the sky, a brooding gloom in
sunshine, a lurid glare under the stars.

JOSEPH CONRAD
(1. from *Youth*.   2. from *Heart of Darkness*)

A ROMAN PILGRIMAGE

The sun was conquering me, and I was looking hope-
lessly for a place to sleep, when a cart drawn by two oxen
at about one mile an hour came creaking by. The driver
was asleep, his head on the shady side. The devil tempted
me, and without one struggle against temptation, nay with
cynical and congratulatory feelings, I jumped up behind,
and putting my head also on the shady side (there were
soft sacks for a bed) I very soon was pleasantly asleep.

We lay side by side for hour after hour, and the day

rose on to noon ; the sun beat upon our feet, but our heads were in the shade and we slept heavily a good and honest sleep : he thinking that he was alone, but I knowing that I was in company (a far preferable thing), and I was right and he was wrong. And the heat grew, and sleep came out of that hot sun more surely than it does out of the night air in the north. But no dreams wander under the noon.

From time to time one or the other of us would open our eyes drowsily and wonder, but sleep was heavy on us both, and our minds were sunk in calm like old hulls in the dark depths of the sea where there are no storms.

We neither of us really woke until, at the bottom of the hill which rises into Acquapendente, the oxen stopped. This halt woke us up ; first me and then my companion. He looked at me a moment and laughed. He seemed to have thought all this while that I was some country friend of his who had taken a lift; and I, for my part, had made more or less certain that he was a good fellow who would do me no harm. I was right, and he was wrong. I knew not what offering to make him to compensate him for his trouble which his heavy oxen had taken. After some thought I brought a cigar out of my pocket, which he smoked with extreme pleasure. The oxen meanwhile had been urged up the slow hill, and it was in this way that we reached the famous town of Acquapendente. But why it should be called famous is more than I can understand. It may be that in one of those narrow streets there is a picture or a church, or one of those things which so attract unbelieving men. To the pilgrim it is simply a group of houses. Into one of these I went, and, upon my soul, I have nothing to say of it except that they furnished me with food. . .

The road was interminable, and the crest, from which I promised myself the view of the crater-lake, was always just before me, and was never reached. A little spring, caught in a hollow log, refreshed a meadow on the right. Drinking there again, I wondered if I should go on or rest ; but I was full of antiquity, and a memory in the blood, or what not, impelled me to see the lake in the crater before I went to sleep : after a few hundred yards this obsession was satisfied.

I passed between two banks, where the road had been worn down at the crest of the volcano's rim ; then at once, far below, in a circle of silent trees with here and there a vague shore of marshy land, I saw the Pond of Venus : some miles of brooding water, darkened by the dark slopes around it. At its hither end a hill, that had once been a cone in the crater, stood out all covered with a dense wood. It was the Hill of Venus. There was no temple, nor no sacrifice, nor no ritual for the Divinity, save this solemn attitude of perennial silence ; but under the influence which still remained and gave the place its savour, it was impossible to believe that the gods were dead. There were no men in that hollow ; nor was there any memory of men, save of men dead these thousand of years. There was no life of visible things. The mind released itself and was in touch with whatever survives of conquered but immortal Spirits.

Thus ready for worship, and in a mood of adoration ; filled also with the genius which inhabits its native place and is too subtle or too pure to suffer the effect of time, I passed down the ridge-way of the mountain rim, and came to the edge overlooking that arena whereon was first fought out and decided the chief destiny of the world.

For all below was the Campagna. Names that are at the

origin of things attached to every cleft and distant rock beyond the spreading level, or sanctified the gleams of rivers. There below me was Veii; beyond, in the Wall of the Apennines, only just escaped from clouds, was Tibur that dignified the ravine at the edge of their rising; that crest to the right was Tusculum, and far to the south, but clear on a mountain answering my own, was the mother of the City, Alba Longa. The Tiber, a dense, brown fog rolling over and concealing it, was the god of the wide plain. There and at that moment I should have seen the City. I stood up on the bank and shaded my eyes, straining to catch the dome at least in the sunlight; but I could not, for Rome was hidden by the low Sabinian hills.

HILAIRE BELLOC (from *The Path to Rome*)

SAN ANTONIO OF THE RIO MADEIRA

Where we were anchored, San Antonio was in view, about five miles up stream. Where at the end of that reach of river a line of tremulous light, which we thought was the cataracts, bridged the converging palisades of the jungle, in the trees of the right bank it was sometimes easy to believe there was a glint of white buildings. But looking again, to reassure your sight, the apparition of dwellings vanished. At night, in the quiet, sometimes the ears could detect the shudder of the weighty rapids by San Antonio; but it was merely a tremor felt; there was no sound. The village remained to us for some time just that uncertain gleam by day, and the rapids but a minute reduction of a turmoil that was far. For in that languorous heat we counted miles differently, and it was pleasanter to suspect than to go and prove, and much easier.

One day I went. When in a small boat the jungle towered. The river, too, had a different character. From the shore, or from the big *Capella*, the river was an expanse of light, an impression of shining peace. Whenever you got close to its surface it became alive and menacingly intimate. Our little boat seemed to roll in the powerful folds of a monster which wallowed ponderously and without ceasing. The trees afloat, charging down swiftly and in what one felt was an ominous quiet, stood well above our tiny craft.

We steered close in-shore to avoid the drifting wood and the set of the current. The jungle's sheer height, confusion, and intensity were more awesome than when seen from the steamer. Not many of the trees were of great beam, but their consistent height, with the lianas in a wreck from the far overhanging cornice, dwarfed our boat to an unimportant straw. At times the forest had a selvage of cane, and growths of arrow grass, bearing long white plumes twelve feet above us, and a pair of fan-shaped leaves resembling palm leaves. . .

The little huddle of San Antonio's white houses is on slightly rising ground, and the lambent green of the jungle is beside them and over them. The foliage presses the village down to the river. Like every Amazonian town and village, it appears, set in that forest, as rare a human foothold as a ship in mid-ocean ; a few lights and a few voices in the dark and interminable wastes. So I landed from our little craft elated with a sense of luckily acquired security.

The white embowered village, the leaping fountains and the rocks, the air in a flutter with the shock of

ponderous water collapsing, the surmounting island in mid-
stream with its coronet of palms, the half-naked Indians
idling among the Bolivian rubber boats hauled up to the
foreshore below, the unexplored jungle which closed in
and framed the scene, the fierce sun set in the rounded
amplitude of the clouds of the rains, made the tropical
picture which was the right reward for a great journey.
I had come down long weeks of empty leisure, in which the
mind got farther and farther away from the cities where
time is so carefully measured and highly valued. The
centre of the ultimate wilderness was more than a matter of
fact. It was now a personal conviction which needed no
verification.

H. M. TOMLINSON (from *The Sea and the Jungle*)

THE GOLDEN JOURNEY

We who with songs beguile your pilgrimage
    And swear that Beauty lives though lilies die,
We Poets of the proud old lineage
    Who sing to find your hearts, we know not why,—

What shall we tell you ? Tales, marvellous tales
    Of ships and stars and isles where good men rest,
Where nevermore the rose of sunset pales,
    And winds and shadows fall toward the West :

And there the world's first huge white-bearded kings
    In dim glades sleeping, murmur in their sleep,
And closer round their breasts the ivy clings,
    Cutting its pathway slow and red and deep.

And how beguile you ? Death has no repose
　　Warmer and deeper than that Orient sand
Which hides the beauty and bright faith of those
　　Who made the Golden Journey to Samarkand.

And now they wait and whiten peaceably,
　　Those conquerors, those poets, those so fair :
They know time comes, not only you and I,
　　But the whole world shall whiten, here or there ;

When those long caravans that cross the plain
　　With dauntless feet and sound of silver bells
Put forth no more for glory or for gain,
　　Take no more solace from the palm-girt wells ;

When the great markets by the sea shut fast
　　All that calm Sunday that goes on and on :
When even lovers find their peace at last,
　　And Earth is but a star, that once had shone.

J. E. FLECKER (from *Prologue*)

FOURTH PART

§1 MOON AND STARS

Canst thou bind the sweet influences of Pleiades, or loose the bands of Orion? Canst thou bring forth Mazzaroth in his season? Or canst thou guide Arcturus with his sons? Knowest thou the ordinances of heaven? Canst thou set the dominion thereof in the earth?

JOB XXXIX. (A.V.)

When in heaven the stars about the bright moon shine clear to see, when the air is windless and all the peaks appear and the tall headlands and glades and from heaven breaketh open the infinite air and all the stars are seen, then the shepherd's heart is glad.

HOMER (*Iliad*)

The massy shoulder of Orion came heaving up . . . first one bright star, then another; then the gleaming girdle. . . . As the constellation rose, so presently new vigour entered into the trees, the sap moved, the buds thrust forth, the new leaf came, and the nightingale travelling up from the south sang in the musical April nights.

RICHARD JEFFERIES (*Bevis*)

§ I MOON AND STARS

THE PROBLEM OF THE HEAVENS

The generations of men observed that the pageant of heaven and the seasons of the year came round in regular succession, and they could not discover the causes of these movements. Hence they sought refuge by leaving all this in the hands of the gods, supposing everything to be guided by them. And they placed the gods' abode in the heavens, because night and moon were seen to revolve through the sky—moon, day and night and night's grave stars, night-wandering meteors, clouds and sun, rain and snow, winds, lightnings, hail, and the loud blasts of thunder.

O unhappy race of men, to charge such doings to the gods, ascribing to them bitter wrath! What groans did our forefathers thus beget for themselves, what wounds for us, what tears for future generations! It is no mark of piety to be seen often with veiled head approaching every altar, falling prostrate on the ground and spreading out the palms before the statues of the gods, or sprinkling their altars with the flowing blood of beasts, linking vow to vow—true piety it is to be able to look upon all things with a mind at peace. Yet, when we lift our eyes to the heavenly regions of the upper world, to the ether filled with glittering stars, and think of the journeys of sun and moon, then another misgiving suddenly arises in our hearts already burdened with other ills—the fear that perchance the gods have an unlimited power over us, if indeed they are able to roll the bright stars in their various motions. And we are sorely puzzled, finding no answer to these questions—whether there was ever a birth-time of the world, whether there is to be an end of it, whether the heavenly ramparts will be unable to endure the strain of this mysterious motion or whether endowed with everlasting existence they can glide on through never-ending time, defying the strong powers of immeasurable ages. Again, what human mind does not quail with fear of the gods, what human limbs do not sink with terror, when the scorched earth shakes with the thunderbolt's appalling shock and the great sky resounds with rumblings ? Do not the nations then tremble and their proud rulers shrink smitten with terror, lest for some evil deed or some proud word the solemn day of punishment be now come ? When too, the utmost fury of a violent wind strikes the sea and sweeps over its waters the admiral of a fleet with his mighty legions and his elephants, does he not beseech the gods' peace with vows, does he not tremble and pray for an end of the storm and for favouring breezes ; but all in vain, since none the less he is often seized by the hurricane and driven upon the shoals of death ? So does some hidden power constantly trample upon us, treading underfoot the noble rods and cruel axes of human authority, holding them in derision. Again, when the earth quakes beneath our feet, and cities rock or fall, what wonder if mortal men abase themselves and acknowledge that the gods have marvellous powers—sufficient to govern all things !

LUCRETIUS (*De Rerum Natura*, V—Trans. A. S.)

THE HARPER OF DIDO

Sweet soundeth the golden harp with the song of the
    long-haired Iopas,
For Atlas the Great was his teacher. Now sings he of
    moonrise and moonset,
Now tells of the Sun and his toiling, of men and of beasts
    the beginnings—
Of lightning and storm, Arcturus, of Hyades wet and
    the Bear-stars;
Why Winter hurries the Sun to his bed in the deeps of the
    ocean,
When nights are so heavy with darkness, so gloomy and
    tardy in passing.

VIRGIL (Æneid, Bk. I—Trans. A. S.)

HOW THE EARTH WAS MADE

A few stars are known which are hardly bigger than the
earth, but the majority are so large that hundreds of thousands of earths could be packed inside each and leave
room to spare ; here and there we come upon a giant star
large enough to contain millions of millions of earths. And
the total number of stars in the universe is probably something like the total number of grains of sand on all the sea-
shores of the world. Such is the littleness of our home in
space when measured up against the total substance of
the universe.

This vast multitude of stars are wandering about in

space. A few form groups which journey in company, but the majority are solitary travellers. And they travel through a universe so spacious that it is an event of almost unimaginable rarity for a star to come anywhere near to another star. For the most part each voyages in splendid isolation, like a ship on an empty ocean. In a scale model in which the stars are ships, the average ship will be well over a million miles from its nearest neighbour, whence it is easy to understand why a ship seldom finds another within hailing distance.

We believe, nevertheless, that some two thousand million years ago this rare event took place, and that a second star, wandering blindly through space, happened to come within hailing distance of the sun. Just as the sun and moon raise tides on the earth, so this second star must have raised tides on the surface of the sun. But they would be very different from the puny tides which the small mass of the moon raises in our oceans; a huge tidal wave must have travelled over the surface of the sun, ultimately forming a mountain of prodigious height, which would rise ever higher and higher as the cause of the disturbance came nearer and nearer. And, before the second star began to recede, its tidal pull had become so powerful that this mountain was torn to pieces and threw off small fragments of itself, much as the crest of a wave throws off spray. These small fragments have been circulating around their parent sun ever since. They are the planets, great and small, of which our earth is one.

SIR JAMES JEANS (from *The Mysterious Universe*)

Each living cell that floats in protoplasm has a kind of protecting membrane round it ; and of such is our intellect to us who float in cosmic protoplasm, and are being perpetually bombarded by stellar and universal influences that, though we know it not, pierce through and through the thinking cell that is man. They come to us by night and by day, the messages and communications for which we have been so ardently longing ; not in the childish articulate language we have sought to impose on the spheres, but in a manner far subtler, more cogent, more irresistible, than if they had been words spoken from the very crown of the sky.

Our earth being poised in the centre of the universe, where all is centre ; living and developing there like a child in its mother's womb, must of necessity be in constant communication, communion, symbiosis with the universe. Nothing can happen there that has not its effect, reverberation, on the earth. In the entire universe the elements are everywhere the same as on our own globe ; few in number and unvarying, however distant a star may be and whatever its temperature. In the whole Cosmos our spectroscope reveals nothing that we have not ; when the presence of unknown gases or substances was suspected, indications furnished by the stars themselves helped our chemists to identify similar bodies on the earth. Behind solid matter, behind gases and fluids that hide it, lurks the electron, perpetual, eternal, universal, immortal ; the most infinitely little of the infinitely little, and yet propelling the infinitely great. The limitless All, with its nebulæ, galaxies, vast hidden spaces that even light cannot reach, with its new worlds that suddenly spring into being, floats in the ether, most inevitable of all the fluids and the one of which we know least ; the ether whose waves will transmit through eternity, through measureless areas of millions of light-years, the flash of light sent by a star so remote that most of the worlds will be dead or extinct before it can reach them.

M. MAETERLINCK
(from *The Magic of the Stars*—Trans. A. SUTRO)

THE MARINER'S BENEDICTION

In his loneliness and fixedness he yearneth towards the journeying Moon, and the stars that still sojourn, yet still move onward ; and every where the blue sky belongs to them, and is their appointed rest, and their native country and their own natural homes, which they enter unannounced, as lords that are certainly expected, and yet there is a silent joy at their arrival. By the light of the Moon he beholdeth God's creatures of the great calm —their beauty and their happiness. He blesseth them in his heart.

COLERIDGE
(from *The Ancient Mariner*—Prose Argument)

VOICES OF THE NIGHT

I remember nothing better than the time when in the south country I was first able to look out night after night over woods and fields, with nothing but one small country town halfway between my window and the

Downs and the sea twenty-five miles away; to hear the fox's bark, the hoot of owls, and the song of nightingales answering one another away down the valley. A vixen's scream is surely the most unearthly of night noises, just as the purr of the nightjar and the stick-and-comb chatter of the landrail are the most homely and soothing; though even the vixen's scream is not much less startling than, heard within a few yards, the screech of the white owl. But the sound of sounds of the night is the hoot of the brown owl. That long-drawn, deep music of the night, the voice and vigour of life unseen, comes from the heart of the wood.

These sounds of night belong to an open window. But to know other sounds, to learn what can be the noise or the silence of darkness, you must walk by night alone. It has fallen to my lot to spend many hours at all times of the night alone, in English woods and fields, and I have heard many sounds and have seen sights I should never have known so well in any other way. The grunts and squeals of badgers at their earth only a few yards away up the hill; rats cracking hazel-nuts in the trees above my head; an otter taking the water of a stream in a place where no otter was ever found by hounds. Songs of birds; I have heard the cuckoo often, and the wood-pigeon once, and snatches of other song, lark's and chaffinch's and robin's, —sometimes it seemed as if the bird sang without thought, sometimes as if it was suddenly angered or alarmed. Mallard on the wing, curlew, whimbrel; the whee-yoh of widgeon, the screwy calls of coot, the lapping noises of duck feeding on ooze, though these, too, may be sounds of the day as well.

Yet they are sounds to be heard more clearly and more separately by night; and as for sights, only he who has walked many hours in the dark knows that there are few nights in the summer when he will not see the horizon leap with lightning, and that winter lightning is not much less common. And that the cold glory of moonlight over wood and field is only part of the night ; the deepness of night is over a man when the moon is down, and he waits under the dome of stars to hear and to see ; to listen for the owl and the fox ; to watch Vega swing behind the naked oak, and Orion with his jewelled sword journeying high above the southern hills.

ERIC PARKER (from *English Wild Life*)

HOUSES OF THE SUN

Thousands of years ago the Chaldean astronomers saw the Sun as a traveller through the heavens who stayed in certain houses on his way, and Job (A.V. xxxviii. 32) gives the name " Mazzaroth" to the great series of hostels provided for this illustrious traveller. Along the curving road which he apparently followed (his orbit or ecliptic) certain groups of stars were seen in association with his movement. This starry pathway across the sky was called the Zodiac or " animal circle " (Greek, *zodiacos*), for all the constellations in it with one exception (*Libra*) were seen as figures of living creatures. Within this zone, it was noticed, lay the track of other lesser travellers—the moon and the five planets known to the ancients (we can now see eight under favourable conditions). So the Zodiac was divided into twelve Houses or " Signs " (one for each month of the year), a twelfth part of the whole circular band being assigned to each of its twelve star-groups or constellations. Each sign was given an appropriate symbol and a name. The names are :

SPRING. *Aries* (the Ram), *Taurus* (the Bull), *Gemini* (the Twins) ;

SUMMER. *Cancer* (the Crab), *Leo* (the Lion), *Virgo* (the Virgin) ;

AUTUMN. *Libra* (the Scales), *Scorpio* (the Scorpion), *Sagittarius* (the Archer) ;

WINTER. *Capricornus* (the Goat), *Aquarius* (the Water-carrier), and *Pisces* (the Fishes). They are easily remembered by the help of this old rhyme :

> *The Ram, the Bull, the Heavenly Twins,*
> *And next the Crab the Lion shines,*
> *The Virgin and the Scales,*
> *The Scorpion, Archer and Sea-goat,*
> *The Man that bears the watering-pot*
> *And Fish with glittering tails.*

Or, if you prefer a more stately measure, by the following verses :

> *Behold our orbit as through twice six signs*
> *Our central Sun apparently inclines :*
> *The Golden Fleece his pale ray first adorns,*
> *Then tow'rds the Bull he winds and gilds his horns ;*
> *Castor and Pollux then receive his ray ;*
> *On burning Cancer then he seems to stay ;*
> *On flaming Leo pours the liquid shower ;*
> *Then faints beneath the Virgin's conquering power ;*
> *Now the just Scales weigh well both day and night ;*
> *The Scorpion then receives the solar light ;*

Then quivered Chiron clouds his wintry face,
And the tempestuous Sea-goat mends his pace ;
Now in the water Sol's warm beams are quench'd,
Till with the Fishes he is fairly drench'd.
These twice six signs successively appear,
And mark the twelve months of the circling year.

The symbols are mostly conventional pictures. Thus, the symbol for *Aquarius* is the Egyptian character for water. The origin of the signs for *Leo, Capricornus,* and *Virgo* is obscure.

The Sun stays for a month (i.e., a solar month, a little longer than a lunar month) in each of his Houses ; or, more properly speaking, he spends this time in passing through each. The House of the Sun on any particular day can easily be ascertained. Imagine the twelve star-groups as represented by the hours marked on the dial of a watch, the first constellation (*Aries*) being one o'clock. If there is a full moon, and the moon is in the second constellation (*Taurus*), then the Sun must be on the *opposite* side of the ecliptic in the eighth constellation (*Scorpio*). If the moon is not full, observe the constellation which is in the south at midnight, and the Sun will be in its opposite.

" The first point of *Aries* " was the Vernal Equinox, when the Sun crossed the equator going north and days and nights are equal throughout the world. This point was fixed according to the position of the *Aries* star-group in relation to the Sun at the time (several thousand years ago) when the ancients provided these Houses for the Sun. It happens, however, that the Sun does not now enter *Aries* exactly in accordance with this old man-made time-table, for the equinoctial points have a continuous westerly motion or " drift," the direction of the earth's axis with reference to the stars changing slowly. Consequently the pole-star of one age is not the pole-star of another. Hipparchus, a Greek astronomer of the second century B.C., discovered that the year of the seasons was shorter than the solar year. It seemed that the equinoxes stepped forward a little (" preceded ") to meet the Sun. This phenomenon, known as the precession of the equinoxes, was first explained by Newton, who found it was due to the attraction of the sun and moon on the bulging equator of the earth. Our planet rotates like a wobbly spinning top, whose slanting axis rotates as the top spins. It takes nearly 26,000 years to make one complete wobble. As a result of this behaviour the signs of the Zodiac no longer correspond to its star-groups. Each sign has " backed " into the constellation west of it, so that the sign of *Aries* is now in the constellation of *Pisces*. The equinoctial points have been moving slowly westward since the ancient astronomers assigned these Houses to the Sun, but it is satisfactory to know that, when a cycle of about 26,000 years has been completed, the Sun will once more enter *Aries* punctually at the Vernal Equinox.

A. S.

THE MAN IN THE MOON

Look out for a dusky form on the western side of the moon when it is eight days old, and if you have the eye of a lunarian you will see the Man in the Moon ; and you will (in such case) also observe the thornbush carried on his back and the small dark figure of his little dog. It is difficult to say how he got there. As to his identity, the popular view common to many nations has connected him with the Sabbath-breaker whose short history is recorded in the Bible. " While the children of Israel were in the wilderness they found a man that gathered sticks upon the Sabbath day" (*Numbers*, Chap. xv). They brought the culprit to Moses and Aaron, and he was stoned to death without the camp. This punishment would seem to be both severe and conclusive. The mediæval mind, however, was not content with it, and embellished the story with the addition of perpetual banishment to the cold regions of the moon, recording a curse pronounced in the following terms : " As you regarded not *Sunday* on earth, you shall keep a perpetual *Moonday* in heaven." These mediæval writers, in whom the historic sense was but feebly developed, quite overlooked the fact that the position of Man in the Moon was already occupied by Cain, who—condemned to be a fugitive on earth—was generally understood to have taken refuge in the moon. It is true that Beatrice " smiled a little " when Dante asked for an explanation of those dusky marks on the moon which made folk on earth " tell the tale of Cain " (*Par.* II). In spite of the learned explanations he then received, Dante later on decorates his verse with this legend, poetically describing moonset in these words : " Cain and his thorns already touch the wave." But, whoever he was, it is clear that there was somebody in the moon with a bush or a bundle of sticks, and Bottom the weaver, preparing his play for Duke Theseus, was careful to provide Moonshine by means of a man with a bush of thorns.

There are some people who see a sort of facial expression on the moon at the full, and to these the Man in the Moon is nothing more than this jolly round face. There are others who object to this view as a derogation of the moon's manhood, since it causes the Man in the Moon to dwindle like the Cheshire cat in *Alice in Wonderland*, leaving us nothing but a smile. Truly, as Lyly says in his Prologue to *Endymion*, " there liveth none under the sun that knows what to make of the Man in the Moon." It is likely that the only people who know the truth of the matter are *lunatics*, properly so called.

A. S.

THE GREAT BEAR

Last night Jones was walking down with me from Staple Inn to Clifford's Inn, about 10 o'clock, and we saw the Great Bear standing upright on the tip of his tail which was coming out of a chimney pot. Jones said it wanted attending to. I said :

" Yes, but to attend to it properly we ought to sit up with it all night, and if the Great Bear thinks that I am going to sit by his bed-side and give him a spoonful of barley-water every ten minutes, he will find himself much mistaken."

SAMUEL BUTLER (from *Note-Books*)

TOM OF BEDLAM

The moon's my constant mistress,
And the lonely owl my marrow ;
    The flaming drake
    And the night-crow make
Me music to my sorrow.

I know more than Apollo,
For oft, when he lies sleeping,
　　I see the stars
　　At mortal wars
In the wounded welkin weeping,

The moon embrace her shepherd,
And the Queen of Love her warrior,
　　While the first doth horn
　　The star of morn,
And the next the heavenly farrier.

With a host of furious fancies
Whereof I am commander,
　　With a burning spear
　　And a horse of air
To the wilderness I wander;

By a knight of ghosts and shadows
I summoned am to tourney
　　Ten leagues beyond
　　The wide world's end—
Methinks it is no journey.

ANONYMOUS

A COMPLAINT BY NIGHT

Alas, so all things now do hold their peace !
　Heaven and earth disturbèd in no thing ;
The beasts, the air, the birds their song do cease,
　The nightès car the stars about doth bring ;

Calm is the sea ; the waves work less and less :
   So am not I, whom love, alas ! doth wring,
Bringing before my face the great increase
   Of my desires, whereat I weep and sing,
In joy and woe, as in a doubtful case.
   For my sweet thoughts sometime do pleasure bring ;
But by and by, the cause of my disease
   Gives me a pang that inwardly doth sting,
When that I think what grief it is again
To live and lack the thing should rid my pain.

EARL OF SURREY (after PETRARCH)

A TALK BY MOONLIGHT

(*Enter* LORENZO and JESSICA.)

LORENZO : The moon shines bright : in such a night as
    this,
When the sweet wind did gently kiss the trees
And they did make no noise, in such a night
Troilus methinks mounted the Trojan walls
And sigh'd his soul toward the Grecian tents,
Where Cressid lay that night.
JESSICA :   In such a night
Did Thisbe fearfully o'ertrip the dew
And saw the lion's shadow ere himself
And ran dismay'd away.
LORENZO :   In such a night
Stood Dido with a willow in her hand
Upon the wild sea banks and waft her love
To come again to Carthage.

655

JESSICA :   In such a night
Medea gather'd the enchanted herbs
That did renew old Æson.
LORENZO :   In such a night
Did Jessica steal from the wealthy Jew
And with an unthrift love did run from Venice
As far as Belmont.
JESSICA :   In such a night
Did young Lorenzo swear he loved her well,
Stealing her soul with many vows of faith
And ne'er a true one.
LORENZO :   In such a night
Did pretty Jessica, like a little shrew,
Slander her love, and he forgave it her.

SHAKESPEARE (from *Merchant of Venice*)

WINTER NIGHTS

Now winter nights enlarge
The number of their hours ;
And clouds their storms discharge
Upon the airy towers.
Let now the chimneys blaze
And cups o'erflow with wine,
Let well-tuned words amaze
With harmony divine !
Now yellow waxen lights
Shall wait on honey love
While youthful revels, masques,
    and courtly sights,
Sleep's leaden spells remove.

This time doth well dispense
With lovers' long discourse ;
Much speech hath some defence,
Though beauty no remorse.
All do not all things well ;
Some measures comely tread
Some knotted riddles tell,
Some poems smoothly read.
The summer hath his joys,
And winter his delights,
Though love and all his pleasures
    are but toys,
They shorten tedious nights.

THOMAS CAMPION

HYMN TO DIANA

Queen and huntress, chaste and fair,
    Now the sun is laid to sleep,
Seated in thy silver chair,
    State in wonted manner keep :
        Hesperus entreats thy light,
        Goddess excellently bright !

Earth, let not thy envious shade
    Dare itself to interpose ;
Cynthia's shining orb was made
    Heaven to clear when day did close :
        Bless us then with wishèd sight,
        Goddess excellently bright !

Lay thy bow of pearl apart,
  And thy crystal-shining quiver;
Give unto the flying hart
  Space to breathe, how short soever:
    Thou that mak'st a day of night—
    Goddess excellently bright!

BEN JONSON

A SONNET OF THE MOON

Look how the pale Queen of the silent night
Doth cause the ocean to attend upon her,
And he as long as she is in his sight,
With his full tide is ready her to honour:
But when the silver waggon of the Moon
Is mounted up so high he cannot follow,
The sea calls home his crystal waves to moan,
And with low ebb doth manifest his sorrow;
So you, that are the sovereign of my heart,
Have all my joys attending on your will;
My joys low-ebbing when you do depart,
When you return, their tide my heart doth fill;
  So as you come, and as you do depart,
  Joys ebb and flow within my tender heart.

CHARLES BEST (1602)

NIGHT-PIECE, TO JULIA

Her eyes the glow-worm lend thee,
The shooting stars attend thee ;
    And the elves also,
    Whose little eyes glow
Like the sparks of fire, befriend thee.

No will-o'-the-wisp mislight thee ;
Nor snake or slow-worm bite thee :
    But on, on thy way
    Not making a stay,
Since ghost there's none to affright thee.

Let not the dark thee cumber ;
What though the moon does slumber ?
    The stars of the night
    Will lend thee their light,
Like tapers clear without number.

Then, Julia, let me woo thee,
Thus, thus to come unto me :
    And when I shall meet
    Thy silvery feet,
My soul I'll pour into thee.

ROBERT HERRICK

MIDNIGHT

All things are hushed, as Nature's self lay dead ;
The mountains seem to nod their drowsy head,
The little birds in dreams their songs repeat,
And sleeping flowers beneath the night-dew sweat ;
Even lust and envy sleep, yet love denies
Rest to my soul and slumber to my eyes.

DRYDEN

A NIGHT-PIECE

——The sky is overcast
With a continuous cloud of texture close,
Heavy and wan, all whitened by the Moon,
Which through that veil is indistinctly seen,
A dull, contracted circle, yielding light
So feebly spread that not a shadow falls
Chequering the ground—from rock, plant, tree, or
      tower.
At length a pleasant instantaneous gleam
Startles the pensive traveller while he treads
His lonesome path, with unobserving eye
Bent earthwards ; he looks up—the clouds are split
Asunder,—and above his head he sees
The clear Moon, and the glory of the heavens.
There, in a black-blue vault she sails along,
Followed by multitudes of stars, that, small
And sharp, and bright, along the dark abyss
Drive as she drives : how fast they wheel away,
Yet vanish not !—the wind is in the tree,

But they are silent ;—still they roll along
Immeasurably distant ; and the vault,
Built round by those white clouds, enormous clouds,
Still deepens its unfathomable depth.
At length the Vision closes ; and the mind,
Not undisturbed by the delight it feels,
Which slowly settles into peaceful calm,
Is left to muse upon the solemn scene.

WORDSWORTH

LUCY

The stars of midnight shall be dear
To her ; and she shall lean her ear
In many a secret place
Where rivulets dance their wayward round,
And beauty born of murmuring sound
Shall pass into her face.

WORDSWORTH

SONNET TO NIGHT

Mysterious Night ! when our first parent knew
  Thee from report divine, and heard thy name,
  Did he not tremble for this lovely frame,
This glorious canopy of light and blue ?
Yet 'neath a curtain of translucent dew,
  Bathed in the rays of the great setting flame,
  Hesperus with the host of heaven came,
And lo ! Creation widened in man's view.

Who could have thought such darkness lay concealed
Within thy beams, O Sun ! or who could find,
   Whilst flow'r and leaf and insect stood revealed,
That to such countless orbs thou mad'st us blind !
   Why do we then shun Death with anxious strife ?
   If Light can thus deceive, wherefore not Life ?

JOSEPH BLANCO WHITE

ALL THROUGH THE NIGHT
(*To an old Welsh air*)

Deep the silence round us spreading,
   All through the night ;
Dark the path that we are treading
   All through the night.
   Still the coming day discerning,
   By the hope within us burning,
   To the dawn our footsteps turning,
      All through the night.

Star of faith, the dark adorning
   All through the night,
Leads us fearless toward the morning
   All through the night.
   Though our hearts be wrapt in sorrow
   From the hope of dawn we borrow
   Promise of a glad to-morrow
      All through the night.

ANONYMOUS

THE PERSIAN MOON

Ah, Moon of my Delight who know'st no wane,
The Moon of Heaven is rising once again :
  How oft hereafter rising shall she look
Through this same Garden after me—in vain !

    EDWARD FITZGERALD
             (after OMAR KHAYYÁM)

THE SLEEPER

At midnight, in the month of June,
I stand beneath the mystic moon.
An opiate vapour, dewy, dim,
Exhales from out her golden rim,
And, softly dripping, drop by drop,
Upon the quiet mountain top,
Steals drowsily and musically
Into the universal valley.
The rosemary nods upon the grave ;
The lily lolls upon the wave ;
Wrapping the fog about its breast,
The ruin moulders into rest,
Looking like Lethe, see ! the lake
A conscious slumber seems to take,
And would not, for the world, awake.
All Beauty sleeps !—and lo ! where lies
Irene, with her Destinies !
O lady bright ! can it be right—
This window open to the night ?

The wanton airs, from the tree-top,
Laughingly through the lattice drop—
The bodiless airs, a wizard rout,
Flit through thy chamber in and out,
And wave the curtain canopy
So fitfully—so fearfully—
Above the closed and fringèd lid
'Neath which thy slumb'ring soul lies hid,
That, o'er the floor and down the wall,
Like ghosts the shadows rise and fall !
Oh, lady dear, hast thou no fear ?
Why and what art thou dreaming here ?
Sure thou art come o'er far-off seas,
A wonder to these garden trees !
Strange is thy pallor ! strange thy dress,
Strange, above all, thy length of tress,
And this all solemn silentness !

The lady sleeps ! Oh, may her sleep,
Which is enduring, so be deep !
Heaven have her in its sacred keep !
This chamber changed for one more holy,
This bed for one more melancholy,
I pray to God that she may lie
For ever with unopen'd eye
While the pale sheeted ghosts go by !

My love, she sleeps ! Oh, may her sleep
As it is lasting, so be deep !
Soft may the worms about her creep !
Far in the forest, dim and old,
For her may some tall vault unfold—

Some vault that oft has flung its black
And wingèd panels fluttering back,
Triumphant, o'er the crested palls
Of her grand family funerals—
Some sepulchre, remote, alone,
Against whose portal she hath thrown,
In childhood, many an idle stone—
Some tomb from out whose sounding door
She ne'er shall force an echo more,
Thrilling to think, poor child of sin !
It was the dead who groan'd within.

EDGAR ALLAN POE

MOON MAGIC

What, there's nothing in the moon noteworthy ?
Nay : for if that moon could love a mortal,
Use, to charm him (so to fit a fancy),
All her magic ('tis the old sweet mythos)
She would turn a new side to her mortal,
Side unseen of herdsman, huntsman, steersman—
Blank to Zoroaster on his terrace,
Blind to Galileo on his turret,
Dumb to Homer, dumb to Keats—him, even !
Think the wonder of the moonstruck mortal—
When she turns round, comes again in heaven,
Opens out anew for worse or better !
Proves she like some portent of an iceberg
Swimming full upon the ship it founders,
Hungry with huge teeth of splintered crystals ?

Proves she as the paved work of a sapphire
Seen by Moses when he climbed the mountain ?
Moses, Aaron, Nadab and Abihu
Climbed and saw the very God, the Highest,
Stand upon the paved work of a sapphire.
Like the bodied heaven in his clearness
Shone the stone, the sapphire of that paved work,
When they ate and drank and saw God also !
What were seen ? None knows, none ever shall know.
Only this is sure—the sight were other,
Not the moon's same side, born late in Florence,
Dying now impoverished here in London.
God be thanked, the meanest of his creatures
Boasts two soul-sides—one to face the world with,
One to show a woman when he loves her !

BROWNING

SOHRAB AND RUSTUM

So, on the bloody sand, Sohrab lay dead.
And the great Rustum drew his horseman's cloak
Down o'er his face, and sate by his dead son.
    And night came down over the solemn waste,
And the two gazing hosts, and that sole pair,
And darken'd all ; and a cold fog, with night,
Crept from the Oxus. Soon a hum arose,
As of a great assembly loosed, and fires
Began to twinkle through the fog : for now
Both armies moved to camp, and took their meal :
And Rustum and his son were left alone.

But the majestic River floated on,
Out of the mist and hum of that low land,
Into the frosty starlight, and there moved,
Rejoicing, through the hush'd Chorasmian waste,
Under the solitary moon : he flow'd
Right for the Polar Star, past Orgunjè,
Brimming, and bright, and large : then sands begin
To hem his watery march, and dam his streams,
And split his currents ; that for many a league
The shorn and parcell'd Oxus strains along
Through beds of sand and matted rushy isles—
Oxus forgetting the bright speed he had
In his high mountain cradle in Pamere,
A foil'd circuitous wanderer :—till at last
The long'd-for dash of waves is heard, and wide
His luminous home of waters opens, bright
And tranquil, from whose floor the new-bathed stars
Emerge, and shine upon the Aral Sea.

MATTHEW ARNOLD

LUCIFER IN STARLIGHT

On a starred night Prince Lucifer uprose.
Tired of his dark dominion swung the fiend
Above the rolling ball in cloud part screened,
Where sinners hugged their spectre of repose.
Poor prey to his hot fit of pride were those.
And now upon his western wing he leaned,
Now his huge bulk o'er Afric's sands careened,
Now the black planet shadowed Arctic snows.

Soaring through wider zones that pricked his scars
With memory of the old revolt from Awe,
He reached a middle height, and at the stars,
Which are the brain of heaven, he looked, and sank.
Around the ancient track marched, rank on rank,
The army of unalterable law.

GEORGE MEREDITH

LULLABY

Lullaby, oh, lullaby!
Flowers are closed and lambs are sleeping;
Lullaby, oh, lullaby!
Stars are up, the moon is peeping;
Lullaby, oh, lullaby!
While the birds are silence keeping,
(Lullaby, oh, lullaby!)
Sleep, my baby, fall a-sleeping,
Lullaby, oh, lullaby!

CHRISTINA ROSSETTI

SONG

Let the red dawn surmise
What we shall do,
When this blue starlight dies
And all is through.

668

If we have loved but well
　　Under the sun,
Let the last morrow tell
　　What we have done.

BLISS CARMAN

THE STATUE OF KING CHARLES AT CHARING CROSS

Sombre and rich, the skies ;
Great glooms, and starry plains.
Gently the night wind sighs ;
Else a vast silence reigns.

The splendid silence clings
Around me : and around
The saddest of all kings
Crowned, and again discrowned.

Comely and calm, he rides
Hard by his own Whitehall :
Only the night wind glides :
No crowds, nor rebels, brawl.

Gone, too, his Court ; and yet,
The stars his courtiers are :
Stars in their stations set ;
And every wandering star.

669

Alone he rides, alone,
The fair and fatal king :
Dark night is all his own,
That strange and solemn thing.

Which are more full of fate :
The stars ; or those sad eyes ?
Which are more still and great :
Those brows ; or the dark skies ?

Although his whole heart yearn
In passionate tragedy :
Never was face so stern
With sweet austerity.

Vanquished in life, his death
By beauty made amends :
The passing of his breath
Won his defeated ends.

Brief life and hapless ? Nay :
Through death, life grew sublime.
Speak after sentence ? Yea :
And to the end of time.

Armoured he rides, his head
Bare to the stars of doom :
He triumphs now, the dead,
Beholding London's gloom.

Our wearier spirit faints,
Vexed in the world's employ :
His soul was of the saints ;
And art to him was joy.

King, tried in fires of woe !
Men hunger for thy grace :
And through the night I go,
Loving thy mournful face.

Yet when the city sleeps ;
When all the cries are still :
The stars and heavenly deeps
Work out a perfect will.

LIONEL JOHNSON

THE BUSH, MY LOVER

The camp-fire gleams resistance
  To every twinkling star ;
The horse-bells in the distance
  Are jangling faint and far ;
Through gum-boughs lorn and lonely
  The passing breezes sigh ;
In all the world are only
  My star-crowned Love and I.

The still night wraps Macquarie ;
  The white moon, drifting slow,
Takes back her silver glory
  From watching waves below ;
To dalliance I give over,
  Though half the world may chide,
And clasp my one true Lover
  Here on Macquarie side.

The loves of earth grow olden
  Or kneel at some new shrine ;
Her locks are always golden—
  This brave Bush-Love of mine ;

671

And for her star-lit beauty,
    And for her dawns dew-pearled,
Her name in love and duty
    I guard against the world. . .

If we some white arms' folding,
    Some warm, red mouth should miss—
Her hand is ours for holding,
    Her lips are ours to kiss ;
And closer than a lover
    She shares our lightest breath,
And droops her great wings over
    To shield us to the death.

The winds of Dawn are roving,
    The river-oaks astir—
What heart were lorn of loving
    That had no Love but her ?
Till last red stars are lighted
    And last winds wander West,
Her troth and mine are plighted—
    The Lover I love best !

WILLIAM OGILVIE

ACQUAINTED WITH THE NIGHT

I have been one acquainted with the night.
I have walked out in rain and back in rain.
I have outwalked the furthest city light.

I have looked down the saddest city lane.
I have passed by the watchman on his beat
And dropped my eyes unwilling to explain.

I have stood still and hushed the sound of feet
When far away an interrupted cry
Came over houses from another street,

But not to call me back or say good-bye ;
And further still at an unearthly height
One luminary clock against the sky

Proclaimed the time was neither wrong nor right.
I have been one acquainted with the night.

ROBERT FROST

THE POOR GIRL'S MEDITATION
(*Translated from the Irish*)

I am sitting here,
Since the moon rose in the night ;
Kindling a fire,
And striving to keep it alight :
The folk of the house are lying
In slumber deep ;
The geese will be gabbling soon :
The whole of the land is asleep.

May I never leave this world
Until my ill-luck is gone :
Till I have cows and sheep,
And the lad that I love for my own :

I would not think it long,
The night I would lie at his breast,
And the daughters of spite, after that,
Might say the thing they liked best.

Love covers up hate,
If a girl have beauty at all :
On a bed that was narrow and high,
A three-month I lie by the wall :
When I bethought on the lad
That I left on the brow of the hill,
I wept from dark until dark
And my cheeks have the tear-tracks still.

And, O, young lad that I love,
I am no mark for your scorn :
All that you know of me is
Undowered I was born :
And if I've no fortune in hand,
Nor cattle nor sheep of my own,
This I can say, O lad,
I am fitted to lie my lone !

PADRAIC COLUM

MOONLIT APPLES

At the top of the house the apples are laid in rows,
And the skylight lets the moonlight in, and those
Apples are deep-sea apples of green. There goes
   A cloud on the moon in the autumn night.

A mouse in the wainscot scratches, and scratches, and then
There is no sound at the top of the house of men
Or mice ; and the cloud is blown, and the moon again
  Dapples the apples with deep-sea light.

They are lying in rows there, under the gloomy beams ;
On the sagging floor ; they gather the silver streams
Out of the moon, those moonlit apples of dreams,
  And quiet is the steep stair under.

In the corridors under there is nothing but sleep.
And stiller than ever on orchard boughs they keep
Tryst with the moon, and deep is the silence, deep
  On moon-washed apples of wonder.

JOHN DRINKWATER

OLD FIRES

The fire burns low
Where it has burned ages ago,
Sinks and sighs
As it has done to a hundred eyes
Staring, staring
At the last cold smokeless glow.

Here men sat
Lonely and watched the golden grate
Turn at length black ;
Heard the cooling iron crack :
Shadows, shadows,
Watching the shadows come and go.

And still the hiss
I hear, the soft fire's sob and kiss,
And still it burns
And the bright gold to crimson turns,
Sinking, sinking,
And the fire shadows larger grow.

O dark-cheeked fire,
Wasting like spent heart's desire,
You that were gold,
And now crimson will soon be cold—
Cold, cold,
Like moon-shadows on new snow.

Shadows all,
They that watched your shadows fall.
But now they come
Rising around me, grave and dumb. . .
Shadows, shadows,
Come as the fire-shadows go.

And stay, stay,
Though all the fire sink cold as clay,
Whispering still,
Ancestral wise Familiars—till,
Staring, staring,
Dawn's wild fires through the casement glow.

JOHN FREEMAN

LOVE'S CAUTION

Tell them, when you are home again
   How warm the air was now ;
How silent were the birds and leaves,
   And of the moon's full glow ;
And how we saw afar
   A falling star :
It was a tear of pure delight
   Ran down the face of Heaven this happy night.

Our kisses are but love in flower,
   Until that greater time
When, gathering strength, those flowers take wing,
   And Love can reach his prime.
And now, my heart's delight,
   Good night, Good night :
Give me the last sweet kiss—
   But do not breathe at home one word of this !

W. H. DAVIES

THE MOON

Thy beauty haunts me, heart and soul,
   Oh thou fair Moon, so close and bright ;
Thy beauty makes me like the child,
   That cries aloud to own thy light :
The little child that lifts each arm,
To press thee to her bosom warm.

Though there are birds that sing this night
    With thy white beams across their throats,
Let my deep silence speak for me
    More than for them their sweetest notes :
Who worships thee till music fails
Is greater than thy nightingales.

W. H. DAVIES

NIGHT RHAPSODY

How beautiful it is to wake at night,
When over all there reigns the ultimate spell
Of complete silence, darkness absolute,
To feel the world, tilted on axle-tree,
In slow gyration, with no sensible sound,
Unless to ears of unimagined beings,
Resident incorporeal or stretched
In vigilance of ecstasy among
Ethereal paths and the celestial maze.
The rumour of our onward course now brings
A steady rustle, as of some strange ship
Darkling with soundless sail all set and amply filled
By volume of an ever-constant air,
At fullest night, through seas for ever calm,
Swept lovely and unknown for ever on.

How beautiful it is to wake at night,
Embalmed in darkness watchful, sweet, and still,
As is the brain's mood flattered by the swim
Of currents circumvolvent in the void,
To lie quite still and to become aware
Of the dim light cast by nocturnal skies

On a dim earth beyond the window-ledge,
So, isolate from the friendly company
Of the huge universe which turns without,
To brood apart in calm and joy awhile
Until the spirit sinks and scarcely knows
Whether self is, or if self only is
For ever . . .

How beautiful to wake at night,
Within the room grown strange, and still, and sweet,
And live a century while in the dark
The dripping wheel of silence slowly turns ;
To watch the window open on the night,
A dewy silent deep where nothing stirs,
And, lying thus, to feel dilate within
The press, the conflict, and the heavy pulse
Of incommunicable sad ecstasy,
Growing until the body seems outstretched
In perfect crucifixion on the arms
Of a cross pointing from last void to void,
While the heart dies to a mere midway spark.

All happiness thou holdest, happy night,
For such as lie awake and feel dissolved
The peaceful spice of darkness and the cool
Breath hither blown from the ethereal flowers
That mist thy fields ! O happy, happy wounds,
Conditioned by existence in humanity,
That have such powers to heal them ! slow sweet sighs
Torn from the bosom, silent wails, the birth
Of such long-treasured tears as pain his eyes,
Who, waking, hears the divine solicitudes
Of midnight with ineffable purport charged.

How beautiful it is to wake at night,
Another night, in darkness yet more still,
Save when the myriad leaves on full-fledged boughs,
Filled rather by the perfume's wandering flood
Than by dispansion of the still sweet air,
Shall from the furthest utter silences
In glimmering secrecy have gathered up
An host of whisperings and scattered sighs,
To loose at last a sound as of the plunge
And lapsing seethe of some Pacific wave,
Which, risen from the star-thronged outer troughs,
Rolls in to wreathe with circling foam away
The flutter of the golden moths that haunt
The star's one glimmer daggered on wet sands.

So beautiful it is to wake at night !
Imagination, loudening with the surf
Of the midsummer wind among the boughs,
Gathers my spirit from the haunts remote
Of faintest silence and the shades of sleep,
To bear me on the summit of her wave
Beyond known shores, beyond the mortal edge
Of thought terrestrial, to hold me poised
Above the frontiers of infinity,
To which in the full reflux of the wave
Come soon I must, bubble of solving foam,
Borne to those other shores—now never mine
Save for a hovering instant, short as this
Which now sustains me ere I be drawn back—
To learn again, and wholly learn, I trust,
How beautiful it is to wake at night.

ROBERT NICHOLS

THE PERSIAN FLUTE

Persian shepherd by a waterfall
Piping to please himself among his goats,
Gave me this flute, that now upon my wall
Hangs, hollow exile, prisoning its notes.

Its heart is broken ; silent are its strains.
I cannot wake the little Persian flute.
It does not, will not, know me ; it remains
Beneath my fingers obstinately mute.

Yet this slim reed, when stars were overhead,
And dusk was vocal with the bleating flocks,
Sent up its pure and melancholy thread
Of music by the river and the rocks.

I thought that I should wake that note again
With one clear echo of the hills apart,
And summon Persia to an English lane,—
I had not reckoned with a broken heart.

Shall we go back together, my flute and I,
To find again the shepherd of Shalil,
And when the planet Venus travels high
Above the myrtle grove of Murdafil

Make each our separate music ? For I too
Am silent sometimes, thinking of those stars,
That solitude, those evenings waning blue,
And the lost beauty of the plains of Fars.

V. SACKVILLE-WEST

NIGHT

An odorous shade lingers, the fair day's ghost,
  And the frail moon now by no wind is tost,
And shadow-laden scents of tree and grass
  Build up again a world our eyes have lost.

Now all the wood is but a murmured light
  Where leaf on leaf falls softly from the height;
The hidden freshness of the river seems
  A breath that mingles with the breath of night.

And time and shade and silence seem to say
  Close now your eyes nor fear to die with day;
For if the daylight win to earth again,
  Will not its beauty also find a way?

And flower and stream and forest, will they not
  Bring back to-morrow, as to-day they brought,
This shadow-hidden scent—this odorous shade?
  Yea, and with more abiding memories fraught.

SEUMAS O'SULLIVAN
(from the French of HENRI DE RÉGNIER)

THE NIGHT WILL NEVER STAY

The night will never stay,
The night will still go by,
Though with a million stars
You pin it to the sky ;
Though you bind it with the blowing
    wind
And buckle it with the moon,
The night will slip away
Like sorrow or a tune.

ELEANOR FARJEON

FOURTH PART

§ II GOOD BEDFELLOWS

They are never alone that are accompanied by noble thoughts.

SIR PHILIP SIDNEY (*Arcadia*)

Good company and good discourse are the very sinews of virtue.

IZAAK WALTON

Please you, draw near!

SHAKESPEARE (*Tempest*)

§ II GOOD BEDFELLOWS

A GIFT OF GOD

A wyf is Goddės giftė verraily ;
Alle othere manere giftės hardily,
As londės, rentės, pasture, or commùne,
Or moeblės, alle been giftės of Fortùne,
That passen as a shadow on a wal ;
But dredėlees, if pleynly speke I shal,
A wyf wol laste and in thyn hous endure,
Wel lenger than thee list, paràventure.

CHAUCER (from *Merchant's Talc*)

A TALK AT URBINO

(*in the year* 1506)

[The Speakers are :—

PIETRO BEMBO (afterwards Cardinal), a Venetian humanist,
called "The Dictator of the Renascence."

CESARE GONZAGA, a kinsman of the Duchess and friend of
Castiglione (the author).

GASPARE PALLAVICINO, a gay young courtier.

EMILIA PIA, a lively companion of the Duchess.

GIULIANO DE' MEDICI, son of Lorenzo the Magnificent and
friend of Castiglione.

ELISABETTA GONZAGA (the Duchess), wife of Guidobaldo,
Duke of Urbino.]

Messer PETER BEMBO *said* : Since the beauties, which we
daily see with these our dim eyes in bodies subject to corruption, that nevertheless be nothing else but dreams

687

and most thin shadows of beauty, seem unto us so well favoured and comely, that oftentimes they kindle in us a most burning fire, and with such delight, that we reckon no happiness may be compared to it, that we feel otherwhile through the only look which the beloved countenance of a woman casteth at us : what happy wonder, what blessed abashment may we reckon that to be, that taketh the souls, which come to have a sight of the heavenly beauty ? what sweet flame ? What great incense may a man believe that to be, which ariseth of the fountain of the sovereign and right beauty ? . .

Then the Lord CESAR GONZAGA : The way (*quoth he*) that leadeth to this happiness is so steep (in my mind) that (I believe) it will be much a do to get to it.

The Lord GASPAR *said* : I believe it be hard to get up for men, but impossible for women.

The Lady EMILIA *laughed and said* : If ye fall so often to offend us, I promise you, ye shall be no more forgiven.

The Lord GASPAR *answered* : It is no offence to you, in saying, that women's souls be not so purged from passions as men's be, nor accustomed in beholdings as Messer Peter hath said, is necessary for them to be, that will taste of the heavenly love. Therefore it is not read that ever woman hath had this grace : but many men have had it, as Plato, Socrates, Plotinus, and many other. . .

Here answered the Lord JULIAN : In this point men shall nothing pass women, for Socrates himself doth confess that all the mysteries of love which he knew, were oped unto him by a woman, which was Diotima. And the angel that with the fire of love imprinted the five wounds in Saint Francis, hath also made some women worthy of the same print in our age. You must remember moreover that Saint Mary Magdalen had many faults forgiven her, because she loved much : and perhaps with no less grace than Saint Paul, was she many times through Angelic love haled up to the third heaven. And many other (as I showed you yesterday more at large) that for love of the name of Christ have not passed upon life, nor feared torments, nor any other kind of death how terrible and cruel ever it were. And they were not (as Messer Peter will have his Courtier to be) aged, but soft and tender maidens, and in the age, when he saith that sensual love ought to be borne withal in men.

The Lord GASPAR *began to prepare himself to speak, but the* DUCHESS: "Of this" (*quoth she*) "let Messer Peter be judge, and the matter shall stand to his verdite, whether women be not as meet for heavenly love as men. But because the plead between you may happen be too long, it shall not be amiss to defer it until to-morrow."

"Nay, to-night," *quoth the Lord* CESAR GONZAGA.

"And how can it be to-night ? " *quoth the* DUCHESS.

The Lord CESAR *answered*: "Because it is day already," and showed her the light that began to enter in at the clefts of the windows.

Then every man rose to his feet with much wonder, because they had not thought that the reasonings had lasted longer than the accustomed wont, saving only that they were begun much later, and with their pleasantness had deceived so the Lords' minds, that they wist not of the going away of the hours. And not one of them felt any heaviness of sleep in his eyes, the which often happeneth when a man is up after his accustomed hour to go to bed. When the windows then were opened on the side of the Palace that hath his prospect toward the high top of Mount Catri, they saw already risen in the East a fair morning like unto the colour of roses, and all stars voided, saving only the sweet Governess of the heaven, Venus, which keepeth the bounds of the night and the day, from which appeared to blow a sweet blast, that filling the ear with a biting cold, began to quicken the tunable notes of the pretty birds, among the hushing woods of the hills at hand. Whereupon they all, taking their leave with reverence of the Duchess, departed toward their lodgings, without torch, the light of the day sufficing.

From *Il Cortegiano* of CASTIGLIONE
(Trans. SIR THOMAS HOBY, 1561)

BITS OF BURTON

Remedies against Discontent

Many grievances there are which happen to mortals in this life and many good remedies to mitigate and oppose them, many divine precepts to counterpoise our hearts, special antidotes both in scriptures and humane authors, which who so will observe, shall purchase much ease and quietness unto himself. I will point at a few :—

Be sober and watch.
Recompence good for evil.
Love one another.
Know thy self.
Beware of " Had I wist."
Speak well of friends.
If thou seest ought amiss in another, mend it in thyself.
Be not proud or popular.
Cast not off an old friend.

Take heed of a reconciled enemy.
If thou come as a guest, stay not too long.
Make not a fool of thy self to make others merry.
Live merrily as thou canst.
Go as thou wouldst be met : sit as thou wouldst be found.

The Advantage of Music

Music is a roaring-meg against melancholy, to rear and revive the languishing soul ; " affecting not only the ears, but the very arteries, the vital and animal spirits, it erects the mind, and makes it nimble." Labouring men that sing to their work, can tell as much, and so can soldiers when they go to fight, whom terror of death cannot so much affright, as the sound of trumpets, drum, fife, and such like music animates. It makes a child quiet, the nurse's song; and many times the sound of a trumpet on a sudden, bells ringing, a carman's whistle, a boy singing some ballad tune early in the street, alters, revives, recreates a restless patient that cannot sleep in the night, etc. In a word, it is so powerful a thing that it ravisheth the soul.

Enjoyment out of doors

The most pleasant of all outward pastimes is to make a petty progress, a merry journey now and then with some good companions : to visit friends, see cities, castles, towns, to walk amongst orchards, gardens, bowers, mounts, and arbours, artificial wildernesses, green thickets, arches, groves, lawns, rivulets, fountains and such like pleasant places, brooks, pools, fishponds, betwixt wood and water, in a fair meadow, by a river side, to disport in some pleasant plain, park, run up a steep hill sometimes, or sit in a shady seat must needs be a delectable recreation.

A Good Friend

Tobacco, divine, rare, superexcellent tobacco, which goes far beyond all the panaceas, potable gold, and philosopher's stones, a sovereign remedy to all diseases.

From *Anatomy of Melancholy* (1621)

MR. PEPYS GOES TO EPSOM

July 14th, 1667. Up, and my wife, a little before four, and by and by Mrs. Turner come to us by agreement, and she and I staid talking below while my wife dressed herself, which vexed me that she was so long about it, keeping us till past five o'clock before she was ready. She ready ; and taking some bottles of wine and beer and some cold fowle with us into the coach, we took coach and four horses which I had provided last night, and so away. A very fine day, and so towards Epsum. The country very fine, only the way very dusty. We got to Epsum by eight o'clock, to the well ; where much company, and there we 'light, and I drank the water : I did drink four pints. Here I met with divers of our town, among others with several of the tradesmen of our office, but did talk but little with them, it growing hot in the sun, and so we took coach again and to the towne, to the King's Head. Here we called for drink, and bespoke dinner. W. Hewer rode with us, and I left him and the women, and myself walked to church, where few people, contrary to what I expected, and none I knew, but all the Houblons, brothers, and them after sermon I did salute. We parted to meet anon, and I to my women, and there to dinner, a good dinner, and were merry. After dinner we all lay down (the day being wonderful hot) to sleep, and each of us took a good nap, and then rose. We took coach and to take the ayre. W. Hewer's horse broke loose, and we had the sport to see him taken again. Then I carried them to see my cozen Pepys' house, and 'light and walked round about it, and they like it, as indeed it deserves, very well, and is a pretty place; and then I walked them to the wood hard by, and there got them in the thickets till they had lost themselves, and I could not find the way into any of the walks in the wood, which indeed are very pleasant, if I could have found them. At last got out of the wood again; and I, by leaping down the little bank coming out of the wood, did sprain my right foot, which brought me great present pain; but presently, with walking, it went away for the present. And so the women and W. Hewer and I walked upon the Downes, where a flock of sheep was; and the most pleasant and innocent sight that ever I saw in my life. We find a shepherd and his little boy reading, far from any houses or sight of people, the Bible to him; so I made the boy read to me, which he did, with the forced tone that children do usually read, that was mighty pretty, and then I did give him something, and went to the father and talked with him; and I find he had been a servant in my cozen Pepys' house, and told me what was become of their old servants. He did content himself mightily in my liking his boy's reading, and did bless God for him the most like one of the old patriarchs that ever I saw in my life, and it brought those thoughts of the old age of the world in my mind for two or three days after. We took notice of his woollen knit stockings of two colours mixed, and of his shoes shod with iron shoes, both at the toe and heels, and with great nails in the soles of his feet, which was mighty pretty : and, taking notice of them, " Why," says the poor man, " the downes, you see, are full of stones, and we are faine to shoe ourselves thus ; and these," says he, " will make the stones fly till they sing before me." I did give the poor man something, for which he was mighty thankful, and I tried to cast stones with his horne crooke. He values his dog mightily, that would turn a sheep any way which he would have him when he goes to fold them : told me there was about eighteen scoare sheep in his flock, and that he hath four shillings a week the year round for keeping of them. So we posted thence with mighty pleasure in the discourse we had with this poor man ; and Mrs. Turner, in the common fields here, did gather one of the prettiest nosegays that ever I saw in my life.

So to our coach and through Mr. Minnes's wood, and looked upon Mr. Evelyn's house ; and so over the common, and through Epsum towne to our inne, in the way stopping a poor woman with her milk-pail, and in one of my gilt tumblers did drink our bellyfulls of milk, better than any creame ; and so to our inne and there had a dish of creame, but it was sour and so had no pleasure in it ; and so paid our reckoning and took coach, it being about seven at night, and passed and saw the people walking with their wives and children to take the ayre ; and we set out for home, the sun by and by going down, and we in the cool of the evening all the way with much pleasure home, talking and pleasing ourselves with the pleasure of this day's work, Mrs. Turner mightily pleased with my resolution, which, I tell her, is never to keep a country-house, but to keep a coach, and with my wife on the

Saturday to go sometimes for a day to this place, and then quit to another place ; and there is more variety and as little charge, and no trouble, as there is in a country-house. Anon it grew dark, and as it grew dark we had the pleasure to see several glow-wormes, which was mighty pretty, but my foot begins more and more to pain me, which Mrs. Turner, by keeping her warm hand upon it, did much ease ; but so that when we come home, which was just at eleven at night, I was not able to walk from the lane's end to my house without being helped, which did trouble me, and therefore to bed presently.

Other Adventures

16th January, 1660.

After dinner we went to the Green Dragon, on Lambeth Hill, and there we sang of all sorts of things, and I ventured with good success upon things at first sight, and after that I played on my flageolet, and staid there till nine o'clock, very merry and drawn on with one song after another till it came to be so late. So parted, and thence home, where I found my wife and maid a-washing. I staid up till the bell-man came by with his bell just under my window as I was writing of this very line, and cried, "Past one of the clock, and a cold, frosty, windy morning." I then went to bed, and left my wife and the maid a-washing still.

25th May, 1660.

Got on shore when the King did, who was received by General Monk with all imaginable love and respect upon his entrance upon the land of Dover. Infinite the crowd of people and the horsemen, citizens and noblemen of all sorts. The Mayor of the town came and gave him his white staff, the badge of his place, which the King did give him again. The Mayor also presented him from the town a very rich Bible, which he took and said it was the thing that he loved above all things in the world.

12th December, 1660.

With J. Spicer to his office and took £100, and by coach with it as far as my father's, where I called to see them, and my father did offer me six pieces of gold, in lieu of six pounds that he borrowed of me the other day, but it went against me to take it of him and therefore did not, though I was a little troubled that I did not. Thence home, and took out this £100 and sealed it up with the other [of] last night, it being the first £200 that ever I saw together of my own in my life. For which God be praised. So to my Lady Batten and sat an hour or two, and talked with her daughter and people in the absence of her father and mother and my wife to pass away the time. After that home and to bed, reading myself asleep, while the wench sat mending my breeches by my bedside.

9th July, 1663.

Abroad, it raining, to Blackfriars, and there went into a little alehouse, and here I kissed three or four times the maid of the house, who is a pretty girl but very modest.

30th November, 1664.

(Lord's Day.) Up, and this morning put on my new, fine, coloured cloth suit, with my cloake lined with plush, which is a dear and noble suit, costing me about £17.

21st February, 1665.

My wife busy in going with her woman to a hot-house to bathe herself, after her long being within doors in the dirt, so that she now pretends to a resolution of being hereafter very clean. How long it will hold I can guess.

25th March, 1667.

(Lady Day.) . . . By and by to dinner, a poor dinner, my wife and I, at Sir W. Pen's, and then he and I before to the King's playhouse; and by and by comes Mr. Lowther and his wife and mine, and into a box, forsooth, neither of them being dressed, which I was almost ashamed of. Sir W. Pen and I in the pit, and here saw " The Mayden Queene," which indeed the more I see the more I like, and is an excellent play, and so done by Nell, her merry part, as cannot be better done in nature, I think.

31st May, 1669.

Up very betimes, and so continued all the morning with W. Hewer upon examining and stating my accounts, in order to the fitting myself to go abroad beyond sea, which the ill condition of my eyes, and my neglect for a year or two, hath kept me behindhand in . . . Being called by my wife, we to the Park, Mary Batelier, and a Dutch gentleman, a friend of hers, being with us. Thence to " The World's End," a drinking-house by the Park; and there merry, and so home late.

And this ends all that I doubt I shall ever be able to do with my own eyes in the keeping of my Journal, I being not able to do it any longer, having done now so long as to undo my eyes almost every time that I take a pen in my hand; and therefore whatever comes of it I must forbear . .

And so I betake myself to that course, which is almost as much as to see myself go into the grave : for which and all the discomforts that will accompany my being blind, the good God prepare me !

From *Diary of Samuel Pepys*

AN INTERRUPTED CONFERENCE

Word was brought that the tea-table was set in the library, which is a gallery on a ground-floor, with an arched door at one end opening into a walk of limes ; where, as soon as we had drunk tea, we were tempted by fine weather to take a walk which led us to a small mount of easy ascent, on the top whereof we found a seat under a spreading tree. Here we had a prospect on one hand of a narrow bay or creek of the sea, enclosed on either side by a coast beautified with rocks and woods, and green banks and farm-houses. At the end of the bay was a small town, placed upon the slope of a hill, which, from the advantage of its situation, made a considerable figure. Several fishing-boats and lighters, gliding up and down on a surface as smooth and bright as glass, enlivened the prospect. On the other side, we looked down on green pastures, flocks, and herds basking beneath in sunshine, while we, in our superior situation, enjoyed the freshness of air and shade.

Here we felt that sort of joyful instinct which a rural scene and fine weather inspire; and proposed no small pleasure in resuming and continuing our conference without interruption till dinner. But we had hardly seated ourselves and looked about us when we saw a fox run by the foot of our mount into an adjacent thicket. A few minutes after, we heard a confused noise of the opening of hounds, the winding of horns, and the roaring of country squires. While our attention was suspended by this event, a servant came running, out of breath, and told Crito that his neighbour Ctesippus, a squire of note, was fallen from his horse, attempting to leap over a hedge, and brought into the hall, where he lay for dead. Upon which we all rose, and walked hastily to the house, where we found Ctesippus just come to himself, in the midst of half a dozen sun-burnt squires, in frocks, and short wigs, and jockey boots. Being asked how he did, he answered it was only a broken rib. With some difficulty Crito persuaded him to lie on a bed till the chirurgeon came. These fox-hunters, having been up early at their sport, were eager for dinner, which was accordingly hastened. They passed the afternoon in a loud rustic mirth, gave proof of their religion and loyalty by the healths they drank, talked of hounds, and horses, and elections, and country affairs, till the chirurgeon, who had been employed about Ctesippus, desired he might be put into Crito's coach, and sent home, having refused to stay all night.

Our guests being gone, we reposed ourselves after the fatigue of this tumultuous visit, and next morning assembled again at the seat on the mount.

Now Lysicles, being a nice man and a *bel esprit*, had an infinite contempt for the rough manners and conversation of fox-hunters, and could not reflect with patience that he had lost, as he called it, so many hours in their company. I flattered myself, said he, that there had been none of this species remaining among us : strange that men should be diverted with such uncouth noise and hurry or find pleasure in the society of dogs and horses! How much more elegant are the diversions of the town!

There seems, replied Euphranor, to be some resemblance between fox-hunteer and free-thinkers; the former exerting their animal faculties in pursuit of game, as you gentlemen employ your intellectuals in the pursuit of truth. The kind of amusement is the same, although the object be different.

GEORGE BERKELEY, Bishop of Cloyne
(from *Alciphron*)

A DISTURBED HOUSEHOLD

" Were one sure," said my father to himself, scratching his eyebrow, " that the child was expiring, one might as well compliment my brother Toby as not—and it would be a pity, in such a case, to throw away so great a name as *Trismegistus* upon him—but he may recover."

" No, No," said my father to Susannah, " I'll get up."
" There is no time," cried Susannah, " the child's as black as my shoe."

" *Trismegistus*," said my father—" But stay! Thou art a leaky vessel, Susannah," added my father, " Canst thou carry *Trismegistus* in thy head, the length of the gallery without scattering? "

" Can I? " cried Susannah, shutting the door in a huff.

" If she can, I'll be shot," said my father, bouncing out of bed in the dark, and groping for his breeches.

Susannah ran with all speed along the gallery.

My father made all possible speed to find his breeches. Susannah got the start, and kept it. "'Tis *Tris*— something," cried Susannah. "There is no christian-name in the world," said the curate, "beginning with *Tris*—but *Tristram*."

"Then 'tis *Tristram-gistus*," quoth Susannah.

"There is no *gistus* to it, noodle!—'tis my own name," replied the curate, dipping his hand, as he spoke, into the basin. "*Tristram!*" said he, &c., &c., &c., &c., so *Tristram* was I called, and *Tristram* shall I be to the day of my death.

My father followed Susannah, with his night-gown across his arm, with nothing more than his breeches on, fastened through haste with but a single button, and that button through haste thrust only half into the button-hole.

"She has not forgot the name?" cried my father, half opening the door.

"No, no," said the curate, with a tone of intelligence.

"And the child is better," cried Susannah.

"And how does your mistress?"

"As well," said Susannah, "as can be expected."

"Pish!" said my father, the button of his breeches slipping out of the button-hole—So that whether the interjection was levelled at Susannah, or the button-hole —whether Pish was an interjection of contempt or an interjection of modesty, is a doubt, and must be a doubt till I shall have time to write the three following favourite chapters, that is, my chapter of *chamber-maids*, my chapter of *pishes*, and my chapter of *button-holes*.

All the light I am able to give the reader at present is this, that the moment my father cried Pish! he whisk'd himself about—and with his breeches held up by one hand, and his night-gown thrown across the arm of the other, he turned along the gallery to bed, something slower than he came.

————————

I wish I could write a chapter upon sleep.

A fitter occasion could never have presented itself, than what this moment offers, when all the curtains of the family are drawn—the candles put out—and no creature's eyes are open but a single one, for the other has been shut these twenty years, of my mother's nurse.

It is a fine subject!

And yet, as fine as it is, I would undertake to write a dozen chapters upon button-holes, both quicker and with more fame, than a single chapter upon this.

Button-holes! there is something lively in the very idea of 'em—and trust me, when I get amongst 'em—You gentry with great beards look as grave as you will—I'll make merry work with my button-holes—I shall have 'em all to myself—'tis a maiden subject—I shall run foul of no man's wisdom or fine sayings in it.

But for sleep—I know I shall make nothing of it before I begin—I am no dab at your fine sayings in the first place —and in the next, I cannot for my soul set a grave face upon a bad matter, and tell the world—'tis the refuge of the unfortunate—the enfranchisement of the prisoner— the downy lap of the hopeless, the weary, and the broken-hearted ; nor could I set out with a lie in my mouth, by affirming, that of all the soft and delicious functions of our nature, by which the great Author of it, in his bounty, has been pleased to recompense the sufferings where-with his justice and his good pleasure has wearied us— that this is the chiefest (I know pleasures worth ten of it) ;

or what a happiness it is to man, when the anxieties and passions of the day are over, and he lies down upon his back, that his soul shall be so seated within him, that whichever way she turns her eyes, the heavens shall look calm and sweet above her—no desire—or fear—or doubt that troubles the air, nor any difficulty past, present, or to come, that the imagination may not pass over without offence, in that sweet secession.

" God's blessing," said Sancho Pança, " be upon the man who first invented this self-same thing called sleep—it covers a man all over like a cloak." Now there is more to me in this, and it speaks warmer to my heart and affections, than all the dissertations squeez'd out of the heads of the learned together upon the subject.—Not that I altogether disapprove of what Montaigne advances upon it—'tis admirable in its way—(I quote by memory).

The world enjoys other pleasures, says he, as they do that of sleep, without tasting or feeling it as it slips and passes by. We should study and ruminate upon it, in order to render proper thanks to him who grants it to us. For this end I cause myself to be disturbed in my sleep, that I may the better and more sensibly relish it. And yet I see few, says he again, who live with less sleep, when need requires ; my body is capable of a firm, but not of a violent and sudden agitation—I evade of late all violent exercises—I am never weary with walking—but from my youth, I never liked to ride upon pavements, I love to lie hard and alone, and even without my wife—This last word may stagger the faith of the world—but remember, " La Vraisemblance " (as Bayle says in the affair of *Liceti*) " n'est pas toujours du Côté de la Verité." And so much for sleep.

———

" If my wife will but venture him, brother Toby, Trismegistus shall be dress'd and brought down to us, whilst you and I are getting our breakfasts together."

" Go, tell Susannah, Obadiah, to step here."

" She is run upstairs," answered Obadiah, " this very instant, sobbing and crying, and wringing her hands as if her heart would break."

" We shall have a rare month of it," said my father, turning his head from Obadiah, and looking wistfully in my uncle Toby's face for some time, " we shall have a devilish month of it, brother Toby," said my father, setting his arms a-kimbo, and shaking his head, " fire, water, women, wind, brother Toby ! "

" 'Tis some misfortune," quoth my uncle Toby.

" That it is," cried my father, " to have so many jarring elements breaking loose, and riding triumph in every corner of a gentleman's house. Little boots it to the peace of a family, brother Toby, that you and I possess ourselves, and sit here silent and unmoved, whilst such a storm is whistling over our heads."

" And what's the matter, Susannah ? "

" They have called the child Tristram, and my mistress is just got out of an hysterick fit about it—No—'tis not my fault," said Susannah—" I told him it was *Tristramgistus.*"

" Make tea for yourself, brother Toby," said my father, taking down his hat, but how different from the sallies and agitations of voice and members which a common reader would imagine ! For he spake in the sweetest modulation, and took down his hat with the genteelest movement of limbs that ever affliction harmonised and attuned together.

"Go to the bowling-green for corporal Trim," said my uncle Toby, speaking to Obadiah, as soon as my father left the room.

STERNE (from Tristram Shandy)

AN EARLY MORNING FRISK

One night when Beauclerk and Langton had supped at a tavern in London, and sat till about three in the morning, it came into their heads to go and knock up Johnson, and see if they could prevail on him to join them in a ramble. They rapped violently at the door of his chambers in the Temple, till at last he appeared in his shirt, with his little black wig on the top of his head, instead of a night-cap, and a poker in his hand, imagining, probably, that some ruffians were coming to attack him. When he discovered who they were, and was told their errand, he smiled, and with great good humour agreed to their proposal : " What, is it you, you dogs ! I'll have a frisk with you." He was soon drest, and they sallied forth together into Covent-Garden, where the greengrocers and fruiterers were beginning to arrange their hampers, just come in from the country. Johnson made some attempts to help them ; but the honest gardeners stared so at his figure and manner, and odd interference, that he soon saw his services were not relished. They then repaired to one of the neighbouring taverns, and made a bowl of that liquor called *Bishop*, which Johnson had always liked ; while in joyous contempt of sleep, from which he had been roused, he repeated the festive lines,

> " *Short, Ó short then be thy reign,*
> *And give us to the world again !* "

They did not stay long, but walked down to the Thames, took a boat, and rowed to Billingsgate. Beauclerk and Johnson were so well pleased with their amusement, that they resolved to persevere in dissipation for the rest of the day : but Langton deserted them, being engaged to breakfast with some young Ladies. Johnson scolded him for " leaving his social friends, to go and sit with a set of wretched *un-idea'd* girls." Garrick being told of this ramble, said to him smartly, " I heard of your frolick t'other night. You'll be in the Chronicle." Upon which Johnson afterwards observed, " *He* durst not do such a thing. His *wife* would not *let* him ! "

BOSWELL (from *Life of Johnson*)

A BALL AT BATH

10th June, 1780.

In the evening was the last ball expected to be at Bath this season, and, therefore, knowing we could go to no other, it was settled we should go to this. Of our party were Mrs. Byron and Augusta, Miss Philips, and Charlotte Lewis.

Mrs. Byron was placed at the upper end of the room by Mr. Tyson, because she is honourable, and her daughter next to her. I, of course, the lowest of our party ; but the moment Mr. Tyson had arranged us, Augusta arose, and nothing would satisfy her but taking a seat not only next to, but below me ; nor could I, for my life, get the better of the affectionate humility with which she quite supplicated me to be content. She was soon after followed by Captain Brisbane, a young officer who had met her in

Spring Gardens, and seemed much struck with her, and was now presented to her by Mr. Tyson for her partner.

Captain Brisbane is a very pretty sort of young man, but did not much enliven us. Soon after I perceived Captain Bouchier, who, after talking some time with Mrs. Thrale, and various parties, made up to us, and upon Augusta's being called upon to dance a minuet, took her place, and began a very lively sort of chit-chat.

Just before she went to dance her minuet, upon my admiring her bouquet, which was the most beautiful in the room, she tore from it the only two moss-roses in it, and so spoilt it all before her exhibition, merely that I might have the best of it.

Country dances were now preparing, and Captain Bouchier asked me for the honour of my hand, but I had previously resolved not to dance, and, therefore, declined his offer. But he took, of the sudden, a fancy to prate with me, and therefore budged not after the refusal.

He told me this was the worst ball for company there had been the whole season ; and, with a wicked laugh that was too significant to be misunderstood, said, " And, as you have been to no other, perhaps you will give this for a specimen of a Bath ball ! "

He told me he had very lately met with Hannah More, and then mentioned Mrs. Montagu and Mrs. Carter, whence he took occasion to say most high and fine things of the ladies of the present age,—their writings, and talents ; and I soon found he had no small reverence for us blue-stockings.

About this time, Charlotte, who had confessedly dressed herself for dancing, but whose pretty face had by some means been overlooked, drawled towards us, and asked me why I would not dance ?

"I never intended it," said I; "but I hoped to have seen you."

"No," said she, yawning, "no more shall I,—I don't choose it."

"Don't you?" said Captain Bouchier, drily, "why not?"

"Why, because I don't like it."

"O fie!" cried he; "consider how cruel that is."

"I must consider myself," said she, pertly; "for I don't choose to heat myself this hot weather."

Just then, a young man came forward, and requested her hand. She coloured, looked excessively silly, and walked off with him to join the dancers.

When, between the dances, she came our way, he plagued her, *à la* Sir Clement.

"Well," cried he, "so you have been dancing this hot night! I thought you would have considered yourself better?"

"Oh," said she, "I could not help it—I had much rather not;—it was quite disagreeable to me."

"No, no,—pardon me there!" said he maliciously; "I saw pleasure dance first in your eyes; I never saw you look more delighted: you were quite the queen of smiles!"

She looked as if she could have killed him: and yet, from giddiness and good-humour, was compelled to join in the laugh.

After this we went to tea. When that was over, and we all returned to the ball-room, Captain Bouchier followed me, and again took a seat next mine, which he kept, without once moving, the whole night.

From *Diary of Frances Burney, Madame D'Arblay*

CAROLUS REX

A pretty severe fit of indisposition which, under the name of a nervous fever, has made a prisoner of me for some weeks past, and is but slowly leaving me, has reduced me to an incapacity of reflecting upon any topic foreign to itself. Expect no healthy conclusions from me this month, reader; I can offer you only sick men's dreams.

And truly the whole state of sickness is such; for what else is it but a magnificent dream for a man to lie-a-bed, and draw daylight curtains about him; and, shutting out the sun, to induce a total oblivion of all the works which are going on under it? To become insensible to all the operations of life, except the beatings of one feeble pulse?

If there be a regal solitude, it is a sick-bed. How the patient lords it there; what caprices he acts without control! how king-like he sways his pillow—tumbling, and tossing, and shifting, and lowering, and thumping, and flatting, and moulding it, to the ever-varying requisitions of his throbbing temples!

He changes sides oftener than a politician. Now he lies full length, then half length, obliquely, transversely, head and feet quite across the bed; and none accuses him of tergiversation. Within the four curtains he is absolute. They are his Mare Clausum. . .

He has put on the strong armour of sickness, he is wrapped in the callous hide of suffering; he keeps his sympathy, like some curious vintage, under trusty lock and key, for his own use only.

He lies pitying himself, honing and moaning to himself; he yearneth over himself; his bowels are even melted within him, to think what he suffers ; he is not ashamed to weep over himself.

He is for ever plotting how to do some good to himself ; studying little stratagems and artificial alleviations.

He makes the most of himself ; dividing himself, by an allowable fiction, into as many distinct individuals as he hath sore and sorrowing members. Sometimes he meditates—as of a thing apart from him—upon his poor aching head, and that dull pain which, dozing or waking, lay in it all the past night like a log, or palpable substance of pain, not to be removed without opening the very skull, as it seemed to take it thence. Or he pities his long, clammy, attenuated fingers. He compassionates himself all over ; and his bed is a very discipline of humanity, and tender heart.

He is his own sympathizer ; and instinctively feels that none can so well perform that office for him. He cares for few spectators to his tragedy. Only that punctual face of the old nurse pleases him, that announces his broths and his cordials. He likes it because it is so unmoved, and because he can pour forth his feverish ejaculations before it as unreservedly as to his bed-post. . .

Household rumours touch him not. Some faint murmur, indicative of life going on within the house, soothes him, while he knows not distinctly what it is. He is not to know anything, not to think of anything. Servants gliding up or down the distant staircase, treading as upon velvet, gently keep his ear awake, so long as he troubles not himself further than with some feeble guess at their errands. Exacter knowledge would be a burthen to him ; he can just endure the pressure of conjecture. He opens his eye faintly at the dull stroke of the muffled knocker, and closes it again without asking " Who was it ? " He is flattered by a general notion that inquiries are making after him, but he cares not to know the name of the inquirer. In the general stillness, and awful hush of the house, he lies in state, and feels his sovereignty.

To be sick is to enjoy monarchal prerogatives. Compare the silent tread and quiet ministry, almost by the eye only, with which he is served—with the careless demeanour, the unceremonious goings in and out (slapping of doors, or leaving them open) of the very same attendants, when he is getting a little better—and you will confess that from the bed of sickness (throne let me rather call it) to the elbow-chair of convalescence, is a fall from dignity, amounting to a deposition.

CHARLES LAMB (from " The Convalescent ")

A " FANCY " OVERTURE

Joe and I could not settle about the method of going down. He said there was a caravan, he understood, to start from Tom Belcher's at two, which would go there *right out* and back again the next day. Now I never travel all night, and said I should get a cast to Newbury by one of the mails. Joe swore the thing was impossible, and I could only answer that I had made up my mind to it. In short, he seemed to me to waver, said he only came to see if I was going, had letters to write, a cause coming on the day after, and faintly said at parting (for I was bent on setting out that moment)—" Well, we meet at Philippi? " I made the best of my way to Piccadilly. The mail coach stand was bare. " They are all gone," said I—" this is always the way with me—in the instant I lose the future—if I had not stayed to pour out that last cup of tea, I should have been just in time ; "—and cursing my folly and ill-luck together, without inquiring at the coach-office whether the mails were gone or not, I walked on in despite, and to punish my own dilatoriness and want of determination. At any rate, I would not turn back : I might get to Hounslow, or perhaps farther, to be on my road the next morning. I passed Hyde Park corner (my Rubicon), and trusted to fortune. Suddenly I heard the clattering of a Brentford stage, and the fight rushed full upon my fancy. I argued (not unwisely) that even a Brentford coachman was better company than my own thoughts (such as they were just then), and at his invitation mounted the box with him. . . . The Bath mail I had set my mind upon, and I had missed it, as I miss everything else, by my own absurdity, in putting the will for the deed, and aiming at ends without employing means. " Sir," said he of the Brentford, " the Bath mail will be up presently, my brother-in-law drives it, and I will engage to stop him if there is a place empty." I almost doubted my good genius ; but, sure enough, up it drove like lightning, and stopped directly at the call of the Brentford Jehu. I would not have believed this possible, but the brother-in-law of a mail-coach driver is himself no mean man. I was transferred without loss of time from the top of one coach to that of the other, desired the guard to pay my fare to the Brentford coachman for me as I had no change, was accommodated with a great coat, put up my umbrella to keep off a drizzling mist, and we began to cut through the air like an arrow. The mile-stones disappeared one after another, the rain kept off ; Tom Turtle the trainer sat before me on the coach-box, with whom I exchanged civilities as a gentleman going to the fight ; the passion that had transported me an hour before was subdued to pensive regret and conjectural musing on the next day's battle; I was promised a place inside at Reading, and upon the whole, I thought myself a lucky fellow. Such is the force of imagination! On the outside of any other coach on the 10th of December, with a Scotch mist drizzling through the cloudy moonlight air, I should have been cold, comfortless, impatient, and, no doubt, wet through; but seated on the Royal mail, I felt warm and comfortable, the air did me good, the ride did me good, I was pleased with the progress we had made, and confident that all would go well through the journey. When I got inside at Reading, I found Turtle and a stout valetudinarian, whose costume bespoke him one of the FANCY, and who had risen from a three months' sick bed to get into the mail to see the fight. They were intimate, and we fell into a lively discourse. My friend the trainer was confined in his topics to fighting dogs and men, to bears and badgers; beyond this he was " quite chap-fallen," had not a word to throw at a dog, and indeed very wisely fell asleep, when any other game was started. The whole art of training (I, however, learnt from him) consists in two things, exercise and abstinence, abstinence and exercise, repeated alternately and without end. . . . We had now but a few miles to our destination, and the first thing I did on alighting at Newbury, both coaches stopping at the same time, was to call out, " Pray is there a gentleman in that mail of the name of P——s?" "No," said Joe, borrowing something of the vein of Gilpin, " for I have just got out." "Well!" says he, " this is lucky; but you don't know how vexed I was to miss you; for," added he, lowering his voice, " do you know when I left you I went to Belcher's to ask about the caravan, and Mrs. Belcher said very obligingly,

713

she couldn't tell about that, but there were two gentlemen who had taken places by the mail and were gone on in a landau, and she could frank us. It's a pity I didn't meet with you ; we could then have got down for nothing. . ."

Our present business was to get beds and supper at an inn ; but this was no easy task. The public-houses were full, and where you saw a light at a private house, and people poking their heads out of the casement to see what was going on, they instantly put them in and shut the window, the moment you seemed advancing with a suspitious overture for accommodation. Our guard and coachman thundered away at the outer gate of the Crown for some time without effect—such was the greater noise within ; and when the doors were unbarred, and we got admittance, we found a party assembled in the kitchen round a good hospitable fire, some sleeping, others drinking, others talking on politics and on the fight. A tall English yeoman (something like Matthews in the face, and quite as great a wag)—

A lusty man to ben an abbot able,

—was making such a prodigious noise about rent and taxes, and the price of corn now and formerly that he had prevented us from being heard at the gate. The first thing I heard him say was to a shuffling fellow who wanted to be off a bet for a shilling glass of brandy and water—" Confound it, man, don't be *insipid* ! " Thinks I, that is a good phrase. It was a good omen. He kept it up so all night, nor flinched with the approach of morning. He was a fine fellow, with sense, wit, and spirit, a hearty body and a joyous mind, free-spoken, frank, convivial—one of that true English breed that went with Harry the Fifth to the siege of Harfleur—" standing like greyhounds in the slips," &c. We ordered tea and eggs (beds were soon found to be out of the question), and this fellow's conversation was *sauce piquante*. It did one's heart good to see him brandish his oaken towel and to hear him talk. He made mince-meat of a drunken, stupid, red-faced, quarrelsome, *frowsy* farmer, whose nose " he moralised into a thousand similes," making it out a firebrand like Bardolph's. " I'll tell you what, my friend," says he, " the landlady has only to keep you here to save fire and candle. If one was to touch your nose, it would go off like a piece of charcoal." At this the other only grinned like an idiot, the sole variety in his purple face being his little peering grey eyes and yellow teeth ; called for another glass, swore he would not stand it ; and after many attempts to provoke his humorous antagonist to single combat, which the other turned off (after working him up to a ludicrous pitch of choler) with great adroitness, he fell quietly asleep with a glass of liquor in his hand, which he could not lift to his head. . . . The morning dawns ; that dim but yet clear light appears, which weighs like solid bars of metal on the sleepless eyelids ; the guests dropped down from their chambers one by one—but it was too late to think of going to bed now.

WILLIAM HAZLITT (from *The Fight*)

THE TRUE GENTLEMAN

It is almost a definition of a gentleman to say that he is one who never inflicts pain. This description is both refined and, as far as it goes, accurate. He is mainly occupied in merely removing the obstacles which hinder the free and unembarrassed action of those about him; and he concurs with their movements rather than takes the initiative himself. His benefits may be considered as parallel to what are called comforts or conveniences in arrangements of a personal nature: like an easy chair or a good fire, which do their part in dispelling cold and fatigue, though nature provides both means of rest and animal heat without them. The true gentleman in like manner carefully avoids whatever may cause a jar or a jolt in the minds of those with whom he is cast;—all clashing of opinion, or collision of feeling, all restraint, or suspicion, or gloom, or resentment; his great concern being to make every one at their ease and at home. He has his eyes on all his company; he is tender towards the bashful, gentle towards the distant, and merciful towards the absurd; he can recollect to whom he is speaking; he guards against unreasonable allusions, or topics which may irritate; he is seldom prominent in conversation, and never wearisome. He makes light of favours while he does them, and seems to be receiving when he is conferring. He never speaks of himself except when compelled, never defends himself by a mere retort, he has no ears for slander or gossip, is scrupulous in imputing motives to those who interfere with him, and interprets everything for the best. He is never mean or little in his disputes, never takes unfair advantage, never mistakes personalities or sharp sayings for arguments, or insinuates evil which he dare not say out. From a long-sighted prudence, he observes the maxim of the ancient sage, that we should even conduct ourselves towards our enemy as if he were one day to be our friend. He has too much good sense to be affronted at insults, he is too well employed to remember injuries, and too indolent to bear malice. He is patient, forbearing and resigned, on philosophical principles; he submits to pain, because it is inevitable, to bereavement, because it is irreparable, and to death, because it is his destiny. If he engages in controversy of any kind his disciplined intellect preserves him from the blundering discourtesy of better, perhaps, but less educated minds; who, like blunt weapons, tear and hack instead of cutting clean, who mistake the point in argument, waste their strength on trifles, misconceive their adversary and leave the question more involved than they find it. He may be right or wrong in his opinion, but he is too clear-headed to be unjust; he is as simple as he is forcible, and as brief as he is decisive. Nowhere shall we find greater candour, consideration, indulgence: he throws himself into the minds of his opponents, he accounts for their mistakes. He knows the weakness of human reason as well as its strength.

CARDINAL NEWMAN (from *The Idea of a University*)

•

DINNER WITH A BACHELOR

I expected Miss Matty to jump at this invitation; but, no! Miss Pole and I had the greatest difficulty in persuading her to go. She thought it was improper; and was even half annoyed when we utterly ignored the idea of any impropriety in her going with two other ladies to see her old lover. Then came a more serious difficulty. She did not think Deborah would have liked her to go. This took us half a day's good hard talking to get over; but, at the first sentence of relenting, I seized the opportunity, and wrote and dispatched an acceptance in her name—

717

fixing day and hour, that all might be decided and done with . . .

She was in a state of silent agitation all the way to Woodley. She had evidently never been there before; and, although she little dreamt I knew anything of her early story, I could perceive she was in a tremor at the thought of seeing the place which might have been her home, and round which it is probable that many of her innocent girlish imaginations had clustered. It was a long drive there, through paved jolting lanes. Miss Matilda sat bolt upright, and looked wistfully out of the windows, as we drew near the end of our journey. The aspect of the country was quiet and pastoral. Woodley stood among fields; and there was an old-fashioned garden, where roses and currant bushes touched each other, and where the feathery asparagus formed a pretty background to the pinks and gillyflowers; there was no drive up to the door: we got out at a little gate, and walked up a straight box-edged path. " My cousin might make a drive, I think," said Miss Pole, who was afraid of earache, and had only her cap on.

" I think it is very pretty," said Miss Matty, with a soft plaintiveness in her voice, and almost in a whisper; for just then Mr. Holbrook appeared at the door, rubbing his hands in very effervescence of hospitality. He looked more like my idea of Don Quixote than ever, and yet the likeness was only external. His respectable housekeeper stood modestly at the door to bid us welcome; and while she led the elder ladies upstairs to a bedroom, I begged to look about the garden. My request evidently pleased the old gentleman; who took me all round the place, and showed me his six-and-twenty cows, named after the different letters of the alphabet. . .

When he and I went in, we found that dinner was nearly ready in the kitchen,—for so I suppose the room ought to be called, as there were oak dressers and cupboards all round, an oven by the side of the fireplace, and only a small Turkey carpet in the middle of the flag-floor. . .

When the ducks and green peas came, we looked at each other in dismay ; we had only two-pronged, black handled forks. It is true, the steel was as bright as silver ; but what were we to do ? Miss Matty picked up her peas, one by one, on the point of the prongs, much as Aminé ate her grains of rice after her previous feast with the Ghoul. Miss Pole sighed over her delicate young peas as she left them on one side of her plate untasted ; for they *would* drop between the prongs. I looked at my host : the peas were going wholesale into his capacious mouth, shovelled up by his large round-ended knife. I saw, I imitated, I survived ! My friends, in spite of my precedent, could not muster up courage enough to do an ungenteel thing ; and, if Mr. Holbrook had not been so heartily hungry, he would probably have seen that the good peas went away almost untouched.

After dinner, a clay pipe was brought in, and a spittoon ; and, asking us to retire to another room, where he would soon join us, if we disliked tobacco-smoke, he presented his pipe to Miss Matty, and requested her to fill the bowl. This was a compliment to a lady in his youth ; but it was rather inappropriate to propose it as an honour to Miss Matty, who had been trained by her sister to hold smoking of every kind in utter abhorrence. But if it was a shock to her refinement, it was also a gratification to her feelings to be thus selected ; so she daintily stuffed the strong tobacco into the pipe ; and then we withdrew.

" It is very pleasant dining with a bachelor," said Miss Matty, softly, as we settled ourselves in the counting-house. " I only hope it is not improper ; so many pleasant things are ! "

ELIZABETH GASKELL (from *Cranford*)

ON GETTING UP ON COLD MORNINGS

Some people say it is a very easy thing to get up of a cold morning. You have only, they tell you, to take the resolution ; and the thing is done. This may be very true ; just as a boy at school has only to take a flogging, and the thing is over. But we have not at all made up our minds upon it ; and we find it a very pleasant exercise to discuss the matter, candidly, before we get up. This, at least, is not idling, though it may be lying. It affords an excellent answer to those who ask how lying in bed can be indulged in by a reasoning being,—a rational creature. How ? Why, with the argument calmly at work in one's head, and the clothes over one's shoulder. Oh—it is a fine way of spending a sensible, impartial half-hour.

If these people would be more charitable they would get on with their argument better. But they are apt to reason so ill, and to assert so dogmatically, that one could wish to have them stand round one's bed, of a bitter morning, and *lie* before their faces. They ought to hear both sides of the bed, the inside and out. If they cannot entertain themselves with their own thoughts for half-an-hour or so, it is not the fault of those who can. . .

On my first movement towards the anticipation of getting up I find that such parts of the sheets and bolster as are exposed to the air of the room are stone cold. On opening my eyes, the first thing that meets them is my own breath rolling forth, as if in the open air, like smoke out of a chimney. Think of this symptom. Then I turn my eyes sideways and see the window all frozen over. Think of that. Then the servant comes in. " It is very cold this morning, is it not ? "—" Very cold, sir."— " Very cold indeed, isn't it ? "—" Very cold indeed, sir."—" More than usually so, isn't it, even for this weather ? " (Here the servant's wit and good-nature are put to a considerable test, and the inquirer lies on thorns for the answer.) " Why, sir . . . I think it *is*." (Good creature ! There is not a better or more truth-telling servant going.) " I must rise, however—get me some warm water."—Here comes a fine interval between the departure of the servant and the arrival of the hot water; during which, of course, it is of " no use ? " to get up. The hot water comes. " Is it quite hot ? "—" Yes, sir."— " Perhaps too hot for shaving ; I must wait a little ? "— " No, sir ; it will just do." (There is an over-nice propriety sometimes, an officious zeal of virtue, a little troublesome.) " Oh—the shirt—you must air my clean shirt ;—linen gets very damp this weather."—" Yes, sir." Here another delicious five minutes. A knock at the door. " Oh, the shirt—very well. My stockings—I think the stockings had better be aired too."—" Very well, sir. Here another interval. At length everything is ready, except myself.

LEIGH HUNT

EL DORADO

To be truly happy is a question of how we begin and not of how we end, of what we want and not of what we have. An aspiration is a joy for ever, a possession as solid as a landed estate, a fortune which we can never exhaust and which gives us year by year a revenue of pleasurable activity. To have many of these is to be spiritually rich. Life is only a very dull and ill-directed theatre unless we have some interests in the piece ; and to those who have neither art nor science, the world is a mere arrangement of colours, or a rough footway where they may very well break their shins. It is in virtue of his own desires and curiosities that any man continues to exist with even patience, that he is charmed by the look of things and people, and that he wakens every morning with a renewed appetite for work and pleasure.

R. L. STEVENSON (from *El Dorado*)

DARK HOURS

In the ordinary way I have to woo my sleep, and that is one reason why I have read so many books, chasing Morpheus down innumerable labyrinths of eighteenth-century moralising or twentieth-century introspection. Those no-sooner-have-I-touched-the-pillow people are past my comprehension. There is something suspiciously bovine about them. When they begin to yawn about half-past ten, as they always do when I am with them (and I make you a present of the inevitable comment,) I feel that they forfeit all right to be considered as fellow-creatures, spirits here for a season that they may exchange confidences at the hour when all the beasts that perish are fast asleep. I do not complain about having to approach sleep so stealthily, tip-toeing through a chapter or so. After all, this is only to prolong the day, and I cannot help thinking that such a reluctance to part for ever from the day, though it be only an unconscious reluctance, is proof of an affectionate nature, unwilling to dismiss a servant, however poor a thing. Nor do I complain—though I like it less—about waking too early, beginning the day before it is fairly ready for me, nothing but a grey little monster with the chill on it and still opposed to all our nobler activities. I have been told that as the years wither me away, I shall have more and more of these early wakings, and I cannot say that the prospect pleases me. But for the moment I will submit to it without complaint, for there are worse things, and all this last week I have been suffering from them. I have been finding myself awake, not at the end of one day nor at the beginning of another, but sometime between them, in the mysterious dark hours.

Now this I do most bitterly resent. I have accustomed myself to prolonging the day, and I will try hard to resign myself to beginning it before it is worth beginning, but this other thing, this awful interloping piece of time, neither honest to-day nor splendid to-morrow, is a horror. You suddenly wake up, open your eyes, expecting welcome daylight and the morning's post and the savour of breakfast, only to discover that it is still dark, that nothing is happening. You roll over, turn back then over again, curl your legs up, stretch them out, push your hands under the pillow, then take them out, all to no purpose ; sleep will not come. You have been thrust, a dreadfully alert consciousness, into some black No Man's Land of time.

Reading, for once, fails as a resource. Frequently your eyes are so tired that the lines of print become blurred and run into one another. But even if you have no difficulty in seeing, it is still hard to read because all the savour seems to have departed from literature. You feel as if you were trying to attack a dish of cold potatoes. Even a new play by Shakespeare would leave you indifferent. I remember spending one very hot night in a London hotel. The place was full and I was a late-comer, so that I was given a tiny bed-room not far from the roof and looking out on nothing but a deep narrow court. I got off to sleep very quickly, but awoke about two and then vainly tossed and turned. There was nothing for it but to read, and I switched on my light. As a rule I have a book in my bag, but this night I was completely bookless, and the only reading matter in the room was that supplied by two evening papers. I had already glanced through these papers, but now I had to settle down to read them as I have never read evening papers before or since. Every scrap of print, sports gossip, society chit-chat, City Notes, small advertisements, was steadily devoured. There I was, in my hot little aerie, reading those silly paragraphs about Lord A leaving town or Miss B the musical comedy star making puddings, while the night burned slowly away. For weeks afterwards the sight of an evening paper made me feel depressed.

J. B. PRIESTLEY (from *The Dark Hours*)

SOME FRENCH COMPANIONS

MONTAIGNE

The True Friendship

I cannot allow other common friendships to be placed in the same line with ours. I have as much knowledge of them as another, and of the most perfect of their kind, but I should not advise any one to measure them with the same rule ; he would be much mistaken. In those other friendships one has to walk with the bridle in one's hand, prudently and cautiously : the knot is not tied so tightly but that it will cause some misgiving. " Love him," said Chilo, " as if you had one day to hate him ; hate him, as if you had to love him." This precept which is so abominable in this sovereign and commanding friendship, is of salutory use in the common and customary friendships to which must be applied the saying that Aristotle was so fond of, " Oh my friends ! there is no friend.".

In this noble intercourse, good offices and benefits, the feeders of other friendships, deserve not even to be taken into account, by reason of the complete blending of our wills. For even as the love I bear to myself is not increased by the succour I give myself in time of need, whatever the Stoics may say, and as I feel no gratitude to myself for the service I do myself ; so the union of such friends, being truly perfect, makes them lose the sense of such duties, and hate and banish from their minds these words that imply separation and distinction : benefit, obligation, gratitude, request, thanks, and the like. Everything being actually in common between them, wills, thoughts, opinions, possessions, wives, children, honour, and life, and their agreement being such that they are but one soul in two bodies, according to the very apt definition of Aristotle, they can neither lend nor give anything to one another. That is why the makers of laws, in order to honour marriage with some imaginary resemblance to this divine alliance, interdict all donations between husband and wife; meaning to infer therefrom that all should belong to each of them, and that they have nothing to divide and share out between them.

If, in the friendship of which I speak, one could give to the other, it would be the one who received the benefit that lays his friend under an obligation. For, as each of them studies above all to benefit the other, it is he who furnishes the matter and occasion that plays the liberal part, by giving his friend the satisfaction of doing that to him which he most desires.

When the philosopher Diogenes was in want of money he used to say that he redemanded it of his friends, not that he demanded it. And to show how that works in practice, I will relate a singular example from antiquity.

Eudamidas of Corinth had two friends, Charixenus a Sicyonian and Aretheus a Corinthian. When on his deathbed, being poor, and his two friends rich, he made his will after this manner: " My legacy to Aretheus is that he maintain my mother and support her in her old age; to Charixenus, that he give my daughter in marriage, and provide her with as good a dowry as he is able to afford; and in case one of them chance to die I appoint his survivor to take his place." They who first saw this testament laughed at it; but when the heirs were informed of it, they accepted it with a singular satisfaction. And one of them, Charixenus, dying five days later, leaving Aretheus at liberty to take his place, the latter supported the mother with great care, and of five talents he had in his estate, he gave two and a half as a marriage portion to his only daughter and two and a half to the daughter of Eudamidas and the two weddings took place on the same day.

This example is very complete, except for one objection, namely the number of friends. For that perfect friendship of which I speak is indivisible: each one gives himself so wholly to his friend, that there remains to him nothing to divide with another; on the contrary he grieves that he is not double, triple, or fourfold, and that he has not several souls and several wills, to confer them all on the object of his love.

Common friendships are capable of being shared: we may love one for his handsome exterior, another for his easy-going manners, another again for his liberality; this one for his fatherly and that one for his brotherly ways, and so forth; but this friendship which possesses the soul and dominates it with absolute power, cannot possibly be split in two. If two at the same time entreated your assistance, to which of them would you hasten? If they required of you opposite services, how would you arrange it? If one of them imparted to you a secret that it would be useful for the other to know, how would you solve the difficulty?

The unique and paramount friendship dissolves all other obligations. The secret that I have sworn not to reveal to another, I may without perjury communicate to one who is not another: that is myself. It is miracle enough to divide oneself into two, and they know not the greatness of it who speak of dividing oneself into three. Nothing is extreme that has its like. And he who supposes that I can equally love each of two, and that they can love one another and me as much as I love them, makes a multiple brotherhood of a thing that is most one and united, and of which even one is the rarest thing in the world to find.

The sequel of that story agrees very well with what I was saying, for Eudamidas makes it a kindness and a favour to his friends to employ them for his needs. He leaves them heirs to his liberality, which consists in giving into their hands the means of benefiting him. And without doubt the power of friendship is much more richly evident in his action than in that of Aretheus.

In short, these are delights which are not to be imagined by one who has not tasted them ; and therefore I highly honour the answer of a young soldier to Cyrus, who inquired of him what he would take for a horse that had just enabled him to win the prize in a race, and whether he would exchange it for a kingdom : " No indeed, Sire, but I would willingly part with it to gain a friend, if I could find a man worthy of such alliance." Not a bad answer, " if I could find " ; for it is easy to find men fit for a superficial acquaintance. But in the other kind, where we exhibit the very depths of our heart and make no reservations, truly all the springs of action must be perfectly clear and true.

A Gascon Library

I never travel without books, either in peace or in war-time. Yet many days, and even months, will pass without my using them. . .

When at home I resort a little more frequently to my library, from which I can quite easily overlook my household. It is over the entry, and I see below me my garden, my farm-yard, my court-yard, and into most parts of my house. There I turn over now one book, now another, without order or plan, in a desultory way. At one time I muse, at another I make notes and dictate, walking to and fro, my fancies, such as these.

It is on the third story of a tower[1]; on the first is my chapel, on the second a bedroom with its accompaniment, where I often lie down, to be alone. Above it is a large wardrobe. Formerly this was the most useless place in my establishment. There I spend most of the days of my life, and most of the hours of the day; I am never there at night. Adjoining the library is a rather neat study, in which a fire may be kindled in winter, very pleasantly lighted by a window. And if I did not fear the trouble more than the expense, the trouble that drives me from every kind of business, I could easily join to each side, on the same level, a gallery, a hundred paces long and twelve broad, having found all the walls raised, for another purpose, to the necessary height.

Every place of retirement requires a place for walking. My thoughts go to sleep if I sit still. My mind will not move unless stirred by my legs. All who study without a book are in the same plight.

My library is circular in shape, the only flat side being that needed for my table and chair; it being rounded I can see all my books at a glance, arranged about me on five rows of shelves. From this room I have three open and extensive views; and it offers sixteen paces of empty space in diameter.

In winter I am not there so continually, for my house is perched upon an eminence, as its name implies, and no room is more exposed to the winds than this, which,

[1] The tower here described is still standing on its hill in Périgord. A. S.

being rather difficult of access and a little out of the way, I like, both for the benefit of the exercise and because I can keep people at a distance.

Pain and Pleasure

We are naturally so feeble that we cannot enjoy things in their native purity and simplicity. The elements we live on are corrupted ; and so are the metals : even gold must be debased with some other matter to fit it for our use. . .

Of the pleasures and good things we enjoy not one is exempt from some mixture of evil and discomfort. . . Our keenest pleasure appears, as it were, to groan and lament. Would you not think it were dying of anguish ? Nay, when we compose a picture of it at its highest point : we deck it out with sickly and painful epithets and qualities, languor, softness, weakness, faintness, *morbidezza*; a great testimony to their consanguinity and consubstantiality.

In profound joy there is more seriousness than gaiety ; in the highest and fullest contentment more soberness than merriment. " Even felicity, unless it be tempered, overwhelms " (Seneca). Happiness grinds us down.

That is the meaning of an old Greek line which says " that the gods sell us all the good things they give us ;" that is to say, that they give us none pure and perfect and that we do not buy at the price of some evil.

Toil and pleasure, very unlike by nature, are however joined together by some sort of natural connexion.

Socrates said that some god tried to mix in one lump and

to confound pain and pleasure ; but that, unable to succeed, he bethought himself to couple them at least by
the tail.

Metrodorus said that in sadness there is some alloy of
pleasure. I know not whether he meant something else,
but for my part I imagine there is a certain amount of
purpose, acquiescence, and satisfaction in nursing one's
melancholy ; I mean besides the desire for approval which
may be mixed up with it. There is a little shade of dainti-
ness and delicacy that smiles upon and flatters us in the
very lap of melancholy.

Of Sleeping

Reason commands us ever to walk along the same path,
but not at the same pace ; and, although the wise man
should not permit his human passions to turn him from
the right course, he may indeed, without prejudice to his
duty, leave it to them to hasten or retard his steps and not
plant himself like an immovable and impassive Colossus.
Though Virtue herself should put on flesh and blood, I
believe her pulse would beat more strongly when marching to an attack than when going to dinner : nay, it is
necessary that she should be subject to emotion and heat.
For that reason I have remarked as a rare thing to see
great men, when engaged in the loftiest enterprises and
the most important affairs, keep themselves so entirely in
trim, as not even to curtail their sleep.

Alexander the Great, on the day assigned to that furious
battle against Darius, slept so profoundly and so late in

the morning, that Parmenion was obliged to enter his chamber, and, approaching his bed, call him two or three times by name to awaken him, the moment to go to battle being so urgent.

The Emperor Otho, having resolved to kill himself, on that same night, when he had settled his domestic affairs, divided his money among his servants, and sharpened the edge of a sword wherewith he intended to take his own life, staying only to know if each of his friends had retired in safety, fell into so sound a sleep, that his chamber-servants heard him snore.

The death of that Emperor has many points in common with that of the great Cato, and particularly that just mentioned: for, Cato being ready to make away with himself, whilst awaiting news to be brought him whether the Senators whom he was sending away had evacuated the port of Utica, began to sleep so soundly that he could be heard breathing from the next room: and when the man he had sent to the port awakened him to tell him that the Senators were prevented by a storm from conveniently setting sail, he sent yet another, and, resettling himself in his bed, again began to slumber until the second messenger assured him of their departure.

We may also compare with that of Alexander his behaviour in that great and dangerous storm which threatened him through the sedition of Metellus the Tribune, when the latter insisted on publishing the decree recalling Pompey with his army to the city, on the occasion of Catiline's conspiracy; which decree Cato alone opposing, high words and violent threats passed between him and Metellus in the Senate. But it was on the next day that the matter was to be put into execution in the Forum, where Metellus, besides being favoured by the common people and by Caesar, then conspiring in Pompey's interest, was to appear accompanied by many alien slaves and desperate gladiators, Cato being fortified by his courage alone. His friends and relations and many worthy people were consequently in great anxiety about him, some of whom spent the night together without any desire to sleep, eat or drink, on account of the danger they saw threatening him, his wife and sisters especially did nothing but weep and fret in his house, whilst he, on the contrary, comforted everybody, and after having supped in his usual manner, retired to his couch, and slept a very sound sleep till morning, when one of his fellow tribunes roused him to go to the skirmish.

The knowledge we possess of the greatness of this man's courage, throughout the rest of his life, may enable us to judge in all sureness that his conduct proceeded from a soul so far raised above such accidents, that he disdained to allow this one to cause him any more uneasiness than any ordinary event.

In the naval battle which Augustus won against Sextus Pompeius in Sicily, when on the point of entering into conflict, he was sunk in so deep a sleep, that his friends had to rouse him to give the signal for attack. This gave occasion to M. Antonius to reproach him afterwards, that he had not had the heart even to behold with open eyes the array of his army, and that he had not dared to appear before his soldiers until Agrippa came to announce to him the victory he had gained over his enemies.

But as to the young Marius, who did still worse, for on the day of his last battle against Sylla, after having marshalled his army and given the word and signal for battle, he lay down to rest in the shade of a tree, and slept so heavily that he could hardly be awakened by the rout and flight of his own men, having seen nothing of the battle; they say it was because he was so extremely spent with fatigue and the want of sleep, that nature could hold out no longer.

On the subject of sleep, the physicians will determine whether it is so necessary that our life depends on it: for we hear indeed that King Perseus of Macedon, when prisoner at Rome, was brought to his death by being prevented from sleeping; but Pliny instances cases of people who lived a long time without sleep. In Herodotus we read of nations where men sleep and wake by half-years. And they who wrote the life of the sage Epimenides say that he slept for fifty-seven years on end.

Is Death an Evil?

Theodorus replied to Lysimachus, who was threatening to kill him, " Thou wilt do a great thing in doing what a Spanish fly could do ! " Most of the philosophers are seen to have either designedly anticipated, or hastened and aided their own death. How many men of the people we see led to their death, and that not a simple death, but attended with ignominy and sometimes with cruel tortures, and exhibiting such assurance, the one through stubbornness, the other through a natural simplicity, that we may perceive no change from their ordinary demeanour; settling their domestic affairs, commending themselves to their friends, singing, preaching, and talking to the people, nay, sometimes jesting and drinking to their acquaintances, as cheerfully as Socrates.

A man who was being led to the gibbet said " For goodness' sake don't go by such and such a street, where I shall run the risk of being collared by a tradesman for an old debt." Another entreated the hangman " not to touch his neck, for he was so ticklish he would shake with laughter." Another replied to his confessor, who was promising him that he should sup that night with our Lord, " You may go yourself, for I am fasting." Another, having called for drink, and the hangman drinking before him, said he would not drink after him for fear of catching the pox. Everybody has heard the story of the man of Picardy who, when on the ladder, was presented with a girl, with the offer (as our justice sometimes permits) that, if he would marry her, his life should be spared ; he, having considered her for a while and perceived that she halted, said, " Tie up ! Tie up ! she limps." The same tale is current of a man in Denmark who was condemned to lose his head ; being on the scaffold he was offered the same condition, but refused it on the ground that the girl they offered him had flabby cheeks and too sharp a nose. . .

Fortune does us neither good nor harm : she only holds out to us the seed and the matter of good or harm, which our soul, more powerful than she, turns and applies as she pleases, being sole cause and mistress of her happy or unhappy condition.

Essays (Trans. E. J. TRECHMANN)

SOME THOUGHTS OF PASCAL

We rate human reason so highly that no matter what privileges we have, we are not content unless we stand well with our fellows. This, we think, is the finest position in the world; and those who place man on a level with the brutes still wish to be admired and believed in by men, for their feelings convince them of the greatness of man more powerfully than their reason convinces them of his vileness.

Man may be overwhelmed by a natural force, but he is nobler than his destroyer; for man knows that Nature has this power, while Nature knows nothing.

Justice and Truth are of too fine a quality to be measured by our clumsy human instruments.

We are conscious of beauty when there is a harmonious relation between something in our nature and the quality of the object which delights us.

Whoever will know fully the vanity of man has but to consider the causes and the effects of love. Its cause is unknown : its effects are over-powering. This unknown something is so intangible a matter that we cannot analyse it. Yet it moves the whole world, princes, armies, and people. If Cleopatra's nose had been shorter, how many countries would have had a different history !

From *Pensées* (Trans. A. S.)

ADVICE FROM AN ARCHBISHOP

(Letter to a Young Nephew, advising him to go to Court)

Jan. 7, 1713

I am not surprised at your disliking it—one feels constrained with people whom one knows but little or not at all, and one does badly that which one is not accustomed to do. Our self-esteem is apt to assert itself when we control our dispositions without making much progress. You are accustomed to a simple life, made easy and acceptable by the friendship of those around you, and this spoils you. You must grow accustomed to mental fatigue in the world as to bodily fatigue in camp. The longer you postpone the labour of making acquaintance with the world the harder it will grow, not to say impossible. You run the risk of very decided failure after a certain age ; and if you give it up entirely, you will spend your life in obscurity, without any distinguished friends, without credit or position, without any reward for your service, or any means of helping your family. So it is important that you should at once break the ice courageously and patiently. Ease will gradually come with practice. You will not be shy when you know everybody and everybody knows you, when you are accustomed to the new ways and are qualified to enter into familiar conversation with those around you. As soon as you have made friends with a few worthy, highly-esteemed people, they will admit you into their society, and by degrees you will get all you want. You will be courteous to every one, you will pay customary civilities to individuals, while for real society you will limit yourself to true

Z<small>B</small>

friends. In these you must look not merely for goodness, but for a certain standing and position. . .

As for Paris, keep some hours to yourself for work; avoid suppers, which are prolonged too late and upset all the next day; try to save some part of your mornings for yourself. Read, and reflect on what you read. I am quite aware that you cannot always be so regular; good nature to friends must sometimes lay you open to invasion, society and the habits of the age demand it; but while giving up something to your friends' amusement, you must rescue those hours without which you would do nothing to make you worthy of their friendship.

FÉNÉLON (Trans. A. s.)

SAYINGS OF LA BRUYÈRE

A fine face is the loveliest thing we can see, and the voice of a friend makes our sweetest music.

The most delightful intercourse a man can have is with a lovely woman who has the qualities of a gentleman.

A delicate thought is the finest product, and, as it were, the flower of the soul.

(Trans. A.s.)

ROUSSEAU

Father and Son

I know not how I learned to read; I recollect only my first reading, and its effect on me. From this time I date my continuing knowledge of myself. There was in the house a collection of romances which had belonged to my mother, and my father and I sat down to read them after supper. My father's object, at first, was merely to instruct me in reading by means of amusing books ; but we both became so interested in these adventures that we read by turns without relaxation, and often spent whole nights in that occupation. We could never stop till we got to the end of the book. Sometimes my father, hearing the swallows outside the window, would jump up, exclaiming " Let us go to bed ; I am more of a child than you."

A Night in the Open

It is certainly a hardship to pass one's nights in the street, and this happened to me several times at Lyons. I decided to spend my few remaining sous on food rather than on lodgings, for I thought I should die sooner from want of food than from want of sleep. I was surprised to find that in this unfortunate situation I was neither sad nor uneasy. I felt no misgivings about the future, and lying on the ground or stretched out on a bench I slept as peacefully as on a bed of roses. I remember one delightful night I spent outside the city, on a roadside by the Rhone or the Saône—I forget which. Above the road some terraced gardens faced the river. It had been a hot day, and the evening was very pleasant. The withered grass was wet with dew. The setting sun had filled the sky with crimson clouds, making lovely reflexions in the river. It was a serene and windless night, fresh but not too cold. The trees above the gardens were full of nightingales calling to each other. I walked about in a kind of ecstasy, giving myself up to delightful sensations, but not without a sigh of regret that I must enjoy this happiness alone. Absorbed in my reverie, I walked far into the night without noticing that I was tired. At length I did so, and lay down on the slab of a kind of niche or false door let into a wall. My bed was canopied by overhanging branches, and a nightingale, perched above my head, sang me to sleep. I awoke refreshed. It was broad day-light, and I beheld again the river, the friendly trees and the pleasant fields. I got up and shook off my drowsiness. I soon felt hungry, and with a light heart I made for the town, resolved to spend the two coins I had left on a good breakfast.

The Nightingale Again

It was on the 9th of April, 1756, that I left cities never to reside in them again. Madame d'Épinay came and took us in her carriage. My little retreat was furnished with simplicity and taste. Although the weather was cold (for there had been more snow) there was already some growth, and I saw both violets and primroses. Trees were beginning to bud, and on the night of my arrival the nightingale sang his first song hard by my window, for the house was on the edge of a wood. After a light sleep, forgetting my change of abode, I fancied myself still in the Rue de Grenelle until the twittering of the birds gave me a start and I exclaimed " At last my wishes are fulfilled."

The first thing I did was to give myself up to the impressions of my rural surroundings. Instead of setting my things in order indoors I began to plan my walks abroad, and by the next day I had become familiar with every path, every grove and every corner of the grounds. The more I explored this delightful retreat, the more I felt satisfied with it. This wild, or rather solitary, spot seemed to me to be the end of the world. It had beauty of a kind hardly to be found in the neighbourhood of a city, and no one suddenly transferred there would imagine that he was within four leagues of Paris.

The Lake of Bienne

I have ever been passionately fond of water, and the sight of it throws me into a delightful reverie, although often without a definite object. When the weather was fine, immediately after getting out of bed, I never failed to run to the terrace to breathe the fresh and invigorating morning air, and feast my eyes on this lovely lake, its shores and its mountains. I can easily understand why the inhabitants of cities, who (surrounded by walls) see nothing but the streets and their crimes, have little faith, but it is not so easy to see how country people—especially those in remote places—can be without it. How comes it that these do not a hundred times a day elevate their souls in ecstasy to the Author of the wonders which they see ? For my part,—especially when I rise wearied from want of sleep—long habit inclines me to this elevation, which does not give me the trouble of thinking. This is when my eyes can behold the ravishing spectacle of nature. In my chamber I pray less frequently, and less fervently, but at the view of a fine landscape I feel myself moved, yet by what I am unable to tell. I have somewhere read of a wise bishop who came across an old woman whose only prayer consisted in the single interjection Oh ! " Good mother," said he to her, " continue always to pray thus. Your prayer is better than ours."

From *Confessions* (Trans. A. S.)

Wisdom is to the mind what meat is to the body.

Perfect valour consists in doing without a witness all that we should be capable of doing before the whole world.

We are much nearer loving those that hate us, than those who love us more than we like.

No person is either so happy or so unhappy as he imagines.

Happiness lies in imagination, not in possession ; we are made happy by obtaining, not what others think desirable, but what we ourselves think so.

The greatest faults are those of Great Men.

To praise great actions with sincerity, may be said to be taking part in them.

AMIEL

A dream is an excursion into the world beyond, a temporary deliverance from our human prison. When we dream we are a theatre in which various scenes are staged, and we are at the same time involuntary spectators of the performance. We are then passive and without personality—the playthings of unknown forces and invisible powers.

A man who lives habitually in a state of dreaming is hardly alive; but a man who never dreams can know his own character only when it is formed, knowing nothing of the genesis of personality—he will be like a crystal without a crystal-gazer. Dreams are rare in old age, for they arise from our vital energy, being indeed, the flower of organic life.

Thought represents the highest point in the series of ascending changes which we call Nature. If our thoughts are turned inward—if we look within ourselves—we shall be fully compensated for what we miss of the outside world ; for our compensation will be no less than that privilege of self-direction which is our true liberty. Our dreams, throwing everything into confusion and removing all limits, make us realise how severe are the conditions of the higher existence. It is, however, by means of our conscious and voluntary thoughts that we are capable of knowing and doing. Let us dream, then, to satisfy our psychological curiosity and our desire for diversion ; but let us not despise thought, which gives us power and dignity. Let us begin like wise men of the East, but let us end like wise men of the West, for each has one half of wisdom.

. . . .

Our greatness depends upon our needs. Tell me what you wish for and I will tell you what you are. You will reply, perhaps, that resignation is better than aspiration. That is true, but not of a resignation which is passive, melancholy, and unmanly—it is true only of a resignation which is compelling and serene, resulting from an act of will. The former is negative, nothing more than regret : the latter is a possession of the mind and includes hope. Consider this, and you will see that your resignation may be in reality an aspiration.

. . . . . .

The surface of the sand is indented with little spots, and heavy clouds hang in the sky. The sea, veined tawny and green, has taken on a work-a-day aspect. It goes about its business without threat and without tenderness. As I walk along the shore I come across a heap of shell-fish about to crumble, and I perceive that the sand dunes may well be the detritus of the organic life of past ages, pyramids built up by millions of generations of little fishes, who have laboured on these shores as good workmen of God. If, then, sand-hills and mountains are the dust of beings who have preceded us, how can we doubt that our death will be as useful as our life—how doubt that nothing that has ever flourished can be lost? A mutual lending and serving seems to be a law of life. But the strong exploit or destroy the weak, and this concrete inequality of parts, in spite of the abstract equality of the whole, leaves us with disquieting thoughts of divine justice.

.   .   .   .

The secret of remaining young in spite of old age and white hairs is to preserve our enthusiasm, and this we can do by means of meditation and goodwill—in short by maintaining harmony in ourselves. When everything has its proper place in our minds we are able to stand in equilibrium with the rest of the world. A solemn enthusiasm for the order and beauty of the universe, an elevated mind and a serene benevolence—these things are, perhaps, the very foundations of wisdom.

From *Fragments d'un Journal Intime* (Trans. A. S.)

SAINTE-BEUVE

A Plea for Quiet Books

A friend who, after having seen much of the world, has withdrawn from it almost entirely, and judges at a distance—as it were from the shore—the swift whirlpool in which the rest of us are tossed about, lately wrote to me about certain rough estimates I had made of contemporary writings: "What you say of our 'sublimities' interests me very much. Certainly they are sublime. What they lack is calm and freshness, as it were a little cold water to cool our burning palates." This quality of freshness and delicacy, this clearness of emotion and sobriety of speech, this soft and quiet shading, as they disappear on all hands from actual life and the imaginative writings now produced, become all the more precious when we meet them in obscurity, and in those pleasing compositions in which they were last reflected. It would be a mistake to suppose that it is a sign of weakness or degeneracy to regret these vanished charms—these flowers which, it would appear, could bloom only in the very last days of an order of society now passed away. The softly-tinted pictures of which we speak presuppose a kind of taste and culture which democratic civilisation could not have abolished without loss, unless something analogous were to reappear later on. Modern society, when it shall have become a little more settled and better defined, will also have its element of repose, its cool, mysterious nooks, its shades favourable to refined sentiment, a few tolerably ancient forests, a few undiscovered fountains. It will admit into its seemingly uniform framework a thousand varieties of thought, and many a rare form of inner life : otherwise it

745

will be, in one respect, far inferior to the civilisation which preceded it, and will hardly meet the needs of a whole family of souls. In a progressive age, in times confused and incoherent like the present, it is natural to aim at what seems most important, to follow the general movement, and everywhere, even in literature, to strike boldly, aim high, and shout through trumpets or speaking-tubes. The modest graces will, perhaps, eventually, come back and come with an expression appropriate to their new surroundings. I would fain believe it; but while hoping for the best, I feel sure that it will not be to-morrow that their sentiments and their speech will once more prevail. Meanwhile, we realise that something is wanting, and suffer accordingly. We betake ourselves, in our hours of *ennui* to the perfumes of the past—a past only of yesterday, which, nevertheless, will not return.

From *Portraits de Femmes* (Trans. A. S.)

FOURTH PART

§ III A SANCTUARY OF QUIET

e la sua volontate è nostra pace :
   ella è quel mare, al qual tutto si move
   ciò ch' ella crea e che natura face.

DANTE (*Paradiso*, III)

Truth hath a quiet breast.

SHAKESPEARE (*Richard II*)

§ III A SANCTUARY OF QUIET

A BALLAD OF GOOD COUNSEL

Flee fro the press, and dwelle with sothfastnesse,
Suffice thine owen thing, though it be small ;
That thee is sent receive in buxumnesse,
The wrastling for this worlde axeth a fall ;
Here is none home, here is but wildernesse.
Forth, pilgrim, forth ! Forth, beast, out of thy stall !
Know thy countrèy, look up, thank God of all ;
Hold the high way, and let thy ghost thee lede,
And truthé shall deliver, it is no drede.

CHAUCER (from " Truth ")

GARMENT FOR A FAIR LADY

Her gown should be of goodliness
Well ribboned with renown,
Purfilled [1] with pleasure in ilk place
Furrèd with fine fashòn. [2]

Her belt should be of benignity
About her middle met ;
Her mantle of humility,
To thole [3] both wind and wet.

Her hat should be of fair having,
And her tippèt of truth,
Her ruffet of good pansing [4]
Her neck-ribbòn of ruth.

[1] Bordered.   [2] Good manners.   [3] Endure.   [4] Fair thought.

749

Her sleeves should be of esperance
To keep her from despair ;
Her gloves of the good governance
To guide her fingers fair.

Her shoon should be of sickerness,[1]
For then she would not slide ;
Her hose of honesty I guess,
I should for her provide.

Would she put on this garment gay,
I durst swear by my seel
That she wore never green nor grey
Suited her half so weel.

ROBERT HENRYSON

MEDITATION IN WINTER

In to these dirk and drumlie days,
When sabill all the hewin arrays
With misty vapours, clouds, and skies,
Nature all courage me denies
Of sangis, ballads, and of plays.

When that the night does lenthin hours,
With wind, with hail, and heavy showers,
My dulè spreit does lurk for schoir [2] ;
My heart for languor does forloir
For lack of Summer with his flowers.

[1] Security.   [2] Cower for dread.

I walk, I turn, sleep may I not ;
I vexèd am with heavy thought ;
This world all o'er I cast about,
And ay the mair I am in doubt,
The mair that I remeid have sought.

I am assailed on every side.
Despair says ay :—" In time provide,
And get some thing whereon to leif,
Or with great trouble and mischèif
Thou shall in to this court abide."

And then says Age :—" My friend, come near,
And be not strange, I thee requeir !
Come, brother, by the hand me take :
Remember thou hast compt to make
Of all thy time thou spended here." ..

For fear of this all day I drowp ;
No gold in kist, nor wine in cowp,
No lady's beauty, nor luif's bliss
May let me to remember this,
How glad that ever I dine or sowp.

Yet, when the night begins to short,
It does my spreit some part comfòrt,
Of thought oppressèd with the showers.
Come, lusty Summer ! with thy flowers,
That I may live in some disport !

WILLIAM DUNBAR

AN OLD CAROL

I sing of a maiden that is makèless ;
King of all kings to her son she owes,

He came all so still
Where His mother was,
As dew in Aprill
That falleth on the grass ;

He came all so still
Where His mother lay,
As dew in Aprill
That falleth on the spray ;

He came all so still
To His mother's bower,
As dew in Aprill
That falleth on the flower.

Maiden and Mother
Was never none but she ;
Well might such a Lady
Goddis Mother be.

ANONYMOUS (15th Century)

THE OBSCURE NIGHT

Upon an obscure night
Fevered with love in love's anxiety
(O hapless-happy plight !)
I went, none seeing me,
Forth from my house where all things be.

752

By night, secure from sight,
And by the secret stair, disguisedly
(O hapless-happy plight!)
By night, and privily,
Forth from my house where all things quiet be.

Blest night of wandering,
In secret, where by none might I be spied,
Nor I see anything;
Without a light or guide,
Save that which in my heart burnt in my side.

That light did lead me on,
More surely than the shining of noontide,
Where well I knew that one
Did for my coming bide;
Where He abode, might none but He abide.

O night that didst lead thus,
O night more lovely than the dawn of light,
O night that broughtest us,
Lover to lover's sight,
Lover with loved in marriage of delight!

Upon my flowery breast
Wholly for Him, and save Himself for none,
There did I give sweet rest
To my belovèd one;
The fanning of the cedars breathed thereon.

When the first moving air
Blew from the tower and waved His locks aside,
His hand, with gentle care,
Did wound me in the side,
And in my body all my senses died.

All things I then forgot,
My cheek on Him who for my coming came ;
All ceased, and I was not,
Leaving my cares and shame
Among the lilies, and forgetting them.

From the Spanish of ST. JOHN OF THE CROSS
(Trans. ARTHUR SYMONS)

A LOVER'S COMPLAINT

If care or skill could conquer vain desire,
Or reason's reins my strong affection stay,
Then should my sighs to quiet breast retire
And shun such sights as secret thoughts betray ;
    Uncomely love, which lurks now in my breast,
    Should cease, my grief by wisdom's power oppress'd.
But who can leave to look on Venus' face,
Or yieldeth not to Juno's high estate ?
What wit so wise as gives not Pallas place ?
These virtues rare the Gods did yield a mate.
    Save her alone, who yet on earth doth reign,
    Whose beauty's string no God can well distrain.
What worldly wight can hope for heavenly hire,
When only sighs must make his secret moan ?
A silent suit doth seld to grace aspire.
My hapless hap doth roll the restless stone.

EDWARD DE VERE, EARL OF OXFORD

FROM " THE FAERY QUEEN "

1. *Care In Heaven*

And is there care in heaven ? And is there love
In heavenly spirits to these creatures base
That may compassion of their evils move ?
There is—or else more wretched were the case
Of men than beasts : but O th' exceeding grace
Of Highest God that loves His creatures so,
And all His works with mercy doth embrace,
That blessèd angels He sends to and fro,
To serve to wicked man, to serve his wicked foe !

How oft do they their silver bowers leave
To come to succour us that succour want !
How oft do they with golden pinions cleave
The flitting skies, like flying pursuivant,
Against foul fiends to aid us militant !
They for us fight, they watch and duly ward,
And their bright squadrons round about us plant ;
And all for love and nothing for reward :
O, why should Heavenly God to men have such regard !

2. *The End of the Passage*

What if some little pain the passage have
That makes frail flesh to fear the bitter wave ;
Is not short pain well borne, that brings long ease,
And lays the soul to sleep in quiet grave ?
Sleep after toil, port after stormy seas,
Ease after war, death after life, doth greatly please.

SPENSER

755

THE PILGRIM'S WAY

Give me my scallop-shell of quiet,
My staff of faith to walk upon,
My scrip of joy, immortal diet,
   My bottle of salvation,
My gown of glory, hope's true gage ;
And thus I'll take my pilgrimage.
Blood must be my body's balmer ;
   No other balm will there be given ;
Whilst my soul, like quiet palmer,
   Travelleth towards the land of heaven ;
Over the silver mountains,
Where spring the nectar fountains—
    There will I kiss
    The bowl of bliss,
And drink mine everlasting fill
Upon every milken hill.
My soul will be a-dry before ;
But, after, it will thirst no more.

SIR WALTER RALEIGH (b. 1552)

THE SCENTED GARDEN

And because the Breath of Flowers is farre Sweeter in
the Aire (where it comes and goes like the Warbling of
Musick) than in the hand, therefore nothing is more fit
for that delight than to know what be the Flowers and
Plants that doe best perfume the Aire. Roses Damask and
Red are fast Flowers of their Smells, so that you may
walke by a whole Row of them and find Nothing of their
Sweetnesse ; yea, though it be in a Morning's Dew.
Bayes likewise yeeld no Smell as they grow ; Rosemary

little ; nor Sweet-Marjoram. That which above all Others yeelds the Sweetest Smell in the Aire is the Violet; specially the White-double Violet, which comes twice a Yeare, about the middle of Aprill, and about Bartholomew-tide. Next to that is the Muske-Rose ; then the Strawberry-Leaves dying, with a most excellent Cordiall Smell. Then the Flower of the Vines ; it is a little dust, like the dust of a Bent, which growes upon the Cluster in the first comming forth. Then Sweet Briar. Then Wall-Flowers, which are very Delightfull, to be set under a Parler or Lower Chamber Window. Then Pincks and Gilly-Flowers, specially the Matted Pinck and Clove Gilly-Flower. Then the Flowers of the Lime tree. Then the Honey-suckles, so they be somewhat a-farre off. Of Beane Flowers I speake not, because they are Field Flowers. But those which perfume the Aire most delightfully, not passed by as the rest, but being Trodden upon and Crushed, are Three : that is, Burnet, Wild-Time, and Water-Mints. Therefore you are to set whole Allies of them, to have the Pleasure when you walke or tread.

BACON (from *Of Gardens*)

CONTENT

Art thou poor, yet hast thou golden slumbers ?
　　　　O sweet content !
Art thou rich, yet is thy mind perplexèd ?
　　　　O punishment !
Dost thou laugh to see how fools are vexèd
To add to golden numbers, golden numbers ?
O sweet content ! O sweet, O sweet content !

Work apace, apace, apace, apace ;
Hence labour bears a lovely face ;
Then hey nonny nonny, hey nonny nonny !

Canst drink the waters of the crispèd spring ?
O sweet content !
Swimm'st thou in wealth, yet sink'st in thine own tears ?
O punishment !
Then he that patiently want's burden bears
No burden bears, but is a king, a king !
O sweet content ! O sweet, O sweet content !

Work apace, apace, apace, apace ;
Honest labour bears a lovely face ;
Then hey nonny nonny, hey nonny nonny !

THOMAS DEKKER

ALMS FOR MORPHEUS

Sleep must be procured, by nature or art. It moistens
and fattens the body, concocts, and helps digestion (as we
see in dormice, and those Alpine mice that sleep all
Winter), which Gesner speaks of, when they are so found
sleeping under the snow in the dead of Winter, as fat as
butter. It expels cares, pacifies the mind, refresheth the
weary limbs after long work. To procure this sweet moist-
ening sleep, it's best to take away the occasions (if it be
possible) that hinder it, and then to use such inward or
outward remedies, which may cause it.—Sacks of worm-
wood, mandrake, henbane, roses made like pillows and
laid under the patient's head, are mentioned by Cardan
and Mizaldus, " to anoint the soles of the feet with the

fat of a dormouse, the teeth with ear wax of a dog, swine's gall, hare's ears " : charms, etc.

Many cannot sleep for Witches and Fascinations, which are too familiar in some places. But the ordinary causes are heat and dryness, which must first be removed ; a hot and dry brain never sleeps well : grief, fears, cares, expectations, anxieties, great businesses, and all violent perturbations of the mind must in some sort be quali- fied, before we can hope for any good repose. He that sleeps in the day time, or is in suspense, fear, any way troubled in mind, or goes to bed upon a full stomack, may never hope for quiet rest in the night. Inns and such like troublesome places are not for sleep ; one calls Ostler, another Tapster, one cries and shouts, another sings, whoops and halloos. Who, not accustomed to such noises, can sleep amongst them ? He that will intend to take his rest must go to bed with a secure and composed mind, in a quiet place : and if that will not serve, or may not be obtained, to seek then such means as are requisite. To lie in clean linen and sweet ; before he goes to bed, or in bed, to hear sweet musick, to read some pleasant author till he be asleep, to have a bason of water still dropping by his bedside, or to lie near that pleasant mur- mur, some flood-gates, arches, falls of water, like London Bridge, or some continuate noise which may benumb the senses. As a gentle noise to some procures sleep, so silence in a dark room and the will itself is most available to others. Andrew Borde commends a good draught of strong drink before one goes to bed ; I say, a nutmeg and ale, or a good draught of muscadine, with a toast and nut- meg, or a posset of the same, which many use in a morn- ing, but, methinks, for such as have dry brains, are much more proper at night ; some prescribe a sup of vinegar as they go to bed, a spoonful saith Aêtius, because it rarifies melancholy, and procures an appetite to sleep. If in the midst of the night when they lie awake, which is usual to toss and tumble, and not sleep, Ranzovius would have them if it be in warm weather, to rise and walk three or four turns (till they be cold) about the chamber, and then go to bed again.

Against fearful and troublesome dreams the best remedy is to eat a light supper, and of such meats as are easy of digestion ; no Hare, Venison, Beef, &c., not to lie on his back, not to meditate or think in the day time of any terrible objects, or especially talk of them before he goes to bed. Ptolemy, King of Egypt, had posed the 70 interpreters in order, and asked the nineteenth man, what would make one sleep quietly in the night, he told him the best way was to have divine and celestial meditations, and to use honest actions in the day time.

ROBERT BURTON (from *Anatomy of Melancholy*)

A GOOD-NIGHT

Close now thine eyes, and rest secure ;
Thy soul is safe enough ; thy body sure ;
   He that loves thee, he that keeps
And guards thee, never slumbers, never sleeps.
The smiling conscience in a sleeping breast
   Has only peace, has only rest :
   The music and the mirth of kings
Are all but very discords, when she sings :
   Then close thine eyes and rest secure ;
No sleep so sweet as thine, no rest so sure.

FRANCIS QUARLES

VIRTUE

Sweet day so cool, so calm, so bright,
The bridal of the earth and sky,
The dew shall weep thy fall to-night,
    For thou must die.

Sweet rose, whose hue, angry and brave,
Bids the rash gazer wipe his eye,
Thy root is ever in its grave,
    And thou must die.

Sweet spring, full of sweet days and roses,
A box where sweets compacted lie,
My music shows ye have your closes,
    And all must die.

Only a sweet and virtuous soul,
Like seasoned timber, never gives ;
But though the whole world turn to coal,
    Then chiefly lives.

GEORGE HERBERT

THE PULLEY

When God at first made Man,
Having a glass of blessings standing by—
Let us (said He) pour on him all we can ;
Let the world's riches, which dispersèd lie,
    Contract into a span.

So strength first made a way,
Then beauty flow'd, then wisdom, honour, pleasure :
When almost all was out, God made a stay,
Perceiving that, alone of all His treasure,
     Rest in the bottom lay.

For if I should (said He)
Bestow this jewel also on My creature,
He would adore My gifts instead of Me,
And rest in Nature, not the God of Nature ;
     So both should losers be.

Yet let him keep the rest,
But keep them with repining restlessness ;
Let him be rich and weary, that at least,
If goodness lead him not, yet weariness
     May toss him to My breast.

GEORGE HERBERT

FLOWERS AND MEN

As many herbs and flowers with their fragrant sweet smells do comfort and as it were revive the spirits and perfume a whole house ; even so such men as live virtuously, labouring to do good, and to profit the Church of God and the commonwealth do as it were send forth a pleasing savour of sweet instructions, not only to that time wherein they live and are fresh, but being dry, withered and dead, cease not in all after ages to do as much or more.

JOHN PARKINSON (from *Paradisus*, 1629)

ON THE SEPULCHRAL URNS FOUND IN NORFOLK

Now since these dead bones have already out-lasted the living ones of Methuselah, and in a yard under ground, and thin walls of clay, out-worn all the strong and specious buildings above it ; and quietly rested under the drums and tramplings of three conquests : what prince can promise such diuturnity unto his relics ? Time, which antiquates antiquities, and hath an art to make dust of all things, hath yet spared these minor monuments. In vain we hope to be known by open and visible conservatories, when to be unknown was the means of their continuation, and obscurity their protection. . .

What song the Syrens sang, or what name Achilles assumed when he hid himself among women, though puzzling questions, are not beyond all conjecture. What time the persons of these ossuaries entered the famous nations of the dead, and slept with princes and counsellors, might admit a wide solution. But who were the proprietaries of these bones, or what bodies these ashes made up, were a question above antiquarism ; not to be resolved by man, nor easily perhaps by spirits, except we consult the provincial guardians, or tutelary observators. Had they made as good provision for their names, as they have done for their relics, they had not so grossly erred in the art of perpetuation. But to subsist in bones, and be but pyramidally extant, is a fallacy in duration. . .

And therefore, restless inquietude for the diuturnity of our memories unto present considerations seems a vanity almost out of date, and superannuated piece of folly. We cannot hope to live so long in our names, as some have done in their persons. . . . To be nameless in worthy deeds, exceeds an infamous history.

But the iniquity of oblivion blindly scattereth her poppy, and deals with the memory of men without distinction to merit of perpetuity. Who can but pity the founder of the pyramids? Herostratus lives that burnt the temple of Diana, he is almost lost that built it. Time hath spared the epitaph of Adrian's horse, confounded that of himself. In vain we compute our felicities by the advantage of our good names, since bad have equal durations, and Thersites is like to live as long as Agamemnon. Who knows whether the best of men be known, or whether there be not more remarkable persons forgot, than any that stand remembered in the known account of time? Without the favour of the everlasting register, the first man had been as unknown as the last, and Methuselah's long life had been his only chronicle.

Oblivion is not to be hired. The greater part must be content to be as though they had not been, to be found in the register of God, not in the record of man. Twenty-seven names make up the first story before the flood, and the recorded names ever since contain not one living century. The number of the dead long exceedeth all that shall live. The night of time far surpasseth the day, and who knows when was the equinox? . .

Darkness and light divide the course of time, and oblivion shares with memory a great part even of our living beings; we slightly remember our felicities, and the smartest strokes of affliction leave but short smart upon us. Sense endureth no extremities, and sorrows destroy us or themselves. To weep into stones are fables. Afflictions induce callosities; miseries are slippery, or fall like snow upon us, which notwithstanding is no unhappy stupidity.

To be ignorant of evils to come, and forgetful of evils past is a merciful provision in nature, whereby we digest the mixture of our few and evil days, and, our delivered senses not relapsing into cutting remembrances, our sorrows are not kept raw by the edge of repetitions. . .

In vain do individuals hope for immortality, or any patent from oblivion, in preservations below the moon : men have been deceived even in their flatteries, above the sun, and studied conceits to perpetuate their names in heaven. The various cosmography of that part hath already varied the names of contrived constellations ; Nimrod is lost in Orion, and Osyris in the dog-star. While we look for incorruption in the heavens, we find they are but like the earth ;—durable in their main bodies, alterable in their parts ; whereof, beside comets and new stars, perspectives begin to tell tales, and the spots that wander about the sun, with Phaeton's favour, would make clear conviction.

There is nothing strictly immortal, but immortality. Whatever hath no beginning, may be confident of no end —which is the peculiar of that necessary essence that cannot destroy itself ;—and the highest strain of omnipotency, to be so powerfully constituted as not to suffer even from the power of itself : all others have a dependent being and within the reach of destruction. But the sufficiency of Christian immortality frustrates all earthly glory, and the quality of either state after death, makes a folly of posthumous memory. God, who can only destroy our souls and hath assured our resurrection, either of our bodies or names, hath directly promised no duration. Wherein there is so much of chance, that the boldest expectants have found unhappy frustration ; and to hold long subsistence, seems but a scape in oblivion. But man is a noble animal, splendid in ashes, and pompous in the grave, solemnising nativities and deaths with equal lustre, nor omitting ceremonies of bravery in the infamy of his nature.

SIR THOMAS BROWNE (from *Urnes found in Brampton Field, Norfolk, anno* 1667)

OLD AGE

The seas are quiet when the winds give o'er ;
So calm are we when passions are no more.
For then we know how vain it was to boast
Of fleeting things, so certain to be lost.
Clouds of affection from our younger eyes
Conceal that emptiness which age descries.

The soul's dark cottage, batter'd and decay'd,
Lets in new light through chinks that Time hath made :
Stronger by weakness, wiser men become
As they draw near to their eternal home.
Leaving the old, both worlds at once they view
That stand upon the threshold of the new.

EDMUND WALLER

ALL IS BEST

All is best, though we oft doubt
What the unsearchable dispose
Of Highest Wisdom brings about,
And ever best found in the close.

MILTON (from *Samson Agonistes*)

THE WISH

Well then ; I now do plainly see
This busy world and I shall ne'er agree.
The very honey of all earthly joy
Does, of all meats, the soonest cloy ;
 And they, methinks, deserve my pity
Who for it can endure the stings,
The crowd, and buzz, and murmurings
 Of this great hive, the city.

Ah yet, ere I descend to the grave,
May I a small house and large garden have ;
And a few friends, and many books, both true,
Both wise, and both delightful too !
 And since love ne'er will from me flee,
A mistress moderately fair,
And good as guardian angels are,
 Only beloved, and loving me !

O fountains ! when in you shall I
Myself eased of unpeaceful thoughts espy ?
O fields ! O woods ! when, when shall I be made
The happy tenant of your shade ?
 Here's the spring-head of pleasure's flood ;
Here's wealthy Nature's treasury,
Where all the riches lie that she
 Has coined and stamped for good.

Pride and ambition here
Only in far-fetched metaphors appear ;
Here nought but winds can hurtful murmurs scatter,
And nought but echo flatter.

The gods, when they descended, hither
From heaven did always choose their way;
And therefore we may boldly say
    That 'tis the way too thither.

How happy here should I
And one dear she live, and embracing die!
She who is all the world, and can exclude
In deserts solitude.
    I should have then this only fear:
Lest men, when they my pleasures see,
Should hither throng to live like me,
    And so make a city here.

COWLEY

FITNESS FOR SOLITUDE

The truth of the matter is, that neither he who is a fop in the world is a fit man to be alone; nor he who has set his heart much upon the world, though he have never so much understanding; so that solitude can be well fitted and set right, but upon a very few persons. They must have enough knowledge of the world to see the vanity of it, and enough virtue to despise all vanity; if the mind be possest with any lust or passion, a man had better be in a fair, than in a wood alone. They may, like petty thieves, cheat us perhaps, and pick our pockets, in the midst of company; but like robbers, they use to strip and bind or murder us, when they catch us alone. This is but to retreat from men, and to fall into the hands of devils. It is like punishment of parricides among the Romans, to be sew'd into a bag, with an ape, a dog, and a serpent.

COWLEY (from Essay on Solitude)

THE REVIVAL

Unfold, unfold ! take in his light,
Who makes thy cares more short than night.
The joys which with his day-star rise
He deals to all but drowsy eyes ;
And, what the men of this world miss,
Some drops and dews of future bliss.

Hark how his winds have changed their note,
And with warm whispers call thee out !
The frosts are past, the storms are gone,
And backward life at last comes on.
 The lofty groves in èxpress joys
 Reply unto the turtle's voice ;
 And here in dust and dirt, oh, here
 The lilies of his love appear !

         VAUGHAN

THE NIGHT

 Through that pure virgin-shrine,
That sacred veil drawn o'er thy glorious noon,
That men might look and live, as glow-worms shine
  And face the moon :
 Wise Nicodemus saw such light
 As made him know his God by night.

 Most blest believer he !
Who in that land of darkness and blind eyes

Thy long-expected healing wings could see
    When thou didst rise,
  And, what can never more be done,
  Did at midnight speak with the Sun !

  O who will tell me, where
He found thee at that dead and silent hour ?
What hallowed solitary ground did bear
    So rare a flower
  Within whose sacred leaves did lie
  The fulness of the Deity ?

  No mercy-seat of gold,
No dead and dusty cherub, nor carved stone,
But his own living works did my Lord hold
    And lodge alone ;
  Where trees and herbs did watch and peep
  And wonder, while the Jews did sleep.

  Dear Night ! this world's defeat ;
The stop to busy fools ; care's check and curb ;
The day of spirits ; my soul's calm retreat
    Which none disturb !
  Christ's progress, and his prayer-time ;
  The hours to which high heaven doth chime.

  God's silent, searching flight :
When my Lord's head is fill'd with dew and all
His locks are wet with the clear drops of night ;
    His still, soft call ;
  His knocking-time ; the soul's dumb watch,
  When spirits their fair kindred catch.

Were all my loud, evil days
Calm and unhaunted as is thy dark tent,
Whose peace but by some angel's wing or voice
    Is seldom rent;
  Then I in heaven all the long year
  Would keep, and never wander here.

  But living where the sun
Doth all things wake, and where all mix and tire
Themselves and others, I consent and run
    To every mire;
  And by this world's ill-guiding light,
  Err more than I can do by night.

  There is in God (some say)
A deep, but dazzling darkness; as men here
Say it is late and dusky, because they
    See not all clear.
  O for that night! where I in him
  Might live invisible and dim.

VAUGHAN

A QUIET SOUL

Thy soul within such silent pomp did keep,
  As if humanity were lull'd asleep;
So gentle was thy pilgrimage beneath,
  Time's unheard feet scarce make less noise,
  Or the soft journey which a planet goes:
Life seem'd all calm as its last breath.

771

A still tranquillity so hush'd thy breast,
As if some Halcyon were its guest,
And there had built her nest ;
It hardly now enjoys a greater rest.

JOHN OLDHAM

FRUITS OF SOLITUDE

Ignorance

It is admirable to consider how many millions of people come into, and go out of the world, ignorant of themselves, and of the world they have lived in.

If one went to see Windsor Castle, or Hampton Court, it would be strange not to observe and remember the situation, the building, the gardens, fountains, etc., that make up the beauty and pleasure of such a seat. And yet few people know themselves ; no, not their own bodies, the houses of their minds, the most curious structure of the world ; a living walking tabernacle : nor the world of which it was made, and out of which it is fed ; which would be so much our benefit, as well as our pleasure, to know. We cannot doubt of this when we are told that the invisible things of God are brought to light by the things that are seen ; and consequently we read our duty in them as often as we look upon them, to him that is the great and wise Author of them if we look as we should do.

The world is certainly a great and stately volume of natural things ; and may be not improperly styled the hieroglyphics of a better : But, alas ! how very few leaves of it do we seriously turn over ! This ought to be the subject of the education of our youth, who, at twenty when they should be fit for business, know little or nothing of it.

Friendship

There can be no friendship where there is no freedom. Friendship loves a free air, and will not be penned up in straight and narrow enclosures. It will speak freely, and act so too ; and take nothing ill where no ill is meant ; nay, where it is, 'twill easily forgive, and forget too, upon small acknowledgments.

A true friend unbosoms freely, advises justly, assists readily, adventures boldly, takes all patiently, defends courageously, and continues a friend unchangeably.

They have a right to censure, that have a heart to help : the rest is cruelty, not justice.

Happiness

We are apt to call things by wrong names. We will have prosperity to be happiness, and adversity to be misery. If thou wouldest be happy, bring thy mind to thy condition and have an indifference for more than what is sufficient.

Religion

Men may tire themselves in a labyrinth of search, and talk of God : but if we would know him indeed, it must be from the impressions we receive of him ; and the softer our hearts are, the deeper and livelier those will be upon us.

WILLIAM PENN (from *Some Fruits of Solitude*)

ON EQUANIMITY

It is certain that to enjoy life and health as a constant feast, we should not think pleasure necessary, but, if possible, to arrive at an equality of mind. It is as mean to be overjoyed upon occasions of good fortune, as to be dejected in circumstances of distress. Laughter in one condition is as unmanly as weeping in the other. We should not form our minds to expect transport on every occasion, but know how to make it enjoyment to be out of pain. Ambition, envy, vagrant desire, or impertinent mirth will take up our minds, without we can possess ourselves in that sobriety of heart which is above all pleasures, and can be felt much better than described. But the ready way, I believe, to the right enjoyment of life, is by a prospect towards another to have but a very mean opinion of it.

STEELE (from *Spectator*)

SONG

How sweet I roamed from field to field,
   And tasted all the summer's pride
Till I the Prince of Love beheld
   Who in the sunny beams did glide !

He shewed me lilies for my hair,
   And blushing roses for my brow ;
He led me through his gardens fair
   Where all his golden pleasures grow.

With sweet May-dews my wings were wet,
   And Phoebus fired my vocal rage ;
He caught me in his silken net,
   And shut me in his golden cage.

He loves to sit and hear me sing ;
   Then, laughing, sports and plays with me ;
Then stretches out my golden wing,
   And mocks my loss of liberty.

WILLIAM BLAKE

FAREWELL TO THE RIVER

I thought of Thee, my partner and my guide,
   As being past away—vain sympathies !
   For backward, Duddon, as I cast my eyes,
I see what was, and is, and will abide ;
Still glides the Stream, and shall for ever glide ;
   The Form remains, the Function never dies ;
   While we, the brave, the mighty and the wise,
We Men, who in our morn of youth defied
   The elements, must vanish ;—be it so !
Enough if something from our hand have power
To live and act and serve the future hour ;
   And if, as toward the silent tomb we go,
Through love, through hope, and faith's
     transcendent dower
   We feel that we are greater than we know.

WORDSWORTH (from *The River Duddon :*
A Series of Sonnets)

Reader, would'st thou know what true peace and quiet mean; would'st thou find a refuge from the noises and clamours of the multitude; would'st thou enjoy at once solitude and society; would'st thou possess the depth of thine own spirit in stillness, without being shut out from the consolatory faces of thy species; would'st thou be alone and yet accompanied; solitary, yet not desolate; singular, yet not without some to keep thee in countenance; a unit in aggregate; a simple in composite; come with me into a Quakers' Meeting.

Dost thou love silence deep as that " before the winds were made " ? go not out into the wilderness, descend not into the profundities of the earth; shut not up thy casements; nor pour wax into the little cells of thy ears, with little-faith'd self-mistrusting Ulysses. Retire with me into a Quakers' Meeting.

For a man to refrain even from good words, and to hold his peace, it is commendable; but for a multitude it is great mastery.

What is the stillness of the desert compared with this place ? what the uncommunicating muteness of fishes ? Here the goddess reigns and revels. " Boreas, and Cesias, and Argestes loud," do not with their interconfounding uproars more augment the brawl—nor the waves of the blown Baltic with their clubbed sounds—than their opposite (Silence her sacred self) is multiplied and rendered more intense by numbers, and by sympathy. She too hath her deeps, that call unto deeps. Negation itself hath a positive more and less; and closed eyes would seem to obscure the great obscurity of midnight.

There are wounds which an imperfect solitude cannot

heal. By "imperfect" I mean that which a man enjoyeth himself. The perfect is that which he can sometimes attain in crowds, but nowhere so absolutely as in a Quakers' Meeting. Those first hermits did certainly understand this principle, when they retired into Egyptian solitudes, not singly but in shoals, to enjoy one another's want of conversation. The Carthusian is bound to his brethren by his agreeing spirit of incommunicativeness. On secular occasions, what so pleasant as to be reading a book through a long Winter evening, with a friend sitting by—say, a wife—he, or she, too (if that be probable), reading another, without interruption, or oral communication?—can there be no sympathy without the gabble of words? Away with this inhuman, shy, single, shade-and-cavern-haunting solitariness! Give me, Master Zimmermann, a sympathetic solitude.

To pace alone in the cloisters or side-aisles of some cathedral, time-stricken;

> Or under hanging mountains,
> Or by the fall of fountains;

is but a vulgar luxury compared with that which those enjoy who come together for the purposes of more complete, abstracted solitude. This is the loneliness "to be felt." The Abbey Church of Westminster hath nothing so solemn, so spirit-soothing, as the naked walls and benches of a Quakers' Meeting. Here are no tombs. no inscriptions,

> —Sands, ignoble things,
> Dropt from the ruin'd sides of kings—

but here is something which throws Antiquity herself into the foreground—SILENCE—eldest of things—language of old Night—primitive Discourser—to which the insolent decays of mouldering grandeur have but arrived by a violent, and, as we may say, unnatural progression.

> *How reverend is the view of these hush'd heads,*
> *Looking tranquillity !*

Nothing-plotting, nought-caballing, unmischievous synod ! convocation without intrigue ! parliament without debate ! what a lesson dost thou read to council, and to consistory! If my pen treat of you lightly, (as haply it will wander,) yet my spirit hath gravely felt the wisdom of your custom, when sitting among you in deepest peace, which some out-welling tears would rather confirm than disturb, I have reverted to the times of your beginnings, and the sowings of the seed by Fox and Dewesbury. . .

Frequently the Meeting is broken up without a word having been spoken. But the mind has been fed. You go away with a sermon not made with hands. You have been in the milder caverns of Trophonius ; or as in some den, where that fiercest and savagest of all wild creatures, the TONGUE, that unruly member, has strangely lain tied up and captive. You have bathed with stillness. O, when the spirit is sore fretted, even tired to sickness of the janglings and nonsense-noises of the world, what a balm and a solace it is to go and seat yourself for a quiet half hour upon some undisputed corner of a bench, among the gentle Quakers !

Their garb and stillness conjoined present a uniformity, tranquil and herd-like—as in the pasture—" forty feeding like one."

The very garments of a Quaker seem incapable of receiving a soil ; and cleanliness in them to be something more than the absence of its contrary. Every Quakeress is a lily ; and when they come up in bands to their Whitsun conferences, whitening the easterly streets of the metropolis, from all parts of the United Kingdom, they show like troops of the Shining Ones.

CHARLES LAMB (from *A Quakers' Meeting*)

WHY DISTANT OBJECTS PLEASE

Whatever is placed beyond the reach of sense and knowledge, whatever is imperfectly discerned, the fancy pieces out at its leisure ; and all but the present moment, but the present spot, passion claims for its own, and brooding over it with wings outspread, stamps it with an image of itself. Passion is lord of infinite space, and distant objects please because they border on its confines and are moulded by its touch. When I was a boy, I lived within sight of a range of lofty hills, whose blue tops blending with the setting sun had often tempted my longing eyes and wandering feet. At last I put my project in execution, and on a nearer approach, instead of glimmering air woven into fantastic shapes, found them huge lumpish heaps of discoloured earth. I learnt from this (in part) to leave " Yarrow unvisited," and not idly to disturb a dream of good !

Distance of time has much the same effect as distance of place. It is not surprising that fancy colours the prospect of the future as it thinks good, when it even effaces the forms of memory. Time takes out the sting of pain ; our sorrows after a certain period have been so often steeped in a medium of thought and passion that they

" unmould their essence " ; and all that remains of our original impressions is what we would wish them to have been. Not only the untried steep ascent before us, but the rude, unsightly masses of our past experience presently resume their power of deception over the eye : the golden cloud soon rests upon their heads, and the purple light of fancy clothes their barren sides ! Thus we pass on, while both ends of our existence touch upon Heaven ! There is (so to speak) " a mighty stream of tendency " to good in the human mind, upon which all objects float and are imperceptibly borne along ; and though in the voyage of life we meet with strong rebuffs, with rocks and quicksands, yet there is " A tide in the affairs of men," a heaving and a restless aspiration of the soul, by means of which, " with sails and tackle torn," the wreck and scattered fragments of our entire being drift into the port and haven of our desires ! In all that relates to the affections, we put the will for the deed ; so that the instant the pressure of unwelcome circumstances is removed the mind recoils from their hold, recovers its elasticity, and re-unites itself to that image of good which is but a reflection and configuration of its own nature. . .

WILLIAM HAZLITT (from *Table Talk*)

AUTUMN THOUGHTS IN ITALY

Noon descends and after noon
Autumn's evening meets me soon,
Leading the infantine moon,
And that one star, which to her
Almost seems to minister
Half the crimson light she brings
From the sunset's radiant springs :
And the soft dreams of the morn
(Which like wingèd winds had borne
To that silent isle, which lies
'Mid remembered agonies,
The frail bark of this lone being)
Pass, to other sufferers fleeing,
And its ancient pilot, Pain,
Sits beside the helm again.

Other flowering isles must be
In the sea of Life and Agony :
Other spirits float and flee
O'er that gulph : even now, perhaps,
On some rock the wild wave wraps,
With folded wings they waiting sit
For my bark, to pilot it
To some calm and blooming cove,
Where for me, and those I love,
May a windless bower be built,
Far from passion, pain, and guilt.
In a dell 'mid lawny hills,
Which the wild sea-murmur fills,
And soft sunshine, and the sound
Of old forests echoing round,

And the light and smell divine
Of all flowers that breathe and shine
We may live so happy there,
That the Spirits of the Air,
Envying us, may even entice
To our healing paradise
The polluting multitude ;
But their rage would be subdued
By that clime divine and calm,
And the winds whose wings rain balm
On the uplifted soul, and leaves
Under which the bright sea heaves ;
While each breathless interval
In their whisperings musical
The inspirèd soul supplies
With its own deep melodies ;
And the love, which heals all strife,
Circling, like the breath of life,
All things in that sweet abode
With its own mild brotherhood :
They, not it would change ; and soon
Every sprite beneath the moon
Would repent its envy vain,
And the earth grow young again.

SHELLEY (from *Lines written among
the Euganean Hills*)

THE OLD PACKHORSE ROAD

Well, people say this hollow track
   Was never made for wheels and springs ;
   But worn by packhorses in strings,
With wares, on ev'ry horse a pack.

Before, by yonder plain and ridge,
   The road was stean'd two-waggons wide,
   Where wheels now spin and horsemen ride,
On high-cast bank and high-bowed bridge.

The road climb'd up, onwinding deep
   Beside the ashes on the height,
   Where elderflow'rs are hanging white
O'er yonder crowds of cluster'd sheep.

And up at Holway men would shout
   " Hold hard," or else would blow a horn
   On their side of the way, to warn
Oncomers back, till they were out.

And then it struck along the glades
   Above the brook, to Rockley spring,
   And meads, where now you hear the ring
Of mowers' briskly-whetted blades.

And then it sunk, the slope to dive
   Through Pebbleford, where uncle took
   His way across the flooded brook,
But never reach'd his home alive.

And then it touch'd the ridgy ground
　　With marks of walls, where Deanton stood ;
　　Though now the houses, stone and wood,
Are gone, with all their tongues and sound.

Our elders there, as we are told,
　　Had once their homes, and doors to close
　　Between warm hearths and winter snows ;
And there play'd young, and there grew old.

WILLIAM BARNES

THE GUARDIAN-ANGEL

(*A Picture at Fano*)

Dear and great Angel, wouldst thou only leave
　　That child, when thou hast done with him, for me !
Let me sit all the day here, that when eve
　　Shall find performed thy special ministry,
And time come for departure, thou, suspending
Thy flight, mayst see another child for tending,
　　Another still, to quiet and retrieve.

Then I shall feel thee step one step, no more,
　　From where thou standest now, to where I gaze,
And suddenly my head is covered o'er
　　With those wings, white above the child who prays
Now on that tomb—and I shall feel thee guarding
Me, out of all the world ; for me, discarding
　　Yon heaven thy home, that waits and opes its door.

I would not look up thither past thy head
    Because the door opes, like that child, I know,
For I should have thy gracious face instead,
    Thou bird of God ! and wilt thou bend me low
Like him, and lay, like his, my hands together,
And lift them up to pray, and gently tether
    Me, as thy lamb there, with thy garment's spread ?

If this was ever granted, I would rest
    My head beneath thine, while thy healing hands
Close-covered both my eyes beside thy breast,
    Pressing the brain, which too much thought expands,
Back to its proper size again, and smoothing
Distortion down till every nerve had soothing,
    And all lay quiet, happy and suppressed.

How soon all worldly wrong would be repaired !
    I think how I should view the earth and skies
And sea, when once again my brow was bared
    After thy healing, with such different eyes.
O world, as God has made it ! All is beauty :
And knowing this, is love, and love is duty.
    What further may be sought for or declared ?

BROWNING

THE IMPRISONED SOUL

At the last, tenderly,
From the walls of the powerful, fortress'd house,
From the clasp of the knitted locks—from the keep
        of the well-closed doors,
Let me be wafted.

Let me glide noiselessly forth ;
With the key of softness unlock the locks—with a
    whisper
Set ope the doors, O soul !

Tenderly ! be not impatient !
(Strong is your hold, O mortal flesh !
Strong is your hold, O love !)

WALT WHITMAN

THE VINE

The wine of Love is music,
    And the feast of Love is song ;
And when Love sits down to the banquet,
    Love sits long :

Sits long and arises drunken,
    But not with the feast and the wine ;
He reeleth with his own heart,
    That great, rich Vine.

JAMES THOMSON (b. 1834)

WHITSUN EVE

The white dove cooeth in her downy nest,
Keeping her young ones warm beneath her breast :
The white moon saileth through the cool clear sky,
Screened by a tender mist in passing by :
The white rose buds, with thorns upon its stem,
All the more precious and more dear for them :

The stream shines silver in the tufted grass,
The white clouds scarcely dim it as they pass;
Deep in the valleys lily cups are white,
They send up incense all the holy night.
Our souls are white, made clean in Blood once shed:
White blessed Angels watch around our bed:—
O spotless Lamb of God, still keep us so,
Thou who wert born for us in time of snow.

CHRISTINA ROSSETTI

THE HOUSE BEAUTIFUL

A naked house, a naked moor,
A shivering pool before the door,
A garden bare of flowers and fruit
And poplars at the garden foot:
Such is the place that I live in,
Bleak without and bare within.

Yet shall your ragged moor receive
The incomparable pomp of eve,
And the cold glories of the dawn
Behind your shivering trees be drawn;
And when the wind from place to place
Doth the unmoored cloud-galleons chase,
Your garden gloom and gleam again,
With leaping sun, with glancing rain.
Here shall the wizard moon ascend
The heavens, in the crimson end
Of day's declining splendour; here
The army of the stars appear.

The neighbour hollows dry or wet,
Spring shall with tender flowers beset;
And oft the morning muser see
Larks rising from the broomy lea,
And every fairy wheel and thread
Of cobweb dew-bediamonded.
When daisies go, shall winter time
Silver the simple grass with rime;
Autumnal frosts enchant the pool
And make the cart-ruts beautiful;
And when snow-bright the moor expands,
How shall your children clap their hands!
To make this earth our hermitage,
A cheerful and a changeful page,
God's bright and intricate device
Of days and seasons doth suffice.

R. L. STEVENSON

TO SILENCE

Not, Silence, for thine idleness I raise
My silence-bounded singing in thy praise,
But for thy moulding of my Mozart's tune
Thy hold upon the bird that sings the moon,
        Thy magisterial ways.

Man's lovely definite melody-shapes are thine,
Outlined, controlled, compressed, complete, divine;
Also thy fine intrusions do I trace,
Thy afterthoughts, thy wandering, thy grace,
        Within the poet's line.

Thy secret is the song that is to be.
Music had never stature but for thee,
Sculptor ! strong as the sculptor Space whose hand
Urged the Discobolus and bade him stand.

.   .   .   .

Man, on his way to Silence, stops to hear and see.

ALICE MEYNELL

THE LEAST OF THESE

Lord, in thy Courts
　　Are seats so green bestow'd,
As there resorts
　　Along the dusty road
A cavalcade,—King, Bishop, Knight and Judge :
And though I toil behind and meanly trudge,
Let me, too, lie upon that pleasant sward—
　　　　For I am weary, Lord.

Christ, at Thy board
　　Are wines and dishes drest,
That do afford
　　Contentment to the best ;
And though with poverty my bed hath been
These many years, and my refreshment lean,
With plenty now at last my soul acquaint,
　　　　Dear Master, for I faint.

But through the grille,
　　" Where is thy robe ? " said He :
" Wouldst eat thy fill,
　　Yet shirk civility ? "

789

" My robe alas ! There was a little child
That shiver'd by the road——" Swiftly God smiled.
" I was that Child," said He, and raised the pin :
　　" Dear friend, enter thou in ! "

OUR HOUSE GOD'S HOME

Thy kingdom come ! Yea, bid it come !
　　But when Thy kingdom first began
On earth, Thy kingdom was a home,
　　A child, a woman, and a man.

The child was in the midst thereof,
　　O, blessed Jesus, holiest One !
The centre and the fount of love,
　　Mary and Joseph's little Son.

Wherever on the earth shall be
　　A child, a woman, and a man,
Imaging that sweet trinity
　　Wherewith Thy kingdom first began,

Establish there Thy kingdom ! Yea,
　　And o'er that trinity of love
Send down, as in Thy appointed day,
　　The brooding spirit of Thy Dove !

KATHARINE TYNAN

LUX IN TENEBRIS

At night what things will stalk abroad,
    What veilèd shapes, and eyes of dread !
With phantoms in a lonely road
    And visions of the dead.

The kindly room when day is here,
    At night takes ghostly terrors on ;
And every shadow hath its fear,
    And every wind its moan.

Lord Jesus, Day-Star of the world,
    Rise Thou, and bid this dark depart,
And all the east, a rose uncurled,
    Grow golden at the heart.

Lord, in the watches of the night,
    Keep Thou my soul ! a trembling thing
As any moth that in daylight
    Will spread a rainbow wing.

KATHARINE TYNAN

THE SEED SHOP

Here in a quiet and dusty room they lie,
Faded as crumbled stone or shifting sand,
Forlorn as ashes, shrivelled, scentless, dry—
Meadows and gardens running through my hand.

Dead that shall quicken at the trump of spring,
Sleepers to stir beneath June's morning kiss,
Though bees pass over, unremembering,
And no bird seek here bowers that were his.

In this brown husk a dale of hawthorn dreams ;
A cedar in this narrow cell is thrust
That will drink deeply of a century's streams ;
These lilies shall make summer on my dust.

Here in their safe and simple house of death,
Sealed in their shells, a million roses leap ;
Here I can blow a garden with my breath,
And in my hand a forest lies asleep.

MURIEL STUART

A CHRISTMAS CAROL

Lacking samite and sable,
Lacking silver and gold,
The Prince Jesus in the poor stable
Slept, and was three hours old.

As doves by the fair water,
Mary, not touched of sin,
Sat by Him,—the King's daughter,
All glorious within.

A lily without one stain, a
Star where no spot hath room—
Ave, gratia plena,
Virgo Virginum.

Clad not in pearl-sewn vesture,
Clad not in cramoisie,
She hath hushed, she hath cradled to rest, her
God the first time on her knee.

Where is one to adore Him?
The ox hath dumbly confessed,
With the ass, meek kneeling before Him,
" *Et homo factus est.*"

Not throned on ivory or cedar,
Not crowned with a Queen's crown,
At her breast it is Mary shall feed her
Maker, from Heaven come down.

The trees in Paradise blossom
Sudden, and its bells chime—
She giveth Him, held to her bosom,
Her immaculate milk the first time.

The night with wings of angels
Was alight, and its snow-packed ways
Sweet made (say the Evangels)
With the noise of their virelays.

Quem vidistis, pastores?
Why go ye feet unshod?
Wot ye within yon door is
Mary, the Mother of God?

No smoke of spice ascending
There—no roses are piled—
But, choicer than all balms blending,
There Mary hath kissed her Child.

MAY PROBYN

FOURTH PART

§ IV LIGHT IN DARKNESS

Holy is the true light, and passing wonderful, lending radiance to them that endured in the heat of the conflict : from Christ they inherit a home of unfading splendour wherein they rejoice with gladness evermore.

The Salisbury Antiphoner (Trans. G. H. PALMER)

He calleth to me out of Seir " Watchman, what of the night ? Watchman, what of the night ? "
The watchman said " The morning cometh, and also the night : if ye will enquire, enquire ye : return, come."

ISAIAH xxi.

There was a man of the Pharisees, named Nicodemus, a ruler of the Jews : the same came to Jesus by night.

JOHN iii.

§ IV LIGHT IN DARKNESS

THE FULNESS OF CHRIST

Christ is a path—if any be misled;
He is a robe—if any naked be;
If any chance to hunger—He is bread;
If any be a bondman—strong is He!

GILES FLETCHER

THE CITY OF GOD

Hierusalem, my happie home,
  When shall I come to thee?
When shall my sorrowes have an end,
  Thy joys when shall I see?

O happie harbour of the Saints!
  O sweete and pleasant soyle!
In thee noe sorrow may be founde
  Noe griefe, noe care, noe toyle. . .

Noe dampishe mist is seene in thee,
  Noe cold, nor darksome night;
There everie soule shines as the sunne
  There God himselfe gives light. . .

Thy terrettes and thy pinacles
  With carbuncles doe shine;
Thy verie streetes are paved with gold,
  Surpassinge cleare and fine.

Thy houses are of Ivorie,
    Thy windoes cristale cleare,
Thy tyles are mad of beaten gold—
    O God that I were there !

Within thy gates nothinge doeth come
    That is not passinge cleane,
Noe spider's web, noe durt, noe dust,
    Noe filthe may there be seene. . .

Thy saints are crownd with glorie great,
    They see God face to face,
They triumph still, they still rejoyce ;
    Most happie is their case. . .

Thy gardens and thy gallant walkes
    Continually are greene ;
There growes such sweete and pleasant flowers
    As noe where eles are seene. . .

Quyt through the streetes, with silver sound,
    The flood of life doe flowe,
Upon whose bankes on everie syde
    The wood of life doth growe. . .

Hierusalem, my happie home,
    Would God I were in thee !
Would God my woes were at an end,
    Thy joyes that I might see !

                              F. B. P. (*c.* 1600)

PEACE

My Soul, there is a countrie
  Afar beyond the stars,
Where stands a wingèd Sentrie
  All skilfull in the wars.
There, above noise and danger,
  Sweet peace sits, crowned with smiles,
And One born in a manger
  Commands the beauteous files.
He is thy gracious friend
  And (O my Soul awake!)
Did in pure love descend,
  To die here for thy sake.
If thou canst get but thither,
  There grows the flowre of peace,
The rose that cannot wither,
  Thy fortress, and thy ease.
Leave then thy foolish ranges;
  For none can thee secure,
But One, who never changes,
  Thy God, thy Life, thy Cure.

VAUGHAN

PRAISE AND PRAYER

All praise to Thee, my God, this night,
For all the blessings of the light;
Keep me, O keep me, King of kings,
Beneath Thine own Almighty wings. . .

When in the night I sleepless lie,
My soul with heavenly thoughts supply;
Let no ill dreams disturb my rest,
No powers of darkness me molest.

BISHOP KEN

THE BREASTPLATE

(from the Irish of St. Patrick)

I bind unto myself to-day
   The pow'r of God to hold, and lead,
His eye to watch, His might to stay,
   His ear to hearken to my need.
The wisdom of my God to teach,
   His hand to guide, His shield to ward;
The Word of God to give me speech,
   His heavenly host to be my guard.

CECIL FRANCES ALEXANDER

A HYMN OF TRUST

Alone with none but Thee, my God,
   I journey on my way:
What need I fear, when Thou art near,
   O King of night and day?
More safe am I within Thy hand
Than if a host did round me stand.

ST. COLUMBA (from the Latin)

LOGIA FROM EGYPT

Jesus saith :—

I stood in the midst of the world and in the flesh was I seen of them, and I found all men drunken, and none found I athirst among them, and my soul grieveth over the sons of men, because they are blind in their heart, and see not.

Wherever there are two, they are not without God, and wherever there is one alone, I say I am with him. Raise the stone and there thou shalt find me, cleave the wood and there am I.

Let not him who seeks cease until he finds, and when he finds he shall be astonished. Astonished he shall reach the Kingdom, and having reached the Kingdom he shall rest.

Strive therefore to know yourselves and ye shall be aware that ye are the sons of the Almighty Father : Ye shall know that ye are in the city of God and that ye are the city.

Everything that is not before thy face and that which is hidden from thee shall be revealed to thee. For there is nothing hidden which shall not be made manifest, nor buried which shall not be raised.

From Papyri found in Egypt (1897–1903)

FROM THE CONFESSIONS OF SAINT AUGUSTINE

1. *Mother and Son*

It came to pass that she and I stood alone, leaning in a certain window, which looked into the garden of the house where we now lay, at Ostia ; where removed from the din of men, we were recruiting from the fatigues of a long journey, for the voyage. We were discoursing then together, alone, very sweetly; and forgetting those things which are behind, and reaching forth unto those things which are before, we were enquiring between ourselves in the presence of the Truth, which Thou art, of what sort the eternal life of the saints was to be, which eye hath not seen, nor ear heard, nor hath it entered into the heart of man. . .

And when our discourse was brought to that point, that the very highest delight of the earthly senses, in the very purest material light, was, in respect of the sweetness of that life, not only not worthy of comparison, but not even of mention; we raising up ourselves with a more glowing affection towards the "Self-Same," did by degrees pass through all things bodily, even the very heaven, whence sun and moon, and stars shine upon the earth; yea, we were soaring higher yet, by inward musing, and discourse, and admiring of Thy works; and we came to our own minds, and went beyond them, that we might arrive at that region of never-failing plenty, where Thou feedest Israel for ever with the food of truth, and where life is the Wisdom by whom all these things are made, and what have been, and what shall be. . . And while we were discoursing and panting after her, we slightly touched on her with the whole effort of our heart; and we sighed, and there we leave bound the first-fruits of the Spirit, and returned to vocal expressions of our mouth, where the word spoken has beginning and end. . .

We were saying then: If to any the tumult of the flesh were hushed, hushed the images of earth, and waters, and air, hushed also the poles of heaven, yea the very soul be hushed to herself, and by not thinking on self surmount self, hushed all dreams and imaginary revelations, every

tongue and every sign, and whatsoever exists only in
transition, since if any could hear, all these say, We made
not ourselves, but He made us that abideth for ever.—If
then having uttered this, they too should be hushed
having roused only our ears to Him who made them, and
He alone speak, not by them, but by Himself, that we
may hear His Word, not through any tongue of flesh, nor
Angel's voice, nor sound of thunder, nor in the dark
riddle of a similitude, but, might hear Whom in these
things we love, might hear His Very Self . . . could this be
continued on, and other visions of kind far unlike be withdrawn, and this one ravish, and absorb, and wrap up its
beholder amid these inward joys, so that life might be for
ever like that one moment of understanding which now we
sighed after ; were not this, Enter into thy Master's joy ?

2. *Sero Te Amavi*

Too late loved I Thee, O Thou Beauty of ancient days,
yet ever new ! too late I loved Thee ! And behold, Thou
wert within, and I abroad, and there I searched for Thee ;
deformed I, plunging amid those fair forms, which Thou
hadst made. Thou wert with me, but I was not with Thee.
Things held me far from Thee, which, unless they were
in Thee, were not at all. Thou calledst, and shoutedst,
and burstedst my deafness. Thou flashedst, shonest, and
scatteredst my blindness. Thou breathedst odours, and
I drew in breath and pant for Thee. I tasted, and hunger
and thirst. Thou touchedst me, and I burned for Thy
peace.

(Trans. E. B. PUSEY)

THE TREASURE OF POVERTY

The wonderful servant and follower of Christ, to wit Saint Francis, to the end that he might in all things conform himself perfectly unto Christ, who, as the Gospel saith, sent his disciples forth by two and two unto all the cities and places where He was himself purposing to go ; seeing that after the pattern of Christ he had gathered together twelve companions, sent them forth by two and two to preach throughout the world. And to give them an ensample of true obedience, he was himself the first to go, after the pattern of Christ who began to do before he taught. Wherefore having allotted to his companions the other parts of the world, he with Brother Masseo as his companion took the road that led to the land of France. And coming one day to a town sore hungered, they went according to the rule, begging their bread for the love of God ; and Saint Francis went by one street, and Brother Masseo by another. But because Saint Francis was mean to look upon and small of stature, and was deemed thereby a vile beggar by whoso knew him not, he got by his begging naught save a few mouthfuls and scraps of dry bread : but to Brother Masseo, in that he was tall and fair of form, were given good pieces, large and in plenty, and of fresh bread. When that they had done their begging they met together to eat in a place without the city, where was a fair fountain and, hard by, a fine, broad stone ; upon the which each set the alms that he had begged. And Saint Francis, seeing that Brother Masseo's pieces of bread were more and finer and larger than his own, rejoiced with great joy, and said : " O Brother Masseo, we are not worthy of such vast treasure " : and when he repeated many times these self-same words, Brother Masseo made answer : " Father, how can one speak of treasure where is such poverty and lack of all things whereof there is need ? Here is nor cloth, nor knife, nor plate, nor porringer, nor house, nor table, nor man-servant, nor maidservant." Quoth Saint Francis : " And this it is that I account vast treasure, wherein is no thing at all prepared by human hands, but whatsoe'er we have is given by God's own providence, as manifestly doth appear in the bread that we have begged, in the table of stone so fine, and in the fount so clear ; wherefore I will that we pray unto God that He make us to love with all our heart the treasure of holy poverty which is so noble, that thereunto did God Himself become a servitor."

From *Fioretti di San Francesco*
(Trans. T. W. ARNOLD)

OF THE FOLLOWING OF CHRIST

Set not much by this—who is against thee or with thee but so do and care that God be with thee.

In every thing that thou dost have a good conscience and God shall defend thee : for him that God will help no man's overthwartness shall be able to annoy.

If thou canst be still and suffer thou shalt see without any doubt the help of our Lord ; he knoweth the time and manner of helping thee, and therefore thou oughtest to reserve thyself for him.

To God it belongeth to help and to deliver from all confusion.

If it seemeth to thee that thou knowest many things and art understanding enough, yet are there many more things that thou knowest not.

Think not highly of thyself but rather acknowledge thine
   ignorance.
Why wilt thou prefer thyself before any other, since many
   other are found better learned and more wise in the
   law of God than thou ?
If thou wilt learn and know any thing profitably love to be
   unknown and to be accounted as naught.
Thou comest to serve and not to govern : know well that
   thou art called to suffer and to labour and not to be
   idle and tell tales.
Here are men proved as gold in the furnace : here may no
   man stand unless he will humble himself with all
   his heart for God.

He hath great tranquillity of heart that setteth nothing by
   praisings or blamings.
He whose conscience is clean, he will soon be content and
   pleased.
Thou art not the holier though thou be praised nor the
   more vile though thou be blamed or dispraised.
What thou art, that thou art ; that God knoweth thee to
   be and thou canst be said to be no greater.
If thou take heed what thou art within thou shalt not
   reck what men say of thee : man looketh on the visage and God on the heart ; man considereth the deeds
   and God praiseth the thoughts.

Study to live so now that thou may in the hour of death
   rather rejoice than dread.

THOMAS À KEMPIS

(from the work commonly called *The Imitation of Christ*,
   —Everyman's Library text, based on the first English
   translation)

THE VICTORY OF PRAYER

(From a Sermon at St. Gregory's, London, 1619)

The children of God must not expect a gentle and soft entertainment in this world, but hard exigents; when to fly from their enemies they are fain to pass through fire and water. Prayer was the Apostles' refuge in the time of affliction. Bernard in a fiction doth excellently express this necessity, enforce this duty. He supposeth the kings of Babylon and Jerusalem (by whom he means the world and the Church) to be at war one against the other. During this hostility a soldier of Jerusalem was fled to the Castle of Justice. Siege was laid to this Castle, and a multitude of enemies environed and entrenched it round. There lies near this soldier a faint-hearted coward, called Fear : this speaks nothing but discomfort : and when Hope would step in to speak some courage, Fear thrust her out of doors. Whilst these two opposites Fear and Hope stand debating the Christian soldier resolves to appeal to the direction of sacred Wisdom ; who was chief Counsellor to the Captain of the Castle, Justice. Hear Wisdom speak : " Dost thou not know," saith she, " that the God whom we serve is able to deliver us ? Is he not the Lord of hosts—even the Lord mighty in battle ? We will despatch a messenger to him with information of our necessity."

Fear replies " What messenger ? Darkness is on the face of the world : our walls are begirt with an armed troop ; which are not only strong as lions, but also watchful as dragons. What messenger can either escape through such an host, or find the way into so remote a country ? " Wisdom calls for Hope, and chargeth her with all speed to dispatch away her old messenger. Hope calls to Prayer, and says " Lo here a messenger speedy, ready, trusty, knowing the way. Ready ; you can not sooner call her than she comes. Speedy; she flies faster than eagles—as fast as Angels. Trusty ; what embassage soever you put in her tongue, she delivers with faithful secrecy. She knows the way to the Court of Mercy ; and she will never faint till she come to the chamber of the royal Presence."

Prayer hath her message ; away she flies, borne on the sure and swift wings of Faith and Zeal; Wisdom having given her a charge, and Hope a blessing. Finding the gate shut, she knocks and cries " Open, ye gates of righteousness, and be ye open ye everlasting doors of glory, that I may enter, and deliver to the King of Jerusalem my petition." Jesus Christ hears her knock, opens the gate of mercy, attends her suit, promiseth her infallible comfort and redress.

Back returns Prayer, laden with the news of consolation : she hath a promise, and she delivers it into the hand of Faith : that " Were our enemies more innumerable than the locusts in Egypt, and more strong than the giants the sons of Anak : yet Power and Mercy shall fight for us and we shall be delivered."

Pass we then through fire and water, through all dangers and difficulties, yet we have a messenger, holy, happy, accessible, acceptable to God, that never comes back without comfort, Prayer. And here fitly I will end our misery, and come to God's mercy. Desolation hath held us long, but our consolation is eternal.

We went through fire, and through water ; but thou broughtest us out into a wealthy place (Ps. lxvi. 12).

The song, you see, is compounded like music : it hath high and low, sharp and flat. Thou causedst men to ride over us, but thou broughtest us out. Sorrow and joy, trouble and peace, sour and sweet, come by vicissitudes. This discord in our music hurts not, but graceth the song. Whiles grief and pleasure keep this alternation in our life, they at once both exercise our patience, and make more welcome our joys. If you look for the happiness of the wicked, you shall find it *in primis*, at the beginning : but if you would learn what becomes of the righteous, you shall know it at the last. Mark the upright man, and behold the just : for the end of that man is peace.

THOMAS ADAMS

THE LIGHT OF THE WORLD

(*From a Sermon at St. Paul's*, 1624)

He brought light out of darkness, not out of a lesser light ; he can bring thy summer out of winter, though thou have no spring ; though in the ways of fortune, or understanding, or conscience, thou have been benighted till now, wintered and frozen, clouded and eclipsed, damped and benumbed, smothered and stupefied till now, now God comes to thee, not as in the dawning of the day, not as in the bud of the spring, but as the sun at noon.

JOHN DONNE

FROM THE BIBLE

Proverbs of Solomon, the son of David

Wisdom crieth without :
She uttereth her voice in the streets.

How long wilt thou sleep, O sluggard ?
When wilt thou rise out of thy sleep ?
Yet a little sleep, a little slumber,
A little folding of the hands to sleep :
So shall thy poverty come as one that travelleth,
And thy want as an armed man.

Wisdom is better than rubies.

He becometh poor that dealeth with a slack hand.

Wealth gotten by vanity shall be diminished ;
But he that gathereth by labour shall increase.

Better is a dinner of herbs where love is
Than a stalled ox and hatred therewith.

Better is a dry morsel and quietness therewith
Than an house full of sacrifices with strife.

The fining pot is for silver and the furnace for gold
But the Lord trieth the hearts.

A friend loveth at all times.

A merry heart doeth good like a medicine.

Even a fool when he holdeth his peace is counted wise.

A brother offended is harder to be won than a strong city.

Death and life are in the power of the tongue.

A man that hath friends must show himself friendly.

It is an honour for a man to cease from strife :
But every fool will be meddling.

Even a child is known by his doings.

Love not sleep lest thou come to poverty.

It is naught, it is naught, saith the buyer :
But when he is gone his way then he boasteth.

It is better to dwell in a corner of the housetop
Than with a brawling woman in a wide house.

It is better to dwell in the wilderness
Than with a contentious and an angry woman.

Remove not the old landmark :
And enter not into the fields of the fatherless.

A wise man is strong :
Yea, a man of knowledge increaseth strength.

The slothful man saith there is a lion in the way :
A lion is in the streets.

Where no wood is, there the fire goeth out :
So where there is no tale-bearer the strife ceaseth.

As in water face answereth to face :
So the heart of man to man.

The wicked flee when no man pursueth.

There be three things which are too wonderful for me,
Yea, four which I know not :
The way of an eagle in the air :
The way of a serpent upon a rock :
The way of a ship in the midst of the sea :
And the way of a man with a maid.

The Virtuous Woman

She openeth her mouth with wisdom ;
And in her tongue is the law of kindness.
She looketh well to the ways of her household,
And eateth not the bread of idleness.
Her children arise up, and call her blessed ;
Her husband also, and he praiseth her . . .
Favour is deceitful, and beauty is vain :
But a woman that feareth the Lord,
She shall be praised.
Her price is far above rubies.

Proverbs (A.V.)

Love

Set me as a seal upon thy heart, as a seal upon thine
arm : for love is strong as death. . . Many waters cannot

quench love, neither can the floods drown it : if a man would give all the substance of his house for love, it would utterly be contemned.

Song of Solomon (A.V.)

The Offering

He hath shewed thee, O man, what is good ;
And what doth the Lord require of thee,
But to do justly, and to love mercy,
And to walk humbly with thy God ?

Micah (A.V.)

Unknown Warriors

Some there be, which have no memorial ;
Who are perished, as though they had never been ;
And are become as though they had never been born ;
And their children after them.
But these were merciful men, whose righteousness hath
    not been forgotten. . .
Their bodies are buried in peace ; but their name liveth
    for evermore.

Ecclesiasticus

Alpha and Omega

He said unto me :
In the beginning, when the earth was made,

Before the borders of the world stood,
Or ever the winds blew,
Before it thundered and lightened,
Or ever the foundations of paradise were laid,
Before the fair flowers were seen,
Or ever the moveable powers were established,
Before the innumerable multitude of angels were gathered
    together,
Or ever the heights of the air were lifted up,
Before the measures of the firmament were named,
Or ever the chimneys in Sion were hot,
And ere the present years were sought out,
And or ever the inventions of them that now sin were
    turned,
Before they were sealed that have gathered faith for a
    treasure :
Then did I consider these things,
And they all were made through me alone,
And through none other :
By me also they shall be ended,
And by none other.   *2 Esdras*

Sacred Songs

The Lord is my Shepherd ; therefore can I lack nothing.
He shall feed me in a green pasture,
And lead me forth beside the waters of comfort.
He shall convert my soul
And bring me forth in the paths of righteousness, for his
    Name's sake.
Yea, though I walk through the valley of the shadow of
    death,

I will fear no evil ; for thou art with me:
Thy rod and thy staff comfort me.
Thou shalt prepare a table before me against them that
trouble me.
Thou hast anointed my head with oil, and my cup shall be
full.
But thy loving-kindness and mercy shall follow me all the
days of my life,
And I will dwell in the house of the Lord for ever.

    .   .   .   .

He shall cover thee with his feathers, and under his
wings shalt thou trust.
His truth shall be thy shield and buckler.
Thou shalt not be afraid for the terror by night,
Nor for the arrow that flieth by day,
Nor for the pestilence that walketh in darkness,
Nor for the destruction that wasteth at noonday.

    .   .   .   .

He sendeth the springs into the rivers
Which run among the hills.
All beasts of the field drink thereof
And the wild asses quench their thirst.
Beside them shall the fowls of the air have their habita-
tion
And sing among the branches.
He watereth the hills from above—
The earth is filled with the fruit of thy works.
He bringeth forth grass for the cattle
And green herb for the service of men ;
That he may bring food out of the earth and wine that
maketh glad the heart of man

And oil to make him a cheerful countenance and bread
    to strengthen man's heart.
The trees of the Lord also are full of sap—
Even the cedars of Libanus which he hath planted
Wherein the birds make their nests
And the fir-trees are a dwelling for the stork.
The high hills are a refuge for the wild goats,
And so are the stony rocks for the conies.
He appointed the moon for certain seasons,
And the sun knoweth his going down.
Thou makest darkness that it may be night
Wherein all the beasts of the forest do move.
The lions roaring after their prey
Do seek their meat from God.
The sun ariseth, and they get them away together
And lay them down in their dens.
Man goeth forth to his work, and to his labour
Until the evening.
O Lord, how manifold are thy works !
In wisdom hast thou made them all—
The earth is full of thy riches.

.   .   .   .

O Lord, thou hast searched me out and known me ;
Thou knowest my down-sitting and mine up-rising ;
Thou understandest my thoughts long before.
Thou art about my path and about my bed,
And spiest out all my ways.
For lo, there is not a word in my tongue
But thou, O Lord, knowest it altogether.
Thou hast fashioned me behind and before
And laid thine hand upon me.
Such knowledge is too wonderful and excellent for me :
I cannot attain unto it.

Whither shall I go then from thy Spirit
Or whither shall I go then from thy presence?
If I climb up to heaven, thou art there:
If I go down to hell, thou art there also.
If I take the wings of the morning
And remain in the uttermost parts of the sea,
Even there also shall thy hand lead me
And thy right hand shall hold me.
If I say, Peradventure the darkness shall cover me,
Then shall my night be turned to day.
Yea, the darkness is no darkness with thee, but the night
   is as clear as the day.
The darkness and light to thee are both alike.

BE STILL, THEN, AND KNOW THAT I AM GOD.
   Psalms (Version of TYNDALE and COVERDALE)

The Preacher exhorteth the Young Man

In the morning sow thy seed, and in the evening
withhold not thine hand: for thou knowest not whether
shall prosper this or that, or whether they both shall be
alike good.

Truly the light is sweet, and a pleasant thing it is for the
eyes to behold the sun. But, if a man live many years and
rejoice in them all, yet let him remember the days of
darkness, for they shall be many. All that cometh is
vanity.

Rejoice, O young man, in thy youth, and let thy heart
cheer thee in the days of thy youth, and walk in the ways of
thine heart and in the sight of thine eyes; but know thou
that for all these things God will bring thee into judgment.

Ecclesiastes (A.V.)

The Prophecy

Be strong, fear not ! . .
He will come and save you.
Then the eyes of the blind shall be opened,
And the ears of the deaf shall be unstopped.
Then shall the lame man leap as an hart,
And the tongue of the dumb sing :
For in the wilderness shall waters break out,
And streams in the desert ;
And the parched ground shall become a pool,
And the thirsty land springs of water :
In the habitation of dragons where each lay
Shall be grass with reeds and rushes.
And an highway shall be there and a way,
And it shall be called The Way of Holiness.

Behold a man shall be as an hiding place from the
wind, and a covert from the tempest, as rivers of water in
a dry place, as the shadow of a great rock in a weary land.

Thine eyes shall see the King in his beauty : they shall
behold the land that is very far off . . . Thine eyes shall see
Jerusalem a quiet habitation, a tabernacle that shall not be
taken down ; not one of the stakes thereof shall ever be
removed, neither shall any of the cords thereof be broken
. . . For the Lord is our judge, the Lord is our law-giver,
the Lord is our King : he will save us.

Thus saith the Lord : In an acceptable time have I
heard thee, and in a day of salvation have I helped thee
. . . that thou mayest say to the prisoners " Go forth," to
them that are in darkness " Shew yourselves." They shall
feed in the ways, and their pasture shall be in all high

places. They shall not hunger nor thirst; neither shall the heat nor sun smite them : for he that hath mercy on them shall lead them, even by the springs of water shall he guide them.

How beautiful upon the mountains are the feet of him that bringeth good tidings of good, that publisheth salvation, that saith unto Zion " Thy God reigneth ! " . . . Break forth into joy, sing together ye waste places of Jerusalem : for the Lord hath comforted his people, he hath redeemed Jerusalem.

Surely he hath borne our griefs, and carried our
    sorrows : . .
Yet we did esteem him stricken, smitten of God and
    afflicted ;
But he was wounded for our transgressions. . . .
He was bruised for our iniquities :
The chastisement of our peace was upon him,
And with his stripes we are healed.
All we like sheep have gone astray :
We have turned every one to his own way ;
And the Lord hath laid on him the iniquity of us all.
He was oppressed and he was afflicted,
Yet he opened not his mouth :
He is brought as a lamb to the slaughter,
And as a sheep before his shearers is dumb
So he openeth not his mouth.
He was taken from prison and from judgment ;
And who shall declare his generation ?
For he was cut off out of the land of the living ;
For the transgression of my people was he stricken.

Behold, the darkness shall cover the earth, and gross

darkness the people : but the Lord shall arise upon thee, and his glory shall be seen upon thee. And the Gentiles shall come to thy light, and kings to the brightness of thy rising. Lift up thine eyes round about, and see : all they gather themselves together, they come to thee : thy sons shall come from far, and thy daughters shall be nursed at thy side. Then shalt thou see, and flow together, and thine heart shall fear, and be enlarged ; because the abundance of the sea shall be converted unto thee, the forces of the Gentiles shall come unto thee. The multitude of camels shall cover thee, the dromedaries of Midian and Ephah : all they from Sheba shall come : they shall bring gold and incense : and they shall shew forth the praises of the Lord. All the flocks of Kedar shall be gathered together unto thee, the rams of Nebaioth shall minister unto thee : they shall come up with acceptance on mine altar, and I will glorify the house of my glory— Who are these that fly as a cloud, and as the doves to their windows? Surely the isles shall wait for me, and the ships of Tarshish first, to bring thy sons from far, their silver and their gold with them, unto the name of the Lord thy God, and to the Holy One of Israel, because he hath glorified thee.

Isaiah (A.V.)

Et incarnatus est

There went out a decree from Cæsar Augustus that all the world should be enrolled. And all went to enrol themselves, every one to his own city. And Joseph also went up from Galilee, out of the city of Nazareth, into Judæa, to the city of David, which is called Bethlehem, because he was of the house and family of David, to enrol himself with

Mary, who was betrothed to him, being great with child. And it came to pass while they were there, the days were fulfilled that she should be delivered. And she brought forth her first-born son ; and she wrapped him in swaddling clothes, and laid him in a manger, because there was no room for them in the inn.

Luke (R.V.)

Sayings of Jesus

If ye forgive men their trespasses, your heavenly Father will also forgive you : but if ye forgive not men their trespasses neither will your Father forgive your trespasses. . . . No man can serve two masters : for either he will hate the one, and love the other ; or else he will hold to the one, and despise the other. Ye cannot serve God and mammon. Therefore I say unto you, Take no thought for your life, what ye shall eat, or what ye shall drink ; nor yet for your body, what ye shall put on. Is not the life more than meat, and the body than raiment ? Behold the fowls of the air : for they sow not, neither do they reap, nor gather into barns ; yet your heavenly Father feedeth them. Are ye not much better than they ? Which of you by taking thought can add one cubit unto his stature ? And why take ye thought for raiment ? Consider the lilies of the field, how they grow ; they toil not, neither do they spin : and yet I say unto you, that even Solomon in all his glory was not arrayed like one of these. Wherefore, if God so clothe the grass of the field, which to-day is, and to-morrow is cast into the oven, shall he not much more clothe you, O ye of little faith ? Therefore

take no thought, saying, What shall we eat? or, What shall
we drink? or, Wherewithal shall we be clothed? (For after
all these things do the Gentiles seek :) for your heavenly
Father knoweth that ye have need of all these things.
But seek ye first the kingdom of God and his righteousness ; and all these things shall be added unto you. . .

Come unto me, all ye that labour and are heavy laden,
and I will give you rest. Take my yoke upon you, and
learn of me ; for I am meek and lowly in heart : and ye
shall find rest unto your souls. For my yoke is easy, and
my burden is light.

Matthew (A.V.)

I AM THE LIGHT OF THE WORLD : HE THAT FOLLOWETH
ME SHALL NOT WALK IN DARKNESS, BUT SHALL HAVE THE
LIGHT OF LIFE.

John (A.V.)

I am the true vine, and my Father is the husbandman.
Every branch in me that beareth not fruit, he taketh it
away : and every branch that beareth fruit, he cleanseth
it, that it may bear more fruit. Already ye are clean because of the word which I have spoken unto you. Abide in
me, and I in you. As the branch cannot bear fruit of itself,
except it abide in the vine ; so neither can ye, except ye
abide in me. I am the vine, ye are the branches. He that
abideth in me, and I in him, the same beareth much fruit :
for apart from me ye can do nothing. If a man abide not
in me, he is cast forth as a branch, and is withered ; and
they gather them, and cast them into the fire, and they are
burned. If ye abide in me, and my words abide in you, ask

whatsoever ye will, and it shall be done unto you. Herein is my Father glorified, that ye bear much fruit ; and so shall ye be my disciples. Even as the Father hath loved me I also have loved you : abide ye in my love. If ye keep my commandments, ye shall abide in my love ; even as I have kept my Father's commandments, and abide in his love. These things have I spoken unto you, that my joy may be in you, and that your joy may be fulfilled. This is my commandment, that ye love one another, even as I have loved you. Greater love hath no man than this, that a man lay down his life for his friends. . .

Peace I leave with you ; my peace I give unto you : not as the world giveth, give I unto you. Let not your heart be troubled, neither let it be fearful.

John (R.V.)

The Vision

And I saw a new heaven and a new earth : for the first heaven and the first earth were passed away ; and there was no more sea.   And I John saw the holy city, new Jerusalem, coming down from God out of heaven, prepared as a bride adorned for her husband. And I heard a great voice out of heaven saying:

> *Behold, the tabernacle of God is with men,*
> *And he will dwell with them,*
> *And they shall be his people . .*

And he that sat upon the throne said, Behold, I make all things new. And he said unto me, Write : for these words are true and faithful. And he said unto me, It is done.

I am Alpha and Omega, the beginning and the end. I will give unto him that is athirst of the fountain of the water of life freely. He that overcometh shall inherit all things ; and I will be his God, and he shall be my son. . .

And there came unto me one of the seven angels, and he carried me away in the spirit to a great and high mountain, and shewed me that great city, the holy Jerusalem, descending out of heaven from God, having the glory of God ; and her light was like unto a stone most precious, even like a jasper stone, clear as crystal. . .

And he shewed me a pure river of water of life, clear as crystal, proceeding out of the throne of God and of the Lamb. In the midst of the street of it, and on either side of the river, was there the tree of life, which bare twelve manner of fruits, and yielded her fruit every month : and the leaves of the tree were for the healing of the nations.

Revelation (A.V.)

A PRAYER OF SAINT DUNSTAN

Kyrie Rex Splendens

O Lord, O King, resplendent on the citadel of heaven, all hail continually ; and of Thy clemency upon Thy people still do Thou have mercy.

Lord, Whom the hosts of cherubim in songs and hymns with praise continually proclaim, do Thou upon us eternally have mercy.

O Christ, enthroned as King above, Whom the nine orders of angels in their beauty praise without ceasing, deign Thou upon us, Thy servants, ever to have mercy.

O Christ, Whom Thy Church throughout the world doth hymn, O Thou to Whom the sun, and moon, and stars, the land and sea, do service ever, do Thou have mercy.

ST. DUNSTAN, Archbishop of Canterbury, 961–988
(Trans. C. WORDSWORTH)

SOME EVENING PRAYERS

I WILL LAY ME DOWN IN PEACE AND TAKE MY REST, FOR IT IS THOU, LORD, ONLY THAT MAKEST ME DWELL IN SAFETY.

Ps. iv. 8.

A Prayer of St. Augustine

WATCH Thou, dear Lord, with those who wake, or watch, or weep to-night, and give Thine angels charge over those who sleep. Tend Thy sick ones, O Lord Christ. Rest Thy weary ones. Bless Thy dying ones. Sooth Thy suffering ones. Pity Thine afflicted ones. Shield Thy joyous ones. And all, for Thy Love's sake. Amen.

For Love and Light

O LORD, give us, we beseech Thee, in the Name of Jesus Christ Thy Son our God, that love which can never cease, that will kindle our lamps but not extinguish them, that they may burn in us and enlighten others. Do Thou, O Christ, our dearest Saviour, Thyself kindle our lamps, that they may evermore shine in Thy temple, that they may receive unquenchable light from Thee that will enlighten our darkness, and lessen the darkness of the world. Lord Jesus, we pray Thee give Thy light to our lamps, that in its light the most holy place may be revealed to us in which Thou dwellest as the Eternal Priest, that we may always behold Thee, desire Thee, look upon Thee in love, and long after Thee, for Thy sake. Amen.

ST. COLUMBA

For Rest

BE PRESENT, O merciful God, and protect us through the silent hours of this night, so that we who are wearied by the work and the changes of this fleeting world may rest upon Thy eternal changelessness; through Jesus Christ our Lord. Amen.

6th Century Collect

Thanksgiving for Repose

O GOD, Who, by making the evening to succeed the day, hast bestowed the gift of repose on human weakness, grant, we beseech Thee, that while we enjoy Thy blessings we may acknowledge Him from Whom they come, even Jesus Christ our Lord. Amen.

Mozarabic Liturgy (7th Century)

A Prayer of St. Richard, Bishop of Chichester (1244)

O MOST merciful Redeemer, Friend and Brother, may we know Thee more clearly, love Thee more dearly, and follow Thee more nearly; for Thine own sake. Amen.

For a Quiet Night

O LORD, the Maker of all things, we pray Thee now in this evening hour, to defend us through Thy mercy from all deceit of our enemy. Let us not be deluded with dreams, but if we lie awake keep Thou our hearts. Grant this petition, O Father, to Whom with the Holy Ghost always in heaven and earth, be all laud, praise, and honour. Amen.

KING HENRY VIII

Thanksgiving and Prayer for Protection

O LORD, our heavenly Father, by Whose Divine ordinance the darkness covers the earth and brings unto us bodily rest and quietness, we render Thee our hearty thanks for the loving-kindness which Thou hast shown, in preserving us during the past day, and in giving us all things necessary for our health and comfort. And we beseech Thee, for Jesus Christ's sake, to forgive us all the sins we have committed in thought, word, or deed, and that Thou wilt shadow us this night under the wings of Thy almighty power, and defend us from all power of the evil one. May our souls, whether sleeping or waking, wait upon Thee, delight in Thee, and evermore praise Thee, so that when the light of day returns, we may rise with pure and thankful hearts, casting away the works of darkness and putting on the armour of light ; through Jesus Christ. Amen.

R. T. BECON (16th Century)

An Evening Commendation

INTO Thy Hands, O Lord, we commit ourselves, our spirits, soul and body. Thou hast created and Thou hast redeemed them, O Lord God of truth. And with us, we commend all our friends, and all our possessions. Thou, O Lord, hast graciously given them unto Thy servants. Preserve our down-sitting and our uprising from this time forth and even for evermore. That we may remember Thee upon our bed and diligently search out our spirit, and when we awake, be still with Thee. We will both lay us down in peace and sleep, for Thou, Lord, only makest us dwell in safety. Hear us and answer us, we humbly beseech Thee ; for the sake of Christ Jesus our Lord. Amen.

BISHOP ANDREWES (1555-1626)

For Proper Sleep

FORASMUCH as it hath pleased Thee to make the night for man to rest in, as Thou hast ordained him the day to travail, grant, O dear Father, that we may so take our bodily rest, that our souls may continually watch for the time that our Lord Jesus Christ shall appear for our deliverance out of this mortal life, and in the mean season that we (not overcomen by any fantasies, dreams, or other temptations) may fully set our minds upon Thee, love Thee, fear Thee, and rest in Thee : furthermore, that our sleep be not excessive or overmuch after the insatiable desires of our flesh, but only sufficient to content our weak nature, that we may be better disposed to live in all godly conversation, to the glory of Thy holy name, and profit of our brethren. So be it !

From a book of Metrical Psalms
published at Geneva, 1556

Thanksgiving

THOU hast given so much to us, give one thing more, a grateful heart; for Christ's sake. Amen.

GEORGE HERBERT (1593–1633)

For Rest and Confidence in God

COMPOSE, O God, our faculties and thoughts that we may be enabled worthily to thank Thee through Jesus Christ Thy Son for all the good with which Thou hast blessed us graciously to-day. This evening we commend our whole welfare and life and all other things to Thy guidance and keeping. Yea, we take refuge from all our enemies in the kindness of Thy Fatherly love and in Thee only do we seek our rest, inasmuch as without Thee is no peace or calm in heaven or earth. Let us be Thine whether we wake or sleep, and work Thou Thyself in us whatever is well pleasing in Thy sight; through Jesus Christ and in the power of His Spirit. Amen.

Weimarisches Gesangbuch, 1873

For all we Love

O GOD, our heavenly Father, we would commit to Thy Fatherly care all whom we love, especially those who are far away. O Lord, remember them for good, be Thou with each one of them, keep them outwardly from all harm, and above all bless and strengthen them in their souls. Pour out Thy Holy Spirit upon them to guide them into all truth. Grant unto each one of us that we may be standing with our loins girded and our lamps burning, waiting for the coming of our Lord. And we also bless Thy holy Name for all Thy Servants departed this life in Thy faith and fear, beseeching Thee to give us grace so to follow their good examples, that with them we may be partakers of Thy heavenly kingdom ; grant this, O Father, for Jesus Christ's sake. Amen.

A. WRIGHT and E. S. OSMASTON
(Prayer Union, 1889)

For Travellers

O GOD, Who didst call Abraham to leave his home, and didst protect him in all his wanderings, grant to those who now travel by land, sea, or air, a prosperous journey, a quiet time, and a safe arrival at their journey's end. Be to them a shadow in the heat, a refuge in the tempest, a protection in adversity, and grant that when life's pilgrimage is over, they may arrive at the heavenly country ; through Jesus Christ our Lord. Amen.

Priest's Prayer Book, 1870

For support here and peace hereafter

MAY He support us all the day long, till the shades lengthen, and the evening comes, and the busy world is hushed, and the fever of life is over, and our work is done ! Then in His mercy may He give us a safe lodging, and a holy rest, and peace at the last. Amen.

CARDINAL NEWMAN (from a Sermon on
Wisdom and Innocence, 1843)

A CHILD'S CAROL

Sweet Jesu, human and divine,
O grant this loving wish of mine ;
Come Thou to wash my heart from shame
And write therein Thy sweetest name :
On all I am or hope to be
Write with the blood once shed for me.

Sweet Jesu, in a stable born,
O come and wake me every morn ;
Come Thou with me along the way,
In all my work and all my play.
Through day and night my comrade be,
That I may wake and sleep with Thee.

ARTHUR L. SALMON
(*Based on an Old Flemish Carol*)

CONCLUSION

Except the Lord keep the city,
The watchman waketh but in vain.
It is but lost labour that ye haste to rise up early, and so
late take rest,
And eat the bread of carefulness :
For so he giveth his beloved sleep.

Psalm cxxvii. (Version of Tyndale and Coverdale)

When thou liest down, thou shalt not be afraid :
Yea, thou shalt lie down, and thy sleep shall be sweet.

Proverbs (A.V.)

NOCTEM QUIETAM
ET
FINEM PERFECTUM
CONCEDAT NOBIS DOMINUS
OMNIPOTENS

THANKS AND ACKNOWLEDGMENT

THANKS

I gratefully acknowledge the debt I owe to the authors or owners of copyright matter included in this book, and heartily thank all who have helped me in various ways. Special thanks are due to Sir Arthur Quiller-Couch for his thoughtful consideration of my scheme and for many valuable suggestions. I am also much indebted to Mr. J. C. Squire for his kindly encouragement. The late Dr. Paget Toynbee revised my text of the letters from Thomas Gray—one of the last acts of a life of many kindnesses. I have received permissions from nearly every publisher in London, and in many cases the publisher's co-operation has extended far beyond the mere giving of consent. The characteristic generosity of English scholars has enabled me to provide a selection of brilliant translations from the literature of the ancient world. All copyright items are included in my acknowledgment, but I would here add a special word of thanks to the Editors of the Loeb Classical Library for placing at my disposal that monument of modern scholarship.

July, 1932.   A. S.

ACKNOWLEDGMENT

I am indebted to the following persons for permission to use the items here enumerated :—

To Miss Eleanor Alexander and Hodder & Stoughton Ltd. for " Epitaph in Derry Cathedral " by Archbishop Alexander and an extract from " St. Patrick's Breastplate " by Cecil Francis Alexander ; George Allen & Unwin Ltd. for William Cory's translation from Callimachus, Ep. II (*Ionica*) ; Mr. G. C. Allingham for " Four Ducks on a Pond " by William Allingham ; Angus & Robertson and The Bulletin Newspaper Co., Sydney, for " The Bush, my Lover " by William Ogilvie ; Mr. Martin Armstrong and Martin Secker Ltd. for " In Lamplight " ; and Association for Promoting Christian Knowledge, Dublin, for the extract from St. Columba's Hymn (*Irish Hymnal*) ;

Mr. Thomas Baker for the letter from St. Teresa (*Letters of St. Teresa* translated by Benedictines of Stanbrook) ; G. Bell & Sons Ltd. for " Morning " by C. S. Calverley (*Verses and Fly Leaves*) and the lines from his translation from Virgil—Eclogue I, two extracts from J. S. Watson's translation of *Lucretius*, an extract from Swift's *Journal to Stella* (*Prose Works*, edited by J. Scott, Vol. II), and two extracts from the *Letters of Cicero* (trans. E. S. Shuckburgh) ; Mr. Hilaire Belloc for " A Railway Sleeper " and " A Roman Pilgrimage " (*The Path to Rome*) ; Ernest Benn Ltd. for " Nanny " by A. P. Herbert ; Mr. Edmund Blunden and R. Cobden-Sanderson Ltd. for " Forefathers " ; Bradbury Agnew & Co., Ltd. for ten extracts from *Punch*, 1914–1918 (reprinted by permission of Proprietors of *Punch*) ; Mr. Ernest Bramah for " Chat with a Brigand " (*The Wallet* of *Kai Lung*) ; Sir E. A. Wallis Budge for an extract from his translation of the *Book of the Dead*; Mr. Thomas Burke and Constable & Co. for "The English Inn" (*The Book of the Inn*) ; Mr. Thomas Burke and Longmans Green & Co. Ltd. for "The Inn of the Future" (*The English Inn*) ; and Burns, Oates & Washbourne Ltd. for "Our House God's Home" and "Lux in Tenebris" by Katharine Tynan and "A Child's Prayer" by Father Tabb ;

Jonathan Cape Ltd. for an extract from the *Travels of Marco Polo* (Travellers' Library), extracts from Charles Doughty's travels in *Arabia Deserta* and "The Great Bear" (*Note-Books of Samuel Butler*); Chatto & Windus Ltd. for "Disturbances at Heilbronn" by Mark Twain, an extract from *El Dorado*, "A Memory of Cummy," "Sayings of R. L. S.," and "The House Beautiful" by R. L. Stevenson; Mr. Padraic Colum, Macmillan & Co. Ltd. and the Macmillan Co., New York, for "The Bat" (*Old Pastures*) and "The Poor Girl's Meditation" (*Dramatic Legends*) ; The Controller of His Majesty's Stationery Office for a letter from the *Calendar of State Papers*; Mrs. Frances Cornford and The Poetry Bookshop for "The Country Bedroom" ; Messrs. Francis Coutts and W. H. Pollock and John Lane The Bodley Head Ltd. for the translation from Horace, Ode I. 9 (*Icarian Flights*) ; Mr. R. G. T. Coventry and "Country Life" Ltd. for "Solitude" ; Mr. Edwin M. Cox for his translation of a fragment by Sappho (*The Poems of Sappho*); and Mrs. Creighton for a saying by Bishop Creighton ;

Mr. W. H. Davies and Jonathan Cape Ltd. for "Love's Caution" and "The Moon" ; Mr. Walter de la Mare for "Nod," "Farewell," and "A Little Sound" ; J. M. Dent & Sons Ltd. for extracts from the Temple Classics texts of Marcus Aurelius' *Golden Book* and the *Fioretti di san Francesco*, Julia Cartwright's translation of the letter from Beatrice D'Este, " The Death of a Bird " by W. H. Hudson and extracts from the " Everyman " text of Thomas à Kempis ; P. J. & A. E. Dobell for " The Vine " by James Thomson ; Dodd Mead & Co., New York, for " In the Heart of the Hills " and " Song " by Bliss Carman (copyright by Dodd Mead & Co., Incorporated) ; Doubleday Doran and Hodder & Stoughton Ltd. for " Makes the Whole World Kin " by O. Henry ; Lord Alfred Douglas and Martin Secker Ltd. for " False Sleep " ; Mrs. Dowden for " A Day's Coaching " by Professor Dowden ; Mr. John Drinkwater and Sidgwick & Jackson Ltd. for " The Midlands " and " Moonlit Apples " (*Collected Poems of John Drinkwater*); and Gerald Duckworth & Co. Ltd. for an extract from *The Sea and the Jungle* by Mr. H. M. Tomlinson, extracts from *Note-Books of Leonardo da Vinci* (trans. E. McCurdy), and an extract from *Bevis* by Richard Jefferies ;

The Editors of the Loeb Classical Library (published by William Heinemann Ltd.) for an extract from Plato's *Phaedrus* (trans. H. N. Fowler), an extract from Philostratus' *Life of Apollonius* (trans. F. C. Conybeare), an extract from *Daphnis and Chloe* of Longus (trans. George Thornley, revised by J. M. Edmunds), " Sulpicia's Birthday " (Catullus—trans. J. P. Postgate), a letter of the Emperor Julian (trans. W. C. Wright), and an extract from a letter of Pliny the Younger (trans. W. Melmoth and W. M. L. Hutchinson) ; The Egyptian Exploration Society for five letters from the *Oxyrhynchus Papyri* translated by Messrs. Grenfell and Hunt and five " Logia " (*Papyri found in Egypt* 1897–1903) ; Messrs. Ellis for " Love Sight," " Sleepless Dreams," and " The Blessed Damozel " by

D. G. Rossetti; the Executors of T. E. Brown and Macmillan & Co. Ltd. for "Vespers," "An Oxford Idyll," and " Dreams " (*Collected Poems of T. E. Brown*); the Executors of J. E. Flecker and Martin Secker Ltd. for the Prologue from *The Golden Journey to Samarkand*; the Executors of John Freeman and Macmillan & Co. Ltd. for " Old Fires " (*Collected Poems of John Freeman*); the Executors of W. E. Henley and Macmillan & Co. Ltd. for " The Late Lark " and " Song " by W. E. Henley; and the Executors of " Saki " (H. H. Munro) and John Lane The Bodley Head Ltd. for " The Matchmaker ";

Miss Eleanor Farjeon for " The Night will never stay "; the Rev. E. H. Fellowes and The Clarendon Press for the text of several old English songs (*English Madrigal Verse*); Mr. Robert Frost and Henry Holt & Co., Incorporated, New York, for " Acquainted with the Night " (*West Running Brook*); Principal Fyfe for " A Prayer to the Boy-God "; and Miss Rose Fyleman for " Temper " reprinted from *Punch* by permission of the Proprietors and from *The Faery Flute* (Methuen) by permission of the author;

Captain Harry Graham and Methuen & Co. Ltd. for " Grandpapa ";

Miss Irene Haugh for " The Valley of the Bells "; Wm. Heinemann Ltd. for " A Child's Laughter " by A. C. Swinburne; Hodder & Stoughton Ltd. for " One World " by H. Van Dyke and The Houghton Mifflin Co., Boston, for " Madonna of the Evening Flowers " by Amy Lowell, the extract from Lafcadio Hearn's translation of " The River of Heaven," " Amor omnia vincit " by James Russell Lowell and two distichs by John Hay (all by permission of and arrangement with Houghton Mifflin Co.); and Mr. Laurence Housman for " Johnnie Kigarrow ";

Ingpen & Grant Ltd. for "Lights Out" by Edward Thomas;

Jackson Wylie & Co. for use of the text of Hakluyt's *Principal Navigations, &c.* published by Maclehose, Jackson & Co., and "In a Meadow" by J. S. Phillimore; Mr. W. W. Jacobs and Methuen & Co. Ltd. for extracts from "A Black Affair" (*Many Cargoes*); and Sir James Jeans and the Cambridge University Press for "How the Earth was made" (*The Mysterious Universe*);

Mr. William Kerr for "Counting Sheep"; Mr. Rudyard Kipling and Macmillan & Co. Ltd. for "The Way through the Woods" (*Rewards and Fairies*);

John Lane The Bodley Head Ltd. for "Summer Sorrows" by Mr. Stephen Leacock (*Winnowed Wisdom*); Sir Harry Lauder for an extract from one of his songs; Miss W. M. Letts for "Wishes for William"; Mr. Sinclair Lewis and Jonathan Cape Ltd. for "An Atlantic Liner" (*Dodsworth*); the Literary Executor of Katherine Mansfield for the sonnet "To L. H. B."; the Literary Executors of Thomas Hardy for "Twilight on Egdon Heath" (*The Return of the Native*); the Literary Executor of Joseph Conrad for the extracts from *Youth* and *Heart of Darkness*; Longmans Green & Co. Ltd. for "Two Dreams" by Andrew Lang (*A Book of Dreams and Ghosts*), "The Spinning Woman" translated from Leonidas by Andrew Lang (*Poetical Works*), the extract from "The Story of my Heart" by Richard Jefferies; the extracts from D. W. Freshfield's *Italian Alps*, "Voices of the Night" by Mr. Eric Parker (*English Wild Life*), the prayer from the *Priest's Prayer-Book* (1870), and "Sport at the Races" by E. Œ. Somerville and Martin Ross (*The Irish R.M.*); and Mr. E. V. Lucas and Methuen & Co. Ltd. for "The Oldest Joke" (*A Boswell of Baghdad*);

839

Mr. J. W. Mackail and Longmans Green & Co. Ltd. for ten epitaphs and epigrams translated by him from the *Greek Anthology* and the extract from the Introduction to his *Selections from the Greek Anthology*; Macmillan & Co. Ltd. for " Priam goes to Achilles " (Homer's *Iliad*—trans. Lang, Leaf and Myers), " Ulysses and Nausicaa " (Homer's *Odyssey*—trans. Butcher and Lang), " The Country Life " (Virgil's *Georgics*—trans. Lonsdale and Lee), " Rest out of Doors " (Theocritus—trans. Walter Pater, from *Greek Studies*), " The Marriage of Pscyhe " by Walter Pater (*Marius the Epicurean*), " Discount for Cash " (*Autobiography of Benvenuto Cellini*—trans. J. A. Symonds), " Lullaby " by Christina Rossetti (*Sing Song*), an extract from Tennyson's *De Profundis* and the extracts from the *Journals* of Dorothy and Mary Wordsworth; the Rev. G. Currie Martin and Mr. Harold A. Barnes for the translation entitled " A Song from Palestine "; Mr. John Masefield for " Tewkesbury Road " (*Salt Water Ballads*, E. Mathews, 1913); Elkin Mathews & Marrot Ltd. for " The Fair Chivalry " and " The Statue of King Charles " by Lionel Johnson and " A Christmas Carol " by May Probyn; Methuen & Co. Ltd. for two sayings of Oscar Wilde (*Aphorisms of Oscar Wilde*); Mr. Wilfrid Meynell for " Chimes," " At Night," " Renouncement," and " To Silence " by Alice Meynell and " Ad Amicam " by Francis Thompson; Professor Gilbert Murray and George Allen & Unwin Ltd. for the translation from Euripides' *Hippolytus*; Mr. John Murray for two sonnets and the prose passage " Night in Venice " from *A Venetian Medley* by J. A. Symonds, " The Noises of Rome " (Martial—trans. W. J. Courthope) and three extracts from the works of Robert Browning; and Mrs. Myers and Macmillan &

Co. Ltd. for " A Cosmic Outlook " (*Collected Poems of F. W. H. Myers*);

Sir Henry Newbolt for four lines from his masque *Dream Market* and "Night is fallen" by Mary E. Coleridge (*Poems by Mary E. Coleridge*, Elkin Mathews & Marrot Ltd.); Mr. Robert Nichols and Chatto & Windus Ltd. for " Night Rhapsody " ; and The Nonesuch Press Ltd. for two letters of William Blake (*Poetry and Prose of William Blake* edited by Geoffrey Keynes);

Professor Okey and J. M. Dent & Sons Ltd. for " A Basket of Bugs " (*A Basketful of Memories*); Mr. Seumas O'Sullivan for " Night " and " The Starling Lake " ; The Oxford University Press for " An Evening in Sussex " by W. J. Courthope (*The County Town and Other Poems*), " The Tryst " and " The Source of Love " by Robert Bridges (*Poetical Works*), the extracts from the Revised Version of the Gospels of St. Luke and St. John, " A True History " (Lucian—trans. H. W. Fowler and F. G. Fowler), and the extracts from *The Questions of King Milinda*, *Aphorisms on the Sacred Laws* and the *Dhammapada* (*Sacred Books of the East*);

The Phoenix Publishing Co. Ltd. for " Lullaby of a Mountain Woman " by Padraic H. Pearse (*Plays, Stories and Poems*); and Mr. J. B. Priestley for an extract from " The Dark Hours " (*Apes and Angels*);

Sir Arthur Quiller-Couch for " The Least of These " ;

Lady Raleigh and Edward Arnold & Co. for an extract from *Writing and Writers* (Edward Arnold & Co.), " Some Thoughts on Examinations " and " Wishes at a Garden Party " from *Laughter from a Cloud* (Constable & Co.) by Sir Walter Raleigh; Mr. Walter Ramal for "The Prince of Sleep " ; Representatives of A. C. Benson and John Lane The Bodley Head Ltd. for " Evensong "

(*Lord Vyet*); Representatives of Marjorie Pickthall and John Lane The Bodley Head Ltd. for " Swallow Song " from *The Lamp of Poor Souls* (John Lane); Representatives of Stephen Phillips and John Lane The Bodley Head Ltd. for " To Milton—Blind "; Mr. Grant Richards as Literary Executor for " Romney Marsh " by John Davidson; Miss Eleanour Sinclair Rohde for " Evening Scents " (*The Scented Garden*); Mrs. Rolleston for " The Dead at Clonmacnois " by T. W. Rolleston; Mrs. Amanda M'Kittrick Ros for extracts from *Irene Iddesleigh*; Miss Naomi Royde-Smith for " At Dusk " by Enid, Countess of Kinnoull; Mrs. Theodora Roscoe for " Washing Day " from *Market Morning* (St. Catherine Press); George Routledge & Sons Ltd. for " A Sonnet to Eternal Slumber " by J. A. Symonds, the translations from the Greek Anthology by Mr. F. A. Wright (*The Girdle of Aphrodite* and *Poets of the Greek Anthology*), and the extract from Mr. W. S. Stallybrass's version of Caxton's text of " Reynard the Fox " (*Epic of the Beast*); and Mr. George Russell (" A. E.") and Macmillan & Co. Ltd. for " The City " and " Promise " (*Collected Poems by "A. E.*");

The Hon. V. Sackville-West for " The Persian Flute "; Mr. Arthur L. Salmon for " A Memory " from *New Verses* (G. T. Foulis); Mr. Arthur L. Salmon and Sir Walford Davies for " A Child's Carol " by Mr. Arthur L. Salmon; Mr. George Santayana and Constable & Co. for three sayings from *Little Essays*; Mr. George Santayana and J. M. Dent & Sons Ltd. for a saying from *Words of Doctrine*; Mr. Siegfried Sassoon and William Heinemann Ltd. for " Falling Asleep "; Mr. Duncan C. Scott and McClelland & Stewart, Toronto, for " The End of the Day "; Miss Bertha Smith for " A Night out in the Dolomites "; Mr. J. C. Squire for " The Happy Night ";

Mr. James Stephens and Macmillan & Co. Ltd. for " In the Cool of the Evening " (*Collected Poems*) ; Miss Muriel Stuart for " The Seed Shop " ; and Mr. Alfred Sutro and George Allen & Unwin Ltd. for the extract from M. Maeterlinck's *Magic of the Stars* ; Mrs. H. M. Swanwick, M.A.C.H., for the recipe for " Stinger " ; and Mr. Arthur Symons for " The Obscure Night " ;

Mrs. Trencham and the Oxford University Press for Mr. E. J. Trechmann's translations (*Essays of Montaigne*) Trustees of George Meredith, Constable & Co. and Charles Scribner's Sons, New York, for " Lucifer in Starlight " ; and Trustees of William Morris for " Inscription for an Old Bed " ;

Miss Helen Waddell and Constable & Co. for " How goes the Night " and " To Babylon by Candlelight " (*Lyrics from the Chinese*) ; Mr. Arthur Waley for " A Dream in Winter " from 170 *Chinese Poems* (Constable & Co.), the extract from " Pillow Book of Sei Shōnagon (George Allen & Unwin Ltd.) and " When Evening Comes " from *Japanese Poetry=the uta* (Oxford University Press) Mr. Hugh Walpole for " Books at Night " ; Lady Warren and Mr. John Murray for " May-day on Magdalen Tower " by Sir Herbert Warren ; Mrs. Watts-Dunton for " A Dream " by T. Watts-Dunton ; the *Wide World Magazine* for an extract from *Adventures of Louis de Rougemont* ; Mr. Harold Williams, Literary Executor of Mr. Herbert Trench, for " Song " by that author ; Mrs. Margaret L. Woods and John Lane The Bodley Head Ltd. for " March Thoughts from England " ; and the Rev. Canon Christopher Wordsworth for an extract from his translation of *Kyrie Rex Splendens* by St. Dunstan ;

Mr. W. B. Yeats and Ernest Benn Ltd. for " The Stolen Child " (*Poems*: T. Fisher Unwin); Major Francis

Brett Young for the extract from "Portrait of Clare"; and Professor Zimmern and the Oxford University Press for the translation of " Pericles' Praise of the Dead " (*Thucydides*).

As regards three copyright poems I have used, after repeated efforts I have been unable to trace the owners, who will not, I trust, resent their appearance in this book. All existing rights not here acknowledged will (if notified) be duly recorded in any subsequent edition.

A. S.

INDEX OF AUTHORS

847

849

851

855

857

858

859

860

861

ANONYMOUS ITEMS

FROM THE BIBLE

FROM THE APOCRYPHA

867

INDEX OF FIRST LINES OF VERSE

(Some short items are omitted)

868

877

Printed in Great Britain by
The Camelot Press Ltd., London and Southampton.